The Importance of
Being Earnest

Charleston Conference
Proceedings 2014

Edited by Beth R. Bernhardt, Leah H. Hinds,
and Katina P. Strauch

An electronic version of the proceedings is available at http://docs.lib.purdue.edu/charleston/

Contents

Collection Development   145

End Users

Management and Administration 357

Scholarly Communication 487

Techie Issues 520

Preface and Acknowledgments

"The Importance of Being Earnest" was the theme of the 2014 Charleston Conference which took place in Charleston, South Carolina, on Wednesday, November 5 through Saturday, November 8, 2014, with over 1,600 participants. The far-ranging and diverse program, which focuses on the purchase and leasing of information of all types and in all available formats, is curated by an able team of Charleston Conference directors headed by Beth Bernhardt and Leah Hinds who have worked long and hard to compile this volume. Thanks are due to Leah and Beth and to all the Charleston Conference Directors who helped in assuring timely and professionally peer-reviewed submissions. Thanks are also due to the Purdue University Press team: Katherine Purple, Managing Editor, Dave Scherer, Scholarly Repository Specialist, Bryan Schaffer, Sales and Marketing Specialist, Dianna Gilroy, Production Editor, and many others behind the scenes.

In 2014, the Charleston Conference included eleven preconferences covering the evaluation of electronic resources, using Excel, content analysis, online learning, the library as publisher, building eBook collections for the long term, campus open access policies, online learning and the library, negotiating with vendors, advanced data analysis, and sustainable strategies for digital resource delivery and access. Ten plenary sessions; several hundred concurrent sessions; and lively lunch discussions, PechaKucha-like shotgun "shorts," and poster sessions spiced up the offerings. In 2013, the Neapolitan format was introduced which allowed three plenary-level speakers to speak in large rooms during the same time slot. This innovation by the Conference Directors was very popular and was continued in 2014. The Conference Directors also continued Charleston Premiers during Saturday morning breakfast which were refereed and allowed companies to make 5-minute presentations about new and emerging products.

The Charleston Conference has a plethora of additional offerings including Juried Product Development Forums for publishers or vendors who want to get feedback from librarians about new or emerging products, Dine Around dinners on Friday night at some of Charleston's well-known restaurants, a Gala Reception on Thursday evening, and a Leadership Award for one of the Conference Directors.

The 2014 lead keynote speech by Anthea Stratigos of Outsell, entitled "Being Earnest is the New Normal," energized us all to consider new approaches in our everyday environments. Other keynote and Neapolitan speakers included Charles Lyons, Bob Nardini, and Nicole Allen discussing the library's changing role in providing textbook content; Todd Carpenter, Bruce Heterich and Brian Sherman and Scott Bernier were interested in discovery and fair linking; Adam Chesler, Jim Dooley, David Parker and Zac Rolnick tackled DRM and intellectual property rights; and John Rennie was interested in developments in science education; Scott Plutchak, Greg Tananbaum, and John Vaughn dissected the scholarly ecosystem; James L.W. West presented a fascinating historical view of price control and the publisher; and Carol Tenopir and Gabriel Hughes concentrated on download data.

There were breaks in the plenary and Neapolitan talks when a lively Oxford-style debate ensued between Rick Anderson and David Magier about whether library collections should be shaped by patrons or librarians. As well, a panel of James J. O'Donnell, Phil Richerme, and Christine Fair were brutally frank about what Faculty want librarians to know.

The Saturday sessions were equally stimulating. Beginning with Premier five-minute refereed presentations by new companies and products, the next plenary/Neapolitan talks were about crowd-sourcing of library services (Ilana Barnes Stonebraker, John Dove, Scott Johnson, and Tim Johnson); unavailable material on interlibrary loan (Jennifer Duncan and Carol Kochan), and Big Data, Retention, and Academic Libraries by Adam Murray.

The Concurrent sessions, Lively Lunches, Poster sessions, shotgun sessions, and the like that were submitted and refereed by the editors are grouped into six categories in this volume: Collection Development, End Users, Management and Administration, Patron-Driven Acquisitions and Interlibrary Loan, Scholarly Communication, and Techie Issues.

In 2014, the Charleston Conference introduced several Charleston Seminars which were held prior to the main conference and preconferences. A Digital Curation Seminar was sponsored by the UNC-Chapel Hill School of Information and Library Science and the Charleston Conference for a full day on Monday, November 3 and a half day Tuesday, November 4 just prior to the main Charleston Conference. The luncheon/seminar on Saturday, November 8, 2014, was also held on the theme "Being Earnest With our Collections: Determining Key Challenges and Best Practices. The luncheon was moderated by Michael Arthur and included Michael Levine-Clark and Rebecca Seger, Jill Grogg and Robert McDonald, Jonathan Harwell and Jim Bunnelle as well as Rick Anderson discussing alternative serial distribution models, transitioning from legacy systems to cloud infrastructure, and future possibilities for ebooks. Information and slides from these presentations is located on the Conference website.

Many new ideas and innovations are implemented and shared at the Charleston Conferences!

Reports of many of the plenary sessions and concurrent sessions are included in this volume, many transcribed ably by Caroline Goldsmith. Archives of many of the papers are also loaded online at the Conference website.

And, of course, the city of Charleston was as beautiful and vibrant as ever!

The next Charleston Conference will be held November 4–7, 2015, with the theme "Where Do We Go From Here?" There will be several new offerings, several preconferences, and Charleston Seminars as librarians, publishers, vendors, aggregators and consultants from all over the world explore important changes within the industry that impact the way in which information is leased, acquired and made available. Charleston Conference information will be updated regularly. For archives and further information, http://www.charlestonlibraryconference.com/

See you in Charleston in November!

Katina Strauch, Founder and Convener, Charleston Conference

Bruce Strauch, Owner, Charleston Conference

Introduction

The Charleston Conference continues to be a major event for information exchange among librarians, vendors and publishers. Now in its thirty-fourth year, the conference continues to be one of the most popular library-related conferences in the United States, if not globally. With record numbers for 2014, conference attendees continue to remark on the informative and thought-provoking sessions. The conference provides a casual, collegial atmosphere where librarians, publishers, and vendors talk freely and directly about issues facing their libraries and information providers. All of this interaction occurs in the beautiful city of Charleston, South Carolina. This is the tenth year that Beth R. Bernhardt has put together the proceedings from the conference and the sixth year for Leah Hinds. We are pleased to share some of the learning experiences that we, and other attendees, had at the conference.

The theme of the 2014 Charleston Conference was "Too Much Is Not Enough!" While not all presenters prepared written versions of their remarks, enough did so that we are able to include an overview of such subjects as collection development, management, end users, scholarly communication, and technology issues. The unique nature of the Charleston Conference gives librarians, publishers, and library vendors the opportunity to holistically examine these and other points of interest.

Katina Strauch, founder of the conference, continues to be an inspiration to us. Her enthusiasm for the conference and the proceedings is motivating. We hope you, the reader, find the papers as informative as we do and that they encourage the continuation of the ongoing dialogue among librarians, vendors, and publishers that can only enhance the learning and research experience for the ultimate user.

Signed,

Co-Editors of the 34th Charleston Conference Proceedings

Beth R. Bernhardt, Assistant Dean for Collection Management and Scholarly Communications, University of North Carolina at Greensboro and Main Conference Director

Leah Hinds, Assistant Conference Director

Plenary Sessions

What's the Big Idea? Mellon, ARL, AAU, University Presses, and the Future of Scholarly Communication

Leila Salisbury, Director, University Press of Mississippi

Raym Crow, Senior Consultant, SPARC

Helen Cullyer, Program Officer, The Andrew W Mellon Foundation

Barbara Kline Pope, Executive Director for Communications and the National Academies Press,
The National Academies

Charles Watkinson, Director, University of Michigan Press, and Associate University Librarian for
Publishing, University of Michigan Library

The following is a lightly edited transcript of a live presentation at the 2014 Charleston Conference. Slides and videos are available at http://2014charlestonconference.sched.org/

Leila Salisbury: Good afternoon. I'm happy to hear it's still lively. This is very nice. It's really good that you're all here to hear a quirky piece I feel will solve our issues in scholarly communications over the next hour, so congratulations for coming here. You'll find this very edifying.

In 2014, both the Mellon Foundation and AAU-ARL taskforce on scholarly communication have encouraged publishers and universities to develop programs for digital projects that would increase access to and reduce the cost of scholarly communications. These funders in scholarly societies are imagining what the future landscape of scholarship might look like and how digital scholarship might be presented and made accessible both within as well as outside the academy. Concerns over issues of cost, access, the free rider problem, and ongoing sustainability for scholarly monographs and their sponsoring publishers, often university presses, are not new issues, but the current work at Mellon and with this AAU-ARL taskforce has the potential to change the conversation and develop some viable solutions and new thinking in the research publication value chain. Critical to such projects will be the involvement of university presses for the processes of selection, development, vending, and publication of monographs. Also key will be libraries who may act as partners in developing new hosting capabilities and channels of dissemination.

Today, we've gathered individuals from both the funding and the publishing side to discuss recent initiatives and to explore how such ecosystem partnerships might function in the years to come. I'll introduce the speakers briefly here. The full biographies are available online. And then I'll begin with a series of questions for our group. It's going to be very much a roundtable discussion. This is going to be hopefully a very lively exchange, and we won't be doing formal presentations, so we really encourage a lot of interaction with the audience as well.

I'll do brief introductions from your right to left. We have Helen Cullyer, who's a program officer in the scholarly communications program at the Andrew Mellon Foundation. She works with the senior program officer, Don Waters, on developing new grant-making initiatives and reviewing grant proposals in the area of scholarly publication, preservation, access, and library services as well as in the evaluation and assessment of grant-funding projects. Sitting next to Helen is Barbara Kline Pope, executive director of communications for the National Academies Press at The National Academies and the current president of the Association of American University Presses. In addition to book publishing, she manages marketing communication programs designed to bring science and engineering to public audiences. Next to her we have Raym Crow. He's a senior consultant with the SPARC Consulting Group and principal of Chain Bridge Group, a consulting firm providing publishing and sustainability planning. Crow specializes in developing plans for collaborative publishing projects and supply-side business models capable of supporting open-access dissemination. And on the end here, we have Charles Watkinson, an associate university librarian for publishing at the University of Michigan Libraries and Director of University of Michigan Press. Prior to moving to Michigan in 2014 just a couple months ago, Charles was director of Purdue University Press and head of Scholarly Publishing Services in the Purdue Libraries for five years. He's been a board member of the AAUP and the SSP and was an initiator of the Library Publishing Coalition.

We don't a have a particular order. People are just going to jump in as they have things they want to share about these particular questions. So I'll start off. From a personal perspective of your organization, what needs are not being met for participants in the scholarly ecosystem? What is one thing you think should be done to get those needs met? Charles? You want to start?

Charles Watkinson: From the perspective of arriving in Michigan, something that really strikes me, as Director of the Press as well as a librarian, is the number of scholars who are now coming to us with digital scholarship. And it's not the people who are self-identifying as digital humanists. It's just everybody. And they often talk about it in terms of the inner companion website or some such thing, but they all have products of digital scholarship. So I think this is a major challenge, and what to do about it. One thing that we're very interested in here we are University of Michigan Press, as a humanities and qualitative social science publisher, we're very interested in leveraging the data repository infrastructure being built by libraries as potentially a monograph platform, certainly a platform for companion and supplementary data because that is a very blurry line between what a monograph is and what a humanities data presentation is.

Raym Crow: What I can speak to is I'm involved in a project that is a result of a taskforce on scholarly communications. And what came out of that project was a whitepaper talking about the scholarly monograph marketplace and what the AAU-ARL taskforce is supposed to do is how do we take this intermediate constructively to encourage the economic viability of humanities publishing while leveraging the maneuverability of digital

communications and digital technologies and networking. Out of that, the discussion around the whitepaper, I did a prospectus and a proposal for an institutional based title subsidy. And just to give a quick outline of that proposal for those of you that haven't read the prospectus, the idea was that institutions with sufficient for the faculty's first books, the effect that's mentioned where you have to be accepted by a qualifying publisher, initially by university presses, who accept based on their current course standards, part of that payment probably will be made available on open access, but the press and the publishers would be able to sell value-added versions of print-on-demand. So that was the, again, we focused on first books. It would be expanded to target that, and we can talk about that in a little detail.

Leila Salisbury: I like the line "at their own risk."

Barbara Kline Pope: So I was introduced as both a publishing director and also president of AAUP, and mostly I'm here today to represent many diverse publishers who are university presses and the associate members of the AAUP, so I just want to make sure you know that. Also want to give you a baseline that all of those 130-some members have very diverse opinions, very diverse data on the plans for pay-to-publish model and other areas. But what I think all of us in university press publishing or scholarly publishing have in common is that we have a dual mission, and that mission is to advance scholarship through connecting readers to authors and authors to readers, but we also have a financial responsibility to our institutions. So I just want to sort of give you a baseline there.

So when I started to think about this first question, I went looking for data. Rather than say what we as an organization or we as a set of publishers can offer scholars, what do scholars want and what do scholars need, mostly? So I went to the Lever Initiative at the Oberlin Group, to that report, and it was pretty clear that scholars are really looking to be published for tenure and promotion. And that a big chunk of that is peer review. So peer review is incredibly important, and I will say that university presses, as compared to for-profit scholarly publishers, are known for peer review. And so I think that that is something that we need to continue as university presses and associate members of the university press community to make sure that we are providing the best peer review for scholars. Also, I think what is being put on the table today with the AAU-ARL and the Mellon Foundation can help scholars in that that same Oberlin study, 80% of scholars said that they get published, and of that 20%, there's certainly quality publication going on there, but there's a certain percentage of those scholars who don't get published. And one of the reasons is because our financial responsibility. Typically, we are publishing books that we lose money on, which we can't do that over and over again, so there is some scholarship where we just can't make the numbers work. And I think that's where these two plans that we're talking about today can really help scholars and help the library community and the university press community.

Helen Cullyer: Thank you very much. So again, Charles, Raym, and Barbara made some really important points and I think I'd like to follow up on all of them, really. As Charles said, the need to publish is becoming increasingly important to scholars in the humanities. And because they're working with a lot of digital collections or data sets, they're using computational techniques. They want to present maps, maybe they're using multimedia. There are a variety of reasons to want to publish in a digital medium. Barbara mentioned peer review. There are not good peer review standards really established for rich multimedia-based, -driven publications, especially those having software tools, and there are certainly not established tenure and promotion criteria in most fields. And so we're trying to address those issues in a number of different ways and especially with tenure and promotion guidelines with the American Historical Association, CAA, College Art Association, and Society of Art Historians to really try and address that because that's one important thing. And in addition to the sort of desire to publish digitally amongst many, certainly not all scholars, but many, there's been the question of who is going to see that scholarship, how it's going to be used. And we came to the conclusion that digital scholarly publications rather than the traditional

monographs in the digital medium or those that bridged more traditional genres really could benefit from being out there on the open web, firstly to generate more readers, and secondly to make those publications more usable, to have them linked to related publications and collections so those publications can be searched, mined, analyzed, along with primary sources and other types of digital data collections. But obviously, to make a large portion of humanities scholarship openly accessible, accessible on an open access basis, is a huge sustainability challenge for the scholarly ecosystem and university presses to realize that. So we started thinking about possible different economic models, and so this is where Raym, right around the same time that the ARL-AAU came up with their first book initiative, we had started thinking very much along the same lines. And we started thinking, "Well, what would happen if instead of pay-to-read model, publishers experimented with a pay-to-publish model," so really meaning the institutions would then cost of their humanities faculty when those faculty are publishing more works. Those works would then be published on an open access basis by publishers according to standard editorial peer-review criteria, vanity publishing. No money would change hands until a contract could be issued, and according to the pretty standard open access licensing terms, and there may be some preservation requirement as well. And we thought possibly we could use grant funding to seed such a program. What we don't know yet is whether that pay-to-publish model is even feasible. Of course, institutions would have to better cost themselves, and there are many possible barriers to that happening. So the current standards of this initiative are that we have two grants pending, and those pending grants would enable three institutions, because one of the grants is collaborative, to really do some pretty serious planning and do a walkthrough of how would this look like from the intuitional, the university college perspective? How would provosts and deans allocate the money to faculty? Which faculty would be eligible? What would be the licensing terms that the universities and colleges would require? Where would the pay-to-publish money even come from? We imagine, of course, this would have to be a reallocation from somewhere. Money doesn't just grow on trees. So we are hoping that these institutions will be able to sort of go through this process and really come up with some conclusions about the feasibility of this model. And based on the outcomes of those studies, we might do some more planning and more research or we might decide to go ahead with some kind of experimental grant program or not. We might just say no, this isn't going to work. So that's where we are. We're also very much thinking about the press side. And as many of you know, we initiated our university presses over the summer. The proposals that would enable presses to develop really shared infrastructure for the publication of digital works, and that includes digital monographs but also some of these more sort of nontraditional forms. And as Charles said, sort of thinking what a monograph is is pretty blurry right now. So there's even a problem with the language. What do we mean by a monograph at this stage? I think I've gone on for too long, and I didn't say one thing; I talked about many things that need to be done.

Leila Salisbury: No, no, thank you. Well, and this leads me to think, I'll ask a question. Is there a crisis in monograph publishing? This is the thing we hear all the time. Or is it more, is it that faculty cannot get these tenure books published or is the problem how the books are being published or is the problem that there may be very limited market once those books are published, or is the problem all of the above? Do you have comments?

Raym Crow: Yes, in the whitepaper they estimated how many faculty would be publishing a first book, try to estimate what the market was and what the cost would be for the institutions participating in it. So in looking at that, just focusing on North American university presses, not looking at Anglo-American presses or looking at commercial publishers, the ballpark was about 85% of faculty, junior faculty's first books and seeking books for tenure could get published. The issue with the first books convention tries to address is the fact that we want to decouple the evaluation of books for tenure from commercial liability. Barbara said presses can't publish everything they might want to publish, especially

if they're very specialized monographs. There's a positive externality for universities to use these books for tenure. They can't be captured by a title's price. So that's the idea of the first books convention was again, it was this convention that covered all the first copy costs of the press. How that would be set is a detail that needed to be worked out, but also the opportunity costs of a press. That's better than the, would actually give more options. There wouldn't be a partial run on presses to do.

Leila Salisbury: Did anyone else have anything?

Charles Watkinson: I think that maybe from an author point of view, there isn't that much of a monograph crisis. And I feel that I'm on delicate ground here, that it certainly is true that we're seeing at university presses a market where we're competing with new and even more aggressive commercial humanities and social science book publishers who are increasing their output every year. And it feels a little bit from the university press side like it's a Dr. Jekyll and Dr. Hyde situation that we're facing where our editorial boards are telling us we have to invest very heavily in the very highly intensive work of producing a monograph, but when they act as authors, they are sometimes choosing speed over those values. So I think from the point of view of, the monograph crisis is for publishers like University of Michigan Press who have high costs are very invested in a very intensive design process and are at risk of being undercut sometimes. And I don't know if they do a good point version.

Helen Cullyer: Okay, I think this is a really difficult question. I think overall, the language of the crisis is probably unhelpful. And scholarly not-for-profit publishing, economic sustainability, and the ability of people to get published I think will always be an issue. I think, we commissioned a study about monograph output in the US, not just books, all monographs. And we received that data. We have yet to go down into it and sort of look at it by discipline and field. I think probably what that will reveal is what we get a sense of anecdotally, that in some fields there really is a problem and scholars do have problems getting published. Literary studies is one we hear a lot. But the flip side of that is, as we've been talking to faculty, some people say, "Well, too many monographs are being published." And by that, they mean that the monograph is not necessarily the most appropriate form sometimes of humanistic scholarship. And of course, the monograph is the most standard of the tenure and promotions. So almost everyone in every humanities field, there are some exceptions, have to publish at least one monograph in their scholarly career. And so I think that the monograph crisis or one of our problems, if there is one, has multiple dimensions. And while I certainly don't think the monograph is dead or should ever be dead as a genre, it's a very, very important form of publication, there are certainly other, maybe more experimental forms that can and should grow up and that should receive vigorous peer review and full credit.

Leila Salisbury: You talked about some of the nuance that we don't necessarily discuss with monographs, and I'm curious, it's sort of the old story that monograph sales can be very limited. I mean, print runs in the low hundreds now at many university press publishers, and I think that sometimes to the outer community, that low number sort of indicated that these are books, and I hate it when people say this, that no one needs or shouldn't be published. And I guess I'd like to talk, dig into that a little more deeply. Is it more a discoverability problem, these things are out there, but in the past, we haven't had the greatest tools for helping these things be discovered, or is it really a money problem? One of the things that I've been hearing in these discussions in the last few days as we're talking more about use data through different types of collection development programs. My sense very much is switching to that it's not that this content's not being used, it's not necessarily being sold in a way that brings the same revenue back to the publishers and may not be sustainable. Can you talk a little bit about these issues?

Barbara Kline Pope: I think I've got to now mention this as well as Director of the National Academies Press. Because I can shed a little bit of light on the discoverability of books and how that changed from when you go from just selling a printed book to posting content in discoverable ways. And then we went to actually posting content in ways that are actually substitutable for a printed book. And we know that opening up the content a bit or opening it up a lot, really more broadly, disseminates the content. We get more downloads of that content as we got more and more open. But it's a scary thing for a press to do that. And luckily, we were part of the National Academy of Sciences. The books that we published are central products of that entire huge institution, and so they put the money there to allow us to do that. So I think discoverability is certainly a great concept to think about when you think about open or public access, but we also need the data, and we need the data for the humanities to determine these kind of scary questions. For the sciences, we collected data. We did it at the beginning of the century, actually. In the year 2000 we looked at this to determine what is the revenue lost of completely free in PDF. What is the revenue lost and the revenue gained in different formats? And we had arguments in the year 2000 before we actually did this research. And in fact, Mellon funded this research for us. And I think now various communities are in those arguments with one side saying it must be open, the other side saying it must be closed. That's because we don't have the data. And what I would like to see is for the humanities, for us to do another study like that, determine really what is the cost and what is the benefit of going open. And I kind of call on Mellon to maybe help us in that.

Raym Crow: I don't disagree with anything you say. I think one of the points behind the supply-side model is to remove the risk of the press of these very specialized monographs that sell a few hundred copies. One suspects with DDA and PDA purchasing are going to get even lower and lower and lower. And so it's a big press goal to gather some of the value from the institutions.

Barbara Kline Pope: And there is a study going on to determine what a true cost is. What is the true value that a university press puts into a monograph? And I think that's really important. But it's also important to look at that as entire cost, overhead cost, and what a press needs to really help scholars not only produce that book but also to help that scholar look at their line of inquiry, get involved in that scholar's life, you know, the role of that petition setter is incredibly important in moving disciplines forward. So I think we need to be very careful about using this data to do it.

Helen Cullyer: I definitely agree with the need to collect data and still be on top of the costs of monographs that Barbara alluded to, what funding is being conducted. To go back to Leila's original question, is discoverability or money really the problem, I do think it's both. I think that both issues, and we're going to come back to the discoverability later this session, but just to make a point now, we're putting something up on the web, on the open web, to make it discoverable. Lots of the things on the open web are really hidden because they don't come up on the first couple pages of a Google search or other kind of search engine.

Charles Watkinson: I do think there's an interesting aspect of the discoverability problem, which is that in the digital space, it feels like monographs haven't been given much of a chance yet. So I think it is a bit of an issue when we, from the press side, look at the general perception that the content that we produce is not used at all. And that is a big narrative. That there may be a strong issue of digital accessibility in there and probably we need to wait a little bit to make those presumptions until we have good data from databases that combine journal and book content in the same space, because anecdotally, there is some good news of some e-book collections that we know of. So that's just one point on discoverability that monographs are not necessarily not used. We just don't really know yet, I think. I could be corrected on that. Just about the money problem, I mean, it is very interesting to talk to colleagues here from libraries, from acquisitions and collections development side and talk about the halving of monograph budgets a few years ago. From the university press angle, we're definitely seeing that very starkly. So at University of Michigan Press, we've seen a decline in revenue of about a third over the last five years, and we're a very heavily monograph-based press. And that's a pretty scary

thing to be seeing. And I think it's a result of those cuts and it's just taken a while to hit us.

Leila Salisbury: Well, this links into something else I wanted to talk about with these OA materials. How can we get data about these open access materials? It's one thing when we can work through vendors that might handle OA content. There is the question of, well, it's OA. How is that worked through the vendor? If the library publishing program is putting together material that some might say, well, it exists in the silo. How is the user data being shared? How is discoverability driven from that one particular institution to other institutions more widely? Can you all talk about some of these questions? I mean, for publishers, if we feel like we want to get into this, we need some answers to show how the work we put into this is going to be meaningful.

Raym Crow: Well, from one perspective, I think the openness will increase use. But kind of the conventional model really captures the value from the institution; it's really the quality of the scholarship that's being validated. And so subsequent use is important, but it's not because it drives the value from the institution's perspective. So again, the idea that this is set at a level where the pressures in different, in that kind of detail, I mean, at this point, it's internal. But the goal in the concept is to alleviate present risks, not increase it. And the idea is that most presses aren't making lots of money on first books. And that's wrong, I think. It's basically saying, in terms of first books, capturing the value of the institutions, so it takes the risk out of it and you don't have to worry about commercial liability and making publishing decisions.

Barbara Kline Pope: I think also discoverability is incredibly important. And as I said before, I'm not representing all university presses when I talk about open access. We do know that sometimes when a book is free, the ratio of free downloads to sales is 100 to one. We do know that that helps, but it doesn't help if you don't actually draw people to that content. And I think what Leila and Raym have been referring to we're going to talk about later is just posting a file and having it be free and expecting people to find it. That doesn't work. And so the knowledge of all people in the marketing groups in these university presses gave them their audiences. They know how to promote these books. They know what awards they should go to. They know what reviews they can get for these books. They know how to generate buzz about these books. And you need that kind of critical knowledge, that kind of critical skills whether the file is free, whether this scholarship is free or whether it's for sale. And I think many of us think that, "Oh, it's free, just post this file." And it is relatively inexpensive as a cost of the next file to post once you have the infrastructure there, but that's not what you want. You really want people to use that scholarship now that it is free.

Helen Cullyer: Okay, so on discoverability, I think there should be many ways, many methods by which publications should be made discoverable in order to reach a wide variety of audiences. Marketing is certainly one of them. Search engine optimization. The role of repositories and aggregators who, as Charles said, can make e-books better go along with journals and other content. Use of the link to open data. And also the role of libraries, naturally, in making sure that for open access publications, there are records for those publications and links to publications in their discovery into things. And I think that's really important because I think there's still a perception in some areas of the academy that, well, it's just out there on the web. It's not a real publication. Sometimes people have a print of a university press. It's silly, but the publications need to be discoverable, open access publications alongside those publications which libraries have acquired for a fee. I think that's really important. On usage statistics, I also think that's crucial. As funders, I don't think we're in a position to dictate what sort of usage statistics presses want and need. I think we need to get that from presses, and we'd certainly be willing to assist if more work is needed in this area. One issue that I think someone alluded to was content that was published under open licenses is just that even if it's distributed sort of by a standard, the publishers might have a bunch of other content, some open access, some not, and so you're getting standardized usage statistics that way. What happens if someone downloads that

content and then republishes it and redistributes it? And how could you get meaningful usage statistics about feedback and published content? We had a conversation with the CEO of Creative Commons a while ago, and he mentioned one strategy that we're thinking of is to actually place some kind of tracking device in seed licenses so that you actually know where that stuff is republished, and I think that would be fantastic. That really would be that openly licensed material, you could actually get pretty comprehensive usage statistics back. I don't know if Creative Commons will do that, but it's certainly something that they're thinking about and discussing.

Barbara Kline Pope: I would think there'd be privacy issues with that as well.

Charles Watkinson: I just want to echo Helen on that. I've been in charge of two educational repositories, one at Purdue and one at Michigan, and all of us involved in the repository movement know that usage stats are the currency of open access. And it is an absolute precondition of any platform that has open access books on it that it needs to have rich usage stats and those need to be pushing out. They're not just things that people go and retrieve. They need to push out to the publisher, to the author, to the funder, and that is the only way sustainable open access monographs are going to happen. It's absolutely essential. The other thing I would say is I think it's particularly relevant to a region like Charleston to really appeal to the aggregators and the jobbers to think very carefully about how open access monographs are going to fit into their workflows. And I would pull also on the librarians to be ready to pay the self-ready fee for an open access book because it is, again, essential if anybody cares about open access that this content is brought into the same environment through the same workflows as all the scholarship that you'll currently find.

Raym Crow: I just want to add one thing. I mean, there's nothing being proposed in the AAU-ARL proposal suggests that open access content would just be put up and then people could trip over it. You sort of mentioned to cover the cost of the market was negotiated. Even in the market now, sort of sell a few hundred copies. So an open system contributes to it if that is a recognized value by institutions.

Barbara Kline Pope: And also, if the open content sits on a publisher's website, that also brings eyeballs to the rest of the scholarship there. It gets additional downloads, gets additional reading and perhaps purchase of other books. So it's important that publishers also have the file not just sitting out there.

Leila Salisbury: If we're looking at really flipping things as we've been short-handing it to a pay-to-publish monograph model, this is something, this is called the "free writer" problem for university presses. And certainly Macmillan is looking at this now, but I think the question may be, where do these institutional grants come from? You alluded to it a little bit. I would posit there may be a fear from university presses, for example, this is a situation where universities say, "Well, we have this key thing, a piece of the pie for scholarly publications," kind of being asked to contribute however many thousands of dollars towards one of these first monographs or monograph initiatives. How can we help ensure maybe that that money doesn't all just come out of a press's institutional allocation or it is just shifting around money, is it going to make things worse to some extent for some of the university presses? Or inversely, I've heard a lot of publishers express fear of even more of a class system or a tiering system among university presses. And I'm sure, Helen, you've probably got some of these issues maybe not answers yet, but if you could talk a bit about them.

Helen Cullyer: Yeah. I would say we don't have the answers yet on where funds would come from at universities and colleges. I think there has to be some different creative thinking about them. When we float the idea, obviously every constituency within the institution is worried that the funds will come from their budget. The library is worried, the faculty are worried the funds might be taken from their research funds they currently get and so maybe they get the pay-to-publish funds but they wouldn't get research funds to travel, to go to conferences, and things like that. So I don't have the answers. And it may be that we conclude that it wouldn't

just be moving money around in a way that's detrimental, but we don't know that yet. University finances are incredibly complicated, and there need to be multiple people involved in the discussions to figure out whether this is actually feasible or not and different institutions may come up with different answers. Another worry is that maybe, and this speaks to the class system for institutions, actually, maybe not for presses, though I'll speak to them in a bit, there may be some institutions that just can't afford to do this. Might there be ways that Mellon can sort of address that problem? As far as the presses go, can you just explain to me again about the class system for the presses and what your particular worry was there?

Leila Salisbury: Well, we're competing for content all the time, and so are projects that come with money being evaluated differently by the presses or are they more attractive to, is everyone going to want to take their publication to one of the big, probably financially healthier university presses? It seems to maybe put smaller university presses at even more of a disadvantage.

Helen Cullyer: It might do. I think to determine that, we have to run some experiments after we determine the feasibility at the university level. And as I'm sure you all realize, I've been talking, we imagine that exploration as potentially a multiyear process. And we certainly don't think it will be possible or wise to try and sort of flip the model, as you put it, overnight. We can't do that, we shouldn't do that. So there have got to be multiple levels of planning and possibly experimentation.

Raym Crow: In terms of the cost, now I'm talking here about the traditional specialized monographs as opposed to the digital projects that Mellon is looking at, the estimate we used coming out of the whitepaper, I'm using a fairly high per title subscription level of $20,000. For a large research institution, on average it'd be about $75,000 a year. And even at smaller institutions, you get down to, at smaller institutions it'd probably be about $2,500 a year because they have fewer faculty looking for tenure. So in terms of it not being affordable, that seems unlikely. So that's one issue. Any attempt to increase that subscription has to increase it, it would still be affordable for first books. In terms of the inequity court for small presses, the idea behind this from the outset was you need to get critical mass of presses participating. Otherwise, you're right, individual presses can't do a lot, really, to do this kind of thing. It has to be most if not all the presses. The economic logic is such in my mind that in the large presses, they don't need it, but still it'd be thought about to take it because they'd be able to use it for their mission. So the economic side of this effort, anybody could do it. And the idea is that if everyone is participating in it, no one's disadvantaged by, painted by the idea that it's bad to be published.

Charles Watkinson: I had to mention some research projects that Mellon might to be considering, and at the University of Michigan and two of the institutions, that's a collaborative project that we've proposed to the Mellon Foundation to look into what happens at the institution level. And I think it's a major concern, or it's certainly a big question mark which we want to get ahead of, which is whether the institutional administration looks at where to take funding from. The press is an obvious place and the library budget is an obvious place. Just to clarify something, I mean, in the proposal rates talking about the AAU-ARL proposal, that is a first books proposal and that is a relatively manageable amount of money; but if we talk about all books, we do not yet know the dimensions of that kind of thing, and it could be substantial. I think that's definitely an issue to look at. Just one thing creates other issues or losses for authors and scholars. So when we started talking about the submission of this proposal to the Mellon Foundation and so on with humanities scholars locally in Michigan, their immediate reaction was, "These kind of systems are going to be fine for us at the University of Michigan, a well-funded research university. But we're very worried about our colleagues in small colleges, and we're very worried about independent scholars, and we're very worried about scholars in our network outside the United States." So I think we know that with open access journal publishing, a whole group of scholars are disenfranchised. And that is a particular concern I

think we need to have as we enter the open access monograph world.

Raym Crow: Well, again, I think that it places the focus on first books because there's really no reason to provide a submission for second and third books. I mean, the market model should work for those books. It's whether there's this positive externality for the institution that's using the first book conventionally. So I think Charles is right, but I think we need to focus on the AAU-ARL proposal for what it is, again, first books makes sense in that.

Helen Cullyer: To go back to what Charles was saying about disenfranchising scholars, that's certainly a concern in addition to independent scholars and adjuncts. I don't think you mentioned adjuncts just now, but we talked about it out in the hall the other week. And we'll see what further research and we'll have to see what the outcomes of research and planning initiatives are. But I think it's highly unlikely that most institutions would say, "Yeah, we'll give our adjuncts these pay-to-publish funds." It's sad, but I think that's the truth. And then we as a foundation and possibly as a fund, we have to think very carefully about the methods by which such funding might be able to be provided to the adjuncts and independent scholars, and this may involve Scholarly Communications.

Leila Salisbury: I'm going to change gears just a little bit. I wonder if I could ask everybody to just briefly, because I do want to leave some time for questions, talk about a couple of things that either your organization or within the Scholarly Communications ecosystem we should stop doing when it comes to how we've traditionally been disseminating the development of scholarly content. So what would not doing these activities do to improve the situation?

Charles Watkinson: I think as university presses, we have to stop creating Rolls-Royces when authors need Toyotas. And you would be amazed how hard that is to manage within a particular university press because there is a strong commitment to quality that is embedded in every university press employee. So it's a hard message, but it's a necessary message.

Raym Crow: And to that point, I'm sure that that's the case because an institution would only want to pay for that level of service that was needed potentially. So in terms of the press, myself, obviously, but what I would like to see people stop doing is looking for others to solve the problem. And I'm not saying anybody's shirking here, but it makes talking to solutions or presses, faculty, and institutions, funders come together to address the situation. And the presses stand for it unilaterally. The faculty obviously can't do it unilaterally, nor can the institutions. So I think there needs to be more talked about.

Barbara Kline Pope: I think from my own perspective, and it could be that the university press community might get there as well, when I read this question from Leila, I had trouble figuring out what she's not doing because I think it's having to break even, and in advanced scholarship, you have to stop doing things in order to make that happen as publishing has evolved so quickly. I mean, this is really fast evolution. So just one of the things we stopped doing a while ago were scientific publishers, and we spent lots and lots of time over the decades trying to talk bookstores into carrying our books. When the web came along and we could connect to our readers directly, we started to put our money in that and stopped trying to talk bookstores into doing that. And I think that while we have a rigorous peer review system and our content is incredibly high quality, our product is more like a Smart Car.

Helen Cullyer: We downgraded from the Toyota to the Smart Car.

Barbara Kline Pope: We had to.

Helen Cullyer: I guess I'll speak from a different question, which is what should we stop funding? And I actually had difficulty with this question because my original answer I realized was slightly problematic, so I'll just take you through my thought process. My original answer was going to be, "We should stop funding, and in many ways we have stopped funding, the cool, one-off digital projects and start funding infrastructure for reproducible forms of digital publication and especially these new forms of interactive scholarly works involving media and data and maps and all those sorts of things." And then I thought, "Well, that's sort of, that's hard to do when those forms haven't yet emerged." And sometimes the cool, one-off little scholarly project, what looks like one may be an example of a new reproducible form. So I think that's where we are. How do you pull project experimentation and really the development of what we think will probably be new genres and on the other hand push on as a funder development of some sort of infrastructure for something that yet maybe doesn't exist?

Leila Salisbury: I think you've described the quandary for many university presses as we think about how to allocate our own funds in exactly that kind of way. Charles, did you have something?

Charles Watkinson: No, I was just thinking about time.

Leila Salisbury: Right, go ahead. We've got about five minutes left. Open it up. Questions from the audience. Got a great set of people here. Thank you.

The Punishment for Dreamers: Big Data, Retention, and Academic Libraries

Adam L. Murray, Dean of University Libraries Murray State University

The following is a lightly edited transcript of a live presentation at the 2014 Charleston Conference. Slides and videos are available at http://2014charlestonconference.sched.org/

Adam Murray: Thank you, everybody for being here. I know it's the Saturday morning of the Charleston Conference, so you guys are definitely the very dedicated group here to hear about some exciting things, assessment. I know everyone loves to talk about assessment. But hopefully we're going to be able to make this a pretty exciting session for you. My name is Adam Murray. I'm the Dean of Libraries at Murray State University in Kentucky. And just to set aside any rumors because this is something the vendors love to ask, no, the university is not named for me. We're going to have a Q&A session after the presentation. But if you don't get a chance to ask your questions or if you think of something later that you'd like to follow up with me, my email address is up here along with my Twitter. I'll have this information again at the end of the slide or the end of the presentation if you didn't grab it at the time. So I look forward to hearing from anyone who has follow up questions after the fact.

Of course the theme for this year's Charleston Conference is based on an Oscar Wilde quote, and so is the theme for this presentation. "A dreamer is one who can only find his way by moonlight, and his punishment is that he sees the dawn before the rest of the world." So I thought this quote was very pertinent for talking about retention and things like student success, because in the context of higher education there is definitely a new dawn coming, a new day coming for higher education. Higher education is under an incredible amount of pressure from a wide array of stakeholders. And assessment is changing. The data is making different methods of assessment possible and libraries have to figure out, they have to find their way by moonlight with little guidance on how to use these assessment methods in order to demonstrate value and communicate impact.

As librarians, we spend a lot of our time focused internally. We think a lot about our services and our resources. We take a look at uses. We spend a lot of time refining our services and resources. So I think it's good every once in a while for us to take a step back and really look at the very broad and complex picture of higher education. Of course everyone knows about decreased state funding. That's the first thing that a lot of people think about when they talk about the pressures that higher ed faces. So we'll talk a little bit about just how much state funding has decreased. But along with that, there are a lot of other pressures coming from the states and from the federal government, including an increased expectation for universal access. Everyone thinks of college and a degree now as the means of access into a career. This is a credential. So we want everyone to be able to do this. This is something that all students coming out of high school should go into college, get an undergraduate degree in order to be able to place themselves in a career. So there's an increased expectation for that universal access. Linked in with that, in order to make universal access a little bit more possible are increasing pressures to keep costs contained and to keep tuition low. Also linked in with universal access is the fact that a lot of our institutions have had drives for enrollment. We're admitting students that probably are not college ready, so we have a lot more remediation that we have to provide. So there's an increased need for students to take classes in order to bring themselves up to the necessary skills that they need to complete college. So those are some of the pressures coming from the state and from the federal government.

Other stakeholders have a very different and sometimes competing expectations for higher education. So for students they expect an idealized social experience. How many of you have been in some of the newer dorm rooms or dorm buildings on your campuses? They're nice, aren't they? They look a lot like a hotel. They're a lot nicer than what I lived in when I was an undergraduate. Students want that idealized social experience. They want what they've seen kind of perpetuated as a stereotype of the college experience: the tailgating, and the nice wellness centers, and fantastic residency experiences. That all costs money, of course. Parents and nontraditional students see higher ed as a credentialing agent for career advancement. They want, parents want their students to go to college to get a degree and to be able to move out and pay their own bills. And nontraditional students come back to maybe complete a degree or to obtain an additional credential or certificate to continue moving up the job ladder. So let's talk about employers. Once those traditional or non-traditional students graduate how are employers of our graduates thinking about the skills that we produce in higher ed? Overall, nationally there's dissatisfaction with student learning outcomes. Employers tend to want students that are able to write effectively, communicate effectively, and demonstrate critical and creative thinking, problem-solving skills. And overall nationally, there's a trend that they are not seeing this in our graduates. And then accreditation is always a fun thing to do, and it's always a constantly moving target. How many of you have had to rewrite some of your own self-studies because you found out some new standards are coming down from your accrediting agency or from some of the discipline level accrediting agencies? So these are a sampling of the pressures and the different constituency groups that have competing expectations for higher education.

Let's talk a little bit about the financial crunch for higher ed. And this really boils down the formula for an institution's funding model to a very simple set of three factors, state funding, tuition as a factor of how many enrolled students there are, and external funding, grants, fundraising, other sources of revenue. So a very simplified model. Nationally, state funding for higher education has decreased by ten billion dollars since 2007. And that money is not going to come back, even as the economy improves that money is not going to come back. And if it does come back it's going to come back in a different way and I'll talk about that here in a second. So tuition as another factor that institutions can use to control their financial well-being. The percentage of educational

revenue that is derived from tuition has climbed to nearly 50% in the last few years. And, of course, this is catching a lot of attention by the federal government and by state legislators. So they are increasing pressures to keep tuition down. So that really leaves . . . of this formula, setting aside the grants and the external funding, of this formula the only item that institutions of higher education have that they can do something about is enrolled students. So, keep getting students enrolled and keeping them enrolled has become a very high stakes endeavor. On the topic of enrollment, there are declining populations of traditional college age students. How many of you . . . I'm curious by show of hands . . . how many of you have heard this kind of rhetoric in your area, that high schools-? Yup, most. High school are not graduating enough students. There are not enough students of a traditional college age coming out of high school if we enrolled 100% of them to keep out institutions afloat. So this creates tremendous competition between our institutions in order to enroll those traditional college students. We try to lure them with these very nice residency halls and these fantastic wellness centers, all of which puts increasing pressure on universities' debt service, both for the university and for the state through bonds, which serves to drive up tuition as well because institutions have to have a revenue stream to serve that debt service.

There's also an increased focus on nontraditional students. And that has a very strong impact on the curriculum. Nontraditional students are again wanting to come back and finish up a certificate, finish up a degree. They're looking for something that is relevant to them and their immediate workforce needs. And so workforce development becomes a very driving factor of the curriculum rather than the traditional liberal arts focus. And there are the increased numbers of students that are not college ready. I know at some of our institutions there have been big pushes for enrollment, simply getting students in the door. And again, that has a pretty significant implication for the amount of remediation that we have to provide just to bring them up to be where they can perform in college. There's another factor in this and that is that the cost of recruiting students is higher than the cost of retaining students. So, think again about your own institutions. How many recruitment officers do you have working in your enrollment management office? How much travel do they have to put in? Institutions put a lot of money into recruitment and not as much into, necessarily, retention. I mentioned earlier as the economy improves, that funding still is not going to come back. And if it does come back, it's going to come back in a different way. And this is that different way, performance-based funding. Again by show of hands, how many of you hear performance-based funding talked about in the rhetoric at your institutions? A good number. I'm sure most of your institutions are talking about this because as of a year ago, 39 of the states were involved in performance-based funding mechanisms coming from the state agency that governs higher education. And I'm sure that there's going to be, with the federal scorecard coming out some time this month, there's going to be continued conversations at the different state level agencies about implementing performance-based funding formulas for determining state allocations and state appropriations. Some of the typical metrics included in performance-based funding formulas are the number of degrees awarded, sometimes for certain populations and sometimes in certain disciplines, the graduation rates, which again comes back to retention, transfer rates, so making sure that our four year institutions are working well with our two year community and technical colleges so that students have a way of getting a two year degree at a lower cost than transferring in and not having to retake courses and incur further debt.

And along the same lines of that theme of debt, the time and the credits to degree, keeping those low, making sure that students don't incur more debt than they need in order to complete a degree. Retention then becomes a critical funding issue really at two levels. You have the direct level, the lost tuition and the axillaries revenue that come from students that may drop out. But then you also have the cumulative effect, the indirect effect of the impact of lost students on institutional state appropriations coming through performance-based funding formulas.

Why does all of this matter to academic libraries? Why this bigger context? How does it impact us? Well, how can you justify keeping vacant lines when provosts and presidents are under pressure to move vacant lines into better revenue generating areas? I know at my institution, and this is just one example and I know that there are other institutions that do this, our VP for Accounting just finished a study where they looked at revenue generation, not at the degree level, not at the program level, but at the course level and correlated that into individual faculty performance. Big data is being looked at and used by accounting offices in order to really move around an institution's resources in order to maximize potential revenue. How can you make a better argument for improved collections funding? I know we've all had great luck at getting inflationary increases, right? So . . . and how can you argue for favorable positioning and campus master plans for renovations or new construction projects?

In this talk, why am I focusing on retention? I'm sure all of you are aware of Megan Oakleaf's report from 2010 that she did for ACRL for the Value of Academic Libraries committee. She outlined a number of different areas, provided a framework for libraries to begin doing better studies, collecting better data in order to communicate value to university administrators in order to speak their language. So, those items included student enrollment, student retention and graduation rates, student success, achievement, learning, the student experience, faculty research productivity. I've heard several sessions about faculty research productivity here at this conference that were great, faculty grant proposals and funding, faculty teaching and institutional reputation and prestige. Why focus in on retention in this particular session? It doesn't . . . you can construct a study on retention in a way that it doesn't rely on self-reported or anecdotal data. I know a lot of us do a lot of studies on what are impact is on different things of institutional importance. But a lot of times we tend to rely on self-reported data and that does not give us the full picture of what we're doing. And through this we can provide evidence of powerful correlations that can be directly tied into institutional performance and well-being. You can put a dollar amount on retention because we all know our tuition rates. In other words, retention is a low-hanging fruit in terms of talking about value and communicating impact.

Now there is a lower hanging fruit and that's GPA. And there are a lot of studies that look into the impact of use of the library on GPA. I chose not to focus on that because GPA at a lot of institutions is inflated. You have grade inflation taking place. And it's not really an indicator or much of anything. We have students that are graduating that haven't learned anything. This is being demonstrated through things like the NSSE, the National Survey of Student Engagement. They've gone through their degree program with minimal work and they're coming out with 4.0s. So a GPA really is not as much of an indicator of true impact. To ground our conversation of retention in some solid theories or models there are two very defining models of retention that have been proposed, starting with Tinto back in the 1970s. And his model is a very sociologically oriented theory. At the opposite end of the spectrum is Bean's model which was put forward in the 1980s and it very much focuses on psychology. There are a huge number of models and theories and studies in between these two kind of primary ones that have tested each of them, tried to disprove or prove elements of each of them, have modified, adopted, blended. There's a huge range of theories in the student retention. But these two are really the foundational theories of student retention.

Tinto's model is the first one, is the very groundbreaking, paradigm setting theory. His model is the model of student integration and again it's sociologically grounded. It's grounded in cost-benefit analysis, economics and in Durkheim's theory of suicide. Tinto reasoned that students that dropped out probably had insufficient integration with the prevailing value patterns of their institutions, and went through a longitudinal series of cost-benefit analyses to determine a point at which it was no longer worth their while to be in higher education and they dropped out or stopped out. This really . . . he has two domains within this theory, academic integration and social integration. The idea being that students that want to finish a degree will

have a goal commitment and that they will be integrated into their curriculum. They'll feel connections with the faculty that teach their courses. They'll be engaged with the content of what's being discussed in their courses. That they are very highly academically integrated. In fact, academic integration can overcome a lack of social integration. If a student is at an institution where they don't really have a peer group, they don't feel connected and this is increasingly the case with non-traditional students who don't spend a lot of time on campus, academic integration and goal commitment can overcome a lack of social integration. Social integration is of course the feeling, the sense that the students are integrated in with their peer groups, that they have a connection with the institution. And this also maps into a concept of institutional commitment. So a student may have always dreamed of graduating from a particular college. That dream of graduating from a particular college may override a lack of academic integration if they don't necessarily feel connected with the faculty or with their degree program. Those are the basic tenets of Tinto's model.

There are a few obvious weaknesses. It does not account for nontraditional students. It assumes that students are going to be traditional, first year, first time, full time freshmen. It doesn't account for minority students and it doesn't account for the impact of external influences, which Bean's Model of Student Motivation does. So moving into the psychological side of the theories, Bean's model argues that dropping out of higher education is a behavior and behavior is psychologically motivated. He mapped out four domains: academic performance, background variables, intent to leave and environmental variables. And the environmental variables are really the key for Bean's model that really sets it aside. This accounts for such things as finances, employment, external encouragement or support from family or friends, whether a student may have family responsibilities for a child or for an aging parent, and whether or not there are opportunities to transfer. Of course, with more and more online degree programs, the opportunities to transfer really begin to overcome some of the geographic limitations, especially for nontraditional students that they encountered in the past. The weakness for Bean's model of course is that it portrays drop out behavior as a pathology because it's grounded in psychology. But between these two models, both of which have a lot of elements that make a lot of sense, there have been a lot of studies into both of them trying to prove or disprove elements of them. Ultimately they have found that really both of them apply, that there are elements of both of them that take place in a student's decision to drop out. Retention is a very complex set of decisions that a student goes through in order to make a decision to stay enrolled or to drop out.

Out of both of these theories and all the myriad of studies and other examinations into retention since then, the concept of engagement has really come out. Engagement is defined by George Kuh as the level of investment in higher education in which students spend significant time and energy on educationally purposeful activities. George Kuh is actually the man who is primarily responsible for the development of the National Survey of Student Engagement, the NSSE. I'm sure many of you have heard of this at your institution because a lot of our state agencies require us now to implement the NSSE on a multiyear cycle. Coming out of the NSSE is also the FSSE and several other related surveys. But building off of the NSSE, which has been around for a while at this point and has accumulated a very large national data set on student engagement, the American Association of Colleges and Universities have adopted ten educationally purposeful activities as high impact practices. They're saying that these are practices that our institutions can put into place that have a very positive impact on engagement, and through engagement on retention.

With retention being such a complex set of interactions between the external environment, resources, family, integration with the institution, there are a lot of factors that institutions of higher education don't have any control over. But the things that we do have control over can be narrowed down into concepts that further engagement. These ten high impact practices include first year seminars, common intellectual experiences, learning communities, writing intensive courses, collaborative assignments and projects, undergraduate research, diversity and global learning, service learning, internships and capstone courses and projects. How do high impact practices relate to academic libraries? Kuh, along with several others that he has worked with on defining these practices, have discussed the fact that a lot of these high impact practices require time spent outside of the classroom in informal academic environments. And they have even indicated the library as such, as an informal academic environment that provides a great place for students to fulfill the practices that further engagement. High impact practices require integration of ideas or information from various sources including diverse perspectives in class discussions or writing, discussing ideas with faculty and students and others outside of class and making judgments about the value of information. All of these should sound very familiar and very relevant to what we do in libraries.

There have been a number of studies already done on the connection between academic libraries and retention. These tend to focus on studies of space or collection use, correlations with expenditures, and the impact of instruction. There are a couple of notable studies, Haddow and Joseph in 2010 and Haddow again in 2013, this was in Australia. Then Soria, Fransen and Nackerud, both in 2013 and 2014. These studies tracked individual use of different library services in order to correlate them with retention. So, Haddow and Joseph in 2010 and Soria, Fransen and Nackerud in 2013 found, by tracking individual use and correlating it with retention, that students that use the library tended to be retained from the fall semester to the spring semester. And then again, Haddow (2013) and Soria, Fransen & Nackerud (2014) found that students that use the library tended to be retained from their freshman year to their sophomore year, or first year to second year. So library use, and within that particular types of library use, tended to correlate with a higher rate of retention than nonuse.

Murray State did a variation of this type of study. We didn't seek originally to narrow it down to retention. We began our data collection in 2012. Our point at the time was to seek to calculate correlations between library use and different types of student success metrics. And ultimately we will continue to look at a variety of different metrics. But when ACRL announced their Assessment in Action program a couple of years ago we put in an application to use our data set and focus in on retention specifically for that project. Our study differed from the previous studies a little bit in that we also looked at the time of the semester that students used different services in our correlations between library use and retention. This particular project was led by Ashley Ireland, our Director of User and Instruction Services, with the data analysis being completed by Dr. Jana Hackathorn at Murray State University. Let me be clear on this. Our data elements track individuals. We track their use. And I know that that is something that sometimes gives librarians a funny feeling in their stomach. We track whether individuals check out an item. We track whether they log into a computer in our computer labs. We track whether they log into an electronic resource or if they log in to Illiad, if they are participating in an instruction session or if they are enrolled in one of our credit bearing information literacy courses. We have a few other elements that we're looping in to what we track, but this is what we started with. This was tracked using individual student ID numbers, was cross-walked through the registrar's database to an anonymous ID number and then lumped in with their retention data which the registrar's office could provide at the individual level. All of this data was then put through a binary logistic regression which allowed us to calculate the odds and odds ratio. What impact did certain library uses have on the odds of a student being retained?

We found some fantastic results. And these results . . . we actually have another set of data still in the hopper, and once we have that completely finalized, we're going to be publishing our findings. So this is still a preliminary set of findings. Overall library users are twice as likely to be retained as nonusers. So to put it another way, use of library resources or services in any way increased the likelihood of retention by 96%. Now that is something that a president and a provost can understand. Delving down into particular services, checking out items from the library increased the likelihood of retention by 36%, so getting back into the root of this conference, looking at collections and the impact that they can have on value. Logging into electronic resources, and this is where our study about the time of the semester factors in, particularly a little bit later in the semester, increased the odds of retention by 24%. And for those of you who love stats out there, these are very highly significant numbers. The statistical significance . . . that's always a mouthful to say . . . is less than .01. So there's less than a one in 100 chance that these findings happened by accident or by corruption of data. And the variance accounted for eight percent, so of all possible reasons a student might be retained, the library use accounts for eight percent of those.

There are actually two studies, the findings of two studies being presented in this presentation. And the second one looked at the perspectives of library deans on the role academic libraries can play in student retention by using those ten high impact practices as a conceptual framework. This was an exploratory study using 271 library deans at the public Master's Institutions in the US, which is all of them. We got a sample of 68. There were a lot of different types of data that we gathered through this survey and we put those through descriptive statistics, calculated Pearson correlation coefficients and also frequency distributions. The primary question was a matrix in which library deans were asked to indicate the degree to which library collections, library instruction, and library facilities were aligned with high impact practices. We know these high impact practices. Many of our libraries have services already in place to support them. To what degree are we purposefully doing that? Are we looking at what our institutions are putting into place to support retention and engagement and specifically trying to address those and support those? This was a Likert scale. Each interaction had a Likert scale drop down option. And just for the sake of displaying the data, there it is. I won't go into all of it but you'll notice that every single interaction between each library scale and each high impact practice, there's a double asterisk beside it, which also means that this is highly statistically significant at the .01 level. So again, less than one in 100 chance that this happened by accident or corruption of data. Pulling out of that some key findings: at a minimum, there was a moderately strong positive correlation between each of the library scales, library collections, facilities and instruction, with each of the ten high impact practices. This confirms what we already know. Libraries are supporting these high impact practices. We are putting our services and our resources into place in order to support these things that help keep students retained.

Of those, library instruction displayed a particularly strong correlation with learning communities and collaborative assignments, again, a finding that makes sense. Likewise, collaborative assignments and projects had an overall higher correlation with each of the library scales, collection facilities and instruction. And library facilities displayed a strong positive correlation with diversity and global learning. So again, our libraries are a place where students from different backgrounds and cultures have a place where they can work together. These findings shouldn't be surprising, but we finally have some justification in saying that this is how we are supporting these particular practices.

There were some troubling findings. That matrix was of course not the only question that was asked in the survey. We asked how library deans are documenting and communicating this impact. And as a big surprise, they're not. So we're doing these things. We are supporting high impact practices. We know from numerous different studies that there is a high correlation between library services and retention. But we're still not documenting it. A lot of them indicated that they didn't know how to go about documenting it. For those that were documenting it, they had very few methods of communicating those results beyond the annual report. Now I know we all put a lot of effort into our annual report and we like to think that it's read, but it's not. It's maybe flipped through by the president and the board. There was a continued overreliance on student learning outcomes as an

indirect measure of impact. And there was also a continued overreliance on self-reported anecdotal and satisfaction data.

To begin wrapping this up, between these two different studies, there are a few key takeaways that I'd like to throw out there for all of you guys. The first of those being enough with relying on indirect measures. With the rise of big data and how we can capture big data, there are changes in how we can assess what we do and how it impacts on things that university boards and presidents and provosts care about, things that are at the very top of their mind. So direct measures are becoming much more feasible. Indirect measures are still very important. We need to gather use data, door counts, download numbers, things like that. That's fantastic. Those help us refine our services internally, but they don't communicate anything to a president or a provost. You can tell door counts all you want, but so what? What does it mean? What does it do? So in order to do this, in order to have a better conversation in your libraries about how to do better direct measure, conduct an assessment audit to align the data that you have, that you already have. We all have tons of data from the services that we provide. Align your data with outcomes and institutional priorities. This can be very complex because we have, again, a lot of data and we have a lot of outcomes that we can impact. To help keep it clear inside the library, develop visualizations of your different services and resources, the assessment strategies that you can use to look at those and how they connect with items of institutional priority and focus. And finally, stop confusing student learning outcomes with measures of retention and graduation. Student learning outcomes are measures of student learning, right? It's an indirect measure at best. There are a lot of responses coming back from the survey that indicated, well we provide instruction and we have an impact on student learning outcomes so we assume that we're positively impacting retention. It is an indirect measure. Student learning outcomes are a direct measure of student learning, which again are very important. We don't need to stop assessing that. Higher education is, after all, about education. We need to have strong methods of assessing student learning outcomes. But we need to not confuse them.

Some other take-aways, use what you find. Close the loop within the library. I talk to a lot of places where they're trying to get a better assessment program started. And one of the things that I consistently hear is confusion about it and some resentment about the complexity of putting together such an assessment program. And a lot of times faculty and staff within the library don't necessarily understand all of the different interactions and all the different types of findings and why we're doing assessment. Communicate your findings within the library. And use your findings to refine your services and resources. Then find new ways to communicate your findings externally. Don't continue to rely on the annual report. Put together a communication or a marketing plan that accounts for all of your different stakeholders. These are just some of them: students, faculty, staff, deans, provosts, president, board. Of course there are others: alumni, community members, I mean whatever is the population in your area and at your institution that has a vested interest in the success of your university. Develop a communication plan for your findings that relates to them and to their needs and their interests.

Of course, there are some concerns with this kind of study. The first that I hear from librarians is on privacy because again, we tracked individual users. We tracked using the student ID number. We worked with our registrar to cross-walk that end with an anonymous student ID number. And we analyzed the data in aggregate. But taking a further step towards maintaining privacy, our data was categorical. It was yes or no. Did a student check out an item? One equals yes, zero equals no. We have no idea what they checked out. We didn't track that. If they logged into an electronic resource, we don't know which one. We simply know that they logged in. So you can structure your data in such a way that you're still protecting content while still looking at individual use. Security is another issue. Obviously this is some sensitive data so we had our data stored on an encrypted drive that was not on a network and the file itself was also encrypted. You'll need to make sure that if you choose to do something like this that you work on appropriate security measures for the data. And then finally, working

with your IRB and your registrar. Our registrar was very supportive of this. And one concern that I often hear, also associated with this kind of study, is FERPA. And our registrar helped us understand that as school officials, that FERPA has allowances for school officials to do this kind of study and look at this kind of data in order to improve the services and resources that we provide. FERPA is not really an issue and our registrar was very supportive. If you're planning to publish as you do this kind of study, of course you need to run through IRB. And our IRB office was very concerned. In fact they freaked out quite a bit. The thought being, yes libraries may have this data but we shouldn't look at it. You know, we may have it but we shouldn't look. Our registrar helped us navigate that process and ultimately the board itself was fine. It was just our IRB coordinator that ended up having the biggest problem with it. But we got approval from them and we have moved forward with it. Have these conversations with your folks on campus, registrar's office, and IRB office and any other entities that relate to the research process to address some of these concerns.

To get back to the original quote, there is a new dawn coming. In an age of big data, increasing accountability, tightened budgets, we have to figure out ways of doing this kind of study. And again, retention is simply a low hanging fruit. All of those other items that Megan Oakleaf outlined in her report for ACRL, we need to figure out ways to address each of those. And maybe for your institutions, depending on the focus of your president or of your institutional culture, retention isn't the one that you would start with. Maybe you need to start with faculty research productivity or grants. But take a look at that and figure out how you can start getting at it using some direct measures. It's very important that we learn to do that because this new day is going to get tougher and tougher in higher education as we have continued accountability standards that we're going to have to meet. And librarians need to be able to speak the language that provosts and presidents are increasingly going to have to use to determine resources. Thank you.

Let's Talk: Bringing Many Threads Together to Weave the Scholarly Information Ecosystem

Laurie Goodman, Editor-in-Chief, GigaScience

Howard Ratner, Executive Director, CHORUS

Greg Tananbaum, Owner, ScholarNext Consulting

John Vaughn, Executive Vice President, Association of American Universities

Moderated by T. Scott Plutchak, Director, Lister Hill Library of Health Sciences, University of Alabama at Birmingham

The following is a lightly edited transcript of a live presentation at the 2014 Charleston Conference. Slides and videos are available at http://2014charlestonconference.sched.org/

T. Scott Plutchak: Good morning. I'm always impressed with the intrepid nature of the Charleston conferees coming into these crowded rooms morning after morning. I'm Scott Plutchak, from the University of Alabama at Birmingham, and what I would like to do is welcome you to what I hope will be an interesting and engaging conversation for the next 45 minutes about some of the issues involved in creating the new scholarly communications ecosystem that we are all involved in.

I want to set the stage with what is commonly called the "Holdren Memo" released by the White House Office of Science and Technology Policy back in February 2013, which directed all of the federal funding agencies to develop policies and plans making the results of federally funded research publicly available. Now the memo addressed both peer-reviewed publications and data and it inspired many in the scholarly communication world to greater efforts and greater activity to try to address these challenges, which many people had been working on for a long time. Now we haven't heard a lot from the agencies since then but there's been an awful lot of activity across the systems since then. Much of which goes far beyond what was called for in the OSTP memo.

What we've convened here is a group of people who have a significant background and interest in these. What I hope we can do over the next 45 minutes is have some stimulating conversation,

bring many of you into that discussion as well. Now within a couple of months after the Holdren Memo came out, the SHARE and CHORUS initiatives were first announced. The two projects were developed independently and many people in the community saw them as being indeed competitive and there is some concern about who's going to win. But what we've seen over the succeeding months is that the people involved in those have really started to see a lot of opportunity for collaboration, a lot of shared interests, and there's an increasing amount of work being done together. And so to talk some about that, we have Howard Ratner who is the Executive Director for CHORUS, Greg Tananbaum who is working as a consultant to help shepherd the development of SHARE. Now I'm going to assume that most of you are basically familiar with the two proposals but I did ask Howard and Greg to give me just a little snapshot of where things currently are. And so, Greg describes SHARE as a "higher education research community initiative to ensure the preservation of, access to, and re-use of resource outputs. SHARE aims to develop workflow policy and infrastructure solutions that capitalize on the compelling interests shared by researchers, libraries, universities, funding agencies, and other key stakeholders to maximize research impact today and in the future. SHARE aims to make the inventory of research assets more discoverable and more accessible and to enable the research community to build upon these assets in creative and productive ways." And it's a joint initiative of the Association of Research Libraries, the Association of American Universities, and the Association of Public and Land-Grant Universities with funding from IMLS and Sloan.

Howard talks about the focus of CHORUS being "to efficiently advance public access to content, reporting on funded research and associated data. Services are available at no cost to funders, researchers, academic institutions and libraries, and the public. It's built on widely used technology thereby simplifying compliance, minimizing implementation costs, and enabling interoperability, text and data mining, and dashboard monitoring. It uses distributed access approach points to the accepted author manuscript or version of record in context on the publication site backed by a trusted archive. Systems currently in production with a commitment from the Department of Energy—they're in discussions with other U.S. and global funders. Project is managed by CHORUS as a 501(c)(3) membership organization with publisher members, affiliate members, funder partners, and academic supporters. It's growing and evolving through a membership drive, collaboration with SHARE, and exploration of connection to data repositories."

Much of the attention in the library and publishing communities has been on publications. The Holdren Memo lays equal stress on data. And it can be argued that the public benefit of access to data will be even greater than the public access to publications. There's been a flurry of activity in research institutions around the challenge of effectively managing research data. And on the publishing side, people really trying to figure out how do we connect publications to the data on which articles are based? To help us sort through some of those issues, we're joined by Laurie Goodman who's the Editor-in-Chief of the journal *GigaScience*. As Laurie pointed out in an email last week, there are basically five primary needs for data availability: release, accessibility, curation, tools for data manipulation, and permanent community-approved databases for all types of reusable data. Each of these has different levels of difficulty and different personnel and financial solutions and so we'll try to weave some of those issues into our discussion as well.

Finally, I want to welcome John Vaughn, whose experience on these issues is broad and deep. He's currently a senior fellow with the Association of American Universities. He was, for many years, the Executive Vice President of that organization, worked on scholarly communication, intellectual property issues, has many interesting scars from the political wars involved in working on that association in DC for many years. I first got to know John when he was the Chair of the Scholarly Publishing Roundtable several years ago. The recommendations from the roundtable, many of which were incorporated into the America COMPETES Act and many of which really informed the Holdren Memo and those requirements. So we're very glad to have John here. I can attest to his ability to walk the tightrope of balancing the needs of competing communities and figuring out how to bring them together to work on common solutions. I want to start with John, and start by asking him, from his standpoint to someone who's worked with the higher education community for a long time, what you see as some of the key issues and points that those of us who are involved in developing systems like SHARE, CHORUS, data issues really need to be paying attention to meet the needs of those constituencies that presumably we are all trying to support?

John Vaughn: Well I, I think, as Scott has said, there's been a long running effort that I've been involved in on a series of versions to try to get these various, and I think it in the past has been appropriate to call them various warring factions, together because within the higher education community, you have multiple perspectives. The broad mission of higher education and of particularly of research universities is the discovery and dissemination of new knowledge, and we have a mission with students, with faculty . . . And I think in many respects, this scholarly communication system has been and is working very well. We produce high quality research. Publishers do a terrific job with peer review. There's broad dissemination. There have been surveys indicating that many scholars think that they have more access to information now than they ever have. But if you look at it from a different perspective, say research libraries, there's been an explosion of cost, and sort of an undercurrent of what's the source of these increased costs, which have really been quite dramatic. There is some evidence in the past, and I think it is largely in the past, not totally, of exploitative pricing policies by publishers, commercial publishers making large profits, not-for-profit society publishers charging prices to generate revenue to run their societies. And that, many provosts see it as, well, tantamount to saying research libraries should subsume their responsibility of funding academic society. Commercial publishers have done a terrific job of providing high-quality publications and using the revenue in a variety of other ways that are very helpful to the community. The societies are extremely important to the university system, but essentially, some of the pricing policies have been saying, "Universities, you give us commercial publishers or societies some revenue that we will generate from the journals you buy and we'll decide how to use that money." And the decisions often have been quite good, but that has been a source of tension. The digital revolution has been seen by many of us as providing a way to increase access, reduce cost, and maintain quality. But as we work through this, and I should say that the increased cost to libraries and universities probably predominantly represents an increase in the explosion of research around the world. Me, I was astounded when we were working with the American Physical Society a few years ago that— and I think it's still the same—two-thirds of the authors of APS journals are outside this country. China, European universities, their governments are pouring money into them. They have seen the advantage to the economy that US universities have provided the increase and innovative capacity. So there's been an explosion in research. That's a good thing! But trying to figure out both in terms of cost and volume of this explosion of information how to manage it is really daunting and I think that's where we see, I think, less a way of reducing costs and more a way of expanding access using digital technologies. What becomes clear, and I think we will hear more today, is no group can do that alone. Universities can't do this alone. Societies can't. Publishers can't. We need a collaboration of publishers, universities, and their libraries, and even government. I say even government because I've over the years watched all too often good government intentions becoming bureaucratic ossification. But this OSTP memo is just terrific and I think that is launching a really good collaboration.

T. Scott Plutchak: I think it has, and I want to pull in Howard and Greg here. There was a lot of work being done, but it, and I know from the publishing community really looking at where does open access fit, understanding the push towards from government mandate, certainly within the university and library communities trying to figure out how to really change the ecosystem, the OSTP memo really sort of lights a fire under everybody. And we start these two independent activities, which have gotten quite broad. Can you talk a little bit about your experience with those and when you started to see those guys are also working on the same problem in a different way and maybe we don't agree with all issues but we really need to start talking to them.

Greg Tananbaum: Sure. I can, I can take first crack at it. Certainly, informed by what OSTP produced but not necessarily a direct result, this notion of SHARE was bandied about in early 2013 and, and John has been an integral part of that since the beginning. And initially, we talked about, in a working graph that was meant to be provocative and evoke feedback, and get the community involved. We talked about the notion of a network of federated repositories to house this public access information that was going to be under the OSTP umbrella. And in talking to a wide range of stakeholders, not just librarians but provosts and vice chancellors to research, and individual professors and publishers, and the funding agencies, and nongovernmental funding bodies, it became apparent to us that discovery is important. Discovery's very important. But there are means to discover content. There are efficient paths to discover content. What was more pressing was understanding, getting a handle on who was writing what and on whose dime? And understanding that in a timely and comprehensive and structured fashion. So all the stakeholders that I just mentioned, in some capacity, want to know that. They want to know in a, again, comprehensive way who is doing what and who's paying for that?

T. Scott Plutchak: And, I don't think many of us, certainly in the library community, realize how big a problem that was.

Greg Tananbaum: Yeah.

T. Scott Plutchak: I think we just assumed the funders are funding stuff they know what's being published and . . .

Howard Ratner: No.

T. Scott Plutchak: . . . that's not it at all!

Howard Ratner: Yeah, no, it's not that way at all.

Greg Tananbaum: And just to conclude this point and I'll turn it over to Howard, the notion that we have all these systems . . . We live in an amazing age, right? There are all these systems. We have institutional repositories. We have CHORUS. We have grant management systems. We have editorial management systems. We have personal productivity tools. But there's this real potential that these become towers of Babel—that they don't talk to one another. So, to the extent that there's an opportunity and a pressing need here, I know the way that SHARE have used it is, if we can apply some rationality to the ecosystem, that will be a service that will be very, very valuable to all of the players.

Howard Ratner: So for me, spending about 30 years in publishing, built a career on interoperation, right? So when I was approached with this problem—and but I wasn't there at the very start, of course but certainly got involved very quickly—I saw . . . There's so much need for interoperation—along the same lines that Greg was just talking about and there are all of these identifiers that I helped create or helped cajole to move along from CrossRef's DOI to ORCID's to other all the things and now, including some of the work that's been going on with FundRef. But they're not being used and they're not necessarily being used as widespread. They're being used in pockets. What CHORUS is trying to do is really try to pull that all together and make all of these different things interoperate and most importantly, make it itself publicly accessible vis-à-vis transparency. Everything about CHORUS is about transparency. Our search is completely

open. Our dashboard's completely open. And so when we started talking to SHARE, I said, "You know, what's the problem here?" Really, you have some very unique pieces of data that publishers don't know about, "research events," as you call them. I think that's a great word. Publishers obviously know about publication events and therefore, they could feed into the system. Everyone wants to understand the data. And the thing that's missing, really, especially in the data space, is good comprehensive data which supplies context. Because it's great, you can hand me your Excel spreadsheet. That's great. It's a bunch of numbers. I have no idea what context it was developed in. I have no idea who you are. Right? I have no idea what experiments were done with it. And so, context around that, again, metadata around the data is key. And so, you're absolutely right that when we started talking to the funding agencies . . . And this got actually started with my ORCID work first. It was so clear to me that they had no idea what happened to the research after they gave the grant. And this is the genesis of ORCID, quite honestly. It's because we said, "This is a huge problem." And first, we thought it was a publishing problem. But then, we opened it up and we called a summit and we had lots of people come from the university, we had lots of people come from the government and we said, "Wow! This actually isn't a publishing problem." The publishing problem is maybe 10 or 15% of the problem.

T. Scott Plutchak: Yeah.

Howard Ratner: It's a huge problem outside of it. And that's why, ORCID in particular, became such a collaborative effort amongst all the different stakeholders and CHORUS is doing the same. But the biggest difference, CHORUS is also about efficient workflows. There's already existing workflow that can channel most of this. That funnel already exists. The researcher pays attention to a lot of metadata when they go to submit a manuscript. So why not reuse that? Why not maximize that? Why not leverage that so you could reduce the burden on the researcher and then, up compliance?

T. Scott Plutchak: Okay. When you talk about efficient workflows and I think about my life in academia . . . Academia's not known for efficient workflows. So again, it is something that is desperately needed. And then of course, you talk about data and as I said, I think, many of us looked at the publications because we've been so focused on open access as the publications. But you start to get in the data, and if you look at the work that Laurie's been doing at the journal, *GigaScience*, it really makes open access to publications look easy. And data is just a mess. The context issue, for example, that the physicist in the previous session said, "Oh, well, you know, we don't need librarians and we don't really need to make our data open and nobody would understand it anyway because it's all just ones and zeroes." Um . . . how do we start to address that practical issue but then also that mindset?

Laurie Goodman: Yeah. There's actually a number of things when you talk about mindset that is where people are like, "Nobody can understand my work." And I'm like, "The whole point of your work is for people to be able to use it and understand it." And in the publishing field, I've certainly had people go, "People have to stand at my side at the bench in order to understand this." And I've said, "Well, that's great for you to put out an advertisement that your lab is doing nice stuff but you have to explain this for people to use it." But data curation, being able to organize the data so that people who are not collecting this, is a major, major issue! And when you talk about metadata, that is the . . . When I look at your zeroes and ones, this metadata tells me what each zero means and what each one means. And librarians are curators of information. And that's really what data is. We were talking last night about how, you know, putting money aside and all that, I'm a strong believer in if it's important, we can figure out a way to fund it. There might be arguments but we can figure it out. Librarians are in a perfect position as already understanding the issues of organizing information and information is data that you can be a driving force for curating this information, for having initiatives within your universities to educate the researchers. You would think the researchers would understand that they have to curate it! But in fact, researchers

say as soon as I put this into the computer and I'm done with it, if you ask me three months from now or next week, I wouldn't be able to tell you what this data means. Well, if you're funding this with your taxpayer dollars, or you have people who are giving money to charities where their children are dying from medical diseases, do you want all of that work just put away in, into a computer and . . . ?

T. Scott Plutchak: As you say, they're focused on their particular thing.

Laurie Goodman: Yeah.

T. Scott Plutchak: I would say, by the way, we'd be happy to, any of you who would also like to join the conversation, come up to the microphone and I'll try to recognize you. You mentioned the money piece and many people who've looked at this said there's enough money in the system to do what we need to do but the challenge is of moving it. You've dealt with universities and moving money. How realistic is it to think that we're going to be able to persuade the people who run the funds in universities to make the kinds of decisions that need to be done to actually address some of these challenges?

John Vaughn: Well, part of the job of universities is to enable bright, energetic, creative researchers to do their work driven by their understanding of the discipline, investigate or negotiate their work, but there has to be . . . There's a point at which you want to enable researchers to follow their own logic but there's a responsibility back, most university research is publicly funded. We have got to be able to make a connection between this work and an eventual advance of knowledge. It may be years away, but unless we can connect what we are doing to societal benefit, we're going to . . . I think most of you are aware of the battles that are going on in Congress now: the assault on NSF and peer review and social science. But universities are really struggling with finding the resources. Research funding in this country has been flat for some time. We've been talking about ways of moving toward open access. That gets you into author pays. Where does that money come from? I think there are funding challenges and that is where I go back to this notion that we've got to have collaboration among the key players. I think the way CHORUS and SHARE are working together is exceptionally important. The government is now working, effectively launched by OSTP But, there's a public responsibility that we collectively have to work on.

T. Scott Plutchak: Yeah. To what extent in the SHARE and CHORUS discussions do you all get into those human factors thing? I know you're focused on the systems and the workflows but we were talking last night about some of the data challenges, and so much of it is getting to change the way that people think about this stuff.

Greg Tananbaum: I think one of the things that Howard and CHORUS have done well, and he alluded to it, is their capturing information at a point where it's in the author's interest to provide it. Right? The author's never more captive or the researcher's never more captive than when they're submitting a paper for potential publication. You know! Just by a show of hands, how many people here work in an institution that has a repository? An institutional repository? Okay, keep your hands up. Now, of you, how many of you have had success in getting authors submit directly to your institutional repository? [laughter] So when we talk about data, uh, for example, this is why, as a fundamental principle, CHORUS knows or SHARE knows or we do together as part of a larger set of activities, capturing that information as organically in the workflow as possible is critical. Because as you said, the moment they're done with it, they're done with it. And trying to get them to retroactively, the researcher, to retroactively go back and put out this information, it's simply not going to happen. So that's a challenge and it's a challenge that we collectively have to face.

Howard Ratner: But there's also capturing and using the data. I mean, publishers have been capturing data and institutions have been capturing data for years. It's not until you start to use it that you see the value it or the inaccuracy of it. So one of the interesting things is because of CHORUS, we're actually pulling that data all the through CrossRef and all the way through our workflow and actually showing it up in our search interface, people are saying, "That's not right!"

And why isn't the Department of Energy showing up there? We know that that's about physics—why isn't it there? And so, the publishers that are part of my group have really been tweaking those interfaces and working with FundRef. And FundRef actually, when it started, had all of—what?—about 2,000 entries? Okay? So this is identifying all the various different funding agencies and departments around the world. It's now up over 8,500 terms worldwide! And again, why is this happening? Because it's being used! If it's not going to be used, it's just going to be dormant and then, no one really knows if it's good. And by the way, that's the other thing that we're doing. It's like we worked with Portico. And for the first time ever, we're saying, "Okay. You know, the publisher says that that DOI or that work is actually archived at Portico." But we actually asked the question. We say, "Here's a bunch of DOIs that we're actually monitoring. Do you actually have this?" And we're making that public to all of you.

T. Scott Plutchak: A question from the floor.

Gail Clement: Hi. I'm not sure it's a question. It may be a comment. And it's also a little plug for a lively lunch presentation later today. I'm Gail Clement. I'm at Texas A&M University in the Schol-Comm office and I work directly, my colleagues and I are the ones that would actually be working at worm's eye view. Where y'all are at about either space shuttle view or . . . you're very high level. And I think when we start to wrestle with how we implement stuff to support our campus authors to be aware and ultimately to comply with policies, mandates, and practices, you know, what I feel is there's this ginormous missing link. That's what we're going to talk about in the Empowering Data (lively lunch session). By the numbers, at the end of the day, the average researcher on campus who knows the most about that data—because they're the ones collecting it, curating it, and best qualified to document it in a rich way so it could be made reusable by others—are the graduate students and the postdocs. You know, I'm going to share this in our lively lunch, but there's 29,000 faculty out there in the US. There's 1.7 million graduate students and there's about 90,000 postdocs. So the scale of not closing this gap . . . And when we start looking at practices around how we treat graduates—I'm going to, specifically with graduate scholarship is what we're going to look at later today but . . . The point is they're being mandated to put their scholarship behind a pay wall. They're being mandated to roll everything up into big, fat, chunky PDFs because that's the most operationally manageable way for most of our campus repositories, whether it's bepress or dSPACE. If you actually look at the problem space for trying to get our campus authors to meet you somewhere in the middle and be able to meet your high level objectives, we've got to close that gap. And I'm not sure our campuses can handle new formats. And it's . . .

T. Scott Plutchak: Yeah. Well, I think some of that is Howard's emphasis on workflows and existing stuff to try . . . And I think SHARE at the same time also looking at how do we leverage those existing things on the ground level? And figure out how to link 'em up? But it's, it's huge and I see Laurie's nodding as you're . . .

Laurie Goodman: I must answer! You know, I see problems as sort of an exciting moment to how can we answer this? I love problems. And one of the things . . .

T. Scott Plutchak: You're in right field.

Laurie Goodman: Yes! One of the fields . . . Well, all fields have problems. One of the things that you're talking about is the grad students are the ones who know what they're collecting. Now, they know what they're collecting but they don't know how to write it down. There are no tools. None! Available for people to properly curate. What if you're out in the field? In the jungle collecting stuff? You don't have a, you know, a PDF maker out there and PDFs aren't searchable. Librarians interacting directly—don't wait for it to come to you! Create initiatives at your university where librarians are engaged with the researchers where you understand what is going on. You don't need the details of exactly how this experiment is going to work but you need to be able to engage in a conversation at the time that they are developing these experiments. Don't wait until they're publishing. I have a bio-curator with my journal

because by the time it comes to us, that data is in a disastrous format and we have someone who walks them back through it. You guys are in that place! You could do it at the beginning.

Gail Clement: Well, can I just do a Part B follow up?

T. Scott Plutchak: Yes.

Gail Clement: Because I really appreciate what you're saying, and I think many of us here are right there with you. The concern and the challenge we face is that in the case of graduate stuff, we know what we would like to see happen. But the problem is that when it comes graduate scholarship in particular, and I would argue probably also postdocs, 1) these are transitory linkages to the data set. They are not the persistent curators over time. So that wouldn't be enough if we don't catch the PI, their faculty adviser, because they have the long term. Postdocs, we now know that "Scholarly Kitchen" Phill Jones piece on the state of postdocs and in some cases, there's more po-, you know. In chemistry, most research is being done by a PI as a postdoc, than as faculty. These are people that don't necessarily have a long-term relationship so we won't get there. The other thing is that administrators are driving the bus. We know what we would like to reach out to them, and many of us are very engaged in outreach and learning, and teaching and learning efforts. But in many of our institutions, those early career people have minimum agency over their choices. They are out of power. And we can talk to them about what it would be nice to do, but I've been on a task force at A&M for now two years just to hash out the IP rights—not only in the dissertation but in all that constellation of research output, you know, the underlying data, and authorship epics. So, until our institutions honor the agency of our early career researchers that are doing the most heavy lifting around creating research, I'm not sure how effective a librarian, who may be also a faculty member in many of our cases, we can go toe to toe as faculty members, but as long as there's no agency with the users . . .

Greg Tananbaum: And some of this, some of this is certainly . . . I mentioned at the outset, workflow infrastructure and policy. And on the policy perspective, if you look at PubMed Central for example. When NIH stepped up enforcement and made it clear that if you didn't comply, you were at risk at not getting future funding, suddenly that became, the numbers jumped up. So there is a policy component. This isn't front and center of what SHARE is doing at the moment but certainly, we talk to lots of folks at the university administration level and at the funding agency level about the impact of existing and potential policies in attracting compliance.

T. Scott Plutchak: Yeah, you know, we're talking here about the need to get these larger communities working collaboratively, but the problem on individual university campuses is huge because they tend to be so siloed. As you were talking, I was thinking, two threads—one is so much of the work that Howard has done even prior to CHORUS is developing those kinds of linkages that can create that persistence through CrossRef, through ORCID. But then also looking at what John has done from the association level is the associations of universities have got to put pressure on their members to recognize that these needs require different interactions on our campuses and there has to be room to develop those extra kinds of agencies that you talk about.

Fred Dylla: Fred Dylla, American Institute of Physics. I want to pick up on Greg's last point. The beauty of the OSTP memorandum was its highly nuanced language that allowed many solutions to boom. The danger of the OSTP memorandum is the same language. And I think the nightmare scenario we all have—whether you're an university, university administrator, a librarian, a publisher—is we'll have 41 different mandates from various federal agencies. I think one possible way—and I'd like to hear your comments on this—to guard against this chaos is for our colleagues in the federal agencies to see the universities and the publishers and the data management community working together to establish a rational way as to move forward. What are your comments on the ability . . .

Greg Tananbaum: I would say, Fred, it's difficult to coax and cajole graduate students and post-docs to do what you want them to do. I don't think it's much easier to coax and cajole agencies

to do what we want them to do. I wish it were, but I think there's a sense—and you can weigh in here, obviously, too—the agencies are going to do what they're going to do. Universities have tried to inform the process by which they've set forth their answers to the Holdren Memo, and publishers have tried to weigh in on there as well. But the publishers are going to do what they're going to do. And of course, that's a, potentially a tremendous burden for many people in this room. I mean, you think about, as you said, from an institutional perspective, if the vice provost for research office, president for research office has to make sure, as a condition of funding, that these mandates have been fulfilled or have been complied with, and there are 41 different ones, and people get funding from multiple sources, the coordination problem is a mess! It's absolutely a mess. So I agree with you. To get out in front of it is important. But ultimately, I'm not sure how much influence we potentially have to move their policies.

John Vaughn: Let me add something there. There was one line that John Holdren put in his memo that to the extent feasible, agencies should try to coordinate their policies. They're aware of this. And I know a goal of SHARE, and I think of CHORUS, is to first . . . There are a lot of behind the scenes conversations with agencies to try to minimize the nightmare you talk about, Fred. And I think there'll be some success there. But the other responsibility we have is to try to protect our researchers from having directly to spend time responding to all these different compliance rules. There was a study recently that indicated that of the faculty members' time in research, 40% of it is spent in administrative compliance. You could argue that that's a generous percentage that is being taken away from created work into bureaucratic work. And I think part of the job of CHORUS and SHARE is to try to minimize that. So we've got to have multiple conversations. There will necessarily be agency differences, sometimes driven by disciplinary differences. But I do think we all need to focus on trying to avoid that kind of nightmare disparity and I think we will have some progress on that.

Fred Dylla: I think that the agencies have admirers. The fact that FundRef started, ORCID started, DataCite started; you ask the typical graduate students down in the trench, they think ORCID's a flower. They never heard of CrossRef. [laughter] So these have to be, as both Greg and Howard have mentioned, behind the scenes thing that take care of that magic moment when a data set is being sent in to DataCite to get an identifier or the manuscript's being sent in. We need to do more of that.

Greg Tananbaum: And to that point, I'll just give a plug for you here. If you are going to walk away with one action item in the audience, evangelize ORCID on your campus. It makes life easier. It makes life easier for publishers, for funding agencies, for institutions. We need to be able to know who is doing what.

Howard Ratner: Right. The . . . But, but ORCID is one thing. And that's definitely a grease in the wheels and that's great. We want more grease in the wheels. We want to make things move along. But actually, with what we're talking about today, much more important than ORCID actually is FundRef. Because if we can't identify the content, actually, the whole system breaks down—and that includes everything along the way. So we need to be able to identify this content. So I would say . . . Yeah, ORCID's great. Do that. Please do that.

Greg Tananbaum: And while you're talking . . .

Howard Ratner: And while you're talking to them, encourage when they submit their manuscripts to fill out those screens that are on every single manuscript tracking system now that say tell us about where you got your grant from. Okay? It's very simple! Usually it's two fields and in some experiments or some articles, it could be as many as five or what have you. But the more you fill that out, the more transparent information we have and data so we can actually make some logical, informative decisions. Because one of the things that I've experienced by talking to these agencies . . . And you're right, they're tough to influence. Right? I'm not even trying to influence them one way or the other. I'm just trying to present them with data that there is data available that they are not even aware of. They

don't know what happens on the institution campus. They have no idea of the publishing workflow. They don't know what CHORUS is. They don't know what ORCID is. Some of them do know about FundRef—the larger agencies do. But we need to really get out there and speak to them so that they understand our language and they understand what we've already built, what we've already worked together on so that they don't redevelop it.

T. Scott Plutchak: But again, part of the challenge on the ground, when you're talking about getting them to fill out the form. On an institute like mine, which is heavily invested in big center grants, any particular paper that author is not entirely sure what he or she is being funded for . . . And again that comes back to those of us on the ground in the institutions doing that educational work to try to keep that going. Question, comment here?

Marilyn Billings: Marilyn Billings from UMass-Amherst and kind of a comment and a suggestion. We've done a lot of work working with our graduate school and with our office research, but one of the comments I hear from our VC for Research is, "I don't see what librarians bring to the table. I don't see what the added benefit is. Why do librarians know about data? Or any of this kind of works?" So, comment to AAU and ARL also is that when we have our programs for our chancellors, our provosts, the research officers, it would be very useful to bring in a panel that would talk to them about all of these elements and what librarians are bringing to that table.

Laurie Goodman: I actually want to speak to that because we're at this meeting where you're all here. And I think what you need to have, absolutely, is each of you've brought up a particular problem. There should be sessions where everybody who has that problem comes together and says what can we do about it? How can we move our academic organization forward? What powers do we have and who do we have to engage? When everybody raised their hand with a database and then lowered it . . .

Howard Ratner: That's the problem.

Laurie Goodman: That's because it's hard to do. But what was interesting was how many people raised their hand for a database. All of you people together have expertise in knowing, creating a database, and not being able to get people to populate it. You're all smart. You should have a group that comes together. I mean, librarians are the ones who created the cross-sharing between libraries! You guys are already organized on getting people to share. And that expertise, I think, is lost a lot of times because it's not directly addressed when every library in the world is here.

T. Scott Plutchak: Right. We're close to end of time. John.

John Vaughn: Just, just quickly to respond to. I think that few of the UMass-Amherst administrators are somewhat idiosyncratic. AAU's now worked with ARL on a task-force for a couple of years that grew out of precisely the meeting you were talking about. We had the head of ARL and the librarian and the publisher meet with our chief academic officers at their annual meeting about three years ago. That led to a task-force that is, some of you heard about this yesterday. We're focusing on trying a new way of handling book publishing. But we also had an initiative on scholarly journals that was turned into SHARE. So I, I think on most campuses, provosts are acutely aware of the key role that research libraries have played and will play even more so in the future. But again, it really is a challenge on these enormously complicated research universities just to get people within a single institution talking to each other.

T. Scott Plutchak: Right.

John Vaughn: But we're working on it.

T. Scott Plutchak: We're out of time. We could go on like this for a long time. I want to thank all of you. I hope what we have done is given you a little bit of a way of thinking about how these things interact, what our various responsibilities are to reach out, as Laurie said, to each other and take advantage of that, but also to reach out beyond into those other communities which are absolutely essential if we're going to get it to where we want to go. Before I end, I need to thank a couple of people who are not here who were very helpful in putting this together. My other colleagues from the roundtable: Fred Dylla who is here, Crispin Taylor, Judy Ruttenberg from ARL helped put this together, Alice Meadows, Liz Ferguson from Wiley, and a big hand for my conspirators up here for participating in the discussion. All right. Thank you all very much.

Being Earnest in the New Normal

Anthea Stratigos, CEO, Outsell

The following is a lightly edited transcript of a live presentation at the 2014 Charleston Conference. Slides and videos are available at http://2014charlestonconference.sched.org/

Anthea Stratigos: Good morning! Good to be with you this morning. It's a pleasure. Thank you, Katina. Thank you, Anthony, for being here and welcoming me to Charleston. I've not been to this event. I've long wanted to be. It's an honor to be here, up in front of you, this morning. So we're going to talk a bit about being earnest in the new normal, and what that looks like. I'm passionate about libraries. I've got an aunt who recently passed away. She worked 40 years at the VA hospital in Sheridan, Wyoming. And I've been a patron of libraries since I was a very little girl. And for the last several years, we have been advising libraries, and advising publishers and information providers, about changing market demands, what's happening with new technology, disruptive competitors, and the landscape, and how it's changing in the information industry.

Katina asked me to spend two minutes telling you a little bit about Outsell. We're a 45-person team. We have about 20 analysts, who research, and track, and analyze the information industry every day. We've been doing this for about 18 years, and we bring insights from our research, from our analysis, from our daily log with you. And I'm going to share our perspective this morning, a topic I'm very passionate about, which is strategic marketing and its relationship to libraries. We're going to move onto that topic now.

But first, I'm going to start with just a little story. A few weeks ago, we just came back from a business trip overseas. And on that trip I had two little vignettes happen that I reflected on later, and realized they were both about libraries. I'll tell you a little bit more about them at the very end, but I'm going to ask you to think about Dewey: Dewey Readmore Books, and *22 Jump Street*. Kind of a brain candy movie, but there's a little twist about

libraries in there, and I want you to hold that thought.

What's happening in the information industry, and what's happening in the big picture? And I'd like to start with, I'm a storyteller. I like to use analogies, and, and give people things to think about that relate to maybe other instances. So I'm going to start with the, a story about an industry that in 1960, the established players had 99% market share. They ruled their industry, and shortly thereafter, came a new technology. A very disruptive technology. The new technology was so sophisticated it had about 600 patents, compared to the technology of the incumbents. Within 20 years, the new disrupters had taken 50% market share, and within another 20 years, had 99% market share. In 40 years, the incumbents went from 99% market share to 5% market share, and the new technology, which now has about 1,000 patents associated to it, completely dismantled the industry. Dramatic (shows slide of cloth vs. disposable diapers).

Yes, yes, I call this the digital diaper story, because what's happening in the print to digital shift is exactly some of the things that happened in this industry. What's happening in brick and mortar? If you're in retail, brick and mortar, their version of print to digital, or cloth to disposable, is e-commerce. So many, many industries face new disruptive technologies. Not just the information industry. And you can see it's everywhere in many different industries. And I use this story to illustrate a couple of things. One, that an industry can be dismantled in a very short period of time, and shift happens.

All right, so, we're seeing shifts in our industry, and when shifts happen in industries, often what happens is they move to a more marketing orientation. So if we think about water, or coffee, or credit cards, Apple, and Virgin Airlines, in many cases they've taken industries that have been somewhat commoditized, new entrants change pricing models, it's happening in the information industry every day. These industries move to strategic marketing. They move to brand. They move to experience. They move to building products that are somewhat superior, but the superiority is really around that brand halo. When we talk about diapers, you know, they're not marketing what really goes on with diapers. They're marketing that parents can sleep at night, because there's no leakage, and there's new pretty things, and Johnny can work better during the day. And we see this at Starbucks Coffee we're talking about coffee. And credit cards we're talking about credit cards, but MasterCard is talking about priceless experiences. And I believe that this is happening in the information industry. That what we are doing, we're going through a shift from print to digital. From commoditization with information everywhere, and sometimes users not understanding value, or stakeholders asking why we're spending so much. And what we need to do is become better at delivering our experience in the library. Our branded experience.

Ladies and gentlemen, I'm going to stand here and tell you today that I believe librarians, and libraries, and library management needs to be better at strategic marketers. Now, you may say to me, Anthea, I've had to learn new technology. I went, I was trained in an iSchool. How am I going to do this? Now you're telling me I have to become a strategic marketer. And I am, because believe that the future of libraries, and the continued success of libraries rests on strategic thinking about our markets, and, looking at the portfolio of what we buy, and build, and deliver through the eyes of our stakeholders, and the eyes of our users. I'm passionate about this topic. I've been speaking about it for many, many years. I'm a marketer at heart, and I believe firmly that as we move forward, we have to think about what we do. And continue to think about what we do, and build on the innovation that's going on in libraries. It's an extraordinary time, a tremendous opportunity, and I am very excited about it, to be here with you talking about it.

Let's take it down a notch. We've talking about shifts. I want to talk about the information industry more broadly for a moment, and place the libraries in the ecosystem. At Outsell, we track

and analyze about $730 billion worth of information industry activity. There are many sectors. It's really a kaleidoscope. What these industries have in common, and these sectors have in common, and they're all in the business of information. Whether they're public or private, whether they have different information categories, whether they're print or digital, whether they're subscription-based, or ad-based. Their business is fundamentally about delivering information solutions, publishing to marketplaces. Libraries do most of their business with a book space, science, technical, medical, education. In this $738 billion ecosystem, the library market is about $25 billion of it. The industry is going through a lot of change, and I want to talk a little bit about what's happening with your vendors. Because it drives some of the decisions I'm going to ask you to be making as you think ahead in the world of libraries.

First of all, vendors are struggling with growth. They're dealing with changing markets, your needs are changing because your stakeholders, and end users, and patron's needs are changing. Talent gaps persist. New product management capabilities. Analytics capabilities. New types of sales talent. Changing cost structures are a big deal. I spoke with one publisher last week, and he said, "Anthea, our business is upside down because the notion of an addition doesn't exist anymore. We built our whole business around additions, how we budget, what our systems look like, how we manage inventory and production, how we quote a sales teams." Their entire business is in a state of paradigm shift because they have to think about modeling their business in completely new ways. Because the notion of addition. An addition doesn't exist anymore for them. Digital transformation is creating these constant shifts, and with it comes stresses on sales teams, global expansion, product development. And, the notion of dealing with business shifts that we just talked about. The vendors are dealing with it as libraries are dealing with it. And that growth arrow is an important factor. I'm going to come back to that in just a quick moment. Libraries, we do our research, we study libraries every year. Katina and I compared notes a little bit before this event. These are key issues that we see constantly rising and bubbling to the top. Many of them you recognize. You're leading the way on many of them as you change and move and innovate in your libraries.

I want point out a couple of things in dealing with these items. One is, number one, your vendors are going through it very similarly. Many of the issues on the two slides are the same. The other is that there's a constant need to innovate, and you can't innovate with all of these things all the time. So part of being a good strategic marketer, and why I'm advocating about being a strategic marketer, is because it helps you make choices about what you choose to focus on. Because we can't focus on everything. There's too much to do with too few resources, and the possibilities are endless. So we choose what we do, we choose our future, based on strategic marketing, understanding our markets, and working backwards. Library budgets are actually fairly stable. They've come back from the downturn. They're growing at about 3%, 3 1/2 %. We're just coming out of the field with our latest benchmark study, and this is preliminary findings. Staffing and content as a percentage are about the same, making up about 80% of budgets. And print spending is continuing to decline in libraries. We're seeing about 29% for print next year, and it's been on a continuous change. That shift is continuing is to happen in our industry. And also, vendors, and they're holding steady. And price increases are coming in at about 3%. We're hearing from libraries that the guidance from vendors is 3%. So here's the rub, ladies and gentlemen. That too many people underestimate and really overlook in thinking about what goes on between some of the vendor and library dynamics.

You've got budget growth at 3 1/2 %, and you've got price increases at 3%. Right away, your budget is pretty much going to content or people. But if the vendors have it their way, it's going to content. At the same time, those vendors need to deliver growth to their stakeholders, and normally, that's around 6%, 10%. If you're private equity backed, or if you're in a large, established society where the publishing arm has been profit engine, the pressure on growth is enormous. And

that's one of the reasons, number one, you see a lot of consolidation, because it's the only way that vendors can grow in some instances. Number two, what it says is that vendors are consistently competing for market share if they're going to get your dollar. And it's very important to understand that dynamic when you're at the negotiating table, or when you're planning, in, in the case of vendors, business planning. Because fundamentally, the market that's available is smaller than those who want to satisfy that market. And that's a dynamic that I think a lot of companies underestimate in the information industry. Budgets are fixed. They don't grow as fast as many publishers need to grow to satisfy the needs of their businesses, and their ownership. And while this is going on, librarians are very ambivalent about vendors. We asked in our studies about their perceptions. And one of the things that we believe is that these are going to be the things that differentiate vendors. Because the good quality content, and the unique content is now a given to be at the table. So better product management, better product delivery, better customer service, transparency about pricing, simplifying licenses. This is the list of things that are increasingly mattering to librarians, and what we want you, as librarians, to be looking for in your relationships. But the startling thing here is, and when we ask about whether librarians agree or disagree with these notions of vendors, they're ambivalent. The big majority of librarians are right in the middle. They're not, and, and if you look at the data, there are very few who strongly agree, or kind of agree. So we've got this problem, if you will, in the relationships. Especially in these competitive times. And librarians are increasingly looking at these factors, and we want you to look at these factors as you're thinking about the solutions that you bring in. Because you're a strategic marketer, and you're thinking about the portfolio and the vendors that are going to satisfy your needs.

I've been talking about strategic marketing. What does that look like? I come from San Francisco, it's been a great week for us. And, really, it's about executing and delivering value. And when you execute and deliver value the first thing that you have to do is have the right team. I'm going to switch gears on you. I'm going to take you on another little trip that our family took in 2008. We went sailing in Greece. My first time, my husband's first time to Greece, we're both of Greek origin. I learned some lessons on that trip about leadership and about marketing. And the first thing that I realized is that you have to have the right team. Just like the Giants did, this team, they had their roles, they had their names. I could go, Jorgos, Spiros, Tassos, Basil, like Bill, Ted, George. Right? So they knew their roles. One was the captain, one was the utility player, one was the engineer, one was the chef, one was the steward. They did not change roles. They knew as a team what they needed to do. Who played what role. They backfilled for each other when they needed to. So when you're in your libraries, and you're thinking about your teams, you got to have those roles and responsiblities. You've got to have the A-team, because in the market climate we're in, B's and C's don't cut it anymore. And I can tell you how many conversations I have, I mention talent on both of those slides about vendors, and about information professionals. Big issue is talent, because it starts with talent. You can't execute, you can't be a strategic marketer, you can't make decisions about your library without the talent at the table that's going to take you forward.

How can a library be a better strategic marketer? There's six steps to value, and you're going to say to me, "Anthea, I can't do all these?" And, I'm going to say, "Start small. Pick something." If you have to start some place, pick understanding your target markets inside your institutions and their needs. That would be where I would start. We'll go through each of these a little bit. But it's really important that you think about these steps sequentially. This is what people do at Proctor & Gamble, this is what people do at Intel, this is what progressive information companies are doing, this is what progressive libraries are doing. And we believe, through our research and the dialogue that we have with the market, there's much more room for improvement in this area. And this roadmap is the mechanism where you're going to be able to make choices, and manage your future in, in changing and dynamic times when shift happens. I'm emphasizing the F, just so

nobody in the back of the room has any problems with what I'm saying.

Let's start first with having a strategy. Ithaka Study, an organization I greatly respect. I've known Deanna for many years, and it startled our analysts when we saw this statistic. That roughly in a three year period, only about 50% of libraries have a strategic plan or a mission. If you don't have a strategic plan or a mission, you do not know where you're going. You don't know where your collections should be, because you don't have a roadmap to where you're going to go. Some missions are around the notion of learning. Some might be around history. Whatever your mission is, and they're all going to be different, because no two libraries are the alike. You have got to have a strategy and a mission. Where are you going? What do you stand for? You can change that strategy just like you change directions, sometimes when you change course on a cross-country trip. Strategies aren't fixed in stone, they adapt. Companies and organizations that we work with that are doing best in class strategy, are doing a rolling 18 month strategy. Very hard to do five years from now. Even in institutions with long, long histories, because so much is changing, you want to keep some agility. But you have to have some direction of where you're going. Building on some of the innovations that we're seeing in the industry and in libraries today. Understanding target markets. So I'm using market speak, and marketing speak, but really this about understanding your patrons. It's an exercise that says, "Who do I serve? Do I serve consumers at a public library? Am I serving administrators, and professors, and students in different schools, in a university? Am I thinking about serving lawyers if I'm in a law firm? Or am I serving administrators and doctors if I'm at a national library of health, or a medical school? Students of medicine, versus medical professors, or both?" So it's a very straightforward way of looking at who are the roles that we serve? What are they, what do they do? Who are those roles? What are the kind of institutions they're in? And it's a very simple framework to just take a look at, who am I serving? And because when you understand that better, it helps, uh, uh, focus again, services and library offerings. So we call it target markets, but it's really about, who are your patrons? Who are your users, digitally, physically, and otherwise? And who could they be?

On that trip to Greece, one of the things that's really important is to understand what users want. The captain and his team, were very focused on us as clients on that trip. They took care of what we needed, including times when they had to shift gears. This was a particular night, we were at a cove in Greece. We didn't want to port. We wanted to stay on that cove in the middle of the evening. And what that meant is the crew couldn't go on shore at night. They said, "No problem, Anthea." They understood what we wanted, and they were very gracious with us about what we wanted. In the world of libraries that translates to understanding those users, those target market users that we just identified, and we're evaluating what they want. How they use us. What they do. So we did some really interesting research not too long ago. I'm going to tell you a statistic that surprised me. We just did a survey of 400 university students up through college students in the U.S. statistically valid sample. Seventy-eight percent of them use the physical library weekly or daily. 83%, males, and they actually use the library more often. Libraries used online, only 44% used digital access to the libraries. So there's actually more use of the physical library than there is of the digital library, according to the study. We're finding in other studies that we've done, that students and professors are actually more tied to print than most other knowledge workers. That includes financial services, professionals, salespeople, purchasing agents, doctors. Huge reliance on print. 86% of students would rather use a print text book than a digital text book. Now, I could go on and on about some of these statistics. The important part of the statistics is that they're going to be unique and different for each of your markets, and you need to understand them. For example, when we asked the question, why do you go to the library? It turns out the biggest reason is to have a quiet place to study. The second reason is to do research, look up books and manuscripts, or write. And we purposely raised the question, separated online databases, because we really wanted to get a sense of what

the physical meant. Now if you are working your way to Starbucks-away your library, you might be making a big mistake if this is your market. Because they don't want the library to hang out and socialize. Trust me, my husband and I put four kids through college, there's plenty of places to socialize on a college campus. Right? So we may be destroying the very thing that our brand stands for. And I'm not saying, "Don't modernize." I'm not saying, "Oh, don't put any coffee kiosks." What I am saying is when you make those choices, make sure that you're doing it with the needs of your marketplace. What if the professors actually said, "We don't go to the physical library. We actually use online more, but we don't like the digital resources." You might make a different decision with your portfolio, but you have to look at your portfolio in terms of different kinds of patrons that you serve, and the users that you serve, because it's the way that you can manage stakeholders, and it's the way that you can manage decisions in how you're actually funding and supporting your library.

It's also important to benchmark. On this trip to Greece, we noticed, oh, there's plenty of big yachts. Those weren't the ones we were on (referring to a picture of a yacht on the slide). There's plenty of better views, and there's plenty of huge houses. So, again, this was 2008. This was before the downturn. Greece is still a beautiful place. I recommend it to anybody. But it's important to recognize that those things that are better, or bigger, they're actually opportunities to benchmark. To assess best practices. To learn how people got to where they are, if you aspire to have something somebody else has or needs. We just believe that benchmarking and understanding best practices is critical. Benchmarking, vendor portfolio. How many content providers do you have for patrons? How many typical users are you serving compared to other libraries and institutions of your size, or nature? What kinds of practices do you have in terms of strategic management that other libraries are using, or aren't using?

We believe that benchmarking your best practices is a really critical practice as part of the strategic marketing repertoire. If you are thinking about running your innovations forward, we see libraries that are continuously strapped with research demands with fixed budgets, with stakeholders that don't understand why budgets are so big. Or why they need to grow, and sometimes having the best statistics are the ways to do that, and understanding patrons is another way to do that, tying it all together. When you understand your markets, when you've had a chance to assess their needs, when you've had a chance to benchmark and evaluate other libraries in relationship to your work, then it's time to establish your portfolio. We constantly see libraries that are going and doing English as a second language, or doing videos, or doing the coffee Starbucks, and they're all great things. I just learned the other day that at San Francisco Public Library you can actually checkout tickets to some of the best museums in San Francisco. Instead of going to checkout a book, or checkout a video, I can check out a trip to the Exploratorium. Huge benefit. And I'm not saying don't do any of those things. I'm actually saying, "Yes, do them all." But do the ones of the all, that matter to your marketplace. So then you know what to drop, what to add, when to add, what to ask money for, what to target to whom. I really believe that in this dynamic time of change, and when shift happens, and is going to continue, that you've got to have the market ammunition around your institution, to work with your vendors strategically, and the collections that you're building, and the research that you're doing, or the discovery support that you're doing, in terms of the scholarly resource cycle. Or whatever you're doing, has to be tied to what's important to your stakeholders and your customers. You got to have a little bit of view on the rearview as you're looking into the road ahead. Then it's time to brand your experience. How many of you brand your library as a wonderful, quiet place to be? What if that's the most important thing? I'm not saying it is to all of your students. These are the students that we say represent some, uh, students in the United States, but yours are going to be different. They're all different. But then you can pick those services that you're going to, the collections that you're going to have, the databases that you're going to have because you know they matter, and you've got the analytics to support it. I know this is a

stretch. In some cases, there are libraries who are also doing it. I believe that it's just best in class practice in this day and age, and it's very important in terms of staying competitive. And having the questions that you can ask and answer for yourself for when you're also having to look for budget, and look for justification for what things that you're choosing to do, and what you might not be choosing to do. So brand your experience.

This is another cove in Greece. When you see pictures of Greece, you don't see all the graffiti in Athens. It's actually very ugly in Athens, sometimes. I love the Parthenon and the Acropolis, you don't see graffiti. You see this. When they're branding travel magazines or talking about Greece, they're getting you into that water, into that experience. So brand your experience for what you want to deliver that's unique to your users and patrons, and, and do it based on the things they've told you that matters. Market in purposeful rhythms. Libraries are under marketed. Go out, sit in stakeholders' offices, ask what matters. Ask what you can do for them? Put teams embedded into end users groups, where you can be better support for them. Have brown bags, use gamification. Make sure that you've got newsletters going out. Make sure that you're part of the community. You know, websites if you're in a public library environment. All kinds of things to do, but market, and market what matters. Not what you think matters, not what you've done to your library, but what you've done to your library that matters to those that you're serving. And make sure that you market. Because people aren't going to necessarily know about you, if they don't know all the things that you offer. I didn't know that my library offered me free tickets to the Exploratorium. I have a grandson that just moved up from Southern California. I want to take him there. I thought, "Great, I'm going to take him to the public library in San Francisco. We'll do something there, and then we'll got to the Exploratorium." I've just learned a new thing, and I more connected to that library as a result.

Deliver wow. This was a secret cove that we didn't know existed. Surprise your patrons. Have cookies in the library. Have book clubs. Make sure that you're delivering wow with whatever you're doing. Have actionable deliverables. When people ask you for research, make sure that you're delivering it in a package that might have visual design elements to it. Not pages and pages of search results, but actually finished product that is decision ready. Stakeholders, especially at the executive level, administrators, city management, they want the bottom line delivered in a way that they can understand it. And users who are doing research, they need to sift and understand the details, at the same time making sure it's easy for them to get what they need, really critical. So make sure you deliver wow.

This was a night that we wanted to go someplace quiet, and if you sail down the side of the sea, you couldn't actually see this port, because it was a secret entrance. It was an optical illusion where you could just see the two sides of the mountain coming together. And the captain just snuck us into this little town called Ieraka, means the hawk. And that was at dusk. It was a beautiful place to be, and he delivered wow, because we weren't expecting it. We didn't even know it existed. That's how you deliver that brand experience.

Very important to measure ROI and value. Very important. We did a study for the Group of Eight, university libraries in Australia, on ROI. There are methodologies to do it. And many of you are in environments where you have access to business students. Those business students need experience. They need internships. There's marketing programs in your university. You can tap into new talent who is dying for experience to do some innovative things, who can do the research, and get you some of the survey work that you need of your patrons. In fact, some leading edge libraries and publishers are actually having students work with design schools to create, and completely disrupt the way they deliver services. And say, "Design, design us for you. Design us the newspaper of tomorrow. The newspaper for your generation." They're in your midst if those of you are in academic environments. Tap into them, they're your market today and tomorrow, as well as the faculties. We're seeing that there is some resistance to change. Text books work, text books work. A lot of

professors still using print. We have to continue to shape the future, and edge people into the new world. Or actually, most change comes from vendors. Comes from information libraries making movements in what you provide, and measure the value that comes with not just usage statistics. Usage statistics don't measure value. They measure volume. Activity doesn't equal results. So you want to ask things about did you save time? Did you save money? Did you minimize risk? Did you get published? Did you discover faster? Did you get product to market faster? Did you solve a legal case faster? These are now called outcomes. You're familiar with them. Your institutions are asking for them. Part of delivering and building a strategy is to tie what you're doing in your library, your part of the institution, to the institution's goals. If somebody is measuring outcomes on student retention, or job placement for graduates, or publishing for scientific and scholarly research, you want to make sure that what you're doing as a library supports that. And you can deliver metrics that help you show that message.

This was an opportune moment. There was a school of fish in the, um, in the local cove, it was about 10:00 in the morning, and the captain went free-hand netted a whole school of fish. Brought them onboard. We were the recipients of the ROI of that experience, because we had a few of them for dinner. And then, because it was 2008 in Greece, they went for about $30, 30 euro a kilo. So our captain made out like a bandit that night, because he went and sold them in the fish market that evening. So, that was ROI for us and for him, and there's ROI in doing metrics and ceasing opportunity about how you look at collecting and building your story of value for your library. Be sure and play and enjoy the results.

There's a couple of definitions about being in earnest on the web and different dictionary sites. And one of them is about being serious, being solemn. That's not my picture of earnest. And there's better definitions out there. I actually put that one away, and went to the one I liked better on Webster. But it's really important in these demanding times, knowing that we have to be productive, that we focus on taking some time for us and our teams. And I'm really thrilled you're taking time to come here, and learn, and benchmark, and get new techniques, and things that you want to continue to deploy in your library. Take some time to enjoy the results, whether it's the dine arounds, whether it's a time to go swimming, whether it's meditation. Whatever it is, make sure in these demanding times, you are taking time for yourself. Because you can't be a strategic marketer, and go through the continuous cycle of updating your plans, and changing to make sure that you're responding to vendors, and responding to your patrons, and users without taking some time for you.

So this gets us back to Dewey and *22 Jump Street*. Any of you know these stories? Anybody know about Dewey? Hands raised. Okay. So on my trip recently, my friend handed a book over to me and said, "You've got to read this." And Dewey, for those of you who don't know, became the kind of patron cat in Spencer, Iowa. He was rescued one winter night as a teeny, teeny kitten on the verge of death, and actually lived about 18, 20 years in that library, and became a rallying point for the community. And that library took on a whole, a whole new aesthetic about it. Dewey was an incredible spirit and added to the ethos of that library. So like Anthony said, "Maybe in my library, I'd have a Labrador." Right? We'd have Labrador in our library. But Spencer, Iowa, had Dewey. A book was written about him. So here I am on this trip, reading the story of Dewey and the Spencer Library. I wasn't yet thinking about the Charleston Conference when this was going on, but I had an 18-hour flight home. And on 18-hour flights, I don't like super serious movies. I don't want to watch planes blowing up or presidential hijackings. So brain candy. I chose *22 Jump Street*, and it's a sequel to *21 Jump Street*. Love the movie. Silly humor. Love these guys. But they are sent back to college as undercover cops to bust up a drug ring, and the drug ring is working through drug trading that's embedded into the dusty books of the library archives. I'm thinking, okay, I've got these library metaphors right in front of me. I'm going to weave them right into Charleston.

It's really interesting because we can choose our future. If we really think about our roadmap, with

our management, and whatever that we're part of a team. And we're building our set of understanding of who are key patrons are, and users, we're going to do some needs assessment. I've got those business school and marketing students handy to do some internships for me and design some studies. And then I'm going to understand needs, and then I'm going to think about my portfolio, and my collections, and what I buy, and what I do, and whether I'm offering tickets to museums, or whether I'm offering ESL, or I'm offering digital or print or anything else. These libraries had two completely different paths, and each of you can have your path. Because you've got the tools to choose your future. And one of the things I loved about the quote in Dewey is is the following: "A great library doesn't have to be big or beautiful. It doesn't have to have the best facilities, or the most efficient staff, or the most users. A great library provides. It is enmeshed in the life of the community in a way that makes it indispensible. A great library is one nobody notices, because it is always there, and it always has what people need." And those needs are different for each of you. You're here to pick up best practices and learn new things, and when you go back, you'll apply some new renovations and new ideas. And I'm excited for you to do that, because you're modeling what's going to take libraries continuously forward. Libraries make a difference, they matter. What we do is a contribution to society, and how we do it is going to be different for every one of us. Because our stakeholders are different, our institutions are different, our teams are different, and the people that we serve are different, and they need different things. So keep that in mind when you're thinking about your library's future, because your library's future depends on the unique choices that you make to make sure that you remain relevant, and remain innovative, and continue to deliver and delight, and deliver wow. Whether you deliver the path of Dewey, the Labrador Retriever, I'm not going to get up here and advocate drugs, that's too far for me. Maybe that's the X, well that's the X of what not to be. Right? Not to be. We don't want to have the metaphor of the dusty archives. So choose your future. Have fun doing it, and with that, I welcome any questions.

The Long Arm of the Law

William Hannay, Partner, Schiff Hardin LLC
Laura Quilter, Copyright and Scholarly Communications Librarian, University of Massachusetts Amherst
Moderated by Ann Okerson, Senior Advisor to CRL, Center for Research Libraries

The following is a lightly edited transcript of a live presentation at the 2014 Charleston Conference. Slides and videos are available at http://2014charlestonconference.sched.org/

Ann Okerson: Good afternoon. Thank you for being here when you could be outdoors on what is one of the loveliest days I've ever seen in Charleston, but you've instead chosen to spend your time with our panel. So thanks for that. We know that we are just a few people standing between you and dining around in Charleston and everything, so we're going to try to be both informative and entertaining to the extent that we can so that you won't regret coming here. We're also joined this afternoon by our annual friend, Kenny Rogers, who comes to the Long Arm of the Law session. [music] Okay.

UNKNOWN: Did you have public performance rights for that?

Ann Okerson: Oh. We each year we invoke fair use on this, you know? What can I say?

Bill Hannay: It's the library exemption.

Ann Okerson: Yeah, the library exemption. Thank you. Our lawyers have spoken. But this is a theme song and maybe, Katina, maybe next year we can get everyone to sing it. Yeah, that would be great.

Now, to be a little bit less entertaining but more informative, I made a word cloud out of the abstracts and the bullet points that the speakers sent us in advance, and what you're going to see is that we're going to focus a whole lot in this session on things like fair use trends, first sale, and privacy, all of which are, particularly privacy, I think, are increasingly important issues for the folks who come to Charleston, the Charleston family, the Charleston community. Now, I exercised some liberty and asked the speakers not to talk about the Georgia State case. The reason I did this was very personal. I feel that this case,

which I thought we were having a nap over for a while, I thought it had taken so much air and energy and money out of various rooms over the last few years that we might just kind of give it a snooze. But then there was this big reveal in the last two or three or four weeks, and we're kind of back where we started from. Well, not quite, but almost. They may choose to defy me and say something about Georgia State anyway. So there you have it.

I'm going to introduce the two speakers right at the outset, and they will proceed in an orderly or not orderly fashion, and after that we will have time for discussion questions and answers. Our first speaker is Laura Quilter, who describes herself on her blog as a "librarian, lawyer, teacher, and geek." Whatever all of that means, I don't know, but I liked it. She's the copyright and information policy attorney librarian at the University of Massachusetts in Amherst. She works with the UMass Amherst community on copyright and related matters, equipping faculty, students, and staff with the understanding that they need to navigate copyright, fair use, open access publishing, and related issues. Laura, while doing all of that, maintains a teaching appointment at Simmons College School of Library and Information Science, and she has previously taught at UC Berkeley School of Law with the Samuelson Law Technology and Public Policy Clinic. She has a library degree, masters in librarianship, University of Kentucky, and a JD, UC Berkeley School of Law. She's a frequent speaker. She's taught and lectured to a wide variety of audiences. I think I will not carry on. I don't know if there are bios in your programs, but Laura's website and her bio are worth your time.

Our second speaker, return offender, is Bill Hannay, whom we have had the fortune of hearing at this conference over the years and in other venues. He is a great friend to libraries, and we are so fortunate to have someone in private commercial practice who really does have a passion for the kind of work that libraries are trying to do. He's a partner in the Chicago-based law firm, Schiff Hardin LLP. He regularly represents corporations and individuals in civil antitrust and complex litigation. He's an adjunct professor at IIT Chicago-Kent School of Law, where he teaches courses in antitrust law and international business transactions. He has held many leadership positions with the American Bar Association. And as I said, we regularly see him here. He's the author of numerous books on antitrust, fair competition, as well as other related aspects published by companies that we also see here, such as Thompson West, Thompson Reuters, ABA, and Bureau of National Affairs. His JD is from Georgetown University. His BA is from Yale. And I too will stop the introductions here. There's much more to say about Bill, but I think opportunities at the Charleston site will be abundant to give him the attention that he deserves as well. So I welcome our two speakers. Laura's up first.

Laura Quilter: Hi, I'm Laura Quilter. It's good to see you all, and I hope that my own voice doesn't give out. I've been wrestling with a cold all week, which is why I have this peculiar frog-like, or one of my friends kindly called it "Lauren Bacall-like" voice. I'm going to be talking about copyright, and I promise to be very brief when I mention the case that I otherwise won't mention right now.

In talking about copyright, I'm going to do it this way: two jokes and then one transformation in analysis. I don't promise the jokes to be funny, but there they are. The first topic will be first sale, because there've been quite a few things happening in first sale. Maybe it's been a little bit more subtle than our perennial favorite, fair use, but this is what I think of when I think of first sale. I think of first sale as something we all love, we don't think much about it because it is perhaps going away. Although we rely on it, it's receding in importance in many respects because of licensing. So *An Affair to Remember*, used bookstores rely on fair use. Here's the first joke, and this is a joke told by Aspen Casebooks of this year. What is a genius way, or maybe not genius, for getting around the used textbook market, right? We all

know that textbook publishers would like to get around the used textbook market, and the traditional way of getting around it is by revising your textbook every year or few years, just enough to change the pagination so that the professors have to change their assignments and a whole new textbook has to be bought. Aspen came up with a new model this year, which was to sell licensed access instead. And they did this with a program called the Connected Casebook. If you're familiar with law schools, how many of you heard about this whole little imbroglio that Aspen Connected Casebook? A few of you. Not so many. I'll tell you.

First of all, casebooks are textbooks in law school, and it's interesting because a casebook is basically largely, maybe 90% public domain material, it is cases, which are public domain. And the cases are annotated, so there's definitely intellectual work that goes into them. They're assembled, they're organized, they're annotated, and there is some smattering of other content, excerpts from articles and so forth. But primarily, they are public domain content, and so students, as you can imagine, are especially not really willing to buy them if they can avoid it. And because they're public domain, you can get your update just by downloading the case these days. And the other thing to know about casebooks is that although they are predominantly by far printed material text, they are just as expensive as those beautifully bound fully color illustrated biology textbooks that are hundreds and hundreds of dollars. So this market is ripe for disruption, and I think one of the ways it's been getting disrupted is students just not buying them and instead downloading cases. Aspen is trying to, on the other hand, disrupt it in another way. They're trying to say, "Well, how are we going to claim this market?" And the way they decided to reclaim it was through their program called Connected Casebook. Connected Casebook involved book rental, and the way they made it a book rental was they said, "We will sell you, we will still give you the print book, but you will return it at the end of the semester, and we will pulp it." They didn't say they would pulp it, but that was the obvious conclusion. "But in exchange, you will have lifetime e-book access to this casebook!" Now, this is perhaps of limited value, right? I mean, some of us lawyers keep our casebooks. Many of us don't because we prefer to get the money and we sell them. A few of us keep them, but they're not really useful references for many people. Maybe for some people, right? So this was something that was perhaps of less value than you might expect. James Grimmelmann, who responded to this whole program by starting a petition, James Grimmelmann said the lifetime access to this site is, these kinds of sites have the lifetime of a gerbil, so not exactly something that people are going to want to have forever. The announcement was immediately followed, literally immediately followed. The announcement came out around the 4th or the 5th of May and was followed immediately, maybe that day or the next, by a boycott which ended up with like 330 law professors agreeing not to use these casebooks, and these are some of the big casebooks in the field. On the 8th, Grimmelmann announced "Triumph! Victory!" because Aspen had issued a correction, a clarification, I believe it was, where they said, "Oh, well, students are not going to be forced into this program. Students will still have the option to buy the hard copy." I'm sure that everybody's thinking about what the next moves are, but I think this is just an illustrative thing case of what you can do with licensing and how the publishers are really trying to think about dealing with these hard issues.

Here's the second joke. When is an electronic good, by which I mean a thing, a copy? All right, if you thought the first joke was funny, then you'll really appreciate this one. When it is electronic. Because in the ReDigi case, how many of you heard of the ReDigi case? All right, a few of you. The ReDigi case was an electronic music market. If you buy your, usually if you buy MP3s through an electronics site, they're encumbered by licensing that says you can't resell them. And Apple did not encumber it in that way. They had various other restrictions, but they didn't say you can't resell. So ReDigi was a company that said, "Hey, let's set up a marketplace so that people can resell it on the marketplace." And that made sense, except to Capitol, who said, "No, you're infringing our rights." And ReDigi said, "No, I have first sale." And the court agreed with Capitol. Why? Not

because they said first sale doesn't exist, but because they said if it's an electronic good, you're necessarily making a copy, and they talked even about the bits. It's not the same bits that it was when you move it. I think there's lots of interesting philosophy here. There were also lots of interesting copyright approaches that could be taken because you could think about the intermediate copyings or different kinds of ways of getting round this. Nevertheless, we're sitting there with this precedent that says electronic goods do not have first sale rights because they are necessarily, inherently copies. This is not a precedent that I personally like. ReDigi rolled with it by rolling out their 2.0 version which, instead of buying it from Apple and then deleting your copy and putting it on ReDigi, instead, you buy it through ReDigi so the bits, the original bits, are on ReDigi's server. And now when you go to sell them, you're deleting your own copies of the bits, but they have the original bits. And they have smart copy control that actually makes sure these things are deleted.

So I said two jokes, and you might think that maybe ultimately, the joke is on us, the users, the people who used to own books, and I think that's kind of where we're going. So what is the future of first sale? More of these textbook and e-book experiments. We're all dealing with them when we are buying, when we're negotiating our contracts for e-book collections. The publishers are definitely trying to figure this out. The libraries are trying to figure it out, where it all goes. We don't know. But the secondary markets that we've all relied on as an important piece of our information marketplace are in jeopardy. I think it's worth thinking about. Licensing continues to be a piece. And the thing I want to flag about licensing here is that it's not just the negotiated licenses that we librarians deal with when we're dealing with our friends, the publishers, but it's also the EULAs that the users often have to deal with on top of those, because you're often seeing, either through software, the people doing the coding or the lawyers getting involved, or some unholy mesh of the two, that oftentimes once the user accesses the resource, they're still being asked to click a EULA which might have different rights or things that they don't know. That's something to flag. I guess the ultimate joke is on us, as I said, because Congress is looking into this question. There're hearings that they're thinking about. We'll look at digital first sale, and I don't have a lot of optimism about that. All right, so that's first sale. And I can't leave the question of licensing and first sale without my favorite XKCD cartoon ever where Mephistopheles says, "I come offering a deal," and the guy says, "Read the sign." And it's like, "By entering this room, you agree to forfeit your own soul rather than negotiate with the mortal residing therein." "Wait! Wait! You can't!" And then he's like, "Too late. You already read it so you have agreed to the terms." And this is "Mephistopheles Encounters the EULA," which is creative commons licensed. So that's my very favorite cartoon on this whole issue.

Then the transformation tale, and I think, how am I doing on time? Am I still good? I'm good. Yeah. That's because I talk fast. Okay. The thing that I wanted to talk about fair use, and I promise to be very brief when I get to the dreaded case, is what's changing, what's transforming about the transformativeness narrative that we've been dealing with for a long time. And for a while, there was so much talk about transformativeness that some people were even saying, "Look, it's just like fair use. It's not a four-step thing. It's practically a two-step analysis. Is it transformative or not? And if it is transformative, then too much or too little or any other thing that you might want to think of." And we have a whole bunch of cases that are telling us that that is the story, that it's all transformative. The first HathiTrust case came out, they talked about transformativeness. Google, the most recent case. And this art program, this art thing called Cariou v. Prince is sort of like this classic example of art criticism that a court was engaging in and saying, "Well, we've transformed, the artist transformed these works," and then it's three pages of art criticism, and I urge you to read it if you like art or are amused by judges doing art. So the Cariou v. Prince case. everybody was saying transformativeness is the key. But I would say in the last year, we really have had a little bit of retrenchment where courts are falling back. And so this is the thing that I want to tell you about in terms of fair use. First of all, there's a lot of question about just what does it

mean to be transformative, anyway? Some people are suggesting that if everything is transformative, if changing the mere purpose or changing the way you use it or doing any of those things are transformative, then it really swallows the whole analysis. That came out pretty clearly in the Seventh Circuit in a case recently about somebody making a satirical t-shirt where this very esteemed judge said in this very snooty way, "We really disapprove of the Second Circuit's," you're nodding. You read this case too, right? "We really disapprove of this, we prefer to stick to the tried-and-true four-factor test." So I think this whole question of what is transformativeness and is it, is just making some courts a little bit uneasy.

What I think we're seeing is that even if it's not transformative, the purpose is really important. And this is very key because if you're in the educational sector or if you're dealing with educational materials or accessibility or any other kind of purpose that is not necessarily transformative, it's really important that we be able to have some power in the first factor as well. The first factor doesn't just stand alone, actually. It interacts with all the other factors. The market effect is still important. That's what the Seventh Circuit said, that's what the, sorry, that's what the recent big case, was that the market effect is still important. So this is my slide for the case which won't be mentioned and is the Fair Use Emotional Rollercoaster that was done in a newsletter that called "Five Useful Articles," which if you ever follow legal issues in IP is well worth reading. I'm clicking because I can't keep watching that. But it's very funny, I think, that GIF. And it was intended to describe how those of us who read this case felt when we were reading the case that I'm still not mentioning. But it kind of encapsulates some of the points that I was making, which is that even though things are not transformative, the purpose is still really important and can be a plus factor. That licensing is very important. We used to think it was just transformativeness that had replaced the whole value of the fourth factor, but no, the fourth factor, the market effects, are still really important. Then finally, the second and third factor actually are not dead letters. They are important. You have to pay attention to the nature of the work and to how much is taken. Those things are there. And now we move on.

There are other cases that have been also really playing around with this same set of maybe organizing principles, which we could call the four factors, that I think are reviving the "four-ness" of the four factors. One case that came out just a few months ago is the White v. West case, and this is Westlaw and Lexis and this attorney who got dumped from a case got upset, copyrighted his briefs, and then used Lexis and Westlaw for including his briefs in his database, which I think was chutzpah. But the court said, lawyers do this. Every year or two there is another case with a similar set of facts. But this one was particularly notable because it generated this nice opinion. The court said, "Look, Lexis and Westlaw, although commercial entities, are transforming the work." How are they transforming it? This is the Second Circuit, so they have this broad view of transformativeness these days, and they said, "They're transforming it because they're using it for a different purpose." And they kind of transformed it a little bit with metadata and annotations. That will be very useful to us librarians to think about that as a transformation. But just the whole different purpose was a transformation. And then, they did pay attention to the other factors. They said the nature of these documents, they're publicly filed documents that were intended to be disclosed. And they talked a lot about the audience. Who is the audience for these briefs? The audience for the briefs originally is the client and the court, and the audience for these briefs in Lexis, Westlaw is a database, is a legal research database and these other purposes. And the important point here is that the purpose shifted the market. So the factors are playing together. We can't just say it's transformativeness; it's how they all work together.

And then there are a whole bunch of these other cases. There's the Fox vs. TV Eyes case, which was an indexing case, another indexing case where TV Eyes is this high, pricy subscription service that makes transcripts of TV news and then sells the transcripts and then gives little clips of the video attached to them if you get the keyword right. That was fair use. The Swatch v. Bloomberg case,

which was where Bloomberg News listen, joined kind of a closed press conference, took a recording of it, and then just sent it out to its subscribers. That was a fair use too. There were four cases filed by the American Institute of Physics and Wiley against law firms for using scientific articles in patent filings. The two that have resulted in decisions both said fair use. The HathiTrust, the Second Circuit said that indexing is a quintessential transformative use, but they said the disability access that you're providing, that's not transformative at all, but it is a highly favored purpose. So those are also more, what I would call indexing and awareness kinds of cases. We've got a whole slew of cases that I think are really, whether they're commercial entities or whether they're more public entities, they're all around the kinds of things that libraries do and educators do, which is providing access to information and organizing it. And all of them are saying, "Hey, even if you're not transforming the content significantly, as long as you're doing it with a different purpose or a different audience, it can still be fair." Notice the different purpose/audience showing up in the first factor, which is the purpose and character, it's showing up in the second factor, which is the nature of the use, and it's showing up in the fourth factor, which is the market substitution, the effect on the market. So it's showing up in all of these places, but it's the same concept. And the purpose on all of these is indexing or awareness, education, accessibility. And taking the whole thing is not a problem in any of them. They're paying attention to the markets. There's a problem in the American Geophysical Union case where people said, "Oh, well any avoided license could be a market harm, and so that is a very circular argument." And courts are really paying attention to avoid that problem.

All right, so this is my gist, and now I'm at my end. So the point is that transformativeness is not the be all and end all. We've been using transformativeness perhaps as a proxy for purpose. I think if we get back to that original concept and just sublimate transformativeness as one of the ways a purpose can be changed or as one of the types of purposes that will help us, I guess, keep transformativeness in its place. It's the transformativeness plus the holistic analysis. The other pieces are actually all still important. Who is the audience? Is the nature of the work? The purpose affects how much is taken. The purpose can affect the market. The purpose can affect everything, whether they're transformative or not. And so that's my upshot. And that's what I have to do to cue up Mr. Hannay, which I'm very excited because I can't wait to hear what we have to say about the right to be forgotten. Thank you, and questions.

Bill Hannay: Well, I guess I have to add my own caveat that my voice is a little hoarse too. So you had Lauren Bacall because of hoarseness. Well, I guess I'm Humphrey Bogart, huh?

I'm going to talk about the right to be forgotten. I'm sure many of you if not all of you have heard of this famous case that occurred earlier this year in the European Union, and we're going to focus on that and then try to spin it a little further beyond that. The right to be forgotten is also known as the right to oblivion. So indeed, it is called the right to oblivion in some of the texts and some of the commentaries and some of the court opinions that talk about it as well. I kind of like that concept. What's the worldwide fuss? I'm going to actually read this out loud because I've got to get through it with the right emphasis on the syllables. So on May 13th, 2014, the European Court of Justice held that the operator of a search engine, Google, is obliged to remove from the list of results displayed, following a search made on the basis of a person's name, links to webpages, published by third parties and containing information relating to that person, if such information is, quote, "inadequate, irrelevant or no longer relevant, or excessive," unquote, in relation to the purposes for which the data was collected or processed and in the light of the time that has elapsed, even if the information is true. So that's what the fuss is about. It is generally perceived as a kind of David and Google-iath kind of a competition. Mario Costeja Gonzalez is the David, and Google is the Google-iath.

So the decision, and this is actually the full name of the case, because it was an appeal by Google in Spain and Google Inc. worldwide against the Spanish Data Protection Agency, which was the

regulatory agency that supported Mr. Costeja Gonzalez's case. And what the case is really about is not so much the privacy itself, because that was really a foregone conclusion from the Data Privacy Directive, which I'll tell you about in a second, but what the case really established as a precedent was that Google, as a search engine provider, was responsible for the results of the searches. And that's what the case was really, really, really about. It's not so much that a person in Europe has a right to get rid of certain information about that. That was kind of a foregone conclusion. But it's the fact that Google, and any other search engine provider, is stuck with the responsibilities that a controller of this information would have, the website provider. So it's big deal in that regard and shifts the responsibilities quite handily.

Quick factual background. In 2009 Mr. Costeja Gonzalez discovered that if you did a kind of internet selfie and ask, "Oh, what are people saying about me? What does my name appear in?" It pulled up two old newspaper articles about him, or really about the fact that he had been in debt for not having paid some governmental tax or something, and so they'd ordered his property put up for sale. Kind of a big deal. I'm sure it was disturbing to him. But he settled it. It all got taken care of 15 years ago. But the newspaper articles lived on in the internet, and if you did a search on his name, whatever else came up, you got these two newspaper articles. So he went to the newspaper and he said, "You know guys, this is old history. Would you please remove them from your archives. Take it down off the internet." They refused. He went to Google and he said the same thing. They refused. So he went to the data privacy agency in Spain, which every in the EU has set up a data privacy regulatory agency pursuant to this Data Directive, and he said, "You got to help me, guys." And they said, "Okay. Si." And they held two things. Interestingly, they said, "Well, the newspaper doesn't have to do anything because it's a legitimate reporter of things that happened." It's a record, a chronicle of what happened. And so it doesn't have to do anything. It properly reported that news. But when Google runs its machine and pulls those newspapers up, now it's got a different responsibility. It's not protected by the equivalent in Europe of the newspaper First Amendment. It's parleying what's on the internet for money, and now they're putting it out there and the court says they're going to be liable for that. They did all this within the context of this Data Directive. In the EU, which you may know, a directive is the word they use instead of "legislation." It's a product of the coresponsible system in the EU, which is a little bit esoteric, but there's a parliament, and they have a council, and the two of them have to go back and forth and agree. It's kind of like the Senate and the House of Representatives. They go back and forth and eventually agree on, compromise legislation, and that's called a directive.

So there's two provisions of it: Articles 6(1) and 12(b). The first one is the one, and you'll recognize this language, that says that member states, member states of the EU, shall, must, provide that personal data must be adequate, relevant, and not excessive in relation to the purposes for which they're collected or further processed. And (d), they must be, (d), accurate and, where necessary, kept up to date. It's a responsibility that the states put upon anybody who is going to be deemed a controller of information. 12 gives the remedy. Member states shall guarantee every data subject, that's me or you, the right to obtain from the controller of this data, as appropriate, the rectification, erasure, or blocking of data the processing of which does not comply with the provisions of this directive, e.g. 6(1), in particular because of incomplete or inaccurate nature of the data. So if you find information about yourself and you are a European citizen, you can, if the data meets this test, this inadequate, irrelevant, excessive, inaccurate, un-up to date, if you can prove this data meets this test or tests, plural, then under 12, you can ask for the rectification, erasure, or blocking of the data.

What's the interplay between these? This is what the court says, is that this "processing of personal data carried out by the operator of a search engine is liable to affect significantly the fundamental rights of privacy and the protection of personal data since that processing enables any internet user to obtain information which potentially concerns a vast number of aspects of an individual's private life and which, without the

search engine, could not have been interconnected or could have been only with great difficulty." So the search engine is the enabler of the publication of the inaccurate, inadequate, ineffective, irrelevant information. And so therefore, the operator of this search engine has got special responsibilities. Now, the court emphasized that there is need for a balance in the process. So when you complain to a controller of data that it's not accurate or adequate or etc., then the operator has to go through a balancing test to figure out whether the data is so harmful to your rights as the subject of the data that it outweighs the public's interest in the information. Now, that's a kind of awesome responsibility, but that's the way the court has figured that this, this is the best way to do it. We're going to let the controller, in this case, Google, make these decisions. The subject of the data applies, says, "I've got this problem. Please take it down," Google thinks about it, they do this balancing tests and somehow, and then they make a ruling. And if they make, in the data user's mind, the wrong ruling and leave it up, then they can go to their local privacy agency, as did Mr. Costeja Gonzalez.

How do you do this balancing? Oh, this is a black box. It depends, "on the nature of the information in question and its sensitivity to the data subject's private life and, on the other hand, on the interest of the public in having that information." Do the public really need to have this information from 1998 about Mr. Costeja Gonzalez's property problem? The court said, "No, not really." And his interests override the economic interest of the search engine. What would that be? Well, that would be, it costs money to run this balancing test. It costs money for us to go and pull this information out and program our computers so it doesn't pop up when Mr. Costeja Gonzalez's name is plugged in. Well, that's too bad. You do this for a living, you got to live with this. And that's the economic interests of the search engine operator and the general public's interest in the data about him.

Where are we in Europe? On request of an individual to remove information about him, the controller must do this balancing test. And, trying to live up to its court-ordered obligations, Google has dutifully published an online form that you can fill out and submit online to request removal of data links. The first day this went into operation, there were 12,000 requests. As of July, there were 70,000 requests. Okay, this, from Google's point of view, there's an economic interest here. There's been a lot, wonderfully a lot, of reactions. I mean, I spent time flipping through all these things and I'm thinking, "Oh, man. I could quote for an hour on either side of this." But here's just a few. Well, first off, Google sent a SWAT team out of scholars and lawyers and others to go around holding seminars in essentially every city in Europe, every major city in Europe, to explain why this was unnecessary, why it was a terrible burden, why it was just a disaster. Wikipedia cofounder Jimmy Wales, who constantly pops up on my screen asking for money, had an interview in a newspaper and he called the EU's decision "deeply immoral" and warned that the ruling will "result in an internet riddled with memory holes." Pretty good imagery. I like that part. Another legal commentator characterized the judgment as "profoundly harmful to the operation of the internet and a betrayal of Europe's legacy in protecting freedom of expression." Ooh. Harsh words. Another guy says it's a draconian attack on free speech. Someone else called it "retrograde," "akin to," and I know you'll like this, "marching into a library and forcing it to pulp books." Who would do that other than the local county board?

But there's lots of positive statements as well. A leader of the UK Parliament praised the decision, saying, "The presumption by internet companies that they can just use people's personal information in any way they see fit is wrong and can only happen because the legal framework in most states," he means countries, "is still in the last century when it comes to property rights in personal information." And a privacy advocate, I mean, I like this phrase too. "Without the freedom to be private, we have precious little freedom at all." I mean, Tom Paine could've said that if he lived in the internet age.

So what do I think? I know you really want to know what I think. I think it's a great decision! A careful and correct application of the EU data privacy law, and it recognizes the need to balance all interests, not just, say, well, whatever the internet controller wants to do. More than that, I see it as a vital first step in trying to bring the insanity of the internet under control. It's already destroyed legitimate newspapers and is now gutting libraries. It's easier to find porn and libel on the internet than Shakespeare. And it's all well and good to worship free expression, but you cannot yell "fire" in a crowded movie theater just because you're expressing yourself. We need to get control of this Wild West now before it gets worse. But hey, it's just me talking.

Who cares about Europe? Europe, Schmeurope. What about the US? Could Google happen here? Maybe, maybe not. We don't have any broad-based law like the anti, excuse me, the Data Directive. We don't have anything in the Constitution that you can hang a hat on and say a data controller has to remove or take down data that's irrelevant or inaccurate. Now, sometimes our legislatures do step in. We do regulate data use and content in one notable area: credit reporting. The Fair Credit Reporting Act imposes certain rules on accuracy, relevance, and obsoleteness. Maybe we need a Fair Credit Reporting Act that's much broader and goes well beyond credit reporting. Is there any other remedy right now? Well, in general in the United States, we recognize a hazy kind of invasion of privacy. Some states prohibit use of a name or likeness for advertising without consent. And there's defamation and slander laws, but those require proof of intent to harm and damages, elements that were not required under the Data Directive in the EU. There's even a tort called intrusion upon seclusion. That's so poetic. But it doesn't get used much because it's kind of a trespass theory. There is another one, and I think it may be the best shot if you were going to try to bring some kind of lawsuit: public disclosure of embarrassing private facts. Well, that would fit.

And how about Canada? You know, Canada's kind of like the US, right? I think it's part of the US. I'm not sure. But there was a judge in British Columbia that ordered Google, poor Google, it's a target again, to block a group of websites from its worldwide search engine. Now the EU decision only relates to Google in Europe, that is to say, only sites in Europe. But this order from this Canadian judge applies to the entire world for Google, and it isn't even a privacy case; it's a trade secrets case where someone wanted an injunction to protect its trade secrets, and the judge perceived Google as in effect being an unwilling and unwitting facilitator of these trade secret violations.

You, my friends, are dedicated to preserving information, printed information in books and periodicals, information on CDs and DVDs as well as e-books. And of course, now every library is filled with computer terminals for patrons and scholars and students to access e-information online. And I know it tears your hearts out to have to discard old books and magazine into the dumpster to make room for the new. But what about bad or private info? What do you say when someone asks you to help them take down false, old, or embarrassing information? A weird guy comes in and asks you to delete a particularly embarrassing photo from the internet. He says he's a different person now. What do you do? Well, you might offer him a Lethe cocktail. Lethe, as you know, is the river in the Greek underworld that when drunk from made souls forget the

sufferings of life. Oblivion, there's that word again, or something to make you enter oblivion and forget. Well, that may not work. But you could try notice and takedown. And certainly all of you may have already had experience doing this. Most online hosts offer procedures for requesting that they voluntarily remove or take down material. You can go on their websites. Go on, for example, YouTube. If that photo was part of a YouTube and some music was playing behind it, I could probably get them to take it down because it's obviously pornography. And in fact, notice and takedown is part of the Digital Millennium Copyright Act for copyright-related violations. But the other thing you can do, and this is really what I'd recommend, is you get on the phone and you call Google, and you say to him (singing):

> "Forget him 'cuz he doesn't want fame. Forget him 'cuz it isn't fair.
>
> Don't let them search for his old data 'cuz they can't find the dirt that isn't there.
>
> Google guy, I'm asking politely, remove those links so they can't see.
>
> Oh, don't you cry now, just be a good guy now. Forget him and guard his privacy."

Budgets, Services, and Technology Driving Change:
How Librarians, Publishers, and Vendors Are Moving Forward

Kittie Henderson, Vice President, Academic, Law and Public Library Markets, EBSCO Information Services
Meg White, Executive Director of Technology Services, Rittenhouse Book Distributors

The following is a lightly edited transcript of a live presentation at the 2014 Charleston Conference. Slides and videos are available at http://2014charlestonconference.sched.org/

Meg White: Well, good afternoon and welcome to one of our Neapolitan sessions here at Charleston. You have come to Budget, Services, and Technology Driving Change: How Librarians and Publishers and Vendors are Moving Forward. So, if that's not the session you want to be in, now is the time. My name is Meg White. I am the Executive Director of Technology Services at Rittenhouse Book Distributors. I am joined this afternoon by Kittie Henderson, who is Vice President, Academic, Law, and Public Library Markets for EBSCO Information Services. We welcome you and thank you for choosing to spend some of your time with us this afternoon.

Over the next hour, in the true spirit of Charleston Conference, we hope to be able to share some industry data that is relevant to all shareholders, librarians, vendors and publishers. No matter which role we play in the information distribution chain, we share a common goal to increase access to scholarly information. Kittie and I both work for a distribution company, so we occupy a pretty unique viewpoint in terms of the information distribution chain. Essentially we are two customers. The libraries for whom we work provide materials and services, but also the publishers whose information it is our job to disseminate as widely and broadly as possible. This perspective allows us access to key data from both of these stakeholders. And Kittie and EBSCO were kind enough to collate some of that data through a survey that's been conducted from mid-September through mid-October of this year. So, very, very recent data. This data talks about and focuses on key financial strategic acquisitions and technology issues. So, it's that data conducted in that survey that we're going to focus on today.

And hopefully, again, in the true spirit of Charleston, generate some Q and A with the audience during the session as well. So, we will save significant time in the end for your questions or comments. Please do take note as we go through and we'll save that for a discussion after we take a look at at the data. With that, I will turn the podium over to Kittie and thank you for your kind attention.

Kittie Henderson: Thanks Meg. Now, I am acutely aware of the fact that we stand between you and a happy hour/poster session. And I mostly believe that this data is just infinitely stimulating. However, I do realize that not everybody might share that so some of these points I'm going to move through fairly quickly. We will be taking questions at the end, so with that let's get started.

First of all, as Meg mentioned, I am Kittie Henderson. I've been with EBSCO for 23 years. I like to say that I was part of the kindergarten recruitment program as some of them are in the room that I have known since I started. But we see tremendous change in libraries and, in the entire information services industry. Numbers have changed drastically in the last decade. So, the talk is divided into a few key points and, we're going to transition through this.

Just an overview of the company, librarian trend data, the key trends, market factors and then focusing on the long term. EBSCO is an acronym that stands for the Elton B. Stephens Company. There really was a Mr. Elton. I'm lucky enough to have joined in the years while Mr. Elton was still very active. If you would like to Google EBSCO Industries you will get the home page for EBSCO Industries and it will talk about some of the elements of EBSCO. As you can see we are ranked 8 of 10 in Google ranking. We have a Dun and Bradstreet rating of 5A1. That is the highest rating available to a privately owned company. Now, there's been a lot of disruption in the market.

There are several sessions here that talk about the situation in the market. I'm not going to beat that because a lot of other people are already talking about it. But 5A1 is the highest rating available. We are also listed each year in the list of the top 200 privately held companies by *Forbes* magazine. So, we are a very large and very financially stable.

As I mentioned, EBSCO was founded my Mr. Elton in 1944. We generate over $2 billion a year in annual sales. The Chairman of EBSCO is family owned. It's owned by the Stephens Company. The Chairman is Jim Stephens. And Tim Collins recently became the fourth president of EBSCO. Tim Collins is the founder of EBSCO Publishing which, is our database division. And if Tim were to be here he would tell you the story of meeting Jim Stephens about 25 years ago when he was doing a little product called Magazine Article Summaries and he was in the basement of his house. Some of you have heard story. So, Tim is a man with great vision, great pride and tremendous energy.

All this, for this presentation we surveyed 200 major academic library customers and we got a 25% response rate. In past years we've done the survey on all market types but this year we restricted it just to academic. As you can see it was pretty evenly divided between college and universities and ARL libraries.

Just like with the libraries survey, the people who responded were the decision makers with nearly half of them being the executive people. Nearly a third being sales and marketing and 21% or 20% being operational people.

I don't have to tell you in this room what the landscape looks like. You know that. That's why you're here. Under the economic situation the library, and in fact, all of the economy did a hard contraction in 2008, 2009. Budgets plummeted. When cash revenue plummets, budgets plummet, orders plummet. The entire market went through a dramatic downsize during that time. In the decade prior to that we got a big deal in the packaging of content. We saw the rise of different metrics to evaluate collections. We had a few ways of finding content in discovery. We have some new acquisitions models in PPV. The open access movement, we're into that.

E-books, we went from having print books to e-books and we're going to talk some about what we did during that time.

Library budgets are never in the discussion. And as you can see, and I'm not going to do this on all the slides, although I do have the data, if any of you want to talk about it. Library budgets, at least for the people responded, of this year, and as you can see the 2013, 2014 most recent data is to the right, 35% of people indicated that they got some sort of budget increase. And this is confirmed by a survey that ARL did last year. I joke that flat is the new up. There for a while if you were flat you were actually doing really good. Budgets are flat. But the good news in this is that, you see the far column to the left, the decreased more than 10% that number is now down to 2% of respondents. This is a good thing because it means that we're starting to stabilize.

Now, we also surveyed publishers and we asked them if their budget was starting to recover from the economic downturn. As you can see, 81% indicated that it was. This is up from 2011. Only 32% of people responded with their budgets were starting to recover. By 2012 that number was up to 50%. So, the good news is that the recovery, while it is not like the tide flowing back into the harbor, things are improving.

Okay, it's not an, an EBSCO presentation without at least one mind numbing chart. Um, and I spared you the 22 years, up to 25 years, of library journals serving this pricing data. I'm one of the coauthors of the library journal's serials pricing article along Steve Bosch at the University of Arizona. Each year we publish this chart with our annual fall price projections and the way we calculate the annual historical price increase by libraries is that we have a sample set of accounts. So, we treat ARL libraries as one group. We treat non-ARL four-year universities as another group, and then include your academic biomedical here because increasingly academic biomed comes under the general. But this tracks the average price increase for that group per year. Now, if some of you have tracked this over the years, you'll know that there is variation each year we go in and we review every library in that group to make sure that they're still appropriate. But, as you can see, there were increases in ARL and college/universities have been about the same with academic medical. Now there, the evaluative tool applied to this is always the consumer price index. I personally don't believe that is appropriate. But as you can see in the 2013 column that library budgets were going up 5.5% when library costs were going up 5.5% and 6.1% .

The consumer price index was 1.5%. I think there's two different sets of market factors in play here. But this is the way people present the data. This translates the mind numbing chart into a line graph. And once again it talks about price increases and annual rate of inflation. What is missing from this chart is the budget data that you saw a few slides ago.

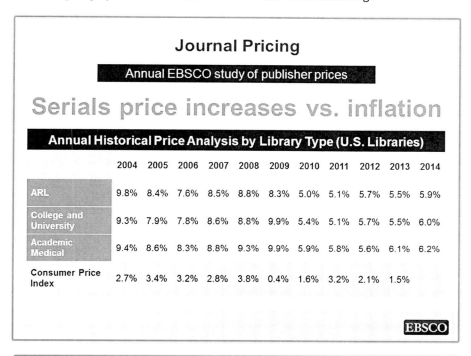

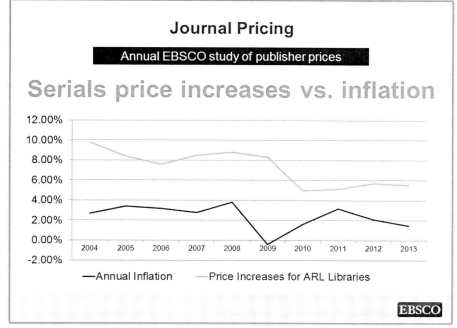

EBSCO handles a lot of e-packages. And, uh, we looked at 3,000 of those and this data is less than a week old. We looked at 3,000 of the e-packages we handle and the average price increase on the e-journal package was 6.6%. Now, I'm not going to belabor all of you about how the, the inflation of e-journal packages work but this has been, I want to use a highly scientific term, nudging up over the last few years. In 2010 the average rate of inflation was 5.1% and in 2013 it was 5.5. So, it's gone up an entire percentage point in a year.

The reason for that is a number of people have been renegotiating e-journal packages, and there is a slide about that later on. But we analyzed the average rate of price increase per package per publisher and yes, the numbers are changed to protect the innocent or the guilty depending upon your perspective. What you're seeing in publisher package A is pressing. So, a shift in the basis of their pricing.

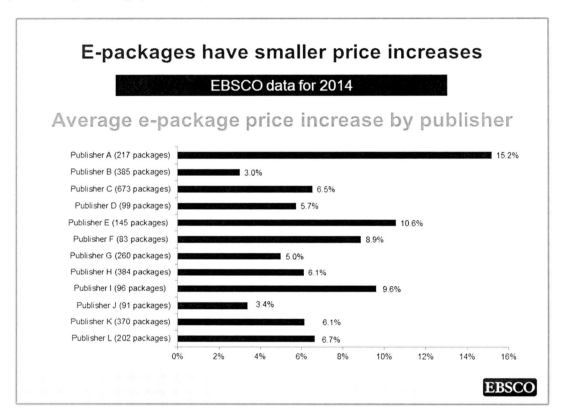

We asked the publishers what they were likely to do in the coming year. And as you can see, and this is not all publishers, 91% indicated that they are likely to increase their prices. This is up from 85% last year. 9% indicated that they, are likely to decrease, they'll have a pricing decrease. And once again, the way this usually happens is with a pricing model change although some people do go through and relay what their pricing model. And if any of you in the room are from publishers and you want to speak to them I'm comfortable with that.

The average expected publisher price increase by 2015 is somewhere between 5 and 7%. And this is pretty much where it's been for the last few years. During 2009, whenever we have recession price increases were at their lowest point. And ever since then they have been slowly building. My colleague Steve Bosch once said, and actually wrote the section of the article last year that said that this rate of price increase was enough to maintain the publishers, but it wasn't too high. I don't know if I agree with it but this has been the way of the profession for the last three years.

People are always talking about what they do in response to fitting into their budgets and how they reallocate their orders of their content so that they can fit into the budget. And as you can see, we asked librarians what they plan to do, what strategies they plan to employ with their budgets. We're thinking of move from print and move to online only. 86%, everyone in this room knows that in North America this has been going on a long time. And most libraries do this every year, they go through, they evaluate anything that can move, a lot of times they do. 46% as you can see indicated that they did not move e-journal packages. This is up from 34% last year. Which is really interesting because if you look at the renegotiated multiyear e-package deals, that is 74%. That is the same number as last year. So, there are a lot of people out there, when their e-journal contracts come due they are renegotiating. And then the alternative OA content, that's up 10% from last year. In a session earlier today we were asked about open access. You don't hear as much about open access right now as you did in the past. About 10% of the librarians who responded to the survey are seeking open access content.

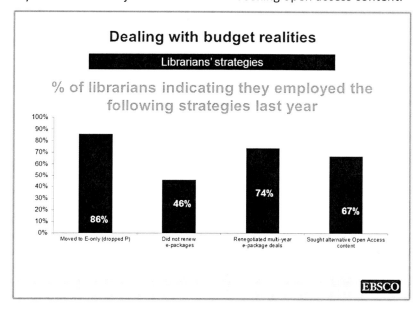

Now, it's not a serials presentation without a slide about the print. And you were supposed to laugh at that. Okay, we once again we surveyed the publishers and we looked at the North American market. As you can see the number of print orders continues to decline. Having said that, print is not dead yet. And I don't think print will disappear in my career. The publishers who run dual systems to produce public print and online still have the double cost. Even though print is declining in North America, that is not necessarily true in all parts of the world. Europe in particular has a different tax structure so, any places without strong internet connectivity, print remains quite strong.

Over the years EBSCO has made a substantial investment in handling the electronic order transaction. And in EBSCO we don't refer to them so much as orders as we do as financial transactions. Because literally that's what we do for you. We transact business. As you can see the print has leveled off. Print P plus E continues to decline as indicated whereas electronic only continues to grow.

These pie charts represent our revenue distribution by format. As you can see in 1999 we were 88% print. And I was with the company then and we thought that 80% that was print plus online, we were cool. Now, as you can see electronic only is 73% of the transactions we handle and print plus online is 11%. So 84% of business that we currently transact has an electronic component. And that number grows every year.

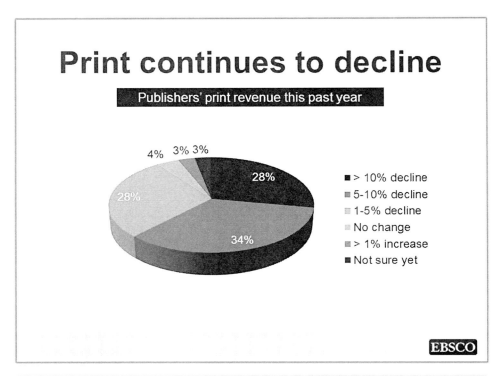

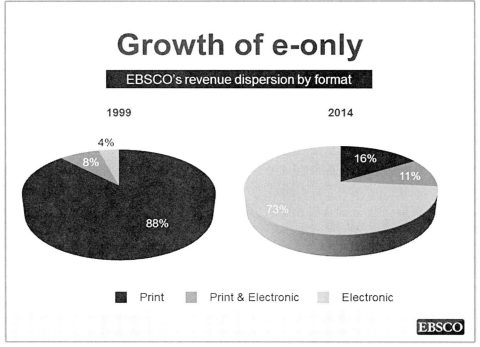

We asked the same question of publishers. And we ask where their business growth was. As you can see, the number of e-journal, individual e-journals is still a substantial part of their market, it's 44%. There is also a substantial increase in the number of packages for which they service orders. So, the largest segment of your business are the packages when they offer them.

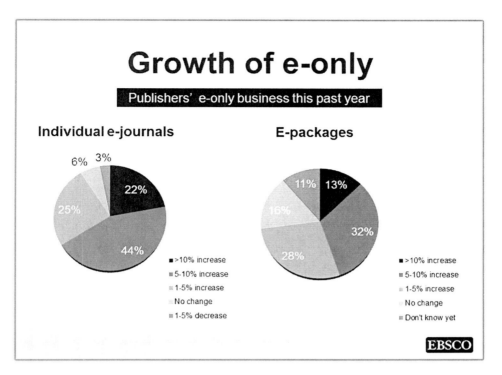

Growth of e-only

Publishers' e-only business this past year

Individual e-journals

- 22%
- 44%
- 25%
- 6%
- 3%

Legend:
- >10% increase
- 5-10% increase
- 1-5% increase
- No change
- 1-5% decrease

E-packages

- 13%
- 32%
- 28%
- 16%
- 11%

Legend:
- >10% increase
- 5-10% increase
- 1-5% increase
- No change
- Don't know yet

EBSCO

Once again, dealing with the budget realities. Once again, the number of people who dropped from print plus online to e-only went up by 6% this year. It was 80% last year. They're renegotiating multiyear deals. You hear a lot in the press about people who dropped out of big deals, wrapping up big deals. You know, it goes in cycles. The reality is, is that while people talk about it they don't really seem to do it a lot. I think publishers have been very responsive to that and I think librarians have also. I think people have worked to meet in the middle.

We asked librarians where they plan on spending the greatest percentage of their budgets this year. As you can see the biggest increase on spending, they think is going to be in individual e-books. And this followed by individual e-subscriptions. Now, go back a slide in your mind and remember that, that number about 74% renegotiating packages. You'll find as you go through this survey that what people say they're going to do, this lady in the front row is smiling. What people say they they're going to do and what they actually do can be two entirely different things. The way that people responded to us. If you are looking at the e-journal packages, at 27%. That actually dropped. It was 41% in 2012. So, if people say they're not going to do it and yet they do it.

Discovery solutions, the 17% is unchanged from 2012. The people who planned on spending money in 2012 on that voted the same way this year. Print books, can you believe print books went up 2% in this survey? How many of you are spending 2% more on print books? Perfect. Never want to hear this discussion prior to this.

Now, this is the slide some of you have been waiting for. This is the publishers' view of the big deal. We asked publishers "Do you think that the big deal will be around in 5 years?" And as you can see, 38% indicated that it was very likely. Interestingly enough, this is up from 29% two years ago. So, it's increased almost 10%. In the somewhat likely category with 44%, that has increased from 33% just two years ago. So, publishers believed that the big deal is, is getting stronger. Unsure, fewer of them are unsure than there were in 2012. In 2012 they were, 10% not sure and now only 6% are not sure. So, people are buying content in packages and that's what the response from the publishers indicate.

We asked what publishers are likely to do because the big deal seems to be continuing. I don't particularly like the term the big deal, but package content and when we asked publishers what they plan to do with this publishers are also very cognizant of library budgets. As you can see, 74% indicated that they plan to offer smaller subsets of their content. This up from 52% in 2012. So, I think that is a significant increase. I think you would agree. A smaller percentage indicated they planned on offering even bigger e-journal packages. And 27% response is exactly what it was two years ago.

So, we asked publishers about the pricing model because when e-journals were born, as you know, it was based on the print model and ever since then everyone in the industry is searching for the holy grail of the perfect pricing model. And people are nodding because I have talked about this with a lot of the people in the audience. There is no perfect pricing model and no matter what pricing model publishers choose someone is not going to like it. But, when they asked this year, 23% said there's a plan to move to a tiered pricing model. That's about the same as it was two years ago. 6% said that they plan to reduce the cost per unit of e-journal packages. That is actually down from two years ago when 12% indicated that they planned to reduce cost. And then on increase in unit cost, 39% is up from 34% last year. So, essentially within a few percentage points it's pretty much the same as it was two years ago.

Publishers content plans. The way publishers grow, as you know, is by either start new titles or they buy them or the buy other companies. There are a lot of comments in the market about the big five publishers. I can tell you that from doing the library journal serials pricing article that we look at this in an amazing, mind numbing level of detail. That, of the publishers in the Morsch ISI indices, more than 60% are from the big five. The big five are truly the big five. They're Exeter, Wiley, Taylor & Francis, Sage, Springer.

The way that they grow, and a number of you are from publishers, is that they add, they will start or acquire titles. The start titles is up from 52%. A 52% response rate just two years ago. So, that is a significant increase. Interestingly enough, we have a slide coming later on about open access and the people who planned on starting new journals that were open access. That was the thing a few years

ago, or even last year. That was where you saw growth in the publishing industry. The publisher's response on this didn't change for this year.

I am always looking for an updated slide on this and those of you in the audience, you and I talk ad-infinitum about the percentage of your budget spent on serials and how this goes up every year and how the percentage shifts. This is an example from the University of Oklahoma library. I chose this because this is this year. But, these percentages are fairly universal across libraries. And I don't have to tell you. I think some of you in the audience can document this far better than me. As serials have gone up over the last decades because it's not always a phenomena. The percentage of your budget can still buy serials increases. And, the amount of your budget can still decrease. That trend is bucked somewhat by e-books, but this the money.

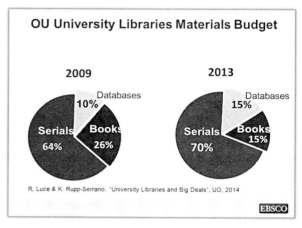

OU University Libraries Materials Budget

R. Luce & K. Rupp-Serrano. "University Libraries and Big Deals", UO, 2014

This is a slightly older slide but it's still is very true. There is concern in the market about the percentage of your budget allocated to big deals because, as I don't have to tell you because you're under contractual relationship you have a percentage of your budget already allocated each year before you even get it. And you're amount of discretionary spending depending on what items with your budget may or may not go up. So, this is a concern, this continues. And what this does is this puts pressure on smaller publishers because when you have to pay the fill in the blank bill, what do you do? Cut 'em. It's the only thing you can do.

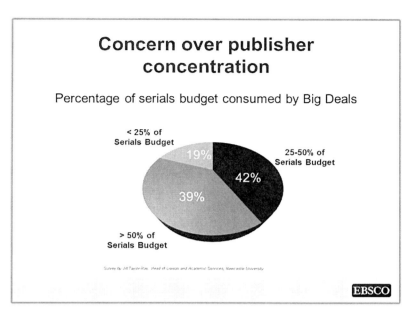

Now, there's a, a widely held premise in e-journal packages that 20% of the content accounts for 80% of the usage. I chose this example because this data was presented at Charleston last year. But in this, just like I'm sure in a lot of your individual cases, 20% of the titles do indeed get 80% of the use. And that is fairly consistent across general academic libraries.

Recent surveys, and frankly a lot of the news videos, talk about the way that we as librarians acquire what content. And this is going to come as no surprise, people in the room: usage, it's all about usage. Use it or lose it all. We surveyed librarians and we asked, "What's the most important metric in making content decisions?" And this year 100% of the people whose, of the librarians who responded indicated that usage and cost per use was one of their main metrics. This is up from 83% just two years ago. Why do you think this is? I think it's a couple of things. I think it is budget pressure. But I also think that it is the maturation of a technology that better provides this data. We have better tools. Interestingly enough, faculty recommendations remains approximately the same. Historical price increases, the number of people who considered that factor went up a little bit, from 38 to 45% but, but not a lot. Value metrics is where there are some changes. In the past this has been things such as the ISI Impact Factor. But now it's

looking at things like alternative metrics, which we will touch on later. It also looks at the way your content is discovered. And as you can see the discovery market, discovery, discoverability, be it through products such as Summit. I'm going to try to name everybody so if I miss somebody go ahead and shout 'em out. So, you've got Summit, you've got Primo, you've got OCLC, and you've got EDS EBSCOhost. And we're the big ones on the market. As you can see, of the people, of the librarians who responded 75% already have have a discovery service. This is up from 41% two years ago. So, that shows the market penetration and the move to discovery services in a very, very short time. And that is what's driving a lot of your usage.

I love the title of this slide. I'd love to say I came up with it, but, publishers get it. They understand that use is driving the the selection and the retention of content. If you'll notice 100% of the publishers who responded indicated that increase in usage was the main priority. And these, these numbers are unchanged from two years ago. So, publishers have understood this landscape for a long time. And you see very good use of the statistics, you see supporting of it. I always point out, and I see a few of my publisher friends in the room, that increasing usage actually ranked above increasing sales. So, you guys were supposed to laugh at that.

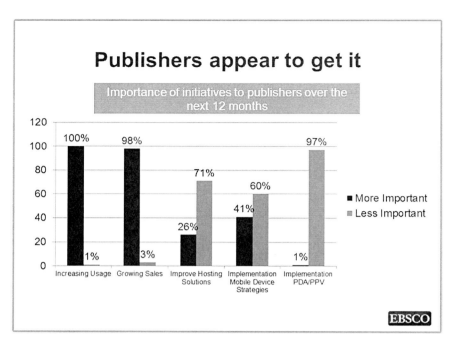

As part of this, we are looking at a new way of evaluating and we've had COUNTER, and we are looking a new things like Altmetrics. These are things like tweets and downloads, and it's tracking the new ways that we use content. Some of you may know that EBSCO purchased Plum Analytics in January, and we are supporting them in their growth, but we're also in the process of integrating the types of growth provided by this.

We believe that as the usage tools become available, you're going to take advantage of all of the data elements that you can get. Because as you know, for a journal to be cited it can take as short a time as two years. It can take a lot longer. So, in that factor is, as a measure of quality can lag. And there are some disciplines where in that factor is simply not a good one. We believe that the article-level metrics and alternative metrics are one of the tools that you can use in the future.

We hear a lot about patron driven and pay per view. And when we surveyed librarians, and I've had this conversation with a number of you in the room, we ask about the percentage of librarians who agree that PDA and pay per view in combination with journal purchases will replace the big deal packages. Now, I reference you back to slide that talked about big deal package sales going up. But, in the responses, librarians talk about pay per view. In this case 69% said that they

thought, that in combination with individual e-journal purchases, this would replace the big deal. This is up from 56% just two years ago. I think that the type of library will determine, well I know a lot of you are doing this already, but your ability to emphasize those options many times will depend on the type of library and the type of clients that you serve. There are, 50% of people who responded to the survey run also indicated that they worried about pay per view budgets being eaten up too quickly by users. So, it is a double edged sword. Most of the pay per view systems have controls on them that control them. But the service philosophy of any content at any time, what the user wants, is impeded or will have limitations on it.

We asked librarians if they currently have a PDA or pay per view arrangement where the library pays all or a portion of the content on behalf of the users. Slightly more than half did not, 45% did. In terms of the libraries who did not, on the list, 71% do not offer any sort library support pay per view in 2012. So, there has been significant growth and there has been a significant shift in the, in the ranks of the people who do. So, this is clearly a collection trend.

Open access. Open access has certainly been in the news the last few years. It's a major movement in scholarly publishing. And yes, if you're thinking you've seen this slide before, you have. I want to call your attention to the last column over on the right. The 67% of respondents who said that they had saw open access content in the last year. That number is up 10% since 2012. So, it is certainly a growing trend. I don't know that it is growing as quickly as, as some people thought it would.

We asked publishers, uh, what about open access? Are you planning to add open access titles for this year? 72% said no, 28% said yes. Would anybody like to venture what, what they said in 2012? Actually in 2012, somebody said it's the other way around. In 2012 the results were exactly the same, which we found interesting.

That being said, open access is a growing movement. All of the major publishers have open access initiatives because, as you know, what open access does is it shifts the revenue model from library subscription to other

agencies on the campus. So, open access is going continue to grow.

A place that is also expected to, that is going to continue to grow is, is e-books. E-books have been a revolution in the last five years and as you can see 56% of the people responded indicate that they are going to increase their expenditures on individual e-books. That is about the same as it was two years ago. Interestingly enough the number on e-journal packages decreased slightly. So, packages may have been a way of rapidly front-loading collections. We will see. But remember, what people respond to in these surveys and what people actually do can be two different things.

We asked librarians about which model of e-books they would like to use. As you can see, one book, unlimited users was the most popular. Wow. That is essentially the same as it was two years ago. The number people who would consider one book, three users column did go up from 72%.

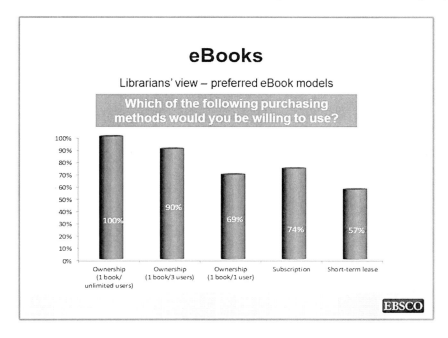

Well, the models that publishers would consider. If you will notice, the ownership column and the way this chart works, is unlikely and not sure. The biggest change in this, I think, is the far column to the right, the short term lease. If you will notice, 55% indicated that they are not likely to consider

that. A number of you may have followed the discussions on this. It's been held in a number of forms and it will continue. This is step four of this pricing model. So, that was the survey of the market.

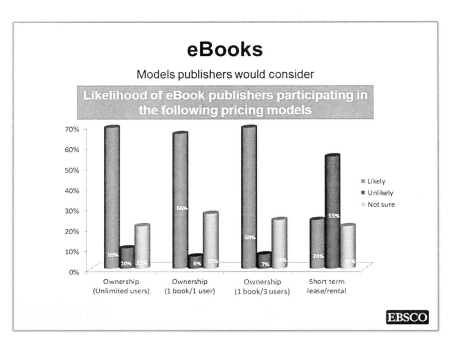

What we are doing at EBSCO is we are focused on the long term. Our financial stability allows us, when we have a publisher, we send payment with order 100% of the time. And particularly with what's happened with the Swets situation, we think that that is important. As mentioned, we focus on the long term. We are privately owned. We don't have to be on the roller coaster of a venture capital firm. We can step back and take a longer view. We are also very highly diversified as you know.

In EBSCO Information Services there is the subscription division and the intermediary services. And there is also the EBSCO publishing platform. With our subscription services we have our established EBSCONET platform that allows you to do everything from order journals to get consolidated usage statistics and analytics. We will be launching AccessNow, which is an institutional pay per view product, next year.

There are more EDS customers than any other discovery service out there. And we plan on continuing with our current indexing and abstracting services such as CINAHL and supporting our Smartlinks technology that allows you, if you ordered it from us we will automatically link you over, at any point for the database on the EBSCOhost platform. So, instead of going and studying an articles list, our Smartlinks technology takes care of that.

And that is the overview. I tried to allow about 10 minutes for questions. Thanks.

What Faculty Want Librarians to Know

Christine Fair, Assistant Professor of Security Studies, Georgetown University
Timothy Johnson, Chair of Classics, College of Charleston
Phil Richerme, Postdoctoral Researcher, Joint Quantum Institute
Moderated by Jim O'Donnell, University Professor, Georgetown University

The following is a lightly edited transcript of a live presentation at the 2014 Charleston Conference. Slides and videos are available at http://2014charlestonconference.sched.org/

Jim O'Donnell: Good morning everybody and thank you for coming out at this hour. Regular Charleston goers will know that, for the last several years, we've done a session on "What Provosts Want Librarians to Know." And, at this point in the conversation, I would be saying something like, "You may not realize it, but provosts are the nicest people in the world and we've brought several of them here." When we went to put together this year's panel, after several years of distinguished and very nice provosts, we discovered we kind of run out of nice provosts. So we decided instead that we would go with, "What Faculty Want Librarians to Know," because faculty, you may not realize this, are indeed the nicest people in the world and we have several of those folks. What we want to do today is have three colleagues do a kind of autoethnography of scholarship in libraries. I've asked these folks to come together, all of whom are scholars closer to the beginning of their career than to the end. The one who chuckled is my former student and, for that reason, he is young and he will always be young, and he should enjoy the luxury of that. But to describe a little bit of what they are and what they do and how they actually use libraries, what their access to library-like information resource is and, where appropriate to talk about, what they're not getting that they'd like to get, and to describe a little bit some of the ways they get things that don't come about simply by going down to their local library. We have one from each of the three traditional domains of scholarship, though each is untraditional in their own way. Phil Richerme, from the University of Maryland, is a Physicist; Tim Johnson, from here, the College of

Charleston, is a classicist; and Chris Fair, my colleague at Georgetown, is a "Social Scientist." I think that's the way we, uh, we put that. She can explain a bit more why. We'll start with Phil. Phil is a high energy physicist at the Quantum Institute at the University of Maryland, and works on simulation of quantum systems at a level that my high school physics would not be able, I'm sorry, to keep up with. I've asked them to hold it to 15 to 20 minutes maximum and I've promised to put snotty notes next to them if they run long so that we can have some time for you to continue the ethnography by interrogation. So let's start with Phil and the world of high energy physics. Phil? Why don't you come on up to the podium.

Phil Richerme: All right. Well, thank you so much, Jim. It's a real pleasure to be invited here and to speak in such a wonderful city. It's such a pleasant time of year. And so, I'll spend a few minutes talking about, "What Physicists Want Librarians to Know." The talk will be in two parts. I'll start with a little bit about who I am and what I do, and then I'll move on to the meat of the talk, as to how I interact with libraries and how I actually go about my daily research, finding information and communicating the information that I find. So, let's start right off with my younger years. So, in graduate school, this was home for me. This is an accelerator hall at CERN over in Geneva, Switzerland. At this building, we were taking in anti-matter particles, which are real and exist. We were taking them in from CERN, we were slowing them down and we were building atoms made entirely out of anti-matter. The goal there was that if you can build an atom made out of anti-matter and study its properties, then you can compare those properties to the properties of ordinary matter and, due to some very deep symmetries in nature and some very deep physical ideas, everything that you measure in anti-matter should be the same as in matter. This would give us a really sensitive test of whether or not these deep theories in physics are correct or not. Now, unlike some of the big collaborations at CERN, which had many thousands of people and find things like the Higgs boson, our experiment is somewhat more human sized and human manageable. So, in, in general, it took about 15 to 20 of us to design and build and operate an apparatus that looked something like this. And, of course, when we found results, we like to communicate those with the community and so we would generally publish. And typically we would publish in journals that are known as being in the top in the physics field, so this would be *Physical Review Letters*. Over the course of this experiment, there would be something like 50 or so articles to come out, two review articles. No books, though, really all journal publications.

Now recently, after graduate school, I've gone onto an atomic physics lab, and in an atomic physics lab, you typically are doing experiments that fit within a room rather than a warehouse. Everything is done on a table-top experiment. The center of a table, you have, generally, some sort of a chamber into which you load a micro fabricated trap. This is very micro engineered and micro machined, so that you can apply very specific voltages to trap individual atoms within. So, here is a picture of 16 individual atoms (Figure 1). We've adjusted voltages in that trap so that all of them lie just along a row and then you can see each individual atom there glowing like stars. Each individual atom there, we can actually program it with lasers and very, very good control to perform computations on very hard problems and, just with that chain of ions right there, we can do a computation that takes a super computer many, many days to figure out. It's a really brand new way of looking at quantum computation, to really solve some of the world's hardest problems. This is a current area of research that I'm interested in.

Bohr and Peace

Figure 1.

As before, we like to publish when we find something novel or, or new and, as before, we'll also publish in *Physical Review Letters* but now some of the journals that we'll publish in have somewhat of a broader reach to not just physicists but also the larger scientific communities, so journals like *Nature* and *Science* as well. Still no books.

That's a little bit about where I've been, but I want to talk now about what it is that I do in a kind of daily basis and how I interact with libraries in the course of a current day. So, in some hypothetical day, we'll start with the physicist's version of reading the paper and having your morning coffee and bagel. The first thing that I do in the morning is to ask, "What's new in the world?" And to do this, my first stop is a website called *The ArXiv*. This is an e-print server. And I need to say straight off that if you or your libraries in any way have developed or supported *The ArXiv* over the years, really from every physicist out there, "Thank you."

Because this is really been a transformative thing in the physics community. As you can see that there, there are really, just tons of different subfields of physics that are represented on *The ArXiv*. The idea is that, whenever there's some new result out there from some group, they will write a manuscript and, at the same time that they submit it to a journal, they'll also upload it to *The ArXiv* and, depending on the size of the field, there could be anywhere from 10 to a 100 new papers per day in each of the subfields. And so that's quite a lot to browse through. Being a quantum physicists myself, I might click on the quantum physics subsection of *The ArXiv* and that'll bring you to a page that looks something like this (Figure 2). You can very easily scroll through all of the day's new news. You can look at all of the titles of the new papers that have come out, see what groups they've been coming from, read all of the abstracts and, if there's a particular paper that catches your interest, you can zero in even further.

The Arxiv-ology of Knowledge

[1] arXiv:1410.4195 [pdf]
High visibility two photon interference of frequency time entangled photons generated in a quasi phase matched AlGaAs waveguide
Peyman Sarrafi, Eric Y. Zhu, Barry M. Holmes, David C. Hutchings, Stewart Aitchison, Li Qian
Journal-ref: Optics Letters. Vol. 39, No. 17, September 1, 2014
Subjects: Quantum Physics (quant-ph); Optics (physics.optics)

We demonstrate experimentally the frequency time entanglement of photon pairs produced in a CW pumped quasi phased matched AlGaAs superlattice waveguide. A visibility of 96.0+-0.7% without background subtra inequality by 52 standard deviations.

[2] arXiv:1410.4257 [pdf, other]
Magneto-optical properties of paramagnetic superrotors
A. A. Milner, A. Korobenko, J. Floß, I. Sh. Averbukh, V. Milner
Subjects: Quantum Physics (quant-ph); Atomic Physics (physics.atom-ph)

We study the dynamics of paramagnetic molecular superrotors in an external magnetic field. Optical centrifuge is used to create dense ensembles of oxygen molecules in ultra-high rotational states. In the presence of n birefringent, which indicates preferential alignment of molecular axes along the field direction. The experimental observations are supported by numerical calculations and explained by means of an intuitive qualitative m molecular axes is mediated by the spin-rotation coupling. We show that the induced magneto-rotational birefringence is more robust with respect to collisions than the rotational coherence, and that this robustness incre

[3] arXiv:1410.4285 [pdf, ps, other]
Negativity of quantumness and non-Markovianity in a qubit coupled to a thermal Ising spin bath system
Zheng-Da Hu, Yixin Zhang, Ye-Qi Zhang
Comments: 7 pages, 5 figures
Journal-ref: Commun. Theor. Phys. 62 (2014) 634
Subjects: Quantum Physics (quant-ph)

We propose a scheme to characterize the non-Markovian dynamics and quantify the non-Markovianity via the non-classicality measured by the negativity of quantumness. By considering a qubit in contact with a critical negativity of quantumness indicate the non-Markovian dynamics. Furthermore, a normalized measure of non-Markovianity based on the negativity of quantumness is introduced and the influences of bath criticality, bath shown that, at the critical point, the decay of non-Markovianity versus the size of spin bath is fastest and the non-Markovianity is exactly zero only in the thermodynamic limit. Besides, non-trivial behaviours of negativity keeping constant are found for different relations between parameters of the initial state. Finally, how the non-classicality of the system is affected by a series of bang-bang pulses is also examined.

[4] arXiv:1410.4297 [pdf, ps, other]
Quantum Bit Commitment Combinbing with BB84 Protocol
Linxi Zhang, Changhua Zhu, Nan Zhao, Changxing Pei
Comments: 4 pages, 2 figures
Subjects: Quantum Physics (quant-ph)

We proposed a new quantum bit commitment scheme in which secret key need not to be provided by other quantum key distribution system. We can get the bit commitment with probability p by adding a waiting time in outcomes can be encrypted by one-time pad with the key generated by BB84 protocol. We can also obtain the redundant secret keys to encrypt other information in this quantum key distribution system

[5] arXiv:1410.4318 [pdf, other]
Experimental implementation of optimal linear-optical controlled-unitary gates
Karel Lemr, Karol Bartkiewicz, Antonín Černoch, Miloslav Dušek, Jan Soubusta
Comments: 7 pages, 5 figures
Subjects: Quantum Physics (quant-ph)

We show that it is possible to reduce the number of two-qubit gates needed for the construction of an arbitrary controlled-unitary transformation by up to two times using a tunable controlled-phase gate. On the platform probabilistically, our method significantly reduces the amount of components and increases success probability of a two-qubit gate. The experimental implementation of our technique presented in this paper for a contro controlled-phase gate is needed instead of two standard controlled-NOT gates. Thus, not only do we increase success probability by about one order of magnitude (with the same resources), but also avoid the need for

Figure 2.

It'll take you to a page where you can, again, see the title in the abstract, click on some of the authors' names to see what else has been published by them in the past and also, on the right, you can see that there's a, a link to download a PDF so that you can read it immediately, you can save it for later, take it on the plane, do whatever you need to do with that PDF. If it's been some later time and this preprint version of the paper comes out in some journal, then you can see at the bottom there's a journal reference. You can click on the journal reference and that'll take you immediately to the so-called version of record. I should also say at this point that *The ArXiv* allows you to update based on referee comments or any other changes that you've made in the paper, and a lot of the journals that are popular to publish in in physics will allow you to upload the final version of record to *The ArXiv*, so long as it doesn't have the publisher's letterhead on the top.

And so really, this is a great source for getting kind of the most up-to-date information that's out there in the physics community. And I mentioned before that this is a really transformative new technology for physics and I'd say that there's really two reasons for this. The first reason has to do with accessibility. *The ArXiv*, at least from the point of view of physicists, it has been free and it has always been free and it will continue to be free for us, so that people from pretty much any country can upload their information to *The ArXiv* and read what others around the world have done. Now, certainly the publishing community has taken note of this. There are a couple of new open access journals in the past few years to spring up in physics. These are really going in the right direction but even still to date, these journals cost about $2,000 per article for the author to publish in, and there's certainly some initiatives and consortia to try and reduce that costs for publishing groups but these consortia are not really universal quite yet and there's still some room to go. I would say that *The ArXiv* at least has been, for 15 years or so, making it free to physicists and will continue to be free.

All right, so, the other big reason that *The ArXiv* has been so transformative is it's really the large amount of time that's saved and the up-to-date information that you get right away by reading it. Just for sake of example, this is a paper that we published in *Physical Review Letters*. You can see right in the byline here that this paper was received in March. It had to go through peer review and publishing and then it came out in September. So, that's five months from submission to it actually appearing in a journal. And it's not just *Physical Review Letters*. You can look at other journals like *Nature*, where a paper is submitted in January and it doesn't appear until July, five-and-a-half months later. Now, on *The ArXiv*, of course, this is submitted at the same time that they go to the journals and so that information is out there now half a year before it comes out in print. And so if I were to kind of look at the hierarchy of how information is communicated in physics, I would say if you want the most leading edge, up-to-date information that's out there, you have to go to conferences. You have to talk to people and often you'll actually see plots or, new ideas from those conferences that haven't made it into publication and, in fact, it's somewhat of a bragging right if you can show a plot in your talk that is only hours old data rather than something that, you know, is weeks old or months old. That's where you really get to that bleeding edge, but when the group's actually make a sellable story, when they have all their error analysis really down and well characterized, then you publish something on *The ArXiv*. And that's immediately how the wider community gets access to what you've done, and then maybe about half a year later or so, that paper will eventually land in some journal; but, by that point, people aren't really reading the journals to figure out what's new. Maybe every so often to figure out what has fallen through the cracks, what you've missed on *The ArXiv*, but, ironically, *The ArXiv* has really now become the medium of communication and the journals have now become the archive.

Okay. So that's, that's how I start my day, is seeing what's new in the world. But now we actually have to go to work and start doing experiments. If we already have an experiment planned, then that's great. We go ahead, we run our apparatus, we take data and life is great. But half of experimental physics is trying to figure out what experiments are we really looking to perform. And for that, just like other fields, we need to start doing some sort of a literature search. And to do a literature search, we start in maybe a number of the interesting places. I've already mentioned *The ArXiv*. Google Scholar is probably the most widely used broad-based search tool that I know about and, and my colleagues also use. Some also use Web of Science. These are really powerful tools for us to use. We can search by author or date or journal or paper title or anything. It'll give us a large list with possible other related papers, and these are all very useful tools. The American Physical Society also has a very broad-based search tool. One of the things that I've notably left out here is the university library site, which I'd say, in some sense, I would say it suffers because it's too comprehensive, and the number of different resources that it pulls up, many, many books included, are usually not the place that we'll first be looking for that sort of information we're interested in. And so if we find a paper of interest, we can read through it, and papers have references and we can follow reference lists all the way through until we're fully exhausted. I pull up this particular reference list (Figure 3) because, as you look through it, you'll notice that most of the references that are in this paper that I pulled out are to journals. But every so often in a reference list, you'll come across something like this entry here, number 24. And this, I believe, is called a book. I had to dig through a number of different papers to find even this one example in a reference list of this book.

Things Fall Apart

[16] M. Piraud and L. Sanchez-Palencia, Eur. Phys. J. Special Topics **217**, 91 (2013).

[17] E. Gurevich and O. Kenneth, Phys. Rev. A **79**, 063617 (2009).

[18] A. Yedjour and B. A. Van Tiggelen, Eur. Phys. J. D **59**, 249 (2010).

[19] M. Piraud, L. Pezzé, and L. Sanchez-Palencia, New J. Phys. **15**, 075007 (2013).

[20] S. E. Skipetrov, A. Minguzzi, B. A. van Tiggelen, and B. Shapiro, Phys. Rev. Lett. **100**, 165301 (2008).

[21] R. C. Kuhn, O. Sigwarth, C. Miniatura, D. Delande, and C. A. Müller, New J. Phys. **9**, 161 (2007).

[22] See Supplemental Material at http://link.aps.org/supplemental/10.1103/PhysRevLett.111.145303 for information on experimental parameters, the speckle autocorrelation, and the stretched exponential fit.

[23] B. DeMarco, J. L. Bohn, J. P. Burke, M. Holland, and D. S. Jin, Phys. Rev. Lett. **82**, 4208 (1999).

[24] J. Goodman, *Speckle Phenomena in Optics* (Roberts and Company, Englewood, CO, 2007).

[25] S. Pilati, S. Giorgini, M. Modugno, and N. Prokof'ev, New J. Phys. **12**, 073003 (2010).

[26] A. Gatti, D. Magatti, and F. Ferri, Phys. Rev. A **78**, 063806 (2008).

[27] M. Pasienski and B. DeMarco, Opt. Express **16**, 2176 (2008).

[28] A. Gaunt and Z. Hadzibabic, Sci. Rep. **2**, 721 (2012).

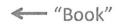 ← "Book"

Figure 3.

Now, unlike a lot of the fields in the humanities, or others, typically when a book is cited in physics, it's because there's a particular equation of interest or maybe a very well worded paragraph or something, but I would say that books, in general, aren't really the medium for breaking new ground in physics. And so, as such, books are really kind of a, an extended review paper. They're a collection of really good references with maybe some more pedagogical explanations of how things work that aren't really condensed in journals, but in general, they're not breaking new ground, which means that the information that we're pulling out of this book, generally, it can be found in about a minute or so and then we're done with it and we're ready to continue on with our literature search. As a result, if we want to look at what's going on in this book and whether or not it'll be of interest of us, probably the first thing that we'll do, rather than go to the library, is to go to Google Books, okay? You have all of these online scanned versions of books and, if you get lucky, then the pages that you want, explaining the equation that you're interested in, won't be blocked by Google Books and you can find it. Sometimes, you're not that lucky and so, of course, then the natural choice is to go to Amazon, look, go to the "Look Inside" feature and try and see what you're interested in. Sometimes that doesn't work either, in which case, probably the next step is to continue searching on the Internet for the particular equation of interest.

Notice here, we have not yet gone to the library to look for this book. And, in fact, it's not just me. I took a poll of the lab in this extraordinarily scientific study, asked them, "Do you know how to get to the physics library?" And these are the results (Figure 4). Okay. That's right. You'll notice there's no error bars, but okay. This is what I found as an informal poll at the lab.

Things Fall Apart

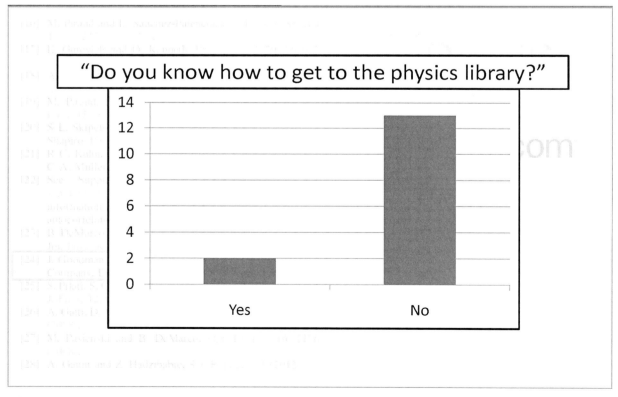

Figure 4.

In my final few minutes, I just want to talk a little bit about analysis. After we've done our literature search, after we've taken our data, we want to analyze it. We want to store that data long term and I often get the question from some librarians as to whether or not archival of this data is something that's interesting to us, something that's wanted by physicists. I'd say the short answer to that is no. Here is a screenshot of all of the data in our folder from the year 2013 (Figure 5). You'll see that all of the data takes up about 100 gigabytes. So, unlike the LHC, and I think they have in-house librarians to deal with archival and all that, a typical experimental group will take about a hundred gigabytes of data per year and if you look at all of the data that we take in our experiment, all the way back to 2008, including every image, every paper that we've written, every everything, it takes about one terabyte on a two terabyte hard drive, something that you can purchase for a hundred to two hundred dollars.

Clearly, this sort of thing is backed up in many places. We have our own on-site backups, we contract with physics IT departments to back it up for us as well. If libraries want to start filling in that role, that's probably fine with us, but we don't necessarily have a need for it right now. I'd also point out that just raw data without any context is not very useful to a broader community. It's a very specialized thing of how to take data and the data that we get is really strings of ones and zeros that we're measuring and, without knowing exactly what experiments you're doing, exactly what apparatus it's coming from, all of that kind of documentation that needs to go hand-in-hand with the data, I think that would really put an undue burden on the physicists themselves to try and make this available to a broader community so that it could be achieved in a library. I think that the burden of that is pretty high in general.

Lord of the Files

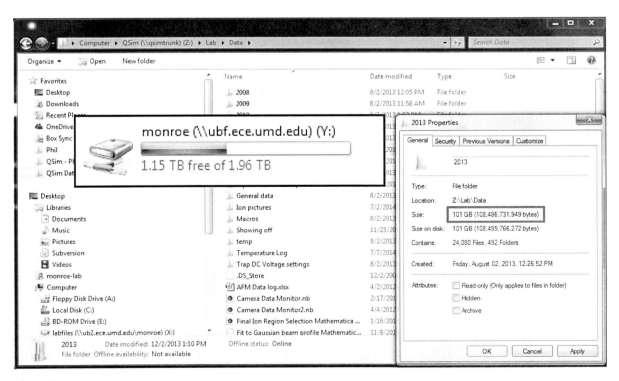

Figure 5.

Just to wrap up with a couple of my key points: if you haven't been able to tell in general, I love books, personally, okay. I think books are great, but the honest truth is that, for physics research, in our day-to-day, they're really no longer a critical resource for how we actually do our work. There would be some better utilization, I'd say, of books if text were available online, but maybe that's not also the best way for librarians and libraries themselves to be using their resources. I would say, by far, journals are the dominant method for communication, both for learning about what's going on in the world in physics and also for communicating with the world what you have done in physics. And I would say to librarians, particularly for things like *The ArXiv*, we need continued access and we need continued support for this tools because these are really how the medium of communication has really turned in the last ten years, and the physics world would be completely different if these tools were to not persist.

And finally I just touched on this point that data archiving, it's not necessarily the realm of libraries for physical data. We only need very modest storage requirements. We can take care of that in-house, or with other IT departments at universities, and the data itself will be useless without context. With that, I'd like to wrap up. So, thank you for your attention.

Jim O'Donnell: Thank you, Phil. Tim Johnson will speak next from the College of Charleston. He's been here in his third year now as chair of the largest department of classics in South Carolina. Before that, Tim was indeed my student a long time ago. He holds his PhD from the University of Illinois, and made his bones in the scholarly world at Baylor and at the University of Florida. He's a recognized and widely published scholar in the field of Latin lyric poetry. He also has the experience of having been involved at the University of Florida in creating and running the first and still the only online PhD program in classics, which had a particular niche. So, I've asked him. You may be able to predict or you think you can predict some of what his needs and experiences would be, but that online experience suggests that he's had to push some envelopes as well. So, please welcome Tim.

Tim Johnson: I must admit that I still cringe to call my professor Jim, because 30 years ago, when he called me on the phone and said, "I don't see any Latin on your transcripts. If you can tell us just a little bit of Latin, I'll be willing to take you into our new post-doc program." And I thought that none qualified for little. So, I answered that question, "Yes." And without that fortune, I would not have the career that I have today. That's one facet of my experience, is starting from behind and learning how to run fast as I could.

The other part of my experience is that I've been fortunate in my career that I've been able to move and, as you can tell by the gray now in my beard, I've been able to move quite a bit. From, in fact, Luther College, a small private institution, to Truman State, a small public institution, to Baylor University, a large private institution, to the University of Florida, a large public institution, to now the College of Charleston, a small public institution. After navigating these moves, I'm now appreciative of the different perspectives that they have offered me. So, I title this reflection, "Books, Databases, and Bodies."

Last week when I was driving home on Savannah Highway in Charleston, once again sitting in traffic, I saw a bumper sticker and it said simply, "I love libraries." Short, pointed, like most bumper stickers, but, unlike most bumper stickers, actually true. I do love libraries, and now that we live and work in a digital world, we can put libraries in places where they never before existed. That's fantastic and exciting. But in 1966, when I first learned to use libraries, access was nothing about logging in, clicking and downloading. At the old Carnegie Library in Paris, Illinois, two blocks down from the town square, a librarian, priceless, took the time to teach this six-year-old to sort through the card catalog and browse the stacks so that I could discover and expand my own interests. Another voracious reader was born that day and the entire act was physical. Walking to the library, hearing its echo, smelling its polish, fingering indexed cards, pulling books off shelves. I work best when my entire person is active. Research, in its fullest experience, is, for me, a collaborative act among my senses and, as such, encompasses my whole being, I hope, mind and body, sight, sound, smell, taste, and touch.

But I hope my learning is not egocentric, my mind and my body. If I remain sole sovereign of my work, then I am most isolated, trapped within my own senses and my own experience, and therefore bound to my own limitations, which I admit, are severe. This, in fact, is what I want most from libraries, to provide me with the others I need and the others I desire who will save me from the disaster of a solitary self. Others research not only touches me but I need to touch their work, to lay my hands on it and feel it, like I would embrace a body. So it is that research begs to be handled in some form. It is tactile. And I must admit that I want it to remain touchy-feely, hands-on. Horace, the first century BC Roman lyricist, when defending his own work against critics, assumes the voice of his poems and books and says, as if he were his own poetry, this, "I, presenting what is new, love to be read and handled by the eyes and hands of those who know what they are doing." And maybe this has something to say about patron driven acquisition. It's fine to be handled, but I prefer it to be handled by those who know what they are doing. I've been touching books and articles all my life and I do not want to stop. I'm far too addicted.

Now, I must say I'm glad that research feels different in my hand now than it used to and is much easier to share in all forms, Kindles, iPads, e-books, JSTOR, Google Books and on and on it goes. And less often now, as given my schedule, just like Phil, I have little chance to walk to the library campus, which is only five minutes from my office. The stacks I browse most often, and I believe most of my students, as the data would suggest, are digital, access driven by search engines. This high speed power is, I would say, part of our challenge. As sophisticated as my students are in handling technological gadgetry, they are surprisingly unsophisticated in constructing meaningful and effective search rubrics. Too often, we do not have the personnel or do not take the time, in this digital age, to do the equivalent of what that mid-western Parisian librarian did for me, teaching learners to search the digital stacks. Consequently, for these

simplistic searchers, conducting a digital browse, arrangement matters more than it ever did. It is not just about finding a particular book or article. It is about what they can find around that particular item on the digital page without their searches instantly becoming too diffuse. Too often still, students come to my office after running a keyword search, and I'm sure you've been there too, with a list of 2,500 entries printed out on 25 pages. It is impossible for them to tell which libraries have which book or if it's just available on Amazon. As a default then, they tend to use only e-books or JSTOR sources and let all others go. So, books are losing out progressively to articles. We do need better and coordinated strategies for once again making our students and ourselves constantly more search literate.

Returning to my first tenure-track position, which I refer to as NPCC, Nearly Post Card Catalog, at Baylor at 1994 to 1999, it was the world now of the private university. Baylor became a first-rate undergraduate classics program, but their library resources in the area, like many, were and are limited. While there then, my research was supported mostly through a visiting courtesy appointment at the University of Texas, Austin, still built on the model of departmental libraries supported by the larger main library, but public, not private, and, therefore, not in the consortium with Baylor. When links between institutions are nonexistent or broken, public versus private, in state versus out of state, fee paying versus non-fee paying client, then researchers are focused or forced to find their own connections. Interlibrary loan, no matter how large the consortium, I have found not to be a workable solution. True enough, my library here, within weeks, can place in my hands almost any needed resource but then, within only weeks, I have to ship it back. And so when I'm working on a long term project, I start to have visions of standing, like we used to, at the Xerox machine. And what saves me mostly are kind librarians at the University of North Carolina Chapel Hill and still the University of Illinois, who are willing to take time and bend some of the rules in order to send me a PDF by email. My experience teaches me that the push that we are undertaking for access, with all of its budgetary implications, security challenges and concern for quality control, is a fight worth picking and winning.

My years at the University of Florida in 1999 to 2011 taught me just how acute the problem of access is. I was privileged then to be a part of a team that created an online PhD program in Roman studies, 2005. We underestimated the demand for this. When we launched this, we anticipated, at most, 25 enrolled and that was immediately at 100. Since then, the program has been tailored back, has learned better parameters and is, I think, of a better quality, but the basic structure of that program has not changed. Students, during their academic year, take two courses online with real-time interaction with the professor and their peers. Then, during the summer, students come to the university and take intensive summer institutes. This structure is very intentional. It creates the face-to-face time needed for directing advanced research and allows the remote students to comply with the same minimum in-resident requirements that every traditional student at the university has to meet. This satisfied the university, which was still, at that time, nervous about distance education, nervous that the quality of the program would meet their standards and that the integrity of their brand would be maintained. But this, however, was not the problem that confronted the students on a practical level. They would be located off campus for most of the year and neither their high school libraries nor their public libraries were even close to providing the resources they needed for their research. If they just happened to be located near a university library, they more often than not could not gain access because they were not enrolled as students. We basically were entirely and dependent on online sources, which is when the real frustration began. Since these students were labeled remote and were technically classified as continuing education, their own university was reluctant to grant them full access for security reasons and the cost of server space. Basically, the students were shut down because of institutional technology. Now, before I turn institutional technology into the outlaws, which is always a favorite sport, the problem was essentially one of coordination and was essentially and eventually

resolved. I'm afraid, however, that this problem still remains, that there are no or few too links between local public libraries, the secondary school library system, and the private and public universities. We and our students too often become stuck when trying to navigate such territorial boundaries when we are utilizing instruments and tools that recognize no such distinct territories. The artificial boundaries that we keep set up between types and stages of students and learning and research, we must question, challenge and continue to breach. We could say that, in spite of the rapid and constant technology driven change in which we now work and play, the end game of our field remains constant. From the time of Horus in 10 BC, from the time he hoped that the books he published would be available for all the hands and eyes who would know what to do with them, we want to put books, resources in contact with human bodies. In that hope, Ovid in 10 AD, an exile from Rome, himself now a remote scholar, used the technology available to him and mailed his book off to Rome, telling it, "My little book, you will go to the city without me. It pains me that I, your author, am not able to go but, my book, greet with my words my favorite places because, through your footprint especially, I am able to touch them."

Like Horus and Ovid and I suppose all other learners, I do have some wishes for bringing my body of work in contact with others and I'll keep these short and end with these because we are busy and my attention span is short. So, here are three of the proverbial wishes that I would have. One, I want versatile space in my libraries. My office is crowded with people and stuffed with administrative paper work and, for my writing, I need space, sometimes to be able to collaborate with others, but oftentimes to be alone and uninterrupted. I find it very hard to find any space to be alone where the conversations of others do not suffocate my creative self. While I was at Florida, they renovated the library and they replaced all cubicles with the equivalent of an open concept house plan and larger rooms for groups.

Two, I want more database projects specifically designed for my research interest. Now, I understand databases can cause problems. They do for my students. I can instantly sit them in front of a computer with, with a TLG and PHIM and give them immediately a searchable database of most all of Latin and Greek literature. The problem with that database, of course, is it assumes too stable a field in the amount of additions at or in, that it takes into account and therefore, the student's perspective is limited, even though they think, "This is so great. It's covering everything." Right? There's a problem with databases but still, I want more. As a model, we can consult the Homer Multitext project, which is an open source data collection giving, if you will, access to the textual tradition of the Iliad and Odyssey within its historical context or the Palace of Nestor project, which is here at the College of Charleston, which is developing 3D images of these tablets which were previously accessible only to a few and then only in Greece.

My third wish, if wishes one and two are going to take a while, and I imagine that they will, for right now, I would simply like more money. Just send cash, because nothing makes collaborative partners become defensive and fight quicker than a poor funding supply. We need more efficiency in the grant cycle and better strategies for convincing funding sources that libraries are not just a heartbeat of our colleges, universities, businesses, research, but the very life source of our culture. And so, at the end, I'm looking back at that bumper sticker, "I love libraries." And I appreciate all its professionals, their dedication and hard work, which do make my work easier and better. Thank you.

Jim O'Donnell: Third and last speaker is Professor Christine Fair from the School of Foreign Service of Georgetown University. I said she's a social scientist in quotation marks because she started life with a PhD in South Asian studies at the University of Chicago, which is probably the best place in the world to do that, but she's had an interesting employment career, working as an analyst for the RAND Corporation for the Institute, US Institute of Peace and as a political officer with the United Nation Assistance Project in Kabul. She

has picked up some frequent flyer miles. Her most recent book, highly controversial in some parts of the world, if not Charleston, South Carolina, is called, *Fighting to the End: The Pakistan Army's Way of War*, for which, among other things, she has to collect information from official Pakistan military, journals not held, I think, in all of your libraries. So, Chris represents the sometime scholar, the sometime political officer, the full-time scholar and social scientist with a significant impact on policy debates and a significant need for good current information of many kinds. Chris.

Christine Fair: Thank you. So, he spared me the indignity of describing myself, but let me say that I actually do need this thing called a physical book. I get a lot of information from journals but, actually, what I often need are these things that are actually published and bound and typically housed in libraries. Unfortunately, they're often housed in libraries that I do not have immediate access to. So, let me explain how I had previously used libraries and how spoiled I became and now how I have to sort of MacGyver my research based out of Georgetown. I have done everything at the University of Chicago. I started out as a scientist, where I lived in the Crerar Library. If there's any Crerar librarians out there from the USC, I love you. Regenstein librarians, anyone in the house from the Regenstein? Anyone? Oh, my heart is breaking. Yay, Regenstein. Yay! I bet your aunt hooked up at the Regenstein, because we USC people love the stack so much that that's where we dated, because we were so busy studying we didn't have time to leave the library to have a social life. So I'm, I love libraries. I love librarians. I love reference librarians. I have been spoiled. When I am sitting there at the coffee shop doing work online, using whatever access materials I have online that I have personally scanned from the Regenstein, I think back to the time when I would actually wander the stacks because, even in the process of looking for a book that I actually wanted, I would find books that were actually more interesting.

Obviously, as someone who works in South Asia, I have been an enormous beneficiary of the PL 480 program. So again, all of you working the entire supply chain from picking books out in Delhi, out in Islamabad, out in Dhaka, Colombo, let me also thank you because my research would not be possible without the PL 480 program. Let me also say very briefly that, even though I primarily work on South Asia materials, many of the countries that I work in Pakistan, well I can't work there now because I'm blacklisted, but when I did, they don't understand libraries. The collections are disastrously organized, they're poorly kept. Ironically, some of the best resources for doing this kind of work is actually here in the United States, at places like the University of Chicago, UC Berkley. In other words, in any school where you have a PL 480 program. This is where these kinds of resources are privileged and they're valued, not only by the people who lovingly cultivate them, i.e., you, but also the users of them, i.e., me.

Also, when I was at the RAND Corporation, I want to say I really, I worked with a lot of economists, so I have an acute appreciation of the value of librarian's times. One thing that really frustrates me when I go to academic environments is that academics have no sense of the value of their time. I can't tell you how many meetings I've been in and people sort of take the opportunity to, I don't know, go on for 40 minutes for no apparent reason. I'm just thinking, "My consulting rate ranges from $350 an hour to $1,250 and I just add up all the money that we've just wasted for no good purpose and it drives me nuts." RAND had a very good way, of course, when I was at RAND, sometimes it bothered me, but RAND had a very good way of monetizing the value of librarians and their contributions to the projects because we had to basically pay for their service, and we would do this, especially at RAND, because, for better or for worse, we had to become masters of multiple literature. When I did a lot of work on military manpower, i.e., how do we recruit, train, retain, a military, which by the way completely transfers to my work on Islamist militants because they're also manning a force, I would have to know the advertisement literature, so, in other words, how much bang for buck do you get out of certain advertisements, how do you instrument bang for bucks. So, I know the advertisement literature. I had to know the labor economics literature and I also had to know the very specialized military manpower literature. And obviously, there's no

way someone like me could master all of those literature. So, for me, the, the RAND librarians were my collaborators and we paid for them on our projects. Acquisitions would be, if there was a product that they couldn't get through interlibrary loan, for example, there'd be a decision. If this was a general use product, RAND's library funds would pay for it which was, of course, subsidized in part by our overhead, which is usurious, I'll be the first to acknowledge, or it would be paid for by the project funds. But, essentially, projects had to endogenize the value that librarians created. And, as a consequence of that, we actually valued them. So, what I find is, as I've transitioned to the university, there's no way of endogenizing librarian's value and this, this affects everyone. So, when my students, and I'm going to conclude with this at the end of my remarks, when my students approach librarians, there's no way of valuing that transaction.

If the librarian wants to treat my student with disregard, which, believe it or not, actually does happen, and it's very frustrating to me because they pay the librarian's bills and they pay my bills. My students are the customer. So when my students, the customers, don't get value, it pisses me off, to put it very bluntly, and so I think this is in part because librarians think they have different missions. But from my point of view, the big mission is servicing the customer who paid, who pays the bills. This is perhaps an interesting discussion best had over mimosas, since we're still in the morning. But my experience with libraries, I would say, I have been generally very, very spoiled with the one exception of when I was at USIP, but I happened to catch the tail end of the debate that was going on about nonresearch libraries.

Let me tell you how someone, a data MacGyverer, the USIP library sucked so much and that's a technical term. Suck is an acronym. It's early, I forgot what it stands for. It sucked so much that I would stroll up to my Alexandrian Public Library to use the resources there. Why? Because they basically had the things that I needed. They actually had databases that allowed me to do a literature search using whatever tools that the library had and they also had interlibrary loans, something that my employer didn't have. I remember saying to my boss, "Sorry, I'm not coming in today. I'm going to the Alexander Public Library, because your library sucks." I think these local resources are really, really important. In fact, I've had students who have worked with me over the summer who didn't have an institutional home. They couldn't use the Georgetown library, so I sent them also to the Alexander Public Library. I'm a big fan of these public resources and I, for one, have benefited from them. I had this great experience and then I came to Georgetown and I love Georgetown. The library experience has not been on the top of my, "I love this stuff about Georgetown." And the reasons for it, I think, I'm not exactly sure what the reason is because I've been to a lot of institutions. I think part of it is there's a very big mismatch. And that is what I do, South Asia, is not something that Georgetown has historically specialized in and therefore, as a consequence, its collections are just completely disconsonant with the work that I need, but, as I said, you know, I'm aware of economics.

Libraries are, in fact, I would argue, the most expensive things in the world. I mean, think about some of the most important libraries in major cities. They are sitting on huge chunks of real estate. So having this thing called a book on a shelf, if you were just to think about the money per book that you spend to essentially rent the home for that book, these are incredibly expensive. So, I would never suggest that a library should have special collections that reflect the need of its scholars. I think that's incredibly economically inefficient and it makes no sense. I'm not expecting that, but echoing the other comments on this panel, what I do expect is that my university has better relations with those universities that do have the collections that I need, so that when I do an interlibrary loan request, for example, for a very specialized book, I actually have access to it. But let me also make a comment about interlibrary loan. A couple of things that Georgetown does really, really well. I'm very thankful for all of its electronic services, the various databases that allow me to do literature search, document delivery is generally very good for journals, have a pretty good success rate with interlibrary loan. Many of the schools on the east coast do have a PL 480 program. So

generally their hit rate is about 80%, but here's the reality. I'm not the only one that said that this morning. "I'm going to go to Amazon." Right? And no one wants the books I want. No one. So, I can usually buy them for $3.99 with shipping. So, by the time I hop in my car and I commute through the jackass parade to get to Georgetown and then find parking, I have just taken basically six months off of my life that I can't get back. So, what do I do? I just hit the buy on Amazon and then, of course, that $3.99 is covered by my research fund. It turns out that I am actually endogenizing my own library. I've had to completely redo my upstairs office with floor-to-ceiling shelves. I've had to spend $15,000 reclaiming what used to be this wet, disgusting, vermin-infested excuse for a basement. So, I have essentially built my own library. And actually, you know, is that efficient? I'm not sure, but it's what I have had to do, and it's actually the only, I don't have any jewelry, I drive a crappy car, but let me tell you, my South Asia collection, don't come near my books.

But going back to the book that I mentioned, so this, if I were the University of Chicago, this would've been an easy project to execute, because it has all of those journals that I needed. And you obviously, when you're doing a project like this, you're actually trying to collect a universe of every single article that's appeared on a certain topic in every single, traceable Pakistani military publication. So, the first thing you have to do is build, basically build an inventory of every single issue of the key journals that you're looking at, right? You're basically creating your universe and then you're going and you're constructing your sample based upon the things that are available. I have access to University of Chicago because I'm an alum. What I don't have access to, unfortunately, is their consortium of research libraries, which is just like two blocks south of the University of Chicago, because I don't have privileges. I have to buy privileges to get there. So, at one point, this is how ridiculous it was. That collection, four blocks away from the midway, and I was already based in Chicago for several days working in the B level, having lots of memories about when I was younger, when the B level meant different things other than looking at journals, um, I realized that there were something like 30 volumes that were right across the street, but there was no way I could get them. So, I had to go back to Washington, DC, and I had to go to UC Berkley because I couldn't use that collection. And I couldn't believe it. I got to go to freaking UC Berkley and I hate Berkley. All those tweekers, just homeless tweekers. That's just hell. It's like a gauntlet of homeless tweekers to get to the library. But that's what I ended up doing. And, of course, because UC Berkley is a public school, they also allow me to have access to the overflow, which is also where many of these journals were stored. And then finally, anyone from the NYU Public Library? Well, I love you if you're out there because, believe it or not, the most difficult to acquire journal issues that I needed were actually housed at the NYU Public Library, which was, again, pretty easy access. But all of this really had to do, I mean all, just required just a bunch of MacGyvering.

It occurred to me how really lucky I am that I am at Georgetown and the School of Foreign Service has been so supportive and they provided me all sorts of funds to basically go out throughout the country and peruse these journals. And the whole question is, how do you actually, if I had to photocopy all this stuff, there would just be, the entire Amazon forest would be depleted. What I ended up doing, and again, this would've been very different if I had done this project 15 years ago, is I have this very small scanner. It's about the size of my laptop and it just plugs into my laptop. So I scanned thousands of pages in libraries that have internet access. I was just uploading it to the cloud so I had it stored in redundant places, both locally on my laptop as well as in the cloud. And then this, of course, was very easy, in terms of organizing it, but I think about how expensive it is to house these journals. I couldn't help but think, "Boy, I just wish that the money were available to make this stuff digital." Because a person who's not at Georgetown, who's not at a university that has such resources, there's no way they would be able to do the kind of research that I did. Clearly if these journals were digitized, it would make this kind of information accessible to everyone. There was one, boy, there was a moment where I came home and I said to my husband, "Why is that library there?"

Georgetown did have this one book. It was an incredibly rare book. It was very rare, very few libraries had it. World Cat showed me which ones had it. They were generally not in the ILL relationships here with Georgetown, but it was held in their special collections. Okay. All right, y'all are gonna have to explain this to me, how special collection works. I, sometimes, I thought for Georgetown, it's like their own special petting zoo, because you just go there and look at the book, pet the book because we were not allowed to photocopy the book because it might be injured. We couldn't even take a picture of it with a camera or a phone. I was just, what in the world is this book doing here? I wanted to put it on my syllabus for Blackboard, which is a whole other issue about the really crappy copies I get for Blackboard. I have to do all the photocopying myself, which is not, that's another side issue. But I had to go back to interlibrary loan and I had to say, "I know that you have this at special collections but I can't use this book at special collections because I have to do this thing called read this goddamn book." I go and I get the interlibrary loan. I then take it and I scan it, which, yeah, we spend a lot of time, I think my ovaries are completely useless from all the radiation from the scanner. Thank God I don't have kids or they'd have like a tail, or a photocopier leaping out of its head. I just couldn't, I honestly couldn't understand what's the point of special collection? If this book is so fragile that it can't be photographed with an iPhone, why is it not being digitized? I almost used a swear word. So, just anytime I see special collections, I just go back to Amazon and I try to find a copy for sale in London, Delhi, wherever. All right.

So, for me, my wish list, just to be very blunt, um, I don't expect libraries to cater to, to my research interest. I, it's just, economically, that's a silly proposition and it's best that schools specialize, right? So that, that we're not having schools, or libraries duplicate, collections. I believe in specialization, but I also believe that this means that as essentially as one library specializes, they're essentially creating a public good, and it's imperative that libraries understand that they benefit from the public goods that other libraries are providing. And if they forge these relationships that allow scholars to go and have access to these various public relation, or to these various holdings. Right now, I feel that that's definitely missing. "Do I miss wandering the stacks?" There is no question. My tactileness as a scholar has been very restricted that I can't just visually go and see, "Well there's this book in Hindi. Um, well, crap, that's a more interesting book in Hindi." That, that part of my scholarship, based upon where I am, is absolutely gone. I so value the electronic databases. I cannot emphasize enough how important that is. Let me say very briefly, how Georgetown, however, organizes the databases, again, drives me to drink. They're just alphabetized, alphabetized. You've got thousands of these things and they're organized alphabetically. So, you have to know what it is you're looking for to go and find it. When I first came to Georgetown, they had them helpfully organized by subjects, so that's at least navigable. But for my students, this is an incredibly overwhelming process. They don't know how to extract value because Georgetown has not organized its resources in a way that allows my students to derive value.

I still, I must confess, when I'm really stumped, I will still call the reference librarian at the University of Chicago although, as the staff turns over and they no longer know me from my graduate student days, that's getting harder to do. "I don't know you and you're that really grousy person that says Pakistan's military supports terror. Do I want to talk to you? Probably not." So, that personal relationship is getting a little bit harder to, so even I'm finding myself a little bit at a loss because Georgetown can't help me there. But most importantly, it's for my students who are not South Asianist. They're just security study students. They really need to understand how to do things like a literature review. They're not learning this as undergraduates. They think a literature review is a Google search, going to Amazon. Trying to explain to them what social science abstracts is, it's almost like explaining Schrodinger's cat to my dog. When I send them to librarians, because they're supposed to be the people that are most effective at sort of introducing my students to what the university can offer, both physically and electronically, I find they seem to be inconvenienced by my students and I hear this so often that I consistently raise it with my programmatic leadership because I don't know. They might have other jobs like acquiring things, but one of their jobs should be helping students understand the value of a library, even if the value of that library isn't just the physical space, but all the other things, like access to information that libraries provide. Thank you.

We Sincerely Regret to Inform You That the Material You Have Requested Is Unavailable via Interlibrary Loan

Jennifer Duncan, Utah State University

Carol Kochan, Utah State University

Lars Leon, University of Kansas

Abstract

This paper outlines the preliminary results of the authors' research study on one consortium's interlibrary loan and collection development practices for returnable items. Local practices and policies that appear to have affected other member libraries are outlined. The audience will consider whether this analysis identifies concerns that they should investigate with their own consortium partners.

Do local collection development decisions have an impact on consortium resource sharing agreements? And does it matter? This study looks at collection development and resource sharing budgets, practices, and policies for returnable items. It considers the possible effects of widespread changes in collection development practices on interlibrary loan operations, particularly within a consortium but potentially across all lending partners.

The most basic collection development goal is to provide the materials that meet the research and teaching needs of the local institution. In terms of providing access to monographic materials, that means buying a (shrinking) core of print and electronic materials prospectively through firm orders and approval plans, leasing appropriate e-book packages that might disappear, and scoping a larger set of materials for potential demand-driven acquisition. Then, at the (ever-growing) periphery is the content that is not have immediately available.

Resource sharing is, for most libraries, an integral part of providing access to the corpus of information resources. However, most libraries make collection development decisions independently of others in their consortium. The ability for resource sharing officers to provide access to that global corpus is predicated on the idea that other collections officers have already identified and purchased materials that they are willing and able to share. Collection development officers claim to be radically scaling back, changing purchasing channels, and shifting

formats. Because some of these decisions (e.g. moving to e-book only purchasing, reducing prospective purchases, considering certain categories of materials out of scope, etc.) may reduce the content available to share with other libraries, the authors wanted to examine what effect these behaviors might have on interlibrary loan activity within a consortium. The assumption is that someone out there, hopefully in a preferred consortium, is surely buying that content and they can loan it. In the rush to move to new collection development models, will libraries have collections that can be shared sustainably? What, will that mean for the ability to provide a robust interlibrary loan service through a preferred consortium?

Utah State University and the University of Kansas are both a part of the Greater Western Library Alliance (GWLA), whose mission is to deliver "cost-effective and high-quality information services to its member institutions and their clientele." Comprised of 33 academic research libraries, primarily west of the Mississippi, GWLA serves over 650,000 undergraduates, 150,000 graduate students, and 41,000 instructional faculty. In 2012 the shared collection was comprised of more than 130 million volumes and member combined materials budgets exceeded $310 million dollars per year.

The Greater Western Library Association has a long history of resource sharing and has developed and implemented policies that both speed material delivery and increase the convenience of the service. For example, GWLA uses expedited shipping and provides a twelve-week loan period. The underlying philosophy is for lenders to "treat other member libraries' patrons the same as their own." (Kochan, 2013)

The GWLA Collection Development Committee also has a history of collaborative projects and group purchasing. More recently it has begun exploring what it might mean to do some kind of collaborative collection development. In determining if the project should be retrospective or prospective or both (or neither), it becomes clear that issues surrounding the unique needs of each institution, the size of the consortium, and the scope of the data for analysis are all very challenging for a group of volunteers to manage.

Methodology

The main investigators discussed possible reasons why some libraries borrowed more returnable items than others and came up with five theories to use to survey consortium members to test these hypotheses:

- Schools with the smallest budgets would be the heaviest borrowers.

- Schools that have eliminated their approval profiles would be the heaviest borrowers.

- Schools with the most restrictive ILL policies would not borrow as heavily.

- Schools that heavily market their ILL program would be heavy borrowers.

The authors developed questions based on these theories, focusing on local policies. Among others, collection development questions included:
1) preference between print and e-books, 2) current purchasing practices (e.g., PDA/DDA, approval plans), 3) types of materials purchased (e.g. textbooks, popular titles, scholarly materials only, etc.) 4) importance of GWLA collections, to your library's collection development strategy.

The authors questions for Resource Sharing focused on: 1) resource sharing policies (e.g. textbooks, popular titles, items held locally, etc.), 2) if it's easy for patrons to discover titles not held locally via a discovery layer, 3) marketing

strategies for resource sharing, 4) open-ended questions that allowed libraries to describe what borrowing activity was occurring.

In addition in order to gather consistently reported numbers on budgets, collection size, and patron demographics, the investigators drew from the longitudinal data gathered by the Association for College and Research Libraries (ACRL) as well as the data included in the Academic Library Survey (ALS), administered by the National Center for Educational Statistics. Consortium-compiled data on interlibrary loan borrowing activity for returnable items are also included. Thirty-two of thirty-three collection development librarians and twenty-nine of thirty-three resource sharing librarians completed their respective surveys.

The initial hypothesis was that by looking at local data and policies, clear ILL trends would emerge, including lending and borrowing rates. The situation is clearly complex, but the investigators assumed that there would be some common indicators that resulted in a school borrowing from other consortium members more heavily— and that these indicators would come from things that were happening in collections policies and practices. However, it became increasingly clear that while some practices may lead to increased or decreased usage to interlibrary loan, there were always exceptions to the rule. No patterns emerged.

Collection Development Issues

First, it is very clear that *there is more to buy and less to spend.* The latest data reported in the 2014 "North American Academic Books Price Index" (covering 2012) indicates an annual price increase 8% (note that this was 4.6% in the previous year) and e-books saw a staggering 23% increase in price (Tafuri 2014). Moreover, examining trends in the numbers year over year, the data reveals an increase in the number of titles produced across most subjects. While prices increase for a growing quantity of content, budgets are failing to keep pace. Reviewing national nonserial materials expenditures for Research I universities in the ALS, with 275 libraries reporting, the expenditures went down 8% between 2008 and 2010. Four years later, in 2012, with 10 additional libraries

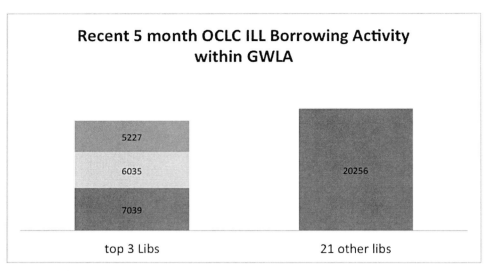

Recent 5 month OCLC ILL Borrowing Activity within GWLA

5227	
6035	20256
7039	
top 3 Libs	21 other libs

Figure 1. All GWLA one-time expenditures.

reporting, the increase in non-serial expenditures was only 4%. GWLA follows this pattern, with nonserial expenditures registering only a 1.5% increase overall between 2006 and 2012.

Next comes the very difficult question of what is the appropriate level of duplication for books in a consortium. Some of the best research on this question comes from OhioLink. In a 2003 study, Rob Kairis determined that OhioLink schools had, as a group, purchased 95% of all approval books and, on average, each title had been acquired 8.46 times (Kairis, 2003). Digging deeper, he discovered that 70% of those copies were available for circulation at any moment, clearly indicating unnecessary duplication. After very laborious attempts to run and analyze duplication reports for GWLA, the Collection Development Committee determined that this work might be too labor intensive for the reward. Conversations to determine what might be a "right" number for duplication have occurred, but there is not consensus what that might be. This number could be used both for local weeding as well as prospective planning.

For the most recent fiscal year, the survey asked the GWLA-CD officers to report how many books came into their collections via approval, firm order, and demand driven channels—both for print and electronic books. For the 17 schools that were able to report these numbers consistently, it was very clear that the vast majority of print titles

were still coming into collections via approval plans. Overall, all but two of the 32 respondents asserted that they still rely on approval plans of one type or another for the majority of acquisitions, even if they were unable to provide firm numbers.

On a related note, GWLA schools have been early adopters of the demand-driven acquisition model, with 22 members purchasing via this channel in 2012 and all but one of the 32 responders to the current GWLA survey doing so now. In an attempt to assess the true scale of DDA implementation at GWLA institutions, the survey asked CD officers to rate the level at which they believed they were acquiring materials through DDA (1-5). Only two schools claimed to acquire the "vast majority" (5) of materials through DDA and most schools seemed more to dabble, with 13 out of 32 ranking this channel as 2. Of course, most DDA plans rely on approval profiling and the corpus of books available via DDA is prescribed to a limited set of content. By increasing duplication through DDA and approval, dollars available to build the GWLA corpus through unique purchases are reduced.

Resource Sharing Assumptions

The premise behind interlibrary library loan is that a library can quickly provide access to patrons to books and other types of returnable items because partner libraries are continuing to build collections that can be shared. As a group, the

Resource Sharing Committee forged strong agreements to speed the delivery of materials amongst the partner libraries.

GWLA has historically used OCLC to transmit requests between libraries. However, last year the consortium began licensing the Relais software to facilitate the discovery of holdings and identification of potential lenders to which to send requests. GWLA calls its version of this system BorrowItNow. Currently almost all libraries are lending through BorrowItNow, and about half (sixteen) borrow via this system. BorrowItNow is not a true shared catalog (e.g. Orbis Cascade). Despite not having a shared catalog, library patrons are readily identifying materials that are needed for scholarship and research. Different libraries in GWLA have selected different integrated library systems and discovery layers. Forty-five percent of the libraries' discovery systems contain book titles that are not held at the local library and 48% do not. Many libraries that do not have information about titles not held locally mentioned that patrons commonly use Amazon, Google Books, and other Internet resources to identify titles. Patrons have increased access to identifying unique item types. While many libraries whose catalogs contained titles not held locally reported increased borrowing activity, this was not the case for all libraries that responded to the survey.

Looking at Policy Questions

In gathering data, the survey attempted to identify how various interlibrary loan policies might increase/decrease activity. It also juxtaposed ILL policies with collection development policies to further look at possible correlations and identify potential problems.

E-Books

First, there is the question of e-book acquisition. There is absolutely no question that GWLA institutions are moving faster and faster in this direction, as are most academic institutions. This is a planned move for most of GWLA schools with almost 70% having at least some form of e-preferred CD-policy according to the survey. Moreover, there is a rapid growth as a percentage

of the GWLA collections of e-book content. In 2006, the corpus was comprised 9% of e-books (data taken from ACRL Metrics). In 2013, the corpus was 17% e-books. For individual members in this group, one school reported to ACRL a high of 38% of his collection is comprised of e-books. What does this mean for a potentially shared collection?

From the resource sharing side, the survey asked if ILL policies allow patrons to order print copies if an electronic copy were already owned locally. The majority, 67%, said yes, they would just order the copy. Only 12% said no, they would not order a title already owned locally regardless of the patron's preference. As GWLA partner libraries continue to purchase e-preferred materials, ordering and receiving a print copy may no longer be an option. Members may need to order outside the consortium, which would usually take longer and might mean shorter loan period for items borrowed outside GWLA. In addition, some loans would incur charges from libraries outside the consortium.

Finally, the consortium needs to know that it can both legally and technologically share this content going forward. A possible solution is being developed in GWLA through the e-book lending technology in Occam's reader. In terms of the licenses, Anne McKee, who negotiates on GWLA's behalf with vendors and publishers, has incorporated the following language into consortium agreements:

> Interlibrary Loan must be allowed. The consortium may supply a single copy of an individual document, chapter or book derived from the Licensed Materials to an Authorized User of another library utilizing the prevailing technology of the day.

Textbooks

As the prices of textbooks have increased dramatically, students are looking for cheaper alternatives. The numbers of patrons wanting to get these types of materials via Interlibrary Loan is also increasing. Many GWLA libraries (73%) have policies against borrowing textbooks, but it is labor intensive to identify and deny these types of requests. A significant number of ILL offices do not restrict patrons and make no effort to screen requests.

Generally, collection development policies at most GWLA libraries do not permit the purchase of textbooks. Only 9% of libraries make it a policy to purchase some textbooks on demand by campus patrons. So even those libraries that do allow ILL for these types of materials will not generally be successful in meeting these needs within the consortium. In many ways obtaining textbooks on ILL is not practical. It is not possible to acquire 400 entry-level biology textbooks on ILL. The solutions for this conundrum are complex and not easily resolved. One positive recent development is the inception of OER textbooks.

Sustainability

Comparing borrowing activity from 2010 to 2014, 68% (seventeen out of twenty-five) of GWLA libraries filled fewer loans from all sources via interlibrary loan borrowing in FY14 compared to FY10. This drop ranged from 2% and 3% for two libraries to 63% each for two libraries who experienced the steepest decline. The average drop across all libraries that saw a decrease was 2,879 loans. However, 32% (eight out of twenty-

five) of GWLA libraries filled more loans from all sources via interlibrary loan borrowing in FY14 compared to FY10. This increase ranged from three libraries increasing 3%, 5%, and 6% respectfully to one library increasing 61%. This upward trend by 1/3 of GWLA libraries continues to put pressure on collections and policies even as 2/3 of GWLA libraries have seen a decrease in ILL borrowing. This impacts consortia partners. Of the seventeen GWLA libraries where overall ILL borrowing is down only three of them increased their borrowing with GWLA. Of the 8 libraries where overall ILL borrowing is up, five of them have also increased their borrowing within GWLA including the three with the largest overall increase in requests.

This wide range of borrowing activity within GWLA continues. In fact, a recent five-month period of time illustrates how wide the need is to borrow from within GWLA. Chart 2 illustrates that three libraries have borrowed from other GWLA libraries the same amount of materials as 21 consortia members. It should be stressed that GWLA does not have a policy related to borrowing levels so no policy is being broken. These totals though do help raise the question as to whether current collection development and resource sharing policies and practices are sustainable.

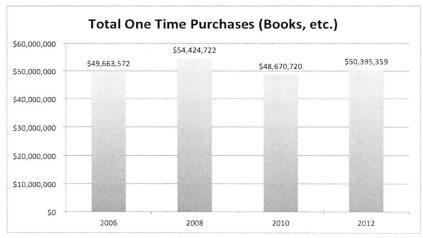

Figure 2. Recent five-month OCLC borrowing activity with GWLA. The top three libraries totals are equivalent to the bottom twenty-one in library activity.

As GWLA libraries collective borrowing power decreases and libraries rely more on DDA and e-format titles, there is some concern that the shared collections will become less diverse and

there will not be as many unique title holdings to meet patrons needs from within GWLA. Most libraries do have a number of resource sharing agreements, but generally speaking it takes longer for materials to arrive from nonpreferred partners. These materials also have shorter loan periods.

Final Thoughts

The solution to these questions remains opaque. A critical question is how much each library really values the building of a cooperative collection. When asked about how much they think about the GWLA collections in terms of their individual CD strategy, only a few outliers said that thinking about the shared collection was absolutely central to their strategy. By far the most common response was that people thought about it a bit. However, libraries still rely on shared collections to meet patrons' information needs, as demonstrated by the volume of borrowing activity.

Although no clear patterns emerged from this survey on how local collection development

policies affect consortium interlibrary loan activity, the study does illustrate that resource sharing and collection development are very closely intertwined. The diversity of GWLA institutions' patron composition, fiscal resources, and local practices make it difficult to identify concrete effects of one unit's activities upon the other. What remains clear is that communication between the two units is essential to stretch limited resources and provide quality services to patrons It is time for libraries to move beyond rhetoric. On the collections side, librarians have stated that it is possible to buy and/or lease everything and on the resource sharing side libraries don't need to buy they can just borrow from their partners. The reality is that no library can buy everything and at least one library needs to buy an item before someone else can borrow it. In spite of the complex results, this survey has illustrated the symbiotic mission and work of collection development and resource sharing.

References

Kairis, R. (2003). Consortium level collection development: A duplication study of the OhioLINK central catalog. *Library Collections, Acquisitions, & Technical Services, 27,* 317-326.

Kochan, C., and Leon, L. (2013). Revisting interlibrary loan best practices: Still viable? *Interlending & Document Supply, 41*(4), 113-119.

Tafuri, N. (2014). Prices of U.S. and foreign published materials. In *Library and book trade almanac, 59th edition* (pp. 432-433). Medford, NJ: Information Today.

From Course Reserves . . . to Course Reversed? The Library's Changing Role in Providing Textbook Content

Nicole Allen, Director of Open Education, SPARC

Charles Lyons, Electronic Resources Librarian, SUNY University of Buffalo

Bob Nardini, Vice President, Product Development Ingram Library Services

The following is a lightly edited transcript of a live presentation at the 2014 Charleston Conference. Slides and videos are available at http://2014charlestonconference.sched.org/

The Evolving Landscape of Course Content

Nicole Allen, Director of Open Education, SPARC

Nicole Allen: Hi, everybody. Nicole Allen from SPARC, the Scholarly Publishing and Academic Resources Coalition. I direct our program on open educational resources. And my talk today here is going to focus on kind of setting the stage of what's happening in the environment right now with course content and textbooks and the solution which SPARC advocates for, which is open educational resources. Before I begin, I do want to apologize for my voice. I'm getting over a cold, so it's probably good that I'm up here rather than among all of you, although sorry. So apologies for water breaks and so on. So I want to start the talk today with a textbook. This is a very popular Physics textbook used in undergraduate Intro Physics courses. And just take a second and think how much does this book cost. How much do you think it costs? So sorry, Beth, to plug UNCG. At UNCG, this books costs $241 to buy it new at the college bookstore. $241 for Introductory Physics where the material is very well established. And of course, you can rent a used copy for $108. So that's better, right? This is what college students face today. Not every course has a $240 textbook, but a lot of them do, especially undergraduate high-enrollment courses. Right now, the average student budget for books and course supplies is about $1,200 a year according to the College Board. And textbook prices have risen more than 80% over the last decade. Actually, that's been as long as I've been out of college, and I thought textbooks were expensive when I was in school. So put this in the

larger context of the rising cost of education. Students are taking on more and more debt to finance their education. And when you think about it, textbook expenses are actually particularly burdensome on students because they're often an out-of-pocket expense. They often come after grants and loans have subsidized the cost of tuition, so students don't feel that expense. But they feel this expense. And of course, we know there are many ways for students to save money, renting, buying used books, shopping around online. I think we all recognize that there's huge potential in moving into digital platforms to reduce costs for students.

So let's see what's going on in the market with that right now. This is that same Physics textbook on the digital published textbook platform started by the main textbook publishing companies. It's called Course Smart. This book on that platform costs $103 to rent an ebook. But notice that you rent it for 180 days. This is a two-semester course, Intro Physics. So 180 days means that this book is probably going to expire before you finish the second semester of the course. At the end of the day, buying the digital textbook is not going to help students save much money, and in fact, it could end up harming their learning. I mean, think about the message that that sends, that the way that we're moving into the digital environment is by actually limiting access and limiting the ability to keep and save and use your books for future reference. The message it sends to students is kind of like this: at the end of the course, zap, poof, the knowledge you were learning from goes away. And that's just not the way it should be in today's world.

With the textbook market right now, what's led to this dynamic is that the market doesn't work like a normal market because students are the ones that have to purchase textbooks, but professors make the decision on their behalf what to buy and don't actually have to buy the books themselves. They're not quite as sensitive to price as they would be otherwise. The result is that students are essentially a captive market, that the publishing industry is able to change these really inflated high prices. And as we think about where to go from here, as textbook publishers are starting to innovate and come up with new types of course content to sell, this is the dynamic we need to work with and we need to find ways to help students not be a captive market because what is happening today is not working.

There's been study after study that has found students are actually not buying their required textbooks because the cost is too high. In this study released earlier this year, it was two out of every three students say they've done that at least once. One out of every two students in another study say they've taken fewer courses because the cost of textbook is too high. So they're not advancing in their degree as fast as they could. The lesson here is that students can't learn from materials they can't afford. As we think about where we go from here in terms of providing access to course content, we need to make sure that it's both high-quality and affordable. And that's where we come to Open Educational Resources, which is the solution that SPARC advocates for. The definition is any sort of teaching and learning materials that are either in the public domain or released under an open license that allows their free use and repurposing by others. It sounds similar to the definition of Open Access for Open Access journals. It contains the same two key parts, which are "free," meaning no cost to the user and no barriers to access, and two, "open," meaning the right to fully use the materials. In the OER world, we typically refer to the permissions that make a material an open educational resource as the "five R's." The right to make and own copies, to use it in any way that you want, to adapt and modify and improve the material, to mix different open educational resources together and share whatever you've created without fear of rebuke.

Many of you may be familiar with Creative Commons licensing, which is the most commonly used form of open licensing. What's happening in the OER space right now? There are really three main pathways for advancing OER. The first is to create new materials and release them under this open license and make them freely available. The most common case of this is open textbooks, so textbooks just like any other textbook that have been released under this open license. They're available free online, free in PDF versions, free in an EPUB version. You can go online right now and access the entire contents of this textbook for free. You can also buy a print copy of this book for $49. It's about this thick, full color, hardbound, and just looks like any traditional printed textbook. But it costs about a fifth of the price. This is what's possible in today's world. This is through a project out of Rice University called Open Stacks College. They're building 20 open textbooks for high-enrollment courses, building tools around those books to support it. Some of them charge fees which help sustain the project. They fund authors and provide compensation with up-front lump-sum payments instead of royalties. And at the end of the day, their books have been used by enough students to save over $30 million across the world. This Intro Physics textbook has already gained at least 5% of the Intro Physics market in the last two years, which is really remarkable.

There's also a public policy side of this. A few years ago, the state of Washington realized that students were spending a lot of their student financial aid to buy expensive textbooks, so they funded a program for faculty to develop and curate high-quality free and low-cost materials for the 81 highest enrollment courses in the state. And then finally, we all know what MOOCs are, but the problem with MOOCs is that the materials that are assigned with them often aren't accessible by the students that are using them across the world. For example, research articles that are licensed by your library aren't accessible in Africa. This is an example of a truly open course produced by Carnegie Mellon University that uses a data-driven approach to actually learn as the student learns and help present the concept that the student hasn't quite gotten yet over and over again until they get it. And they also use the data to go back and improve the material over time, which is something that's only possible when you have the permission to do so under an open license.

The second pathway is sharing OER. And of course, sharing is what education is all about. That's why institutions of higher education exist is to share knowledge. This is what MIT recognized in the early 2000s with their Open Courseware program, which allowed faculty members to share the resources that they're already creating through their teaching with the entire world, including lectures, videos, course materials, and the like. And there're actually over 200 institutions across the world that have programs set up like this. There are also online repositories, for example, OER Commons, that allow anybody anywhere who has educational materials to share them freely under an open license, and you can go there to search for materials. And then again, on the public policy front, the U.S. government has, in a number of grant programs, recently required open licenses on federal grants, on the outcomes of federal grants like this $2 billion grant program through the Department of Labor that's creating workforce training materials. All of the materials come out of it are under a Creative Commons attribution license. It makes sense, because we don't need to create five open nursing curriculums. Really, we need to create one and then enable other schools to adapt it.

Then finally, the pathway of supporting OER. Because open educational resources, even though they're out there, they're not necessarily easy to find or easy to use. There are a number of startup companies that have popped up to support the use of open educational resources, for example, Lumen Learning, which actually contracts with institutions of higher education that want to expand the use of OER on their campus and gain the benefits of it. Also, at the University of Minnesota, they've curated a catalog of open textbooks where any faculty member can go and search for materials, and they're actually collecting reviews of the books by faculty members to help assess the quality. And this is a realm where SPARC is really interested in working with and engaging and supporting our member libraries to provide support on their campus for open educational resources, whether it's helping to find materials, helping to publish materials, or a combination of the two. But I will leave it to my colleagues to delve into that a little bit more.

So by way of closing, I just want to illustrate a couple of the impacts and the things that are possible with open educational resources. So first, at Tidewater Community College in Virginia, they've assembled an entire two-year business administration degree that uses open educational resources in every single course. So a student can literally graduate without spending a single dollar on textbooks. So imagine how much faster students get through their degrees, how much faster they're able to get into the workforce. And while this doesn't necessarily work at a four-year institution, imagine a gen-ed curriculum knocking out the 101 courses using all OER. Another example is at Mercy College in New York, the math faculty there replaced their developmental math curriculum with open educational resources, and they saw a 12% jump in the students passing the course with a C or better. So imagine that at your institutions, imagine that with the materials that you create. That's enormous. And it's not likely that those materials are that much better. It's because the students have access to the material starting day one of the course.

Moving forward, when you look at what the medieval lecture looked like, medieval universities, it hasn't changed much since then. So today we're on the cusp of the ability to use today's technology to advance openness and open education and do what we do more effectively. So that's the kind of stage that I want to set for the conversation today.

Five Myths Librarians Should Know about Textbook Affordability

Charles Lyons, Electronic Resources Librarian, SUNY University of Buffalo

Anthony Watkinson: Thank you so much. While Charles is just getting his notes together, can I just say that Charles Lyons has done the latest *Against the Grain*, which is in your pack, though you may not have looked at it yet. There's a massively good, really impressive collection of essays on this topic. It's one of the best things of its type I've ever seen, Charles.

Charles Lyons: Oh, wow. Thank you very much. And you've stolen a bit of my thunder, so I save a little bit of time. Nicole did a great job of explaining the really devastating impact that high-cost textbooks are having on higher education today. And my role in 10 minutes is to convince you that libraries can do something about this. My role is to convince you all that we can work with the teaching faculty on our campuses, that we can work with students and we can work with textbook authors and we can work with our university bookstores and we can work even with commercial publishers to make a difference in textbook affordability. So with that, I'll get started here.

In 1901, the *New York Times* published this article describing the controversy that occurred when the law library at New York University decided to stop circulating textbooks to students due to high costs. And in the article, they cite the fact that a single textbook at the time could cost, I apologize for this, up to $5 in 1901. So it puts it in a little bit of context. And the interesting thing I find about this article, and it's not simply that the *New York Times* found this newsworthy, but that in the 113 years since this article was published, not a lot has really changed in the way that libraries handle textbooks. Of course, besides ignoring or avoiding textbooks, we've always put textbooks on reserve, and I think reserves do provide important access points for many students on our campuses. Especially if we use data, interlibrary loan data and circulation data and course enrollment data to identify the courses that can really benefit from having textbooks on reserve. But certainly two-hour in-library use, one student at a time access to textbooks on reserve has certain limitations that are always going to limit the value that reserves can provide. So the question is, can we do more?

At the University of Buffalo for the past two years, we've been running a series of e-textbook pilots in which we've been negotiating with commercial publishers for discounted pricing on the electronic versions of the textbooks that are being used at the University of Buffalo. And we've been having mixed results, some significant discounts and some not so significant. And we're at the point now where we don't know about the sustainability of our initiative. But one of the great things about doing these pilots is that we are awash in data about student preferences and student attitudes towards textbooks. And in the surveys that we run, one thing that is always very abundantly clear is that the library is not even on students' radar screens when it comes to textbooks. We're pretty much at the bottom of the list when they're looking for access to their textbooks. And maybe that's how it should be, right? Maybe given the way our policies towards textbooks over the past 113 years or so, that's appropriate and that's okay. I'm not being critical of the way we've handled textbooks either, but what I am suggesting is that the time is right for change. Given the proliferation of open education resources, given the evolution of e-textbooks, given the fact that the dynamics of the textbook market have just gotten so unsustainable, the time is right for all of us in this room to sort of reassess our position on textbooks.

Many librarians are already doing this and finding that they can play significant and impactful roles in the way that textbooks are used on their campuses. And, as Anthony mentioned, many of those roles are highlighted in the current edition of the *Against the Grain* newsletter that's in your conference tote bag. I won't go into too many of them, but the thrust of most of the initiatives is, as Nicole mentioned, substituting high-priced textbooks with open education resources. And with that is some context. I thought I would explain or say the five things I think are important for any librarian to know who might be interested in getting more involved in textbook affordability.

The first thing is that as you go around your campus and start talking to instructors, your entreaties will not fall on deaf ears. This notion that faculty are unaware of textbook costs or unconcerned by textbook costs is a thing of the past. I know in the past publishers were not 100% transparent about disclosing the cost of textbooks and so forth, but today every single instructor worth their salt is aware of textbook costs and wants to do something about that. I genuinely believe that. We can find exceptions to the rule, of course, but instructors are sensitive to this issue and they will be receptive when you come talking to them about doing something about it. The main challenge is not that they're unaware but that doing something about it is difficult, right, that swapping out a high priced, commercially published textbook with things like open education resources, open textbooks, open courseware, or substituting a high priced book with library licensed resources like e-books and journal articles is hard. It's challenging. It's time consuming. It's a daunting endeavor, and this is new territory for many people, for instructors and librarians alike. But many librarians are finding a role in providing support to instructors with helping them identify relevant open education resources, helping assess the quality of those resources, helping curate and customize those resources so they can be used effectively in the classroom.

The next myth is that all textbook authors are only in it for the money. And I'm not saying that royalties are unimportant or insignificant. This particular textbook is a broadly adopted, widely used introductory economics textbook that's written by a respected Harvard economist named Gregory Mankiw. And usually the information about the sorts of royalties that authors get is kind of hard to find and not disclosed, but because Cengage, the publisher, recently filed for bankruptcy, they had to disclose that they actually owed this author $1.6 million in royalties. I say that just as the "wow" factor, but this really isn't the norm, obviously. There's a group of high-impact blockbuster textbooks that make a ton of money for the authors and for the publishers, but by and large, most authors are not making a killing off their textbooks. But incentives are important, right? Mainly, the people who write these books don't get the same sort of recognition that they might get for writing a scholarly monograph or for publishing a scholarly journal article, so the money is important. Many libraries are recognizing that and they're setting up incentive and award programs at their schools. So at San Jose State University, they have a program set up where faculty are rewarded with a $1,000 grant, if you like, or an award, to support their making this

shift from a traditional textbook to an alternative textbook that costs less money. Temple has a similar program. UCLA has a similar program, and UMass Amherst has a similar program.

Another myth is that as you embark on your textbook affordability initiative, the bookstore is not your enemy. They probably are not the most affordable option for students for buying textbooks, but in my experience, bookstores are starting to get the message and they're starting to embrace textbook affordability and they are partnering with organizations all across their campuses, including libraries, to support textbook affordability initiatives. One example of this is at San Jose State University where the bookstore provides the library each semester with a list of all the textbook adoptions that are being used each semester. The library runs that list through their ebook holdings and then they identify the ones that are already available through ebrary and EBL and EBSCO ebooks and so forth for use for students for quote, unquote "free." And the really radical collaboration with the bookstore here was that the bookstore put a little sign up in their store next to the books that were available for free in the library, indicating to students, "Did you know you can access this book for free in the library?" So be aware that the bookstore may be an important partner, an important collaborator for textbook affordability initiatives.

And finally, this is perhaps the most mildly controversial myth that I'd like to say. Anthea said, "Mention that 86% of students prefer print textbooks over electronic textbooks." And yeah, it's true that currently at this point in time, most students do prefer print. On the surveys we've been doing at the University of Buffalo it's probably about 70/30. But that's taking a poll in a vacuum, and that's with all things being equal. And we know that in real life, all things are not equal. So in the surveys that we've been administering at the University of Buffalo, we ask students, "So if the price is equal, e-textbook and print textbook is equal, which would you prefer?" 70% prefer the print. What if the e-textbook is half off, 50% cheaper? The numbers actually flip flop. 70% would choose the e-textbook, and 30% would choose the print. So when we're doing these surveys in a vacuum, you're getting results that can only be used in a vacuum, and I think the reality is not that print is king and that students hold print sacred, but that they see value in both. There's positives to print and electronic and choice is really what's paramount here.

In closing, I like to just remind people whenever I do a presentation like this that the economics of the textbook market tends to get the most attention, and I know that in my initiatives, I tend to pay most attention to affordability and prices and so forth, but it's important to remember that it's equally important that we focus on learning outcomes and creating better textbooks. So as you begin to pursue textbook affordability initiatives on your campus, remember that it's also important to improve learning outcomes and create better textbooks. Thank you.

The View of a Library Content Vendor

Bob Nardini, Vice President, Product Development Ingram Library Services

Bob Nardini: My name's Bob Nardini. I work for Ingram, and I'm the business guy up here. And like many of you in traveling to a conference like Charleston, I sometimes get into conversations on airplanes with my seatmates. Usually that ends up with somebody asking me, "What kind of business are you in?" and I say, "Well, I work for a company that sells books to libraries." And without fail, the reply is, "Oh, you sell textbooks." And my answer is, "Well, yes. Well, no. Well, not really." And it ends up being a very short conversation. But it could be a longer conversation, it really could, if my seatmate were interested in having it, which they usually would not be. And you can see that conversation in all its facets today *in The Chronicle of Higher Education*, especially in their forums where you can find pretty much any point of view you're looking at, you want to find having to do with print versus e, as we've talked about already, we've heard. Having to do with commercial textbooks versus open textbooks, you can find a range of opinions there. And here's the one statement that I saw in the *Chronicle* that I think everybody would agree with, that there's a lot of answers these days and no single answer. If you look in the journal literature, you can find the

same thing, varying points of view on whatever question it is you want to study.

Can we agree on this much, anyway, that e-textbooks are greener? Well, actually not. Thanks to the *Chronicle*, there's a study that proves that they're not really very different when you take into account all the various costs associated with the two types of textbooks. But one thing we do know. We do know this. Students have more options than ever before. And I have this on impeccable authority. Here are some of the options. Here are some of the commercial options. And this is just a few of them. This is campus book rentals. One of my sons, when I asked him about where he got his textbooks, he got most of his textbooks from this company, he rented them. Let's not forget about Amazon, nor Apple. Flat World Learning was one of the early pioneers in trying to develop print and low-cost e-textbooks. Lumen, already mentioned by Nicole, a consulting company. Chegg, a pioneer in rental of textbooks, moving in a digital direction. Follett now offers on the BryteWave platform of theirs textbooks from the K-12 through higher education spaces. Courseload, another company. Rafter was a pioneer in textbook rental. Now they're referred to what their business as "digital," as "course materials management" is the way they're referring to it. And we have Akademos, works most closely with bookstores, helping bookstores to develop virtual stores. So those are some of the commercial spaces.

Other choices are the open choices, and Nicole mentioned some of these. So did Charles. Open Textbook Library, Open Course Library, Open SUNY Textbooks. We have the Open State College. We have Wikibooks. We have The Orange Grove in Florida. We have the Ohio Digital Bookshelf. We have Affordable Learning Solutions in California, very well-known, associated with Cal State. And we have the Maricopa Millions, also in California. And Merlot, which is associated with Affordable Learning Solutions. That's a repository of low-cost or free textbooks. So it is a crowded, confusing space. There's no answers, there's a lot of entrants, a lot of potential answers.

How's it going to go? We think it's going to go in every direction. We think there's going to be a mixture of print and e and commercial and open. It's not going to be one or the other. I will say this, though, that even free textbooks are not free. It's very expensive to produce a textbook in terms of time, in terms of money, in terms of talent. Somebody's paying something somewhere in one of those currencies for even a free textbook. So we see a mixed future, and we're seeing that already.

Here's an example from last year when Chegg announced that they were going to be working directly with Open Stacks. There's a commercial company and an OER organization working together. Here's an announcement from last, this is a news report having to do with Pearson on their project, Blue Sky, which enables professors to develop course content combining commercial content with open content. Ingram, the company I work for, has a lot of interest in textbooks. We don't publish textbooks, but we sell a lot of them. The book part of Ingram actually began as a textbook company, and the Tennessee Book Company, this is an early picture here, is still part of the business. It's the K-12 book repository for the state of Tennessee. That has evolved, that origin in our textbook business, to VitalSource, which is our ebook platform in higher ed, which is the world's largest ebook platform. We have over 500 publishers, over three million users on 6,000 campuses, and the largest list of textbooks in the world. We also sell a lot of print textbooks. On the left, you'll see a photo of our warehouse. Those are mostly used textbooks, which we sell or rent to students. On the right is a shot of one of our Lightning Source facilities, our print on-demand facilities, where some of the largest textbook publishers and many other publishers too print their books, one at a time, via Lightning Source as needed.

Customization of textbooks. We've mentioned the disruption already: used, new, rental, used. Customization of textbooks is probably going to disrupt everything. When every textbook in every class is a one-off object, a material assembled by the professor, that is really going to be disruptive. Ingram has a piece of software too just recently introduced called Ingram Construct that will allow people to put together textbooks from different

sources. So each textbook is not a unified thing; it could be customized by a professor for a class. Aggregation is another one of the qualities that a company like ours brings to the textbook market. When you aggregate, you can have many thousands of textbooks from many, many publishers in one place. Giving the institution, in this case, in Brazil, a consortium of 70-some institutions that represent three million students, the ability to offer over 5,000 textbooks to their students in one place and to negotiate a good deal to moderate the price of textbooks. So here in Brazil, students were paying approximately $800 to $900 per year for their textbooks. Now they're paying $200 or less per year for those textbooks thanks to the deal cut because of the aggregation we were able to offer.

In California, with Affordable Learning Solutions, which I already mentioned, VitalSource is one of the preferred vendors. And because there's a negotiation, a central negotiation with those institutions and the publishers, we were able to enable discounts to students that go up to 40%. And sometimes, depending upon the publisher, students who wished to have print with their e-textbook, and we've heard about the different choices, the different preferences that students have, they could have a low-cost pure, just black and white, very plain print textbook to go with the online textbook if they prefer to use both. Very inexpensively produced textbook from a major publisher. It looks like that. No bells and whistles, but very serviceable. That would come off of Lightning Source. Individual institutions too, if they negotiate centrally, can offer very good deals to their students. Southern New Hampshire University, I used to live nearby there. I would drive by them all the time. It was this sleepy little institution that about 10 years ago got a new president who decided the only way we're going to grow and survive is to become an online sort of institution. So this is a nonprofit institution, but they behave like the private, profit-making higher education institutions. And Southern New Hampshire today has 40,000 online learners around the country, and because they centralize negotiations, have been able to offer very good discounts to their students. So here again, aggregation has enabled a moderation of the price of textbooks.

In some parts of the world, the UK being one, this photo is from the UK, Middle East being another, this centralization of negotiation with textbooks is more common. This is a popup bookstore in the UK where the negotiations for the textbooks, print in this case, are made centrally. One company is chosen to deliver them all, they put up a popup bookstore on the campus. We have some experience in this, there are other companies that have more than we do, but we expect that institutional licensing of online textbooks is going to be more and more prevalent. And that's an area where librarians have expertise, the licensing of online resources. So we expect that the content on campus, which in the past has been separately negotiated, purchased, talked about in libraries, in the bookstore, with the academic departments, we expect more centralization of negotiation and a blending, a blurring of the different types of content and the business discussions that surround them in the future. We expect librarians like Charles to be involved in that. We expect to be involved too.

Pearson, whom I've already mentioned, huge textbook publisher, as you all know. They began in the 1840s as a construction company doing projects like this, which was Tower Bridge in London. Ingram began as a river transportation company. This is a photo from the 1940s of an Ingram barge. Still an important part of the company, by the way. So in closing, I would just like to say don't underestimate the ability of a smart, agile company to be open to change and to new ideas. So thank you very much.

Hyde Park Debate—Resolved: Wherever Possible, Library Collections Should Be Shaped by Patrons, Instead of by Librarians

Rick Anderson, Associate Dean for Scholarly Resources and Collections, University of Utah
David Magier, Associate University Librarian for Collection Development, Princeton University

Opening Poll: 42% agreed with the proposition, 58% disagreed with the proposition

Opening Statements

IN FAVOR: Rick Anderson, Associate Dean for Scholarly Resources and Collections, University of Utah

The resolution before us is that, wherever possible, library collections should be shaped by patrons rather than by librarians.

Not every library is in a position to undertake a patron-driven acquisition program. And, of course, not every book published is available for purchase under a patron-driven acquisition program. There are situations in which, for a variety of reasons, it may not be possible to undertake a patron-driven program. So to be very clear, supporting the present resolution does not mean saying that librarians should never select books for library collections. Wherever politically and structurally possible, however, I believe that it is better for the collection to be shaped by patrons than by librarians, and I therefore speak in favor of the resolution.

In this as with most other issues, we need to distinguish between means and ends— the things we *do* in libraries are the means, and the things we *hope to accomplish* by doing them are the ends. In libraries, where we have done the same things for a very long time and, in many cases, gotten very good at doing them, there is always the risk of getting means and ends confused—of coming to believe, for example, that the purpose of the catalog is to present perfect information about our collections, or that the purpose of interlibrary loan is to share, or that the purpose of the collection is to be comprehensive and balanced and coherent.

There is a wonderful children's book that some of you may have seen, called *A Hole Is to Dig*. It was

written by Ruth Krauss in 1952, and it compiles responses from small children to questions like "What is a hole?" and "What are eyebrows?" The answers are sweet and hilarious and tend to follow a common circular pattern: "A hole is to dig," "a face is so you can make faces," "a castle is to build in the sand," and my favorite, "grass is to have on the ground with dirt under it and clover in it." The phrase "a hole is to dig" comes to my mind frequently when thinking about and discussing collection development. Too often, I think, we succumb to the temptation to believe that a collection is to collect—that it justifies itself by being a collection, and by being good.

So when it comes to collections, what are the means and what are the ends? To put it more simply, *why* do academic libraries have collections? I would argue that the ultimate purpose of the collection is very simple: it is to give students and faculty access to the documents they need in order to do their scholarly work. Its purpose is not to showcase the erudition and wisdom of librarians, nor is it to ensure the library a high ranking among its peers. Nor is its purpose even to represent a coherent and comprehensive monument to human knowledge. The collection may, in fact, do all these things—but its size and coherence, its organization and its comprehensiveness, are all means to an end, not ends in themselves. Scholarship is the end. An academic library collection is better or worse to the exact degree that it makes the scholarly work of its stakeholders possible. This fact makes patron-driven acquisition—which is to say, the building of collections in response to real-world scholarly needs as expressed in the real-world use of books—a fundamentally superior approach to collection-building than an approach by which third parties (librarians) attempt, at great expense and very often erroneously, to guess and anticipate what books their patrons will need in order to do that work.

I have heard (or can anticipate) a number of different objections to this position, and I will try to answer five of them preemptively.

The first is about relevance over time: an academic library serves more than just the students and faculty who are present at the moment. It also serves those who will come in the future. For this reason, letting its collection be shaped by the immediate needs of today's patrons is short-sighted.

My answer to this objection is to point out the absurdity of trying to anticipate future needs. And if anyone here feels "absurdity" is too strong a word, I invite you to walk the stacks of any large academic library and look at the books that were purchased 20, 30, 40, or more years ago. A few of them remain relevant and useful today. A very large percentage of them do not. A few of them are timeless classics. The great majority of them are not. Some are actually embarrassing. Here's the problem: the further you look into the future, the broader becomes the spectrum of possible scholarly needs, and therefore the greater the likelihood that we will guess incorrectly what our future scholars will actually need. We're kidding ourselves if we think we can guess today which books and other resources scholars of the year 2024 (let alone 2064) are going to need. We can do a pretty good job of guessing what will stand the test of time in terms of *quality*; predicting what will remain *relevant* is a roll of the dice, and an increasingly expensive one.

The second objection is about the quality and relevance of library collections in the long term: Library patrons may know what seems useful to them today, but they don't know what will stand the test of time.

This objection is based on the assumption that the purpose of an academic library collection is to act as an enduring monument to scholarship. I think that assumption, while not entirely without merit, is problematic. The primary goal of a library is to make possible the scholarly work of its patrons. A book that will stand the test of time but is not

relevant to the needs of today's patrons represents, at the very least, a purchase the appropriateness of which should be questioned, given our manifest inability to anticipate what will be relevant to tomorrow's patrons—and given the fact that libraries have no choice but to forego the purchase of high-quality books every day, given budget and mission limitations.

The third objection is specifically about quality in the here-and-now: library patrons may know what they want, but they don't necessarily know what they need. Academic libraries do not exist to please the customer, but to provide access to the best scholarly resources possible. Patron-driven acquisition is the intellectual equivalent of giving your kids Twinkies for breakfast because that's what they think they want.

To this objection I have two responses. The first is that intellectual Twinkies can easily be (and routinely are) excluded from a PDA profile. When setting up PDA programs, librarians can (and invariably do) set broad parameters for what will be offered while still allowing patrons to shape the collection by their scholarly behavior. So the intellectual Twinkies are a red herring. Second response: we librarians have gotten away for far too long with the arrogant stance that we know better than our patrons what they need in order to do their work. In some cases, we may well know better; in others, we don't. And we can't possibly hope to know better than they do, consistently, across all situations and for all of the thousands of students and faculty we serve.

The fourth objection is about the impact of PDA on overall collection quality: librarian-driven acquisition creates a coherent and intelligently crafted collection, because it is guided by a conscious program and a team of trained bibliographic professionals. Patron-driven acquisition creates a disjointed and incoherent mishmash of resources that are guided by no overarching program, including the curriculum.

In response to this objection, I refer again to the question of the collection's purpose. Does it exist to showcase the skill of the librarians who built it, or to serve the scholarly needs of the students and faculty for whose use it's intended? A collection may be coherent and intelligently crafted and nevertheless fail to meet the needs of its users. The best way to ensure that it will fully support the scholarship taking place on campus is to provide access to as many relevant and high-quality documents as possible. In an environment of strictly limited resources—which is the environment in which the vast majority of research libraries are operating—the ability to offer a very large number of such documents and then acquire only those that are demonstrated to meet real-world needs is much more likely to result in a relevant and useful collection than a program of prediction and guesswork. Notably, by offering a far greater number of books than could possibly be purchased preemptively, a PDA program also provides far richer opportunities for serendipitous discovery than traditional collection-building programs possibly could.

The fifth objection is not philosophical, but practical: patron-driven acquisition risks letting spending run out of control.

This is one of the most obvious concerns about patron-driven acquisition—if you put the patron in the driver's seat and tell him to drive as fast and as far as he wants, how do you keep the gas tank from emptying out before all needs have been met?

This concern can be dispatched quite quickly: there are many mechanisms available to regulate the rate of spending on PDA, from the cordoning-off of dedicated and limited budget lines to what is called risk-pool management, whereby the number of books offered is decreased as the amount of money available shrinks. The bottom line, though, is simply that putting the patron in the driver's seat does not mean giving him the option of driving as fast as he wants for as long as he wants; mechanisms exist and are easily applied to manage the rate of PDA expenditure.

Those who have been paying attention may have noticed a common thread among the objections to patron-driven acquisition that I have laid out here: they tend to be library-centered, indeed collection-centered, rather than patron-centered. Those who oppose PDA, or who believe that it should have only a marginal place

in our collecting strategies, seem to me very often to be motivated by a fear that their work as professional librarians will be moved to the periphery by a system that uses scholarly behavior (rather than librarian expertise) to shape our collections. This fear is rational and legitimate. It is not, however, a suitable foundation for a collection development strategy. It is not our students' and researchers' job to keep us happily doing the work we like best. It is their job to learn and to produce scholarship, and our job to make that possible. If we are truly professionals, we will do whatever it takes to further the scholarly work of our institutions and patrons.

For all of these reasons, I stand in favor of the resolution before us today.

AGAINST: David Magier, Associate University Librarian for Collection Development, Princeton University

Point one: I am not against patron selection. PDA can be a cost-effective tool for exposing high-use core materials that librarians would have selected anyway, getting them into collections without the need for selector review. The basic premise of PDA seems almost unassailably logical and "democratic": instead of trying to guess what patrons want, let them choose for themselves and you can't go wrong. Who could argue with that? OK, I concede from the beginning that PDA *is* a useful tool.

A Philips-head screwdriver is also a useful tool: it allows us to efficiently apply maximal torque and rotational pressure to drive a screw into a hard surface with a minimum of force. It is truly a marvelous device, optimal for its task, and we should all be thankful for its invention! How much better the Phillips-head screwdriver is than "traditional" methods of attaching things in the old pre-Philips days!

But should we therefore conclude that the Philips-head screwdriver should be used for all tasks? You could try to use it for cleaning a fish, scraping snow off your windshield, combing your hair or eating your mashed potatoes. But *should* you?

By elevating the role of a special-purpose tool to a broad collection-development *principle*, giving it the *evangelical* force of the word "should," and promoting a dogma that all libraries ought to seek this path to perfection, the proposition leads us down a garden path that would ultimately deprive the entire community of research libraries of the ability to meet their mission and serve their patrons. Notice, critically, that I am not arguing that another useful tool—*librarian*-driven acquisition (LDA)—should be the universal way all collection shaping takes place. We should deploy the right tools for the right tasks. A flexible toolkit gives us maximum scope for meeting our mission. The proposition is false because it presents patron selection as the single best approach for collection-shaping—a false panacea.

Point two: I want to get rid of some myths, false distinctions, caricatures, intentional mis-characterizations and rhetorical straw-men that are raised whenever this topic is discussed. The corollaries of the proposition, which I use to shoot it down, apply equally to the shaping of collections in print and electronic forms, in libraries with large and small budgets. Contrary to the rhetoric my opponent has deployed before, the argument is *not* old-fashioned print-based thinking doggedly resisting the forward-looking visionaries the modern world.

Let's unpack the terms of the proposition in detail:

1. Libraries *should* take those actions that best support their mission of connecting patrons with the content they need.

2. Libraries provide content to patrons in three ways: we *buy* it, we *license* it, and we *borrow* it. The collection is what we purchase or license.

3. *Shaping* a collection means choosing what to collect versus borrow. Librarians engage in a balancing act, deploying limited resources strategically for current and future needs. Librarians look at cost-benefit ratios and trade-offs for their patrons every day:

   - Should we license this content or purchase it?

- Should we get the big-deal package or select title by title?

- Multiyear contracts or a year at a time?

- How many simultaneous users?

- Get it ourselves or buy in the consortium?

- Buy individual articles, subscribe to the journal, or purchase the backfile?

- Maybe don't collect it at all: maybe we could borrow it for our patrons as needed?

- And so on.

In contrast, the life of the patron is simple: "I look at what's available; I pick what I want." The hard questions don't arise for them. Today's proposition is all about *who* should make these hard collection-shaping choices. Should we really take the librarian out of the shaping business altogether?

1. Notice the proposition uses the hedge *"wherever possible"* It is always possible (though not always advisable) to have all choices made by patrons, just as it is possible to eat potatoes with a screwdriver. There already are some libraries following this dictum, eliminating librarians in favor of PDA, and the world has not come to an end . . . *yet*.

What kinds of collections result from patron selection? What gets in and what gets left out? Let's look at the roles of profit, discovery, availability, and cooperation to see the impact of going to PDA.

1. Profit and patrons

PDA systems are arranged with vendors and aggregators supplying sets of records which libraries expose to patrons in a discovery system, from which patrons select by clicking. These systems are optimized for *mainstream, commercial content*, with libraries letting vendors market their wares directly to their patrons. In theory, there's nothing wrong with that: we know lots of mainstream commercial content is precisely what patrons want anyway, right? So far so good.

But what about all the noncommercial, noncore research content (print, digital and other formats) excluded from the mainstream because it is less profitable? Research needs and commercial viability are not always the same thing! Think of datasets, global government documents, NGO publications, think tank reports, grey literature, maps, digital ephemera, print ephemera—all kinds of *specialized research material*. What if all our libraries simply stopped collecting all these because they were not profitable for commercial PDA?

I hear you thinking, "*If these things really mattered, why wouldn't vendors sell them in PDA? Doesn't demand drive supply?*" The answer is no; the market can ignore these needs because it is harder to make a profit on them. The costs of acquiring this kind of content may be too high, projected constituency too specialized, demand too low, market too small.

Would original research really be possible in a community of libraries that simply gave up the long tail of lower use, specialized, noncommercial content?

Until a few weeks ago, Ebola was a distant obscurity. Now it's "Whoa! Where the heck did that come from?" If Liberian public health documents—in English mind you—are available to academia at all, it is only because they were collected by research libraries shaping their collections—before the outbreak hit the headlines. Trust me: these materials will not make their way into your commercial PDA: they are not commercially viable. Vendors thrive on selling as many copies as possible of the same thing: their profit lies in duplicate sales at the high-use end of the spectrum, ignoring the long tail.

Just a few weeks ago, no one had heard of ISIS. Turns out it's a well-equipped army of 30,000 fighters controlling vast areas of Syria and Iraq. "Whoa! Where the heck did that come from?" Content to answer that question exists, but it's in Arabic, a "squiggly language," highly specialized, not commercially viable, not in the "mainstream"

and certainly not coming to you under PDA. If we all adopted the proposition "wherever possible," this kind of material would be absent, not discoverable, let alone accessible. By the time someone had figured out what's needed on ebola or ISIS, libraries would be unable to acquire such material—it would no longer be available.

The same is true with new trends in academia that require us to strategically shape collections: so many fields now adopting *quantitative* methodologies; student research assignments requiring new types of microdata, financial and social/demographic statistics, maps and GIS data, etc.; new cross-disciplinary *global* concerns such as energy and environment entrepreneurship in applied science, climate change and human rights, *internationalization* across the campus; traditional language-and-literature departments with new emphases on cultural studies, film, popular culture, mass social movements, and so on.

Patron selection alone simply will not get us there.

2. Discovery and availability

Patrons can only request what they can discover. The largest source of discovery is the aggregate of library catalogs. But here's the catch-22: if libraries only collect what patrons select, the long-tail just won't make it in. They can't discover it, can't request it, and libraries won't acquire it. And then, too often, it's simply too late: it's no longer available. A tremendous portion of current use of our collections consists of materials no longer in print, no longer found on the web, and available— if at all—only by borrowing from a library that had the foresight to collect it back when it was available. *Collection shaping means being pro-active on behalf of your patrons.*

3. Cooperation in the community of libraries

Abdicating responsibility for shaping collections nullifies the cost-efficiency of collection sharing. All over the country, library consortia are pushing the envelope for more efficient collection sharing with print and electronic delivery, optimized shared repositories, integrated shared discovery and request systems, negotiated consortial deals and new kinds of licenses for shared electronic content, and so on. Collaboration has enabled us to pursue *coordinated* collection development, leverage our resources as a community, enrich the collective collection, reduce unnecessary duplication, and redeploy resources strategically.

But all this coordination disappears if shaping is done exclusively by patrons.

Patrons do not wear this collection development thinking cap.

Relying only on PDA would result in massively duplicated vanilla collections, accumulated with no intelligent design other than greatest profits for vendors, and no provision for patrons actual needs.

I know many of you are thinking, "Oh, they can do that at Princeton, but how could we afford it?" This logic is false. The tighter the money, the more strategic, careful and collaborative you have to be in deploying it. Your patrons can't do that for you on their own. Giving up on the hard task of making priorities and choices means giving in to the panicked psychology of scarcity: it's the tunnel vision that leads to long-term surrendering of the ability to support research in higher education. I say, work with your partner libraries *and* your patrons.

Remember: patron-driven librarians can shape collections, patrons on their own cannot.

RESPONSE STATEMENTS

Rick Anderson

My worthy opponent has, I believe, successfully refuted the proposition that patron-driven acquisition is the best way to build a collection. That, however, is not the resolution that we are debating here today. To argue in favor of this resolution is not to say that PDA is the best way to build a great collection. It's to say that the greatness of the collection is not the point—the point is to support scholarship.

What David has not done, in my view, is demonstrate that librarian-driven collection building is the best way to accomplish that task.

In fact, if connecting students and faculty with what they need in order to do their scholarly work is the task, then librarian-driven acquisition is a demonstrably poor tool for it, since it invariably means guesswork and prediction about which resources will actually meet scholarly needs—which is a bit like using a screwdriver to eat mashed potatoes: it involves a huge amount of wasted energy, not to mention wasted money.

David's points about profit and patrons are not incorrect, but neither are they particularly relevant to the resolution we are addressing today. He's right to point out that there are (and surely always be) documents that patrons need in order to do their scholarly work, but that are not available for acquisition on a PDA basis. If the resolution under debate were "No one except patrons should ever shape library collections," or "Libraries should only collect materials that are available on a PDA basis," then his point would constitute a powerful refutation of it. But neither of those is the resolution under debate. Clearly, if we need documents that can't be acquired through PDA, then we need to get them in some other way. The fact that PDA will not always be possible is explicitly accounted for in the resolution.

Last point: David seems to have confused the idea of patron-driven acquisition with patron selection. The two concepts are very different. PDA doesn't call on patrons to make selections. It provides what patrons experience as a larger collection than what librarians could possibly provide based on speculative purchasing, and then simply invites the patrons to do their work. The patrons don't make selections; they do their work, and the work they do then generates selections. David is right that books in the "long tail" of relevance may not make it into the collection by this mechanism. Some will, and some won't—but this is true no matter how we buy books.

Let me close by pointing out a fundamental point on which David and I very much agree: "The tighter the money, the more strategic, careful, and collaborative you have to be in deploying it." This is why libraries like mine—a library whose entire operating budget is barely larger than Princeton's annual expenditure on collections—have been relatively enthusiastic about embracing PDA. Buying, housing, and caring for books that our patrons don't need may be a great way to build a wonderful collection—but it's no strategy at all for allocating strictly limited resources in support of the scholarly work on our campuses.

David Magier

1. Without identifying a single good thing about PDA, Rick devotes himself instead to a new low of dismissive stereotyping and character assassination, a completely fictionalized librarian straw man to shoot down. He trivializes and slanders the work of librarians, calling us childish ("*a collection is to collect*"), vain and self-centered ("*monuments to our own wisdom*"), absurd and delusional (tilting towards "*comprehensive*" collections for the *distant future*), and wasteful and self-interested (*valuing our own jobs over the interests of patrons*). This cartoon character villain doesn't actually exist: no library would tolerate it. So let's dispose of these distractions and hot air and look at the real world. We librarians *are* patron-driven: engaged closely with faculty and students every day. We engage in collection-shaping with and on behalf of our patrons, because failing to do so produces negative impacts right here and now, not 40 years in the future!

2. Because of potential bad outcomes from PDA, even Rick is forced to hedge his bets. Pay attention to these rhetorical hedges: they reveal something fundamental about the argument he would rather you didn't notice. For example, where he says mysteriously "We have ways of slowing down expenditure," he's really talking about slowing down the patrons through *quantitative squeezing:* decreasing the number of books offered as the money runs out. Well, who selects which records to suppress and which books to hide from patrons so they can't trigger purchases? Even under PDA, it's

the *librarians* who make these choices, just as they chose the profiles of records to expose in the first place. But this is precisely collection shaping: what to include and exclude. Knowing that *bad things can happen* when PDA runs wild, Rick hedges by covertly acknowledging that librarian collection-shaping is necessary after all!

3. Did you notice the biggest hedge, where Rick is forced to argue my side of the debate? Some places maybe can't go with PDA due to "political" reasons . . . Well, what are these mysterious political reasons? Again, it's not that these libraries *couldn't* do PDA, it's just *not politically advisable* because bad things can happen that get the library into trouble! *If you over-deploy the screwdriver, someone gets screwed*! Faculty know this and they exert political pressure to prevent it. So Rick tries to reduce the proposal to a logical zero: "Collections should be shaped by PDA, *except where they shouldn't.*"

4. Finally, Rick ignores the largest fallacy of PDA: it deprives libraries of their primary tool for leveraging limited budgets: coordination. All of us exist in an interdependent ecosystem of cooperation, a whole greater than the sum of its parts, making accessible the long tail of lesser used content without which research is impossible. Even we at Princeton have to borrow lots of what we don't have. Coordination requires strategic shaping by librarians. Otherwise, we'd all have the same 2500 monographs.

CLOSING POLL RESULTS: 50.2% agreed with the proposition, 49.7 % disagreed with the proposition.

Remember: You don't have to collect everything your patrons need. But you do need to have other libraries out there ready to lend what you can't collect. The PDA proposal would make such coordination impossible.

Crowd Sourcing of Reference and User Services

John G. Dove, Former CEO
Tim Spalding, Founder, LibraryThing
Scott Johnson, CEO, ChiliFresh
Ilana Stonebreaker, Assistant Professor of Library Science, Purdue University

The following is a lightly edited transcript of a live presentation at the 2014 Charleston Conference. Slides and videos are available at http://2014charlestonconference.sched.org/

John Dove: Hello, everybody. Welcome to the session on Crowd Sourcing of Reference and User Services. Some of this content is actually based on work that is reported in case studies in the book that Dave Tyckoson and I coedited for the Charleston Insight Series, but we actually have speakers for you today not just from there. So, now, first, my name is John Dove. I'm formerly with Credo Reference and who knows where I'll be next? My father would be really proud of the fact that I was involved with this, but also that as an industry are talking about crowd sourcing.

Now, I'm used to the fact that now many of you have a reference source right with you all the time, so that you can go and Google "Dove" and "Unicorn" and you'll see what my father's most famous work is, but if you went to Credo and looked up his name and his entry, you would find that one of the things that he thought was his life's work, he was a geneticist who then became a social scientist involved in logistics in World War II. In fact, one of his logistic innovations was something that we at Credo applied for a patent for, it's called Diversity Preference Ranking, and he defined this with something he called Agra Descendants. So, Agra Descendants is basically a way to properly manage with the diversity of group. It creates a better quality than any individual element of that group and that's sort of the core basis of what crowd sourcing is all about.

Now, crowd sourcing has a long history and a distinguished history in libraries and in reference. The National Union Catalog, 758 miles, I describe it as the only reference work that you can actually see from the moon. Come to the Boston Public Library, you can see the room, that's about as big

as this room that is lined with [inaudible]. I even said that, actually, if all the printed works before 1956 in libraries in Canada and the United States, World, as of 2008, only had 75% of those books. So, there's another 25% that, only if you went into those dusty old volumes, would you find, but clearly, the main thing about crowd sourcing these days is the example of Wikipedia. I've got two comments later about Wikipedia, but what I mean, the Oxford English Dictionary is an example of a crowd sourced reference work. For decades, they collected, basically, from amateur readers, who would be reading old volumes, examples of uses of words and there's a wonderful book, if you haven't seen it, called *The Professor and the Ant Man*, where the editor of the Oxford English Dictionary decided he should go visit the doctor who was his most prolific contributor, who was a doctor at the insane asylum for the criminally insane and what he discovered when he got there is that the doctor wasn't really a, he wasn't a doctor, but he was actually a patient in that insane asylum. So, that sort of brings up the old questions about madness and crowds and I'm going to get into that a little bit, but, indeed, the central challenges in terms of effective crowd sourcing, and you're going to hear some different answers on this one from our panelists and I hope that we generate some debate, but I'd like you to just hold questions until the end of all three speakers, and then we'll have time for some questions.

So, major challenges are some of the curation that you get when you just let everybody contribute, how to avoid systematic biases that might be there, and very important is how you get the crowd into the crowd sourcing, because we can come up with many ideas that if all if only we all contributed, we could create something of great value, but if you don't make the contribute process fun and meaningful in its own right, you'll end up with a ghost town.

If you haven't read either of these two books . . . I'm going to introduce these two books. In this case, hopefully it's a contrast. *The Wisdom of Crowds*. This title comes as a reference to the madness of crowds, a book about how crowd behavior diminishes moral responsibility. So, you end up with mob behavior and what James Surowiecki did was building on that phrase, talked about what circumstances are there where the crowd doesn't become diminished intelligence, but actually ends up with enhanced intelligence and Surowiecki actually identifies multiple, a couple of key factors of what distinguishes between wisdom and madness. If you've got a group process, contributing groups actually independent of each other, because if they're not independent, then you won't get the benefit of independent outlook and you will end up with, eventually, systematic biases and you can look at any crowdsourced effort and say "Gee, this has some blind spots that are automatically inherent in the way that it's set up." Introducing a fair way of summing up the inputs of the individual elements that go into the crowd. So, it can be crowd source decisions, so to speak, and Cass Sunstein has written a book called *Infotopia*, *How Many Minds Produce Knowledge*, and he goes into a number of things that come from actually decision theory, one of which is the Condorcet Jury Theorem and the Condorcet Jury Theorem is very powerful. If you go by its assumptions, and that's the nub, you get 100% correct answers. So, if it turns out one of those assumptions is that if everybody in a jury has a 51% chance of getting it right and if you fairly sum up the inputs of that jury, you very quickly, it converges on 100% right. The dark side is if it's only 49%, it converges on zero. So, you have to build very carefully about whether you're assuming that all kinds of inputs are good or not, and I know if you put together a jury to discuss the question of whether Paris Hilton's jail time did damage to her career, if you put my wife and I on that jury, we don't know what career she had before, since, or after, so, I'm not sure you'd come up with the right answer to that question.

Now, with Wikipedia being the most famous example of crowd sourcing today, if you look at this from sort of these description and the requirements of, these are, it needs either, you know, systematic biases or independent inputs. What is this, the summing up mechanism? One of the formal aspects of Wikipedia actually leads you to madness. I mean, last in, first out is probably not the best judicial description of what constitutes quality, but you have to look also at all of the other apparatus the exists in terms of Wikipedia, the nonformal parts, the Wiki-manias, the organization of the community and that community's principles, and some of the adherence to those principles, because those are the things that actually take what otherwise, mechanically, would be madness, and turn it into something of real value.

You have to be careful as you do this evaluation. Two good examples of curated crowd sourcing is actually what the editor of *Birds of North America* calls "Wiki with gates," had a 19-volume Encyclopedia of *Birds of North America* and he came up with an outline version and what he did was describe how to actually build a whole community of bird watchers and ornithologists and the gates are the ornithologists. So, bird watchers can contribute observational data. They can't define a new species and, similarly, the *Encyclopedia of Life*, which is based on Wilson's TED Talk from a number of years ago, solicits and credits curators who will curate the inputs that then go into *The Encyclopedia of Life*. So, as you look at these panelists, think to whether, "Gee, are they, um . . ." Let me, back up a second.

I want to talk about the crowd when you're crowd sourcing. How many of you have ever actually written a Yelp or a Zagat review at a restaurant? Oh, a good number. Well, you can see that most of your colleagues have never done it and yet, I'll have, how many of you have used a Yelp or Zagat review? Yeah, it's just about everybody. It needs to be enough to write these reviews or otherwise there wouldn't be value for the rest of us. So, that's this key question about how you develop a proper crowd.

When you look at each of these panelists, think through these questions about have they creatively solved this update problem, by making it valuable to the updater to actually do the contributions that we've come to value and have they had an effective, found an effective way to curate an input. You mention the Zagat reviews; you've got restaurants here who want to write great reviews and you've got his competitor down the street who wants to write really negative reviews. So, you've got to be able to have some mediating mechanism that allows you to have that negative and avoid various individual biases and systematic biases.

So, now, I want to hear this Tim Spalding, and Tim is going to talk about LibraryThing. I tried this experiment. Go to a cocktail party and go up to a stranger and say, "hey, I just found a great website where you can catalog your own books," and see if they don't roll their eyes.

Unknown Speaker: You go to the wrong parties, John.

John Dove: Indeed, then. I'll tell you what he said, when he started to do it, I put in my professional libraries that I maintained at Credo up on LibraryThing, so that people could see what's in it. It's like, you know, it's books I've collected over the last decade and a half, about reference and weird, murky reference books and I was putting in my first hand, I was using this little device you can get that reads an ISBN, you can get from LibraryThing, and in the first half dozen books I put in, I decided to look at one of the features they have, you can look and see who else has this book, because everybody puts their, not everybody but, you know, lots, most people put their library collections online, and one of the books I put in was only in two libraries in the world. One of them was from South Africa, under the name Jenny B. Walker, which many of you know, because she's been a frequent attendant at Charleston, so, it's just the kind of quirky thing that LibraryThing does. So, Tim? Shake my hand.

Tim Spalding: I'm shaking. All right. All right. Let me see what I can do in eleven minutes. Okay. I want to talk about LibraryThing. So, LibraryThing is personal cataloging, as John mentioned. If everyone catalogs together on a site that everyone shares, it becomes something called

social cataloging. If everyone does it, then it becomes social networking. Now, LibraryThing also makes a product for libraries, which I'm not going to be talking about at all, for risk of seeming commercial, but you can Google LibraryThing for libraries. The ladder of engagement is about how people climb the site, about how members for the site and I hope to show you these and other things, like quality engagement and about how you might go about adding crowdsourcing to whatever you want to do.

Personal cataloging is the basis of everything on LibraryThing. We started with the idea that it would only be personal cataloging, go out, you could catalog your books. Not only do people do it, as something else emerged. Here's my catalog. I add books. I use a scanner. I use the scanner to add tags to my books. Tags are the best way to catalog your books, to categorize your books, better than shelves. Members do this by the millions and LibraryThing has added over 112 million tags from users, which means that we have tens of thousands of people using the tag "romance." We even have tens of thousands of people using the tag "paranormal romance." You can say "romance zombies," "romance YA Greece." When you have this enormous combination of tags, something can emerge which nobody intended in the first place. People tag for themselves, and something emerges out of that. There are 393 covers that members have added for Harry Potter and the Sorcerer's Stone, four million covers overall. And here's the trick. They're not adding it to help other people, primarily. You can't add a cover unless it's on your own volume. You're adding for yourself, so you have all these covers and when you look at your catalog, it looks pretty. It looks like your books. Right? Well, the result of that is an enormous collection of covers. Exhibitionism and voyeurism. This was a photo that was submitted for one of our contests. Exhibitionism is, look at my library. Okay? There's lots of different ways of doing this, posts on Facebook, etc. Voyeurism is, "Hey, let's look at that person's library." Right? It's pretty low level with social interaction, but it is social interaction. Self-expression is the next step on the ladder and the idea here is, I'm not just going to share what I have. I'm going to talk about it. So, here's, for example, is *The Hunger Games*. Members have written 2,600 odd reviews on *The Hunger Games*, categorized by language and Mockingjay in general has 2.3 million reviews. Now, this wouldn't happen if it wasn't something people wanted to do on the site. Okay? There have been many attempts to do reviews in library catalogs. My opinion is that most of them have failed quite miserably, because standing at a terminal is not the time you want to be entering a review. Not to mention it's a waste of time when you haven't read the book yet. You're looking for the book, okay? So, if you look at the ChiliFresh thing, you'll see that ChiliFresh has nine reviews for *Gold Finch* that he ordered in '96 and it's because people in LibraryThing actually want to do it, whereas in library catalogs, including the products that we make for library catalogs, they're just not that interested in doing it.

Social cataloging. Now, social cataloging is, in some ways, where things get interesting. It is cataloging on shared data. LibraryThing members want to have series rights. Series is one of the things that libraries generally don't do well. So, the library data we get and the Amazon data we get is not good enough for most users. This is the series page for *Star Wars* that members have settled by cataloging the series on their own books. Now, it's pretty awesome that there's 946 books in the *Star Wars* series but what's really awesome is the thing on the right, which is that there's more than 180 subseries of the *Star Wars* series, *Star Wars: Republic*, *Star Wars: Tales of the Jedi*, right? This is more information about how *Star Wars* books link to each other than any library in the world has or should have, okay? This is the power of people in their underpants at 2:00 in the morning, who care more about *Star Wars* than anyone in this room and that's great, okay?

Here's the example. We have a system called Common Knowledge. You can see some of the things you can enter: series, canonical title, original publication date, characters, races. You can do, for authors, you can say when they were. Okay? And this system has more than six part formulated edits. It's a fielded wiki. So, imagine Wikipedia, but every single field is a Wikipedia page, okay, which is acute data abundance, but it

produces this amazing abundance of cool data. Okay. LibraryThing members do all of the authority control on the subject. That may scare the hell out of people, but it's true. All of the work-edition dissemination, what's called Ferberization, right, are these two editions part of the same world, is done by members. They've done more than four million acts of dissemination. All of the combination of separation of authors, right, Stephen King, Richard Bachmann, all of the homonymous author division. There are 39 John Smiths. LibraryThing members have figured it out. Okay?

Tag disambiguation. So, on LibraryThing, members combine tags. It's one of the weaknesses of tags, is there's all these different parts, and on LibraryThing, on some level, the tag World War II is also WW2, WWII, because members have made that come together. This is, well, does it work? It works really well. It, we put our information in OCLC in 2008. It's even better now. Here's some organizing all the John Smiths in the world by works. Okay.

Policing and helping. At some point, people get invested enough that they want to police and help. That's an essential part of the LibraryThing experience, is a group devoted exclusively to fighting spam. There's a group devoted exclusively to work combination issues, which is mostly shutting down people who are doing it wrong. And there's people who really spend their lives on LibraryThing, improving the data and, but God bless them. I don't think of them like, "hey, you work for us," is just, it's interesting for them, so they do it and that's how we do it.

The top level of the ladder of engagement is collaborative cataloging. So, this is LibraryThing members that catalog the libraries of more than 250 dead people. The rule is they have to be dead and they can't be [inaudible]. So, Tupac Shakur to Thomas Jefferson, Jackie Gleason, Marilyn Monroe, books that Darwin had aboard the Beagle, right? Huge number of presidents and all kinds of random celebrities, too, and this really has no personal value to anyone, but once you get into LibraryThing, once you start enjoying it and you run out of books, right, you still want to do it. You start getting into projects like this. Another time, members cataloged all the books that were in the movie *Dr. Horrible's Sing Along Blog* by freeze framing and cataloging in LibraryThing all the fictional mastermind's of the singing superhero.

The ladder of engagement moves in different ways. It moves from the personal to social, it moves from the love of the thing, and don't underestimate the love of thing. Love of thing is everything. Use your map to mark the other. The love of self to altruism.

LibraryThing is a social network with the primary connector between people is the stuff that their interested in. Right? That's not how everyone works. Right? That's not what makes the world go 'round in general, but, there are a lot of people who want to talk about books they have, even with people they don't know, a lot of people who want to work together on books, because they love them. Low interest people or high interest people. Uh, many, few, right? So, every time you step up the ladder, people drop off. There's a lot of people, about half the users of LibraryThing only use it to personally catalog and don't do anything else, right? Now, in, this is bad in some ways, but it's also good in other ways, because as you step up the ladder, you tend to get geekier, more committed, smarter people, okay? And, you know, the reviews on LibraryThing are just written really well because the people on LibraryThing are people who love to write reviews, the cataloging and so forth on LibraryThing, and somebody who will really, really care about it.

Here are the lessons. Last slide. Secure the bottom of the ladder. The bottom of the ladder is the most critical thing. If you want to do something in crowdsourcing, you need to start with what you're going to get and all the wonderful engagement that people are going to have with each other, you will not get to the top of that ladder. You can build it rung by rung, but when you build it rung by rung, you should think about it rung by rung. Each rung needs to make sense. Most of all, in library context, crowdsourcing is not a feature. If there's one line I want you to take away from this, is that it's not a feature. Over and over again, things like tagging are added to library catalogs. Look, we have

tagging! No one's using it. It's worthless. That tagging is worthless if you've got 20,000 tags. Okay? So, above all, it's not what you get, it's not about what you get, it's about what you're giving to the people who do. Thank you very much.

John Dove: Thank you, Tim. I'm going do something that's really scary, because I made a mistake this morning and actually got the wrong slides for Scott. So, I'm now going to pull up the right slides for Scott. And Scott is somebody who actually, no matter what slides you'd have in here, he'd be able to hold all of our attention. So, but I mean, he should have the benefit of the slides that he wanted, so . . .

There we go. Now, now that that's done, I'm going to introduce you. So, ChiliFresh. A lot of people haven't heard about ChiliFresh, and yet it's in 4,000 libraries and it's actually done some very creative things in terms of how to deal with the curation. If you're going to allow input from various patrons, you know you're going to have problems in the sense of, this is Nazi trash and somebody else will say, you know, so, you've got to be able to say, is this a commentary that you really want to continue to have in your social media or is it something you want to discourage or, more likely, it actually does something that is really good and then the local librarians, they would promote that to the community of the 4,000 libraries that have ChiliFresh, so that everybody, every library benefits. And one of the things that ChiliFresh has had to do in order to make that possible is that they, a lot of people talk about user experience, and mainly they're thinking about features, which are clearly very important in terms of the user experience, but if you're going to ask librarians to do some additional work, then you better really think through how the user experience is for those librarians. And not only that, but you probably want to think about how, in fact, the work that they might be doing for you might actually augment work that they're already doing for the general purpose that they have.

So, ChiliFresh has done a really good job in terms of thinking about how their involvement in a library can enhance the very activities that librarians are already doing. I think it's been a real secret to its success, so, Scott.

Scott Johnson: As he said, my name is Scott Johnson. We're actually in Kansas City. How many of you have not heard about ChiliFresh before today? I like that. You can't answer the question that way tomorrow. Let me tell you why that's interesting to me. Because we don't brand what we do. Our brand doesn't exist in your catalog or in your library anywhere. Our brand only exists in the concept, meaning that your users, your students, your patrons, they never see the word ChiliFresh. They never see who we are. They only see the functionality and they only see the platform now.

So, before I get into it, I want to talk a little bit about crowd source and the importance of that, that collaborative data. As I look around the room, I think I'm probably the oldest one here. One question that I have is how many of you remember the 1970s? Not how many were there, how many remember it? I remember a little bit about them. Most of you were probably in diapers. I was riding my bicycle. How many of you had a waterbed in your house in the 1970s or 80s? How many of you knew people who had a waterbed? What was that all about? At the time, waterbeds made it to 20% of all the households in the United States. Today, how many of you know somebody with a waterbed in their house? Oh, there's two people. That's funny to me. If the internet existed in the 70s and 80s, if there was a review system allowing people to read and write their comments about waterbeds, you think waterbeds would have reached a 20% penetration? I don't know the answer to the question, but I also know that during the 70s, everybody on my street had a station wagon. Do you remember that? Everybody had a station wagon. How did this happen? I believe, and the question was asked, I believe that the wisdom of crowd sourced information is also the madness of crowd sourced information.

I also believe that each one of your users are seeking to connect with other people, with data, and with this crowd sourced message when they go to your catalog and this is how I know. We exist, ChiliFresh exists because I was standing behind a reference desk at a public library. As I was standing behind the reference desk, the reference librarian was sitting there. There was nobody in front of her, she wasn't helping anyone. She had her computer on and there were two windows open on her screen. One on the left was a Searcy Dynex catalog. The one on the right was Amazon. And I watched curiously from behind her, because I really didn't understand what she was doing. And I walked around front, I knew her, her name's Sarah. I said, "Sarah, what are you doing?" She said "I'm just looking for my next read." And I looked at her a little weird. I said, "I don't get it." And I won't, granted, I'm a simple man. You work at the library, but you're going to buy this book at Amazon? And she said "No, no. No, no, no, no. I look through the catalog here and then I read the reviews about what people say about the book and that's how I decide if I want to take a book home." My next question was, I think it was fairly obvious, "Well, why aren't your reviews in the catalog" She looked up at me, like I had spiders on my face, and she said, "That's not possible." And you know, I took that message home and I learned very quickly that it wasn't possible, and the reason I saw that is because of what Tim discussed earlier about this critical mass and the same thing that John talked about. How do you get enough people to do this?

Just after we started ChiliFresh, one of the largest library systems, not only in North America, the world, by circulation, King County, called me up and says "We need your product. We need to put patron reviews in our catalog." And I opened up their catalog while I was talking to her and, and I said "You've already got reviews in there." She said "Yeah. It's a contained system. It's just our patrons writing reviews." And we did some math. We learned that, if keep the system going like it is, it'll be decades before they reach any kind of critical mass. And so what we did is we created a collaborative database of reviews that allows a library to participate in this database of reviews that connect to an ISP or any unique identifier to catalog. So, there's somebody in Seattle, in King County writes a review, that review's visible in a library in Miami or Salt Lake County, or in Australia or in the UK. And all of a sudden, it made all the sense in the world. It solved a lot of our problems, like whose going to be posting reviews? Well, the truth is, everybody wants to read 'em, and this many people will write them. I mean, you proved that by raising your hands earlier.

So, what we've done is we've kept all of this in catalog. Every review in the ChiliFresh system has been written by a library patron in a library catalog and it's been moderated by a librarian. I'm not sure there's many libraries that want to have a Viagra commercial in their catalog or a school librarian who wants the F word showing up in the catalog, but every public school in the state of Ohio has the ability to allow their students, empower their students, to read and write reviews. The system can be as open or as closed as they want. That means that they only want to show reviews from their schools. A library may want to show just reviews from the US. Maybe they're just like that. So, anyway, we've moved past all of this, trying to figure out what is community, because community, I think, is key in this crowd sourcing.

Back to the 1970s, when I was riding my bike, community was about as far as I could ride my bike. There was a grocery store, there was, there was a police station and there was the library. That was my community. My parent's community was their workplace. That's as far as they stretched. Every once in a while, they'd go on vacation. They'd read books to try and create community. Well, community today is completely different. Because of the internet, our communities are interspaced. They have to do with our hobbies, our reading interests. It has to do with where we travel. It has to do with so much more. I swim every day. I like to try to talk to other people that like to swim. Well, there aren't that many of them, but I can find them online. You might like to do other things too that you connect with people.

So, let's talk about this for just a minute. What is the power of the opinion? And we're talking about a group opinion here. The power of the opinion, in my humble opinion, is as strong as any. Every revolution in the world took place because of the crowd. Every change in the world took place because of the crowd. So, we have to share his collaborative data, but how do we know that it's

good? How can we tell if it's good? I think that, as somebody looks through this, they can see very simply. It's why, when we buy a new computer, we're not taking it home with us until we read about somebody who already has it under their arm. How many of you ever bought a washer and dryer without reading a review on it? And it's like every one of your users, if you don't have the ability to read and write reviews in your catalog, everyone of your users, students, it doesn't matter, researchers, it can be patrons, they are all seeking peer comments of what they want to do. And they will open up Amazon or decide to go open up other sources. These activities should be taking place in the catalog. So, we move this a little bit further. This is what the review content looks like here. The way we have done this and the way we have been able to put ChiliFresh content and functionality in libraries is by integrating into the library, the IOS software. And this is really key. And when you talk about personal cataloging, imagine your catalog is the place that not only houses your connection and your information, but it empowers your patrons to catalog their stuff right beside it and share their stuff right beside your collection and then communicate with other users on a global scale, based on common literary interests. That's the power of what we're doing. We never drive your patron out of your catalog. We only build functionality into your catalog that empowers them to communicate and connect on a global scale. This is an example of how it's integrated into the [inaudible] catalog. A person can put in their profile information, they can, they've got bookshelves, which is cataloging. They've got friends and followers.

I can just go through these again. When somebody logs into the library catalog, it automatically logs them into the ChiliFresh network. They don't have to go to ChiliFresh.com to do anything, ever. They only see a connection inside your catalog. I'll just click to a user kind of quick. There's ways to add things to their catalog and to their bookshelf. There's ways to tag things and comments they can share and here's what happens. When people start communicating and making recommendations back and forth and it's a global communication that's going on, we capture that data and make it available to you that you can use in your collection development. You'll also find that our review engine appears in Brodart's catalog, when you're buying your stuff. It appears in Ingram's Catalog when you're buying stuff. It appears in . . . some of these, so basically, we also have functionality that interacts with your users where they live. This all lives in their pocket with mobile apps. It lives on their Facebook page. Your catalog alongside their catalog in all of these places. You want to keep them in your ecosphere, because that's what's important. Thank you for your time.

John Dove: Thank you, Scott. Now, I've got to switch back to the other presentation. Now, what about the idea of crowd sourcing reference or health questions itself? This has got to be kind of personal, given the questions about what is the competency of people who can provide answers to people in the library systems. I've been giving a number of talks over the last few years about user centered designed and online reference systems. A common question I will ask early in the talk is where do people turn first when they have a reference question?

Unknown Speaker: Their friends.

John Dove: Who else? Very few people ever say their friends. People will immediately say "Oh, well, Google" or "Wikipedia" or "the library's website" or, but in fact, if you look at this anthropologically, people first turn to whoever's within shouting distance that they haven't annoyed yet. "Hey, who won the World Cup in 2008?" You know, so, or "How do I make this thing work?" It just happened to me this morning. So, Ilana Stonebreaker's going to describe a very interesting approach to crowd sourcing of questions in the library, too.

Ilana Stonebraker: Before I get started, it's Saturday morning, and you guys are here and I really appreciate it, so we're going to watch a short video. Have, do, are any of you people familiar with the Vlog Brothers? Yay! Okay, that's it. It's an online community out there. And we're going to watch a short clip of jokes.

Video: It's been over a year since the last time I told you jokes, which means that it's time for me to try to beat my record again. This time, 54 jokes, and I'll do it in four minutes. What's the difference between a cat and a compound sentence? One has claws at the end of his paws. One has a pause at the end of its clause. What's the difference between a tuna and a piano? You can tune the piano, but you cannot piano a tuna. The difference between the moon and Julius Caesar? The moon is rocky and full of craters and Julius Caesar is dead. Why do you think was "Civil Disobedience" such a fantastic essay? Thorough editing. Thoreau. What cell phones do traveling nuns use? Virgin Mobile. And how come her cell phone bill was so high? She was a Roman Catholic. Why did they kick Cinderella off the baseball team? She kept running away from the ball. And the mermaid. That was weird. What was she wearing in Math class? Oh yeah, an algae-bra. Why was the sand wet? Because the sea weed. The sea, it weed. What happened when the butcher backed up into his meat grinder?

Ilana Stonebraker: Okay, all right. So, that's, that's the video, and you may be asking yourself, how is my library like the video "54 Jokes in Four Minutes?" The answer is that the Vlog Brothers is a very active and vibrant online community, does a lot of crowdsourcing, a lot of crowd funding and things that they do like "54 Jokes" video, which may seem trivial, are part of supporting a larger community. So, the things that you do above the water, when you answer reference questions, when you, you update your catalog, are supporting a large community of learners that are bound to the library. So, I would say that each and every one of you supports online community and I would say online community, because a huge amount of what you do supports communities which may have never spoken to each other or you may have never seen in person but, nevertheless, is very vibrant. Some examples of some online communities that you may support. So, you are probably physically located somewhere and, your library is, and you support online community about your city, your school or organization, there are many reference questions you may probably answer about your school or organization. Your alumnae or retirement base.

You may support them. The fan, people who are just fans of libraries, like Neil Gaiman, who's always talking about his love of libraries. People who are just fans of reading who want to contribute to these systems that you gentlemen have talked about. And also your collection strengths, the things that you collect, creating community as well. And so you support these online communities. So, what I'm going to be talking about is some specific ways that we've looked at some specific problems involving reference in a R1 large academic library.

I'm going to start with four not shocking facts. So, everyone uses the internet, our patrons are part of a community, and they are, we are supporting, and then students don't read manuals, and the majority of reference questions are lower level. Where do I find this? Where are the printers? Those sorts of questions, but there's also lower level online questions, right? This doesn't work. Why doesn't this work? Where should I check for this person? So, what's supposed to happen at a reference desk is that students develop questions about which they ask the librarian about. The librarian, at a one-to-one level, answers that question dazzlingly well and then the student rocks that, so the next point is, thanks the libraries forever and gives the library a million dollars. What actually happens, and you can start this at any level, is the student starts their path, they find that they can't do whatever it is, they find at least one resource that works for them and then they try and like make that work for all their projects, that's the cat trying to get into the box. And the cat in the box is very important, because I think that, when they look at what sorts of resources they're using, they may not be aware of what even their other students have found.

How many of you guys have had the experience at a reference desk, where you have a long line and the students start helping each other? You know, they're like, "Oh, I had that English 106 class last week." "Yeah, what'd you do?" You know? And that's what we want to happen. When we create our online reference transactions, we're not allowing the line help to happen. So, also, reference service models only assume that the librarian can get to that answer, which is not

always true. People turn to their friends, to other students within the class, to the professor, to give them all sorts of different types of answers. Our questions are also all treated alike. The majority of reference questions, like I said, are lower level, but they're also context-based. People don't generate questions about nothing. They question, they generate questions, especially in academic environment, because they're all part of some sort of online community, be it a class, be it a group of projects, and the process of reference decontextualizing those questions from the environment in which they were asked. If you don't then put that context back in and the use, they don't utilize graduate students, instructors who may have additional information or may be able to answer the question more specifically for the user. And it neglects to think about that we live in an information ecosystem, where we give excellent answers but we don't exist, the library doesn't exist just to answer questions. We're trying to provide help; we're trying to help our users get things done faster. So, we want to use all the information to help us that we can.

And then there's a really excellent book out on MIT Press from 2013 called *Crowdsourcing* and it has a really excellent definition of crowdsourcing, which is an online distributed problem-solving and production model that leverages the collective intelligence of online communities to serve specific organizational goals. So, you need a specific organizational goal and you need a specific community. The crowd is not just the crowd. The crowd is your community. Additionally, the locus of control regarding the creative production of goods exists between the organization and the public. So, you don't own your crowdsourcing and neither do your users. It's rather collaboration between you and this is an excellent place for libraries because libraries are deeply collaborative. Projects of collaborative cataloging have been going on for as long as I've been, well, I'm very young, but you can, you know, if you've been, it's been, the important elemental part of our mission is being collaborative. So, I think that we're a really great location for crowdsourcing.

I'm going to talk about a specific example, which is an IMLS-funded project over the last year over at Purdue. Our community was the students, staff, and faculty at Purdue University. Our specific goal that we're trying to do with crowdsourcing was provide contextual answers for students and also alumni questions. So, when they wanted to know when the school mascot got from this big to this big, or where they can buy a bobble head, or when the next football game is, and where people are tailgating, that's the sort of questions that we're interacting with as well, to strengthen alumni networks, which are also part of our community. So, this is CrowdAsk. It's very similar to, if anyone uses Fact Overflow, it has similar gamification and packaging. You log in using a variety of different types of providers, and this is also, we really, this is open source on GitHub, so you can download this as well and we've branded it with all of our information, so this is a lot of Purdue gold and silver. You can ask a question on the system and you can ask a question. You can also assign a bounty to that question. So, it's a point system. So, you can give out more of your points to get an answer faster. You can assign a category, be it, we launched it in a group of lower level English classes and information literacy classes, so students could work together, as well as we had launched it through the alumni networks for Purdue History, in collaboration with the special elections. This is an example of a question within the system. It's citing references using APA format. You see that users can vote on answers and questions. You can see that one of their, the number one voted answer, which goes to the top, is a link to Purdue Owl, which is a very well-known Purdue source and they, and the students may say that that is probably the best, and other people have also given other sources they use for citing in APA format as well. So, this is also an example of what a user page looks like. You can see this student has a number of badges. There are badges that are implemented, such as good question, knowledgeable, good answer, type-thing. These all have to do with different cases of it. Additionally, this is a meritocracy, so, the more points you get the higher badges you get, the more power you have within the system. So, this is encouraging students to be really good at answering each other's questions.

So, next, I want to talk about some, some stats, because usage is important. So far, since we've launched it, we've had 184 users post questions and 129 users post answers. This is all within the last year. 257 people voted. There are additionally more questions, so people are repeat users. The most views on a question is 182. I think it's still the MLA question. The most answers on a question is 16, the most votes is 48. Additionally, something interesting, and if you do any studying of online communities, there's a whole group of people that are lurkers. So, a lot of you guys would have that on Yelp as lurkers. So, you use the system, but you don't contribute to the system. But, you can see that the average amount of time, from Google Analytics, is six minutes and seven seconds, which means that people just hang out on the page and we had a lot of users, of people who were just getting answers from the system, in addition to contributing, which, lurkers are a very important part of online communities. They build knowledge and they lurk to market that community.

We did usability tests of four students, two novices, who'd never used it before, and two expert users, who were really into it. What was really interesting to us when we asked the expert users why they contributed is their motivation wasn't the points, though the points were cool. What they wanted was reciprocity. They said, and I quote one of the users, "Someone helped me and I wanted to help someone else." So, I think that use, I think there's a lot of optimism. There's the, there's some very earnest users out there who have been helped who want to help other people. Reciprocity seems to be a much more powerful tool than gamification when it comes to crowdsourcing. They want to help each other. They want to be part of a community. So, this is part of kind of a larger goal, and within this is our, once again, our first speaker talked about it, crowdsourcing not being a feature. I totally agree with that. Our goal is to develop sustainable user engagement and community involvement as part of the Purdue University's Library website, not to just answer the questions or to load off some of the late night reference to students who are all working at that time, but it's also just to cultivate a community of learners who help each other, who can answer each other's questions and ask better questions, because they have engaged in a reference interaction from both sides. Yeah, thank you.

So, as I'm kind of finishing up, I just wanted to reiterate that crowds are, you get this idea, when people talk about crowdsourcing, like they're this mass of kind of infectious zombies that just come out of nowhere. I think that, really, crowds are probably people you know. Crowds are helpful students who really love the library. They're people that you know that want to help and this is merely an invitation for them to do so, to be part of the system, as well as strengthen your relationship with your community, to move some of that iceberg above the water mark. Some keys that we found, overall for crowdsourcing reference help, the stronger the online community for the update problem, the stronger the user base. The stronger that community is, so classes are a very strong community but for a very short amount of time. Alumni bases are very strong communities, so finding those communities and then cultivating those resources. Crowdsourcing can also work to strengthen an online community, by bringing people together who did not necessarily know that they had common interests. And I think the library, as a conduit for that interaction, is a fabulous contribution to our mission. And then, once again, reciprocity is important to these communities. They want to give as well as to take. So, what this means is students, even students, even alumni, they want to feel as if they can feel the impact of what they do. They want to help people. So, we need systems that can make that more clear. I think it's an important part for those users. So, this is an ongoing project, so if you're excited about crowdsourcing and you want to help or you want to help develop further, once again, it's an open source code, so if you want to develop it or just do interesting things with it, if you have a community which is, you want to try it out on, or even if you want to come up here and tell me that your users would never use this. I'm interested, and I love to talk to you guys afterwards and talk about possible weaknesses, threats, opportunities, any of those things. Please, I'd love to have this be much more a conversation, so we can talk about better ways to kind of strengthen our online communities. So, that's it. Here's a link to our code and a short video on CrowdAsk. Thank you.

Science Education Gone Wilde: Creating Science References That Work

John Rennie, Editorial Director, Science, McGraw-Hill Professional

The following is a lightly edited transcript of a live presentation at the 2014 Charleston Conference. Slides and videos are available at http://2014charlestonconference.sched.org/.

John Rennie: Okay. Well thank you very much, I appreciate that very much, and I, first of all, am hugely honored to say that you recognize how important a figure I am here in the United States, although that puts you in a very specialized company. I assure you. But thank you very much.

I am John Rennie. I am the Editorial Director of McGraw-Hill Education's general science reference AccessScience. For 15 years I was also the Editor-In-Chief of *Scientific American*, and I've been involved in science journalism, and so forth, for gosh now thirty years. Yikes. I have to say that this is first time coming to a Charleston Conference and looking at the program and seeing a dizzying number of choices, and problems confronting modern librarians and the modern scholars, and the students that depend on them is very impressive. I'm very honored to have been selected to come and speak to you today, but I have to say that when I look at all those matters I could not begin to claim expertise in many of them or any of them. So, I will happily entrust your attention to a lot of the other speakers on a lot of those matters. What I would like to discuss though, in this time, is a little more specific to the creation, selection, and acquisition of good science references and texts; ones that truly do serve the needs of today's scholars. And I am going to, maybe idiosyncratically, look at this on the basis of my own experience.

I think if I were to make a distinction between a lot of what we've already heard about today, there's been a lot of discussion of platforms, and metrics, and of business models, and new ways of approaching it, and they're all very relevant to your concerns. I, though, may look at this a little more from a content creation standpoint, and sort of the question of what should we be looking for in these science texts and science references.

What would help us distinguish the good ones from the bad ones? So, I am partly going to be speaking about science in education, but I'm also going to speaking about the way we speak about science in education. I'm hoping that, if nothing else, some of what I have to say will have some sort of value to you, value to you in maybe helping you to select certain kinds of works in a new way, or evaluating them in a different light. And, for those of you who are in the publishing side of things, maybe to help to reinforce the most sound intuitions you have on this subject so far. Of course, in the spirit of the Charleston Conference, the theme it has thrown down, I am indeed going to try to discuss all of this by, by using Wilde's play, *The Importance of Being Earnest* as a jumping off point. I am picking up the gauntlet as it was thrown down.

Now, the choice of the *Importance of Being Earnest* might seem rather an unpromising starting point on all of this. I'm sure, as you all know, this is widely considered to be Wilde's masterpiece. It's also famously like a Victorian-era version of Seinfeld. It is a play about nothing. It is a comedy of manners. It is filled with false and mistaken identities and the pose of seriousness being more important than reality. It all builds up to the word play which we see in the last lines. In which, Lady Bracknell says, "My nephew, you seem to be displaying signs of triviality." To which Jack, one of the protagonists says, "Well, on the contrary Aunt Augusta, I've now realized, for the first time in my life, the vital importance of being earnest." By the way, Anthony, I apologize now for venturing anything that resembled a British accent.

To my mind, science education suffers from more than a little bit of its own problem with earnestness and triviality. As politicians and education reformers, and social critics are constantly pointing out, STEM literacy is crucial to the nation's well-being. Not simply as an economic driver, but because average citizens must increasingly grapple with the practical and ethical impacts of new science and technologies in their lives. So there's a lot of effort given to all this, but quite frankly, as you know, US students lag embarrassingly in international assessments of math and science achievement and this problem is likely to have serious repercussions for our national competitiveness and well-being. When we look at the state of the public discussion on climate change, and GMOs, and so many other sorts of topics, it's clear that the grasp of science by the public is not all that we might hope. I mean, for example, we can just take as one example of a failure of public science communication, the current Ebola crisis. There is this monstrous confusion, not just among the public, but also politicians, and news commentators, and others about the dangers of the disease, and the advisability of quarantines, and so much of this confusion is really very largely attributable, to my mind, to the failures of the news media to have adequately explain the difference between infectiousness, the efficiency with which viruses will spread throughout the body, and contagiousness, the effectiveness with which disease is actually transmitted from one person to the next. Two rather different things.

As Oscar Wilde joked in *The Importance of Being Earnest*, "The whole theory of modern education is radically unsound. Fortunately, in England, at any rate, education produces no effect whatsoever." But in the 21st-century America, we are not laughing about that. I think a contributing cause to this is that most conversations about science education and indeed most educational science works themselves come wrapped in this mantle of earnest gravitas and weighty importance. Which is a shame because I think it only reinforces this joyless, eat your vegetables, they're good for you, with which many people in the public and particularly students regard science. It makes students approach their science with this sort of dutiful, doomed resignation. This is not a formula for success. I think there's value in breathing more vitality and fun into science lessons, and doing more to help students connect with the natural curiosities, and enthusiasms that they have about the world around them. That's an approach to science that can inspire and entertain us, as well as illuminate. Now many science

communicators, particularly those in the general popular media have read about this problem and they do try this, this sort of lighter approach to explain science, often with good results.

In the world of television, I don't know if you think about this, but what is one of the most commercially successful of all science related brands on television? MythBusters. Because they blow stuff up. And people are interested in watching that kind of thing. Now the danger, of course, in a lot of these situations is that this sort of approach can flirt with a kind of triviality. They may succeed in making science seem appealing, but the risk of portraying science then is that it may come across as a kind of carnival of fun, but disjointed facts. But I'm not recommending that science texts need to change into some kind of nonstop laugh riot, nor even that in the name of popular outreach we should give in to some sort of fanciful sensationalistic nonsense like the cable TV shows that are claiming, with a straight face, that there are mermaids and pyramids built by aliens. Rather what I'm trying to suggest is that a bit of fresh air and sunlight might end the gloom, might help inspire students with their science studies, and there are ways for us to do this very responsibly by availing ourselves of communication techniques that work well in lots of other situations outside of science. My hope is, in talking about some of my views about science communication, and why it succeeds and fails, I'm hoping that can be of some value to you in making some of the kinds of choices that you will be making, and also helping to inspire publishers to do better as well.

If we're going to try to understand this deadly earnestness with which we've often approached traditional scientific references, let's consider what have traditionally been prized as core virtues in those kinds of works. Now, I am . . . by the way, everything I'm about to say, I will be speaking in gross generalities and probably unintentionally defamatory statements, so please forgive me for all of that. But the excellence in science communications often involved correctness, obviously, and accuracy, credibility, and authority, and thoroughness; a notion of completeness. The precision or exactness of the presentation of data;

timeliness, or currency, things being up to date, and, of course, clarity. Though, if we're honest with ourselves, we'd have to say that we've sometimes tolerated some great lapses in clarity in service to conveying the rest of those. We have counted on science texts and reference works to fully and accurately capture the expertise of their authors because this is what the students or scholars turning to them would want or expect. The experts were the final authorities themselves; the librarians and publishers were the gatekeepers to a lot of this information. And, although great and sincere efforts were made to help students find text references that were appropriate to them, the bottom line has typically been that students had to meet those texts on the ground that the authors and the publishers selected for them. Not every work was for everyone. Basically, it was expected that scholars approaching a particular work would rise to the occasion of being able to read and use it, and if they couldn't . . . well too bad; look again. This makes for an intimidatingly formal and intellectually unforgiving system, and if it were a person, I dare say it might be one who would embrace the description in Wilde's witticism, "If I am occasionally a little over-dressed, I make up for it by being always immensely over-educated."

It should probably, of course, go without question that there is nothing wrong with upholding the importance of accuracy and the rest of those kinds of scholarly virtues, but today I would submit they are not enough. They define a certain kind of excellence in, in scientific information, but they don't guard against what makes for the worst kind of reference. Because make no mistake, the worst reference isn't one that's wrong. It isn't one that's incomplete. The worst reference is one that people won't use even if they know, in theory, it could help them. The untouched text is our greatest failure. So, we also need to take very seriously this sort of danger that here, in the era of the internet, that there are dangers associated that simply didn't exist when reference libraries were more closed curated collections. Exclusively, the risk on the internet is that the people could start to consult allegedly scientific works that are in fact misleading or misinforming, but which might actually be more accessible and more

appealing than the better informed ones that we would like them to consult. This great trifecta of challenges that presents itself to all science communication, popular and scholarly alike, is this: the three problems are boredom, confusion, and other priorities. Now boredom, we often blame people for being bored, but it's not just a matter of short attention spans, or some kind of innate dullness in the material. Readers get bored when they fail to see the relevance or significance of a subject, and why it matters to them. Confusion; there's always a central issue for something as, as potentially taxing as a lot of scientific subjects to become confusing, but assuming that readers want to really try to learn about a subject, they may still have trouble digesting the sense of it as it is presented. And, of course, other priorities.

Those other challenges don't play out in a vacuum. Readers can't help but constantly question whether their time might not be profitably invested by attending to other needs that they have. Now these have been problems in all kinds of media, not just scholarly ones, and indeed a lot of popular media have had to come to terms with these early because of course we've heard of about the sort of disasters that have been setting the popular media on their ear. It has always been easy for audiences to try to go to something else and particularly, outside of scholarly needs, where there isn't even a compulsion for them to attend to any one thing in particular, but it's something now that scholarly publications are also very sorely challenged by.

Let me show you something. This, which you can't see very well, but this is a paper that was published in *Nature* back in 1992; it's the growing inaccessibility of science. It's kind of a remarkable paper because it takes a look at the state of the difficulty of reading various scientific journals over the decades. And it makes a rather interesting, a rather interesting point, which I hope you'll be able to see with this. It uses measurements of lexical difficulty in a variety of them, and so, for example, this graph shows how it is the journals *Nature* and *Science*, but also *Scientific American*, how they became harder to read over that period of 1930 up through 1990. And, as you can see, they've all been rising for quite some time, but that particularly once you started to get into the 60s and 70s you really started to see more of a rapid rise in all of that. That represents a real challenge for helping people to be engaged with this kind of content, and it's something that's not just restricted to those journals. It's something that we would see actually, well, across a number of other blurry journals [referring to slides], but I assure you it makes a very similar point about the level, the constant increase, largely because of the increasingly specialized terminology that would be used in the scientific works themselves. It's a great problem with all of that. Now the scholarship in these published papers, it may be revealing all sorts of important truths about how the universe works, but as Oscar Wilde reminds us: "The truth is rarely pure, and never simple." And, it's too bad that our journals and other works have so often not done anything or not done enough to push back against that.

I have a unique perspective, an introduction to a lot of these sorts of problems, during that time, as Editor-in-Chief of *Scientific American*. If you'll indulge me, let me give you a sense of a kind of thing that happened with *Scientific American* over time. We have to jump way back in time to understand just how that's the case. *Scientific American*, established back in 1845, the oldest continuously published magazine in the United States; curiously enough, it started off, as you can see, as this broad sheet of new patents and philosophical reflections, the occasional poem, news of technical and scientific advances. And it followed actually a variety of different sorts of formats and looks up through the balance of the 19th century. Then halfway through the 20th century, it was reinvented back in 1947 and 1948, and that's when it actually became the magazine that most of us think of as *Scientific American* now. That's when it because this magazine which educated readers could find descriptions of science in the words of the scientists who were responsible for that. This turned out to be brilliantly successful; far more so than the reinventors of the magazine had ever intended for it to be. In retrospect, it's not hard to see just why that is; part of it came from the fact that, that they did a great job of making the magazine look

and sound like it was the embodiment of the attitudes that people had toward science. It was cool and austerely white like some sort of Grecian temple. It was a place for contemplation of pure ideas and objective truths, unsullied by merely human opinions and personalities. Science at that time was obviously regarded as this kind of ideal, better than humans. Now, this is what so many of us grew up with and came to love about *Scientific American*.

We all can understand sticking with a good thing, but sometimes sticking with a good thing too much can be a bad idea, and to understand that let's take a look at *The Atlantic* magazine during the same stretch of time: from 1950 through the 1990s. What you could, in theory, see from that is during this time, *The Atlantic* actually experimented with a number of different logos and looks. These are just the covers, but you get the sense that this was a magazine that was constantly reexamining itself, constantly checking whether or not its methods of trying to reach out to its audience worked appropriately. Take a look at *Scientific American* during that same stretch of time. *Scientific American* changed almost not at all for really the better part of 40 to 50 years. It was astonishingly static, partly because readers loved it, they loved it exactly that way and, and people were afraid to tamper with that. But, the problem is that is a formula that when you think about that problem of the rising lexical difficulty, it increasingly became a formula that worked for a certain number of die-hard people who loved the magazine exactly that way, but it did not work for new generations of people who were coming along. And so the mission for *Scientific American*, as glorious as it was and as well-loved as it was by many of us, in that form it still was something that was not working for new generations of students. And, so, that meant that then starting in the 90s we had to start to reexamine this, and we had to make a number of different sorts of changes looking back at it, and we did start to open up to new different kinds of formats, and new approaches to articles. We had to do things like make some of them shorter and use different, more contemporary designs, and visuals. We started to open up to different kinds of voices within the narrative of the magazine, and a more prominent presence of personalities as such. What we came to discover was that it was possible to uphold a proud intellectual tradition without slavishly repeating the exact same content formulas all the time, and the audience agreed with this. Which paved the way not only for an improvement in the original magazine's critical and financial fortunes, but also the expansion of the brand into another magazine, *Scientific American Mind*, and a strong online presence. So, it's possible to make these sorts of changes and to rethink how we do, in a reasonable and sober way, still approach science well, but not let the soberness of the subject overwhelm the fun that can possibly connect to it.

If we go back again to that notion of some of those underlying great virtues: correctness, accuracy, and the rest, they all still apply. We all still want those in text and science references, but real excellence now isn't just a matter of trying to make sure that those are there. You can't just tick those off and expect that you actually still have, in effect, an excellent science work that people will relate to anymore. Instead, the emphasis needs to be on successful learning by the user rather than on the successful capture and display of accumulated knowledge by the author. Learning is this sort of dynamic process; there's always more to learn. So, it can't be measured in just how much has been told, but in how much has been absorbed, and so we should use any and all tools available to us. To that end, including a spirit of joy and wonder that might help inspire the readers of this material to engage with it. The absolute imperative is we need to understand one's actual audience; not just the intended audience, but who are the people who we are actually reaching with these sorts of works, and it's not just the vital importance of being earnest about who they are, it's, it's even more. It's about anticipating that audience's needs and expectations.

Publishers, smart publishers, realize that they can't just know what their users expect; they have to anticipate it, especially with digital products, because when it comes to digital a satisfying experience makes all the difference in the world. When they have a question about the information

they've been provided, or they want to improve a set of return search results, or whatever else, users don't want to have to try to remember at that point how an interface works, or have to consult a help option to try to do it. The appropriate options for further information or for linked resources, or facets for filtering, or whatever else, they need to be prominent and self-explanatory in the moment and ideally they should sink back to a less prominent position when they're not needed in the same way. Anticipating users' needs and their questions is, at every point, an interactive process, and is highly important in crafting a successful online experience. Now, some of the questions that they're going to have will have a lot to do with the context and relevance of the subjects that they're looking at. Context, of course, refers to how that information fits within a field or multiple fields, and relevance is going to point out how that information may therefore have direct or indirect bearing on that person's life or interests. Yes, it can sometimes get sort of wearisome to constantly be bringing things back down to individuals in this way, but remember that problem of the other priorities. Users need to be reminded and ultimately they want to know why it is that they should be making time to learn this information.

Speaking of priorities, I will throw this out, potentially as a controversial point: accuracy, completeness, and clarity of meaning are all very important, but of those ensuring the clarity of the presented information trumps the others. Within a reasonable margin, the user is better off with a confident understanding of a scientific message that is slightly off or incomplete in its details than with only a foggy grasp of extensive, painstakingly precise data. It's a function of human psychology. Human psychology is also what prompts me to make this other point: although we don't often talk about it in discussions of science references, the vast experience of the human race, and, in fact at this point a not insignificant body of psychological literature, teaches us that good stories and strong narratives have always been the best way to convey meaningful information to people. There are studies that suggest that people can remember facts embedded in narratives and retain that more than 20 times as well as they can just isolated sets of facts. So, not only do such narratives automatically hook into issues of relevance and context for the users, but these kind of stories also evoke faculties in their audience. Readers and listeners, they start to learn and they learn about it in a way that, again, there's nothing else that just a flat presentation of information can possibly hope to match. There's actually, while I was putting this talk together, this paper in *Science* actually just came out a couple of weeks ago and it made an interesting point. It showed that narrative fiction, people reading that, that it spurred the readers, their theory of mind capabilities. It, basically it allowed them to understand character's motivations at a much richer, more visceral level than they could with just a simple outside presentation of facts. That is a phenomenon that we in the world of science communication need to try to take advantage of.

Now most of my examples, I'm sure it's not lost on you, have come from the more popular world, but I can absolutely assure you that these more congenial editorial presentations are very much an issue among the editors of journals themselves. They recognize these problems of ensuring the professionals will want to be sufficiently prioritizing their journal engagement as a way of staying current. That rise of lexical difficulty is still always a problem even within fields, and remember that is mostly a barrier to lay people and people who are coming from the outside of a field, but a lot of the most exciting, most important science that's happening these days is exactly at these areas of interdisciplinary collaboration where it's the biologists working with the physicists, or the material scientist working with the biologist. That's the sort of thing that we want to most enable. We need to get past the problems the rising terminology itself.

These are certainly the kinds of things that I and my colleagues working at AccessScience have been very involved with. I'm not going to try to spend a lot of time about the details of what we've been doing in that area, but we definitely, you know, the roots of AccessScience may lie back in the, the encyclopedias of science and technology that McGraw-Hill published in the

past, but we've been working to try to make sure that AccessScience is itself a new product; one that is appropriate to this kind of digital sphere. So, it still has that encyclopedic view of science, but it is richly connected to the underlying resources, and that we are trying to make sure that it is something that students and others who will be using it will get the most possible out of it. One of the things that we do when we move in to this area of digital products and what's so exciting about it is, is that it does allow us to do things that we could never adequately do in print. As you all know, this is a higher area of, of adaptive learning, you know, my colleagues over on the McGraw-Hill higher education side, they have been developing their smartbook program and these kinds of instructionals are really very fascinating because they can develop different sorts of probes that don't just look at what students know on the basis of the presentation of the material, but they can also test the confidence with which they know that and how well they can use that information, how they can turn that over into some sort of skills. Those are exactly the kinds of insights that can be used to individualize the review of material and so that it helps students concentrate on what it is that they most need to study and move more briskly through anything else. That means that students are going to be less bored, they learn more and retain more of what they learn, and those kinds of improvements can actually be documented. Which is something that can then be useful in trying to justify the sorts of investments that would then be made about them.

The other kind of thing I'm very excited by is the uses of these kinds of adaptive heat maps which are based on being able to watch users' eyes as they are reading on screen. We can see precisely where it is that they are running into passages that they are having problems with because that is a guide to those of us on the publishing side of where we can go back and can improve that. It's a great, new, highly detailed granular way to look at updating and revising and improving text, moving on in the future.

We're all familiar, obviously, with the great resources that Cross-Ref and so many others here have been developing. I mean I think that kind of digital innovation is something that needs to be there. It's something we're all looking for, that much more in this case, just the fact that it does so much to help make clear the kind of underlying linkages in subject matter, and authorship, and funding, and that they become more visible and measurable to those of us that are involved with this sort of work. It's why I'm so excited to be here and to be learning more about the kinds of opportunities for that.

But I'd also like to note, at least in passing, that there is at least one other way in which a lot of us can be doing things to try to improve products that has nothing to do with technology and everything to do with humanity. We in the publishing side of things, in service to including only top authorities as authors, it's very, very easy to default back to featuring an overabundance of old, white, straight men. And it's very easy to justify that kind of choice because they are the ones who do have most of the honors and the seniority and the fame at this point, but we, particularly in the content creation side of this, we need to be aware of the fact that there are tremendous numbers of accomplishments being done by other kinds of people, and that this is not being well enough represented in the scientific works we are presenting. We are in a position to take those extra steps to include a wider diversity of different sorts of people, and you know, the outreach scientist Danielle N. Lee has said, "Perception paves progress and one way to broaden the audience for STEM works is to broaden the image of who does STEM." And that's something that we do by just including a greater diversity. It's true to the facts, it's not something we should feel we're being pushed to do, but I will tell you audiences increasingly want to see that, and that more and more science-savvy audiences of students and others, when they look at works and they're aware of a deficit of women or people of color or others then that starts to turn them off those works and they look for other things.

All of us here today want to create and make available better science texts and references. Ones that don't just inform, but also truly engage and inspire. We want students to appreciate how the universe of scientific information is unified by our curiosity, and that directly or indirectly everything really is connected. We want serious scholars to be able to traverse this cosmos of knowledge as effortlessly as their own questions will occur to them. Making that happen is going to involve an enormous amount of work, and collaboration, and active partnership by the scientists themselves, by the publishers, by the librarians, and by the end users, but we have the tools now for being able to bring everyone into that discussion far better than we did in the past. It is a lot of work, but it's work best pursued with a sense of its own fun and reward and not the gravitas of science being so important. If we're going to be earnest about anything, let's be earnest about that. That, thank you very much, and I'll happy you take your questions.

Online Learning, MOOCs, and More

Franny Lee, Co-founder and VP Business Development, SIPX, Inc.
Deanna Marcum, Managing Director, Ithaka S+R
Moderated by Ann Okerson, Senior Advisor, CRL

The following is a lightly edited transcript of a live presentation at the 2014 Charleston Conference. Slides and videos are available at http://2014charlestonconference.sched.org/

Ann Okerson: Good afternoon and welcome to this Neapolitan Plenary on online learning, MOOCs, and more. Yesterday, Franny Lee, who's on the platform here as a speaker, and I had a chance to organize a half-day preconference on libraries in support of distance learning. And that was more a series of case studies and dialogue about how this kind of support is proceeding on campus. Today we're going to do something a little bit more structured and a little bit different. Knowledgeable panelists are going to present studies that they have done that address key measures about MOOCs and online learning. They will talk about subjects such as completion, pedagogical success, certification, infrastructure, what does it cost, and what could we expect next. All of these kind of studies and researches are helping us to understand, in real hard facts, what this emerging environment looks like. And one of the things that we agreed on yesterday in the pre-conference is that in our libraries, in our publishing institutions, in our universities, we are just going to see more and more of this kind of activity and we should be prepared to support it as best we can.

All I'm going to do here really is introduce each of our speakers in turn as they speak. So our first speaker is Ithaka's Strategy and Resource Managing Director, Deanna Marcum. She leads the research and consulting services that assist colleges, universities, libraries, publishers, and cultural institutions in making the transition to the digital environment. Deanna is probably one of the best known people in library circles but I'm just going to list a few of her major accomplishments. I think when I first met her, she may have been Dean at the Library School at the Catholic University of America. She then went on

to become President of what is now the Council on Library and Information Resources or CLIR. And from 2003 to 2011, she served as Associate Librarian for Library Services at the Library of Congress—a considerable job managing 53 units, 1600 employees who are responsible for the entire range of services at the Library of Congress. For the last year or so, Deanna has been the lead on a study conducted by Ithaka S+R with the University of Maryland looking at their distance education programs and she is going to report their recently published results of that effort. So, Deanna . . .

Deanna Marcum: Thank you. Good afternoon, everyone. I'm delighted to see some people in the room. I thought, "Ugh, 4:30?" (laughs) Long day, lots of talks . . . You're probably ready to call it a day. But I'm glad you're here. And I want to talk about two studies that we've been doing at Ithaka S+R that have to do with online learning. Just to explain, in the beginning, Ithaka has been really focused on libraries and publishers for the last many years. But as we think about how technology is changing higher education, we thought if we're really interested in how scholars are going to fare in the digital environment, how teaching is going to change in the digital environment, and how libraries support these new roles, it's really important that we learn more about online learning itself. And that's what this presentation is all about. I'm going to talk about a study we have done for the Public Flagships Network, and then I'm going to talk about the University System of Maryland study that we did; talk about the findings in that study, and then the implications for higher education more generally. And if there's time, I'll be happy to answer some questions as well. I want to leave plenty of time for Franny in this presentation.

I mentioned that Ithaka is interested in thinking about digital technologies as they affect scholarship and higher education and, Ithaka is made up of JSTOR, Portico, and Ithaka Strategies and Research, just to give you some context for who we are and what we do. Let me talk first about the Public Flagships Network. You probably haven't even heard of it. It's a, a new consortium, relatively new. It's made up of 17 of the largest public research universities. And we worked with 10 of those in thinking with them about their strategy for online learning. What we did in this study, we identified 10 of the 17 institutions. A team of two of us went to each campus for three days and interviewed the President, the Provost, the Director of Online Learning, and 10 Department Chairs. We, we spent an hour with each person. We ended up talking to 214 individuals over the study. So we got the President's perspective down to the faculty perspective. What we were trying to understand is what do administrators think online learning is going to do for them, and how do faculty think about online learning? It was absolutely a wonderful, immersive course in higher education doing this study. The only thing I regret is that we did the study between January and March of this year and you remember how cold it was last winter? And Public Flagship universities are hard to get to cold places. That's one of the things I learned. It was below zero in most of the places we visited.

So the findings: we really looked at several things. We looked at how students are consuming courses and credits. We looked at how state policies are affecting what's happening on those research university campuses. We looked at the articulation agreements that many states have written to help students go from community college to any state-funded institution to the major flagship university rather seamlessly and how that's affecting what's happening on those flagship campuses. We found that, without exception, on the 10 campuses we visited, the state budgets have really affected what's happening on those campuses. The subvention funds have dropped precipitously and the flagship universities have had to find other ways to make up that difference between state funding and what the tuition brings in. The articulation agreements that have been signed have very much affected the campuses in that students are

doing comparison shopping. They have general education courses they have to take. They can take them anywhere in the state on most of these campuses. And they shop for the lowest price for taking these general education courses and the result is the humanities departments on these campuses are suffering a lot. Because they're no longer providing the service courses for the campus. Those have been taken care of by the community college in many cases. So the faculty in the English department, the History department, don't have those courses to teach any longer. And they're tenured and it's causing real budget stress for those departments. Still, the administrators on these campuses have great hopes that online learning will be the key to broadening access to higher education in their states.

Many of the chancellors or presidents have made promises to their state legislatures about the number of citizens they are going to educate over a certain period of time. And they are doing everything they can to bring higher education to more people in the state. I mentioned we talked to 10 Department Chairs, and they often brought some of their faculty with them in the interviews. Faculty have quite a different take on this. They believe that personal interaction with the student is the ideal and many, many, many faculty and department chairs said to us, "I can teach my students better because I know them. I know what their needs are. I know how to teach them. I don't want any other kind of learning for my students." They do not believe that online learning can reduce costs. On the other hand, those faculty who've had experience with developing online courses and teaching online courses have much more confidence in what online learning can do. Because they've seen it. And they've seen that, for some of their students, it makes a huge difference. They're able to learn in a different way. They have exposure to different kinds of learning styles. And it's a great help for those students.

One of the purposes of our study for the Public Flagships Network was to find out, because administrators believe that online courses could be created in one place and used on another campus elsewhere thereby, reducing cost. Faculty were almost uniform in saying, "I'd be happy to make my online courses available to other faculty to use, but no thanks, I don't want to use materials that have been developed by someone else." [laughs] So I think we have quite a long way to go in being able to share those kinds of resources. I give you this as background because it was such a broad landscape review of what's happening, at least, on a particular type of campus.

Now, let me talk about the University System of Maryland study of MOOCs. This was a Gates-funded project in which we asked for volunteer faculty from the University System of Maryland, any faculty member who was willing to try using an existing MOOC in his or her classroom—to see if learning outcomes could be improved and to see if costs could be reduced. That was the purpose of the study. It was an 18-month study. We had these research questions: how can MOOCs be used in the traditional classroom to improve student outcomes? Can they be used by faculty who didn't create them? How do MOOCs compare to other online learning resources? We were particularly interested in the kinds of implementation issues that were created for faculty trying to use them and understanding how those challenges might be overcome and really thinking with the faculty about how these tools might be used over time. So, we had 22 faculty who agreed to do this. Ultimately, we chose four side-by-side comparisons. These were hybrid courses using MOOCs that could be compared to the traditional classroom experience because there was a traditional classroom comparison to make. And in cases where there weren't the one-on-one matches, we did case studies. There, we simply followed the faculty member around and looked at how he or she used the MOOC and tried to write an analysis of how it worked.

Just mentioning that we had tremendous support from the University System of Maryland, from the highest levels of administration through all of the faculty. Coursera was a wonderful partner in this study. Coursera gave us access to the courses without a fee. Coursera helped us work with the individual faculty who had created the courses to

gain their permission to use them. Recognizing that this won't always be true, this was true for our study, but we are indeed grateful to them.

So what did we find? You probably can't read the numbers, but three of the professors used an entire MOOC for the classroom experience, 13 of them used some portion. They either used the quizzes, or the videos, or the discussion forums, or some part of it. Two of them used the video lectures only. Just to give you a sense of what they used from the MOOCs. Maybe it's no longer a surprise, but I think earlier it was surprising to many faculty to learn that learning outcomes are pretty much the same in hybrid courses as they are in the traditional classroom courses. You see here that the final test scores and the pass rates for the hybrid courses and the traditional courses are almost identical. So we conclude from this study that learning outcomes are the same in both cases. What's interesting is, not only are those learning outcomes the same but they are almost identical for all the subgroups. We looked at those who had SAT scores of 1,000 or higher, those who had under 1,000, first-year students, not first-year students, African American and Hispanic students, white and Asian students. You see that there's a little bit of a negative finding for those students who have lower SAT scores and from minorities and yet it's not statistically significant. So we concluded that all subgroups do about the same in the traditional classroom and in the hybrid sections.

These are all the things we tested for. Do parents have undergraduate degrees or not? What is the family income? And in all of these cases, there is no statistical difference in any of the subgroups for how well these students did in the two sections. Interestingly though, students liked the hybrid classes less even though they performed as well as they would have in a traditional classroom setting. They thought the hybrid courses were harder and they thought they learned more in the traditional classroom than they did in the hybrid classes. And the overall rating was just generally higher for the traditional classroom. In talking to students who went through this, more often than not they said, "But college is supposed to be sitting with your professor, learning in the classroom. This is the way it's supposed to be." So part of it is based on what the expectations are. But, but it remains the case that they didn't like this as well. The students who participated in those courses for which we did case studies—that is, the professors that created something new using a MOOC but it didn't have an analogue in the traditional classroom world—did a little better. Most of them rated the courses above average. Difficulty is just a tiny bit below average but the rest are a little bit above average so they fared little better.

What did faculty do with the MOOCs? A variety of things. One, they replaced lectures. They used the MOOC video lectures—the students watched them on their own time. And then, they used the classroom time for discussion or for solving problems that were very difficult for the students or talking about related things. But a lot of them used the MOOCs just to replace lectures. They also used the MOOCs for supplementary material. Many of them found that some portion of the MOOCs did a really good job of explaining a concept or one aspect of something they were studying. And they used it in the way that we would typically use a textbook or some sort of supplementary reading.

This is a quote from one of the professors who was taking part in the study. He said, "I felt that the video lectures were brilliant. They fulfilled a need for course materials that integrated a lot of specialized information in accessible, fun way without having to buy or rent expensive DVDs or other textbooks . . . Using the MOOC raised the level of my class." He was really enthusiastic about this, and one of the outcomes of this study is that the University System of Maryland has begun to think about ways to reduce the cost of textbooks for students by using more of these kinds of materials because this was so successful. Not surprisingly, faculty are often asked to teach a course for which they lack complete confidence in their expertise. It's sometimes a new subject for them or it's slightly tangential to their concentrated expertise. They found that some of the video lectures from the MOOCs were really helpful in filling in those gaps that they had concerns about. Several of the faculty talked

about the MOOCs being an excellent way to expose the students to other styles of teaching and class discussion. They liked the different ways that others presented material and found that very useful for their students. This was particularly true for faculty on the smaller campuses where there isn't quite as much variety in teaching styles as you might find on a very large campus. Several of them used the MOOCs to reinforce skills, things like critical thinking, but also problem solving of various kinds. They found it easier to use the MOOC so the student could go back and repeat the work as often as he or she needed to really grasp the concept without wasting a lot of time in class doing that. And they talked a lot about how online courses really help students learn in a different way. Several faculty said, "Yes, the students are very good with digital technology. They know how to use it. They're expert in social media but they don't really know how to learn online." And participating in this program helped them teach students how to learn in that way.

Let me talk just a minute about the benefits for faculty that, that we observed in this study. Working with the MOOCs proved to be a professional development opportunity for instructors. They were able to think about how they taught their courses in new ways. They were able to think much more systematically about what the learning outcome should be for a course because they had to think about that upfront, and just designing the online course proved to be an important professional development opportunity. For some of them, developing these courses in advance also gave them some relief from time pressures during the semester. They had to figure it all out in advance and some of them talked about how helpful that was. But mostly, they commented on the flexibility of new approaches to teaching their classes. And they found that invigorating and professionally rewarding in many cases.

But I don't want to underestimate the challenges. There are many. It was really hard for the professors to find a MOOC that exactly fit what he or she wanted to cover in the class. And so, just finding the right content proved to be a great challenge. Sometimes they thought the lectures were too inaccessible. Sometimes they thought they were too easy. It wasn't always possible to match exactly where their students were. And they were concerned very much about the lack of assessment. If you've looked at a MOOC, you know that many of them use a lot of impromptu quizzes—mostly to see how students are tracking with the content. That's not a really good way to assess what the students are learning. Often, those are just one question multiple choice answer and you go on to the next portion of the content. The greatest challenge for many of the faculty was the integration between the technology that was on the campus and the Coursera technology. How does Coursera interface with Blackboard, for example? And finding people on the campus who were able to support the technology component of the MOOC was not so straightforward.

There were lots of intellectual property questions. While the professors had granted permission for us to use the courses in this study environment, they are not going to be so willing to simply turn over the courses for anyone to use in any way he or she wishes. And universities have signed different kinds of agreements with Coursera. So sometimes the intellectual property is defined well on that campus. Other times, not so much. So there are lots of questions there to be addressed before this study could be taken to some larger interaction on campuses.

And then, there's the question of student engagement. Many students were tired of watching the video lectures after a fairly short time. It's always a challenge for professors to figure out the best way to engage students but, many of them commented that students weren't so engaged with these talking heads on their computer screens. And finally, the impact on cost. One of the reasons for conducting this study was to see if it is possible to use MOOCs that have been created elsewhere to reduce costs on a local campus. This chart simply looks at the number of hours faculty spent preparing the course using the MOOC. And you can see that the average time spent by faculty was 100 hours. The median was 58 hours. One professor reported spending 400 hours developing the course. If you spend 400

hours developing the course, it's probably not a cost-saving technique. [laughs] But interestingly, when faculty were asked do you think using MOOCs can have an influence on reducing cost on this campus, six of them said yes, seven of them said no, and five said, "Not this time, because this is the first time we've done it, but in the future, I can imagine that this would save money."

I know I'm out of time, so this is my last slide. Some of the implications of, of this study. It's no longer a surprise that student learning is comparable in online settings and the traditional classroom. Faculty report that there are some qualitative benefits for their students. It depends upon where the student happens to be and what he or she needs to learn. But there are some notable benefits for students being able to look at lectures as many times as they need to. We know that there have to be better ways to support faculty in using MOOCs. There have to be better mechanisms for IT support. Faculty are going to have to have a different incentive structure to use some of these new technologies that are coming along. And intellectual property issues are going to present long-term problems. So with that, I will stop and, I'll answer questions after Franny has talked. Thank you.

Ann Okerson: Just a quick introduction of Franny Lee, my coconspirator. She's Vice President of Business Development and Co-Founder of SIPX. And I don't know . . . Were you a newcomer to Charleston last year or was it the year before?

Franny Lee: This is my third one!

Ann Okerson: This is her third one. So she's a new and very important face among us. She has a very interesting background to bring to her work. She was originally a composer and a jazz musician and was drawn into the fields of copyright and digital communication through experiencing firsthand their effects on the music industry. She's worked on a variety of complicated copyright issues over the last 10 years. And most importantly to me, Franny is both a Canadian and a US citizen—as am I! And she is a qualified lawyer in both countries and, you know, as I've already said, I think she brings a great deal not just to the Charleston audience but to the start-up that she is a leader in.

Franny Lee: Thank you, Ann. Just let me flip ahead here. So I'm going to take a slightly different approach than what Deanna has taken in terms of talking about MOOCs. And I'm not going to focus on the use of MOOCs in the classroom, but I'm going to focus more on what's happening right now on the front lines, on the ground level in the creation of MOOCs. The data I'll present is aggregated from actual system through SIPX. We supported a number of different MOOCs by now. And it's also going to contain anecdotal reports that we've collected from our conversations with schools, from our conversations with instructors, and from the people who are actually creating these courses. I do want to emphasize that although I do start the talk by focusing on MOOCs, that online learning is much broader and is a much bigger base than just MOOCs and I don't want online learning in general to get lost in the MOOC hype.

I will start by talking about specifically MOOCs and the data we see through that. But then I'll talk about how some of the schools are looking ahead and starting to take some of these early experiments they're doing in MOOCs and applying them to different types of online learning, either in the more traditional approach of distance education, or continuing studies that have online learning components, or in some of the new innovative projects that we see happening. Flipped classrooms, multischool or multicampus or international course collaborations and things like that.

On that note, I did want to start with a little bit of background on SIPX, because I don't know if everyone in the audience would be familiar with us. We are fairly new. I'll take a moment to describe the system because I think it helps everybody understand how SIPX is being used right now and where this data that I'm going to talk about is coming from. SIPX itself is an interface that allows whoever's using that interface in creating the course readings in that interface to get real-time information about what they're selecting. So if they're selecting a reading, for a classroom, faculty will be able to know, for

example, if this is a library subscribed reading, what the cost of it might be. If it's a $2 versus a $25 reading and bringing them that kind of information at the point at which they're making these decisions. Part of how we've built the system has created a very large cost savings for students as well. And part of the data we've run before has been to measure what that effect was. So in looking at all the transactions that run through our system and being able to bring it into platforms that, for example, have not been able to recognize library licenses in the past like bookstore course packs. We've been able to showcase savings of between 20 to 35% for students because of the mere fault that you're already recognizing this library subscribed content. It is fully copyright compliant. It's built to automate all the manual publisher communications and permissions applications that have to be sent back and forth. And it does this using database technology so it is scalable. And one thing that we as faculty who are at Stanford building this ourselves, one of the things that we felt very strongly about is you can't really convince faculty to go and use outside platforms and retrain for those platforms. So we had to make sure that our technology could connect into whatever existing workflow that that school had set up for faculty or that faculty had chosen for their students. And because it's information technology, it does have the ability to report back a new level of analytics and it has the ability to be able to un-bundle elements of what used to be a full course pack into individual readings like iTunes. And that brings a new breed of consumer usage for the students and reports back different kinds of information to the schools as well. And how we do that is we connect in with a variety of different sources. It's a very large range. We'll harvest library subscription information from the universities and their libraries. We'll connect with open access resources and open educational resources. To service that, in the same set of search results as, as publisher paid material so that whoever's making the decision in selecting those readings can make the right choices.

We provide connections with publishers as well as the Copyright Clearance Center to make sure this is a comprehensive experience as well. A professor has the expectation of a Google search these days. You put in what you're looking for and everything in the world will show up to you and you don't have to hop around to different websites and navigate different flows in order to find that. At the end of the day, we are in a position to be able to connect to all of these platforms and showcase a wide variety of different benefits. And how we're seeing that being used right now in the online learning, in the MOOC space is to deal with one of the many, many challenges that exist when a creator comes in and tries to make, for example, a MOOC. It's a maze for an instructional designer, or a professor, or someone who's running a department head, or a program manager to come in and try to figure all of the different pieces that are necessary to create one of these courses. So on one hand, nothing happens without money. You have to figure out where you're going to get your funding from. You have to figure out the grant application and the timelines, you know, what department or what programs you have to apply to. There are video assets that have to be prepared as well. And it's not just about, you know, some of them have talking heads on a screen but other MOOCs try to create a different kind of experience. So you have higher production value and you're thinking about scripts for the professors who aren't used to sitting still and communicating in a television camera. They're used to pacing back and forth in a classroom so in some of these cases, I've heard stories where the program managers have to almost tie the professors to a chair and teach them not to fidget because they look like children that are kicking under the table at the kitchen table.

So there's all of these different kinds of work elements that are required to produce a high quality communicative MOOC. On top of that, Deanna talked a little bit about the technology challenges. You know, first, you need your school to decide well what kind of platform are they going to invest in? Is it EdX? Is it Coursera? Is it FutureLearn? Is it NovoEd? There are contracts that come along with that. And then you have to either teach your department head or the professor themselves or their T.A.s to create and

navigate the course materials themselves on that website. You need T.A. support because who's going to look after these 50,000 students? Are all those emails going to go to the professor's inbox? Who's going to monitor discussion boards to see if there are questions that need to be fielded? Who's going to grade? If you have assignments, who's going to grade these assignments and give feedback to people so they feel like they're being responded to? Tons of administration—forms to fill out, IP issues, approvals to get from department to department to department, and school policies to . . . perhaps, you know, perhaps you don't know. And then, where SIPX comes into play is this tiny little component as well about the pedagogy. What are you actually going to teach? Right? What are the lectures you want to deliver? What are the lessons and the messages you want to communicate here? And then within that, there are going to be content and copyright issues. And we come into play just into this one component - to be able to help people manage some of this content copyright stuff. But you can imagine how an instructor, a math professor, for example—a math professor cannot do this! [laughs] And if you ask them to navigate this on their own without significant infrastructure or resources or help to at least point them to who they could get to help them do some of this work, they're right now at a space, at the ground floor on the ground levels. They are racing to put this stuff out there and they are drowning. And they don't know what they don't know.

At this stage, we often see that the copyright issues come in as an afterthought. And, and these are things that could create significant liabilities for the professor and the school. I echo what Deanna was saying as well. I think the reason that a lot of schools are putting themselves through this pain right now is they're trying to find more effective methods for education. And the only way you can do that is to try to measure what you're doing and see if it's creating an effect, an improvement. But the last thing that the professors who are in this situation right now are thinking about is how to measure the results. They're desperately thinking about how they're going to get their films filmed and, and their grant funding approved and they're not going to be thinking—unless their grant funding is contingent on assessment—they're not going to be thinking about how do I measure the results for my students. Where we come into play is in this content aspect. And I want to share where we're getting our data set from.

To date, SIPX has run 30 MOOCs through our system that we've supported. And these are, you know, think of traditional course readings. The course readings are delivered through SIPX's system. We've had 20 new courses and 10 of what I call "reruns." Those reruns are very interesting as well because we're seeing what changes the instructors are making between the versions. They're from a wide range of institutions across all different types of platforms and disciplines. And in terms of our data set total, we're looking at—I'll explain what the transactions mean here. Transactions is when a student actually comes in and purchases that reading or they don't all have prices to them so . . . When they engage in that reading and they've actually retrieved it. So in total, between the last two years, we've done 48,000 of those transactions and you can see the split between what people will pay for and what people are able to access at $0. There's a couple of different reasons why they might be able to get $0 transactions. One is either the publishers or the rights' holders have said, "This won't cost them anything. Please put it up there." Or it's because there are other benefits that our system has been able to bring to that student. Some publishers, for example, engage in geo-pricing and offer discounts sometimes up to 100% for people in developing nations or whatever factors they want to put in play there. Or sometimes it's because the libraries for the purchasing student have subscriptions that apply for that student and have brought that cost down to zero.

In terms of the types of content we see being selected in MOOCs, the number's a wide range. I present this data not to say we can draw any conclusions, but just to say out of these 30 MOOCs, this is what has happened and I don't want to draw any trends yet. But we do see that subject matter, how the instructor wants to teach, all of this will affect the number of readings that go in and how those students engage with it. In terms of range, we've seen MOOCs that have only used one reading and we've used MOOCs that are more of a traditional course pack list that have used up to 24. Median-wise, about nine and a half each. In terms of the type of reading, we don't try to tell the instructor what they choose. The instructor chooses what they choose. We've seen about 36% come from journals and about 63% come from books. Across the range, we've got about 350 active readings in these MOOCs. They were selected from 53 different publishers and there have been five independent authors in there that were selected. In some cases, we've seen schools choose to put their own materials, things that the professor or the school has put together as the rights' holder and sell those within the course as well. And we've seen that as self-generated readings used in three different MOOCs.

In terms of the pricing, there are some new things being experimented with by publishers and what I was explaining before, contextual pricing or geographic-based pricing. We've seen 25 of our 53 publishers participating in that kind of new differential pricing-based initiative. The discounts that they have offered have ranged from between 50% off to 100% off their base price. The most common type of context-based pricing was 50% off for purchasers who are coming in from developing nations. The way that the tool can be . . . I mean there's a lot of different things and, and publishers right now, we see them taking baby steps in. So we could imagine how as things grow out, you might want to offer your alumni one price, or you might want to offer different geographic-based prices, not just developing versus developed nation but UK gets this. Canada gets this. Whatever it is you want to do there. In terms of the base prices, we saw that the readings ranged from between $0 to $22. I don't want to draw any averages out of this either because these readings are set up by the instructor. They range. They vary greatly in the type of content that's being selected. Sometimes it was one article. Sometimes it was one school business case. Sometimes it was 10 chapters from a book. So I don't think there's anything we can draw right now in terms of averages. The size, the source, the type of reading varied too greatly there. But this is just to give you a sense of how much people are putting up for sale in the MOOCs. 18% of our readings were $0 readings as base price.

Even before discounts were added, there were a lot of materials that professors put up there to track—even if there was no price and they didn't need a commerce component—they wanted to see what happened with those readings. Where we saw engagements from students coming from was all over the place. And each course performed very differently and again, factors vary wildly. The transactions per course ranged from somewhere maybe 100 transactions in that course to somewhere over 15,000. Of the 48,000 transactions, we saw transactions coming in from 183 countries. I've put the top 30 up there just to give you a sense of the divide. But what we do see, I think what's interesting to see here is the US is under 50% right now. We did the same kind of measurement about a year ago. We didn't have as many MOOCs. We only had about five then. But we did the same measurement about a year ago and it was over 50% at that stage and now, I think we're somewhere between 40, 45%? So it is changing and I don't know if you can draw a conclusion just based on 30 MOOCs but this is just what we're seeing right now.

In terms of why there's such a range between 100 readings to 15,000 transactions, I think the way that instructors present materials to their students has a huge effect on this. Some people will put it in there as like a last afterthought bibliography and some people make it very forefront and say, "I think that this is a reading that's very critical to the way you learn. If you want a deeper engagement, here it is." And they build it into their course lessons with our links. What we've always seen is the instructor-generated materials are always highest performing in that course. And, and we do see that—there's no surprise—the cheaper something is or the more zero cost that reading is, the higher the transaction engagement tends to be.

We've been looking at different things that have come into play. So for example, we've been able to show that if, this example we're seeing here is a Case Western Coursera MOOC, but I have signed in as a University of Arkansas student taking this

Coursera MOOC. I'm able to get the second reading here in—this is actually a course of 24 readings—I'm able to get a large number of these readings in the course for free. We saw that students tended to go in and get some of the free stuff to and pick and choose on some of the paid stuff. In terms of participation rates per course, what we do see—and, and again, I don't really want to draw conclusions. This is just a sample of what's happened in one particular course. This was a liberal arts college course out of UT Austin and they published these results regarding . . . This is a total enrollment versus this is how many people received the certificate. And our last line here is what SIPX contributed, which is how many readings were consumed by those students. We're trying to see if there are corollaries. The numbers are about the same, but again, I wouldn't draw trends until we have more data.

What we are seeing though is, you know, I love showing these examples. And I'm showing someone else's work here. This is the liberal arts college from UT Austin, not my survey. But they did a post-MOOC survey after they ran it the first time. They were asking very different questions from what you typically see, thinking about how to measure successful educational experience for a university course. They weren't asking how many students completed that course. They were asking, "Hey students! Tell me what you found most useful about this course." They had identified the video lectures, the homework, it's the assignments. They also asked the students what were you trying to get out of this course. Right? Were you trying to learn about the MOOCs? Are you taking this because you're interested in it? Are you taking this because your job is making you? You're asking them the last question here which is "Well, do you feel like you accomplished what you came in to do? Did you measure, did you find a measurement of success there? Did you take this course because you wanted to earn a certificate or did you take this course because you wanted to learn one new topic item?" Because if you did that, right? Even if you didn't complete the course, to a student who's in a free voluntary learning environment, they've achieved success. And we have to really think about the way we define and apply traditional four-year degree application of success to this type of new voluntary learning kind of experience.

I like to show this because I think they're asking the right questions. They are new questions. And they're using these kinds of questions to pick up what has really helped that student achieve educational effectiveness in this course. We're seeing people not necessarily using the whole course, but using these kinds of questions to identify what components of the entire whole did you find successful? And let's see if we can extract those and apply them in different context. I know this particular MOOC had plans to extract the video components, and the homework, and the readings that had been successful for their students and put them into continuing studies programs that were revenue generating. So it's a new way to think about how to unbundle the educational experience, and unbundle that MOOC experience, and take only the pieces you need and push them forward if you think they've been successful for students in this environment. It is early in the maturity cycle.

What we tend to see is, is it's very rare that after these MOOCs, nothing happens. It's an extremely expensive financial commitment for a school to create a MOOC and they want to do something with it after. What we do see, it's common to see that something happens with that course. Either they're going to re-use the whole thing, they'll either rerun the MOOC, or use it in a new context where it might be a system-wide course offering. Or they might put it into, we've seen some of these MOOCs being used as proprietary materials for undergraduate courses coming in. Or, what I was talking about in terms of extracting and unbundling the successful components and re-using those in different context. So if this video lecture was really good at explaining this element, that's almost a reading for a flipped classroom setting or a distance education setting. We've seen some of these MOOCs have video lectures that were extremely engaging, high production value, and they've extracted that from the MOOC and repackaged it as like a PBS learning asset that they could sell.

We are seeing lots of different activity happening on the ground floor right now. There's a lot of innovation and creativity about what people can do. But to draw it all back to the beginning, we've got to think about making people understand that assessment is important, to be able to identify and move this kind of initiative forward. And we've got to make sure that they have the resources and the infrastructure to create the high quality assets they need to. That's all I've got. [laughs]

To Boldly Go Beyond Downloads: How Are Journal Articles Shared and Used?

Carol Tenopir, PI, Chancellor's Professor, School of Information Sciences, University of Tennessee, Knoxville

Gabriel Hughes, Senior Analyst and Program Director, Elsevier

Lisa Christian, Research Associate, Center for Information and Communication Studies, University of Tennessee, Knoxville

Suzie Allard, CO-PI, Professor, School of Information Sciences; Director of Center for Information and Communication Studies, University of Tennessee, Knoxville

David Nicholas, CO-PI, Director of CIBER; Adjunct Professor, School of Information Sciences, University of Tennessee, Knoxville

Anthony Watkinson, Principal Consultant, CIBER

Hazel Woodward, Board of Directors for Project COUNTER; Director of Information Power; and retired Librarian of Cranfield University

Peter Shepherd, Executive Director of Project COUNTER

Robert Anderson, Graduate Research Assistant, University of Tennessee, Knoxville

Abstract

With more scholarly journals being distributed electronically rather than in print form, we know that researchers download many articles. What is less well known is how journal articles are used after they are initially downloaded. To what extent are they saved, uploaded, tweeted, or otherwise shared? How does this reuse increase their total use and value to research and how does it influence library usage figures? University of Tennessee Chancellor's Professor Carol Tenopir, Professor Suzie Allard, and Adjunct Professor David Nicholas are leading a team of international researchers on a the project, "Beyond Downloads," funded by a grant from Elsevier. The project will look at how and why scholarly electronic articles are downloaded, saved, and shared by researchers. Sharing in today's digital environment may include links posted on social media, like Twitter, and in blogs or via e-mail. Having a realistic estimate of this secondary use will help provide a more accurate picture of the total use of scholarly articles.

The speakers will present the objectives of the study, share the approach and avenues of exploration, and report on some preliminary findings. Furthermore, the speakers will discuss how the potential learnings could yield benefits to the library community.

Introduction

Through the efforts of publishers working with Project COUNTER, measurements for downloads of articles have been standardized. The COUNTER reports are now widely used by publishers and by libraries to monitor how many articles from specific journals are downloaded and to compare download amounts across platforms, titles, and time (Shepherd, 2004). Project COUNTER standards have given libraries and publishers a proxy to measure usage, however, tying usage to downloads in order to, in turn, measure value derived through reading misses an important aspect of usage and value of scholarly material. Articles are also shared without downloading by sending links or author's copies following the first instance of downloading (Interviews and Focus Groups Report, 2014). Sharing digital content by email, internal networks, cloud services, or social networks is now widespread (Harley, Acord, Earl-Novell, Lawrence, & King, 2010) (Cheng, Ho, & Lau, 2009) (Interviews and Focus Groups Report, 2014).

This secondary type of usage may be reducing the accuracy of existing value and usage measures, as these existing measures fail to capture secondary sharing. For instance, widespread sharing may lead to a decrease in repeat downloads or, if only links are shared, an increase in downloads. The extent of this problem is unknown and both downloading and sharing varies by stakeholder group (faculty, postgraduate students, undergraduate students, and nonacademic researchers). What are download counts missing? What is the true or complete value of articles and their access and how might that be measured?

Beyond Downloads: Background to the Research

Gabriel Hughes

Institutions, academics, and publishers all have a common interest in better understanding secondary usage via sharing and related behaviors. Elsevier in particular has been investing in technology which facilitates secondary usage, notably their 2013 acquisition of the Mendeley reference management and collaboration platform. Elsevier is therefore keen to support independent public debate and high quality research about the measurement problems presented by these developments in usage behavior, and is sponsoring this research project conducted by the University of Tennessee.

The measurement problem is that usage data is taken as a proxy measure for actual readership behavior by researchers and yet this relationship is influenced by changes in article sharing behavior. It seems reasonable to assume that downloading of full text articles correlates with subsequent reading of those articles by the person who has downloaded them. It also seems reasonable to believe that sharing behavior would amplify this relationship, as any downloaded article which is shared can lead to more reading events, for example, reading by colleagues of researchers who have downloaded articles and shared them. We strongly suspect that this amplification effect due to sharing is changing over time, and that the assumed proxy relationship between usage measured as downloads and actual readership is unstable and breaking down.

The reason for hypothesizing that sharing behavior is growing is simply the wider context of enormous worldwide growth and transformation in network, social, and cloud technologies, in all areas of human activity. It is now easier and much more common for anyone to share digital content with anyone else via web, mobile, and network platforms. There is already evidence that the research community is subject to these same trends.

In early 2014 Elsevier conducted its own private survey of researchers in which they found that 65% agreed with the statement that they "access or share articles from a shared folder or platform" an increase of 6% against the same response to a survey in early 2013 (the 2014 base was a representative sample of 611 academic researchers, and in 2013 a sample of 1,468). High quality public research is needed to better validate and explore sharing behavior and explore what this means for usage data and the analysis of download and reading behavior.

Beyond Downloads: The Study

Carol Tenopir

There are many methods to share articles. For the purposes of our study, we have divided these methods into two basic categories: formal methods and informal methods. Formal methods are platforms specifically designed to share academic material (such as journal articles) and citations within the researcher's existing research activity and community. Some of the formal methods identified so far include Blackboard, CiteULike, EndNote, Dropbox, Google Docs, Zotero, ResearchGate, Academia.edu, Mendeley, Wizfolio, and RefWorks and newer and better systems appear all the time. These methods fit into a scholar's worklife, while making the process of saving, citing, and sharing easier. They are a positive evolution and aspect of scholarship.

Informal methods, on the other hand, are those methods not specifically developed for article management, citation, and sharing. As we discovered in interviews and focus groups, they are widely used for these (and other) purposes. Some of the most frequent informal methods include: Twitter, blogs, email, Facebook, and LinkedIn.

Methodology

Measuring, or at least estimating, the amount of use and value from both formal and informal methods is not an easy task. To start this process, a two-prong approach has been used. The first prong included interviews in the United Kingdom and focus groups in the United States. Focus group and interview analysis helped inform the development of the second prong of our study: an international survey. This survey is currently deployed and as of December 3, 2014, we had 985 responses.

The aim of the international survey is to gain further insights into the sharing of a scholar's own work and the works by others. We also want to explore if there is a way to estimate or calculate the average amounts of sharing by various methods and to look at differences by discipline. Our survey questions examine: download and postdownload behavior, different methods of sharing, perceptions of sharing behavior in regards to technology, embargo periods, and copyright, as well as differences based on disciplines, years in academia/research, level of education, and geographic location.

Results from Interviews and Focus Groups

Since the interviews and focus groups are completed, this presentation will mostly focus on results from the first prong of the study. Interviewees and focus group participants ranged from senior researchers and academics to doctoral students. We had 15 interviewees and 14 participants in four focus groups for a total of 29 participants. Twelve participants were from the sciences and 17 participants from the social sciences. Most participants (20 of 29) held a PhD in their field and the average years of experience of working in their field was 11.07 years. In terms of age, most participants were in their thirties (10), while only two participants were in their twenties. Six participants were in their forties, five in their fifties, and six at were more than 59 years old. The mean year of birth was 1968.

Types and Methods of Sharing

Two main types of sharing emerged among participants. The first is sharing just a citation or link to an article. This may actually be the most common way to share. Fifteen participants reported sharing a citation or a link to an article. This presents an interesting situation since if the citation or link goes back to the publisher's site, their download stats will capture it, but the library from which the sending scholar originated will not. The link that is shared may not be to the author's own work; often is to another's work.

The second means of sharing is to send the full text, most often as a PDF. This is more likely to be the sender's own work. In the focus groups and interviews, most participants who share their own full texts say that they also upload their work into institutional or subject repositories (although we all know this varies widely by subject discipline.)

Informal sharing through email or an internal network or sharing print email by personal exchange was the most frequently mentioned method of sharing in both the United Kingdom and the United States. A focus group participant labeled this type of sharing as "bootleg" sharing, suggesting their concerns about copyright violations in this type of sharing. Many participants, particularly those from the focus groups, mentioned copyright concerns. Often, they may pass on the citation or link, but more rarely, the article. In light of these concerns, one participant said that he only shared open access journal articles.

Though "bootleg" sharing may not be strictly legal in regards to copyright or licensing agreements, convenience often trumped uneasiness for many participants. A social scientist often working in collaboration with others explains, "If I have got it, I will just share it. It is easier than having them go track it down, even if I have got the citation. The citation is relatively easy to find, but if I have got it, I will either just share it in a Dropbox [folder] or attach a file and send it. It saves them trouble." In fact, Dropbox was the most frequently mentioned tool for complete document sharing with collaborators or within a research team, and

Twitter was the most frequently mentioned social media tool for sharing links or citations.

We asked participants with whom they most commonly shared material. Not surprisingly, colleagues topped the list at 93%. The circle of colleagues is growing, as the number of coauthors grow and big science projects require big teams. Not far behind is sharing with other researchers. Over 80% of participants said they share articles or links with other researchers. Sharing material with students is also a common practice (79%).

Reasons for Sharing

Academics and researchers share material for a variety of reasons. After all, sharing is a natural part of scholarship and most participants maintained that they share material to further scientific and academic discovery. Participants also share what they feel is good or noteworthy—that is, to promote the reading of their own or someone else's work.

One participant in the social sciences explains his reasoning for sharing material, "I think sending articles is one of the ways to maintain a relationship with the people in my professional network. So if I find something I would send it to my PhD, someone in my PhD whom I have studied with or someone I met at a conference and I might say, 'You might find this interesting.' So, I think that is an excellent way to maintain rapport at the same time show that you care about their research and that you want to be part of their research." People will often then share relevant things with you. In other words, as he elaborated, you build a network that then becomes "your passive information seekers." Essentially, sharing material builds goodwill among potential future collaborators.

The second most common motive, again of an altruistic nature, was to fulfill an information need, especially for researchers who lack access. These top reasons, reflect the very nature of scholarship and both formal and informal systems that make it easier to do are widely adopted. One researcher noted, "I'll have people contact me separately, people outside the United States and internationally who don't have access . . . And I

feel very comfortable, and I don't know if I should, but I feel comfortable sharing my work." Another social scientist explained, "Generally, I have some people outside the country when they have difficulty accessing articles, so I can give them some satisfaction and if they cannot find it, they ask me [and] sometimes I send them a pdf."

Nearly all participants viewed having one's own work shared by others positively. One scientist contends, "It is a stamp of how you are measured and evaluated," while another said, "I would be delighted if my work was known by more." After all, as many note, it is good for citations and reputation. It is also good for feedback and critical review. Although one interviewee is unaware if his work has been shared, he wouldn't mind; in fact, he "would be pleased." Another is "comfortable and trusting of colleagues who share his material."

However, many participants expressed reservations about sharing. For example, can I share a pdf legally? Does it violate intellectual property rights or copyright? One social scientist asked, "So you are published in a journal so now do I have a right to put it in my CV, to put a link to it? I have a pdf of it, but can I share that?" But, the general feeling was even if they might be in violation, they do not think of it as purposefully violating copyright. As a social scientist in the United States explained, "You don't even think [that] usually you are breaking copyright laws. You're just thinking, 'Well, I just trying to be academic. I'm trying to promote this or whatever.'"

Some participants made a distinction between formats in discussing their sharing habits. Sharing their *articles* was viewed mostly positively, sharing their *books* was not. Some participants worried about the effect upon royalties and sales when sharing books. A social scientist noted, "I have a book out and I have to stop and think I want royalties too, right so . . . why would I download somebody's book for free when I wouldn't want that done to myself?"

Moving Forward

In conclusion, Beyond Downloads aims to define ways to measure usage beyond downloads, look at the relationship between COUNTER downloads and additional usage, and to develop practical ways to average or estimate total usage. Our goal, therefore, is to provide a more complete view of value. We also wish to initiate discussion across various communities reading these issues. Our overall question that we would like to posit: Is a COUNTER-like measure or calculator possible?

References

Shepherd, P. T. (2004). COUNTER: towards reliable vendor usage statistics. *VINE, 34*(4), 184–189.

Harley, D., Acord, S. K., Earl-Novell, S., Lawrence, S., & King, C. J. (2010). Assessing the future landscape of scholarly communication: An exploration of faculty values and needs in seven disciplines. *Center for Studies in Higher Education.*

Cheng, M.-Y., Ho, J. S.-Y., & Lau, P. M. (2009). Knowledge Sharing in Academic Institutions: A study of Multimedia University Malaysia. *Electronic Journal of Knowledge Management, 7*(3), 313–324.

Beyond Downloads Research Team. (2014). Interviews/focus groups white paper. Center for Information and Communication Studies. (White paper).

Driving Discovery: Do You Have the Keys to Fair Linking?
(It's About Knowledge and Library Control)

Todd Carpenter, Executive Director, NISO

Bruce Heterick, Vice President, JSTOR/Portico

Scott Bernier, Vice President of Marketing, EBSCO Information Services

The following is a lightly edited transcript of a live presentation at the 2014 Charleston Conference. Slides and videos are available at http://2014charlestonconference.sched.org/

You Can't Browse the Stacks In A Digital Library: Indexed Discovery, Fair Linking, and NISO's Open Discovery Initiative

Todd Carpenter, Executive Director, NISO

Todd Carpenter: Good morning, everyone. We're going to talk about discovery services and indexed discovery services and fair linking. And I'm going to be touching briefly on the NISO Open Discovery Initiative. I'll start with how many people are familiar with NISO? Oh, fantastic. I love that. This helps to me make a very efficient in getting through 25 slides in 12 minutes.

I'll just start with a short history of library discovery and how we got here. Does anybody still have these in their library? My wife asked if anybody still had one of these. Oh, two, three? I mean, actually in the stacks, not just in an art exhibit. So for probably a century we were using these cards to navigate discovery in library systems. They were very useful when libraries used to look like this. Unfortunately, many of our libraries still have these things, but most of the content that we have in most of our libraries is electronic. There was a transition into catalog services and moving all of the card catalogs and discovery services or acquisitions management and content management and serial circulation management, which became a computer interface to the users in order to access the print stacks. In 2000-ish, early 2000s, we began work on something called a Metasearch Engine Initiative where services would search out electronic resources and then search results would be filtered or represented to the user in the order in which these servers responded, which is probably not the best way to present search results. In the last, say, three, four years, we've moved to a system of indexed search engines where the search engines go out and they collect as much information about resources as they can and create an index in the center of that, which is then queried by the users. And these have become very popular in the last several years to search and discover materials. There is also a small company out in California, but we won't mention them, that has driven a lot of interest in index discovery as well.

As these systems have evolved and developed over time and over the last several years, they're indexing a tremendous range of content. They're accessing both commercial and open access content, all of the journal literature, e-books, as well as nontraditional content, nontraditional web content as well. They've been adopted by probably thousands of libraries worldwide, impacting millions of users. There's also been some significant research results that point to increased usage of resources based on the usage of these systems. So everything's fantastic, right? Well, except for several key problems. Years ago, I don't know any librarian who would purchase an A&I system if they didn't know what was in it, if they didn't know how things were added to it, if they didn't know the content that was included. Unfortunately, that's not always the case with indexed discovery services. There isn't a lot of clarity in terms of what's included in these systems. There isn't a lot of clarity about how things should engaged and what the discovery services would do with that content, how is data exchanged. There's a lot of concern about how things are ranked. Now, a lot of this is proprietary information, but there are also concerns about bias and how things are ranked in this result stack.

Any good business relationship, be that between publishers and libraries, publishers and software providers, software providers and the library community, all these relationships need to be based upon trust. We certainly don't want to be dealing with the used car salesmen of the world. I think it's important that we also not just trust but we also have a sense of verification, that we understand what the information is that we're getting and how and why. And this is where standards of community practice come into play. Standards can be used to, on a functional level, exchange information between one system and another, make sure they work together. They can also be ensured that we're doing things in the same way, that we have a common understanding of definitions and approaches in terms of how things are done, in what ways that things can be done, help the consumer understand what they're getting. Do you know what you're getting when you purchase a product? It builds trust between the suppliers and consumers if they're based on community best practices. This is where NISO came into this space regarding the index and discovery services. I mentioned we've been doing work, obviously, we've been doing work with MARC records back in the 60s and 70s, we were doing work with Metasearch in the 2000s, and work in index discovery was something that seemed a natural evolution of that.

About two-and-a-half years ago, we pulled together a very diverse community of libraries, publishers, and service providers to explore best practices to help people understand how these systems are working and how they can be improved so that we can all trust their work. That large group was broken into subgroups, and they focused on four particular areas. One was on technical recommendations for the data format and the exchange of information between publishers and service providers. Another was focused on communication of the information in those systems to the library community. Another team was focused on the issues of fair linking and how do you exchange information and prioritize results. And then another looking at usage and reporting assessment. We did not have a broad agreement with this particular group. Whenever we extend a working group to work on every

possible issue, we never get anything done. So we focused, we set aside the issues of performance, features, user interfaces. We didn't want to get into the areas of relevancy ranking and define relevancy ranking, because we think that that's best handled by the service providers and best assessed by the library community in their review of the different products. We also think that while it's probably important that there be work done on APIs and automated data exchange, that wasn't something that this working group focused on, so APIs and protocols for data exchange were set aside.

Over the 24 months of the project, the working group developed a variety of things. There is a standardized vocabulary now, a formal recommended practice for content providers, for discovery service providers, as well as focus on education and conformance. The ODI recommendations were published in June. That's the URL. You can get to it by going to the workrooms section on NISO's homepage. It's free and openly available, as are all of the other resources from this project. I'm not going to go through all of the metadata recommendations, but they exist. Please go look at them. We have metadata recommendations for what a content provider should provide to the library about who they're sharing the information to, we have metadata recommendations for the publishers to provide to the discovery service providers, and we also have metadata the discovery service providers should be providing to the library community. And again, here's just some more examples of what the metadata is. I know you can't read it, but the slides will be posted, I will post them in my slide share, and they will also be part of the record for Charleston. We also talked about the recommended metrics for assessing the work, the performance of these systems, things like the total number of searches per month, total number of unique visitors, unique click-throughs, things along those lines. A very important element of this was not that we define what "fair linking" was, but we thought it was more important to focus on the issue of disclosure.

Discovery service providers should offer affirmative statements of the neutrality of their algorithms, and they should also affirmatively note any business relationships that they have with content providers that may impact their search results. We didn't want to take a position on these as to whether or not it would be appropriate or inappropriate so long as there's disclosure about that behavior. And the library community can then determine, based on those disclosures, what's in the best interests of the patrons.

Another issue that we spent a lot of time on was the issue of nondisclosure agreements and the worry that some organizations might wrap their contractual relationships up with a nondisclosure agreement that says that there had been some prioritization of content of search results, but we can't talk about it because it's covered by an NDA. So we added an element to the recommendation that focused on this issue of nondisclosure agreements saying that licenses and contracts between publishers and discovery service providers should not have nondisclosure agreements that cover any potential bias in the search rankings.

I want to end here with more of a comment about process and the implementation of these discovery systems. Now, there's certainly technical issues related to how the data exchange is provided. There's certainly technical issues that need to be resolved. I think the ODI work has advanced some of that. But there are also very important social aspects to these systems. There are very important setup issues, how your library is implementing these systems, that can significantly impact the search results that you're seeing. I want to end with the point that not every problem is technical and that some of these issues can be addressed through other social or setup issues that at least the library community should be aware of.

For more information about the project, this is the webpage for the ODI group. We just launched a standing committee that's going to be doing some education and training work on these initiatives as well as further developments related to open discovery as we move forward. So if any of you have any questions or comments, feel free to reach out to the standing committee. They

appreciate your feedback. Thank you, and I will pass it on to groups. And as I said, we'll take questions and discussion, hopefully a lively discussion, at the end of the session.

CSI: Discovery

Bruce Heterick, Vice President, JSTOR/Portico

Bruce Heterick: Thank you, Todd, very much. I want to thank Todd and everyone who's been part of the ODI work. When I was on the board at NISO and serving with Todd, that was one of the real important things that I think we got started. I'm glad it's continuing forward. I think he's still got quite a bit of work to do on the disclosures and getting information out to the libraries or to the providers; I can sit here as a provider today, and say that that still needs quite a bit of work.

For those of you who were here last year at this session, I talked a lot about this 18-month Discovery, CSI: Discovery effort I had been under at JSTOR, trying to understand that the power of content was being used. And it brought a whole range of things out that were really quite interesting, and we've been working on those diligently since that time. It's still amazing to me that so many people are still engaged in this topic. It's just says a lot about all the work we have left to do, to do it.

I'm going to talk a little bit today about a content provider and kind of what I'm seeing and what we've found over that 18-month vigil that went on recently. I will say up front, I have engagement exhaustion. I am exhausted from this work because it's relentless. And I think that's one of the things we all have to come to grips with. In some sense, I think discovery has been the great job creator of the library community here in the last two years because I know, at least at JSTOR, we've added positions, we have added resources. We're probably spending close to half a million dollars this year just on trying to manage our discovery efforts with the big four discovery providers. And as an accountant, we're dealing with Google and Google Scholar and all this other stuff. So it's expensive. I think libraries are starting to understand that in order to not just implement these things but actually maintain them at the level they need to be maintained, it takes quite an investment. That can't be caught short when you're taking back your total investment in these services. I think it's really important.

I'm from Southwest Virginia, so I tend to think of things in very simple terms. So I'm going to kind of talk about the three-legged stool here. We never figured out how to put four legs on a stool in Virginia, so I'm going to talk about three-legged stools. I've been here the last few years talking about this topic. And at the beginning, we were really talking about the discovery providers and really pushing them to be more transparent and to talk about things in a particular way, and I think that's alright. I think we need to continue to do that. The last year or so we've really been focusing on the content providers: what are they doing? Are they providing the right metadata to the services? Are they doing the things they need to do to make their content function well within the systems that have been created for this so that libraries can help, it can help libraries leverage that investment that they've made. And I think that needs to be continuous, but I know at JSTOR we still have a lot of work to do.

A lot of things that I talked about last year in this meeting, there were a lot of them, and we're trying to implement them as we go along here. But there's a long list of them that we need to do if we're going to actually be really effective inside of the services. I think now we need to begin talking about what libraries' responsibilities are here, and I think it's really important that libraries need to take more responsibility here about not only how these things are set up but how they maintain them in an ongoing fashion. That's not an easy thing to do, particularly for libraries that don't have a lot of staff to actually maintain these things at the level that they would probably like. We have to start looking at that. We have to start. I think libraries can start looking at themselves, saying "What can we be doing?" too, because I can tell you from the work that I did last year, there were a lot of things that we thought libraries could be doing differently to really help these services work better, and frankly, trying to define exactly what they're trying to do with these services. What are you actually trying to

accomplish with them and how are you measuring that? And those are really important questions.

One of the things that came out of our research last year is that libraries are, a lot of libraries are simply putting these things up, and they're not spending a lot of time in the configuration process, either of the discovery service or the link resolver in the space. And one of these became very clear to us at JSTOR is that we need to create something, we're calling them "quick-reference guides," to provide to people who are putting up these services about what steps they need to take within their discovery service and within their link resolver in order for, if they want the content on JSTOR platform to actually surface and be discoverable in these areas. And let me tell you, I mean, I have to say, the discovery providers were across the board awesome in helping us because they're looking for the same thing, quite frankly, I think. They really want to help with this. But it's very complicated. I bumped into a lot of things that were, you know, you'd get down the road and say, "Oh, I didn't realize this was happening. We need to go back to the discovery provider and talk to them about that." So at the end of this, I was really hoping to have these out in March, and we just got these out about two weeks ago. I'm hoping people are going to find them useful. Our goal here was for people who do want their JSTOR content to show up in these services, to give them a guide on how to do that. If that's not what you want to do, that's fine, but we just didn't want people putting services up and seeing that the JSTOR content wasn't showing up and not understanding why. And so we really want to sort of guide that way.

We have these quick-reference guides for EDS and for Primo and for Summon, and we're building one now for OCLC. We also built them for the major link resolvers, because those two things go hand in hand. And people need to understand that sometimes one overrides the other and they really need to understand how these things work hand in hand. We try to build them in a way that you can configure them. If I've got Primo, then I'm using LinkSource, or I've got Summon and I'm using SFX, you can look at these guides in that way. I know IEEE, I think SAGE, I think there's a number of other publishers who are starting to do this, and I think it's really important that more publishers spend time on this because I think it can only help. But I do think, I hope this is at least a first step for us in working more closely with libraries on how these systems are configured.

Okay, well I can't do one of these presentations without putting some data up. So I apologize to all of you in the back. These slides will be available, I'm sure, on the website soon. I want you to see we actually see referrals coming. This is across JSTOR. And you can see JSTOR, Google, Google Scholar, and then you see link resolvers or, we're not quite sure what they are. They're a mix of things. You see serialsolutions.com or exlibrisgroup.com or ebscohost.com or ebsco.com, right? One of the problems we have right now, and I'm going to skip to the punch line. But the thing that says "category gain percentage" is indexed discovery services, and it's at 0%. This is the amount of accesses that we see coming from these referrals. Now, that's not exactly right, all right? Actually, if you look down here at this academic, 22%, some portion of that is indexed discovery services. However, as a content provider, I cannot tell, right? Because when somebody starts an EDS or somebody starts at Primo or someone starts at Summon, they come through the link resolver. That gets obfuscated when it comes through the link resolver, so it looks to us like it's coming through SFX or Serial Solutions or someone else, we can't tell the original origin of that, right? And that's a big problem for us in trying to understand what the impact of these services is on our usage.

Let me carry that forward. We're a not-for-profit organization trying to figure out where we make investments that we're going to make. When I see this chart, when my board sees this chart, they're saying, "Why are we spending so much time on something that's driving 0% to the usage? Why aren't we spending more time on figuring out how to make the JSTOR interface better, or how to improve our indexing on Google Scholar and Google?" It's a little harder to improve your indexing on Google because you have absolutely no control over that. You have a little more control over index discovery projects because

they want to work with you, and that's very encouraging. But I think the real issue, I'm looking at Todd on this because I really think NISO need to get part of the best practice, we need to have persistent referrals that come through that can see as a content provider to understand, because when it comes to making investments, we're data-driven just like you and libraries. Where do we make these investments? And it's really important that we understand that.

I'm going to go back to where I was before. This is the referral domains that we see coming to JSTOR. It's actually a little bit different about which referral domains actually drive actual usage at JSTOR, okay, so they're a little bit different. One of the really interesting things is that the link resolvers have a much higher capacity to drive actual usage. So the referrals that come from link resolvers drive usage, where as Google, we get a lot of referrals from Google, but they don't necessarily drive usage on the JSTOR platform at such a high degree. So it's really important to us that we really work with the link resolver and discovery providers because they do drive good traffic in that regard. Now, are we seeing increasing or decreasing traffic from institutions who have implemented these things? The jury's out. As I reported last year, for JSTOR, it's not all that encouraging, but that may just be a matter that we don't know exactly what is being driven to us from these discovery providers. And until I really have a better sense of that, it's going to be really difficult for us to have a real measured conversation about it because we're just kind of guessing at this point.

I would stop there. I was kind of laying some groundwork for some questions to come up, and I'll turn it over to Scott as I finish off this part of the presentation.

Fair Linking and Library Choice: A Discussion of Custom Full-Text Link Set Up

Scott Bernier, Vice President of Marketing, EBSCO Information Services

Scott Bernier: Good morning, everyone. Thanks, Bruce. Hope everyone's having a great conference. I'm excited to be here this morning.

My name is Scott Bernier. I'm head of market research for EBSCO, and this is something that I've been wanting to talk about that I started to dive into quite a bit over the last several months and worked pretty closely with Bruce after having seen some of Bruce's presentations in the past. I'll get into a little bit more specifically what brought me here in a moment, but I want to dive a little bit more specifically into how things work to clarify and to start to get into an understanding of the way the links set up, how can you control them, what can you do to optimize. Again, we have, I think, a lot of work to do as a community to understand best practices.

This is an interesting term. I was lucky enough to be part of the ODI community. The biggest piece in my mind was metadata sharing, how do we do this thing. But then there's the other part, or a large part of what we had was about fair linking. And so I actually have the feeling that maybe the word "fair" isn't so fair. What does it mean? In simplest terms, though, what is fair linking? In my mind, it's the vendors taking a step back and giving the options to what it is that you want to do when it comes to linking to the full text. It's fairly simple. We get out of the way and turn those keys over to you. Hence the name of the session today. It's really about driving. Driving your discovery and having the keys to the car and have control. But I think the key is, then, how do you get into the specifics of it? You have the keys to the car and you drive it, but how do you adjust things? What's the best way to optimize the links and how your users interact with the full text? I think its key, and Bruce touched on this, is that we all want the same thing. Content providers, discovery providers, publishers, libraries all want more usage, more value, repeat customers, greater library experience, so we can continue to move this thing forward. But there's really no driver's manual, per se. There have been studies that touch on some of these things, but maybe best practices on how do we set up these links need to be things that we consider and do studies around. Some of that has been touched on from a user perspective and otherwise. But I think the key thing for me today, and hopefully that folks get out of this is that if we can collectively understand how this stuff works, we're in a better position to

make it work better and all moving in the same direction.

That gets me to sort of where or how I came to be here today. As part of the ODI committee, we were right in the stages of being ready to post the file document of ODI. And at the same time, I was behind the scenes with some of my colleagues at EBSCO, pushing and driving for EBSCO to do the metadata share. We need to push that out there for folks to use in their discovery services and take it. So I was excited that that was happening. We got an announcement, yep, ODI was out, and I called someone that I've become closer friends with since then, and I said, "Hey, we're excited about this. I'm thinking we're excited about this." And he says, "Well, I'm just really interested in what EBSCO's going to have to say about fair linking." And I said, "Okay, what do you mean by that?" He said, "You know, EBSCO's biased for their own content." I said, "You know how this works, you choose the links, you choose how it gets to the full text, you choose how it works. The library gets it, does it on their own." And he said, "I've heard it all before." I was kind of peripherally involved, I'm not the linking guru at EBSCO, so I said, "Let me go figure this thing out." So I started to dive into it. I called Bruce and said, "Bruce, I want to learn and I want to get together on this, make sure we're both kind of hearing and seeing the same thing. I'm going to dive into this thing and figure it out and then we'll talk about it because I'd really like to understand maybe what your concerns are, because I've heard you have concerns." And so that's kind of what got me diving down this path. I want to share some of the things that I've learned.

Really, when it comes to discovery records and the discovery experience would be a two-part equation. And the first thing, really, is that the results come up on the list, whatever those results may be. So it's the relevancy ranking of a particular record. That has absolutely nothing to do with the full text that your user might get to from that record. The second part is the full text. How do I set up? How do I go from the result that you just presented to me to the full text? It's completely decoupled. When the results come back, you choose how the user gets to the full text, how, where, when, how that displays, and so on. I tell you that here so we talk a little bit about both sides of that equation.

First step: relevance ranking. Our search team comes from MIT, and we're really every day pushing and driving towards saying what's the best possible result we can put in front of the user. But I tell you, the search team at EBSCO has one goal, and it's really to make sure that the end users have the best possible results for every search query every time. One thing to note, they don't care at all where that record comes from. They want the best one. They don't care about the provider, they don't care about the source. It's not part of the equation. Now, the level of data that we have is important. We need to be able to make decisions, as a relevance algorithm needs to be able to make decisions, and the only way you can make the most refined, best decisions is to have more information to go on. So think about doing a study. You're going to write a research paper, are you going to study and look at one article and someone else gets the luxury of looking at all sorts of different things, they're probably in a position to make better decisions. So those are just some pieces. I'm not going to drive into all this, but there's some different portions of the relevancy algorithm. It's getting tweaked every day, really, to try and find and improve. We put this stuff out to be as transparent as we can possibly be about how relevance works. So this is the relevance ranking ingredients, matching word frequency, metadata field weighting, value ranking, I'll talk a little bit about. You've probably seen some of this from EBSCO. We care a lot about subject indexing. We don't care necessarily about browsing by subject; we care about leveraging that really rich subject index to push the best possible results in the private screen and other things. This was a slide I put together in a conversation I had with Bruce is that each available data field that we have only improves our sort of response, if you will, to be able to make better decisions. I told the groups that no matter what it is, it's only beneficial to the content provider to make sure we have as much data as we can to base those decisions on. So we do a lot of usability testing, we do a lot of user research. We have a full group at EBSCO dedicated to user research. And one of

the things that we do is we watch the users and we say, "What are they looking for? What makes them click on something? What are they trying to find?" And we learn a lot about that, but it also influences part of how we put results on the screen. We influence or we analyze value ranking, and the value ranking is an additional part of the whole relevancy or painting those results on the screen, but some of the value ranking pieces that flow into things like publication data, for example. If all things are equal, the most recent article may be more valuable to users, especially in assigned research and so on. Plus, of course, they were looking for something from the 1800s or whatever it may be. So just a little blurb on relevance ranking. We hope to put more information out there for you. We have a lot of detail that you can find some of the basics at a high level on the relevance, but hopefully you'll see more from us in that.

Part two of the equation is full-text linking. I'm going to use EDS examples. That's what I know, that's what I studied. But to show you, I'll talk about full text. And I think P is the library choice. So I talked to somebody just before here and they said, "Why should the library have a choice? Shouldn't the users have that choice?" That's a good point, an excellent thought. How do we make that work? A different question and other things that got interesting. So full-text links in EDS, we have this notion of customization. And basically that allows you to control the way the links work in three different ways. Which full text displays. You might have three of the same articles in different places, the same article in three different places. Which full text do you wish to display? The order in which the links may appear. I like one, two, three, that kind of range. And then, do you want all three of those, for example, to appear at the same time or do you just want your top preference to appear? I have this record, it just follows through, it says number one is available. Do I want to show one and three, because those are both available, or do I just want to show number one? Again, the library's choice. This is just a mocked up screen just to give you the sense that this is essentially EBSCO and the pieces of administration behind EDS. You go in and you see, what are your holdings, how do I want to rank them? Then all the way down the list, you have this option at the bottom that says, "Just show the first available text, link only?" We actually recommend that from user testing. User, "Why do I have four options? I just want this article." Silly library, you know? That's the other choice here. You're coming through, you label all, put all your records in or your contact in, and you rank them, and then you decide if you want to show them all versions or a single version.

This is an interesting piece. Because customers choose their links and link order preferences, the provider or source of the record itself has no bearing on which full text link appears. Again, it's that idea of decoupling one from another, and I'll show you what I mean by this. I'm sure everybody likes beer, right? All right, so this is just the result. And in the second one, if you look at the second one, this is actually a business source complete record. And a business source completes a fairly strong index in addition to the full text, but it's a strong index. And we have this in here. It ranks up. In this particular search, it says, "All right, this source is an article for your search," and has the full text there. But if you as a user said, "You know, I know I have the full text in EBSCO, but I'm a library administrator, and I want to suppress that because I prefer JSTOR. If I have the JSTOR, show me the JSTOR." Even in the EBSCO's database, you can do that. You have the full text link to JSTOR. Now, I put that up like that. You could put it up like this or however else you want. We give you the ability not only to customize the link but then how it displays. Bruce said something I thought was interesting and I thought about the night before and somebody said to me again recently: "Well, if those have, a PDF look to it across all the resources that we have, maybe it wouldn't be so confusing for the user. Maybe it would be easy. Maybe they'd click on that more often." Yeah, you have those options. I think part of it is understanding those options and then deciding, "How do I organize this thing?" and then maybe together we can do some of that research to figure out what does the user interact with more, because we're trying to get more usage. They click on a link resolver here and they're used to seeing a JSTOR full text or used to seeing a PDF.

How does that work? What's the best way for me to use that? Questions that still come up for me. Options. Does EBSCO default into their own full text? No, we don't, there is no default for the linking. We don't know what you have. So when EDS gets set up, we don't just say, "Here it is. Have a good time. Here's EDS." This configuration is work that goes into actually pulling in your contact. What do I own? What do I link to? How's it going to work? How do I configure this thing? How do I customize the screens and the interfaces and the links and the whole bit? And that's a process, and I'm sure anyone who's embarked on discovery service knows that there's a process and that they're all probably a little bit different, but they're all probably fairly extensive. But there are no default settings. The idea is that we've got to enter your collection first, then you decide, well, how do I order this thing, how does it appear, and the whole bit. IIf we did include collections in advance, if it's default and you just don't have those things, your users are going to run into paywalls. Don't have this collection. It links to it, now I have a paywall. Probably not ideal. Probably not the user experience you're looking for.

One of the things we talked about was what if we look at your collections beforehand? Because right now what we do is our team goes and talks to you and says, "What do you got for collections?" and that's not necessarily that easy or simple of a process. We may not have the resources to do that very well. Everybody's a little bit different. But what if we knew the collections in advance? I talked to Bruce about this. Sorry to keep using him as a reference, but Bruce, well, what if you knew your customers in advance so that when the University of ABC comes to us and says, "All right, we're going to set this thing up," we already know that they have these JSTOR collections and we can say, "All right, I want to continue these things." He said, "I'm not giving you that info." And then he talked to me a couple weeks later and he said, "Maybe that's a good idea." We haven't determined what's going on here. So one exciting thing about it, well, should we provide some type of default? Well, we can't provide a default, but maybe we can provide a sushi menu, if you will. Let's list them all in here, and then you can at least go in and pick and choose, because right now, you're only going to add them in. Or maybe it would be a little bit easier, just take one step further and say, "Here's a bunch of options that you may have." Maybe it's easier or simpler to go in. We haven't done this yet, though. It's just something to think about.

Now, normally we raise things up differently. We offer these custom links. And if you're not familiar exactly what a custom link is, it's the idea you can go directly from a record to some other spot. And that idea is, you know, maybe I say, "I want to go directly to this publisher." But it also, a custom link is also to your link resolver, if that's what you choose to do. So you could have, in the series of options, you can see link resolver is pointed at the bottom. Some books do this. In the last resort, I'm going to show you my link resolver. But it's not always what's right or why do I send some direct and some to the link resolver, and I chose to only show one link when I have the full text and the custom links, but then when I do the link resolver, they get five. I don't know. We need to take a closer look at that on a customer by customer level and think about what's the best way? How're you going to drive usage and the better user experience? I think everybody's seen this kind of thing. Hey, we brought a new resolver and we just launched a new one, but there are inherent issues with link resolvers, right? If we could bypass it, the experience is better and the end user gets to what they want faster and easier and better and comes away saying, "Nice. The library was great to me," maybe we need to think about that.

When do we use the link resolvers? I think there's some approaches to that. Determining best practices, what the user tells us. They want consistency and familiarity and simplicity. We talked about this. If the link says "full text" versus some custom-branded link resolver that you show, they say, "I don't know what that means as a user," perhaps, etc. Okay. So SmartLinks Plus. This is one thing that I learned, that this is the idea that if you buy journals from EBSCO, you can automatically turn on a direct link. These things don't interact, and I learned through this conversation, they don't, these are sort of legacy.

We offer them for EBSCO Host customers to say, "I can link EBSCO's database to the journal that I purchased through EBSCO. You can automate that." Great. It's wonderful. But in the context of discovery, it works outside the realm of our custom links, which means if you've decided, "I want to show the JSTOR link first," and you have the JSTOR record, if you turn on SmartLinks Plus, they both show up. And so I saw that and go, "Maybe that's why people think we're doing this thing."

We actually have a project right now to change that so these interact perfectly well with your custom links that you can get in the site. I talked to Bruce about a bunch of stuff. We looked at the JSTOR specific links just to give them a sense of how people are setting up your JSTOR stuff. We got 6,000 plus sites using EDS. On the academic side, there's almost 8,000 profiles. And that's where you can look at the specifics of linking, so we looked at those, and we realized that somewhere in the 70% of the customers don't link to any purchased JSTOR records from a customized EDS. They may go to the link resolver, but they don't do it in a custom. Just got to skip through. We looked at some of this. Well, how do they rank them, then? Here's some of the, this is generally where they rank the JSTOR stuff. Of course, there's no links at all over on the right-hand side. But what is this? It's an opportunity maybe for people to review and look at their setup. Maybe for Bruce to say, "Hey, can we move some of those 3,700 over to the higher ranking?" No? That's not EBSCO's game to do that. We leave that to you. But something to consider and think about. So we can look more closely at these things, get a little bit better at it. There's some opportunities for our content provider partners. Providing full-text data for searching. We don't do that. It's helpful. E-book chapter-level detail? If you have it, it's helpful. So Bruce talked about documentation guides that you created, which is great. We're trying to make sure this stuff is as accurate as possible. Then we created a how-to video. So this is how it works. Go dig into it. I appreciate the time.

DRM: A Publisher-Imposed Impediment to Progress, or a Legitimate Defense of Publisher/Author Intellectual Property Rights

Adam Chesler, Director of Library Relations, Business Expert Press/Momentum Press
Jim Dooley, Head of Collection Services, University of California/Merced
David Parker, Vice President, Editorial and Licensing, Alexander Street Press
Zac Rolnik, President and Publisher, NOW Publishers

The following is a lightly edited transcript of a live presentation at the 2014 Charleston Conference. Slides and videos are available at http://2014charlestonconference.sched.org/

Adam Chesler: All right, thank you all for coming up to the Gold Balloom here for our presentation about DRM. We have four, as you can tell, panelists up here and you have all of our bios are in the programs so we won't bore you by giving too much detail about ourselves other than to give you the order of presentation. We'll be starting with Jim Dooley from the University of California at Merced. Zac Rolnik is with NOW Publishers. David Parker is with Alexander Street Press and I am Adam Chesler from Business Expert Press and Momentum Press. So we're going to try and keep our presentations reasonably brief with a goal of leaving plenty of time for some questions and some discussions so there is at least one, possibly two microphones in the room and at the end of the talks here if you have questions please step up to the mike and remember to provide your name and affiliation because context is important. Without any further ado I'm going to let Jim get started.

Jim Dooley: Okay, thanks. I'm Jim Dooley, I'm the head of collections services at the University of California Merced and I thought I would start off today just with a definition, and this is one definition from Wikipedia, of what DRM is and some context of what we're talking about. This definition says it's a set of access control technologies used by hardware manufacturers, publishers, copyright holders and individuals to control the use of digital content after sale, and it's the after sale that's one of the important things here, because this is technology that sits with the content literally forever and controls all the way downstream what the user can do with

that content. The intent is to control executing, viewing, copying, printing, and altering of works or devices. This one working definition of what DRM is. I'm sure there are others. When we get to the questions perhaps some of you in the audience may have somewhat different definitions.

I want to talk today, particularly since I'm the librarian on this panel, of the problems that DRM poses from the perspective of individual librarians and also libraries as an institution. The first problem is a very simple one. Libraries today, whether they're whatever type of institution they are, provide a large number of different types of electronic resources from a significantly large number of publishers and some of these are without DRM, some of them have DRM regime A which does some kind of limitation on printing, copying. Others from different publishers have DRM regime B. You have C, D, E, etc. This is extremely confusing to the library user who has to try to figure out, "Okay, what can I do with this and why can I not do with this particular thing what I was able to do with this other one?" And that kind of confusion and difficulty for the user obviously affects library services and so reference librarians, instruction librarians spend an inordinate amount of time trying to explain to users, particularly freshman and sophomores, "Okay, you can do this here but you can't do that. You can do this with something else but you can't do that." And a great deal of time and energy is wasted.

One of the other things I've noticed over the years, particularly from public service librarians, is whenever I, or anybody else in collections, say we have this new electronic e-book package, journal package, whatever, many times I get this sort of deer in the headlights look from my colleagues of,

"Oh blank, here's another one of these things I have to learn and I have to learn what it does and what it doesn't do." And one of my arguments here is that this is not helpful to the adoption of electronic resources generally in libraries. Looking at it from the point of view of libraries as an institution, I think there are several issues, problems with DRM. The first is it certainly has the potential, depending on how it's used, to prevent preservation and archiving of content by libraries and libraries, museums, cultural institutions generally have a long history of preserving content and if you have DRM that makes particular electronic content go away after a particular period of time or limits the number of uses and then it goes away, obviously this has significant impact long term on the ability of libraries to preserve that content.

DRM also has the possibility often times the reality of preventing legitimate uses under the Copyright Act. It prevents users from exercising their fair use rights in their use of particular electronic content. This again I think is particularly problematic. One of the things that I've seen over the last, oh three or four years particularly, is that publishers very often, now particularly in the e-book market will use DRM essentially as a marketing tool. The pitch is, "Okay, we will make this content available on our platform DRM free but if you want to get this same content through, for example an aggregator then it's going to have various kinds, flavors of DRM on it." So, that leads me to the conclusion that in many cases publishers are saying, "Okay, we don't really need DRM here. We can give it up provided it's a way of getting us some sales," and the result of that for libraries is that the presence or absence of DRM has become part of the criteria by which we evaluate offers and we try to make judgments about, "Here's this package from a publisher without DRM. Do I want all of those titles? Am I willing to pay for a significant number of titles I don't really want so that my users can get DRM free access or would I rather, for example, use DDA through an aggregator and accept the fact that there's going to be DRM on that content?" These are the kinds of judgments we have to make regularly and so I'll just wrap it up here by saying that at least by the library perspective DRM

has various negative effects on scholarship and on the ability of libraries and librarians to provide service to our users and to do the things long term that libraries have traditionally been able to do. Thank you.

Zac Rolnik: Hi, I'm Zac Rolnik from NOW Publishers and actually when David and Adam asked me to be on this panel I immediately said, "Yeah, sure, great." Then I realized "Gosh, I don't do DRM on my content," and I was like "Wow, I wonder why they picked me?" So, I hope I make some sense here.

Since my publishing company does not put a DRM wrapper on its content, I just put together some talking points that I thought I would raise with you and then actually as it occurs to me as it relates to DRM. And some of these are like, do we, and we're talking about proprietary content not licensed content where the licensor might require you to put some DRM around it to protect their content and we're also not an open access publisher so, but we have the question of, as a publisher we want to maximize the distribution of our content and the same time we want to control access. Those are sort of conflicting points of view and it's one of the reasons we don't put DRM on our content and we give our authors the PDFs, we want them to distribute it; we think it helps promote the product of a new publisher and is one of the questions I always have.

The next is the impact on the user experience and just as you know, if you have your user names and passwords for all these different sites you go to, DRM is even more complicated and we know how much we hate to remember all of our user names, all of our passwords and from my perspective I want the user of my content to have the most pleasant experience getting to it. I don't want them to be cursing as they're trying to get to the content. So that's another issue that always occurs to me about DRM.

The next is the cost to implement and manage DRM. Our feeling was that the benefits of protecting the content are not nearly as great as the cost to implement, administer, manage that DRM so, and lastly I kind of feel isn't some seepage of our content okay and even good? It's almost impossible to prevent it if you just take a title of an article or of a book you put it in quotation marks and put it into Google, you're going to find that article for free somewhere. It may not be the version of record; it may be a version given at a conference or a copy on the author's website but our feeling is actually, that seepage is good. We want people to sort of say, "Hey, oh, I never heard of this publisher, I never heard of this journal, I've never heard of this book," and getting that access so for those reasons alone I always question as the publisher of primary proprietary content what is the value to me of DRM? And then I actually looked at DRM in the STM space and I'll also include not only STM but also academic publishing in the fields of humanities and social sciences and when I looked online I saw that and I think that this is correct but it may not be but that Elsevier, Springer, Wiley Blackwell, their e-books, at least purchased directly, have no DRM on them. And so I'm wondering where is all this DRM and I know David mentioned that to me for a lot of his content they're actually required by the licensor to actually put DRM around it.

The next thing is, and I know this is not true but, you know, the idea the big deal is that everybody has everything. So, if everybody has everything why put DRM on it? Since if you assume that, you know, the majority of institutions are currently participating in big deals or consortial deals, is DRM really of any value. It also flies in the face of open access. Now again, I'm not an open access publisher, but, given the rise of interest in open access I just don't see the, there you would not have DRM at all.

And lastly, as Jim mentioned, is the issue of fair use and DRM also there kind of makes it difficult in certain circumstances to apply fair use as the patron of the content to share with other people. So for those reasons I kind of wonder is DRM really an issue amongst the, both for publishers I can see from Jim's comments the impact it has on the library and the library user but as a small STM publisher we really don't see much value for ourselves in DRM. We don't think that it would add to our business and we don't think that we're

actually losing business because we don't have DRM. Those are just my brief comments, thanks.

Adam Chesler: So, you've already heard a couple of reasons why people don't think too much, too highly of the notion of DRM, but I thought it would be useful to explain at least, or at least to give some kind of sense or why might a publisher or a provider want to implement DRM regime. We can talk about how it is a marketing component and there's no such thing as bad publicity and it's a good thing when people find out about content by using it or sharing it but I think that there are plenty of good reasons why a publisher, and I'm using that in a generic sense, not one particular kind of publisher or one publisher in particular, would want to protect its assets and would want to make sure that there was some way of, we were talking the other day and the phrase that came into my mind was controlled maximization which is, "How do I make sure that I have some control over the way I'm getting this content out there while ensuring that it's used as much as possible?" And what DRM can do is enable the publisher to manage that process. For instance, if content is freely distributed then it's tough to track the usage. I don't mean in an NSA way track usage, but I mean, how do I know how much usage there's been? How do I go back to the customer at the end of the year and say "Hey, this is how much the content has been used, is this something you want to buy again going forward?" Because we can actually look at that and say "Here's how much it was used because it wasn't shared freely." There wasn't a lot of lost tracking of the usage so there can be a creation of additional sales opportunities.

Jim mentioned the marketing component of that which I think is a good point. Speaking as a small publisher, if all I did was sell stuff indirectly I'd go out of business, so how do I drive people, the buying community, to buy from me directly? Well one of the ways I do that is by offering a better version or a better value for coming to me directly so there are going to be reasons why some publishers are going to apply DRM in certain circumstances because it's part of a business model which is how do you direct the traffic to the place you want it to be? In finding that middle ground, finding that balance of course is important. It may not work for everybody but there are some good reasons why a provider is going to apply DRM or use DRM as part of a strategic plan as opposed to it just being a knee-jerk response to the fear of distribution in the wild.

Having said that, what I wanted to briefly talk about a little bit were some of the administrative ramifications of DRM because if you want to implement one of these regimes it's not simply a matter of pushing a button. We, for instance, Business Expert Press use and Momentum Press use SERU. I would be a little bit concerned about using something like SERU if I had a really strict DRM regime in my content because I'd want to be taking care to ensure that everyone knew exactly how restricted the usage was going to be once they purchased the content. The ramifications of that is that I don't have a large staff. In fact, when I started working at BEP I think I was the third full-time employee that was hired, maybe the fourth. I didn't have time to negotiate licenses and to worry about that so not having to deal with that was an important consideration for us. We simply didn't have the time and resources to have enduring legal discussions about our content. We needed to drive revenue as quickly as we possibly could so eliminating that as a concern, never mind that it was appealing to our community it was also something that made sense for us on an internal basis because I didn't have to worry about it.

Zac mentioned the cost associated with this, especially on a technology front, and Jim talked about how there could be different flavors of it, to have to administer all that, to have to develop it and then to have to keep track of it and understand how this platform might be enabling this but another platform might be enabling something else, having to explain that to every single customer or every single user, to every single author, is a time consuming process, one which we didn't feel we had to take. These things make it harder and one of the things, you look at our website it says we're easy to buy, easy to own, easy to use and it's the only way we could do it effectively was to not get tied down with these different layers of security. I don't want to monitor users. I don't want to monitor my partners. I don't want to worry about who's using it, how they're using it, why they're using it, I just want them to use it and, as Zac pointed out, by not implementing these sophisticated or challenging or complex restrictions we ensure that people can get access to the content as quickly as they can and can use it as much as they want to and how they want to use it and it's really important for us to get the word out so people are distributing this stuff and sharing it. That's kind of a good problem for me to have at this juncture. If I wake up someday and find out that someone downloaded 500,000 articles from my website overnight I will worry about it but I will probably secretly be really happy to know that that many people care that much and think there is that much value in my content. It will be the start of, it will be a problem but it will be an indication of a good problem for me to have and that's certainly not something that I'm especially worried about. As I mentioned before, there's a sales cycle that we want to accelerate, not slow down, and if our sales team has to spend a lot of time explaining to each customer exactly what they can do, and how they can do it, and when they can do it, and what restrictions there are, as opposed to how easy it is, then they're going to be spending a lot of time doing things besides selling and moving on to the next customer. So, when we added all that up and we looked at the ramifications of not just from, David's going to talk a bit about the author perspective, when we thought about it from how we build our program and what our strategic plan is for our type of content, and I think that this is something that other publishers look at, too, it became clear to us that restricting access, building in all of these technological hurdles, would probably be something that will actually slow down our development and not accelerate it. So you get the marketing component that Jim talked about and we try to use DRM I think selectively in an effort to build a larger program and a larger strategy for our company. So, with that I'm going to turn it over to David who's going to talk a little bit more about the people who are actually writing this stuff.

David Parker: Do we have any authors here who've actually published a book and had it posted as an e-book? Anybody? How many e-book publishers do we have here? I might say some things that mean I have to run for the doors. Let me know if I need to hide. I was a publisher of e-books books for a long time and the assumption we generally started from was that as a publisher our interests were closely aligned with authors on DRM. Over time I've come to see that rather differently and I want to look at three reasons today where I think author and publisher interests are not aligned around DRM.

The first is the issue of the platform. The e-book reader platform, the e-book reader itself within which the e-book resides and then the e-book platforms on which they reside are multiple and many. The result is that you've got almost a double layer of trapping of knowledge creation around the content that can't get out, it cannot be found and in a world of gold and green open access where we're all talking about, in the journal world, how do we access not just the information but also the knowledge generated by the information that second- and third-level commentary on the content we can't get it inside of an e-book reader platform. So if you're an author that's written a book, you're proud of it, it's a scholarly work and you have it published inside of a DRM laden e-book reader and e-book reader platform, that peripheral knowledge is never getting out, it's trapped, it lives there forever and I think that's a fundamental problem that I didn't really understand until I started working with hundreds and hundreds of scholarly authors who were disincentivized to publish books over journals and largely because they couldn't see the dissemination of a conversation around their content that they created. That's number one.

Number two is pricing. E-book delivery inside of DRM pricing models are really just an extension of print pricing models and I came to realize over time, particularly in my work at BEP that we might actually generate greater royalty, greater opportunity for authors by deviating substantially from print pricing models and in fact envisioning pricing models that were entirely rooted in a born digital world where there was no recourse to print pricing so I don't have answers today, what's the

right pricing model, but I'm afraid that we're not even engaging in the conversation around e-books because DRM is so closely linked to that original pricing model driven by print and it just eliminates the conversation and more importantly it eliminates the creativity that could come in pricing.

Last is piracy. We all have seen, I guess all of you have kids like I do, I've seen my daughter download songs from bit torrent and share them with thousands of her friends, and I mean thousands, she has thousands of friends in her social media network, and I know that that scared us all as publishers and it scared authors a lot. They thought "Wow, my book is just going to fly out there and I'm never going to see a sale," but I think what we've actually seen in the scholarly and learning space is that the piracy hasn't really happened to the degree that we thought it might have happened, but the argument continues to be perpetuated with authors and having been on the side of negotiating contracts with hundreds and hundreds, if not thousands, of authors every time it's the first point they bring up. "Well, how are you going to protect my content against piracy"? And I have to go and show them that the instances of piracy of scholarly and learning content are simply not significant to the point that you need to be worried or concerned about this, and in fact, the instances of piracy for scholarly and learning content are actually good because it's usually Professor John sends Professor Mary a version of an article or a book that they saw that they think that they should be aware of, which increases exposure of the content, exposure of the publisher, and ultimately exposure to greater sales opportunities. Anyway, that's my shtick and we'll turn it over to you now for questions.

Adam Chesler: There has to be at least one.

Unknown Speaker: Hi, this question is for David. You mentioned that you show authors that piracy is not pervasive. Can you maybe go into a little more detail about that because that's a question that I encounter as well?

David Parker: Sure, and keep in mind I'm speaking about scholarly and secondary learning content. You know, I'm not talking about an introductory to biology textbook but the experience we have with authors is we would actually, this is prospective authors, we would take them on the web and we would start showing them examples of books that we had published and been available for two or three years and try to find version—

Unknown Speaker: We can't hear you.

David Parker: Is that better? Sorry about that. So, what we did with prospective authors is that we would take them onto the web and we would start trolling illegal file sharing sites like bit torrent and others and try to find versions of books that we had had in the market for a couple of years that were readily available as pirated copies and we would have to go through two or three, four, five, six, seven, eight entries in our catalog before we'd find one and we would have to search multiple sites unlike music and that's why I use the example of music. I can type in any song from my favorite band Dire Straits and I can find 1,000 places where you can quickly steal that cut that you want to hear so that's how we would show them.

Unknown Speaker: Hi, I'd like to strongly disagree with the last gentleman's point that stealing of digital content is not pervasive. I work for a journal and our content is stolen every day. It's put on a site in Russia called Cyhub and our journal is completely reproduced on that site. Not only ours but almost every journal. This site comes from a library's proxy server by either stealing passwords or on a proxy from another user. They have, they take the library's journals, all of them, and they also reproduce PDFs on a site called Livegen from India so it is a real problem for at least scholarly journals, I don't know about e-books but digital piracy is pervasive.

Adam Chesler: Do you guys have DRM on the content?

Unknown Speaker: No we don't. I'm not familiar with technology that would, you know, because we want the users to use our content. I'm just not familiar with any technology that would not allow for this reproduction but would also allow our legitimate users to use it properly but if I did find such technology we probably would implement it.

Adam Chesler: I think that that's part of the tension that exists, and Jim addressed it and we talked a little bit about that, is how do you find that middle ground where you can liberate the content just enough to satisfy the business needs as well as the user and the community needs? And I don't think any of us would pretend that the perfect answer exists right now, or that if we could figure out a way to control this a little bit more without restricting it and preventing fair use etc., etc. We would like to avoid that too so it's part of the challenge I think that each institution, each organization has to make a decision about what's going to work for it and what works for it for now, or for BEP, is not necessarily going to work for Alexander Street Press, and it may not work for you guys and that's part of the challenge right now.

Zac Rolnik: My feeling about piracy, though, is the people who typically will look for pirated copies would never buy your content anyway, they're not your customers and we're too small to chase down all the pirated versions, whether it's Rapid Share or this site or that site. We do go to those sites and we tell them please take it down but I really don't think, I have no evidence that it is significantly stealing business from us. I simply think that those are people who probably wouldn't buy your content anyway.

David Parker: I just wanted to thank you for disagreeing with me because that validates that it should be one of those main points we're discussing.

Unknown Speaker: I just had a question, I was curious, how does the DMCA, Digital Mime Copyright Act, interfere with publisher's plans to use DRM as a marketing tool or as a tool to control use or does it just dovetail with it?

Jim Dooley: Well again, speaking from the librarian perspective or the user perspective obviously if we attempted to disable DRM on any of the content that we have purchased or subscribed to we would be violating DMCA and presumably the Feds would come after me or whoever was doing that but again I'll defer to my colleagues on whether there is anything regarding DMCA from their perspective other than it does, at least section 1201, make it a crime to disable electronic controls on content.

Adam Chesler: All I'll do is plead ignorance and say that I'm not really sure that we've had to address anything with DMCA. We haven't had to deal with the DMCA and maybe it's because we don't use DRM but I really can't, I wish I could give you an answer to that, a better answer to that. I don't, we haven't run into any issues with it.

Unknown Speaker: Hi, I'm wondering if you can talk a little bit more about your ideas for separating the e-pricing models from print, especially if you think that the e-prices would go down below print or any of your ideas.

David Parker: I think we were on that topic last night at dinner for two-and-a-half hours. I'm just going to, in the interest of time, I'm going to make one comment in response to your question from last night's conversation that I think would be a fertile area for discussion for all of us and that is as DDA programs grow and libraries and universities look for more diverse kinds of content, particularly high use content that did well in the print world, I think we should be open to discussing very, very high unrestricted access DRM free per unit prices through DDA models. For example, at Alexander Street Press I have a clip or a segment that I know would be viewed 2,000 times a year by students on your campus and I was willing to give it to you unrestricted access, would you give me $10,000 for it for that one piece of content? You'd probably say "No, no way, no way," but it's a conversation we don't seem to be engaging in and I think that that's what DRM does. It stops that conversation.

Unknown Speaker: I just wanted to address the comment about pirated materials not being utilized by your potential customers and that may be true about the libraries' but I'm not certain that it's true of the student who's referred to or used to utilizing pirated songs, movies and if they're utilizing pirated journals or books the library might not then be purchasing them, so.

Zac Rolnik: Well, I think that is actually correct. I mean one of the problems without having DRM on your content is as all the librarians in the room know that you're looking at the usage of our content to justify purchasing or renewal of the content and without DRM there's nothing to prevent a professor from downloading it and then just emailing it their students. There's no violation of a license there but the result is rather than getting 25 downloads for that particular piece of content you're getting one download of that piece of content but at the same time I just kind of like the idea that people have no problem accessing the content and in terms of those students who are finding the pirated content I will again say that they're not going to buy it, they're not going to spend, whether it's $39.00 for an article or $35.00 for an e-book or whatever it might be, if it's not free. Even if it was $2.00, they're still not going to buy it.

Jim Dooley: And I'd just like, again from the library's perspective, many of us have become, and I will admit this, certainly slaves to usage numbers to determine whether something is of value and whether we want to resubscribe to it. I think that many of us, and I'll speak for my colleagues here at the University of California, we have spent a goodly number of years, and I think we're about ready to put all of this stuff out for public comment, trying to develop much more sophisticated metrics to enable us to determine value rather than simply the number of downloads but I'll admit this is a problem. If you get pushed in a corner and you have no money, just usage numbers, raw usage numbers is an easy way to go but I would hope just from the librarian's side that we can become a bit more sophisticated than that and to try to understand exactly what we've been saying here that, yes, there is leakage. Yes, usage, raw usage numbers by themselves are not a particularly good metric for value.

Adam Chesler: I think that there's, what Jim's touched on there is actually, it's kind of like the holy grail of pricing models which is how do we determine value or rather how do you determine value because I can establish a price but you're going to determine the value. You're going to or the users are and trying to figure out a way to measure, monitor and to meter that is one of the ongoing challenges we have. I think a lot of the people up here and certainly the publishers in this room have gone through pricing model exercises in trying to figure out, "Alright, what are we going to do, peers or usage or FDEs?" or "How are we going to assess this?" and I don't think we know. I think we're still trying to experiment with that and that's where I think some constructive dialogue, independent of things like DRM or the print world or whatever, how do we assign value to this and how do we then fit that into a budgetary model that the budget model that you guys have with the material, with your materials budget which of course is growing, if growing at all incrementally, it's not leaping. David mentioned if he had some incredibly useful piece of content you could easily say, "Yeah, it's probably worth that." But, if, you know, if that's going to cost you $10,000 and you're budget is $20,000 can you really afford one article for that kind of money even if you're spending a few dollars to download? That's part of the ongoing challenge. How do we figure out what that value metric is and how do we apply that broadly if it's only going to be on a, if the publisher has something different?

Unknown Speaker: Zac, if widespread access is a desirable outcome for your content does that bring you closer to contemplating becoming an open access publisher either partially or fully with the titles that you're publishing?

Zac Rolnik: We've actually, well we have two types of products. Our primary product we actually pay our authors and we pay our reviewers. Our authors tend to be for that product tenured and shared professors and in addition to that the fields we work in, business, economics, electrical engineering, are not wellsprings of open access, it's not a really open access environment so for that reason all these foundations and trends and even for our regular journals, we've thought about it but it's not a model that we have decided to move towards.

David Parker: And the complete counterpoint to that, Zac will beat me up later for this, is I think content and information is getting more rather than less open. I think that's sort of a fundamental fact that I hope it's not debatable. I think everything across my 20-year career shows content is more rather than less open and as publishers, if we don't experiment with open access, if we don't dive deeply or dive shallowly into open access and play around with the opportunities it presents to new business models than we might miss the boat.

Zac Rolnik: I just want to make one, nothing to get into, we actually, we are green open access. We provide authors with the PDFs, they can post them on their websites, on institutional repositories, the version of record, there's no embargo period on that, so, I guess in some ways we are open access but we still are publication model. Our business model is a subscription based model rather than an APC model and again part of it is just the environment that we're in. If you look at biomedical publishing my guess is 75% of research is, at least 75% is federally funded. I can tell you in business and economics probably less than 5% is federally funded. The environment, it's just a very, very different environment. There are no grant monies to be able to pay for these APCs and in business and economics, I'm aware of only one very successful open access journal and actually that has migrated toward a subscription model also.

Adam Chesler: No other questions? Well, we're wrapping up about five minutes early today so on behalf of the panelists up here I'd like to thank you all for joining us and for your questions and I'm sure all of us who are here will welcome follow up feedback if you care to share it with us after the conference. There are evaluations; please fill them out. Enjoy the rest of the show.

Collection Development

Taming the Wilde: Collaborating With Expertise for Faster, Better, Smarter Collection Analysis

Jacqueline Bronicki, Collections Coordinator, University of Houston Libraries
Cherie Turner, Chemical Sciences Librarian, University of Houston Libraries
Shawn Vaillancourt, Education Librarian, University of Houston Libraries
Frederick Young, Systems Analyst, University of Houston Libraries

Abstract

The importance of collection assessment and evaluation has been a hot topic due to increasing budget restrictions and the need to prove worth to stakeholders through evidence-based evaluations. More robust collection analyses, like comparisons of holdings usage to ILL requests, and gap analyses, are increasingly embraced by the library community. Less thought, however, has been given to how to best conduct these analyses to ensure that the cleanest data is used and that the data tells the right story. The data to do these types of analyses often reside in complex systems and web-environments, which may not be fully understood by the collection managers or subject librarians. The University of Houston Libraries embarked on a large-scale gap analysis of the collection by subject area. The key component to success was quickly, accurately, and properly mining the data sources such as Sierra and the electronic resource management system. Our collection team contends that collaboration with expertise in the Resource Discovery Systems Department allowed the team to more quickly develop complete and accurate datasets, and helped to shape the analysis conducted. This paper discusses the challenges of defining project scope, the process of forming methodology, and the challenges of collecting the data. It will also review how experts were able to contribute to each step of this process. Finally it will outline some initial findings of the analysis, and how this research was accomplished in a realistic time frame.

Background

The University of Houston's MD Anderson Library serves a large student, faculty, and research population. The collection strives to support 12 academic colleges, an interdisciplinary Honors College, and a diverse offering of over 120 undergraduate majors. In order to ensure a consistent level of support for this broad university community some collection analysis was necessary.

The Collection Management Committee, which oversees collection development, recognized a need to better understand the content of the current collection and to identify any potential subject gaps in the collection. In September 2013 a project team was formed to define the research questions, develop appropriate methodology, and collect and analyze data to assess the breadth and coverage of both print and electronic resources.

In recent years the library has not undertaken any efforts of this scale to benchmark the print and electronic collection. The scope of this project required a large amount of data to be collected from the many systems that maintain our holdings and act as repositories for different formats. This large scale data collection proved to be especially time consuming and problematic for public services librarians who lack expertise in the systems that store the data, and made the assistance of experts necessary.

Methodology

The primary objective of this project was to determine the depth and relevance of current UH main campus library collection. The methodology was based on a print collection analysis done by Cornell University Libraries (2012), which provided a detailed benchmark for their print collection. Modifications were made in the University of Houston Libraries project to address differences in library services platform and electronic management systems, but the core methodology and many assumptions are identical. To determine gaps by subject area, Library of Congress call numbers were used as a proxy for subject.

Initially, the team wanted to include and benchmark all formats in the collection (print monographs, e-books, print journals, databases and electronic journals). However, based on a lack of call numbers for e-books and the multidisciplinary nature of databases, these two formats were excluded. This paper focuses solely on the phase of research dedicated to print monographs. The team chose to begin the analysis with this format with the expectation that monograph record data would provide the least complexity, the greatest opportunity for scalability, and a reusable model for other more complex formats.

Research Questions

The project team identified two main research questions to guide the research process and determine data collection variables:

1. What are the best measurements for evaluating the current scope of the collection?

2. What subject areas are not adequately covered in the current collection?

Population

In order to best answer our research questions and benchmark the collection at a point in time,

data was collected for the entire population of print monograph records with valid LC call numbers. The Systems Analyst most familiar with the library services platform developed a query to generate a list of print monographs in the collection based on three parameters: a location code designating our campus from the others in the system, print monograph designation, and status indicating availability.

This data output resulted in over 1 million records (N=1,048,575) and represented the catalog as it existed at the time of parsing, January 31, 2014. The Systems Analyst provided the raw data in a .csv file. Records were removed during cleanup narrowing the final dataset to 889,825 records that met the criteria for inclusion and supported the research question.

Initial Findings

The analyses presented at this conference focused on distribution of monographs per LC class and subclass, shown as Figure 1, as well as a ratio calculation of percentage of holdings and usage between print monographs and ILL borrowing requests which is shown as Table 1. The ratio calculation, based on an analysis conducted by John Ochola at Baylor University (2003), was used to identify and flag potential "gaps" in the collection. The details of the ratio calculations and other analysis done on this dataset are explained in another forthcoming paper (Bronicki, Ke, Turner, & Vaillancourt, in press).

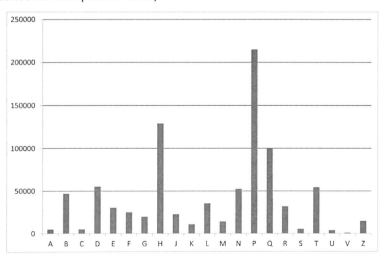

Figure 1. Distribution of monographs per call number.

LC Subclass	Percent of Holdings	Percent Usage	PEU	Holdings Usage	Percent of ILL Borrowing	RBH	ILL Usage	Action
B	1.32%	1.43%	1.08	Overused	0.79%	0.6	Underused	No Changes
BC	0.09%	0.08%	0.82	Underused	0.05%	0.51	Underused	Ease Off
BD	0.24%	0.20%	0.84	Underused	0.24%	1.01	Underused	Ease Off
BF	1.22%	1.78%	1.46	Overused	2.00%	1.64	Overused	Growth Opportunity
BH	0.07%	0.09%	1.29	Overused	0.05%	0.68	Underused	No Changes
BJ	0.22%	0.27%	1.21	Overused	0.18%	0.79	Underused	No Changes
BL	0.42%	0.65%	1.56	Overused	0.69%	1.65	Overused	Growth Opportunity
BM	0.10%	0.07%	0.67	Underused	0.09%	0.95	Underused	Ease Off
BP	0.13%	0.26%	1.95	Overused	0.34%	2.57	Overused	Growth Opportunity
BQ	0.04%	0.10%	2.63	Overused	0.32%	8.05	Overused	Growth Opportunity
BR	0.36%	0.33%	0.91	Underused	0.70%	1.96	Overused	Change Purchasing
BS	0.22%	0.16%	0.73	Underused	0.36%	1.62	Overused	Change Purchasing
BT	0.16%	0.13%	0.85	Underused	0.40%	2.53	Overused	Change Purchasing
BV	0.18%	0.15%	0.86	Underused	0.44%	2.49	Overused	Change Purchasing
BX	0.52%	0.29%	0.56	Underused	1.69%	3.23	Overused	Change Purchasing

Table 1. Holdings usage to interlibrary loan usage comparison for LC subclass B.

Challenges in the Development Phase

The team faced many challenges during the development of the methodology. Most of our initial struggles stemmed from the team's lack of expertise with the library services platform and interlibrary loan system. Records were, in many cases less complete than our inexperienced team anticipated, so priorities and expectations had to be revaluated. We had to scale our expectations about what the systems could deliver, and be cognizant of errors inherent in systems that require manual data entry, specifically the print monograph records. Developing a realistic strategy to collect this data became a major outcome of the research. In the end, collaboration with the Systems Analyst in our Resource Discovery Services department allowed us to collect the raw data in a timely and accurate manner and allowed us to focus more closely on data analysis. In many ways the process of collecting relevant and accurate data has been far more enlightening than the findings.

We presented the challenges from two viewpoints, the project team of the four public services librarians and the systems analyst doing the data mining in the library services platform.

Challenges from viewpoint of the Project Team:

1. The project team lacked necessary understanding of the infrastructure of the systems containing the data.

2. Defining input and output variables that could be reasonably and consistently parsed was more complicated than the team anticipated.

3. A deeper understanding of the MaRC record was necessary to ensure that the right data was gathered.

4. The scope of the project did not initially scale well with the timeline and the realities of obtaining this type of data.

5. Due to limitations of the library service platform, input errors in the records, and missing data in records, it was often a challenge to gather the most relevant and accurate data.

Challenges from viewpoint of the Systems Analyst:

1. The Systems Analyst was brought in after the project was underway, and after the research questions has been developed.

2. A recent migration from a Millennium ILS to the Sierra library services platform presented some benefits and challenges to gathering the requested data.

3. The scale of the proposed project did not match the types of data library system can provide.

Choosing Output Criteria

Once a method to obtain relevant and accurate data was finalized, some decisions could be made about what information to retrieve from our identified records. Our analysis needs, and therefore our output criteria, are shaped by the need for some way to meaningfully denote subject over this very large and broad collection. In addition, our research questions focus around two central ideas: scope of the collection, and adequate coverage. By researching the scope of the collection we hoped to understand what our current collection contains, and by researching adequate coverage we hoped to understand whether our collection is meeting user needs.

We initially planned to gather the fields shown in Table 2, which were selected by the project team with a very basic understanding of the data in our library's records.

Bibliographic Record	
	Call Number
	Subject Headings
	Publication/Copyright Date
	ISBN
	Record Number
	Title
Item Record	
	Copy Number
	Total Number of Checkouts
Order Record	
	Status
	Order Date

Table 2. Planned output criteria.

We planned to use the call numbers as the primary subject proxy, and if necessary utilize the subject headings to fill in any gaps. The publication date was intended to show how materials of different ages are collected and used. ISBN and the bib record number were each intended to be used as unique identifiers. The title was chosen for the benefit that it would provide

to a deeper analysis within a smaller dataset, which we hoped would follow our analysis. The copy number would provide us with an understanding of how many copies of each title were feeding our usage data, and the total number of checkouts would serve as our proxy for use. Finally, we selected the status of the item to ensure that we were focusing our efforts on items that were in our circulating collection, and planned to use order date to get an idea of how the order date related with the item's age and the subject.

After having many conversations with the Systems Analyst and others with more expertise in our library's records and management systems our output criteria shifted to account for that new knowledge. In some cases we found that the fields we originally intended to capture were just not as meaningful as we had hoped. In others the data was unavailable, or not available in a form that would be useful to our analysis. The final output criteria, which are substantially different from those we began with, are displayed in Table 3.

Bibliographic Record	
	Call Number
	Publication/Copyright Date
	Record Number
	Title
	Publisher
	Catalog Date
	ISBN
Item Record	
	Call Number
	Total Checkouts
	Last Year Checkouts
	Year-to-Date Checkouts
	Location

Table 3. Final output criteria.

Subject headings, copy number, status, and order date from our final criteria. Subject headings were removed primarily because it would have been very complicated to shape the data in this field into a meaningful subject proxy. Copy number was found to be unnecessary because our final search was based on the item record rather than the bibliographic record as we originally planned. Status was also incorporated into our search parameters, and order date was not found to add significantly to our analysis.

Several fields were added, including publisher, catalog date, item call number, year-to-date checkouts, and location. Publisher was added to allow for analysis based on publisher, which could be the basis of a future analysis by subject librarians. Catalog date was intended to serve as a more meaningful version of our prior order date category. The item call number was necessary to supplement the sometimes missing bibliographic call numbers. Last year and year-to-date checkouts were intended to provide an idea of what our current usage is like. Finally the location field provides information on where our collection is actually located and was intended to serve, in part, as a way to confirm circulating status.

Transforming the Data

Finally, with the data collection as complete as possible, our focus shifted to cleaning and normalizing the data. Once again we realized that we needed to consult with our experts to make sure we understood the data. In particular we needed clarification on how MaRC records were structured and used locally in order to ensure that we were accurately interpreting each field, and accounting for any gaps in the data based on our MaRC records.

Bibliographic record numbers initially seemed to be problematic because they appeared to be missing a digit, complicating the project team's plan to use them as unique identifiers. Fortunately the missing digit was found to be a random character which would not impact our use of the field as unique identifier. After noticing some strange numbers in our Last_yr_checkout field we sought help from our Systems Analyst for clarification, and discovered that this field was not in use and therefore that data was meaningless. This was a particularly significant discovery as we would have used this data for analysis, perhaps assuming that these strange numbers were just outliers or corrupted records. Having a stronger understanding of the data allowed us to move forward with an appropriate view of what needed to be fixed or modified to be usable.

Cleaning consisted of identifying potential issues in the record and then verifying that these issues did not cause further problems in other parts of the data for a given record. For example, if diacritics were used in the record, they would often not parse out correctly when the records were downloaded and delineated. Therefore, we checked records that had these in the title to make sure that other parts of the record were not corrupted as a result. The most common issues were titles with diacritics, dates that had not been sorted into the correct fields, and items with future cataloging or publication dates, presumed to be data entry errors. For the very few records where errors were detected, we manually checked the record and corrected the errors.

We also examined the ISBNs at this stage. The original plan had been to use them as a unique identifier for items; however, we found that there was so much extraneous information included in the field that cleaning it would have been more work than it was worth. Instead, we deleted the column and solely used bib record numbers as our identifier.

Larger issues in the data cleaning phase required the removal of larger chunks of data that were likely to become problematic in our analysis. By reviewing the location code information we were able to identify 142,823 records that should be removed. Some of these records were items located at other campuses that were not removed by the parameters of our initial search, but most were:

- Government documents cataloged using SUCOC numbers instead of LC call numbers, making analysis by subject impossible.

- Theses and dissertations cataloged with local numbers which identify the college in which the document was written rather than the subject.

- Microform materials not cataloged with an LC call number.

An additional 14,894 records were removed based on a review of the call number data. Most commonly this was because a call number was not available from the fields which were accessed during our data export phase. We also found additional government documents, former reserve materials, and dissertations that were not in the usual locations for these materials and did not have a valid LC call number for us to use.

Because not all bibliographic records included a call number, we opted to pull call numbers from both the bibliographic record and the item record. In most cases an item would have only one of the two, or would have two matching call numbers; however, in some cases both call number fields included data but the call numbers did not match. For records with non-matching call numbers it was decided that the item call number should be used as this would be the call number with which students were most likely to interact. Once this cleaning was completed the analysis could be done.

Planning for Analysis

Given our clean data set of meaningful variables we did a wide range of analyses. Benchmarking analyses included the distribution of our collection included as Figure 1, more detailed LC subclass distributions, analyses of usage by call number and by age, and analyses of age by subject. To learn more about how our collection fits with user needs we used our usage data alongside our interlibrary loan data from a two year span. A subset of the findings of this analysis is shown in Table 1. While our analysis and our findings are not the focus of this presentation, these do help to provide some context for our analysis. Our analytical plan and our findings are closely linked to our data collection strategies.

Future Work

While our findings have been interesting, and promise to help us improve our collection, the project team has found the process of data gathering and of preparing for analysis the most enlightening. For the project team there have been many important lessons.

Lessons Learned

1. Collaborating with experts is essential to gathering data that has meaning.

2. Local practice shapes what data is available and how it can be used.

3. A deep understanding of the infrastructure of our systems is needed to effectively collect data.

The project team is currently working on a related analysis of print and electronic serials, which is encountering some of the same challenges experienced in our print monographs analysis. It is also encountering some new and exciting challenges, like adjusting to the many different systems in which the needed data is stored, understanding what information is available in a serial record, finding meaningful ways to show holdings, and deciding whether to deal with aggregated content as opposed to our own subscriptions.

References

Bronicki, J., Ke, I., Turner, C. Vaillancourt, S. (in press). Gap analysis by subject area of the University of Houston Main Campus Library Collection. *Serials Librarian.*

Cornell University Library. (2012, November 22). *Report of the Collection Development Executive Committee Task Force on print collection usage.* Retrieved from http://staffweb.edu/system/files/CollectionUsageTF_ReportFinal11-22-10.pdf

Ochola, J. H. (2003). Use of circulation statistics and interlibrary loan data in collection management. *Collection Management, 27*(1), 1-13. http://dx.doi.org/10.1300/J105v27n01_01

Collecting and Acquiring in Earnest
(The 14th Annual Health Sciences Lively Lunch)

Wendy Bahnsen, Executive Director Library Services, Rittenhouse Book Distributors
Yumin Jiang, Department Head, Collection Management, University of Colorado Health Sciences Library
Ramune K. Kubilius, Collection Development/Special Projects Librarian, Galter Health Science Library, Northwestern University
Emma O'Hagan, Medical Librarian, Western Michigan University Homer Stryker MD School of Medicine
Andrea Twiss-Brooks, Co-Director, Science Libraries, University of Chicago

Abstract

In this year's sponsored but no holds barred lunch, host Wendy Bahnsen (substituting for colleague Nicole Gallo) offered a brief greeting, and Ramune Kubilius provided the traditional "year in review" synopsis of developments since the last Charleston Conference. Panelists then shared insights and led discussion on earnest attempts to meet users' information needs and satisfy administrations' budget and other expectations. No matter how information has become repackaged, two formats remain important in health sciences communication: books and journals (articles). Speakers focused on library experiments with these formats. Is PDA a solution? Bahnsen contributed highlights and findings from a survey by Rittenhouse on health sciences customers' experience with the R2 PDA program. Yumin Jiang shared some impressions on the experience of her institution with a few e-book PDA/DDA (patron-driven or demand-driven acquisition) packages. Suggestions were made about best practices in e-book collection building with PDA programs. What conclusions can be reached from experimentation with and implementation of on-demand article acquisitions? Emma O'Hagan shared insights and experience with journal article "on demand" and "pay per view" services at two institutions. Andrea Twiss-Brooks fielded questions and moderated discussion with session participants about the services and programs described by panelists, ranging from discussion about specific programs and models to broader collection and service implications.

The 2014 sponsored but no holds barred Lively Lunch began with words of greeting from host Bahnsen who stepped in for her colleague, Gallo. Kubilius provided the traditional Lively Lunch "year in review" synopsis of developments since the last Charleston Conference. (The handout was posted in the conference site and included as a supplement here). She brought participants' attention to items on the list, including seven health sciences focused articles that made up the special April 2014 issue of *Against the Grain*. In the past year, there were a number of publisher anniversaries, a preponderance of news items about big data, more open access initiatives and new publications.

Panelists shared insights and led discussion on earnest attempts to meet users' information needs and satisfy administrations' budget and other expectations. No matter how information has become repackaged, two formats remain important in health sciences communication: books and journals (articles). Speakers focused on library experiments with providing access to information in these formats, concluding with audience questions and discussion.

How is PDA being implemented? Bahnsen shared highlights from the R2 customer survey, conducted in May 2013 (to be posted in the company's site). Of R2 e-book purchases, about 65% were firm purchases and 35% came through the PDA process. Library customers have selected from 2 to 4500 titles for the PDA program but more often, about 400, or 10% are selected for PDA. Overall, 27% of the titles that migrated to the shopping cart were purchased. The R2 PDA model is a mediated program, enabling libraries to customize their collection for patrons. There is no automatic purchase; titles are moved to the shopping cart after three full-text accesses and the library has 30 days to evaluate for purchase.

Jiang shared some insights about three e-book PDA/DDA (patron-driven or demand-driven acquisition) programs. The library's goals in trialing these were to increase access to e-books, build up subject collections outside core collection areas, and to experiment with "just in time" acquisitions. Assessment included examination of usage, cost per use, continued use after purchase, and users' involvement and satisfaction. The first experiment (with MyiLibrary) in 2012 involved shared purchase and access among five libraries. Selections were focused on sports medicine and public health; books mostly were available for unlimited concurrent use. The second experiment in 2013 (with R2) involved mediated purchase after three uses. The third experiment (with Ebsco) began one month before the conference. These different PDA programs offer different options: the short-term loan option, purchase after one significant use, automatic purchase after three uses, and mediated purchase after three uses. Availability of books in *Doody Core Titles* was an appreciated selection feature. Recommended issues to consider for PDA included: the importance of setting up a library profile, devising a workflow (print, e-book packages, and PDA), determining access and cataloging matters, investigating possible consortial deals, devising assessment metrics (e.g., renting vs purchase), and making weeding decisions. Lessons learned? It's not easy to balance three different providers' PDA programs at the same time. Overlap is inevitable (and overlap with print can occur, too). Manual searching may be warranted. Consortial deals can serve as a good experiment for adding breadth to a collection. Publisher usage based packages are also worth investigating, but a minimum deposit requirement can be a challenge

What conclusions can be reached from experimentation with and implementation of on-demand article acquisitions? O'Hagan shared insights and experience with journal article "on demand" and "pay per view" acquisitions at two institutions. The institution at which she currently works opened as an all digital library in the summer of 2013 and the first medical school class (of 54) entered in August 2014. The Get It Now

delivery service is optimal because articles are available to requestors (who can order via a link resolver unmediated or through library mediation) in under two hours and the color pdfs are high quality. Her former institution (University of Alabama at Birmingham), a large research institution, charged users for document delivery, while the current institution caps the number of requests per day to five and encourages "thoughtful use" by including a note in the library's website. Problems encountered? Multiple individuals may need the same article for a class, and the library may reconsider a note on link resolver pages about costs of the service (to the library) that may discourage use of the service. Another experiment, not set up in the article linker yet, is the implementation, primarily though library promotion and library discovery, of ReadCube's institutional model (initially limited to one publisher but since grown to two). Another delivery service, Reprints Desk, is not seen by users, but allows the library staff in a mediated fashion to acquire some older content not available through Get It Now.

Twiss-Brooks not only added insights, but also moderated audience questions and discussion, including queries about the promotion of both PDA and article on demand (trials and as an established service), the availability of turnaway statistics information from PDA providers, requests through mediated services of articles already available in library-licensed journals, usability, browsing, downloading availability of various PDA and article on demand, assessment, usage studies, and surveys.

Final questions and comments ended the session about broader collection development and management implications. Initial decisions about PDA should not be engraved in stone. Program implementations may need to be adjusted (e.g., moving from short-term loan to a purchase plan instead). The initial or primary goals of implementing an on demand acquisitions service may be to supplement or build a collection area, but analysis can also help justify a subscription cancellation or addition as well.

Appendix 1

The 34th annual Charleston Conference: November 5-8, 2014

Collecting and Acquiring in Earnest (The 14th Annual Health Sciences Lively Lunch)
Moderator: **Andrea Twiss-Brooks** (Co-Director, Science Libraries, University of Chicago);
Presenters: **Wendy Bahnsen** (Executive Dir. Library Services) substituting for Nicole Gallo (Executive Dir Sales & Marketing, Rittenhouse), as host/presenter;
Yumin Jiang (Dept. head, Collection Management, University of Colorado Health Sciences Library);
Emma O'Hagan (Medical Librarian, Western Michigan University Homer Stryker MD School of Medicine);
Annual update: **Ramune K. Kubilius** (Col Development / Special Projects Librarian, Galter Health Science Library, Northwestern University)

Synopsis of some developments since the 2013 Lively Lunch
Compiled by Ramune K. Kubilius

Coming in early 2015

- Elsevier is the new publisher of **JADA** (Journal of the American Dental Association).
- *Science Advances* (AAS): new OA publication spanning science, technology, engineering, mathematics, and the social sciences.
- **Biomed Central** no longer requires paid subscriptions to 7 additional content journals.
- **De Gruyter Open** will publish & turn to OA 8 (STM) Central European journals formerly subscription & distributed by Springer.

Coming December 2014

- Final retirement of **MD Consult**, "superseded by" ClinicalKey (requiring new/different licenses).

2014 anniversaries:
PeerJ- 1
Scopus- 10
Cochrane – 20
EMBASE- 40
ISI's Science Citation Index- 50   /   MEDLARS® (Medical Literature Analysis and Retrieval System)- 50

November 2014

- **Scopus** cited references pre-1996 first content starts to appear. (*Cited References Expansion Program* was *announced in March 2014*).
- Launch of Society for Neuroscience (SfN) new OA journal, *eNeuro* (*including* reviews and commentaries to negative results).

October 2014

- **Scopus**: expansion of the *h*-index publication window to 1970 (previously 1996 onwards).
- **Embase** enhanced to support the retrieval of medical device information (supports comprehensive post-market surveillance and device safety as well as the development of novel devices).
- EBSCO announcement about *PEMSoft*, a pediatric medical reference tool for pediatric questions at the point of care.
- **John Wiley & Sons, Inc. and ReadCube** announce the platform-wide integration of ReadCube Checkout technology across all Wiley journals (Wiley now offers rental, cloud and downloadable article access options for the majority of journal articles – offering individual readers "the choice to select the level of access that best fits their needs...").

- **Open access to Author Insights survey** of 30,000 authors by Nature Publishing Group and Palgrave Macmillan.
- **McGraw-Hill eCollections** in YBP's GOBI (1,050 titles available in pre-assembled perpetual access collections).

September 2014

- **Wolters Kluwery's Lippincott Procedures** (online medical-surgical nursing procedures) extensively review by the Academy of Medical-Surgical Nurses (AMSN). ¼ of 395 AMSN-endorsed procedures included in October update with remainder to be released quarterly through July 2015.
- **ClinicalKey** enhancements (intuitive topic pages, a design easily viewable on any mobile device, and multi-layered search functions).
- Zynx Health has announced the general availability of *ZynxCarebook*, a mobile platform designed to profoundly improve care team collaboration across the healthcare continuum.

August 2014

- Thompson Reuters and DataCite produce **Data Citation Index**: access to quality research data sets from multi-disciplinary repositories around the world.
- Final **NIH Genomic Data Sharing (GDS) policy** : way to speed the translation of data into knowledge, products and procedures that improve health while protecting the privacy of research participants.
- Release of 12 new **EBSCO eBooks Subject Sets**, which increases the total number of subject sets to more than 200.

July 2014

- **Springe**r celebrates the milestone of 200,000 open access articles published to date (the articles, published across BioMed Central, and SpringerOpen are freely available and published under a Creative Commons (CC) license)...

June 2014

- *BMJ:* A new name, logo, website design, and homepage address (thebmj.com). 175 years old in 2015.
- **OCLC and Elsevier partnership** to ensure ScienceDirect holdings data kept up-to-date in WorldCat without library intervention.

April 2014

Against the Grain 26(2), April 2014: Trends in Health Sciences and Biomedical Sciences Information and Services Provision
- Introduction & issue compiler (Ramune K. Kubilius)
- Librarians Without Borders: Building In-Country Research and Information Provision Capability (Carla J. Funk, J. Michael Homan, Lenny Rhine)
- Health Association Libraries: The Spackle Needed for Member Societies (Mary A. Hyde)
- Cultivating Scholarship: The Role of Institutional Repositories in Health Sciences Libraries (Lisa A. Palmer)
- Libraries Take on Policy: Support for Open Access and Open Data (Anneliese Taylor)
- Basic Biomedical Scientists: The Rediscovered Library Users (Susan K. Kendall)
- Where to Start? Opening Day Collections and Services for a Newly Founded Medical School (Elizabeth R. Lorbeer)
- Disruptive Technology: Librarians Must Think Heretical Thoughts to Adapt (Michelle A. Kraft)

March 2014

- **PLOS** has set a new policy, requiring authors to make all data behind their published results publicly available.
- **DOAJ** launches a new and much extended form for journals wishing to be included in the DOAJ.
- **Elsevier's Reference Module in Biomedical Sciences** announced (will provide access to reference content updated as science progresses). Other science modules were launched Sept. 2013.

February 2014

- **HighWire Press and Altmetric LLP** agree to offer altmetrics integration to publications hosted on the HighWire Open Platform.
- **Elsevier** opens its papers to text-mining.

January 2014

- *Doody's Collection Development Monthly (DCDM)* premiers: free service for subscribers to Doody's Review Service and Doody's Core Titles-includes website and a monthly e-mail newsletter (4th Tuesday each month).
- **ISNI and ORCID** strategic partnership: ISNI2ORCID tool for ORCID registrants to import data from ISNI profile to ORCID profile.
- **NIH** takes steps to improve reproducibility.
- Decker publishes *Scientific American Medicine* (established 1981; known as *American College of Physicians Medicine 2004-2013*).
- **EbscoHost, Elsevier, Thomson Reuters**: increase of provider/ vendor links in Google Scholar and in Google.

December 2013

- NLM adds over 400 NLM publications and productions dating from the 1860s to the 1990s to its **Digital Collections**.

November 2013

- **IEEE statement** on appropriate use of bibliometric indicators in evaluation of scientific publications.
- **Elsevier and Ex Libris Group** announce a collaborative initiative to use the source normalised impact per paper (SNIP) and SCImago Journal Rank (SJR) metrics in calculating relevance ranking for Primo search results.
- Migration of more *JBJS* titles to the HighWire Open Platform announced (in addition to *JBJS Reviews*).
- **Radiological Society of North America (RSNA)** announces full-text journal apps for *Radiology* and *RadioGraphics* (provider: Sheridan).

The Buck Stops Here: Assessing the Value of E-book Subscriptions at the Columbia University Libraries

Melissa J. Goertzen, Columbia University
Krystie Klahn, Columbia University

Abstract

Over the past four years Columbia University Libraries (CUL) has seen exponential growth in electronic book (e-book) purchasing. These purchases have not only increased the depth and breadth of the collection, but they have also created new opportunities for remote learning and instant information access. In turn, this new push for purchasing electronic has created new demands in assessment to understand the true benefit of these resources, most notably in regards to annual e-book subscriptions.

In 2013, a new position aimed at developing an e-book strategy for CUL was devised. Shortly thereafter, a position was created in the Science and Engineering Library Division (SEL) that focused on assessment. These two positions fall in line with CUL's mission to support research and learning through evidence based decision making.

This paper explains an assessment methodology used within the library system at CUL to evaluate the cost-benefit of e-book subscriptions. By appraising several databases, we were able to analyze cost and usage to determine the actual value of these resources. The findings yielded a savings of approximately $60,000 for the 2015 fiscal year. This is an ongoing initiative that will help us document the e-book landscape and build data sets that will inform collection development decisions.

Introduction

The dawning of the Digital Age revolutionized the way information and knowledge are created, produced, and disseminated in the academic community. The rapid integration of technologies with research, teaching, and learning activities has changed both information and access needs of user communities. A new reliance on electronic content coupled with the pressure of reduced stack space for print collections are factors that contributed to a new focus on electronic book (e-books) acquisition initiatives in academic libraries. Librarians now face the challenge of assessing and evaluating this new format in regards to the value it offers to users.

Columbia University Libraries (CUL) is one of the top five academic research library systems in North America and serves a community of over 3,750 faculty members and 26,000 full-time students at the Morningside Campus and Medical Center. The collections are housed across twenty-one campus libraries and include over twelve million volumes, 160,000 current journals and serials, and an extensive collection of manuscripts, rare books, microforms, maps, and audiovisual materials. In 2004, CUL began purchasing e-books in an experimental capacity. Due to positive reception by faculty and students, CUL began expanding e-book collections to support research, teaching, and learning activities across campus. Currently, CUL provides access to more than two million e-book titles and expenditures comprise 25% of the total book budget.

As the e-book collection continues to grow, CUL is developing a unique strategy and vision for e-book collection development, programs, and initiatives. To achieve this goal, the Collection Development Department launched the E-Book Program Development Study in 2013. This assessment project centers on the collection of essential data to drive the development of policies related to e-book acquisition, discovery, and access. In 2014, the Science and Engineering Library Division (SEL) created the position of Collection Assessment and Analysis Librarian in order to promote regular and standardized assessment of existing collections.

In 2014, 96 active e-book subscriptions were identified at CUL. The objective of this paper is to describe an assessment methodology used to evaluated the cost-benefit of these e-book subscriptions across the entire library system, and then within SEL. By appraising several databases, we were able to analyze the cost, usage, and value of these resources. This work involved conducting cost analysis, examining usage trends, and conducting title overlap analysis. The study was guided by the following four principles outlined in the CUL/IS Strategic Plan 2010–2013:

1. User-focused design.

2. Data-driven decision making.

3. Continuous assessment of results.

4. Flexible and adaptive response to user needs (Columbia University Libraries, 2010, p. 8).

The assessment method described in this paper was applied on two separate occasions in the Collection Development Department and SEL between November 2013May 2014. In both cases, the method provided actionable results and contributed to the standardization of e-book assessment and negotiation strategies across campus. The findings yielded a savings of approximately $60,000 for the 2015 fiscal year. Since savings are tied to subscription packages, they will carry forward into coming years. In addition, both studies resulted in discussions with vendors regarding price negotiation and platform performance. Finally, we gained a deeper understanding of how resources can be allocated to best support the needs of user communities. The ongoing evaluation of e-book subscriptions will allow for evidence based decision making and assist in the continued documentation of the e-book landscape at CUL.

E-Book Program Development Study

The E-Book Program Development Study is an ambitious, two year assessment project aimed at gathering essential data to drive the development of policies related to e-book development programs. It aligns with CUL's mission to support the development and delivery of high-quality services that facilitate research, teaching, and learning across campus and within the wider scholarly community. The results will provide a set of recommendations and policies for internal and external stakeholders as they collaborate on the development and implementation of e-book projects and programs.

The objective at the heart of the E-Book Program Development Study is to develop a strategy and vision for e-book programs and collections at CUL. Essentially, the set of recommendations that result from study findings will create a bridge between the current landscape and CUL's vision for future e-book initiatives on campus. A large part of this work involves the development of methodologies that examine how e-book resources are allocated, evaluate current subscriptions and packages, examine usage trends, and build collaborative relationships with vendors. The data that was gathered while developing these methodologies will be used to inform recommendations and policy statements regarding e-book collection development and management on campus.

The reality that the e-book landscape is constantly evolving was factored into decisions regarding the overarching assessment framework guiding this study. The research design was created so that it can be replicated regardless of how e-books evolve in the coming years. Because the design is flexible and adaptive in nature, it promotes continued assessment, evaluation, and strategic planning as a regular component of e-book programs.

As part of this study, a large-scale cost analysis project was completed between November 2013–March 2014. The goal of the project was to collect quantitative data that will inform e-book collection development policies in regards to fund allocation and preferred business models. While the study examined both e-book subscriptions and purchases, for the purposes of this paper, the discussion will be limited in scope to e-book subscriptions.

After discussions with the Director of Collection Development, and the Head of Electronic Resources Management, it was determined that e-books are most often purchased on the EO fund code. To collect financial data for all e-book subscriptions, a Voyager (CUL's integrated library system) query was run for all library funds ending in EO. After running the cumulative query, we created a base list of all e-book subscriptions at CUL. Given the enormous size of this data set and the time restrictions placed in the study, data collection was limited to subscriptions that had fund activity during the 2013 fiscal year (FY2013). This limited the base list to 96 e-book subscriptions. Next, subscription fees in FY2013 were totaled, and calculations were made to identify the top 70 per cent (bulk) and bottom 30 per cent (tail) of purchases within the budget. Statistical analysis was also conducted to determine the total, average, median, high, and low costs.

To examine usage trends, the top four subscriptions (ranked by cost) were selected and corresponding title lists were collected from the Continuing and Electronic Resources Management (CERM) Division. At the same time, the corresponding BR2 COUNTER report was pulled from the vendor website. At this point, we encountered an unexpected challenge; in several cases, multiple collections from the same vendor are purchased as separate items on the EO fund code. However, there is no apparent way to filter COUNTER reports by collection. At this point, we considered analyzing the data by vendor instead of by collection, but decided that this method would skew results because of the discrepancies in cost, size, and use. Instead, we filtered the data for a second time by matching the 2013 title lists with COUNTER report data. Next, we adapted a cost

analysis framework used by the University of Western Australia to analyze DDA models (Davies & Morgan, 2013, p. 172). After examining our data set, we calculated the number of titles loaned, number of loans, percentage of titles without use after purchase, the average cost of an e-book, and cost per use (see Table 1). Please note that the results were calculated using confidential data. For the purposes of this paper, the numbers were changed and percentages are not exact, but they reflect the trends discovered in the actual study findings.

After analyzing the cost and usage data of the top e-book subscriptions, it was determined that the cost per use of Subscription D was high ($9.00 per use) compared to Subscription A ($0.20 per use), Subscription B ($0.20 per use), and Subscription C ($0.75 per use).

The results were presented to the E-Resource Usage Data Working Group (ERUDWG) at CUL. The consensus was to conduct a second analysis of Subscription D based on the following criteria: evaluation of content, overlap analysis, and interface analysis. The results indicated that Subscription D contained a large number of outdated technical manuals (96 per cent published before 2011), a high number of titles available through other platforms, and incomplete multivolume sets.

Next, a team of librarians from SEL examined the title list and identified 394 high use titles (more than 20 page views). Of this subset, she discovered that 196 titles (49.75%) are available through other platforms at CUL. Then, she

	Subscription A	Subscription B	Subscription C	Subscription D
2013 Cost	$50,000.00	$20,000.00	$15,000.00	$60,000.00
No. of titles	80,000	6,000	125	11,000
No. of titles loaned	34,000	2,100	90	1,600
No. of loans	2,500,00	11,900	22,00	6,500
% of titles without use after purchase	62%	65%	25%	85%
Average cost of e-book	$0.60	$3.00	$140.00	$5.00
Cost per use	$0.20	$0.20	$0.75	$9.00

Table 1. Recalculated results of the e-book subscription cost and usage analysis.

searched GOBI for the remaining 198 high use titles and discovered that the vast majority are available for individual purchase. Based on this analysis, it was determined that Subscription D does not contain a significant amount of unique content. A decision was made to cancel the subscription.

One unexpected outcome of this analysis was the opportunity to speak with the Vice President and a team of sales representatives managing Subscription D on three separate occasions. The company requested feedback from CUL regarding how to improve the platform interface and content, and were provided with study findings. After a series of negotiations Subscription D was renewed for one year at an 80% discount, resulting in a cost savings of $50,000. At the end of FY2014, Subscription D will be assessed using the same methodology to determine if it will be renewed the following year. At this time, we are also investigating a number of marketing initiatives to promote content and will monitor usage rates to determine if there are noticeable changes over the next twelve months.

E-Books in the Science and Engineering Library

The Science and Engineering Library Division (SEL) at CUL was once comprised of eight different libraries. Over the past few years there have been a series of library closures, with the most recent being the closure of the Engineering Library in June of 2014, bringing the total to four libraries. The closures have physically reduced library space and have forced the consolidation of a majority of print books to off-site storage. In addition, these closures coupled with the strong acceptance of electronic content by faculty and students have made SEL the perfect subject for e-book development. There is now a preference policy to purchase electronically when available. This in turn has led to the desire to learn how cost effective electronic collections are and if new models of purchasing would be beneficial.

In recent years, the SEL has moved away from subject specialist roles to focus on a functional role structure. This structure will allow our positions to evolve in a seamless manner

regardless of how the landscape at SEL changes in the coming years. While there are still purchasing and liaison responsibilities related to specific subjects, librarian roles focus on division wide functions. For example, in May 2014 a new position was created to focus on collection assessment and analysis of materials for the entire science division. This new position allows for the designation of much needed time towards the evaluation of our large collection of electronic and print content.

With regards to electronic content, increased cost trends that are inconsistent with library budgets provided the catalyst for initiating the new role. There needed to be a systematic and concentrated effort on assessment to ensure collections warranted purchase and were seen as valuable to the collection. Thus this position allows for the justification of purchases as well as cancellations. Moreover, continued analysis is beneficial in maintaining quality curation of collections. It can highlight under-utilized content as well as reaffirm valuable resources. In-depth looks at electronic content can even point to discovery or access issues, thus addressing silent threats.

The first assessment project for this role analyzed several subscription based e-book packages from one vendor (Vendor A). Vendor A provides access to over forty e-book subject collections. In 2014, CUL subscribed to eleven of these collections. Over the past few years each collection has seen a four to seven per cent cost increase annually, and overall usage of these e-books dipped in 2013. It was also noted that Vendor A reserves the right to drop content from collections without adjusting the price. Instead, they add content which is not always comparable. Before renewing these subscriptions, we needed to find out if each collection was still worthwhile for our library. We decided to conduct a cost analysis to prove or disprove benefit.

We were able to acquire usage data from COUNTER compliant BR2 reports posted on Vendor A's admin site, which aligns with our preference mandate to collect standardized data sets. When we compared usage statistics against fund data gathered from Voyager, we found that the eleven collections seemed like a good deal with a low cost per use ($2.24), which is in line with comparable electronic subscriptions at CUL. However, we also needed to account for the fact that CUL does not subscribe to the eleven collections from Vendor A in one lump sum, but rather subscribes to each on an individual basis.

During assessment, we also discovered a 27% overlap of titles across the eleven collections we subscribe to from Vendor A. This per cent overlap increased between each package and some overlap reached as high as 66 per cent. Upon further investigation, we also found that this content overlapped with titles available through other e-book platforms at CUL. This discovery prompted a deeper analysis of content available through Vendor A, and we discovered a long tail of use with a handful of titles receiving heavy use and the majority receiving low (in many cases zero) uses. In total, our patrons used approximately 25% of collection content. Although this is a common trend in e-book subscriptions, we flagged the collections for further investigation nonetheless.

We also noticed that the cost per use for each collection ranged from $.38 to $11.21. While some collections were well worth the purchase price, others seemed to be far too high a cost. After breaking down the purchases, there were three collections highlighted as questionable (see Tables 2 and 3).

These findings were presented to our colleagues in SEL as well as ERUDWG for discussion. Open conversations with these groups helped us to further analyze the subscriptions and compile feedback that was presented to Vendor A. As a group, we decided to cancel the two lowest used collections and we negotiated a flat percentage increase for two years with the remaining nine collections. With the flat price increase, we will see a savings of $10,000 annually and believe these collections will be sustainable and cost effective going forward.

Conclusion: Library as Advocate and Negotiator

Our findings demonstrate that standardized usage reporting in the form of COUNTER reports are

	Vendor A Subscription	Questionable Packages		
		Package F	Package J	Package K
# of Titles in Database	9161	717	713	238
# of Titles Overlapped	2444	471	241	121
% of Overlap	27%	66%	34%	51%

Table 2. Results of the overlap analysis for Vendor A (FY2013).

	Vendor A Subscription	Questionable Packages		
		Package F	Package J	Package K
Cost	$ 50,000.00	$ 6,000.00	$ 3,000.00	$ 2,500.00
Unique Usage	22324	841	351	223
% Used	25%	27%	11%	21%
Cost Per Use	$ 2.24	$ 7.13	$ 8.55	$ 11.21

Table 3. Recalculated results of the cost and usage analysis for Vendor A based on BR2 COUNTER data (FY2013).

beneficial to the assessment of collections. The reports allow "the usage of online information products and services to be measured in a credible, consistent and compatible way using vendor-generated data" (ProjectCOUNTER, 2012, p. 1). Information such as title, publication year, and unique identifiers like DOI help librarians understand the genuine usage patterns at their institutions. When vendors are compliant with COUNTER it makes assessment more manageable and meaningful by standardizing what is considered use. Therefore, we are no longer comparing apples to oranges but rather apples to apples.

The decisions that were made using this assessment methodology will not only affect our budgets but also the content in our collections. We learned that it is important to present data and findings to library divisions as well as committees or working groups to weigh options and provide feedback. Different viewpoints can point out issues that may have been initially excluded from assessment plans. In addition, discussing findings can increase awareness of initiatives, such as marketing collections to promote discovery, which may result in greater buy-in from stakeholders, thus increasing the value of e-book collections.

The idea that the term "librarian" is not synonymous with "negotiator" must be changed. We need be our own advocates, make informed decisions, and demand change if change is needed. Large price increases that are inconsistent with subscription use should not be tolerated. Assessment projects such as the one described in this paper, prove the true value of resources and can be effectively used to negotiate acceptable price tags based on use.

The reality that the e-book landscape is constantly evolving was factored into decisions regarding the overarching assessment framework. The research design was created so that it can be replicated regardless of how e-books evolve in the coming years. Because the design is flexible and adaptive in nature, it promotes continued assessment, evaluation, and strategic planning as a regular component of e-book programs. This study proves that this methodology can be used on varying collection sizes and provides actionable results.

In closing, systematic and routine assessment of collections is important in determining the true value of resources for our user community. It is imperative to make informed decisions when negotiating renewals rather than passing the "buck." We hope that the experiences and findings outlined through this paper will help others implement an assessment program at their institution.

Acknowledgments

We would like to thank Daisy Alcron at Columbia University for her assistance with data collection from Voyager, Serial Solutions, and COUNTER usage reports.

References

Columbia University Libraries. (2010, January). *Strategic plan, 2010–2013*. Retrieved from https://culis.columbia.edu/content/ dam/staffweb/admin/strategicplanning/ 2010 –2013/CULIS_Strategic_Plan_2010–20131.pdf

Davies, T., & Morgan, M. (2013). E-books down under. *Proceedings of the Charleston Library Conference*. http://dx.doi.org/10.5703/1288284315253

ProjectCOUNTER (2012, April). *The COUNTER Code of practice for e-resources: Release 4*. Retrieved from http://www.projectcounter.org/r4/COPR4.pdf

E-Book Rights: Advocacy in Action

Katy Gabrio, Macalester College
Whitney Murphy, MyiLibrary/Ingram Content Group

Abstract

E-book rights advocacy efforts began nearly from the moment the format appeared. The topics have evolved over time but significant issues and the need for ongoing discussion and negotiation remain. To this end, Macalester College published an E-Book Advocacy Statement in 2013. Since then several libraries have signed on. Most importantly, productive conversations with e-book providers and vendors have ensued. These conversations have led to a better understanding of the library, publisher, and e-book provider points of view as well as helped strengthen library/vendor relationships that are rooted in a willingness to deeply engage on these topics while appreciating one another's knowledge, needs, and realities that may serve as a launching point for positive change. The paper summarizes the statement's genesis and an open dialog between Macalester and a representative from Ingram's MyiLibrary discussing the terms of the statement from both points of view. Even though the parties do not agree on all issues, and the library is not actively purchasing e-books, both have committed to continually learning together so that in time we will both be able to fully meet the needs of our organizations and communities.

Background

Macalester is a small liberal arts college in St. Paul, Minnesota. Most of our students live on campus, although a large percentage of students study abroad at some point in their time here at Macalester. The majority of our classes are taught on campus. So far Macalester has offered a single online course to its students. Although we are a small college, as a library one of our aims is to provide our patrons with a research library experience by connecting students, faculty, and staff to the resources they need to be successful with their scholarship and teaching. We use a variety of methods to do this and interlibrary loan plays a large role in this effort.

Over the last few years we began to notice a few things that prompted us to have more conversations about our e-book collections. We had begun acquiring a significant amount of e-reference materials. We also began circulating Kindles and iPads as well as seeing more and more devices being used by our community. We noted an increase in the number of ILL lending and borrowing requests for e-books—all of which were denied primarily because of licensing restrictions, but also due to undeveloped or cumbersome procedures for facilitating such loans. We were also receiving questions from confused patrons and library staff about how to access e-books they discovered in our catalog. At that point we formed a small group in the library to begin looking more closely at issues surrounding e-books—primarily getting a better handle on how to access the e-books we had, educating ourselves about the licensing restrictions for each collection and learning more in general about the different business models in the marketplace.

Our consortium also began conversations with Ingram about opportunities for the eight schools to share e-books on the MyiLibrary platform. While it looked like a possibility at the outset, we quickly realized the complexities involved, as we would need to work on agreements with each individual publisher for every title we wanted to share. The consortium changed our approach and began engaging publishers (instead of platform providers) in conversations about basing e-book pricing for the consortium by looking at us as one institution with an FTE equivalent to our combined FTE instead of looking at us as eight separate institutions and requiring us each to buy an individual license to the e-book.

Finally, one of our colleagues came back from a Charleston Conference and reported on conversations at the conference where many libraries mentioned that they are not displaying holdings for their e-books in OCLC. This spurred more discussion among our group at Macalester. If all libraries are building collections that we no longer set holdings for in OCLC, what impact does this have on the services we offer and how we provide our patrons access to content? Does our aim to provide a research library experience for our patrons have a future in an environment where libraries are building collections of materials that they cannot lend?

Macalester's E-Book Rights Advocacy Standards

(http://www.macalester.edu/library /changingebooksforlibraries/index.html)

As we asked ourselves these questions our focus began to shift. Our initial intention was to educate ourselves about the e-book collections we had and clarify how we were able to use and provide access to those collections. Educating ourselves was important, but the group also felt drawn towards the role of advocate. Our next step was to identify the issues for which we were advocating. This resulted in a list of twelve standards (listed immediately below) to which we are asking publishers to adhere. We plan to give preference to publishers who most fully meet these standards and we do not plan to invest heavily in building an e-book collection until the e-book marketplace provides us the option to build a collection that helps us to fulfill our mission as a library to act in the public good by enabling access to information.

We have used the advocacy document as a tool to start conversations with colleagues at other libraries, publishers, and content providers. MyiLibrary is one of the content providers that we have engaged in conversation with about this topic.

The Standards

1. Libraries must be able to lend the entire contents of e-books to other libraries in a manner that is not cumbersome to our operations and patrons.

2. Electronic transfer of content between libraries should be permitted to facilitate efficiencies and minimization of paper usage.

3. Libraries should be able to control the parameters of circulation functions: loan periods, renewals, recalls, etc. This includes libraries limiting access to a single user at a time if the content is not authorized for multisimultaneous users.

4. There should be no limits and no additional costs related to the number of times an e-book can be accessed over time.

5. There should be options for archival and perpetual access. This could be accomplished by license agreements, facilitated through a third party, or by selling content outright to libraries.

6. Content should be downloadable and accessible on multiple, standard-use platforms and devices.

7. No patron data should be used or shared if it allows for the identification of an individual without the individual's permission.

8. Libraries should have the option to purchase titles individually, separate from a bundled package.

9. An option for allowing unlimited simultaneous users, for short-term or long-term periods of time, should be offered at fair prices.

10. Copy, paste, and print functionality should be available.

11. Accompanying metadata should be allowable in library systems and discovery layers.

12. Meet ADA accessibility requirements, including allowing the use of text-to-speech engines.

Ingram Content Group Background

Ingram Content Group is a private, family-owned company that has been in the book business for almost 50 years. Ingram is a progressive company that got its start as a textbook depository but has grown and transformed to become the leader in our industry. As the world's largest and most trusted distributor of physical and digital content, Ingram is committed to developing technology solutions that make physical and electronic books available to readers around the world.

The MyiLibrary e-book platform began in 2004, as a web-based portal for academic libraries in the UK. Ingram acquired MyiLibrary in 2006 and MyiLibrary continued to grow, first to US libraries and then worldwide. Today, MyiLibrary serves over 3,000 libraries worldwide, from academic to public and offers more than 530,000 active titles.

MyiLibrary continues to help libraries develop innovative ways to deliver e-books as well as assisting libraries with their community initiatives. Through ongoing strategic discussions with forward-thinking institutions, such as Macalester College, MyiLibrary will continue to offer the premier e-book experience in the library market.

Summary from Conversation with Attendees

This Lively (Lunch) Discussion session offered an opportunity to demonstrate ways library staff could engage publishers and content providers in conversation about issues that are of importance to their library. The session also provided an environment for all attendees to share ideas, priorities and concerns about the current e-book marketplace. Below is a summary of the conversation that took place with the session attendees.

Option to Purchase Titles Individually, Separate from a Bundled Package

From the library perspective, we believe that it is important to have options when selecting and providing content for our patrons, especially while budgets continue to remain very tight. Journal publishers have figured this out over time. For example, libraries have options to provide their patrons access to article content via subscriptions to individual print and/or electronic journals,

subscriptions to bundled journal packages, and aggregated content in databases and via interlibrary loan and/or pay-per-view. Each library can determine which options best meets the needs of their community as well as the demands of their budget. Are e-books such a different animal that we have to treat them vastly differently? Or can e-book models be built on some variation of these journal models?

Many academic libraries also enlist the expertise of departmental faculty to select materials for the collection that best support the curriculum and their research. With bundled packages we lose that freedom along with scarce collection dollars by paying for individual titles we want as well as many other titles that we would not normally select for our collection.

In addition, libraries have internal considerations to puzzle through, which include implementing a decision tree for staff that do the actual ordering of content. Policies for selecting which format and/or business model to purchase need to be considered when developing an effective decision tree, so that the library is getting the right value for its expenditures.

Some publishers are already offering DRM-free content with the ability to lend entire e-books via interlibrary loan if you purchase bundled collections hosted on their platform. However, if a library wants to select title-by-title, the individual titles are hosted on a different platform that usually has more restrictive DRM. So by selecting title-by-title you lose the DRM-free environment and the ability to lend these titles. We understand that managing the business end of title-by-title selection is complex and takes some investment on the publisher's end to the degree that it may prohibit the publisher from providing title-by-title-selection on their DRM-free platform.

Technology continues to be developed that allows for a more graceful way to "chunk" e-book content, so that e-books can be broken down and offered on a chapter-level basis. This technology encourages flexibility in usage, which is married nicely to the "e" format.

Again, for libraries, it comes down to having options. We are seeing an increased use of our e-book titles. Some faculty are using these titles in their courses as one of the textbooks. Some of the e-books are highlighted during a library instruction class and see higher use immediately after an instruction session. The technology allows for unlimited simultaneous users. We believe it makes sense to provide it as an option and we are willing to pay a fair price for it.

From the side of the content provider, we see that the explosion in e-book popularity has really changed the landscape surrounding e-book lending and acquisition. In balancing the shift from "p" to "e," arriving at the fairest price is not always a simple calculation. In order to help the dialogue, libraries may consider providing as much information as possible, which includes usage, concurrent users, and estimated duration. At times, when trying to negotiate between library and publisher, we are literally starting from scratch, which makes the dialogue more extended and not as productive.

Related to this topic is the need for improved metadata and more transparency, provided by e-book providers (either aggregators or direct from publishers), so that libraries are full aware of any restrictions in purchasing and providing access to the content. Having clearly defined remarks regarding the usage make it easier for libraries to buy what they need and to help reduce confusion among their patrons and staff.

No Limits and No Additional Costs Related to the Number of Times an E-book Can Be Accessed Over Time

The e-book marketplace is still in flux. Publishers and content providers are trying out different models to determine which is "the one." In the print environment there is a revenue stream due to purchasing of replacement copies. There is no equivalent need to purchase replacements in the electronic environment. We understand that this may cause publishers to be more cautious about the business models they offer. However, we do not believe that it makes sense to price the content in the electronic format based on the limitations of the print format.

We also recognize that publishers are trying to develop inventive sales models, in order to address the unique complexities associated with e-books. So, as the market matures and trends develop, we believe that publishers and libraries will find more common ground, with respect to e-book pricing, so that all sides feel that they are getting the right value for e-books.

Ability to Lend the Entire Contents of E-books to Other Libraries in a Manner That is Not Cumbersome to Our Operations and Patrons

As a library we see lending content to other libraries as part of our mission—acting in the public good to enable access to information. Due to space and budget constraints, we depend heavily on interlibrary loan to help support our community's teaching and research needs. As more and more libraries spend larger portions of our collection budgets on e-book collections, we are creating a silo of resources that can no longer be shared with patrons outside of our institution. This has significant implications on how we serve our patrons as well as for the role libraries play in the community at large.

Some publishers are allowing us to lend entire e-books electronically via interlibrary loan. There is work underway to develop tools to make this process more streamlined and efficient. We have seen and experienced proof that this can indeed happen and we are hopeful that in time more and more publishers will be comfortable with including the right to lend entire e-books via interlibrary loan in their license agreements.

Conclusion

It was clear that many libraries, publishers, and content providers are still wrapping their arms around e-book business models and licensing terms. There are many pieces to sort through, but we believe that with open and respectful conversations among library staff, publishers and content providers we will continue to find more common ground to help all parties best meet the needs of their communities and organizations.

.

Are E-Book Big Deal Bundles Still Valuable?

Aaron K. Shrimplin, Miami University Libraries
Jennifer W. Bazeley, Miami University Libraries

Abstract

The academic e-book market has undergone significant change in the last five years. E-book availability has greatly increased as library demand has grown, with an increasing percentage of library acquisitions preferring electronic rather than print format. E-book acquisition models like patron-driven acquisition and short-term loan have now become commonplace and available from a multitude of consortia, publishers, and aggregators. With the wide availability of these models, is there still value in buying e-books through package deals?

To help answer this question, we will present the results of a usage-based analysis of Wiley e-books. Since 2012, Miami University Libraries have purchased Wiley e-book collections through a consortial OhioLINK contract. Previously purchased OhioLINK e-book collections have been accessible to patrons through both OhioLINK's Electronic Book Center platform and the publisher platform. The Wiley e-book purchase deviates from previous practice by being available to patrons only on the publisher platform and our analysis is therefore focused on COUNTER e-book usage reports from the Wiley platform. We also augment the usage data with title-level information, such as subject and book type. This preliminary study focuses on the 2012 Wiley collection and its use over a three-year period (2012-2014) and will include data-driven findings presented in visually useful ways.

Introduction

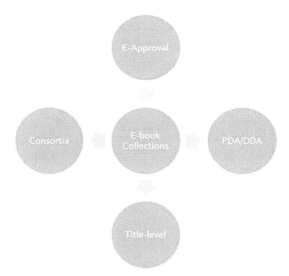

Figure 1. Acquisitions models.

Miami University Libraries have been purchasing e-book packages through the OhioLINK consortium since 2008. In 2010, when the patron-driven acquisition (PDA) model became widely available for e-books, Miami began experimenting with that purchase model locally. Following the success of PDA purchases, librarians were given the ability to firm order e-books on a title by title basis from ebrary and EBSCOhost. Purchasing models and options continued to expand in early 2014 with the addition of e-book approvals in the science and social science approval plans, as well as the addition of additional e-book platforms to our firm order buying options (JSTOR, Cambridge University Press, and Project Muse).

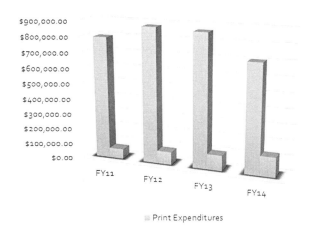

Table 1. Print versus electronic book expenditures.

This graph represents Miami's expenditures on print and electronic books (local only; not consortial purchases) over four fiscal years. While we have seen an increase in e-book purchases over four years, we only saw a comparable decline in print book purchases in the last two years. The slowness of this change is due in part to waiting for easier and more efficient workflows for e-book purchasing through our third party vendor, YBP.

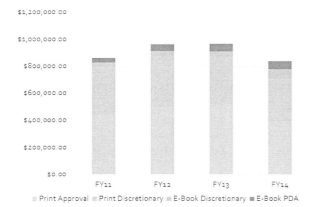

Table 2. Total book expenditures by order type.

This graph compares total expenditures in four different purchase models over four fiscal years. While e-book purchase models have grown over four years, there is more significant growth in e-book PDA and discretionary purchases between fiscal year 2013 and 2014. Users and librarians are becoming more comfortable with selecting and using e-books, and a greater number of titles are becoming available in electronic and print format simultaneously.

The Big Deal Approach

The OhioLINK consortium has purchased large e-book packages from Springer, Wiley, and Oxford University Press over the last several years. In previous analyses, the presenters have analyzed Springer and Oxford University Press e-book use. Because the Wiley e-book package is the newest of our consortial e-book purchases (2012-2014), analysis of Wiley e-books was on hold until three years of data became available. The question which arises from all three analyses is whether the e-book package is still a viable purchase model. Note that the Wiley e-book platform has no digital rights management (DRM) and is packaged by

section or chapter as PDFs. Wiley e-books are unlimited user. Also note that usage data for Wiley e-books requires some clean-up due to the presence of usage for free content included along with usage for subscribed or owned content.

Methodology

This study presents the results of a usage-based analysis of Wiley e-books. Beginning in 2012, Miami University Libraries have purchased Wiley e-book collections through a consortial OhioLINK contract. Previously purchased OhioLINK e-book collections (e.g., Springer and Oxford University Press) have been accessible to patrons through both OhioLINK's Electronic Book Center (EBC) platform and the publisher platform. The Wiley e-book purchase deviates from previous practice by being available to users only on the publishers platform. This preliminary study focuses on the 2012 Wiley collection (927 titles) and its use over a three-year period (2012 through July 2014). Usage data are compiled using standard COUNTER BR2 reports. The COUNTER compliant data are merged with a e-book title list available from the Wiley platform. Merging the two data sources together provides us with additional title level information such as subject information and cost. Usage analysis is done using SPSS and Microsoft Excel. Data-driven findings are presented in visually useful ways a variety of tools, including R (a free software programming language) and Adobe Photoshop.

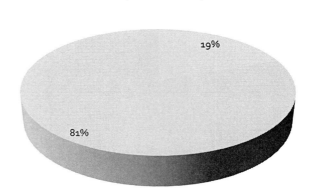

Table 3. Title use 2012-2014.

Findings

Of 927 e-books, 19% had use and 81% had no use.

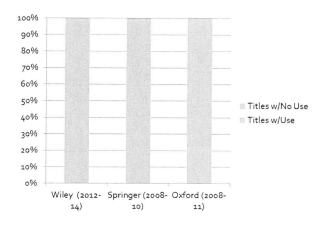

Table 4. Title use comparison.

Analyses of all three consortially purchased e-book packages show very similar usage percentages that hover just above or below the 20% mark.

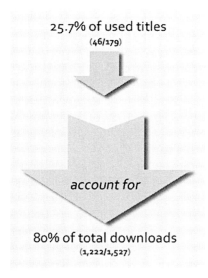

Figure 2. Pareto Principle.

Of the total titles that saw use in the Wiley e-book package (179), 46 of them (or 25.7%) accounted for 80% of the total downloads. This 80/20 split, also known as the Pareto Principle, is evident across packages, and across different analyses.

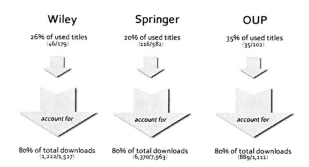

Figure 3. Pareto comparison.

Springer e-books (and to a lesser extent, Oxford University Press e-books), also showed an adherence to the Pareto Principle when examining how many e-books accounted for total downloads.

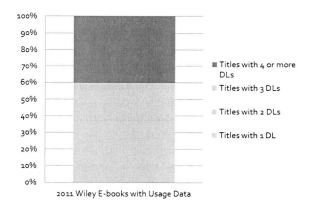

Table 5. Long tail.

Wiley e-books with a publication date of 2011 showed a few high-use titles as well as a long tail of titles that only had 1 download.

Figure 4. Few high-use titles dominate.

Like previous findings (Springer e-books, in particular), several of the highest use titles are clearly textbooks or textbook-like in nature. Given the high cost of textbooks, this high usage is expected, and it's possible that publishers will find a way to capitalize on the use of books like this within packages.

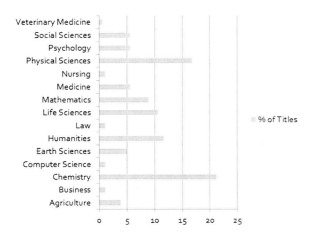

Table 6. Titles with usage by subject.

Titles with usage by subject correlates both to subject areas that are very highly represented in Wiley (STEM) as well as the disciplines that are very research-intensive at Miami University (social sciences, psychology, physical sciences, life sciences, chemistry).

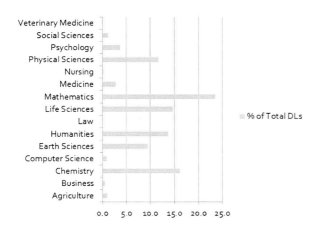

Table 7. Percentage of total downloads by subject.

The percentage of total downloads by subject correlates somewhat with research-intensive subject areas at Miami University, and perhaps also with the subjects that rely more heavily on monographs than on journals (mathematics).

Value Proposition

The cost of the Wiley e-book package for Miami University is not commensurate with the usage. However, like other e-book packages, the bundle of titles enjoys a better value over time. Owning this e-book content in perpetuity means we are prepared for the "just-in-case" usage scenario over many years. However, it has become more difficult to justify this type of reasoning as budgets remain flat or shrink, and package costs rise.

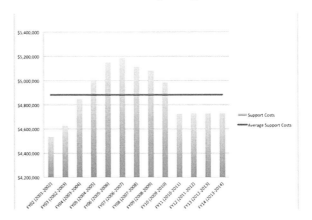

Table 8. Miami University Libraries budget.

Miami University Libraries have had a flat budget since FY11 and remain below a thirteen year average.

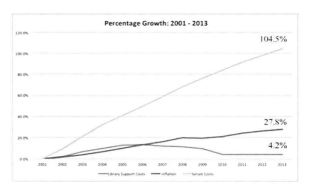

Table 9. Percentage growth.

The rapid rise of serials costs along with nearly flat library budgets year after year result in a significant erosion of purchasing power.

Cost per download for these e-books is very high, at approximately $30 per download. High-use titles that are textbooks or used as textbooks obviously have a better value than other monographs in the collection, but their high-use does not give a lot of additional value to the package as a whole. If Miami University were to purchase the 179 titles with use at list price (approximately $29,588), we would still be further ahead than we are in purchasing the package.

Conclusion

Milton Friedman was found of saying "what is unsustainable will not be sustained." Our analysis of 927 Wiley e-books over a two-and-a-half-year time frame finds 81% of the titles were not used by library patrons. Of those titles that were used, 25.7% account for 80% of all downloads. We also find that a few high-use titles dominate usage and the long tail accounts for a very small percentage of the total downloads. Miami University is known for it's exceptional undergraduate teaching and learning, so it makes that textbooks or books used as textbooks are in high demand relative to other titles available in the 2012 Wiley e-book collection. Demand does vary across subject areas, allowing for the possiblility to preference some subject areas over others in future negotiations. Preliminary results of this study suggest that e-book collections do underperform as an asset class. Flat budgets and rising serials costs contribute to an erosion of purchasing power. This "new normal" has made it more difficult to justify the acquisition of e-books that demonstrate little to no use.

Collection Development, E-Resources, and Meeting the Needs of People With Disabilities

Axel Schmetzke, University of Wisconsin – Stevens Point
Cheryl Pruitt, California State University
Michele Bruno, Cengage Learning

Abstract

Access barriers do not only exist in the physical environment but also online. Just as certain architectural design features make it possible, or impossible, for people with certain disabilities to move about independently, so does design of the electronic environment, which includes all the library e-resources, creates either enabling or disabling conditions for certain individuals. Recently conducted research reveals a rather grim picture: while policy statements issued by professional library organization call for inclusive selection and procurement procedures, books on collection development do not cover the issue adequately. When librarians make decision about the selection of specific e-resources, the needs of people with disabilities are rarely on their radar screen. Collection development policies requiring conformance to established accessibility standards, Section 508 and WCAG 2.0, are the exception rather than the rule. One of the exceptions is California State University (CSU). Driven by CSU policy, a systemwide Accessible Technology Initiative has been put into place to remove access barriers over time. Profit driven database vendors such as Cengage Learning are extremely sensitive to what current and prospective customers want. Responding to demands for accessible products, the company seeks to conform to WCAG 2.0. For efforts to continue, it is important that vendors hear from their customers. Generally speaking, vendors appreciate specific suggestions on how to improve their product. As with all suggestions, prioritization is a matter of competing pressures. The more often vendors hear about certain issues, the more likely these are to gain priority over competing demands.

Introduction

Access barriers do not only exist in the physical environment but also online. Just as certain architectural design features make it possible, or impossible, for people with certain disabilities to move about independently, so do certain design components in the electronic environment, which includes all the library e-resources, create either enabling or disabling conditions for individuals. Hence, when librarians get together and decide to procure a specific online information resource, they not only determine what new content is to be put out there, but also (often unknowingly) who will, and will not, have access to this content.

In order to create an accessible online environment, it is important that librarians

- Adopt a policy in which accessibility is included among the selection criteria.

- Actually consider accessibility during the selection process.

- Inquire about product accessibility when communicating with vendors.

- Provide feedback to vendors about the reasons why a product got selected or not (especially if accessibility was a factor).

Librarians might also want to

- Add an accessibility requirement to the licensing agreement.

- Collaborate with the assistive technology unit on their campus to obtain a vendor-independent assessment of a product accessibility/usability.

Accessibility Awareness among Collection Developers

Several professional library organizations have recognized the need to include accessibility among the criteria to be considered during the selection process or to address it in the licensing language. For example, in 2009, the American Library Association (ALA) Council issued a resolution demanding that "all libraries purchasing, procuring, and contracting for electronic resources and services require vendors to certify that they comply with Section 508 regulations, Web Content Accessibility Guidelines 2.0, or other criteria that become widely accepted as standards of accessibility evolve." ARL endorses model licensing language "designed to permit libraries to make content in their collections fully accessible." The same organization also published a *Report of the ARL Joint Task Force on Services to Patrons with Print Disabilities* (2012), which urges libraries to exercise their buying power to motivate vendors to make their product more accessible and suggests that including "language in publisher and vendor contracts specifically addressing accessibility requirements could have a significant impact if broadly adopted."

Unfortunately, recent research indicates that consideration for the needs of people with disabilities is the exception, rather than the rule, when collection decisions are made. While no data are available that would show whether the collection development courses taught at our nation's library schools cover this aspect of selection, a recent content analysis of pertinent books on the subject reveals that, for the most part, its readers—students enrolled in collection development classes as well as already practicing librarians—are unlikely to receive adequate guidance (Schmetzke, in preparation). Of the 46 books included in the study, published between 2000 and 2014, only 19 address the issue of accessibility at all, and there is no clear indication that things have improved over time. Among these 19 books, Jacobs (2007) stands out in that it includes a whole chapter on "The Electronic Resources (ER) Librarian & Patrons with Disabilities" (Riley, 2007). The remaining 18 books do not address accessibility consistently or in sufficient depth, or include mistakes indicating the authors' unfamiliarity with the subject. A few examples shall suffice here to illustrate this point:

The book by Curtis (2004) is laudable in that it contains a three-page section on "Serving users with Disabilities, covering equipment, accessibility standards, and product compliance." However, Curtis disappoints when she includes a sample of an "E-Journal Collection Policy for Paid Subscription" which lists only aspects of accessibility that have nothing to do with the absence of barriers for people with disabilities (e.g., accessible by IP recognition, accessible to walk-in library users, easy to print and download). In Wikoff's (2012) book, this inconsistency goes the other way. While the author includes "ADA-friendly" among the selection criteria in his sample policy, she does not explain its inclusion in either of the two pertinent chapters: "Acquiring Electronic Resources" (Chapter 2) and "Evaluating E-Resources" (Chapter 6).

Evans and Saponaro (2012) acknowledge a potential conflict between DRM and accessibility, but without explaining it. Elsewhere in their book, when discussing the needs of users with disabilities, the authors seem to lack an understanding of the concept of barrier-free, universal design; their suggestion for fund allocation planning implies that access issues involving digital materials and library websites are to be solved through human assistance. Awareness concerning the importance of universal design, which would foster independence and render human assistance unnecessary, is also lacking in Gregory's (2011) work. Her two-page discussion of ADA-related issues focuses exclusively on alternative formats, such as large print and video, various hardware and software, and the services offered by the National Library for the Blind and Physically Handicapped. Johnson (2013) mistakenly considers Section 508 to be part of the American with Disabilities Act (p. 30).

In light of the inadequacy observed in the literature, it comes as no surprise that, with a few exceptions, the needs of people with disabilities tend not to get considered at academic libraries when the procurement of specific online resources (e-books and online databases) is discussed. At least this is the picture drawn from survey data collected from the libraries at Public

Liberal Arts Colleges (COPLAC) institutions (Schmetzke, unpublished data, 2013). Of the 24 libraries included, on campuses with an enrolment between 1,600 and 6,500 full-time students, only one library, Sonoma State University, had a collection development policy that addressed accessibility among its selection criteria. At some libraries accessibility had been considered at least once during the selection process despite the lack of an adequate policy guiding them to do so. However, the number—seven—was relatively small. A survey of the libraries on comprehensive campuses within the UW system—10 of 11 participating—showed a more positive picture: Four of the 10 libraries had a collection policy with an accessibility component. Three of the six remaining libraries reported that accessibility was considered at least once when having selected e-resources.

To summarize this section: while the survey data cannot be generalized, they suggest that accessibility tends to be overlooked during the selection of e-resources at small-to-medium libraries—even though there are some pockets, where accessibility is clearly on the radar screen, such as at Sonoma State University, which is part of the California State University to be discussed in more detail in the next section, and within the University of Wisconsin system. This situation exists despite the policy guidance issued in recent years by a number of different professional library organizations. The dissatisfactory manner in which accessibility for people with disability tends to get addressed in the collection development/ management literature is probably a contributing factor. Books on collection development, often used as textbooks to guide practicing librarians and to train the next generation of librarians, do not cover the issue adequately, if they address it at all.

Accessibility Efforts at California State University

The California State University (CSU) is comprised of 23 unique campuses located throughout the state of California. Student enrollment of all campuses is approximately 450,000 students and amongst this population, there are over 13,500 verified students with disabilities enrolled as well (*Services*, 2014).

It is the policy of the CSU to make information technology resources and services accessible to all students, faculty, staff, and the general public regardless of disability (Reed, 2004). Eliminating access barriers in electronic and information technology (EIT) benefits all people, not only persons with a disability. For example, providing captioned videos can help students with differing learning styles or English as a second language (ESL) learners (Collins, 2013; Morales, 2013). Furthermore, the cost to provide accommodations for students, faculty, staff, or the general public often can be reduced or even eliminated by considering accessibility at the time of purchase.

In 2006, the CSU Accessible Technology Initiative (ATI) was established to target the elimination of accessibility barriers with a focus in three areas: web-based resources, instructional materials, and the procurement of all resources to support teaching and learning. The CSU ATI implementation guidance articulates key strategies, which include establishing strong administrative/executive support, ensuring continuous quality improvement, prioritizing projects/activities, identifying specific goals/success indicators, documenting each campus's progress, and driving vendor improvements to product accessibility support (Smith, 2013).

The ATI implementation activities take place on individual campuses and throughout the CSU system. In order to support the CSU system, the ATI office has established the CSU Accessible Technology Network (ATN) which leverages campus experts across the system who work together to provide accessibility services and consultation.

Selection of systemwide ATI implementation activities are driven by impact of the activity on the campus population and weak areas shared by several campuses as identified in the CSU ATI Annual Reporting process. One area that was originally identified as high impact and a challenge for campuses was the procurement of accessible

EIT products. As a result, the CSU Accessible Procurement Process was developed as a collaborative effort among stakeholders from six CSU campuses and the Chancellor's Office as part of a systemwide effort to integrate accessibility requirements into a standardized accessible procurement process that could be adopted or adapted by each of the 23 CSU campuses.

Key success factors for establishing an accessible procurement process begins with gaining and sustaining campus executive-level support and hiring or appointing an ATI Coordinator or ATI Project Manager. The accessible procurement process includes four major process steps to integrate accessibility into the existing procurement process, the establishment of eight campus roles with associated responsibilities, and standardized forms for information collection and documentation of the process verifying that key accessible considerations are addressed during the procurement process (Professional, 2009).

Applying the CSU Accessible Procurement Process to the acquisition of accessible library materials would alert the vendors of the needs to serve students with disabilities with their products. A typical procurement process could be the following:

A librarian assumes the role of the purchase requester. The purchase requester selects the most accessible library acquisition that meets their functional requirements. This is documented by the purchase requester completing the EIT Pre-purchase form which lists the technical and functional requirements, intended users of the product, and also includes the results of any market research done to compare suitable products. The purchase requester is also responsible for obtaining any product accessibility documentation (e.g. Voluntary Product Accessibility Template (VPAT), test results that verify the claims on the VPAT, and Accessibility Statement). The completed Pre-purchase form and the accessibility documentation are then submitted to the campus ATI Coordinator for review.

The ATI Coordinator then initiates the EIT Review form which collects information to help the

coordinator to determine product impact on students based on information in the Pre-purchase form and then determines the type of product review (e.g. VPAT review, Vendor Demonstration of accessibility features, Automated Testing, Manual Testing, or Code Review).

It has been the experience of the CSU that the review usually uncovers accessibility issues that are not addressed in the VPAT. Based on the results of the review, the ATI Coordinator will request an updated VPAT and an Accessibility Roadmap from the vendor. The purpose of the Accessibility Roadmap is to have the vendor prepare a remediation plan that addresses the accessibility issues with a timeline for repair. The updated VPAT and Accessibility Roadmap are used by the ATI Coordinator, Purchase Requester, and Disability Services to create an Equally Effective Alternate Access Plan (EEAAP) to seamlessly serve students who may be adversely affected by product accessibility barriers.

Frequently, the vendor requests a meeting to discuss updating the VPAT and preparing the Accessibility Roadmap. The CSU/vendor meetings have been very successful in educating vendors about the impact of accessibility barriers on students, the importance of a timely product remediation schedule, and the importance of accurate accessibility documentation for the preparation of the EEAAP.

The CSU Accessible Procurement Process can be successfully applied to select the most accessible product that meets the needs of all users. On occasion a product cannot be purchased until significant accessibility barriers are removed by the vendor. In many instances commitments by the vendor to remove barriers and the preparation of a campus EEAAP are sufficient to allow the purchase to be made. Product accessibility improvements made as result of this process are benefiting all campus users.

The CSU Accessible Technology Network is currently using this process to review the CSU systemwide library core collection contract renewals. The goal of the CSU ATN library acquisitions review is to raise the level of accessibility of library resources across several large vendors.

Librarians who are making collection purchasing decisions can apply parts of this process even if their campus does not have a formal accessible technology effort. During the purchasing process librarians can ask questions about accessibility, require a VPAT, ask for a demonstration of the product that includes how the product works with assistive technology, and work with the purchasing department to include accessibility requirements in contracts. These actions will send a strong message to vendors that accessibility is required and serving all students is part of the campus mission.

A Publisher's Perspective on Accessibility

Not all e-resource vendors address accessibility equally. This section describes, within a historical framework, the accessibility features and services provided by one of the leading companies in this area, Cengage Learning.

Cengage Learning is a leading provider of innovative teaching, learning and research solutions for the academic, professional and library markets worldwide. Its products and services are designed to foster academic excellence and professional development, increase student engagement, improve learning outcomes and deliver authoritative information to people whenever and wherever they need it. Through its unique position within both the library and academic markets, Cengage Learning provides integrated learning solutions that bridge the library to the classroom. In addition to Gale, Cengage Learning brands include Brooks/Cole, Course Technology, Delmar, Heinle, South-Western, Wadsworth, among others.

Prior to the accessible e-book revolution, when the company received a request from a customer on behalf of a student with a print disability, it provided the textbook source file upon request, at no cost. As with most information technology, the format that customers asked for changed over time. In the late 90s, ASCII files were the most requested format. They were copied onto compact discs and dropped in the mail. The

customer would typically receive the CD in about 14 days. By 2003, the demand for ASCII format had dropped, while Word became the most requested format with a notable increase in the number of requests for students with print disabilities. In 2008, PDF saw a sharp uptick as the most requested textbook source file, and today PDF format is still the overwhelming majority. Overall, the demand for accessible electronic versions at the institutional level had increased tremendously. Striving to meet its customers' needs, Cengage Learning adapted its workflows to these changes. Today, the company provides for efficient web-based support via an online form for customer requests. Many of the source files can be easily downloaded almost immediately.

While this helped bridge the gap for accessible textbook accommodations for the print disabled, Cengage Learning also needed to keep in mind the evolving accessible digital landscape and plan for the convergence of the print world with the digital world. The industry's shift towards digital instructional material coincided with the rapid evolution of the World Wide Web. Starting in 1991, the need for guidelines to make Web content accessible to everyone soon became clear. The Web Content Accessibility Guidelines (WCAG) published by the W3C and Section 508 issued by the U.S. government were important milestones in this process. Initially seeking compliance with Section 508, Cengage Learning today strives to conform to the more stringent WCAG 2.0 Level AA guidelines.

Once again, hearing the customer's voice the company responded to their needs with the production of their first digital e-book. We now have more than 99% of our print textbooks available in an accessible digital format on CengageBrain.com.

Cengage's standards for creating e-books include proper heading structures to permit users who are print impaired to use their screen readers to navigate a page of content just like their sighted peers. In this way they can skim major sections of text without necessarily needing to read each paragraph within.

Cengage Learning ensures that links to other areas of content consist of meaningful, descriptive link text so screen reader users know where the link will take them, rather than hearing the infamous "click here." For images that are critical to the learning experience, text describing the purpose of the image is provided so the print disabled as well as those users with certain cognitive impairments have the same learning experience as users who are sighted—unless the description of the image is already in the surrounding text. The company has policies in place to require close captions and transcripts for audio and video content.

Striving to serve a wider range of users, Cengage Learning considers not only the needs of readers with print disabilities in its design of e-books. For example, products are designed so that the needs of users who have mobility impairments and cannot use a mouse are met. They, too, can successfully navigate the company's digital products using standard keyboard keys. Focus feedback lets them know where they are on a page. For users who have low vision, Cengage Learning provides sufficient foreground and background color contrast so the text can be easily read.

While Cengage Learning strives to make digital e-book solutions that would work for anyone, anywhere, the company is faced with ever-changing technology. Taking a closer look at a few major components of the changing technological landscape helps set the stage for some of the challenges the company faces when designing accessible material. Developing accessible content that works seamlessly on all operating systems poses a major challenge. Similarly, different browsers on the market today have varying levels of accessibility. Assistive Technology has varying support for accessibility. For example, some screen readers, like certain versions of JAWS, can speak Basic Math content, while other screen readers, such as NVDA, cannot speak complex

math content. Likewise, some mobile devices have more support for accessibility than others.

One of the fundamental challenges for Cengage Learning as it continues to move towards better accessibility is to make its content work with all these other components. This environment presents challenges and opportunities. As part of its forward-looking efforts, the company employs upstream accessibility efforts, communication, outreach, and collaboration as important strategies. Cengage Learning continuously seek to identify and evaluate opportunities for improving the accessibility and usability of our all of our digital products.

Cengage Learning integrates accessibility into product development activities. It has an established standard iterative assessment and remediation program to consistently and continuously move the dial towards better accessibility. It conducts ongoing progressive audits performed by disability experts.

A critical driving force for product development at Cengage Learning is the voice of the customer. Comments and suggestions about the accessibility of its products are valued and encouraged via a dedicated accessibility e-mailbox. Real users with disabilities test the products and the company invites users of all abilities to share their suggestions for improving the accessibility of its digital products.

Cengage Learning invites industry accessibility experts to train its staff, and it requires accessibility conformance from its vendors. The company seeks collaborative solutions with others in the industry by remaining active in the accessibility initiatives of the National Federation of the Blind and other accessibility advocacy groups. It continues to build relationships with the accessibility community and those committed to accessibility by telling its accessibility story.

References

American Library Association Council. (2009). *Purchasing of accessible electronic resources resolution* (ALA Council document #52 revised). Retrieved from thttp://www.ala.org/aboutala/governance/council /council_documents/docu_inventory_acmw2009

Association of Research Libraries. (n.d.). *Model licensing: accessibility*. Retrieved from http://www.arl.org/focus-areas/scholarly-communication/marketplace-licensing/2548-model -licensing-accessibility

Association of Research Libraries. (2012). Report of the ARL Joint Task Force on services to patrons with print disabilities. Retrieved from http://www.arl.org/storage/documents/publications/print-disabilities -tfreport02nov12.pdf.

Collins, R., and Collins, R. (2013). Using captions to reduce barriers to Native American student success. *American Indian Culture and Research Journal, 37*(3), pp. 75-86. Retrieved from http://aisc.metapress.com/content/025wr5k68l15021q/?p=41af08e70dd246d3917604db448d1768 &pi=5.

Curtis, D. (2004). E-Journals. *A how-to-do-it manual for building, managing, and supporting electronic journal collections.* New York, NY: Neal-Schuman Publishers.

Evans, G. E., & Saponaro, M. Z. (2012). *Collections development basics* (6th ed.). Santa Barbara, CA: Libraries Unlimited.

Gregory, V. L. (2011). *Collection development and management for 21st century library collections: An introduction*. New York, NY: Neal-Schuman Publishers.

Jacobs, M. (Ed.). (2007). *Electronic resources librarianship and management of digital information: Emerging professional roles*. New York, NY: The Harworth Information Press.

Johnson, P. (2013). *Developing and managing electronic collections: The essentials*. Chicago: American Library Association.

Morales, J. (2013, October 14). Video captions improve comprehension, professor finds. *SF State news.* Retrieved from http://news.sfsu.edu/video-captions-improve-comprehension-professor-finds.

Professional development for accessible technology in the CSU. (2009). *CSU accessible procurement process*. Retrieved from http://teachingcommons.cdl.edu/access/procurement_process/

Reed, C. M. (2004, December 20). *Executive order no. 926*. Retrieved from http://www.calstate.edu /AcadAff/codedmemos/AA-2013-03.html

Riley, C. (2007). The electronic resources (ER) librarian and patrons with disabilities. In M. Jacobs (Ed.), *Electronic resources librarianship and management of digital Information: Emerging professional roles* (pp. 83-98). New York, NY: The Harworth Information Press.

Schmetzke, A. (in preparation). Collection development and barrier-free access to electronic information: A content analysis of 46 pertinent books published between 2000 and 2014.

Services to students with disabilities. (2014). *The California State University*. Retrieved from http://calstate.edu/sas/disabilities.shtml

Smith, E. P. (2013). *Accessible technology initiative memorandum*. Retrieved from
http://www.calstate.edu/AcadAff/codedmemos/AA-2013-03.html

Wikoff, K. (2012). *Electronic resources management in the academic library: A professional guide*. Santa
Barbara, CA: Libraries Unlimited.

Keeping it Real: A Comprehensive and Transparent Evaluation of Electronic Resources

Karen R. Harker, MLS, MPH, University of North Texas Libraries
Laurel Crawford, MLS, University of North Texas Libraries
Todd Enoch, MLS, University of North Texas Libraries

Abstract

There will be a time when your library will need to evaluate all of your electronic resources. How would you do it? In response to a cut to our materials budget, we have developed a method that condenses a large amount of information into a few select criteria. In this day-long workshop, we walked through the process using the Decision Grid process developed at the University of Maryland at College Park (Foudy and McManus, p. 533-538) as a starting point. The workshop leaders first demonstrated each step of our process, and then the participants worked in small groups (5-7) using their own experiences and a sample data set of their own. The steps covered included selecting and defining the criteria, gathering and analyzing the data, and determining how to make final decisions. We covered some technical aspects of gathering and analyzing data, including using Excel functions. We also included discussions about the criteria and ways of eliciting honest and useful feedback from librarians and patrons. The participants received a flash drive with Excel templates that included formulas, as well as completed sheets with sample data, and the presentation files.

Introduction

The dual financial pressures on libraries has been well documented (Kolowich, 2012; Tillack, 2014; Lowry, 2011), with relative reductions in funding (Cuillier & Stoffle, 2011; Kelley & Lee, 2011; Powell, 2011) and relative increases in serials costs (Baveye, 2010; Fowler & Arcand, 2005). Individual libraries have developed their own responses to these pressures, including diversifying their funding models and reducing hours and staff. It is probably not surprising the most common response, though, has been to reduce resources, particularly subscription resources, whose expenses must be met year after year (Weir, 2010). Once considered a minor portion of the collections budget, serials and databases have come to be the second biggest expense for a library, after salaries and benefits (Baveye, 2010). Although serials and databases can be low-hanging fruit, they are often also forbidden fruit, viewed as a measure of collection quality by stakeholders.

There may be as many methods for deselecting resources as there are libraries. Unfortunately, many of these methods are based on historical practices (and thus, historical information), qualitative reasons that are difficult to articulate, or the volume of protest (actual and/or expected). With the infiltration of business practices in the field of higher education and public administration, there is a growing expectation that such decisions would be based more on documented evidence or information or data, and less on ill-defined and difficult to document perceptions.

Towards that end, the members of the Collection Development Unit of the University of North Texas (UNT) Libraries conducted this workshop to present the methods they used in a comprehensive evaluation of subscription resources for the express purpose of selecting resources for cancellation. Our goal was to describe our methods, explain the purposes of the methods and measures, and enable other librarians to apply the broader methods to their own collections.

Background

The UNT Libraries has been faced with cuts to its collections budgets for three of the last four fiscal years. Between 2010 and 2015, our budget has been more or less flat; combined with an average 7% inflation rate on materials (particularly high for subscription resources), this is an effective decrease of 32%. In late 2013, the Collections Management Division was advised to prepare for yet another $1M cut. While efforts had been made in previous years to, essentially, "cut the fat" by eliminating duplicate subscriptions, print or print plus online, and highly irregular continuations, we knew that this impending decrease would be "cutting bone." Our goal was to base our decisions on data that most closely matched the Libraries' values.

While researching methods, we found and distributed amongst ourselves copies of the article written by Gerri Foudy and Alecia McManus, "Using a decision grid to build consensus in electronic resources cancellation decisions." Although published nearly ten years before (2005), the article provided the foundation for a method that we believed would be most useful to us. The authors, from the University of Maryland at College Park, developed a rubric for evaluating their databases, with criteria based on aspects of their collection that they considered important, including accessibility, cost-effectiveness, breadth and audience of the content, and uniqueness of the content (Foudy & McManus, 2005).

UNT and the University of Maryland at College Park are similar institutions, with similar enrollment and funding models, and most, importantly for our project, similar goals for our respective projects. We were able to modify the method to fit our own collection development model and adjusted the criteria to include more objective measures, rather than subjective ratings. Workshop participants were encouraged to similarly "tweak" the method to address local concerns and to balance subjective and objective evidence.

Selecting and Defining Criteria

As mentioned above, we wanted to base our deselection decisions on the values of the UNT Libraries. These values were derived through an examination of the strategic plans of both the university and the libraries. Three core values were identified: an emphasis on undergraduate and graduate education over the faculty's individually driven research; the need to demonstrate the cost-effectiveness of our collection; and the need to view the collection holistically and not as a sum of separate subject-based collections.

Based on these values, and using the Foudy & McManus article as a foundation, we established the following criteria for evaluation: cost-effectiveness, ease of use, breadth and audience, and uniqueness of content. While the authors included ease of use in the criterion for access, other aspects of "access," such as format and technical reliability, were either no longer relevant (all subscription resources under consideration were online), or did not vary enough to be a factor (nearly all were reliable).

While Foudy & McManus rated resources on cost-per-search and being (or not being) a "rapid inflator," they did not detail how they developed these ratings. Rather than convert data that is already quantified into a subjective rating, we used the actual cost-per-use and change in price as the raw "score."

For the other three criteria, our criteria was fairly closely aligned with those described in the article. Ease of use, breadth and audience, and uniqueness of content were all rated subjectively by subject-specialist librarians based on a three-level scale. Unlike the University of Maryland, who used small teams of librarians in broad disciplines, we asked all of the librarians to rate all of the resources, except for those that would be totally irrelevant to their fields. We wanted the broadest opinions, and we also viewed it as a learning opportunity for our librarians, who often are not aware of the possible relevance of these resources. While the librarians were required to provide one of the three ratings for each resources, we did encourage them to provide notes or comments about their score, if they wanted to qualify their score. For the overall rating, we used the mode (most common rating), and we included all comments in the final list.

Regarding these measures, we quickly realized that both the scale and the direction of these ratings or scores were not the same. Typically, for scores, higher is better (as in 1, 2, 3, etc.), and for ratings, lower is better (1st, 2nd, 3rd, etc.). Furthermore, the scales were very different, with the cost-effectiveness scores ranging from near zero or even below zero for changes in expenditures to upwards of hundreds; whereas, the rating scales were set from 1 to 3. To ensure that all the measures would be comparable for each resource, we used the distribution of the resource within the entire list of resources *of its type*. Using the percentile as the score for each measure provided the same scale (0 to 1) and same direction (higher is better) for all measures.

Gathering and Analyzing Data

The decision to make before actually gathering and analyzing the data is where to store the data. There are a myriad of options, from within the integrated library system (ILS) or your electronic resources management system (ERMS) to more open systems, such as a wiki or intranet. The most important decision is to designate one tool or file as the "master repository." This file should contain the final forms of data from all the other sources. After this decision is made, then the titles of the resources should be collected, and other relevant information (such as subject area, type of resource, and type of subscription) and a unique identifier selected. This last item is key to linking all the data together across all the other files or repositories. The other relevant information can be used to analyze deselections by subgroups.

Most librarians who evaluate electronic resources include cost-per-use in their analysis. It is clear that neither cost nor usage alone can provide the contextual information needed to make rational decisions. As indicated above, however, we needed to be clear regarding the definitions and sources of each of these key parts of the cost-per-use equation. While there are multiple sources for cost (e.g., ILS, publisher's quotes, subscription agents,

Ulrich's) and multiple measures of usage (sessions, downloads, etc.), we realized that using the same source and the same measure was most important when evaluating these resources. Important aspects to consider when gathering the cost-per-use is the use of pro- or super-rated prices or one-time discounts or credits, changes to titles or platforms, and lack of usage data altogether.

Another important aspect of the cost-per-use calculation is which usage measure to use. We knew usage measures varied greatly by resources, but we wanted to use the measure that was closest to the end user's experience. We quickly realized that this "highest and best use measure" depended upon the type of resource, notably e-journals, e-books, indexing databases, online reference resources, and audiovisual streaming. With a few exceptions, the resources in each group reported the same use measures; for instance, all e-journals and packages reported full-text views and downloads, while most indexing databases reported record or abstract views. Once the data is gathered and vetted, however, calculating the cost-per-use in Excel is quite easy—by dividing the cost by the usage.

Gathering data on the more subjective criteria was only slightly more difficult than gathering usage and cost data. For our purposes, we developed a rubric (see Figure 1) of three levels on each of the three criteria: Ease of Use, Breadth/Audience, and Uniqueness to the Curriculum. The levels were defined by the Collection Development Librarian, based loosely on the definitions used by Foudy & McManus. While there was no piloting of this rubric or other methods to test validity, we agreed it would suit our purpose.

Rating	Ease of Use	Breadth of Audience	Uniqueness
1	*Easy* Most students can use both simple and advanced features without assistance; students routinely successfully find and access information.	*Interdisciplinary audience* The primary user group is very broad; it is used by students across several disciplines. The number of students who would be affected by cancellation would be high. It has a high impact on curriculum and teaching.	*Totally unique* This resource contains curriculum and teaching information not available anywhere else.
2	*Moderate* Students can figure out simple tasks on their own, but need coaching for advanced tasks; students have some difficulty finding or accessing information without help.	*Disciplinary audience* The primary user group is limited to the discipline. It may impact curriculum and teaching.	*Somewhat unique* This resource contains curriculum and teaching information which can be found elsewhere; or it contains the same information but has a uniquely useful search interface or metadata.
3	*Difficult* Students require coaching for even the simplest tasks; only expert, experienced users are able to find and access information without assistance.	*Niche audience* The number of students who would be affected by cancellation would be limited. It has a minimal impact on curriculum and teaching; it may be used only for faculty research.	*Not unique* This resource contains curriculum and teaching information widely or freely available elsewhere.

Figure 1. Rubric.

We had learned some lessons from previous attempts to gather librarian and faculty input. For instance, each serial item is assigned to a fund code representing a certain subject area; that fund is overseen by a subject-specialist librarian. In this round of feedback gathering, we asked our subject-specialist librarians to rate not only resources purchased using "their" funds, but also interdisciplinary or multidisciplinary resources that may be relevant to their fields. In addition, we used data validation techniques to ensure that the librarians provided one and only one of the three levels for each criteria, instead of variations thereof (e.g., 1.5 or 2a, 2b, 2c or even color codes). We emphasized that they had the opportunity to provide as much additional information as they liked in a text box, and that such information would be taken into consideration.

The primary purposes of analyzing data are to look for patterns and outliers, and to apply context, comparing like against like. Because of their inherent differences, particularly in measures of usage, we grouped the resources by broad types: individual e-journal subscriptions, e-journal packages, literature (or indexing) databases, and online reference resources (which included streaming media, given there were so few of these). The resources would be compared only to others of their own kind, thus avoiding the difficulty of comparing apples with oranges.

Because of the issues related to scale and references mentioned above, we decided to use percentile distributions or rankings to show where any one resource falls among others of its type. The Excel formula PercentRank.inc enables easy calculation of the percent rank of any one value within a list or "array." Simply calculating the percentile ranking was easiest for the cost, usage, and cost-per-use measures, with one exception. The direction of the scales differed among these three measures. While higher usage was better, lower cost and cost-per-use was better. To adjust for this discrepancy and make all the measures in the same direction, we subtracted the percentile rank for cost-per-use (and subsequently, the cost) from 1, which effectively reversed the direction, making those in the highest 75th percentile the best performing.

Additional calculations would be needed for the subjective measures, due in no small part to the very narrow range (1 to 3). We realized that of the three criteria mentioned above, uniqueness to the curriculum was most important to us, followed by breadth/audience, then ease of use. Thus, we weighted these ratings accordingly (3:2:1), and generated a weighted average. This composite score resulted in a wide enough range to apply the percentile rankings.

While percentile rankings do provide an efficient method of comparing resources, we added one more element to make our job easier. We used Excel's feature of "conditional formatting" to apply a color scale to the values using a similar approach as the percentile rankings. The resulting spreadsheet (Figure 2) provides a quick example of the final list of resources with all of the data necessary to start making final decisions.

	A ORDER#	B TITLE	C Renewal Price	D Subject	E Resource Type	F Liaison Ratings Composite Percentile Rank Reversed	G Inflation Score Percentile Rank Reversed	H CPU Percentile Rank Reversed	I Composite Score	J Status	K Modified Price	L Savings
24	0274630x	Database 14	$2,638.49	Communication Studies	Database	0.52	0.79	0.71	0.67	Keep	$2,638	$0
25	03378147	Database 15	$15,846.56	Communication Studies	Database	0.9	0.24	0.86	0.67	Keep	$15,847	$0
26	04686421	Database 36	$4,236.61	Dance & Drama	Database	0.77	0.15	0.48	0.47	On Table	$4,237	$0
27	0125425x	Database 21	$4,659.03	Economics	Database	0.52	0.14	0.65	0.44	On Table	$4,659	$0
28	01048910	Database 45	$13,334.84	English & Literature	Database	0.9	0.41	0.74	0.68	Keep	$13,335	$0
29	0103845x	Database 6	$13,136.60	History	Database	0.16	0.27	0.40	0.28	On Table	$13,137	$0
30	01050072	Database 34	$13,136.60	History	Database	0.16	0.27	0.31	0.25	drop	$0	$13,137
31	01583657	Database 42	$3,867.11	Learning Technology	Database	0.77	0.53	0.68	0.66	Keep	$3,867	$0
32	01774554	Database 44	$1,887.32	Mathematics	Database	0.16	0.8	0.95	0.64	drop	$0	$1,887
33	0314690x	Database 75	$9,345.15	Mathematics	Database	0	N/A	0.08	0.04	drop	$0	$9,345
34	03762518	Database 49	$3,771.63	Philosophy & Religious S	Database	0.52	0.76	0.28	0.52	On Table	$3,772	$0
35	0446803x	Database 10	$3,006.69	Philosophy & Religious S	Database	0.52	0.02	0.59	0.38	Keep	$3,007	$0
36	01832098	Database 74	$5,619.09	Political Science	Database	0.16	0.67	0.23	0.35	Drop	$0	$5,619
37	04582354	Database 53	$1,750.05	Political Science	Database	0.77	0.6	0.98	0.78	Keep	$1,750	$0
38	04699154	Database 73	$5,354.42	Political Science	Database	0.16	0.03	0.00	0.06	Drop	$0	$5,354
39	02403018	Database 56	$55,563.87	Psychology	Database	0.52	0.34	0.81	0.56	Keep	$55,564	$0
40	03629739	Database 33	$2,429.62	Psychology	Database	0.52	0.37	0.53	0.47	Keep	$2,430	$0
41	03642665	Database 54	$47,906.25	Psychology	Database	0.52	0.28	0.78	0.53	On Table	$47,906	$0
42	0377384x	Database 55	$1,799.62	Psychology	Database	0.04	0.38	0.87	0.43	Keep	$1,800	$0

Master List | Ejournal | Packages | Databases | RefSources | Avg % Rank of Criteria by Subj. | Renewal Cost by Subject

Figure 2. List of resources for final decisions.

Making Final Decisions

While it may seem easiest to evaluate resources based strictly and solely on the objective data, we understood that subjective information would be needed to make difficult decisions. We also recognized the importance of both objective and subjective information to meet our goal of holistic planning, through which we hoped to balance the needs of all stakeholders. Such planning requires trust between the collection development decision makers and the library's patron groups. To foster confidence in our actions, we planned ahead to enable smooth, clear communication and transparent decision making.

For this major deselection project, we found it very helpful to have a way to view big-picture effects as decisions were made, alongside a means to envision progress toward our goal of a specific savings amount. Using a single Excel file containing all the relevant data needed to make title-by-title decisions will enable you to develop different scenarios regarding what to cut to reach each target. In our case, a "Status" column for each item under consideration showed either "Keep" or "Drop"; and if "Drop," a calculation was automatically made to show the new price ($0) and the savings (the renewal price). Additionally,

we developed summary tables of costs and savings by format and/or subject area to aid in reaching our goals of transparent and fair distribution of cuts. Excel offers a number of tools to help with this, including the SumIf function, which sums a value based on a specific criteria. In our case, we used SumIf to add up the savings for all items with both a status of "Drop" and certain fund code. This allows you to change the status of any number of resources and see the effect of these changes in real time on the distribution of costs and savings across the subject areas (see Figures 3 and 4). These features of Excel provide the tools to make it easier to communicate and negotiate with the key stakeholders, whether they are "squeaky wheels" or silent users. Communicating with our stakeholders was a major challenge. We needed to communicate with and consider the points of view of students, over 30 subject departments, subject librarians, the university administration, the library administration, and even vendors. There is also the silent user, the undergraduate student user, who is not always considered in such decisions. Compiling the data was immensely helpful. Most patrons, when shown the data that went into the decision, were supportive. Many were surprised by data, like low use, that contradicted their impressions of importance; a few were able to point out flaws in our data or different ways to access the same information. Thanks to the data we collected, we were able to make our stakeholders understand our reasoning, even though they did not always agree with our conclusions. The real-time scenario planning tools we created in Excel were also invaluable as we negotiated with stakeholders and incorporated feedback.

Department	Total Renewal Price for Department	Total Savings for Department	Total Percent Cut for Department
Biology	$ 109,969.34	$ 16,349.16	15%
Business	$ 456,458.07	$ 10,890.65	2%
Chemistry	$ 182,255.14	$ 15,876.74	9%
Dance & Drama	$ 21,747.65	$ -	0%
Economics	$ 12,173.22	$ 2,152.50	18%
Education	$ 76,178.97	$ -	0%
English & Literature	$ 50,462.14	$ -	0%
Geography	$ 17,188.99	$ 2,369.88	14%
Government Documents	$ 222,427.32	$ 98,158.37	44%
History	$ 36,643.37	$ 1,595.20	4%
Interdisciplinary	$ 2,125,336.87	$ 708,721.99	33%
Journalism	$ 2,079.85	$ -	0%
Library & Information Sciences	$ 38,118.10	$ -	0%
Mathematics	$ 70,404.30	$ 45,457.27	65%
Music	$ 42,462.85	$ 8,575.96	20%
Physics	$ 212,903.55	$ 42,486.33	20%
Political Science	$ 39,837.63	$ 7,263.89	18%
Psychology	$ 157,636.11	$ 11,499.98	7%
Sociology	$ 60,656.33	$ 12,815.68	21%
Visual Arts & Design	$ 61,626.79	$ -	0%

Figure 3. Distribution of savings by subject.

Total Savings	Total Modified Price	Total Renewal Price	% of Renewal Price
$ 984,213.62	$ 3,012,352.97	$ 3,996,566.59	33%

Figure 4. Sum of all savings and costs.

Conclusion

Data-driven decision making takes planning, coordination, and documentation. Combining objective and subjective data is difficult and time-consuming, but it's worth it in the end. We do not believe you could do a very good job with just one or the other.

This type of project is detail-oriented, but also allows you to get a holistic view of the entire picture. You're considering not only title-by-title, but also the entire collection, by departmental and interdisciplinary needs, by acquisition method and item type, and, of course, by price.

References

Baveye, P. (2010). Sticker shock and looming tsunami: The high cost of academic serials in perspective. *Journal of Scholarly Publishing, 41*(2), 191-215. http://dx.doi.org/10.3138/jsp.41.2.191

Cuillier, C., & Stoffle, C. J. (2011). Finding alternative sources of revenue. *Journal of Library Administration, 51*(7), 777-809. http://dx.doi.org/10.1080/01930826.2011.601276

Foudy, G., & McManus, A. (2005). Using a decision grid process to build consensus in electronic resources cancellation decisions. *Journal of Academic Librarianship, 31*(6), 533-538. http://dx.doi.org/10.1016/j.acalib.2005.08.005

Fowler, D. C., & Arcand, J. (2005). A serials acquisitions cost study: Presenting a case for standard serials acquisitions data elements. *Library Resources & Technical Services, 49*(2), 107-122.

Kelley, M., & Lee, M. (2011). Miami-dade county budget cut 30 percent. *Library Journal, 136*(18), 12-15.

Kolowich, S. (2012, February 21). Smaller servings for libraries. *Inside Higher Ed News.* Retrieved from https://www.insidehighered.com/news/2012/02/21/library-budgets-continue-shrink-relative -university-spending

Lowry, C. B. (2011). Year 2 of the "Great recession": Surviving the present by building the future. *Journal of Library Administration, 51*(1), 37-53. http://dx.doi.org/10.1080/01930826.2011.531640

Powell, A. (2011). Times of crisis accelerate inevitable change. *Journal of Library Administration, 51*(1), 105-129. http://dx.doi.org/10.1080/01930826.2011.531644

Tillack, T. J. (2014). Pressures, opportunities and costs facing research library acquisitions budgets: An Australian perspective. *Australian Library Journal, 63*(3), 206-219. http://dx.doi.org /10.1080/00049670.2014.915498

Weir, R. O. (2010). Trimming the library materials budget: Communication and preparation as key elements. *Serials Review, 36*(3), 147-151. http://dx.doi.org/10.1016/j.serrev.2010.06.003

Successful E-Resource Acquisitions: Looking Beyond Selecting, Ordering, Paying, and Receiving to Discovery and Access

Denise Branch, Virginia Commonwealth University

Abstract

E-resource acquisitions began as a complex process and libraries struggled to manage it. When e-resources first arrived, librarians spent considerable time determining how to acquire these resources. A movement ensued to generate the best methods for selecting, ordering, negotiating licenses, choosing content, and paying. Libraries were prompted to develop new workflows. Time has passed and acquisitions functions have mostly been standardized. However, with the acquisition of e-resources comes the challenges of discovery, access, and user needs. Now that many libraries feel more comfortable in acquiring e-resources with the help of technology, cloud-based services, and task coordination, they are moving beyond acquisitions and focusing on discovery and access. It takes much time and great effort to efficiently manage e-resources so that there is seamless discovery and access.

The transition from print to electronic is a continuous process for most libraries as they allocate funds for electronic serials and books. Workflows are being developed that incorporate, not only new technology, but also, new staff skills and knowledge. This paper will introduce new workflows and technologies that VCU libraries have adopted to provide discovery and access. A discussion of how workflows have changed since the implementation of Alma and Primo and the influx of e-resources is included. Ideas for identifying successful methods for moving e-resources beyond acquisitions will be shared. Readers will be exposed to a number of ideas for improving the management of e-resources and opportunities that are available for adding value to their library.

Introduction

For many years the acquisition of resources has been the focal point for most libraries. Workflows focused on acquiring content that was considered suitable for the collection, which was mostly print. MARC records, OCLC WorldCat, and OPACs were the mechanisms for acquiring, organizing, delivering, and documenting collection information on library users' behalf. Technical services staff developed skills for successfully acquiring these resources and have become quite proficient in acquisitions. They know how to efficiently order, quickly receive, and accurately describe materials for users to easily locate them in the catalog. Many years of development have attributed to some of the most efficient acquisitions workflows. Technical services staff have discovered inconsistencies, resolved problems, refined workflows, strengthened standards, and enhanced operations. Unbeknownst to the users, they have relished in some of the best services that libraries could offer.

Libraries are changing and technical services will be at the pinnacle of this change. Technical services divisions are transitioning from acquisition of content to discovery and access. Movement is shifting from the traditional role of ownership to access. New technologies are bringing opportunities for libraries to develop roles that will identify, preserve, and deliver electronic resources in response to users' needs. This paper will provide a snapshot of activities and technologies that the VCU Libraries have implemented in their shift from acquisitions to delivery and access.

Tradition Dissipating

The traditional technical services models that libraries are acquainted with are quickly dissipating caused by the erosion of e-resources, budding technology, and tech-savvy users. These dramatic changes are rapidly transforming technical services. Focus is moving away from acquiring and building collections to providing access through new discovery tools. Focus goes beyond selecting, ordering, receiving, paying, and transitions to discovery, access, and users.

Emerging E-Resources

Around 2003, many libraries started acquiring vast numbers of e-resources and technical services has never been the same. E-resource acquisitions began as a complex process and libraries continue to struggle in managing it. Management of this emerging format became another responsibility for technical services staff and engulfed much more processing time than print. Workflows were complex and inefficient. With the rapid acquisition of e-resources and with most libraries not having the advantage of new hires, staff were inundated with unfamiliar tasks. The linear workflow for acquiring print resources was used on e-resources and found lacking in efficiencies. Considerable time was spent determining how to acquire them. Libraries had to consider IP addresses, authentication, license negotiations, pricing, and other business and technical aspects that affect successful acquisition. There was a prompting to develop new workflows. A movement ensued to generate the best methods for selecting, ordering, negotiating licenses, choosing content, and paying.

With extreme determination and hard work, acquisitions staff managed to cope with the electronic workload increase as print activities decreased. Technical services began experimenting with new workflows to subdue the electronic beasts that were disrupting existing technical services models. Over the years, workflows have been standardized and efficiencies created.

Librarians realize that even with successful acquisitions workflows, challenges still arise with e-resource management. Prices fluctuate. Access comes and goes. Publishers and platforms change. New technologies emerge. Users' needs shift. There will never be a perfect workflow for managing e-resources, but libraries are putting forth their best efforts to make processes work efficiently. These challenges are not all bad. Some present opportunities for reconceptualizing the management of information and how that information can be discovered and accessed.

Time Has Passed

Over ten years have passed since the influx of e-resources brought havoc to acquisitions workflows. Since this time workflows have been developed to incorporate e-resources into the daily routine of technical services. What was once a convoluted acquisitions process has turned into a standardized process except for the budget predictions that haunt libraries every renewal cycle. New technologies have been implemented to incorporate e-resource acquisition into workflows. Staff are now comfortable with the acquisition of these resources and have developed skills for successfully researching e-resources, negotiating pricing, reviewing licenses, identifying publisher platforms, and providing IP. They know that processes can shift each time an e-resource enters into the acquisition workflow. There is an understanding that effective acquisition may require the expertise of a group of staff and collaboration. Staff have always been good at embracing change and can quickly shift gears when necessary without too much disruption.

Today's Challenges

Today's technical services face different challenges than what was faced over ten years ago. The concern of acquiring an e-resource has decreased dramatically and in its place is an increasing awareness of the need for providing discovery and access. Libraries are subscribing to thousands of e-journals plus various other resources such as print, digital, and media. Sophisticated technologies have now reached libraries presenting opportunities for reenvisioning of responsibilities and workflows. Users are seeking some kind of result from technology whether for need or entertainment. Technical services can successfully acquire an e-resource, but how can they facilitate the discovery of that full-text article or digital media that is being sought? Libraries find themselves performing new functions and fashioning new services to help users discover and access the information they seek. Technical services divisions can reimagine and redefine themselves.

Background of VCU Technical Services

At VCU, technical services are centralized. Until recently, we had a mostly traditional division called Collections, Technical Services and Information Systems (CTSIS) which was organized into five departments: Acquisitions, Cataloging, Collection Management, Library Information Systems, and Preservation.

The Acquisitions Department ordered, paid for and received materials, negotiated licenses, and managed the e-resources. The Department consisted of three units: Order, Firm Order and Accounting and Serials.

Each of the three units had core responsibilities. Order Unit acquired all materials for the library. They navigated to OCLC where bib records were imported into our local ILS for order creation. The Firm Order and Accounting Unit was responsible for processing invoices and receiving monographs. The Serials Unit performed tasks of checking-in, binding, claiming, and managing electronic serials.

The Cataloging Department worked extensively with computer records. Staff created, edited, and maintained the computer information that assisted users when they search for books, periodicals, DVDs, compact discs, computer software, and a wide and growing array of electronic resources. They ensured that online catalog information described library material accurately, had appropriate subject headings and were given call numbers that located them with similar resources in the Libraries' collection.

Transformation

VCU Libraries' technical services have been evolving over the past ten years to address the changing climate brought about by new technologies, e-resources, and user needs. It has implemented new technology, reorganized, and developed functional positions to support discovery and access of content. Discovery and access are now the focal points since these functions facilitate research and scholarship, both of which are essential to the earnest library user. Users expect simplicity when seeking information and want information that can be seamlessly

delivered just in time. The Libraries want to fulfill that need and provide a one-stop service for discovery and access of the rich resources to which they have invested in.

Is content being used to its full potential? Where does a user start a search? Does he go to Google to perform a search and find thousands of hits and only looks at the first page possibly overlooking relevant information scattered among the results? Or does he go to the library environment where he can discover local, regional, and international resources without having to encounter thousands of results that are not relevant to his topic? VCU Libraries wants to ensure that all content in their collection is easily discoverable and accessible. This is crucial in managing a library particularly when budgets are tight.

Library Technology

From 2003 until 2012 Aleph was the integrated library system. All e-resources were managed in Aleph until SFX was brought up in 2004. The Aleph OPAC was the discovery interface for e-resources. Orders were manually created in Aleph and URLs were added one by one for e-resources. There were multiple records in the catalog when a title was in multiple collections. Holdings had to be updated in Aleph, OCLC, and DOCLINE. It was a very time-consuming process to perform these tasks. Titles and platforms were constantly changing. URLs required constant babysitting and holdings regularly needed updating. E-resources were not as easily discoverable and accessible to users as the library had hoped because of time consuming tasks such as downloading bib records, creating and placing orders, setting up publisher access, and adding URLs and holdings in Aleph, OCLC, and DOCLINE. Workflows were complicated and there were disconnects in processes as resources were handed off from one staff member to another for processing. The Libraries had all these rich resources, but no truly efficient method for providing easy access.

Once SFX was implemented in 2004, serials staff worked diligently to activate titles and update holdings, thereby connecting users to electronic full-text in a timely manner. Aleph and SFX were not integrated and work in one system did not carry over to the other system. However, Serials staff did not have to wait for Order Unit staff to create orders in Aleph before activating titles or collections in SFX. As long as a title had been ordered with the publisher or vendor and access was turned on, activation could take place in SFX. For Serials staff, electronic workflows improved greatly and SFX helped to bring seamless access to users.

In 2011 Primo was implemented as the discovery layer. It is a single interface which allows users to easily find the information they need, including print books, e-books, print and electronic articles, digital media, and other resources. The system was found to be intuitive and integrates licensed, local, and open access resources. Users are presented with a single search box that provides more exposure to not only e-resources, but also, information that is local and widespread. It brings attention to the Libraries' unique collections that may not ordinarily be discovered. Primo improved the way the Libraries arrange, retrieve, and present holdings.

Implementation of the cloud-based unified management system, Alma, began in 2011. Aleph had been the ILS for many years and it was no longer providing quality performance that could be offered by some of the new systems. After being on the verge of buying two new servers to support library operations, Alma was found to be a good return on investment. The Libraries had already implemented the Ex Libris discovery system, Primo, and felt that Alma, another Ex Libris product, would be a good match. Upon showing interest in the product, VCU was invited to become an early adopter in 2011 where a commitment was made to help with final development of Alma before its general release in 2012. After intense training, testing, configuring, meetings, webinars, trial, and success, VCU Libraries went live on October 24, 2012.

Alma has proven to be a good investment for the Libraries. It has streamlined workflows for ordering and managing e-resources. Order Unit staff can perform an OCLC search in the Metadata Editor of Alma, locate a record and import the record into Alma without ever leaving the system.

MARC records can be loaded into Alma which automatically create order records. Staff can easily go to the Community Zone, which incorporates the knowledge base, a community bibliographic catalog, and global authority files to activate titles and collections which puts them in the local catalog where materials can be managed. Titles can be activated at the collection level without having to activate title by title and upon activation materials are discoverable in Primo.

Primo Central Indexing is an Ex Libris cloud product that the library subscribes to as part of the Primo discovery and delivery solution. This index provides aggregation of the library's articles, e-books, and open access resources that are harvested from publishers and aggregators. It facilitates easy searching, discoverability, and access. The single search box allows users to search across open access, local, international, and regional collections. VCU Libraries is able to define the scope of its resources that are relevant to its users and determine how results display. Users are connected to unique local collections. Primo will then show results through relevancy ranking and users can access resources that are of interest to them.

Reimagining of Technical Services

Reimagining of technical services at VCU Libraries occurred when functional responsibilities were added to two of the technical services departments to apply expertise in the area of metadata and digitization. These are functional areas that support discovery and access. Responsibilities focus on identifying unique local collections and making them discoverable.

In 2006 the Digital Collections Systems Librarian was hired in the former Library Information Systems Department (Digital Technologies) within the area with functional responsibilities for raising awareness of the Libraries' unique collections and open access resources and making them discoverable and accessible. This position, along with several other staff, digitizes special collections and archives materials. They work closely with the Metadata Catalog Librarian, ensuring that data is accurately described and digitized for easy discoverability. They also work closely with VCU faculty to identify articles that are published in open access journals and can be added to the institutional depository called Scholars Compass.

In 2007 the Metadata Catalog Librarian was hired in the former Cataloging Department (currently Metadata and Discovery), providing metadata for digitized collections and harvesting of electronic ETDs. Most of the digital collections come from special collections that have been digitized and include images, monographs, newspapers, oral histories, comics, cartoons, medical artifacts, yearbooks, university publications, and alumni publications. A data dictionary is developed before each collection is cataloged, which is a framework for the fields that will be included in the metadata for the item or collection. A metadata specialist assists this librarian to ensure that items and collections are added to the appropriate place for discovery, such as Firstsearch, WorldCat, CONTENTdm, Flickr, and Wikipedia.

Reorganization of Technical Services

VCU Libraries has gone live with two new powerful systems (Primo and Alma) that are supporting discovery and access. The Libraries recognized another opportunity that arose for reimagining technical services and promoting discovery and access.

The Head of Acquisitions decided to retire in April 2013. After study, collaborative work, and planning, the VCU Libraries decided to reorganize technical services. The division was renamed Information Management & Processing (IMP). The Acquisitions Department was split. The Serials Unit joined the newly named Metadata and Discovery Department (formerly Cataloging). The Order Unit and the Firm Order and Accounting Unit joined the newly named Collection Analysis and Investment Department (formerly Collection Management).

The Libraries identified six reasons for reorganization. They are:

- New technologies being introduced that provide opportunities for creating efficient workflows (Alma, Primo, WorldCat Knowledge Base, WorldCat Discovery Services).

- Change in leadership will create a knowledge gap that needs to be filled. Knowledge gap with the retirement of the Head of Acquisitions and other senior management considering retirement in the near future.

- Collections are changing. Materials the library collects is changing, which affects how material is acquired, processed and stored. There are e-books, e-serials, streaming media, large sets of materials. There is a decreased need for traditional processing and an increased need for off-site storage and physical preservation.

- Older organizational model. Analyzing workflows has proven that older model does not work as well as others that can be designed. Check-in is becoming a thing of the past with resources being frequently licensed rather than purchased.

- Aspiration to elevate position among research libraries. This opens new opportunities for changing what we are currently doing.

- Historical workflows less compelling. As we have worked with our current organizational model, there are some things that made sense when we first started doing them and are now stagnant as we enhance skills and gain knowledge. For example, it makes sense to have metadata production with the unit that is creating the digital object rather than having to handoff to another department.

A MAD Journey Begins

The newly organized Metadata and Discovery Department is positioning itself to provide strong support for discovery and access. Staff are aware that they must keep pace with new technologies as implementation occurs and users' needs change. They are learning Alma, Primo, and other discovery systems. Continuing Resources staff (former Acquisitions) are collaborating with Cataloging staff to bring about quick resolution to e-resource issues. Continuing Resources staff are learning how to perform some cataloging tasks and Cataloging staff are learning some continuing resources tasks, eliminating time-consuming handoffs. For example, Continuing Resources staff have learned how to process continuations and added volumes, a task formerly performed by Cataloging. Cataloging staff have learned how to activate titles in Alma, which saves time from having to hand off this responsibility to continuing resources. A buddy system within the department allows staff to pair off to resolve issues and complete tasks. Successful task coordination is occurring with the aid of Alma, which provides logical task lists and guides the efficient workflow of materials. Staff have been introduced to a diverse range of discovery tools, such as WorldCat Knowledge Base and WorldCat Discovery Services, that support discovery and access. They are becoming well-versed in a wide range of activities that empower them to enhance skills and increase knowledge. They are learning to successfully manage knowledge bases, activate resources, create Google documents, maintain a link resolver, and troubleshoot access issues. They are learning key concepts such as web-scale discovery, central index, discovery layer, harvesting, and relevancy ranking.

Future

We have asked ourselves what does the future hold for technical services as traditional acquisitions models dissipate and we move forward in the areas of discovery and access. As we glance back at the past, organizational models can be found that have been in place for decades. Acquisitions, cataloging, collection management,

serials. Sound familiar? At one time you could walk into a library and find common names and similar patterns. Things are changing. You can now walk into a library and see different patterns arising. Metadata, digitization, discovery, access. Technology, e-resources, and users are driving change. Libraries are trying to find the perfect model for their particular library as they explore ways of organizing.

Libraries need to keep abreast of change and be able to flow with it. One method is to understand change. Analysis needs to be brought in to understand the environment. Rapid data export out of systems like Alma and Primo needs to occur to help determine performance so libraries can position themselves to evolve with the environment. How can libraries track analysis? New applications are developing for this purpose. For example, Altmetrics, which uses social media and newspapers, can be used to discern scholarly impact. Plum Analytics can measure research for individuals or groups and track different kinds of information like articles, books, videos, and data sets. Libraries need to pick the best method for them in order to align their workflows and services to address change.

Conclusion

The focus in technical services is changing from acquisitions to discovery and access. When a print book, e-book, electronic journal, letter, university publication, or any other type of content is acquired, it has no value if it can't be discovered and accessed. The technology we are implementing and the services we are providing can improve discovery and access and make our collections work for us. We just have to ensure that we are successfully moving with change. Change is always a challenge, but it can also be an opportunity.

Moving Librarian Collecting from Good to Great: Results from the First Year of a Librarian Liaison Collaborative Monographic Purchasing Project

Genya O'Gara, James Madison University
Carolyn Schubert, James Madison University
Lara Sapp, James Madison University
Michael Mungin, James Madison University

Abstract

As Collins (2001) found in his evaluation of how companies evolve from "good" to "great," one of the key components of such a transition is to focus less on continuing tasks, and more on NOT continuing tasks. Today's librarians are juggling instruction, reference, collection development, outreach, and the need to develop new expertise in emerging areas, such as data curation, multimedia resources, institutional repositories, and more. Librarians cannot responsibly continue all traditional tasks while facing shifting budget priorities and new responsibilities. As noted in ARL's Issue Brief (2012), "never before have we been required to grasp so many dimensions of research in order to make wise decisions" (p.1). In order to meet needs on campus that do not fit within traditional collection models or siloed subject collection practices, the James Madison University Libraries committed to evaluating and implementing more flexible approaches to collection development. These proceedings detail JMU's Applied Health Sciences Librarians' adoption of a collapsed monographic acquisition model. The model's ability to address sustainable and flexible approaches to selection, reduction of duplication of efforts, alignment of collecting practices with budget priorities, and cross-disciplinary campus needs are explored.

Introduction

As Collins (2001) found in his evaluation of how companies evolve from "good" to "great," one of the key components of such a transition is to focus less on continuing tasks, and more on NOT continuing tasks. Today's librarians are juggling instruction, reference, collection development, outreach, and the need to develop new expertise in emerging areas, such as data curation, multimedia resources, institutional repositories, and more. Librarians cannot responsibly continue all traditional tasks while facing shifting budget priorities and new responsibilities. As noted in ARL's Issue Brief (2012), "never before have we been required to grasp so many dimensions of research in order to make wise decisions" (p.1). In order to meet needs on campus that do not fit within traditional collection models or siloed subject collection practices, the James Madison University Libraries committed to evaluating and implementing more flexible approaches to collection development. These proceedings detail JMU's Applied Health Sciences Librarians' adoption of a collapsed monographic acquisition model. The model's ability to address sustainable and flexible approaches to selection, reduction of duplication of efforts, alignment of collecting practices with budget priorities, and cross-disciplinary campus needs are explored.

Background

In January 2013 James Madison University (JMU) Libraries again faced a flat materials budget and rising costs for continuing resources. Format and subject prohibitive collection development workflows impeded a nimble response to emerging collection development needs. Concurrently, the Libraries' had a large number of new subject librarians, a restructured collections department, and a new Director of Collections. The time seemed right to examine existing collection development models, the allocation structure, and to explore alternate methods of content development.

JMU develops circulating collections through several avenues, including firm departmental allocations for single purchase requests, approval plans, and a continuing resources budget. Departmental allocations, approvals, and purchase-on-demand acquisitions comprise 17% of the budget, with the majority of the materials budget (80%) devoted to continuing resources, and the remainder going to preservation, digitization, and information access and interlibrary loan costs. Subject librarians manage one-time purchases and approval plans. To promote collaborative collection development and management of continuing resources, the Libraries' selectors are divided into four subject clusters (Social Sciences,[1] Arts and Humanities,[2] Sciences,[3] and Applied Health Sciences[4]). An elected representative from each cluster serves on the Collection Development Committee (CDC), which is chaired by the Director of Collections. The CDC evaluates and approves continuing resource requests that have been reviewed and priority-ranked for purchase by the subject clusters, or are general and interdisciplinary in nature.

The project began by evaluating the Libraries' collecting framework. Although the largest part of the budget is reserved for continuing resources, the majority of subject librarians reported spending the bulk of their collection development time on title-by-title selection.[5] If where the Libraries spend money is reflective of what JMU values, than there was a steep imbalance where subject librarians expended collecting energies. This was one signal that practices needed to be reevaluated. Further, the Director of Collections, the Director of Acquisitions and Cataloging, and CDC were fielding requests each semester to shift funds from allocations to support alternative academic content, such as datasets, digitization, archival manuscript purchases, streaming media, tablet accessible medical resources, and more. And while some subject areas were overspending allocations, others were having trouble expending

funds. The Collections Department commits to making data-driven decisions to build responsive collections across disciplines, and the data suggested the current model was no longer working. Further, it wasn't allowing enough space for busy librarians to explore new methods of content development. CDC took on the job of examining current allocations, preparing for database and journal reviews, and surveying alternate models of collection development.[6]

After examining different models, CDC determined that a collapsed fund model would fit well at JMU; particularly attractive for the committee was the potential in this approach for collaborative selection across interdisciplinary fields. Of the allocation models examined the ones that paralleled the institutional structure were the most compelling to the committee. This move would cause the budget to reflect changing constituent and curricular needs at the college level, with the added benefit of more closely aligning collecting priorities with those of the university. Further, this would allow the vendor to work out any bugs, and for the Libraries to streamline internal workflows between selectors, collections, and acquisitions. Since subject clusters are already loosely based around colleges, this would also support future allocation and approval profile revisions to be more reflective of campus organization.

The Applied Health Sciences (AHS) cluster members possess a series of characteristics including size, diversity in positions, and years of collecting experience that made it ideal for this collaboration. The cluster consists of 5 subject librarians across 7 departments. Three are full-time subject librarians and 2 are part-time subject librarians with large administrative responsibilities. The AHS cluster librarians also

---

[1] Business, Education, Social Sciences, Communication and General Education.

[2] Music, Theater and Dance, Art and Art history, Media, History, Philosophy, Religion, English and Writing, Rhetoric and Technical Communication.

[3] Math, Sciences, Engineering, Geographic Science, Geology & Environmental Science, Integrated Science & Technology, and Computer Science.

[4] Nursing, Health Sciences, Psychology, Kinesiology and Communication Science Disorders, and Social Work.

[5] 15 of 19 subject-liaison librarians completed a brief anonymous survey about their collection development habits. Respondents included 8 full time liaisons and 7 with liaisons' duties in addition to functional responsibilities.

[6] Including conversations with the University of Guelph, review of Penn State's Collections Allocation Team documentation, and literature review of allocation approaches.

vary in their experiences with collection development from novice to expert.

In addition to the cluster members, the creation of the College of Health and Behavioral Studies encouraged new ways of thinking about how to collect and collaborate in support of the new interprofessionally focused College. This new College consists of the seven departments covered in the AHS cluster.[4] Each of these departments continues to expand enrollment to meet the 19-38% anticipated job growth and increasing workforce demand (U.S. Department of Labor, 2014). For example, the Health Sciences department grew 160% between 2000-2010 to a size of 1680 students, making it "larger than some colleges within the university" (Birch, Deaton, DuBose, Frazer, Lambert, Schoenfelder, & Wunderlich, 2012, p. 2). This growth creates new demands on librarians' time for supporting instruction, reference, and collecting; necessitating the need to think about other ways to be more flexible in the Libraries' support to address new or emerging needs. One response has included more team-based liaison support.

Methods

The first step in establishing the pilot was coordinating the initial conversation with the cluster and the Director of Collections to gauge interest and address concerns about the collapsed funding model. Given the diversity in terms of department size and specialization, the AHS librarians had several concerns. For example, while noting some overlapping subject areas, other subject areas did not need to be reviewed by more than one or two librarians. Finding a workflow that would allow maximum openness to all slips and subject specific filtering was necessary. Another concern centered on the long-term implications of this decision. Recognizing the need for flexibility, it was agreed that the pilot would last for one year with the opportunity to adjust back to the previous model if the collapsed project became too burdensome.

Given each subject librarian's instinctual regard for his or her departments, other general concerns centered around balanced spending across the departments and how to communicate

changes effectively. With a single shared fund librarians were concerned about tracking spending by department. Other questions included whether safeguards should be developed to prevent areas from being over or under supported. In response the AHS cluster identified the need to evaluate spending trends after the first year. Beyond internal workflow and balanced spending, librarians were concerned with how to communicate this change back out to the departments.

The Libraries worked with the approval vendor to collapse AHS slip plans into one fund while leaving the book approvals untouched. Conversations with the vendor enabled tweaking of the processes to meet cluster needs. One challenging aspect was the implementation of a mechanism to allow librarians to see all AHS slips while still being able to filter to those most related to their department.

From an acquisitions standpoint, collapsing the funds meant monitoring one account instead of many, fielding all requests through the same fund, simplifying reporting procedures, and having a cleaner audit trail. Since most of the AHS funds are spent on firm selection, the cluster had to collaborate to establish individual purchasing expectations and meet acquisition order request deadlines.

Results

In late spring Collection Management began the process of documenting the results of the 2014 collapsed model pilot. Data gathered and charted aimed to address questions that arose during the pilot, such as workflow impact, spending distribution by department, and spending distribution by LC classification. Results were reviewed in comparison to the previous year to identify similarities and differences.

Comparison of spending patterns during the collapsed model year and the previous year was one initial indicator of the sustainability of the pilot. In total for 2014 the AHS cluster had a firm fund of $97,260. Throughout the year the AHS cluster worked on selecting titles and expending funds along the prescribed expenditure timeline: 30% by

October 11, 80% by January 31, and 100% by March 28. As of January 24 only 31% of firm funds were spent, requiring the cluster to collectively address the spending need. Forty-seven percent of funds were expended by late February and, by the March deadline, 94% of funds were expended. In comparison to 2013 spending, each firm fund varied widely in total amount spent by the January deadline –ranging from 0% to 101%, with the average being 51% spent. And by the March

deadline only three funds were fully expended, bringing the average to 92%.

Collection Management visualized firm fund spending across departments for the 2013 and 2014 year to compare spending supporting each department, as represented in Figure 1. Health Sciences, Nursing, and All Other increased spending amounts while Psychology, Social Work, Kinesiology, and Communication Sciences & Disorders decreased.

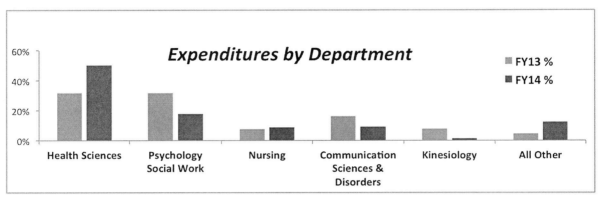

Figure 1.

When comparing spending to department FTE the drop in Communication Sciences and Disorders in the collapsed model appears more reflective of departmental size than in previous years, as

represented in Figure 2. Others, like Health Sciences and Nursing, became more in-line with departmental size and new programs.

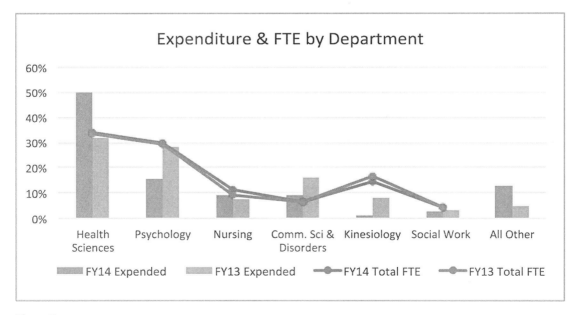

Figure 2.

In a closer look at "All Other" spending (Figure 3), Collection Management charted the percentage distribution of purchases across the Library of Congress (LC) classifications.

LC Classification	% Spent
R - Medicine	67.89%
B – Philosophy & Psychology	7.05%
H – Social Sciences	6.79%
Q – Science	8.41%
P – Language and Literature	4.44%
T - Technology	2.86%
G – Geography, Anthropology, & Recreation	1.07%
L – Education	0.55%
K – Law	0.49%
Others	0.46%

Figure 3.

Discussion

To better understand the impact of this new collecting model, the cluster identified first-year and third-year tiered evaluation points. The first-year analysis included reviewing the cluster's ability to meet spending deadlines, selection ease, an initial comparison of programs to expenditures, and an analysis of spending patterns between the previous year, contrasted with the collapsed year. The cluster also identified different aspects of collecting to assess, such as subject librarian workflow and acquisitions staff workflow. Based on these parameters, the pilot addressed and improved many of the issues previously plaguing firm title acquisition. However, the cluster must consider additional work to improve workflows and ongoing evaluation of the collection's usage before defining complete success.

First-Year Successes

The pilot achieved the first requirement for success by completing the expenditure of firm funds as a cluster even with an increased allocation from the prior year of $15,000. Despite this significant change in budget, the cluster expended their firm funds on deadline.

Throughout the year, evaluation of acquisitions, collections, and subject librarian workflows were all important factors, and required frequent adjustment before the cluster settled on determinations of success. The Monographs Manager in particular found this approach streamlined her financial and audit reporting processes. In comparing 2013 and 2014 spending patterns results, the collapsed fund appears to normalize spending patterns and alleviate the shifting of monies between funds seen in previous years. Acquisitions and collections workflows benefited from a more consistent purchasing pattern throughout the year.

Many subject librarians anecdotally noted the impact of a team-based approach influencing their investment and engagement. Instead of five different people purchasing independently, the single cluster representative managed deadlines and spending status, which allowed the other librarians to focus on collecting. The cluster also communicated more frequently and shared recommendations for purchasing lists. This approach to collecting created flexibility; instead of each librarian debating purchases of a particular resource, librarians were empowered to purchase resources based on his or her understanding of users and departments. No longer were books about autism spectrum disorder, for example, waiting for the Health Sciences Librarian or the Communication Sciences & Disorders Librarian to discuss the purchase.

To address the earlier concern about hoarding funds, the cluster reviewed the overall AHS monographic collection distribution and budget. The budget for the cluster's firm monographic titles increased significantly between the 2013 and 2014 purchasing cycles due to the statewide consortium assuming the cost for a key Psychology collection. Therefore, the changes in firm fund spending require additional interpretation to avoid accidentally assuming that Psychology was underserved in this new model. Instead, the new model allowed for greater flexibility to shift funds to other areas. Tradeoffs like these allowed for collecting in emerging areas like anatomy, neuroscience, and genetics in Sciences; health policy in Law; and leadership in Social Sciences. This collapsed model was less problematic than a permanent reversion of funds for those that underspent.

First-Year Challenges

While there were successful outcomes related to workflows, challenges did emerge; these included retraining librarians, revising larger collections-related procedures across the library system, and clarifying library vendor workflows.

Librarian retraining focused on new methods of collecting, identification of titles within the system, and an understanding of how decisions within the system impacted others. Titles that

were profiled by the vendor prior to the collapsed profile were coded with the previous fund codes (e.g., pre-publication profiling of not-yet-published titles). This meant there were multiple fund codes in the system at the beginning of the pilot, causing confusion for the librarians about the new filtering procedures. Similarly, by collapsing the firm titles altogether, AHS librarians now had a significantly larger number of slips to review. After a few months, the Director of Collections and the vendor were able to develop a workflow for filtering titles. Subject librarians also had to master how decisions were documented or tracked in the vendor system. Since each librarian saw a separate list, rejection decisions were not obviously indicated.

By collapsing the funds, other aspects of the collections lifecycle needed to be considered and clarified, such as individual title replacements and collection promotion. Throughout the year as newer editions arrive, subject librarians are asked to retain or weed older copies. With the new process more than one person could be responsible for this decision. Similarly, monthly collection promotion on the library homepage was tied to specific call numbers or fund codes. While this provided a shorter list of resources it failed to provide for effective interdisciplinary cross-promotion across subject areas.

Future Steps

Based on success of the initial pilot the collapsed purchasing pilot will continue with the AHS cluster and expand to the Social Sciences and Science clusters. The AHS cluster will revise its approval profile collaboratively this upcoming year, rather than individually. Collapsing the separate approval profiles will help with the eventual expansion of the project from collapsed firm funds to collapsed approval funds. An evaluation of the acceptance and rejection rate of approval and slips titles will inform this process. Expansion of the percent of titles that come within adjusted approval profiles will both better align current collecting practices and reduce time spent on title-by-title selection.

For the AHS cluster, the next step is considering what other areas across the collections lifecycle are impacted by this new approach. On a broader scale, the collapsed purchasing model pairs with larger ongoing holistic collection assessments, including revision of allocation formulas to more closely align with colleges, and the completion of a yearlong review of the libraries' continuing resources. Initial CDC discussions concerning the allocation formula will continue with a goal of developing a more nuanced approach, that acknowledges the diversity of formats, materials, and shifting campus needs.

It has been determined that a minimum of three years of data is necessary to discern any patterns in spending practices that emerge with this new model and in order to compare the utility of the model across subject clusters. However, the initial results are promising and the preliminary success of this model is already helping the organization to think outside the box for creative ways to align collecting practices with users needs, recognize the Libraries' capacity for change, and most importantly, empower librarians with more time and more fluid resources to meet the shifting content needs of the JMU campus.

Acknowledgments

We would like to acknowledge the contributions of all of the members of the Applied Health Sciences Cluster (David Vess, Stefanie Warlick, Lara Sapp, Michael Mungin), as well as the critical feedback and data visualizations provided by Cheri Duncan, Bob Martin, and Shirron Ballard.

References

Association of Research Libraries. (2012, March 10). 21st century collections: Calibration of investment and collaborative action. (Issue brief). Retrieved from http://www.arl.org/storage/documents/publications/issue-brief-21st-century-collections-2012.pdf

Birch, D., Deaton, M., DuBose, K., Frazer, G., Lambert, V., Schoenfelder, K., & Wunderlick, R. (2012, March 28-30). Department of Health Sciences academic program review: External team report. Harrisonburg, VA: James Madison University.

Collins, J. (2001). Good to great. New York, NY: Harper Collins.

U.S. Department of Labor. (2014, January 8). Healthcare occupations. *Occupational outlook handbook*. Retrieved from http://www.bls.gov/ooh/healthcare/

It's Not Just About Weeding:
Using Collaborative Collection Analysis to Develop Consortial Collections

Anne Osterman, Virtual Library of Virginia

Genya O'Gara, James Madison University

Leslie O'Brien, Virginia Tech

Abstract

From fall 2013 to the present, the Virtual Library of Virginia (VIVA) has undertaken a pilot collection analysis project with Sustainable Collection Services (SCS). This pilot has involved analyzing the main stacks holdings of 12 of the VIVA member libraries, a total of almost six million records. As is usual for an SCS analysis, the project involved comparing the pilot libraries' holdings with each other, the consortium as a whole, the state, and the United States, as well as with HathiTrust, the internet archive, and selected peer library groups.

The goals for this project were varied, but unlike most library groups, which have used SCS analysis services to inform collaborative print preservation and deselection projects, a primary interest for VIVA was to use the analysis to inform future collection development. The hope was that learning about titles that had been acquired and used across this representative cross-section of the consortium could be effectively translated into collaboratively acquiring e-books in a more thoughtful, data-driven manner, in addition to other collection development initiatives. This paper presents four different collection development approaches that have been applied to this shared data set.

Introduction

The Virtual Library of Virginia (VIVA) is a consortium of 72 nonprofit, academic libraries in Virginia. It includes both public and private colleges and universities, ranging in size from large doctoral institutions to small, specialized institutions, and the Library of Virginia. Central funding for the consortium is provided by Virginia's General Assembly, but there is also extensive cost-sharing by members to acquire products. The consortium is grounded in the coordinated collection development of online resources and an extensive resource sharing program, and more recently it has undertaken significant analysis of some of the member institutions' physical format materials.

In the fall of 2013, VIVA began a pilot collection analysis project with Sustainable Collection Services (SCS). This pilot involved analyzing the primary circulating holdings of 12 of the VIVA member libraries, a total of almost six million records. The project compared the pilot libraries' holdings with each other, the consortium as a whole, the state, and the United States, as well as with HathiTrust, the internet archive, and selected peer library groups.

The goals for this project were varied. Unlike most library groups that have used SCS analysis services to inform collaborative print preservation and deselection projects, a primary interest for VIVA was to use the analysis to inform future collection development. The hope was that in understanding the makeup of circulating collections, and how they were being used across this representative cross-section of the consortium, the consortium could effectively translate this information into collaboratively acquiring e-books in a thoughtful, data-driven manner, and that this would open up new opportunities for future collaborative collection development.

Background: Data Used

The 5.8 million bibliographic records analyzed in the project included all circulating, English language, LC-classed print monographs in the main stacks of the participating libraries. Not included in this analysis were theses and dissertations, reference materials, government documents, special collections, juvenile literature, e-books, musical scores, microform, audio-visual materials, serials, withdrawn materials, or those found in specialized libraries on the participating institutions' campuses such as law and medical libraries.

As there is no shared integrated library system (ILS) within VIVA, there were challenges for SCS in working with a diversity of systems (Alma, Voyager, Sierra, Millennium, and Symphony) and of library practices and policies. For example, a Google Book digitization project at the University of Virginia added extra circulation counts that could not be filtered out from regular check outs.

Background: The Collection Development Discussion

As mentioned above, collaborative collection development was of interest in this project from the very beginning. It was represented as one of the five basic project goals:

- Pilot a coordinated, consortial approach to collection assessment.

- Use the data and analysis to inform future, collaborative collection development.

- Identify scarcely held titles in need of protection.

- Begin a discussion about the possibility of reducing unnecessary duplication and saving local space through strategic weeding.

- Provide remediated and enhanced records back to the participating schools.

At first, this collection development goal was explored through conversation at an in-person meeting. Ruth Fischer from SCS was at this meeting, and she helped guide the conversation toward practical possibilities for data analysis. Many areas were determined to merit further

analysis after that meeting, including the four that will be discussed in this paper:

- Look for local disciplinary strengths in both uniqueness and general holding levels to inform the possibility of distributed, collaborative acquisitions.

- Examine widely held and highly and recently circulated books to determine shared factors such as key publishers.

- Examine shelf life (how long after purchase/publication date do books in different subject areas tend to be used by patrons) as a means of informing the acquisition model selected for new e-books.

- Focus on the print holdings of publishers recently acquired by the consortium in e-format to see if usage patterns were similar.

Local Disciplinary Strengths

During this analysis, SCS was able to provide VIVA with a comparison of subject collection size by percentage, distributed across the pilot libraries, as well as a comparison of unique-in-Virginia titles held by the pilot libraries that participated in this project. This initial snapshot enabled the task force to ask a few key questions about VIVA's consortial monographic holdings:

- What does the whole collection look like distributed across the pilot libraries?

- What do our uniquely held titles tell us about our collections?

In general, there was a fairly wide (if not even) distribution of LC classes, although there were a few notable exceptions. Figure 1 shows the classes for which the percent distribution of total collections is most equitably shared, and an example of how that SCS presented that data.

Subject Distribution

Classes where the percent distribution of total collections is widely (more evenly) shared: B, C, D, E, F, G, H, J, L, M, N, U

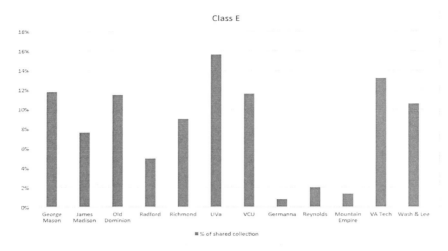

Figure 1.

For the classes where the total distribution of collections was not as widely shared, as detailed in Figure 2, there was often an explanation. For example, although some unlikely schools showed great relative strength in R (Medicine), the medical libraries at a number of participating schools had not been included in the analysis. Similarly, since reference collections were not included in the analysis, the A (General Works) category could be distorted by institutions that had moved more of their traditional reference materials into their main stacks.

Subject Distribution

Classes where the distribution of total collections is *not* as widely (evenly) shared: A, P, Q, R, S, T, V, Z

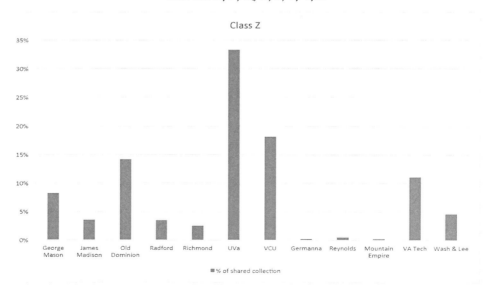

Figure 2.

Finding that the pilot libraries had a wide distribution of general subject strengths was critical to understanding VIVA's capacity to embark on future collaborative collection projects. The second piece of the puzzle was to examine how the depth of collection strength was distributed across the state. To look at this, the task force analyzed the percentage of unique titles at the pilot institutions and compared this to the percentage of total holdings in a given subject among the libraries. This tested the assumption that the collections were deepest where they were expected to be, e.g., where libraries had historic or current institutional disciplinary strengths.

Some things were quickly obvious. For example, in looking at all the data it was clear that the University of Virginia (UVA), one of the oldest and largest public research institutions in Virginia, held the majority of the unique titles across all of the collections analyzed even though the distribution of collections was more evenly distributed across the institutions. This can be seen in Figures 3 and 4, which illustrate the collection distribution by institution across the B (Philosophy, Psychology, Religion) and C (Auxiliary Sciences of History) classifications compared to the percentage of unique titles held by individual pilot libraries. In class B, for example, although there is a wide distribution of general holdings across institutions, UVA has 70% of the unique holdings.

Class B

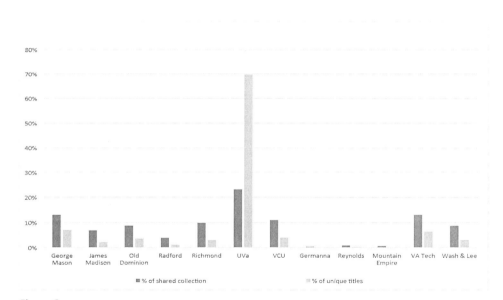

Figure 3.

Even though UVA holds the majority of the unique titles across all institutions, there were many examples of other institutions with high percentages of unique titles by LC class. For example, as seen in Figure 5, Virginia

Commonwealth University (VCU) and UVA together hold around 60% of the unique art titles in the state, a total of over 20,000 titles. This was not surprising considering VCU's disciplinary and historical institutional strengths in art.

Class C

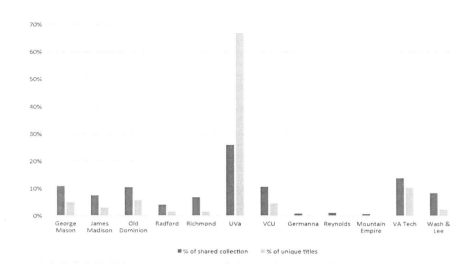

Figure 4.

Class N

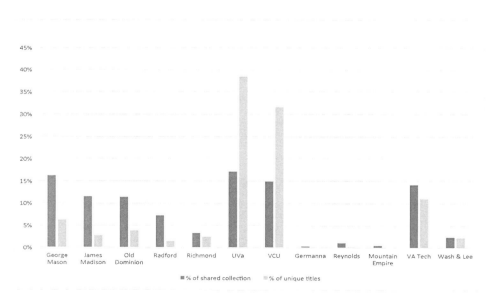

Figure 5.

Similarly, Virginia Tech (VT), as seen in Figure 6, shows depth in agriculture by holding 11,000, or over 75%, of the unique agriculture titles in circulating collections within the state. Again, this was in line with historical and current institutional strengths, but important to be able to visualize.

Class S

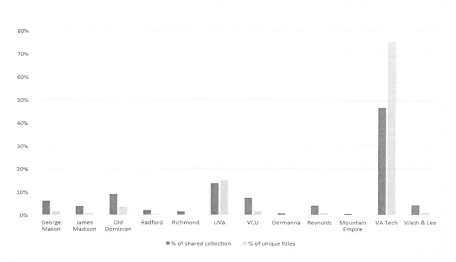

Figure 6.

Occasionally there were surprising results. For example, as seen in Figure 7, although James Madison University (JMU) is far from being the largest holder of education titles by LC class among the pilot libraries, it holds the largest number of unique titles in L—almost 30%. Not a surprise from a disciplinary point of view, in that education is historically a flagship program of that university, but surprising in number of unique titles and the resulting implied depth.

Class L

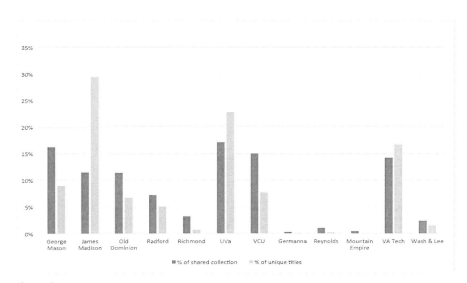

Figure 7.

These initial results gave the task force confidence that a potential future project of building on existing subject strengths within the consortium, where particular institutions could more formally become collectors for specific subjects on behalf of the other institutions, would have merit.

Widely Held and Highly and Recently Circulated Books

As there is no shared ILS or discovery system within VIVA, this collection analysis presented the special opportunity to look at a representative sample of the consortium and see which books were both widely held and highly used. E-books are still a relatively new acquisition approach for VIVA, and the hope was that this analysis might show patterns that would inform what kind of e-books would be useful for VIVA in general.

In order to do this, the task force set some benchmarks for these criteria and asked SCS to generate a list of ISBNs (and other data, such as titles, publishers, and publication years) of books that were owned by 10 or more VIVA libraries (in any edition), had more than 10 recorded uses, and had a last charge date after 2007. This list of just over 175,000 "widely held and highly and recently used" titles was then used in a variety of ways including:

- The ISBNs were sent to ProQuest's Title Matching Fast service to see which products matched up as good fits for VIVA.

- The ISBNs were matched to a standardized list of publishers using an in-house approach that had been used for similar studies in the past.

This second approach was useful in seeing patterns of publishers that might be appropriate for broad acquisition within VIVA. Over 3,200 publishers were matched, but, as can be seen in Figure 8, only around 150 had more than 200 titles in the list, fewer than 40 had over 1,000 titles, and only seven had more than 3,000 titles.

Title Count By Publisher

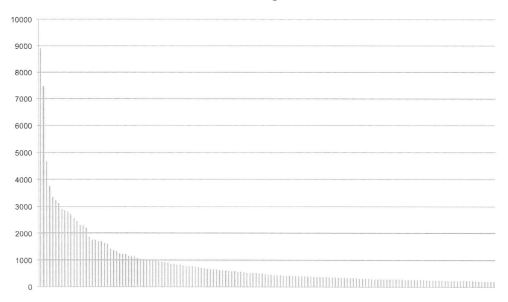

Figure 8.

The top publishers in this list were then included in a survey to collection development contacts that asked which e-book publishers they would like to have VIVA negotiate with for packages. This combination of evidence through analysis and institutional opinion gave clear direction toward a few publishers that merited further exploration, and some interesting discoveries arose from this analysis. For example, when the top ten publishers were reviewed more closely regarding holdings and usage (Figure 9), the data showed that although average holdings were higher for university press (UP) publishers, average recorded uses were higher for the commercial (Comm) publishers, at least relative to their holding levels.

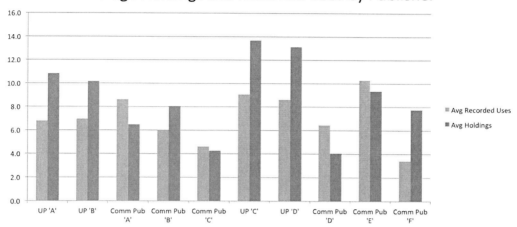

Figure 9.

Because the data included VIVA-wide holdings, not just the pilot library holdings, it was also demonstrated that this data could foster a discussion about how many copies have historically been held by VIVA in print, which could be used in pricing negotiations. A specific
.

publisher is shown as an example of this in Figure 10. This publisher shows an overall average of 7.5 holdings in VIVA that becomes, with a general decline in print holdings over time, an average of only 6 holdings between 2008 and 2012.

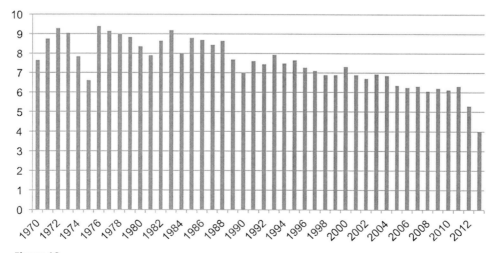

Figure 10.

Visualizing this level of duplication also led to deeper discussions about consortium-wide print holdings. It has been shown by other studies that academic libraries that rely on approval plan purchasing typically buy many of the same titles, and this did seem to be the case for VIVA. Data about duplication was used to guide recommendations about a distributed print repository or archive and establishing a voluntary threshold for new print copies, discussed further at the end of this paper.

Shelf Life

As e-books are still relatively new to the consortium as a shared purchase, also new has been the decision of what kind of acquisition model to use—perpetual access purchase, subscription, or demand driven. Although many factors play into this kind of decision, most notably pricing, the task force wanted to see if this analysis could inform a consortial preference of acquisition model, particularly for different subject areas of e-books. In order to do this, the task force focused on shelf life—or how long books are considered to be useful by patrons.

The task force examined the average number of years between publication year and last charge year for titles with the following criteria:

- Added to catalogs during or after 1990.
- Published in 1980 or later.
- Having a charge date.

Three LC-based subjects were considered: H (Social Sciences), N (Fine Arts), and Q (Science). These were chosen as they could potentially provide basic guidelines for the acquisition of e-books as either leases or perpetual access purchases in the three major divisions of Social Science, Humanities, and Science.

As shown in Figure 11, the global results of this were in line with general industry expectations— N had the longest shelf life, followed by H, and then Q. It is often the assumption made that Science titles "expire" in their usefulness sooner.

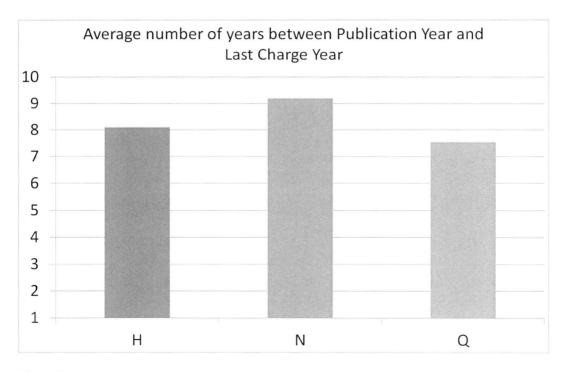

Figure 11.

When looked at in more granular detail (Figure 12), a distinctive higher pattern of titles with extensive years of usefulness in the N class can be seen, while a much greater higher percentage of titles in the Q class had only been used in their first year on the shelves.

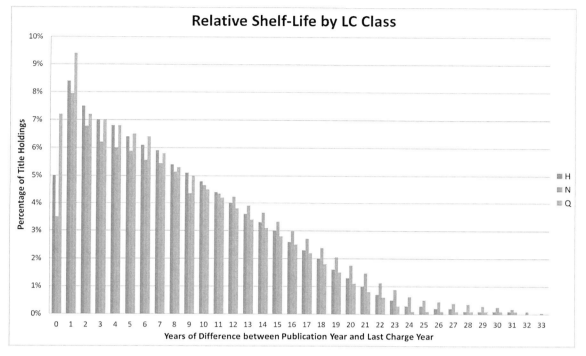

Figure 12.

When viewed at the subclass level, however, as in Figure 13, it can be seen that there is great variety within these broader classes. Some of the subclasses within H such as H, HA, HQ, HS, and HX had long shelf lives. One of them, HS (Societies), was above any other, including the N subclasses.

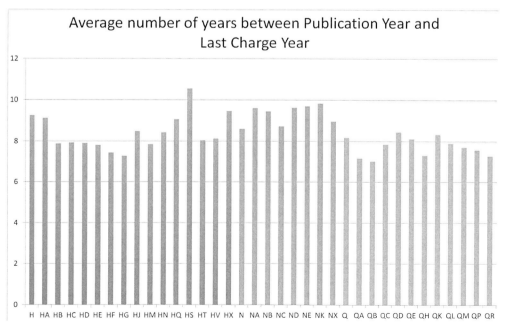

Figure 13.

It was generally recognized that this shelf life approach could be useful in informing future acquisition model decisions. For example, although the consortium's demand driven acquisition e-book pilot had been discontinued after a year due to a lack of state funding, if it were to begin again, different trigger-to-purchase levels could be set for different subjects. Similarly, as the publisher-based discussions progress, the subjects areas that a publisher is strongest in could inform a lease versus purchase decision.

E and Print Usage Comparison

STEM-H e-books have been of key interest in VIVA for the past few years, largely because the consortium received new General Assembly funding for STEM-H e-books in the FY13-FY14 biennium. This print analysis seemed like an excellent opportunity to look more closely at how the books from these publishers had been used in print and how that compared to their usage in the electronic format.

In order to enable this analysis, SCS provided individual records based on keyword searches in the publisher field. (It was fortunate that the three publishers of interest had names conducive to this process.) The task force then matched these holdings up to the shared electronic holdings using the ISBN and sometimes an intermediary match of print to electronic ISBNs. In order to maintain a fair playing field, only the 2013 resources were used in both formats.

As Figure 14 shows, the electronic format had higher levels of the proportion of available titles used. Likely due to the wider availability (across the consortium compared to a presence in only a few libraries), even in a small window of time the electronic format's impact was larger.

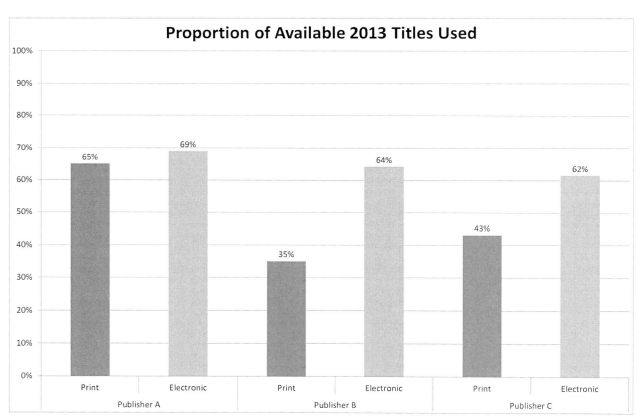

Figure 14.

An examination of the titles held in both print and electronic format by discipline (Figure 15) showed the overlap of what kind of usage was present by format. One of the most interesting results was an especially strong preference for the electronic format within R (Medicine). Only a few shared titles in this discipline had usage only in print.

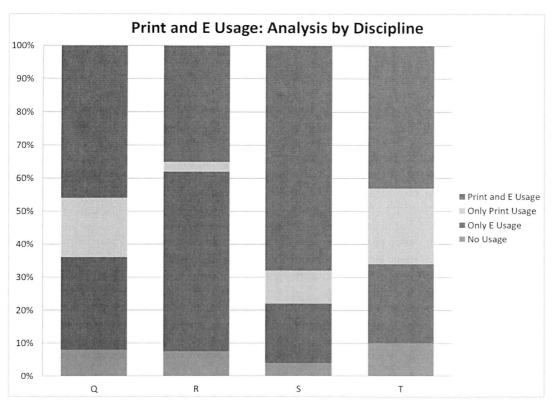

Print and E Usage: Analysis by Discipline

Legend: Print and E Usage, Only Print Usage, Only E Usage, No Usage

Figure 15.

Recommendations

Based on these collection development and analysis discussions, three major recommendations have gone forward from the task force and have been approved by the VIVA Collections and Steering Committees for further study:

Recommendation 1: Collaborative Retention of Widely Held Monographs

One of the early outcomes of this pilot had been the formation of a Memorandum of Understanding (MOU) for the Cooperative Retention of Rare and Unique Monographs. During the project, it was determined that there were over 72,000 main stacks books (in any edition) held by the 12 pilot libraries that were unique in Virginia and held by fewer than 10

libraries in the United States. Based on the MOU, each library will review the list of their titles and identify those worthy of retention, then add a note to the catalog for these titles to ensure their continued protection.

The discussion about collection strengths and duplication of titles across the pilot groups led to conversations about extending the retention project to widely held monographs to allow for safe deduplication within the consortium. If specific copies were set aside from individual institutions and protected from weeding, it would allow other institutions to more safely weed and reduce concerns about getting rid of the last copy or copies available in the consortium of particular titles. Such a project could incorporate the subject strengths seen in the collections by taking these strengths into account when allocating retention copies.

Recommendation 2: Establish a Recommended Threshold for VIVA Holdings as New Purchases

The duplication of title holdings across the consortium also led to discussions about how to prevent this level of duplication in the future. In line with similar projects done at the Orbis Cascade Alliance and OhioLINK, it has been recommended that VIVA member libraries buy print monographs on an individual basis, but in consultation with each other, to cut down on the number of holdings per title across the participating institutions. A common acquisition system, such as YBP's Gobi or Coutts' OASIS, could make this cross-consortium view possible, and at this time both systems are being explored.

Recommendation 3: Collaborative Publisher-Based E-Book Acquisition

The widely and highly and recently used title analysis showed strong patterns of key publishers that would likely be relevant across VIVA. This led to a recommendation that VIVA focus its collaborative e-book acquisitions on content from particular publishers as identified by the collection analysis as well as the survey of the VIVA collections contacts.

Conclusion

Overall, the pilot has provided VIVA with a wealth of data to mine. For a consortium without a shared library system, this project has enabled a view into print monographic data that was simply not possible before.

Cooperative Collection Development Requires Access: SALToC—A Low-Tech, High-Value Distributed Online Project for Article-Level Discovery in Foreign-Language Print-Only Journals

Aruna P. Magier, South Asia Librarian, New York University

Abstract

Foreign-language journals are an essential component of interdisciplinary area studies collections at research libraries but are, by definition, low-use materials. Librarians who select them seek to broaden these collections, reduce duplication, and enable shared access to them. The challenge is lack of article-level discoverability: these are print-only journals, not covered in online indexing/abstracting services. If users cannot discover these articles, then how can cooperating libraries share them, and distribute responsibility for collecting them, which is essential to coordinated collection development?

The SALToC project collaboratively address this issue by creating simple, centrally browsable tables of contents for target journals, through a low-tech, low-cost distributed process that benefits users at all participating libraries. For journals not available online nor included in article databases or indexes, this kind of discovery facilitates research by enabling scholars to use previously undiscoverable holdings of other libraries: they can now issue interlibrary loan, document delivery, and/or offsite retrieval requests, with full citations for desired articles. (Many libraries provide article document delivery, if the requester has a citation). Coordinated collection development (via planned reduction of duplication coupled with broader collective coverage) becomes supportable in the research library community only when shared access (and its prerequisite—discovery) is provided. The South Asian Language Journals Table of Contents (SALToC) project represents a proof-of-concept demonstration of the value of this approach. This paper shows how simple, "grass-roots" distributed efforts can contribute significantly to discoverability of hard to discover resources, thereby making coordinated collection development cost-effective, popular among users, and sustainable.

Introduction and Rationale

It is well understood that for any given unit of content that libraries make available to their patrons, the actual ability to use that content depends on discovery. If you can't discover that it exists, you can't locate it, can't request it, retrieve it, or use it. As many have observed, discovery is a prerequisite for access.

In the same way, if parts of a library's collections are not exposed for discovery, they also cannot effectively be shared with other libraries—because they cannot be requested by patrons at the partner institutions. In other words, discovery—or the lack of it—*delimits* what libraries can share with each other or borrow from each other. Stated from the patron's perspective, the key benefit of shared collections (access to more needed content) can only be derived for materials exposed for discovery.

In recent times, many libraries have responded to tight budgets by cutting back on their own collecting, relying more heavily on the collections of other libraries to help fill their users' needs. When groups of libraries that engage in collection sharing then coordinate their collection development going forward, they can reduce unnecessary duplication, redirect resources to broaden the scope of the community's aggregated shared collection, and increase the likelihood of being able to respond to their patron's needs on the whole. But the entire premise of coordinated collection development relies on access to one another's collections, which, as I have said, presupposes discovery.

But discoverability is not a yes-or-no characteristic. There are various kinds of exposure that libraries can provide, for different kinds of material, yielding different *degrees* of discoverability, and requiring different amounts and kinds of investment to make the discovery possible. For example, at the low-investment end of the spectrum, simply having a book or journal issue present in the open stacks makes its content at least theoretically discoverable via browsing. At the other end of the spectrum, full-text digital presentation of collections of content, with full-text indexing, multiple descriptors and added-value access points, cross-referenced authority files and thesauri, etc., exposed through an intuitive interface for searching and browsing, with facets for narrowing or broadening one's search, relevance-ranking of results, presentation of related materials, and so on, all make the units of content much more discoverable. But, of course, creating the metadata and mechanisms that underlie that kind of discovery costs much more money!

In this paper, I explore the relationships between discovery and cooperative collection development. I focus on a particular category of content for which libraries have traditionally not invested much in its discovery—if they collect it at all. I am speaking here of foreign language journals, and especially print-only journals.

Many countries of the world publish a broad range of journal literature of importance for research, in the languages of their regions. While the best of these are considered to be an essential component of interdisciplinary area studies collections at US academic research libraries, they are often, by definition, low-use, "obscure" material, and it makes sense for the librarians who collect them to seek to broaden these collections in a coordinated way, reducing duplication nationally, and enabling shared access to them. But the problem has been lack of discoverability of the articles in these journals: they are print-only, not covered in online or printed indexes or indexing/abstracting services. If users cannot discover the articles in these journals (except via physical browsing), then how can cooperating libraries share them, and distribute responsibility for collecting them, which is essential to coordinated collection development?

The rise of e-journals in general has enabled vast increases in discovery at the article level. Before

e-journals existed, libraries created title-level discovery of the journal itself through creation of a single bibliographic record, with subject headings, etc. A patron could discover that a journal on a certain topic existed, but the only way to find individual *articles* was to physically browse the holdings. Occasional printed author- and subject-indexes brought out by a journal's publishers enhanced article-level discovery, later followed by third-party indexing and abstracting services that enabled article-level discovery across multiple journals. By and large, such bibliographic-only databases have been supplanted or made redundant by the rise of full-text e-journals with publisher-level cross-journal article discovery through the publishers' or aggregators' interface, and integrated discovery systems across all those systems at the higher end of the spectrum as described above.

But each improvement in article-level discovery along that continuum left some journals behind, as discovery-providers deemed that content not worth the investment needed to bring it up to the current high-end. The journals generally left furthest behind in the process are foreign-language journals in general, and those that are not publishing online in particular. Articles in print-only foreign journals are all too often stuck back in the dark ages of discovery.

Even where libraries have continued to collect them for the inherent research value of their content (and to suit the local research and teaching priorities), bibliographic access at the article level has only been possible by physical browsing. While there are large differences from country to country, due to differences in the penetration of online publishing, area studies librarians report that vast swaths of this kind of content is not only not online, it is not even indexed anywhere. For example, my colleagues among Middle East Studies librarians report almost none of the periodical literature from that region is online or indexed (in print or online fashion). The same is largely the case with journals in the languages of Africa, South Asia, Southeast Asia, much of Eastern Europe and Central Asia, the Caribbean, and even parts of Latin America.

Because this content is in foreign languages, of course, its usage is much lower than that of journals in English or other commonly taught languages. But even those students and scholars who can read those languages, and whose research would benefit from access to these articles, tend not to use them because discovery is so difficult compared to our growing expectations of keyword searching or "click-and-read."

Not surprisingly, libraries respond to low usage in several ways: if the constituency for the content is complacent, the library may simply stop collecting these journals, and withdraw the backfiles to save space. Or, perhaps less radically, they will move these print journal runs to compact, off-site storage, for retrieval on request. But for an unindexed print-only journal, this solution enacts a self-fulfilling prophecy of zero usage. Held offsite where they cannot be browsed, no one will discover any articles in these journals, no one will use them at all, and a history of nonusage will inevitably lead to withdrawal, to save on the costs of storage.

To the extent that foreign print-only journal content has value for research, one could say that leaving these journals behind—so to speak—is a shame. If one wanted to address the problem, a number of approaches might be possible. For example, working with the professional organizations of area studies librarians—such as the Journals Subcommittee of CONSALD (Committee on South Asia Libraries & Documentation), JSTOR has been seeking to identify print journals from abroad that are priorities for negotiation with publishers to get their runs digitized and included in JSTOR. JSTOR's coverage of foreign journals from places like South Asia with vast print-only publishing industries has thus been growing gradually in recent years. But even there, the growth has been in English-language journals (the largest language of publishing in South Asia, as in many parts of the world). So the foreign language journals yet again get left behind.

The question then arises of whether or how to create article-level access to these print-only orphaned journals. Attempts have been made in this direction, sometimes through cooperative efforts of librarians who try to create some of the same kind of indexing and abstracting value seen in an earlier era for English-language journals. But, creating article-by-article metadata for such databases is quite expensive, especially when you consider the need for language-expertise to go along with the indexing or cataloging skills needed to do it.

In an era when even large research libraries working together are having trouble securing the human resources to do original cataloging of their backlogs of books and journals, how likely is it they could prioritize the indexing or abstracting of the vast number of individual *articles* in all those demonstrably low-use, specialized foreign language journals? With some notable exceptions (like HAPI, Hispanic American Periodicals Index published out of UCLA), these attempts have been spotty, limited in scope and/or hard to sustain. The cost-benefit analysis tends to make these efforts hard to justify.

I am now going to provide a case study of another new, experimental approach being undertaken by a collaborating group of South Asia librarians, targeted at a selected group of print-only journals in languages of South Asia. It is called SALToC: the South Asian Languages Cooperative Tables of Contents project. It was designed to be a low-tech, low-investment, distributed online project to enable article-level discovery towards the low end of the discovery continuum: discovery by online *browsing*—which is certainly incrementally better than no discovery, and which provides, as I will show, quite valuable benefits for access and cost-efficiencies for coordinated collection development.

A distributed low-cost system of creating simple, centrally browsable tables of contents in a sustainably accessible infrastructure with low-institutional barriers can facilitate research by finally enabling scholars to make use of these previously undiscoverable journal holdings. Discovering articles this way makes it possible for them to issue interlibrary loan requests, document delivery requests, and offsite retrieval requests, with full citations for the desired articles. While many libraries do not send lend print journals on interlibrary loan, many do offer article-level document delivery on request, but only if the requesting institution provides a *full citation*.

The "grass-roots" distributed nature of the SALToC approach I will describe here offers a proof-of-concept demonstration that coordinated collection development and reduction of unnecessary duplication can be sustainable, popular among users and cost-effective in the research library community through the shared access made possible by this low-lying discovery layer.

Let us look at the SALToC model in some detail to see how it works, and what its values and weaknesses might be.

Goals of the Project

The group of South Asia librarians, representing the needs of their respective South Asian Studies constituencies, worked with me to develop a set of operating criteria and goals for a joint project. The main goal of SALToC was to enable article-level discovery of vernacular language journals from their collections that were identified as not otherwise discoverable, because they are not online and not included in existing full-text or bibliographic databases. Key objectives included:

- Enabling patrons to identify and access articles in their own collections or request them from other libraries through standard ILL.

- Enabling patrons to use citations to request journal articles from offsite storage.

- Enabling cooperating libraries to provide digital document delivery ("scan and deliver" service) for articles in these vernacular journals, just as they already are doing for print journals in English.

- Providing an online substitute for physical browsing.

- Enabling offsite storage decisions for these low-use journals.

In contrast to other, more expensive discovery systems for mainstream materials, we also decided to clarify what SALToC is *not* meant to be. It is

- Not a journal article indexing project.

- Not an indexing and abstracting service.

- Not a searchable, structured database of citations.

- Not a table of contents alert service.

Process

The concept was to find a way to keep this as low-tech and low-cost as possible, while still providing real discovery value. The steps are simple, and do not require any special skills or highly trained staff at each stage of the process. Once the infrastructure was set up, the actual ongoing production is carried out almost entirely by student assistants who do not need to know the relevant languages.

1. Each participating library makes simple page-image PDF files by scanning the table of contents of each issue of the target journals they are contributing.

2. They annotate each issue's PDF file with a couple of basic fields pulled from their existing catalog record and volume holdings: title, imprint, volume, issue number, date.

3. These annotated PDFs are sent to me at the central SALToC repository at NYU.

4. At NYU, these SALToC tables of contents files are stored as part of the University's institutional repository in the DSpace platform, with a separate permanent URI for the separate landing page for each journal, with its accumulating tables of contents, and acknowledgement of the contributing library.

5. A link to permanent URI for each journal's landing page is then added to the regular catalog record for that journal in the contributing library's own OPAC (to

enable discovery of the ToCs by their own local users).

6. NYU catalogers then update the WorldCat record for each SALToC journal to add the same link to the ToCs there (to enable discovery of the ToCs by everyone else).

7. A simple DSpace collection page for whole SALToC project, listing and linking all the journals included, is also maintained in NYU's repository, to allow the participating librarians to promote and highlight SALToC to their patrons (through LibGuides, bib instruction, etc.), beyond the linkage for each title provided through OPACs and WorldCat.

Participants

Current participating libraries contributing ToCs to SALToC include University of Hawai'i, University of Pennsylvania, Princeton, Columbia, Yale, University of Chicago, University of Washington, Center for Research Libraries, and Library of Congress overseas field office in Islamabad. Several other libraries are now preparing to start contríbuting ToCs as well. The home of the SALToC project is New York University, whose contribution to the collaboration is hosting SALToC on their existing DSpace platform as part of their institutional repository, and having students add each new ToC to the collection as it comes in.

Workload

The distribution of production work among the participants is simple. Contributing libraries scan the ToC of each issue of their journal as received (about 10 minutes), and submit it to NYU. They also—just once for each journal—have their catalogers update the local OPAC record to add the 856 link to the permanent URI for that journal (less than 5 minutes).

At NYU, the ongoing workload is just adding each PDF file to the DSpace repository as it is received from the contributors (less than 5 minutes). The one-time work for setting up each journal title in SALToC is just creating its permanent landing page in DSpace (containing the brief bib info from the annotation, a link to the WorldCat record, and acknowledgment of the contributor), which takes about 10 minutes, and updating the master record for the journal in WorldCat (less than 5 minutes).

Sustainability

Our goal was sustainability. Among other reasons, we wanted to make sure that the catalogers' one-time-per-journal work of adding links into OPAC and WorldCat records (simple as it is) would not need to be updated or revised later. While catalog links to web content are notoriously ephemeral, and tend to go out of date and become dead-end links very quickly, we wanted to reassure the catalogers that they were linking to permanent content at a permanent address. We addressed overall sustainability in several ways:

- SALToC uses a light-weight, low-tech maintainable infrastructure.

- It requires minimal resource investment in terms of human workload and system resources.

- It provides demonstrable value for our patrons.

We also managed to avoid reinventing the wheel. We created what is undeniably a niche product (that fills a specific need not otherwise filled for South Asia vernacular journals), but *not* based on a separate niche infrastructure. Basing SALToC in the University's DSpace required no specialized programming, workflow, database, or server maintenance. It uses a system already put in place and maintained to do what the University is already committed to doing anyway: a permanent repository for faculty, with long-term institutional commitment for permanence and permanent URLs. So SALToC gets to leverage the value of that existing infrastructure without adding any extra cost.

Scalability

How scalable is this model? What are the potential limits on its growth? SALToC is scalable because contributor institutions add as much or as little as they want. The barriers to entry are exceedingly low, and so far, the decisions about making these minor investments have been kept very close to the "grass roots" level (i.e., the front-line area studies librarians who work most closely with the scholars who benefit from SALToC). But each contribution (table of contents) adds *incremental* value to SALToC, creating permanent discoverability for the corresponding articles in the libraries' print holdings, via the links in the OPACs and in WorldCat records. Now that this infrastructure is in place, the work to insert each successive contribution is negligible: it is completed in mere minutes by nonspecialist staff and students.

So SALToC seems to be both sustainable and scalable. In contrast, projects that have attempted to create discovery at higher points on the continuum, for example by creating searchable, structured databases of full article citations (like LAPTOC, the Latin American Periodical Table of Contents project) require actual data entry for each article at each participating institution. This dramatically increases the cost of production, making the project less sustainable or scalable. Similarly, the South Asian Periodicals Index at University of Wisconsin is also a manually constructed article-by-article citation database. It ceased production after six journals (all but two of them in English).

Learning from projects such as LAPTOC and SAPI, participants in SALToC chose to use meet the needs of discovery through *browsing*: mere page images, with no data-entry and no language skills required. After only six months in production, SALToC already contains about 300 tables of contents files in six languages of the Subcontinent.

Going forward, the South Asia Librarians have been conferring together to develop consensus criteria for selecting and prioritizing additional journal titles from their collections: periods of coverage and completeness of holdings, target subjects, target languages, and soliciting faculty input to identify specific high-value titles for inclusion.

Conclusion

In designing the SALToC model, we have tried to find an appropriate value point between the ideal and the real. Recognizing that article-level discovery is a matter of degree, and that the high-end of the continuum (the ideal) would require high levels of investment that would skew the cost-benefit ratio making the whole enterprise unsustainable in institutional contexts of constricted resources, we sought instead to create something much more modest, of incremental value that could be sustained because it is unlikely to fall to the cost-cutting axe.

It is too soon to conduct a full-scale evaluation and accounting of fully loaded costs and values, costs-per-use, impact factors, etc. And we have already heard from some that comparing SALToC to other resources they are familiar with (for example, JSTOR), it clearly seems home-grown and improvised, and lacking in features they love in those high-end productions. On the other hand, we are also receiving enthusiastic reports of use cases of how SALToC is enabling scholars to delve into the journal content we are collecting for them across our cooperating institutions, in ways that seem to validate the premise of coordinated collection development. So we are encouraged to stick to our SALToC slogan: *Don't let the excellent be the enemy of the good!*

References

SALToC: South Asian Language Journals Cooperative Table of Contents Project. https://archive.nyu.edu/handle/2451/33560 (accessed 12/5/14)

Magier, Aruna P. 2014. Cooperative collection development requires access—SALToC (Charleston 2014 presentation SlideShare). Retrieved from http://www.slideshare.net/arunamagier/aruna-magier -charlestonpowerpoint

Wilde About Weeding: An Earnest Effort in Collection Development

Melissa Johnson, Georgia Regents University

Abstract

In an effort to create more student space, provide ease of access to resources, and strengthen their collection, a medium sized academic library at a recently consolidated university undertook a major weeding project in 2014. A weeding plan was developed for both the monographs and the serials. Since it was important to get immediate results in removing items from the collection, the print serials section was the first area selected for weeding. Through a step-by-step process that involved all members of the library staff, items were evaluated on electronic availability, availability at the other university libraries, the content, the condition, and the length of run.

In January 2013, the University System of Georgia (USG) approved the consolidation of eight system universities into four. One of these consolidations was between two institutions in Augusta, Georgia, i.e., Augusta State University and Georgia Health Sciences University, home of the Medical College of Georgia. The resulting institution, Georgia Regents University, is "one of only four public comprehensive research universities in the state" (USG, n.d., Overview section, para. 1). In addition to the two campuses in Augusta, now designated the Health Sciences Campus and the Summerville Campus, "the Medical College of Georgia includes a partnership campus in Athens, Ga., and satellite campuses in the Georgia cities of Albany, Rome and Savannah" (USG, n.d., Overview section, para. 1).

The two campuses in Augusta are distinctly different. The Health Sciences campus is the medical campus for the university and attended predominantly by professional graduate students. It is home to the Medical College of Georgia, College of Allied Health Sciences, College of Dental Medicine, the Graduate School, and the College of Nursing. This campus is serviced by the Robert B. Greenblatt, MD Library. The Summerville campus is predominantly an undergraduate campus serving a liberal arts mission with a limited number of graduate programs. It is home to the College of Education, Pamplin College of Arts, Humanities, and Social Sciences, the Hull College of Business, and the College of Science and Mathematics. This campus is serviced by the Reese Library. The total student FTE for the university during fall 2013 was 8,995, with the majority (5,645) of these being

undergraduates. Each of the University Libraries maintains unique collections that support the curriculum on their respective campuses. The Director of Libraries oversees the overall administration of both Reese and Greenblatt Libraries, and a Head Librarian manages the operations for Reese Library.

In some of the other University System of Georgia consolidations, there were overlapping programs, such as two English Departments, two Math Departments, and the like. However, one of the unique features of the Georgia Regents University consolidation was the difference between the two legacy institutions. The only overlap was a nursing program on the Summerville campus that consolidated with the College of Nursing on the Health Sciences campus. The program and its faculty were transferred to the Health Sciences campus. As a result, the nursing resources in the Reese Library were evaluated; with some transferred to the Greenblatt Library while others were weeded from the collection entirely. Reese Library maintained 312 monographic nursing titles that were later removed from the Library. There were also 95 nursing journal titles removed.

Upon the transfer of the program, a comparison of serial titles was made between the holdings of the Greenblatt Library and the holdings of the Reese Library. This comparison looked at runs of journals, journals held at Reese and not at Greenblatt, duplicates, holes in collections, and online availability. There were 33 titles (178 volumes) transferred from Reese Library to Greenblatt Library. There were 62 duplicate titles

(1,251 volumes) between the two libraries. The duplicates were weeded from the Reese Library.

The consolidation of nursing resources was the consolidated libraries' first foray into weeding. A bigger weeding project where the collections of both libraries could be evaluated was planned for 2014 and a weeding plan developed for both libraries. The purpose of this weeding plan is to ensure a relevant collection that supports the university's mission. It will make active items more visible, attractive, and accessible, ensuring the most efficient use of existing, limited space. In addition, shelf space for new additions to collection will be created (Reese, 2014). Space in both libraries is limited and weeding the collections will also allow for the creation of more student areas.

The weeding plan establishes some criteria for both monographs and serials for use in determining whether or not items can be weeded from the collection. For monographs, the criteria for weeding includes those items that are badly worn or mutilated. If an item is important to the collection, however, it will be mended instead of weeded. Duplicate copies of seldom used items are also on the list for weeding.

It is important to note how the collection was originally developed. In an effort to obtain materials to quickly build the collection in early years of Reese Library, many books were acquired in lots. Some of the acquired materials were tangential to the curriculum, but filled the shelves and added volumes to the statistics. For example, being a primarily liberal arts campus, there are many monographs in classic literature that are very old and have never been checked out.

Items determined to be inappropriate to the mission of the University or not relevant to current or planned curriculum needs are also listed in the criteria for weeding. A check-out report was run in Voyager to determine the check-out frequency of items. Those items that have not been used recently, within the past ten years, have also been marked for weeding. Items determined to be obsolete, which is especially important for science and medicine, have been selected for weeding, and monographs that have

not been catalogued, unless determined to be vital to the collection, are also marked for deselection. Superseded editions and unsolicited donations that do not support collection needs are also on the list for weeding. At the start of the weeding plan, the Reese Library's holdings included approximately 352,000 titles.

In an effort to expedite the weeding process, serials were selected as the starting point or the project. Serials weeding presented a different set of challenges. Criteria established for the deselection of serials included the same requirements as monographs, but other factors had to be evaluated, as well. Any serials that are still received in print were removed from the possible weeding list. Since there were two libraries who had print subscriptions to journals, the serials were evaluated for duplication (Thomas & Shouse, 2012). When the catalogs for both libraries were consolidated, print serials available in both Libraries show up in the holdings record as "multiple locations." When the holdings are reviewed, the record indicates that there are volumes available in the Reese Library Serials Area, along with the volumes held in the Greenblatt Library bound journals area. By reviewing the holdings for each library, the librarians determined which library has the most complete collection. Serials from the other library can be used to fill any holes in the run. The final location for the print serial is determined by which campus's program would be best supported by maintaining the serial.

Journals with short runs were also considered for serials weeding. Those serials with fewer than 10 volumes were examined closely to see if they were essential to the collection. Thomas and Shouse recommend removing journals where a low number of volumes are maintained (2012). Sometimes these short runs make finding articles more difficult for patrons as the EBSCO Discovery tool recognizes the journal title in the catalog and sends the patron on a search to find the journal.

One of the key determining factors in weeding the serials is online availability. In fact, this was one of the first criteria used in deciding whether a serial could be weeded. Thomas and Shouse state that "online access reduces a library's need to keep the print copies in browseable stacks" (2012, p. 93). In order to identify the print serials that were available online, a Voyager report was run. It listed all the print serials available at Reese Library. There were 3030 print serial titles. Included in this report were the title and holdings. Since the serials at Reese Library had not previously been available for checkout, the checkout history was not applicable to print serials.

The report run in Voyager included the title and holdings. It was transferred into an Excel file with an added column for online availability and a column for a weeding inquiry. The report was divided into 20 sections and distributed to 20 different library staff members. Each employee checked the Journals A-Z list to see if there was online availability. When the serial was available electronically, the staff member listed the database where the serial could be found, the dates of availability, as well as any embargoes that were put in place. The staff member would then ensure that the links were working to the database, clicking on the link and checking three different volumes and issues to confirm that the serial could be accessed online and text was complete. A benefit for checking the online availability of each title was correcting proxy server issues that remained as a result of the consolidation.

When each employee completed their section of the report, they returned it to the Electronic Resources and Serials Librarian. She reviewed the holdings information in the catalog and compared it with the electronic accessibility to ensure that the print holdings were covered by the online. Print serials that were image-intensive were retained. Also, valuable historical collections that supported the current academic curriculum were kept. The Library boasts possessing volume 1, issue 1 of *Library Journal* from 1876, as well as 100 years of print that the Library does not have online access to. When checking for online availability, depending upon the database where the online version was found, the licensing agreement was reviewed for post-cancellation rights.

The Electronic Resources and Serials Librarian also identified duplicate holdings. In conjunction with the Chair of Content Management at the other Library, items that were available at both libraries were looked at individually to determine which library and which campus should maintain the physical print. Despite there not being overlapping programs, due to the subject matter of the journals, some of the resources in the fields of biology, medicine, chemistry, kinesiology, and psychology were duplicated on both campuses. When there were duplicate holdings, they were reviewed to ensure that any holes in the existing collection were filled before weeding the rest of the journal run.

Once the Electronic Resources and Serials Librarian determined if a title could be weeded, another spreadsheet was created with that information. The title and dates of coverage were listed. If it was a title crucial to the curriculum, the electronic access was added to the catalog. OCLC was checked to ensure that the title and volume weeded was not the "Last Copy in Georgia." Then the print catalog record was withdrawn from the catalog, the record suppressed, and the holdings also removed from OCLC.

The serials were boxed up and labeled with the journal title, volumes, and dates included, and this information was included in a separate spreadsheet that was sent to the University's Asset Management department. Since GRU is a state school, any materials that are weeded must go through the Asset Management Department so that they can be sent out for surplus. This department checks with other universities in the system to see if they want to add the weeded materials to their libraries.

Several issues that the Library did not take into account when the weeding project began were staffing issues and expenses. Due to staffing shortfalls, the weeding process took longer than anticipated. Occasionally, a student worker was available from other departments to help with the weeding process. When additional workers were available the number of journals removed from the collection increased. It was necessary to set up a staging area in the technical services department of the Library to prepare for both journals and monographs that were to be weeded. Shelves were cleaned off to make room for the items selected for removal. The Library has two catalogers who were responsible for removing items from the collection. They began investigating ways to make the removal process go smoother. They implemented location changer software which drastically increased the speed with which they could remove items, using the bar code to select items for removal. Since the majority of the serials in the Reese Library were not able to be checked out prior to consolidation, they did not have bar codes.

Another issue to consider is the cost of boxes. The weeding project began at the end of last fiscal year when there were no funds available to purchase boxes. The Library made connections with some of the local vendors who were willing to give their boxes to the Library after they received a shipment. Once the new fiscal year began, funds were allocated to the purchase of boxes for weeding.

Thus far the Library has removed 503 serial titles. This includes 8947 volumes in 9259 pieces, with 858 boxes sent off to surplus. Through the end of October 2014, 16 of the initial serials spreadsheets distributed to the Library staff have been fully evaluated. The letters P through Z are still awaiting evaluation. Throughout the process, the availability of resources and the ease of access for patrons were forefront in the decision making. As this project continues, an earnest effort is being to ensure the creation of more student space and the remaining resources will be more relevant to the curriculum.

References

Reese Library (2014). *Reese Library—Weeding the book collection and journals plan*. Georgia Regents University, Augusta, GA.

Thomas, W. J., & Shouse, D. L. (2012). Rules of thumb for deselecting, relocating, and retaining bound journals. *Collection Building*, *31(3),* 92-97.

University System of Georgia. (n.d). *Georgia Regents University*. Retrieved from http://www.usg.edu /inst/profile/georgia_regents_university

Staring Into the Whale's Mouth:
Large-Scale Journal Deaccession at a Small University

Jennifer Dean, Siena Heights University
Renee Bracey, Siena Heights University
Peggy Hlavka, Siena Heights University

Abstract

Large-scale journal deaccession is an all-consuming project requiring considerable planning and staff time. The Library team at Siena Heights University, a small, Catholic, liberal arts university in rural Southeast Michigan, recently completed such a project. Project is a keyword—a large project like this is not business as usual, and must be managed as a project with appropriate staff from throughout the organization. Further, journal deaccession on this scale is not simple—it involves a change in what libraries have always done. Staff need time to absorb the changes, and to understand all of the ramifications on their future work. Perspectives from both librarians and paraprofessional staff are essential for a multifaceted view of the organizational, historical, operational, and emotional concerns involved in a large-scale journal deaccession project. This paper outlines how one small institution's journal deaccession project was managed, from initial conception to getting it done, including which staff should be involved, steps necessary to complete the project, how to talk about the project internally and with stakeholders, potential pitfalls, and how to deal with problems as they arise.

Siena Heights University —Background and History

Over the years Siena Heights University, a small, Catholic, liberal arts institution sponsored by the Adrian Dominican Sisters, has migrated from a religiously based women's educational institution to a comprehensive University offering multiple degrees and fields of study and hosting a significant population of athletes. The Library has been in a state of transition throughout, changing from a "fill the shelves" mindset to one of discretion in collection development.

Library staff began weeding the book collection several years ago, when the University started a football program and the institution envisioned an enrollment increase as the program attracted more students. The Library was asked to give up a floor of the stacks to help provide classroom space to accommodate the expected growth. Ultimately, staff weeded over 35,000 books from the general collection. When the decision was made to weed the collection, staff started with the general collection and then moved to specialty collections, using criteria that included use, age, duplication, and fit with the current curriculum, making exceptions as appropriate.

Siena Heights University's Journal Deaccession Project

As little as four years ago, the Library was focused on completing collections of bound journal titles. As budgets grew tighter, staff looked to cut subscriptions, which were still primarily in print, to keep pace with inflationary increases. Initially, the director made difficult decisions to cut content, but duplication occurred as the Library's electronic subscriptions grew. Combined with the directive to clear a floor, documenting this duplication cleared the way for this project to take shape. Using the Library's EBSCO A to Z tool, Library staff ran comparisons of the journal subscriptions to online holdings, taking note of embargos and verifying full-text access to articles in reliable databases. Periodical records in the Library's Horizon automation system were updated, including donation notes, retention periods, binding instructions, location information, and online subscription information. Some of this work was done in the stacks using iPads, but use of printed records allowed for both extensive and informal notes. Data compiled and used to make decisions included who was using the title, use statistics, online database availability, relevance to curriculum, historical relevance, and relevance to the institution. Prior to this large project, staff weeded the bound periodicals three times and cut print journal subscriptions from 350 to about 175 titles. This review will continue in subsequent renewal periods. On the other side, online journal content continues to grow, far exceeding historical print offerings. The Library currently has access to over 45,000 titles online.

The Library team was familiar with the logistics of large-scale deaccession from their experience weeding the book collection previously. Like many libraries, staff chose Better World Books to recycle discarded books, taking advantage of free shipping and a share of the proceeds from any books sold. However, significant labor was still required—Library staff even enlisted the football team. The book deaccession project required gaylords and pallets for shipping books in volume and extensive trial and error and cooperation with maintenance to find the right gaylord fill level and pallet size to fit the Library's small elevator. The project required a floor jack on each level and a forklift to load the trucks.

All of this experience made the journal deaccession project less daunting at first. Although the timeframe was tighter with the journal project, the time-intensive process of collecting and using the data to determine cuts had been finished, and all that was left was finding a recycler. Better World Books does not take journals, and no company would pay us for the content. Initially, staff worked with the University's waste company, who had never expressed a concern with Library recycling previously. As the supply of containers for sending the recycling slowed to a trickle, University custodial staff investigated, only to find the waste company had decided not to take the journals because of the labor involved in separating the hard covers from the print blocks. After a number of phone calls and helpful advice from Library colleagues, the recycler used by the University of Michigan agreed to take on the

project at a cost of $75 per pick-up. The recycling company provided the gaylords and the pallets for Library staff to load.

A cooperative relationship with the University's maintenance department was essential to the success of this project. The maintenance crew removed door frames so the gaylords could pass. Pick-ups were carefully orchestrated to ensure someone was available to drive the forklift when the truck arrived. The maintenance garage proved useful for storing the loaded gaylords until they could be picked up. Borrowed tools, gloves, tarps, and floor jacks made the work go smoothly.

Organizational Considerations

It is essential to think about weeding on this scale as a project. Assemble a team—collections staff might lead it, but they need thoughtful and targeted input from everyone in the Library, particularly those who work in reference, ILL, and stacks management. All Library staff will need to be ambassadors for the project with students and faculty. Those involved in the labor will need support, and they will need time away from their usual work. This is an all-consuming project—it is mentally and physical tiring.

Think about the rationale for making this change to your collection, and how to communicate it in the library and outside. Use data about your collection to justify decisions, and talk with colleagues from other libraries who may be able to share similar experiences and help add credibility to the project. Often an exciting new initiative will precipitate a project like this, something that will bring library staff together to complete the project and create excitement for the campus community. But, this is not always true, and plans can change. Further, while libraries have always weeded, deaccession on this scale may be inconceivable for some library personnel. From their perspective, it simply is not what academic libraries do, despite evidence to the contrary. Project leaders must be given the time and space to think about the project and make peace with it. They will almost certainly be questioned throughout the project, and as the project progresses, decisions may need to be made quickly.

Ronald Heifetz's (1994) book *Leadership without Easy Answers,* available in ebrary's Academic Complete collection and recommended by library leadership expert Maureen Sullivan, provides a leadership model for working through a significant change. Heifetz writes about the difference between adaptive and technical change. Technical change is relatively easy. If the light bulb is out, replace it. A leader is generally not needed for this job.

Adaptive change doesn't have a solution. In an adaptive change situation, leaders can't fix the problems, although those who look up to them will want them to due to the disequilibrium caused. In this type of change, those involved and impacted by the change need to learn. They need time and space to do this. Leaders need to ask the questions that help people understand and come to terms with their situation, create the space to let them explore, celebrate and mourn the milestones, and pace the work. On the surface, deaccession projects are simple: weed the collection. But when undertaken on a large scale, they challenge the very core of what libraries have always done, acquire and preserve the best material. A project like this bears careful thought. Even some fairly progressive library thinkers are troubled about these projects. Libraries are engaged in a process called organizational learning (Argyris & Schön, 1978). Those two words are seemingly at odds with each other— organization implies order, while learning is messy. The organization learns when the people in it learn and apply this knowledge to what they do, changing the organization as a result. Administrators and project leaders must make space for organizational learning to occur. This is essential to the well-being of the library team and increases the likelihood the changes will stick.

Large-scale deaccession projects also involve a long transition, before, during, and after the project. Mitchell and Bridges-Mitchell (2000) have written about leading in transition, outlining a process and describing the supports a transition leader may need. Understand this project will be difficult. All members of the team will get tired at some point. They'll be unable to go back, but they may not be ready to take the next step forward.

However, this transition time helps people come to terms with the situation in their own way. Don't be too quick to solve problems.

Preparing for a Project

For those leaders just thinking about a project with no pressure to do it immediately, take the time to design it carefully. In an ideal world, the project will be orchestrated by the library. Talk with others in your institution to gauge the level of acceptance a project may have and what opportunities the project may help the institution realize. Many projects are happening—just like librarians, chief academic officers talk with one another and attend conferences. Take advantage of the opportunity to set a project in motion in a way that best benefits the library and those who rely on it. If you are tasked with this project by your administration before you are ready, think about how the project can benefit the library and the students and faculty it serves. Administration may have an overarching objective, but they are relying on their library team to make it work. Look for advantages and avoid victim mentality. Present the library as a partner and take ownership. Just saying no probably will not work. Get all the input you can early on, as once you've begun you must continue. This can make decision-making easier, but it doesn't mean the decisions themselves will be easy.

If the project must move forward before the library team has reached agreement, understand that being in opposition to other staff will cause great stress for those working on the project, particularly when their work is criticized. On the other side, for those who disagree with the project, watching it move ahead despite their best efforts to stop it will also cause great stress. All members of the team will need support. Think about how to make opportunities early on for everyone to be involved, even those who would rather not. Sometimes it is easier for staff to see how to contribute when the request is framed more specifically; for example, thinking about how the changes will affect ILL. Reflect and think about how to respond in pressure situations. When things don't go as planned, be honest and apologize if necessary. Mistakes will happen. Having many voices involved in the initial phases will help you avoid the obvious ones . . . but even the best laid plans go awry.

Lessons Learned

This final list includes tips from the Siena Heights Library team. Logistical and communication issues are unique to each library and institution, but these final thoughts are offered in hopes they will benefit others.

- THINK AHEAD!

- Think about the members of the library team, their personality and preferences, and how to empower them to make decisions.

- Include library staff from all areas in the planning process, especially reference, ILL, and stacks management. Talk to administration, students, and faculty.

- Broad involvement is necessary in the early stages. In the action phase, fewer voices involved will help the work progress smoothly.

- Take time to build trust across your organization so that those responsible for making decisions and carrying out the work can keep moving. Someone must have the final say when disagreements arise.

- Communicate, both inside and outside the library.

- Check for duplication between your print and online collections—Siena used EBSCO's A to Z tool. Collect and use data that will help staff make and justify decisions.

- Start with an accurate volume count and keep track of your removals for reporting and auditing purposes.

- Storage may be an option rather than permanent removal for volumes and shelving, whether on or off campus. If timeframe and staffing allow, exchange sites for periodicals may be an option.

- Find a recycler to work in bulk. Better World Books works well for books, but is not an option for journals.

- Give maintenance and custodial staff a heads up.

- Know your building inside and outside. Are door frames wide enough? Will you use an elevator?

- Gauge the project's scale. Will it take large gaylords on pallets or small boxes? A pick-up truck or a semi? A two-wheeled dolly, a pallet jack, or a forklift? A couple of people or a football team?

- Make sure you have sturdy book carts. They will be abused during this process. Cloth-sided bins worked well at Siena.

- Think about what to do with extra shelving. Is there time to donate them to another library? Is metal recycling an option?

- Be mindful of possible damage to floors. Siena's floors were dented, with several broken tiles once the shelves were removed. Sun and wax had changed the color of the surrounding tile.

- Be willing to make exceptions. If someone asks for discarded materials for their office, perhaps these materials should actually stay in the collection.

Conclusion

Planning is essential for a successful large-scale journal weeding project, regardless of the time frame. If possible, take time to lay the groundwork and find partners before starting. Help others take ownership of the project. The library team will change as a result of this project—the work will eventually come to an end, but staff will be just getting started. Once they've completed something big, especially if it required a change in thinking, the library team will see opportunities everywhere, opportunities to continue to streamline or improve or think differently. Embrace it—a learning organization is an exciting place to be.

References

Argyris, C. & Schön, D. A. (1978). Organizational learning: A theory of action perspective. Reading, MA: Addison-Wesley.

Bridges, W., & Bridges, S. M. (2000). Leading transition: A new model for change. *Leader to Leader*, 30-36. Retrieved from http://www.hesselbeininstitute.org/knowledgecenter/journal.aspx?ArticleID=28

Heifetz, R. (1994). *Leadership without easy answers.* Cambridge, MA: Belknap Press of Harvard University Press.

Adios to Paper Journals—Removed and Recycled—One Mile Long and 75 Tons

John P. Abbott, Coordinator, Collection Management and Professor, Belk Library and Information Commons, Appalachian State University

Mary R. Jordan, Collection Management Library Technician, Belk Library and Information Commons, Appalachian State University

Abstract

This presentation uses Appalachian State University's experiences as a stimulus for discussing how we have, and others may, successfully remove in a single swoop several thousand linear feet of little used bound periodicals. This effort opens library areas for new services and spaces. The program will be a resource and guide to others interested in large-scale deaccessioning projects and includes three deaccessioning projects using online back files from 1) JSTOR; 2) ScienceDirect, Wiley, and Sage; and 3) journals outside of these packages.

Introduction

Space constraints limit many midsize and small academic libraries wishing to implement new services. The largest occupant of library square footage is the paper collection: a collection declining in use. With the rise of ejournals and extensive digital archives, the most dramatic fall off in use has occurred in the bound journal stacks. Can large swaths of space be confidently reclaimed by identifying and disposing of bound journal content now held in online archives? What will the campus reaction be and how can it be managed? What is involved in project planning and implementation? What content was rescued from withdrawal?

In the summer and fall of 2014, Appalachian State removed more than one mile and 75 tons of the bound paper journal collection. This is our story.

Preparation, Preparation, Preparation

Setting: Appalachian State University (ASU) is classified as a Carnegie Master's/large institution having 18,000 students, with 10% of those in graduate programs. ASU offers a doctorate degree in education, and 185 undergraduate and graduate majors. The library is only 10 years old and demand for new services and space combined with low use of the bound periodicals indicated an evaluation of those stacks was timely. The bound periodicals are shelved in alphabetical order in compact shelving and occupy 10,000 square feet and eight linear miles of content.

Months of thorough preparation helped ensure success. The first step identified the online journal back files owned by ASU which appear stable and complete. A review of the literature indicated academic libraries engaged in similar projects had chosen JSTOR titles for deaccessioning. JSTOR digital content is redundantly archived in dispersed servers and through agreements with major universities to retain the paper holdings. Additionally, JSTOR participates in the PORTICO dark content archive. JSTOR met our criteria for stability and the extent of the JSTOR holdings would yield the significant clearing of paper volumes we sought. Appalachian State University has bought JSTOR content from the early 2000s, including all the JSTOR Arts & Sciences collections as well as other science and business collections.

After completion of the JSTOR project, further examination focused on other journal back files also owned by Appalachian State University. A second examination of the literature indicated many other libraries had completed deaccessioning projects based on owned major publisher back files. We determined our back files from ScienceDirect, Wiley/Blackwell, and Sage met our criteria for sufficient stability and extent. ASU has not yet considered any broad deaccessioning projects based on aggregator database full text holdings, e.g., Academic Search

Complete or others. The stability of aggregator title lists and holdings is unknown.

After identifying suitable candidate back files, the real work of the preparation began in systematically comparing ASU's bound journal holdings with the holdings information available from JSTOR or the publishers listed above. The following section briefly outlines the steps to remove these bound periodical sets from the collection. The steps were similar for all phases of the deaccessioning projects.

In step one, we exported the JSTOR or publisher's holdings from either their website or our license amendments. Using the print identifier (print ISSN), three students added our holdings beside the online archive holdings on a master Excel spreadsheet, what we called, "the alpha list." In the second step, the collection management librarians prescreened the alpha list for a priori "must keep" titles. The "must keep" titles were usually titles of regional interest or containing illustrations or advertisements not well captured online. A few dozen titles were removed. The third step was to reformat the master alpha list for a campus faculty review.

A fourth step was quality assurance. Student workers using the alpha list opened a full text article at the beginning and at the end of each title's online archive holdings. This assured us sufficiently that the complete content we proposed to withdraw was available online to the campus.

This thorough preparation took more than three months for JSTOR and it gave us firm footing to present the project to the campus through the dean of libraries and several outreach mechanisms including an extensive FAQ in a LibGuide built for the projects. The LibGuide contained a link to an appeal form for faculty to

ask for the removal of titles from deaccessioning. The provost sent out the notification of the project to all faculty.

After a three-week opportunity for faculty review, the fifth step removed the titles appealed by faculty from the alpha list. We were able to honor all requests; there were fewer than 15 appealed titles. The sixth step pulled the first volume of each journal title for the catalog maintenance unit's use to remove or suppress the bibliographic records and holdings.

After pulling the first volume, we indicate selected date range for the journal for removal by flipping the periodicals down on their spine. During summer and fall break, a team of student workers under close supervision by two staff members pulled those indicated bound volumes for recycling. The quantity and type of paper from the project that entered the campus recycling stream proved to be a problem for the existing system to accommodate and required negotiation with the recycling coordinator to complete the project.

The project was an overwhelming success. Approximately 1/8 of the unused or underutilized bound periodical stacks were opened up to be used in allocating new spaces for new or expanded services. Thorough early preparation around holdings and access gave the project integrity. Effective communication with Academic Affairs and directly to the faculty population reduced faculty concerns to only a handful, all of which had good resolutions.

We plan to expand this presentation into an article-level treatment presenting an in-depth discussion of concerns, detailed methods, and further outcomes. To view the LibGuide used for the project visit www.library.appstate.edu, go to Library Guides for Research, and search for JSTOR Duplicate.

Condition Considerations: An Inquiry Into Recording Conditions in Consortial Collections for the Purpose of Selecting (and Deselecting) Shared Print Copies

Mike Garabedian, Whittier College

Abstract

Following preliminary discussions about a shared print network among Statewide California Electronic Library Consortium (SCELC) institutions in which he determined that artifactual condition would not be a criterion for retention, the author developed an online survey instrument for the purposes of verification. The survey was utilized in a condition survey of mutually held book copies at eight SCELC institutions. More than 3,400 book copies were examined. Findings indicated that although the majority of books are in "good enough" condition for a shared print network, because just 1/3 of the copies have paratextual elements, it is probable that random deselection of books would result in deaccessioning "duplicates" with artifactual value.

Why I'm Here and What I'm Doing

People who know my library is not actually one of the SCELC institutions that expressed even a mild interest in shared print and therefore not one of the pilot cohort involved in the first round of collection and use analysis have asked me what a librarian from Whittier College is doing on our consortium's Shared Print Working Group, anyway. I think the main reason SCELC Shared Print Chair Bob Kieft asked me to participate is because in the informal online and in-person discussions about shared print that led up to the formation of our working group, I raised a point I thought important enough to repeat on several occasions. I first broached this subject in an October 2012 listserv posting wherein Bob sought advice from resource sharing network participants regarding his institution's (Occidental College's) large-scale deaccessioning plans:

> I wonder if anyone knows offhand if, in discussions about recent deaccessioning procedures and/or resource sharing (especially in regards to shared print book repositories), practitioners have given consideration to the potential artifactual value of the printed books in our general collections? . . . [I]f in going forward, just one or two . . . copies [of a given edition] are going to be part of our shared print repositories, won't we want to make certain that the copies we retain . . . are the most complete documents we can find?

Since in many ways the impetus for our consortium's shared print efforts can be traced back to that 2012 message to which I was replying, in one sense paying attention to the condition and completeness of shared print copies has been part of conversations about a potential shared print agreement from the first. And since in response to my reply more than a few member librarians said that in thinking about a consortium-level shared print agreement they favored a policy whereby "best copies" would be identified and retained for sharing, I became our Shared Print Working Group's representative condition person.

Of course, simultaneous to expressing a desire to retain best copies, colleagues were also quick to identify significant obstacles to considering book conditions for the purposes of retention and deselection. Karen Schneider of Holy Names University zeroed in on one of the main impediments to using condition as a criterion for shared print, writing "I agree with 'best copy' [but] am thinking that we have at best very limited tools for this (versus online bookselling where noting condition of copies is routine)." Meanwhile, consultant Lizanne Payne expressed others' legitimate concern that developing tools to assess and record condition beyond a simple kind of yes/no validation, and then deploying such tools, would likely be too time-consuming, and too costly an undertaking, for the purposes of shared print. (K. Schneider and L. Payne, personal communications, October 2012).

At the same time I was thinking about how we might use condition as a measure by which to identify copies to share, I became eligible for a summer research sabbatical that would allow me to test on a small scale the feasibility of the kind of condition analysis I was proposing. In short, my project was to define the physical attributes condition validation would include, but also to undertake the more difficult tasks of developing the procedures by which condition would be assessed and recorded and then actually to put these procedures into practice by assessing the condition of mutually held copies at several SCELC member libraries.

Why It's Important

Because of the ambiguity of the term but also because it informed my survey instrument and analysis, I want to distinguish what I mean by *condition.* For the purposes of shared print certainly it is imperative to identify damaged books or books with missing pages, for example, or to exclude from consideration book copies whose poor conditions might mean a copy would have to be conserved before it could be used again. For this reason existing shared print networks have developed basic validation criteria to identify and reject copies in really bad shape, and indeed, this is in general what practitioners who work in circulating collections think of when then think about a book's condition. However, as we begin to think about the exigencies of shared print, I argue it's as important to ensure the copies we select for sharing are the most artifactually complete copies we can identify. In this sense "best copy" means mutually held title whose physical form is closest to the book in its original state. So for example, given three copies of a mutually held book where one copy has been rebound in library buckram, one is yet in its original publisher's binding, and one is yet in its original dust-jacket, the "best copy" would be copy #3.

Librarians who work in general collections are of course not used to thinking about books in this way. Traditionally, the physical or artifactual value of books is something to which our colleagues in special collections give attention and prioritize.

Former University of Pennsylvania Curator of Research Services Daniel Traister has written, "the root of the sense of the difference between general and special collections" has to do with preservation versus access: whereas in circulating collections access and the intellectual content of books is emphasized, in special collections preservation and artifactual value take precedence (para. III.2). And indeed, to the extent we "do" preservation in general collections, it is not to preserve the objects in which information is embedded but simply to ensure these objects last longer, even if this means destroying parts of the originals (e.g., rebinding books in buckram boards), or using surrogates (e.g., microfilm, or digital facsimiles) in their place. Additionally, in general collections we weed books based on criteria like circulation and condition, something that doesn't happen in special collections. In the preservation/access binary practitioners like Traister have posited, then, general collections librarians come down firmly on the side of access: for us a book's intellectual content or "intrinsic value" trumps its format or artifactual value, which is why there's such a thing as library bindings in the first place.

In recent years more than a few librarians and bibliographers, including Robert Bee, Michelle Cloonan, and G. Thomas Tanselle—and perhaps more (in)famously, bibliophiles like Nicholson Baker and Nicholas Basbanes—have challenged the general collections prioritization of access and intellectual content at the expense of original objects. The most well-known of these challenges is articulated in *Double-Fold: Libraries and the Assault on Paper* (New York: Random House, 2001), wherein Baker argues original objects should *never* be weeded, noting that more often than not surrogates—whether digital or otherwise—fail to reproduce original objects in accurate, adequate ways. Tanselle made similar arguments a few years before the publication of *Double-Fold,* suggesting that "when it is understood that access to physical evidence is an essential kind of access, and that books must *therefore be preserved in as many copies as possible,* the questions of ownership and care remain significant" (para. 5, emphasis added).

Of course, in addition to its not being entirely objective, *Double-Fold* was written more than a decade ago, during the earliest days of digitization, and this may be one of the reasons that today Baker's and Tanselle's positions seem not only extreme but also untenable. However, it's not the only reason: Roger C. Schonfeld and Ross Housewright note that Baker's argument to save (nearly) everything "cannot possibly be feasible when libraries hold hundreds of thousands of ill-used copies, far beyond the number required for access or preservation purposes" (p. 8). Instead, they suggest a strategic approach to deaccessioning print journals based on "a clear set of community preservation goals . . . that ensures preservation" (p. 9).

Although print monographs present different preservation issues than do print journals, like Schonfeld and Housewright I hope we can develop a thoughtful and rational preservation-centered strategy for the large-scale withdrawal of books likely to obtain in the wake of a shared print agreement. To this end I suggest adopting an artifact-focused view of preservation allied more closely with special, not general collections. For if one of the goals of shared print is to allow participating libraries to deaccession duplicate copies in order to free up space, then in a real sense we are creating scarcity where none existed before. In other words, whether shared copies will exist in a storage facility or not, in essence a shared print network will constitute a kind of new, special collection whose originals will have to be all things to future consortium member library researchers, including researchers interested in books as artifacts.

Developing the Survey Instrument and the Methods

In developing the survey instrument for my project I wanted the instrument to gather information about completeness of and damage to mutually held book copies in several consortial collections, but also about key artifactual elements of these items. I sought above all to keep my apparatus complex enough to capture significant artifactual, paratextual information, but simple enough for work study students to deploy, and short enough to make analysis efficient and cost-effective. To help shape my questions I looked to some of the well-known published condition surveys undertaken in circulating collections at Yale, the University of Illinois, and Syracuse in the mid- and late-1980s; more recent surveys from the Universities of Kansas and Southern Mississippi; and a condition survey apparatus employed by the preservation unit at the University of California at Los Angeles. In part because my goals of hypothetical deselection of mutually held copies for shared print were different than the goals in these surveys (i.e., extrapolating conditions about entire collections, and prioritizing volumes in a single collection for preservation), without exception the survey instruments in these studies comprised far too many questions. However, the responses in the published studies informed my ultimate apparatus, which represents a kind of stripped-down version of these more complex surveys. (See http://tinyurl.com/conditionsurvey to view the instrument.)

The survey instrument I created is composed of five primary entries. Upon scanning an item's barcode the respondent is presented with three forced-response dropdown questions, two of which are followed by optional specifiers. Dropdown menus include nominal values describing the type of binding the item has, as well as 4-item Likert scales describing external and internal condition with options ranging from "very good" to "poor." The respondent is then asked whether to retain or discard the item, and a space for optional notes or comments concludes the instrument. Thirty-seven scripted responses to the five primary and four optional specifier entries would make data collection more efficient and data analysis easier, and also allow the respondent to make more explicit, objective claims about somewhat subjective Likert scale options.

The survey information was input directly into a web-based database created in Google Forms. I designed the form so that the barcode entry, forced-response dropdown questions, and up/down validation entry were required, obviating accidentally missed questions.

Additionally, for the sake of consistency I included explanatory notes for all but eight responses, which I deemed straightforward enough to stand alone.

Given concerns about the time (and cost) needed to undertake item-level condition analysis, it bears noting that leveraging Google Forms to design a survey instrument that fed directly into a web-based database, in addition to using barcodes as unique identifiers, made the process of data collection and analysis far easier and more efficient. Google Forms allowed for a simple, clean, and instructive data form. Scanning barcodes rather than inputting this information manually—or inputting another kind of unique identifiers like call number, title, author, or imprint information—saved inputting time. It also allowed me, post-survey, to draw out information about book copies from existing ILS item records and to manipulate this data for the purposes of comparing mutually held titles.

Before the survey could begin, a sampling method needed to be developed. I had significant help from USC Associate Dean for Collections John McDonald and SCELC Program Manager Jason Price. From an existing dataset of OCLC numbers of holdings at SCELC member libraries, McDonald derived a convenience sample of nearly 42,000 titles at my institution, Whittier College, that were published before 2010 and also held at two or more other SCELC libraries. Next, Price, McDonald, and I met at the SCELC offices to consider the feasibility of my Azusa Pacific University, BIOLA University, the Claremont Colleges, Loyola Marymount University, Mount Saint Mary's College, Pepperdine University, Whittier College, and the University of La Verne. See http://tinyurl.com/kjos29w for a map of the institutions.

It was determined that to generate statistically significant results, a final sample of approximately 4,000 items was necessary; and because the eight institutions hold these titles to varying degrees, items were sorted into categories based on the number of libraries in which they appear (3, 4, 5, 6, 7, 8). I strove to examine titles from each category in equal amounts, requiring the sample to include approximately 667 items per category.

This evenly distributed final sample was achieved by sorting the existing sample of available titles at the selected institutions by imprint date followed by call number, and then selecting every *nth* title in each category, where *n* was determined by dividing the total number of titles in each category by the number needed to result in the examination of 667 items. The sample was distributed thus:

Number of SCELC libraries that own	Titles count	Copies count
8	87	696
7	94	658
6	112	672
5	134	670
4	168	672
3	223	669
Total	**818**	**4037**

Survey Implementation, Data Collection, and Manipulation

I began with an Excel file generated by Price with each title listed in 818 rows, and whose 11 columns included OCLC #, Author, Title, and then a listing of the eight SCELC institutions; if a given title was held at a member library, this cell was marked with an "X." In order to isolate holdings at each library, I sorted the column that corresponded with the school I was visiting, deleted the remaining titles, and then sorted by call number. Next I printed these sheets out use as a checklist while I was implementing the survey.

Following a first survey conducted at my institution in late May, I visited the remaining seven SCELC libraries between July 14 and July 27, a period at most places when books are not as likely to circulate. Prior to arriving at the libraries I contacted directors and staff to explain my project and arrange my visit, noting that for my purposes I would require a library cart for my laptop and scanner and the wireless password in order to access my Google Form, Worldcat, and local catalogs. With the exception of one institution— Loyola Marymount University, whose student workers pulled and shared titles prior to my arrival—at each library I set my laptop and scanner on a borrowed cart, then proceeded to locate each item in the stacks, scan its barcode, examine the book and record the data in my form, then reshelved the book before moving on to the next title. (See http://tinyurl.com/nrcfk32 to see a few setup examples in situ.)

Following data collection, from the survey results spreadsheets I isolated the barcodes for the items I scanned at each institution. I then emailed these barcodes back to staff at each of the eight survey institutions, where systems librarians used review files to associate the correct author, title, and OCLC number with the barcodes, as well as the circulation data for these items, and then exported this information into a text file which they sent back to me. Next, I pasted this information into the survey results spreadsheets from Google Forms, color coded the data for each institution, and finally aggregated all the survey results in one spreadsheet. Arranging the data by OCLC number resulted in groupings of mutually held copies.

Results

In total I examined 3,429 book copies, spending two days at six libraries and one day at two libraries, where the average time to find and examine mutually held book copies was 90 seconds, i.e., around 40 books per hour. The majority of book copies I was not able to verify (i.e., locate in the stacks) were checked out to patrons or, as in the case of Azusa Pacific University, in the midst of a relocation. In the coming months I intend to return to three institutions in order to examine those copies I did not verify in this initial investigation. After examining and recording the conditions of these 3,429 copies, I compared mutually held titles in my aggregate spreadsheet. Three findings are, I think, worth sharing:

First, I discovered that the vast majority of the copies I examined are in what we might call "good shape." In other words, only 2% of all books I examined had external conditions I regarded as poor, and only 1% of all books I examined had poor internal conditions. In short, I determined

that 98% of all the books I examined reasonably could be candidates for use in a shared print repository. This was somewhat surprising, especially after reviewing condition survey literature from several decades ago which led me to believe that a far greater number of books would be damaged or brittle.

Second—and perhaps unsurprisingly—though not a strong one, there is a correlation between the frequency a copy circulates and the extent to which it is damaged.

Third, and I think more importantly, when I plotted total copies against those copies that had what I designated "paratextual value" (i.e., original dust-jackets, original paperback binding, or facsimile paperback binding), then grouped by "total copies," a clear trend emerged: overall, 31% of the copies in the groupings have paratextual value, which possibly indicates that if a title exists in less than 3 copies, *any* deselection has the potential to remove artifactually valuable copies from the shared print collective.

(See http://tinyurl.com/p4jt9pn, http://tinyurl.com/oee25rg, and http://tinyurl.com/ps6s8qd for graphic representations of these findings.)

Conclusions

For the purposes of a shared print agreement, from a condition perspective rooted in the culture of general collections where access to information is paramount, the overwhelming majority of the books examined for this project were good enough to retain. However, data also indicated that just one-third of the books in each copy grouping had paratextual value in the form of elements like original dust-jackets or publisher's paperback bindings. This finding is significant from a more artifact-centered position that seeks to retain mutually held copies that have the most artifactual value, as it indicates not only that the majority of books in the study did not have paratextual elements, but also that random deselection is likely to result in the loss of artifactually significant copies.

References

Schonfeld, R. and Housewright, R. (2009). What to withdraw? Print collections management in the wake of digitization. Retrieved from http://www.sr.ithaka.org/sites/default/files/reports /What_to_Withdraw_Print_Collections_Management_in_the_Wake_of_Digitization.pdf

Tanselle, G. T. (1998) Texts and artifacts in the electronic era. *21stC,* 3.2. Retrieved from http://www.columbia.edu/cu/21stC/issue-3.2/tanselle.html

Traister, D. (1998). Is there a future for special collections? And should there be?—A polemical essay. Retrieved from https://www.english.upenn.edu/~traister/future.html

Shelf Ready Doesn't Always Mean Ready for the Shelf

Stacey Marien, American University Library
Alayne Mundt, American University Library

Abstract

The Acquisitions and Cataloging Departments at American University have embarked on a partnership whereby an acquisitions specialist uses a cataloging checklist to check various aspects of shelf ready records for correctness and accuracy. Any books that don't meet the requirements of the checklist are automatically routed to the Cataloging Department for additional copy cataloging. Over the course of several years of refining the checklist, the number of approvals bypassing Cataloging has gone from 24% to 60%, which has freed up the Cataloging Department to work on more original and complex cataloging work. This has also led to other collaborations between the two units.

About American University Library

American University is a private, coeducational institution in Washington D.C. with an FTE of approximately 11,000 students. It is known for its programs in international service, public policy and public affairs, and international law and human rights. The library is a member of ACRL but not ARL.

In 2009, the library decided to broaden our services with the book vendor Blackwell to provide us with shelf-ready processing for our approval plan books. Blackwell would attach the spine label, apply the bookplate and property stamp, add the security strip and attach the barcode. At the same time, the library contracted with OCLC Worldcat Cataloging partners to provide us with MARC records for these shelf-ready approval books. Once the books arrived into the library, the Acquisitions Receiving Specialist would receive the books and review that all the pre-processing was done, and then divert all of the titles to the Cataloging Services Department for the record to be reviewed.

Once the shelf-ready program was up and running, we discovered that shelf-ready and computer selected MARC records did not mean books were consistently ready to be put on the shelf. All the books were being routed to Cataloging. However, Cataloging did observe that many books coming in through this workflow had no problems with their records and could have been sent directly to Circulation to be shelved

after the item record was created. At this point, in 2009, the Acquisitions and Cataloging Departments entered into their first collaborative effort to streamline this workflow.

In 2010, with Blackwell's bankruptcy, the library decided to use Coutts (now Coutts Ingrams) as our primary book vendor. We wanted to continue shelf-ready processing approval books with them as well as the collaboration we had established between the two units

The Idea

If the Receiving Specialist was already receiving the approval book and checking that the shelf-ready processing was complete, why couldn't she also check that the book's bibliographic record was complete enough to by-pass cataloging? This was the idea that the heads of both Acquisitions and Cataloging decided to explore. We needed to make sure that the Receiving Specialist had the time, knowledge and attention to detail to ensure the MARC records would be thoroughly checked and that it was done in such a way to make Cataloging staff feel comfortable with not examining every bibliographic record for newly acquired approvals books. It was decided that Cataloging would develop a checklist that the Receiving Specialist would follow. If the book and record matched everything on the checklist, the barcode would be scanned to add the item to the record and the book would be routed to Circulation. If the book and record did not match even one item on the checklist, the book would be routed to Cataloging for review.

The Specifics

Cataloging developed a checklist that is used by the Receiving Specialist to check for bibliographic errors in records for shelf-ready approval books. Elements of the checklist include a physical check for processing, instructions for routing non-standard books including folios, multivolume sets, literature that needs reclassification according to local practices, or books that should be sent to our music library. The Receiving Specialist initially checks the encoding level (Elvl) of the record, so that books with full-level ("I" or "_" [blank]) records are eligible to go through this checklist. The checklist includes basic matching checks of elements on the book and in the record. This includes:

- ISBN.
- Existence of 035 in record with OCLC prefix.
- Call number on the vendor-provided spine label matching the 050 and/or 090 in the bibliographic and holdings records.
- Matching publisher information in the record and on the piece.
- Matching dates in the 050 and/or 090, 260 or 264, and DtSt field in the 008.
- Pagination.

The checklist also includes more complex elements to examine, such as a check for variant titles (246) in records and more extensive instructions on how additional contributors such as illustrators and editors to a book can be reflected in a record. It should be noted that because of the sometimes complex aspects of these elements can't be fully covered in the checklist, it means that sometimes titles are routed to Cataloging for work when they have otherwise good quality records.

Any books with errors or missing information in their records are routed to Cataloging for correction and enhancement. In 2014, the Receiving Specialist who performs this work was

trained to check and compare encoding levels in OCLC and in our ILS. She was trained to import and overlay full level OCLC records onto our existing Voyager record in order to update them from prepublication or minimal level to full level. She then applies the checklist to the newly imported record.

The Results

When we began this workflow in 2009, it initially resulted in 24% of approvals bypassing Cataloging, but with additional refinements and additional training of the Receiving Specialist who performs this check, we have increased this number by approximately 10% per year over the course of the past four years, raising the total number of approvals books bypassing Cataloging to an average of 60%. The Receiving Specialist's accuracy in checking these books was typically 96% to 97%.

More Collaboration

Since collaborating on the shelf-ready approval project (the library also has firm order books pre-processed but these titles always go directly to Cataloging. This may be a future project to analyze, to see if we can apply the checklist to these titles), the Cataloging and Acquisitions Departments have worked together to improve workflows by Acquisitions' contribution to a long-term move to storage project in which we are moving approximately 100,000 volumes from our library's main stacks to a shared storage facility that is part of our consortia, WRLC. The purpose of this move to storage project, which will move approximately 15% of our main stacks to storage, is to make space for increased student study and programming space, as well as being part of a renovation of the library. The renovation of the library is somewhat dependent upon creating space in the library based on this move, so moving items has needed to happen at a rapid rate, at times being the Cataloging unit's number one priority since the project began approximately two years ago. As part of the move to storage process, we confirm that the cataloging record and barcode match the item in hand, make corrections to bibliographic records that are incorrect, correct holdings statements as needed, and examine materials for damage or mold.

One Acquisitions Specialist in particular has contributed significantly to this project, accounting for nearly 35% of the total volumes relocated to storage over the past year. In addition to performing the database maintenance and cleanup aspects of this position, she has also reviewed the work of acquisitions student workers who have been trained to work on this project during their down time and also serves as a point person for answering student questions. Although she initially only worked on single volume monographs and titles that were considered the easier part of this project's workflow, she has, over time, learned additional skills and works to correct problem titles routed to us that have errors in bibliographic, holdings, or item records. This has allowed us to move significantly more titles to storage and has given Cataloging more leeway to focus on projects requiring higher-level cataloging knowledge and skills.

Bender Library's Processing Department is located in the Acquisitions Department, and the Processing Specialist has provided Cataloging Services staff and student assistants training to identify which materials that are moving to storage as part of this project need to be routed to her department for repair, and has trained staff on how to identify mold so that these materials can be isolated and appropriately handled.

Another way the two departments have collaborated has been with e-book cataloging. Over the past five years, we have shifted to purchasing more e-books than print books. The Acquisitions Department is responsible for ordering all e-books that are one-time purchases (The Electronic Resource Management unit orders subscription e-book packages). Acquisitions has one dedicated staff member who handles the bulk of e-book ordering and importing of records. Initially, he would send a list of titles to Cataloging in order for them to review the records. That staff member suggested that since he was already in the MARC record changing the URL field, why couldn't he just check the record to make sure it was correct? Thus was born another collaborative effort. Cataloging developed an appropriate checklist and several staff members in Acquisitions were trained on using it. This collaboration has resulted in the elimination of the backlog of e-books to be checked.

Onward

Often times in libraries, various units in Technical Services do not necessarily work together. These units may create their own silos and may not be involved with work other units are doing. At American University Library, the heads of the units in Technical Services have worked hard to foster the idea that we are one unit, working for the same cause—to provide the best access to the material for our users. It has been very useful for the acquisitions unit to learn what the cataloging unit looks for in a good record. This has provided us with a shared vocabulary and understanding. Cataloging staff have also been trained to work in the acquisitions module of Voyager. This has helped in the demystification process for everyone. We can do this by collaborating on projects that get the materials out to the user in a timely manner. Our staff members have also been eager to learn new skills and to get a better understanding of what work is done in each unit, and how something Acquisitions does may impact the work in Cataloging and vice versa. One positive outcome has been an increased respect for work done in our units.

Digital and Physical: Coevolving Formats in Today's Research Libraries

Cynthia Sorrell, University of Maryland Libraries

Abstract

Academic libraries have been at pivotal crossroads for some years as deans and their staffers realize the perplexing shortage of shelf space for print volumes while at the same time determining the optimum balance of physical resources on shelves in light of the exploding world of online digital information. The question of what is the best format for the library users' research, teaching, and scholarship continues to be analyzed, assessed, and discussed. As a result, new and innovative library business models are evolving that consider dramatically "revisioning" floors of library space to accommodate the ever-changing needs of library users while at the same time providing a limitless quantity of research resources. Various methodologies, as it relates to library collections, have emerged from pioneering thinkers affiliated with such organizations as OCLC, ITHAKA with its JSTOR & Portico initiatives, the HathiTrust Digital Library, and the Committee on Institutional Cooperation (CIC). There are a host of challenges and possibilities as library systems collaborate and dialogue with each other and with these organizations' representatives. When actions are implemented to effectively accommodate what the evolving society of information-seeking users must have for their educational and research needs, then positive perceptions of a library's critical role in higher education can and will surface. The University of Maryland Library System, one of the newest members of the CIC, has been able to take enormous strides in its evolving business model. Perfecting the coevolution of formats—print and digital—thus meeting the demands of an ever-growing number of users, paired with the libraries' renewed confidence in reducing the physical collections' redundancy based on the notion of shared print repositories (SPR) have been tested and the new model is working. This discussion will center around the various stages, some of the challenges, and a few promising outcomes resulting from co-evolving information formats at the University of Maryland Libraries—one of the CIC's east coast "hubs of collective collections."

Presentation

One of the newest members of the Big Ten (actually the Big Fifteen) is the University of Maryland Libraries. It would have been a most pretentious concept to consider this state university as a collaborative colleague of such an established group of mostly Midwest institutions about 10 years ago. Since 2012, the University of Maryland Libraries have contributed to the innovative, dynamic models of academic libraries affiliated with the Committee on Institutional Cooperation, better known as CIC, the academic arm of the Big Ten universities. This library system joins a growing corpus of research libraries that view the cooperative sharing of available resources, whether digital or print, as the intellectually prudent approach in providing users, at all levels of learning, with necessary resources. Not reliant upon physical proximity, our users can now access over 90 million books that represent the combined collections of the 15 CIC university libraries. The "unmediated consortial" service known as UBORROW has made this a reality and has dramatically improved the system of delivery of books on loan while minimizing the need for libraries to invest in multiple copies of requested titles.

Additionally, CIC members are fortunate to have a remarkable remedy for the space limitations that all of us face or will encounter in the future. Attempts to maintain and house dated journal backfiles that are occasionally pulled from shelves for research, along with thousands of books and sometimes their second and third copies that may no longer be essential for current or upcoming university courses, have been challenges for today's libraries. CIC's answer to this dilemma is its shared print repository that has ingested over 93,000 volumes of journal backfiles to date. It is estimated that by 2016, the Committee on Institutional Cooperation's Shared Print Repository (CIC-SPR), with its first host site at Indiana University's Auxiliary Library Facility (ALF), will be able to ingest some 250,000 volumes.

These titles are fully secured. Gaps in the journal holdings are currently supplied by various CIC members, including the University of Maryland Libraries. Our representative on this initiative recently reported sharing a list of some 13,000 piece items for consideration as potential "gap fills" for missing issues in CIC's Shared Print Repository.

More than ever before in the history of libraries as information providers, users need and require research libraries to 1) evolve into businesses that effectively create better utilization of spaces that include a host of necessary research services, 2) experiment with new models of service and delivery of those services, 3) work in collaborative, consortial environments to discover solutions and best practices for libraries' known unknowns, and most importantly, 4) provide a balance in available resources, namely, the coevolution of digital and physical collections.

The major focus of this presentation centers on significant factors that continue to shape the University of Maryland Library System's journey as it assesses the benefits of providing both digital and physical resources to its users. The journey is far from nearing its destination as Greek poet Constantine P. Cavafy suggests in his metaphorical poem on life experiences entitled ITHAKA. Not surprisingly, the mission statement of ITHAKA makes reference to this Greek poem. ITHAKA is one of the organizations whose research continues to stimulate discussions with insightful answers to such questions as, "how do we creatively do what we know we know to match the needs of the libraries' users, *and* how do we do what we need to do as a consortium to affect changes in libraries?" ITHAKA relates the symbolisms in Cavafy's poem to its organizational standards by which work is performed and services are delivered. Thus ITHAKA is offering solutions substantiated by research results to the complex questions surrounding the changing approaches to the various services and the work of libraries. Odysseus's journey in Cavafy's poem was arduous as he conquered each obstacle on his eventual triumphant return back home. Throughout the course of any journey, with its many knowns and unknowns along the way,

Cavafy reminds the reader of the importance of attaining much wisdom and abundant joy through every experience. The flagship's library system has experienced many accomplishments in a short period of time through its leadership, through paradigm shifts in doing the business of libraries, and through joining the CIC.

The following statement is apropos to Cavafy's poem. "Reports that say something hasn't happened are always interesting to me, because as we know, there are known knowns; there are things we know we know. We also know there are known unknowns; that is to say we know there are some things we do not know. But there are also unknown unknowns—the ones we don't know we don't know . . . the latter category tend to be the difficult ones." This was a response by the former United States Secretary of Defense Donald Rumsfeld in a 2002 news briefing regarding the incident involving weapons of mass destruction and Iraq. It was considered one of his controversial "foot in the mouth" statements. http://www.defense.gov/transcripts/transcript .aspx?transcriptid=2636

While "unknown unknowns" may have presented Rumsfeld with difficulties in solving the country's critical defense issues, libraries have taken the unimaginable unknowns and put into practice many revolutionary ideas that have challenged and dramatically transformed the status quo in the library world. His statement will be referenced throughout this presentation to characterize the various transformational stages that have brought the University of Maryland Libraries to our present phase of the journey.

By testing unprecedented concepts of delivering information content to users based on solid analytical results from many years of joint research conducted by ITHAKA and OCLC, in particular, those prior "unknown unknowns" to libraries ten years ago have been turned upside down with what OCLC's Constance Malpas states as "scholarly reliance on full-text electronic resources" and how libraries are taking the lead in implementing with confidence an impressive number of digital resources. What a powerful assertion, especially in light of several fast facts that the University of Maryland Libraries posted on its 07/2014 web site. Known knowns at present include the number of physical volumes (4.3 million) in the collections with an ever-increasing number of e-journals (17,000), e-books (900,000) and databases (352+). This "eight-library system ranked 10th in electronic resources as a percentage of total library materials." In comparing these recent collections statistics to a 1998 report that cites 2.4 million books and 20,425 periodicals with no mention of digital resources, one can definitely grasp the seismic changes that have occurred within a short period of time in libraries across the United States. The University of Maryland Library System is no exception. Academic libraries have now swapped out areas that were once dominated only by physical collections with key necessities in today's libraries—uniquely designed study spaces with accompanying services tailored for a valued commodity—their users.

The concept of what I will refer to as the coevolution of digital and physical resources has by no means compromised the wealth of available research collections for our users as is evident based on the collections' statistics for 2014; however, in many ways, the expansion of digital resources that are available has simply presented researchers at every level of study with a countless quantity of information resources with beneficial choices of formats. Pragmatic improvements to the management of collections, joined with cooperative networks of collegial providers, and the expanded availability of digital research information at the click of a key stroke are shaping creative academic enterprise models for conglomerates of libraries nationally, globally, and virtually. No longer can an academic library system appear intractable in providing the merger of physical and digital research information or ignore cooperative collecting. The subject of relevancy on academic campuses in 2014 and beyond will necessitate libraries demonstrating their prominence, their versatility, and their ability to develop remarkable strategic plans for successful business management models. Library administrators contend periodically with relatively flat budgets that must be stretched beyond the limit to handle skyrocketing costs associated with maintaining a library system's print resources.

Whether it is the space factor for storing, the human factor for shelving and reshelving, the inevitable replacement factor for lost titles, or the boxing-binding-patching preservation factor, the physical collection's annual upkeep, alone, is monumentally expensive.

A major event some six years ago mobilized deliberation into action, as the University of Maryland Libraries faced several challenges with maintenance of the print collections in light of an emerging availability of digital surrogates. One of the projects underway just prior to 2009, which remains a central objective currently, involved members from the UM Libraries' Collections, Acquisitions, and Technical Services Units. The members of the group were tasked with continuing to diligently investigate and eventually procure JSTOR collection packages that represented digital surrogates to many of the libraries' print periodicals. Needless to say, this decision would by no means reduce the availability of research content. It would, however, allow the library to replace rows and rows of cumbersome physical bound periodicals, which occupied countless shelves on every floor of the main library. The work and tireless efforts of these units now provide users with access to hundreds of thousands of journal articles directly online. JSTOR, as educators, researchers, publishers, and institutions now realize, "is a shared digital library created in 1995 . . . providing full-text access to core scholarly journals in the arts, humanities, law, business, social sciences, medicine, as well as science and mathematics, is a not-for-profit organization" and is a member of the ITHAKA family. Since the UM Libraries were investing heavily in e-resources, especially with the ever-increasing number of periodicals available in JSTOR collections that adequately included a wide range of subject areas, it was only logical to begin planning for better use of spaces throughout McKeldin, the main library on campus.

This work would lead into the University of Maryland Libraries selecting Patricia Steele as its new Dean in 2009. A "known known" became strategically significant to the flagship campus's library system. Prior to accepting this position, Dean Steele was at the helm of a library system that was and still is involved in various member activities of the Committee on Institutional Cooperation (CIC). Adding to her portfolio was a direct involvement in digital initiatives. Steele was "cofounder of the HathiTrust, a shared digital library of leading research libraries." It was only logical that the University of Maryland Libraries would announce its HathiTrust membership in November, 2010. With new leadership in place and Steele's philosophies regarding the influence of digital formats and their discovery on the future of research collections, the UM Libraries would be committed to exploring, discussing, and then accomplishing methodologies that could dramatically advance serving library users on and beyond this campus with not only physical but also the expanded role of digital resources. The whirlwind of change continued when the established consortial experiences that the new dean brought to the position would be especially beneficial as the University of Maryland Libraries would indeed join the CIC in December of 2012. Joining CIC was a known unknown in 2009 for the University of Maryland Libraries when new leadership came aboard with new plans for progress. I suspect that in the back of her mind, Dean Steele knew that this future stage of the journey in 2012 would propel UM Libraries into an innovative multifaceted engagement in providing digital research to users on a larger scale than the physical research collections could offer the users locally and globally. A press release from CIC on the newest consortium member stated that this library system is positioned to "save money, share assets, and increase teaching, learning, and research opportunities."

http://www.cic.net/news-and-publications/news/maryland-and-rutgers-to-join-cic/announcement

In 2010, Dean Steele would announce the first of many "user-centered" plans that would involve a major renovation of McKeldin Library's second floor. While there is much to be accomplished at this state institution's library system, let me emphasize that our university constituents—some 37,000 undergraduates, graduate students, and faculty—have found a more "study-oriented, laptop-friendly" main library for the university, in large part, due to what is known as the Terrapin

Learning Commons. Commonly referred to as "TLC," users can find multimedia workstations, lockers for students' use, a MakerSpace lab for creative projects, rooms for individual and group study activities for students, faculty, and organizations on campus along with very inviting seating and a total number of nearly 400 computers available in the TLC and throughout McKeldin Library.

A better balance of digital resources alongside print collections has made it possible to replace hundreds of stacks with their tightly packed bound periodicals with comfortable furnishings for study areas throughout the main library's seven floors. Without a doubt, JSTOR will continue to provide libraries with digitally available surrogate resources that facilitate discoverability of journal articles in an ever-expanding number of disciplines. As this occurs, a larger body of research becomes available to users in digital format. Libraries, including the University of Maryland, will continue to reduce the physical footprint of periodicals as a result of the reliable digital alternatives available through JSTOR, known as "one of the world's most trusted sources for academic content."

Conservatively speaking, JSTOR's titles that are now available online have replaced some 910 identical physical titles (including many title continuations), that required over 3500+ linear feet of floor space!

If your travels take you to the University of Maryland for one of the Big Ten athletic games or if you are planning a road trip to our nation's seat of government, Washington, DC, do stop by College Park and tour Maryland's flagship campus with a stop at McKeldin Library and in particular, the 2nd floor's TLC. It is an impressively designed floor plan that provides users with the most requested services and a host of technological gadgets available through a no-fee loan program for their scholarly work.

With less than two years of active engagement in the CIC, the University of Maryland Libraries are taking advantage of some dynamic posits put forth by researchers that work closely with the consortium. As was previously mentioned, ITHAKA

S+R, part of the ITHAKA family, "is a strategic consulting and research service [that identifies issues facing libraries and] focuses on the transformation of scholarship and teaching in an online environment."

Positioned with ITHAKA S+R and JSTOR, Portico is the third leg of the "service stool" within the ITHAKA family. Such an unimaginable service some ten to fifteen years ago has taken the likely unknown unknown of perpetual access out of the equation. Portico ensures preservation for JSTOR's digitized scholarly content by providing "long-term digital access [beyond] defined trigger events that lead to loss of access." In other words, the Portico Archive, ITHAKA's preservation strategy for academic institutions, will provide post cancellation e-access to materials that are unavailable through other sources. With the use of "technical metadata" and other cutting-edge features, "Portico assesses and ultimately mitigates risks to assets in the archive." ITHAKA and OCLC (Online Computer Library Center) research, with proven results from pilot projects with CIC institutions, have been instrumental in providing the evidence for known knowns, known unknowns, along with unknown unknowns, that allow libraries to seriously incorporate the innovative and pragmatic coevolution of print with digital resources with reliable confidence in their future availability.

Successful breakthroughs at the UM Libraries have not been without challenges or as Rumsfeld would say, "unknown unknowns." An earthquake in 2011 that toppled 13,000+ books off shelves was followed by a mold outbreak in 2013 in McKeldin Library, which required the disposal of some 10,000+ severely damaged books. One could say that there was a bit of irony when comparing the uncanny book count during these two unforeseen events. While both unpredictable, unknown events would delay the JSTOR project, the latter incident dramatically altered the mindset of staff with respect to the print duplication situation in the stacks. The JSTOR project has demonstrated the value of the digital format especially with the vulnerability of print collections. JSTOR will continue to offer collections that increase the plethora of digital

information that replaces its physical counterparts on library shelves. We will embark on reducing duplication of monographs with remarkable acceptance and cooperation by our fellow colleagues. How exciting it will be to read the report, Successful Reduction of Physical Duplications, that will highlight major results of the next phase of the University of Maryland Libraries' collections journey. Based on the continuing research conducted by ITHAKA S+R and OCLC in collaboration with CIC member institutions, along with the growing digital resources now available in HathiTrust, this groundwork is well on its way. I want to also envision a time in the near future when the dilemma regarding the Federal Depository Library Program's (FDLP) print Government Documents will have constructive solutions to this overwhelming space situation for libraries. The next stage of research work that ITHAKA S+R and OCLC have embarked upon entails the colossal task of critically scrutinizing physical collections and the broad dimensions and possibilities with the notion of digital hubs of collective collections. Additionally, another future journey of research libraries will concentrate upon the reduction of identical collections of monographs throughout the CIC membership.

Conclusion

What an exciting period in the history of libraries. The progressive stages that have advanced libraries' users with physical as well as digital resources are phenomenal. Methodologies that have been successfully tested by CIC associates and this newest member are dramatically transforming the business models for delivery of information and the view of libraries from within and without their physical and virtual walls.

Two seemingly disparate statements from various centuries that were referenced earlier can be uniquely applicable as one analyzes the innovative happenings and mishaps in today's research libraries. Concrete, scientifically proven methods in cooperative and collaborative settings have and will continue to inform how the business of information in libraries and its discoverability for users are achieved. Rumsfeld's dubious quote in the face of war during the 21st century, and the

20th century Greek poet's work entitled ITHAKA brilliantly connects the body of research that will continue throughout this journey. At this point in time, with respect to the co-evolution of digital and physical formats, libraries are possibly nearing the midway point of a long journey. Libraries do indeed face many challenges in attempting new ways of doing business but we have many discoveries yet to be revealed, researched, and implemented within the partnerships of known knowns, ITHAKA, OCLC, HathiTrust, and the CIC.

Appendix

Resources

Lavoie, B., Malpas, C., & Shipengrover, J. D. (2012). Print management at "mega-scale": A regional perspective on print book collections in North America. Dublin, OH: OCLC Research. Retrieved from http://www.oclc.org/research/publications/library/2012/2012-05.pdf

Malpas, C. (2011). Cloud-sourcing research collections: Managing print in the mass-digitized library environment. Dublin, OH: OCLC Research. Retrieved from http://www.oclc.org/research/publications/library/2011/2011-01.pdf

http://about.jstor.org/10things

http://en.wikipedia.org/wiki/Constantine_P._Cavafy

http://www.grc.nasa.gov/WWW/k-12/airplane/newton.html

http://www.lib.umd.edu/about

http://www.lib.umich.edu/database/jstor

http://www.oclc.org/about.en.html

http://www.portico.org

http://www.sr.ithaka.org/

Good Things Come in Small Packages: Getting the Most From Shared Print Retention and Cooperative Collection Development With a Small Group of Libraries

Teri Koch, Drake University
Cyd Dyer, Simpson College
Pam Rees, Grand View University

Abstract

In June 2013, the Central Iowa Collaborative Collections Initiative (CI-CCI), inspired by a Charleston preconference on data-driven shared print collections, was established. CI-CCI went from being just an idea to a formal, MOU-governed organization in just six months. It is consists of a group of five mid and small central Iowa private academic libraries. Members are Central College, Drake University, Grand View University, Grinnell College, and Simpson College.

Unlike other collaborations of this nature, the initial primary focus of the group was identification of titles for retention, as opposed to identification of weeding candidates. Because retention was of major concern to the group, each library did a retention verification project. Each assigned retention title was physically verified on the shelf and marked as a retention title. A web application was built, using MySQL, to facilitate the retention verification process.

The second primary focus of the collaborative is the development of the "shared collection" approach via prospective collection development. The group is beginning to turn its attention to this phase of the project. It will be challenging due to the fact that we do not currently share a common catalog or vendor. Nor do we currently have the same level of interest and utilization of e-books or DDA.

There are both advantages and disadvantages of a collaborative of a small group of libraries, which are discussed in this paper as well as tips for beginning such a collaboration.

Project Background

Two academic librarians in Des Moines, Pam Rees, Library Director at Grand View University, and Teri Koch, Collection Development Coordinator at Drake University, initiated the collaboration. While Iowa libraries have a long history of collaboration, there had not been a shared print monograph collaboration involving private academic libraries. The following academic libraries from central Iowa agreed to participate: Central College, Drake University, Grand View University, Grinnell College, and Simpson College. To initiate the process, Pam Rees and Teri Koch developed a set of guiding principles for the proposed collaboration which was shared with and agreed upon in principle by the group:

1. Evaluate shared print monograph collections.

2. Decisions would be data driven.

3. 24-hour delivery of materials.

4. Coordinate acquisitions to eliminate all but the most critical duplications and maximize local budgets.

5. Secure commitment by senior administration at each institution to the project.

The next step was to iron out the Memorandum of Understanding (MOU), which was largely modeled after the Michigan Shared Print Initiative (MI-SPI) version. The group created two addenda to deal with specific and unique issues related to ILL and acquisitions/collection development. The MOU was signed just six months after the project was initiated. It was signed by the Library Director and the Chief Academic Officer/Provost of each institution in order to insure institutional commitment to the project.

CI-CCI Group Characteristics

1. Fairly homogenous (in size, location, mission). FTEs range from 1388 to 4400.

2. Long-standing history of cooperation (all are members of the Iowa Private Academic Libraries Consortium) and mutual trust.

3. Strong commitment to project goals and the importance of decisions to mutually benefit all group members.

4. No project manager.

5. No outside funding.

6. No shared catalog.

7. Once-per-month agenda-driven conference calls.

8. Governance is by directors (with involvement of some of their librarians).

9. Web site was created by Drake for key project documents, including MOU: https://ci-cci.org/

Project Phase I: Data Analysis/Retention Verification Project

After the MOU was signed, the collaborative hired Sustainable Collections Services (SCS) to analyze the data for the group. The group's combined holdings were slightly over 1 million records. About one-half of those titles were unique within the group.

CI-CCI members were in agreement that the data analysis should initially focus on retaining and preserving items rather than on identifying withdrawal candidates. This may seem like a distinction without much difference, but in fact, it turned out to be a significant factor in the analysis.

The group considered multiple factors (usually referred to as "scenarios") in developing the list of preservation/withdrawal candidates. The scenario ultimately chosen by the CI-CCI group used the following criteria:

- Published before 1991.

- Zero (0) recorded uses since 2005.

- At least 1 non-CI-CCI library in Iowa also holds a copy.

- Retain 1 title-holding within CI-CCI.

Given the group's desire to focus on retention/preservation we decided early on that the only way to truly accomplish this would be to do an actual "Retention Verification" project.

The retention verification project involved several elements:

- Verifying the physical location of each assigned title.

- Inspecting the physical condition of each assigned title.

- Assigning a status to the item (more on that below).

- Stamping each book with "CI-CCI 2013" to indicate that the book was a retention title and should not be withdrawn.

- Modifying the item's bibliographic record to indicate that it was a retention title (as of this writing, this step has yet to be completed).

CI-CCI ended up with 143,294 retention titles as a group. SCS attempted to, as much as possible, evenly distribute those among the group members relative to collection size. We all agreed that we would not begin looking at potential weeding candidates until the verification process was accomplished by each institution.

Project Phase I: Data Analysis/Retention Verification Project: Web App Design

Drake decided early on to employ the skills of its Library Applications Developer to build a web application to facilitate the verification process. The collection data from SCS was imported into a database, to be used by the web application, and care had to be taken to account for minor differences in the data between institutions. Due to the amount of data involved, proper indexing and table design were critical to achieving good performance. The data is stored in a MySQL database—a common product for projects like this—and freely available. The applications developer paid particular attention to the creation of indexes, which improved database performance time.

The front-end web application was designed with one purpose: making it easy to record the verification at the shelves. For this it was essential that the user interface be responsive. In other words, it had to function effectively on any device with any size screen-from phones, to tablets, to laptops on carts. There was no way to know what devices users at the member institutions would use, and putting any restriction on what they could use would run counter to the idea of making verification easy. The responsive design was made simpler by using a freely available CSS and JavaScript-based user interface library called "Bootstrap," which was designed with these features in mind.

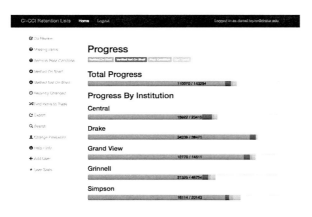

Figure 1. Display of web application used to facilitate retention verification project.

Most of the group members had student employees perform the verification process. At Drake, students went into the stacks with netbooks on carts. Using a dropdown menu in the web app, students assigned each item a status:

- *Verified On Shelf* if the item was found on the shelf.

- *Poor Condition* if the item was found but needed repair.

- *Missing*.

"Verified on Shelf" was the category into which the majority of the items fell. The "Missing" and "Poor Condition" categories were transitory categories. Each school investigated the titles on these lists to determine their true status. Each school investigated "Missing" titles to determine whether they might be checked out or misshelved, and many were eventually located and marked "Verified On Shelf." "Poor Condition" titles were, for the most part, repaired sufficiently to move to "Verified On Shelf." Ultimately, every title needed a status of either "Verified On Shelf" or "Verified Not On Shelf." The web app showed real time information regarding how many titles were in each category for the institution.

Reclaiming Project ("Horse Trading")

As with any project such as this, not every title assigned to an institution for retention is able to be retained by that institution. Some of these title are in poor condition, but most are just missing. Thus, these titles need to be reassigned to a different institution within the group so they end up being retained. We often hear this process referred to as "horse trading" whereby each institution claims titles for retention that were not originally assigned to them. There were a total of 2,601 such titles (2%) across all institutions in the CI-CCI group.

It was important to all that the smaller libraries have a chance to "pull their weight" in this process; thus the group decided to proceed with each institution attempting to claim at least the same number of items that it had marked "Verified Not On Shelf." For one of the libraries, that was not possible, and the other libraries have claimed more. The reclaiming project proceeded with the smaller libraries claiming first, followed by the larger libraries.

Drake's applications developer extended the functionality of the existing web app to provide a reclaiming mechanism. This primarily involved the identification of availability at institutions other than the original assigned institution, which was among the data SCS originally provided. He also added a feature that showed each institution's items that were unclaimed from other institutions and that were only held at their institution. This became the logical place for each institution to start the reclaiming project.

In the screen shot below, Central College was the original institution to which this title was assigned. Drake is the only other institution that has it, so if we can locate it we will claim this title for our retention list by scanning the bar code into the web app.

Figure 2. Display of web application used to facilitate retention title "horse trading" process.

One issue that came up during the claiming process involved call number agreement; three of the libraries in the group use LCC and two use DDC. This created some extra work for each institution during the reclaiming project since it required looking up the catalog record in the web app to determine shelf location for those titles in the classification system not used. For example, if one library uses DDC they had to look up the catalog record for the shelf location of any unclaimed LCC titles. The same was true for libraries that use LCC; they had to look up shelf locations for unclaimed DDC titles. This caused some concerns about back-and-forth in the stacks, but ultimately the group proceeded. As of this writing, the group is in the process of wrapping up this project after another (hopefully final) round of claiming.

CI-CCI: The Simpson College Experience

Dunn Library at Simpson College had a program review in 2011 and a vision study with concept design document completed in 2012. Some of the renovation plans relied on compacted collections. Due to building engineering, we cannot use compact shelving. So how do we gain more student learning space without losing materials

needed by the academic community at Simpson and beyond? The call from Teri and Pam came at just the right time for us.

The five institutions in CI-CCI, by way of over a year's worth of emails, conference calls, and coming to consensus, have formed a true collaboration. All had input to the MOU, the addendums and the website. All participants continue to be prompt in responding to any issues that arise. All of our decisions to date have been data-driven and not based on speculation.

Signing of the MOU by a chief academic officer made it a true institutional commitment. The cost for data analysis and use of staff time are well-worth the data-driven results we are seeing. Faculty members have responded favorably to each phase of the collaboration. They are pleased about proposed 48 hour turnaround of interlibrary loans and extended loan periods. For acquisition of new monographs, staff is now checking OCLC. If two members own the requested item, we check back with faculty to see if it is required to own in-house.

Through the verification and reclaiming projects, we found several perks to physically verifying titles. Students went to the shelves using printed lists from the Drake database; these lists were useful for follow up. Staff then updated the database. In the process of this impromptu shelf-reading, we found misshelved items, identified additional missing items, and repaired or replaced books in poor condition. Soon we will withdraw long missing or never-used items.

I have truly appreciated the openness, humor and professionalism among higher ed "competitors" in Iowa.

Project Phase II: Prospective Collection Development

Prospective collection development has been a primary objective of the collaborative since the outset. It has been well understood that this is where the future payoff will be for us as a group, as well as potentially collaborating on other big picture issues such as technology. The CI-CCI MOU directly addresses this as one of the key project goals: "to coordinate acquisitions with the goal of developing a 'shared collection' among the participants to reduce duplication, leverage acquisition funds, and to reduce the frequency for the necessity to do data refresh."

The Acquisitions Addendum to the MOU spells out how this is to work initially: "Ultimately, the intention of this agreement is to have a shared vendor for acquisitions to enable efficient coordination of future purchases. In fiscal 2013-2014 the group will employ the following procedures: Prior to ordering a title each participating library will check OCLC for CI-CCI holdings. If 2 or more CI-CCI libraries already own the title, the others will not purchase it unless it is specifically required onsite."

Several of the smaller CI-CCI libraries have begun employing this method. Some have not yet begun doing so because of concerns expressed by faculty. Most of the concerns relate largely to the guaranteed turnaround on a loan request. When the collaborative was in its infancy the "24 hour" weekday turnaround was one of the "guiding principles." This is not currently being achieved due largely to the difference in carriers. CI-CCI is currently exploring ways to ensure faster delivery times, including potentially working with the regent institutions. Additional concerns about the shared acquisitions approach include length of checkout for faculty. This issue has already been addressed and the loan period has been extended from 10 weeks to 120 days.

As the collaborative transitions to the collection development phase of the project, we are considering whether to merely coordinate our acquisitions so as to minimize duplication, or to go a step beyond and actually develop our collections in a coordinated manner whereby institutions develop subject specialties. The subject specialty approach seemed to be of particular interest to some of our faculty.

CI-CCI currently has two task forces that are looking at some of these issues. One task force is looking at print acquisitions. They are surveying vendors to inquire about their ability to provide accessible, real-time order data, including circulation notes, as well as experience with

PDA/DDA and print-on-demand. Vendor demos and an RFI will follow.

The second taskforce is looking at ebooks. This group has administered a survey to CI-CCI participants to gather information on how each schools acquires ebooks and makes them available as a precursor to seeking options for a potential shared ebook package or purchase agreement.

The group realizes that prospective collection development will be a challenging endeavor given the differences in budgets and subject specialties. The varying degree of adoption of ebooks and patron driven acquisitions is also a factor in our considerations. We hope to come up with an approach that will meet the needs (to varying degrees) of all of the participants.

Project Next Steps

1. Implement a common vendor for print monograph acquisitions. We will invite presentations from key vendors. This is the first step in furthering the goal of coordination of acquisitions.

2. Determine next steps for sharing collection development efforts (shared purchases, subject emphasis by school, etc.).

3. Work to improve ILL delivery time between CI-CCI schools. This is a key component if we wish to improve faculty buy-in to the philosophy of the "shared collection."

4. The University of Northern Iowa has announced plans to join the collaborative this fall. UNI is one of the three state regent institutions, they have an FTE of approximately 11,000 (which is more than double that of Drake). The group must decide how to incorporate a new member into an existing group who is already well along in the process. UNI is employing SCS (as CI-CCI did), and will have a stand-alone data set since incorporating it with the CI-CCI data would require a data refresh by the entire group (and subsequent costs). Despite

the challenges, the CI-CCI group is thrilled at the prospect of bringing in a larger regent institution especially as we begin to look at prospective collection development.

5. Each school must decide how/if to approach weeding at their institution. At Drake we will consider whether to incorporate a condition survey into the process. That is, a physical inspection of books prior to weeding looking for any contextual information that may preclude weeding (such as note margins in literature, etc.).

6. Implementation of an OCLC Shared Print Symbol to record the retention titles in OCLC. We are currently in the process of implementing this.

7. Updating of MOU to reflect current practices and new members.

8. Long-term management of collaborative. This potentially includes formulating a plan to develop a budget, grant opportunities, and perhaps a project manager.

Advantages of a small collaboration:

1. Geographically close; within 30-mile radius.

2. Fairly homogenous (in size, location, mission). FTE range of 1388 to 4400.

3. Long-standing history of cooperation (all are members of the Iowa Private Academic Libraries Consortium) and mutual trust.

4. Strong commitment to project goals and the importance of decisions to mutually benefit all group members; flexibility key

5. Once-a-month agenda-driven conference calls.

6. Governance by Directors and by consensus (with involvement of some of their librarians).

Disadvantages of a small collaboration:

1. Not grant funded; budgeting is an issue.

2. When and how will we do "data refresh" given budget constraints.

3. Disparity in member budgets results in different priorities when it comes to prospective collection development.

4. No project manager.

5. Need better method for determining group leadership roles.

6. Group shared holdings are limited in number.

Tips for starting a similar type of collaboration:

1. Work within existing collaborative structure (if it exists).

2. Determine need and interest via personal contact.

3. Get a philosophical commitment before attempting a formal agreement.

4. Survey the literature and internet for documentation (including MOUs) on similar collaborative projects. No need to reinvent the wheel for common elements.

5. If possible, secure the support of the Provost/Chief Academic Officer for each participating school (and have them sign the MOU).

6. If possible, determine the leadership roles of group members early in the process.

Changing Library Operations

Allen McKiel, Western Oregon University

Jim Dooley, University of California Merced

Robert Murdoch, Brigham Young University – Utah

Carol Zsulya, Cleveland State University

Abstract

The following article was presented in a panel discussion which explored library operational adaptations to the changing technologies of information distribution and usage. The librarians on the panel presented glimpses of the changes occurring in their library operations as they transition to services without print. The librarians explored, through the evidence of their changing library operations, a range of topics, for example: trends in e-resource acquisition and usage; changes in consortia; processing and organizational changes; and developments in open access publishing and library e-publication. After initial presentations, the panel and moderator encouraged questions, comments, and discussion with attendees.

Jim Dooley, Head, Collection Services, University of California, Merced

The University of California, Merced (UC Merced) opened in 2005 as the tenth University of California (UC) campus and welcomed its tenth freshman class in August 2014. From 875 students and thirteen faculty in 2005, UC Merced has grown to 6,300 students, including 350 graduate students. Currently there are 207 tenured or tenure-track faculty and an additional 140 lecturers. When the campus opened in 2005 only the library building was operational. Currently there are six academic buildings, a seventh under construction and residence halls housing over 2,000 students. The campus hopes to receive a Carnegie Classification as a Research University-High Output in 2015. The current strategic plan envisions that the campus will grow to 10,000 students, including 1,000 graduate students, by 2010. Space for the expansion will be obtained through a public-private partnership with a commercial developer that will construct a series of mixed-use buildings on a site adjacent to the current campus.

For the UC Merced Library the collection philosophy remains access vs. ownership or just-in-time vs. just-in-case. The goal is to meet an information need in the most appropriate way regardless of format or means of acquisition. It doesn't matter if the information resource is purchased, rented, or borrowed; only that the need is met. One manifestation of this philosophy is the heave reliance on demand-driven acquisitions (DDA) and subscription databases to provide access to locally licensed e-books. Collection funds provide access to the largest possible number of titles, not to purchase a much smaller number of titles in order to build a permanent collection.

Currently the library collection is approximately 92% electronic. This includes journals, e-books, databases, and U.S. government documents. The library subscribes to the Marcive Documents Without Shelves service which provides bibliographic records with links to electronic U.S. government documents to enable it to be a Federal Depository Library. The high percentage of electronic resources in the collection is not a result of favoring access over ownership. Rather, the high percentage results from the library being opened in 2005 when the transition from print to electronic was well underway.

The collection is a combination of electronic resources licensed by the California Digital Library (CDL) for all or a subset of UC campuses, as well as locally licensed electronic resources and purchased print books and DVDs. Despite its name, the CDL is a part of the University of California Office of the President and provides negotiation and licensing services as well as technology development and management to the UC libraries. Although negotiation and licensing services for electronic resources are provided by the CDL, these resources are not "free" to the campus libraries. Each UC library pays a proportional share for access to these resources. Currently 60% of the UC Merced Library collection budget goes to provide access to CDL-licensed resources.

At the UC Merced Library the transition from print to electronic is almost complete for serials. Currently the library provides access to approximately 112,000 online journals (most through CDL-licensed packages) and 20 print journals. The print serials are all in the humanities and currently unavailable online. The print subscription would be cancelled if any were to become available electronically.

Acquisition of print books has been through approval plans supplemented by firm orders at faculty request. The print collection has also been supplemented by various gifts of books. Except for gifts, all books in the collection were published in 2003 or later. From the opening of the library there have been two approval plans: one for humanities, social sciences, and arts, and one for science. At the beginning both approval plans were rather broad because academic planning was unfocused. As programs developed, the scope of the approval plans has been progressively narrowed to focus on areas of campus research and teaching. Early in 2014 the science approval plan was shut down completely due to a combination of decreasing circulation and budget pressures. The social sciences, humanities, and arts approval plan remains. Currently there are just over 118,000 print books and 2,600 DVDs in the collection.

When the library opened in 2005, probably few would have predicted that e-books would become such an important part of research library collections in a decade. Very few e-books were available through UC systemwide licenses. While there never was an intention to replace print books with e-books, the library began experiments with e-books soon after opening. The first was a subscription to ebrary Academic Complete which provided access to a growing collection of academic titles, now over 116,000, at a very low cost per title as long as the subscription

was maintained. The largest number of locally licensed e-books are available through demand-driven acquisitions (DDA) plans with EBL (300,000 titles) and MyiLibrary (50,000 titles). Under the EBL plan, titles are purchased on the fourth access after three short -term loans (STLs). The MyiLibrary plan does not employ STLs; titles are purchased on the second access. During the past ten years large numbers of e-books have become available at UC Merced through UC systemwide agreements including both stand-alone packages (Royal Society of Chemistry, ASME) and e-books linked to journal packages (Springer, Wiley, Elsevier). The result is that the library now provides electronic access to 1.05 million titles: 580,000 through systemwide packages and 470,000 through local licenses. This is currently nine times the number of print titles in the local collection.

Because approximately 30% of available e-books are accessed through a DDA plan with STLs, the library has been significantly affected by the increases in STL rates announced by certain publishers in the summer of 2014. The timing of these increases so close to the start of the fiscal year was decried by many libraries and library consortia. The Boston Library Consortium wrote an open letter published in *The Chronicle of Higher Education* strongly objecting both to the timing and size of these increases. (http://chronicle.com/blogs/letters/ebook -pricing-hikes-amount-to-price-gouging)

While the timing of these increases is certainly an issue, the effects on the UC Merced collection are also significant. The monthly spend for the EBL DDA plan has remained relatively constant for the past several years in spite of significant yearly enrollment increases. After the STL increases, spending increased 50%, even though enrollment for 2014-2015 had been held at last year's levels. The number of STLs increased slightly for these months compared to the corresponding months in the previous year, but the costs increased out of all proportion to the increased usage. A hypothetical example illustrates the problem. A STL at 10% for a book with a $200 list price is $20; a STL at 25% for the same book is $50.

As a result of these increases, the content of over a dozen publishers has been completely removed from the DDA plan in stages during the past months and a $30 cap on STLs was instituted in September. The cumulative effect of these actions has been to remove approximately 100,000 titles from the EBL DDA plan. This is content that will not be acquired by the UC Merced Library through other means. It remains to be seen if these actions were sufficient or if further steps need to be taken to control costs.

Several observations concerning collections can be made after ten years of operations. There is a string acceptance of electronic journals by UC Merced faculty and students. There have been no requests to acquire any journals in multiple formats or the substitute a print subscription for an electronic one. Acceptance of e-books is following the same trajectory but influenced by disciplinary preferences. Humanities and arts faculty still prefer print books while science and engineering faculty, to the extent that they use books rather than journals, prefer e-books if available. The library clearly needs to respond to the desires of humanities and arts faculty for print books. One way would be to significantly increase the size of the local print collection. Budget realities, however, make it highly unlikely that the UC Merced Library will ever be able to accomplish this. A more realistic approach is to continue to work with the other UC campuses to improve an already successful internal ILL operation so that UC Merced faculty will have improved access to the 38 million volumes in the UC Libraries collection.

The availability of e-books has resulted in a significant decrease in anticipated ILL costs. Given the size of the print collection, the expectation had been the UC Merced Library would be a net borrower for many years. The reality has been that the UC Merced Library has been a net lender to every other UC library for several years. If one-third of the STL requests for e-books had instead been ILL requests, the library would have been a net borrower in every year. This represents a significant savings in ILL costs.

As the controversy over STL rare increases has shown, e-book business models remain problematic. E-books can be acquired directly by libraries through individual and package purchases as well as through various evidence-based DDA plans and DDA plans that do or don't include STLs. DDA plans using STLs continue to work well for libraries while there is agitation against the use of STLs in various quarters of the publishing community. Regardless of the details concerning STLs, publisher business models need to align with library budget realities.

Allen McKiel, Dean of Library Services, Western Oregon University

Cooperative Collections

This article views the Orbis Cascade Alliance's cooperative collection development efforts, which are central to its mission and vision. "We bring multiple perspectives together to challenge traditional thinking and elevate our ability to deliver outstanding services, programs, and collections . . . to strongly promote the success of students, faculty, staff, and researchers."

Optimizing the expansion of mission relevant information resources is integral to the development and delivery of the services and programs of libraries. Collections are the content. Services and programs assist in their use. Implicit in any discussion of content is its integral requirement of effective access. Optimizing the volume of content must be viewed in the context of the services that provide relevance and means of access. For example, a catalog serves relevance and access to the collection as does a building to house the collections and a program of instruction in the use of a catalog. The objective is effective access to the content. This article will survey the Alliance's efforts in optimizing access to shared information content through its services and programs. The Alliance Shared Content Team is charged with providing "broad oversight and leadership in the sharing of library-selected content. As experts for the consortium, the team continually assesses, manages, and develops initiatives that broaden access by providing cost-effective sharing, licensing, and description of such content."

Consortia, like the Alliance, extend the services and programs of libraries to the network operational level. The initial focus was sharing physical books. Consortia shared local access to their book collections through the development and maintenance of union catalogs and the ongoing provision of local systems of distribution. The Orbis consortium initiated its union catalog in 1995 with 12 Oregon libraries and began a borrowing program in 1996. They initiated a courier system in 1998 to expedite access to their collective holdings for their combined patrons. The Washington-based Cascade consortium initiated a union catalog in 1997 and migrated to INN-Reach, the Innovative Interfaces software for expediting interlibrary loan, which improved access to the collective holdings of the 7 participating libraries.

In 2002 Orbis and Cascade joined to pool the then 26 collections of the Orbis Cascade Alliance using INN-Reach to share access to what was named Summit. Expansion of content through access currently includes nearly 9 million unduplicated titles of the shared 28 million volumes with delivery time within 24 to 48 hours for the 37 libraries serving over 275,000 students. Western Oregon University's (WOU) accessible collection (within 2 days) increase over that time was somewhere around 4,500 percent. Annual growth rate for WOU's individual collection over that period of time was approximately 1%. Individual ownership changed marginally while access improved dramatically even though there is a time delay compared to the immediacy of local access. Last year's Alliance Summit usage was 37% of total WOU book circulation.

The coordinated services that provided access to the collection included the implementation of the union catalog, courier system, and INN-Reach software. All of these were needed to provide more effective access to the shared content primarily with respect to time but also load balancing between institution. The Alliance has attempted to further optimize access by a suggested limit to duplicate copies. The effort was facilitated through the common utilization of Gobi, a management tool that permits selectors to view consortium-wide title purchasing processes. The system was jointly adopted by all Alliance members in 2008. The effort was intended to decrease unnecessary duplication and has instead

resulted most recently in a slight increase in the average number of copies purchased. It seems to have increased duplication with a very slight loss to title expansion. An individual's need for immediacy often trumps the librarians' concerns for shared collection size. Librarians are forever adjudicating between immediate need and general comprehensiveness in their striving to optimize use of limited funds.

The Alliance infrastructure for optimizing access to content has most recently been enriched through the implementation of Ex Libris Alma and Primo. The single system for all 37 libraries provides the technical infrastructure for enriched user access to content through cooperative management of network level bibliographic data, discovery technology, data driven collection development through usage and cost assessment, and vendor data and software coordination.

E-Books

In the realm of e-books, optimizing access to content primarily involves increasing volume of content to increase the probability of a search term providing relevant content. The effort to share e-books in a manner similar to ILL is an unwieldy construct that makes the price negotiation over e-book distribution more complicated. The concept has maintains viability because print and electronic formats compete and e-distribution has an advantage. The price for e-copy production and distribution is zero. E-books do not need to be produced or transported. The costs are artificially imposed for e-books primarily to allow competitive print distribution. A more cynical consideration includes the privileged advantage of access via premier university libraries.

The imposed cost/value appears in acquisition/access models brokered by vendors between librarians and publishers. For instance, the imposition can be seen in the restrictions to access enforced by publishers via an embargo for front list titles in a subscription database. It is, in a sense, subsidizing the sale of front list title prices. The imposition also shows up as the cost of concurrent accesses (multiple copies) to an e-book. Patrons must wait their turn as they would have for a print copy. It is manifest in the provision of access to a collection through short term loans and purchases of perpetuity after an agreed upon number of loans. The negotiated value of access and timeliness to e-books is linked to the need to subsidize the general costs of publishing for e or p publication but also the cost of print production, warehousing, shipping, and handling.

E-Book Consortia Collection Development

A more complex iteration of the "imposed" framework for negotiating access to e-books involves consortium access to a shared collection. As an example, WOU is a member of the Orbis Cascade Alliance and is participating in the cooperative DDA through YBP and EBL. The intent is to provide access to a shared collection as one entity through our combined patron selections. We are working on the evolution of the details of the model. An overview from Western's vantage point of the benefits of cooperative collection development of e-books

can be demonstrated through a look at Western's return on investment for FY 2014. Western's share of the annual cost was $7,547. Approximately 18,000 titles were available in the pool to Western's faculty and students. Of those, 738 titles were purchased for their use. Costs per title availability and purchase were 42 cents and $10.23 respectively. Total usage for the year numbered 2,877 browses or a short term loans (STL) for Western with a cost per use of $2.62 per use. This arrangement is far superior to access that could be provided in print. It would likely be improved if separated from the physical and conceptual constraints associated with print distribution. Facilitation of access through browsing, short term loans, multi-institution access, and subscription are evolutionary steps toward distribution models that stretch toward ubiquitous access that increases use and thereby decreases cost per use with a net gain for all involved. This is the typical expression of technological innovation that first disrupts and then replaces the less efficient technology. They must coexist through a period of adjustment.

Cost/Benefit Analysis	
Cost to WOU - FY14	$ 7,547
Titles in Pool - 18,000	
Cost / Title Available	$0.42
Usage – Browse, Loan - 2,877	
Cost / Use	$2.62
Titles Purchased - 738	
Cost / Title	$10.23
Titles added annually – approx. 6,000	
Cost/ Title available	$1.26

Table 1. FY 2013-14 Cost/benefit analysis of Alliance DDA for Western Oregon University.

	Owned Browse	Owned Loan	Unowned Browse	Unowned Loan	Total
WOU	740	558	1,039	540	2,877

Table 2. FY 2013-14 Western Oregon University Alliance DDA usage.

Library operations occurring at the network level for the provision of cooperative DDA requires an additional layer of complexity. Negotiation and management entails multi-institutional assessments of faculty and student need with respect to institutionally relevant content. This is generally facilitated by adjudicating available content through assessing institutional usage. Relevant systems for assessment need to be devised and data needs to be accumulated and analyzed for ongoing maintenance of cost effectiveness and equanimity. The single bib record in the shared Ex Libris catalog provides more efficient management of the collection for everybody albeit with additional coordination complexity.

Journals

The consortia role in the provision of access to the online journals evinces as cooperative purchasing of access to databases like EBSCO's but there is also a preservation advantage to cooperation. The dramatic online shift has spawned growing concern for its consequent encroached upon ownership, control, and preservation of content. The struggle is manifest in ongoing deliberations and negotiations among librarians, authors, publishers, vendors, lawyers, lawmakers, and organizations promoting a variety of preservation and access schemes for e-journals. This will eventually be sorted out through a mix of competition and cooperation on a global scale among all of the stakeholders. The individual library is no longer the primary agent and guarantor of the preservation of the written word as it transitions to electronic format. Preservation of physical archival copies is still their domain. In the persistence of their electronic offspring, libraries collectively have only a significant voice.

Given the problem of diminishing shelf space particularly for the larger institutions, cooperative preservation has been a core issue in the Alliance's pursuit of cooperative collection development. The issue has been prominent in Alliance strategy discussions of a possible joint project to procure a cooperative storage facility. A practicable plan for a building never materialized owing to a variety of factors including the logistics of financing, the retreating number of print books

and journals being procured, the majority of smaller libraries for whom it was not critical and seemingly out of reach, and the possibilities latent in the alternative of cooperative preservation through shared facilities distribution.

In keeping with the primacy of the library's role in the preservation of physical archival copies of journal articles, the Alliance in its collection development and management undertakings created a cooperative distributed print repository for journals. The initial Alliance endeavor to create a distributed print repository was formally proposed in 2005. The Summit union catalog of the Alliance provided the core mechanism for shared collection development and with it the means for creating a distributed print repository for preservation and for the requisite potential expansion needed for shared collection development. A cooperative repository provides preservation assurance that permits withdrawal of duplicated resources, primarily journals but also monographs.

The Alliance had approved and mostly implemented the proposal for a distributed repository by 2008. The particulars of the shape of the collection included 241 journal titles of the combined JSTOR Arts and Sciences I and II database collections and the 33 titles of the American Chemical Society journals. The broad ownership among Alliance members of the paper back-files along with subscriptions to their electronic counterparts provided the key selection criterion. The titles also provided long journal runs in the humanities, social sciences, and sciences. Nearly all Alliance members hold, and are responsible in perpetuity for, a portion of the titles. Two complete runs of each title are held; one copy circulates. The Alliance effort eventually merged into an agreement with the Western Regional Storage Trust (WEST) in which all of the Alliance member libraries are participants.

Other Content

Books, e-book, and journals are central content for library consortia operations however; as with success in these areas, uniquely held collections both print and online have become more central to Alliance deliberations. Materials in print, online, archives, publications, exhibits, etc., will be increasingly considered for cooperative use. The Alliance has mapped out operational structures for cooperation across a fuller range of content managed by four administrative teams and five program area teams. The administrative teams include assessment, center of excellence, finance, and policy teams. The program area teams include collaborative workforce, content creation and dissemination, discovery and delivery, shared content, and systems teams. All content access is facilitated through library operations, which requires organizational structures for cooperative use at the network level. The Alliance is stretching the limits of consortia operations to facilitate more pervasive levels of content access.

Carol T. Zsulya, Business and Government Documents Librarian and Collection Development Coordinator

Michael Scwhartz Library, Cleveland State University

Universities and colleges are undergoing a transformation. The question of sustainability of universities and colleges is a top priority for the administration, faculty, and staff in higher education as far as competition for funding, students, academic staff, quality requirements and accountability demands. Universities and colleges are now measuring student outcomes relative to course development, course expectations, quality of teaching, and student retention.

The role of academic libraries continues to evolve. Traditional librarian roles are being tested, students and faculty still require research assistance and resources still need to be purchased. However, many academic librarians are asked to be more flexible and adaptable as far as their additional duties. Academic libraries now include the familiar reference librarians, instruction librarians and technical services librarians. Digital initiatives librarians are also being added to the organizational structure. Skill sets that are becoming more in demand include digital content management, electronic resources management, instructional designers, and one of

the newest skill sets (in both academia and the business sector) is business data analytics.

Many academic libraries are destinations for group study, silent study, and subject-specific labs or designated areas of study (such as a math emporium found both at Kent State and Cleveland State). Academic libraries have become prime real estate on many campuses. Print collections have, in many institutions, become obsolete with little, if any, usage. In some cases, this may be true, as the rise of e-resources continues.

The weeding of print collections continues to be a top priority among many academic libraries and even regional depositories as well.

Librarians now purchase fewer books and, if given a choice of books over journals, purchase journals/subscriptions over the books. Yes, e-books are being purchased—as collections or individually. However, reductions in academic library budgets often occur year-to-year (not always at the same percentage rate).

OhioLINK has provided a strong connection for 91 academic institutions in Ohio to share resources. (Waiting for some additional information regarding OhioLINK that will be included in slide presentation.) Journal subscriptions remain the most valuable commodity among the OhioLINK libraries. E-book packages are being considered even though publishers are not as willing to allow consortial sharing of e-books and e-book packages.

One thing that hasn't changed is the agreement that there are still benefits to belonging to a consortium that include sharing resources, collection management collaboration, purchasing products in packages, particularly as academic libraries budgets continue to shrink. In a consortium, as in OhioLINK, there are discussion about maintaining local, special collections, de-duping collections, assessing the role of state-wide depositories and what should be retained.

Other points that will be discussed are the rise of MOOCs and other online courses of study; uses of tablets, e-readers, and mobile phones as the norm for college students; the population of incoming freshmen and how universities (CSU in particular) are dealing with decreasing population for college students; and what CSU is doing to retain and graduate.

Finally, the use of open access materials, institutional repositories (including Engaged Scholarship@CSU) and open access textbooks was discussed.

Library of Congress Recommended Format Specifications: Encouraging Preservation Without Discouraging Creation

Ted Westervelt, Library of Congress (Author)
Donna Scanlon, Library of Congress (Presenter)

Abstract

The Library of Congress has a fundamental commitment to acquiring, preserving and making accessible in the long term the creative output of the nation and the world. The Library has devised the Recommended Format Specifications to enable it to identify what formats will most easily lend themselves to preservation and long-term access, especially with regard to digital formats. The Library is doing this to provide guidance to its staff in their work of acquiring content for its collection, but we also seek to share this with other stakeholders, from the creative community to vendors to other libraries, each of which has a need and interest in preservation and access. To ensure ongoing accuracy and relevancy, the Library of Congress will be reviewing and revising the specifications on an annual basis and welcomes feedback and input from all interested parties.

Why the Library of Congress Developed the Recommended Format Specifications

Throughout its history, the Library of Congress has been committed to a goal best described in its mission statement "to further the progress of knowledge and creativity for the benefit of the American people." At its core, the Library's ability to advance the nation's progress has depended upon its collection, which in turn embodies the knowledge and creativity of the many authors, composers, journalists, artists, and scientists whose work is contained there. The quality of the collection reflects the Library's care in selecting materials and the effort it invests in preserving them and making them accessible to the American people for the long term.

To build such a substantial and wide-ranging collection and to ensure that it will be available for successive generations, the Library relies upon a wealth of expertise. In order to maximize the scope and scale of the content in the collection, the Library calls upon the knowledge in languages, subject matter and trends in publishing and content creation provided by the specialists who identify and acquire material for the Library's collection.

But knowledge of the technical characteristics of the production of creative works is required as well. In the past, the lasting power of the collections depended exclusively upon the endurance of such materials as the paper, ink, and binding of a book; the acetate or paper coated with gelatin in a photograph; or the shellac, vinyl, and coated polyester that comprise a sound recording. Although these materials remain in use today, creators and publishers have also begun to employ a wide array of intangible digital formats, as well as continuing to change and adapt the physical formats in which they work. The Library needs to be able to identify the formats that are suitable for large-scale acquisition and preservation for long-term access if it is to continue to build its collection and ensure that it lasts into the future.

To do this in the past, the Library of Congress has relied upon the specifications included in the copyright regulation known as the Best Edition Statement.[1] This has offered clear guidance to Library of Congress staff on the hierarchy of preference between certain physical characteristics in creative works. For example, it states clearly that when it comes to printed textual matter, "hard cover rather than soft cover." The detail in the Best Edition Statement

---

[1] United States Copyright Office. (2012). Best edition of published copyrighted works for the collections of the Library of Congress. Retrieved from http://www.copyright.gov/circs/circ07b.pdf

has been extremely useful for the Library for decades; however, it has some serious drawbacks. Since it is a regulation, the Best Edition Statement is not revised or updated frequently and there are preferences within it that no longer keep up with changes which have taken place in the creation of tangible media, such as the decline of the use of diskettes. Even more importantly, the Best Edition Statement does not address digital content at all, with the sole exception of online serials. For an institution with the broad goals and remit of the Library of Congress, having guidance that fails to address at least half of all formats in use will not work. Specifications are required that cover the whole range of content it intends to collect and that means digital content at least as much as analog.

In response to this need, in 2011 the Library began a process that would lead to the development of the Recommended Format Specifications (www.loc.gov/preservation /resources/rfs/index.html). The Library began its work by examining the Best Edition Statement, which enabled it to work closely and collaboratively with its colleagues in the Copyright Office (http://www.copyright.gov/) and take advantage of their input and unique expertise. Yet it was not merely the Best Edition Statement that provided a base from which to carry out the group's work. For digital formats, the working group took full advantage of the work done by Library of Congress staff with regard to its work on digital format sustainability (http://www .digitalpreservation.gov/formats/index.shtml) to provide it with a starting point.[2]

Between these two established fields of endeavor and sources of expertise, the Library had a strong basis on which to build the Recommended Format Specifications.

Parameters of the Recommended Format Specifications

Before discussing the specific aims the Recommended Format Specifications attempt to address, it is best to make clear what they do not

attempt to do. The specifications which the Library is now publishing do not replace or supersede the Best Edition Statement, which provides guidance to publishers and creators in fulfilling their obligations with regard to the registration or deposit of their works under the terms of the Copyright Law. It seeks to complement that work, building upon the knowledge gained from working with the Best Edition Statement and providing a broader set of recommendations, aimed at providing guidance and clarity in a creative world, which is rich with both potential and problems and which affords numerous competing options for content format or container.

Likewise, the creation and publication of the Recommended Format Specifications is not intended to serve as an answer to all the questions raised in preserving and providing long-term access to creative content. They do not provide instructions for receiving this material into repositories, managing that content or undertaking the many ongoing tasks which will be necessary to maintain this content so that it may be used well into the future. Tackling each of those aspects is a project in and of itself as each form of content has a unique set of facets and nuances. These specifications provide guidance on identifying sets of formats which are not drawn so narrowly as to discourage creators from working within them, but will instead encourage creators to use them to produce works in formats which will make preserving them and making them accessible simpler. Following these specifications helps make it realistic to build, grow and save creative output for our individual and collective benefit for generations to come.

Developing the Recommended Format Specifications

In 2011, a working group comprised of stakeholders from across the Library was established to examine the existing Best Edition Statement and determine a structure upon which the Library could model its own specifications. The

---

[2] Library of Congress. (2014). Sustainability of digital formats: Planning for Library of Congress collections. Retrieved from http://www.digitalpreservation.gov/formats/index.shtml

Library identified six basic categories of creative output, which represent significant parts of the publishing, information, and media industries, especially those that are rapidly adopting digital production and are central to building the Library's collections: Textual Works and Musical Compositions; Still Image Works; Audio Works; Moving Image Works; Software and Electronic Gaming and Learning; and Datasets/Databases. Technical teams (http://www.loc.gov /preservation/resources/rfs/contacts.html), made up of experts from across the institution bringing specialized knowledge in technical aspects of preservation, ongoing access needs and developments in the marketplace and in the publishing world, were established to identify recommended formats for each of these categories. These technical teams also engaged other subject matter experts throughout the Library, and where appropriate, at other organizations (though not for public comment). The teams also reviewed the currently available formats of published materials—both print/tangible and digital—in their categories, as well as the Library's other guides to selecting collection materials (such as the Collections Policy Statements (http://www.loc.gov/acq/devpol /cpsstate.html) and Sustainability of Digital Formats guidelines).[3] The results of their work are the core of the specifications, which seek to provide a framework within which creative works should have the flexibility to grow and develop, and also help ensure that these creative works be accessible and authentic into the future.

The Recommended Format Specifications seek to provide structure without being enslaved to it. Like the Best Edition Statement, the Recommended Format Specifications use hierarchies for the physical and technical characteristics of creative formats that will maximize the chances for survival and continued accessibility, though in the case of the specifications they are comprehensively digital as well as analog. Yet the hierarchies are not so rigid as to make them unworkable. Each basic category is broken down in logical ways—print text and

digital text (http://www.loc.gov/preservation /resources/rfs/textmus.html), print photographs and digital photographs (http://www.loc.gov /preservation/resources/rfs/stillimg.html)—but these divisions are determined by the specifics of the category and subdivision, not by a forced attempt to fit them in identical boxes. While for text and photographs, it makes sense to have sections for print text and digital text, print photographs and digital photographs, for audio works the key subdivisions are "On Tangible Medium (digital and analog)" and "Media-independent (digital)" (http://www.loc.gov /preservation/resources/rfs/audio.html). This carries through when identifying the specific characteristics of types of works, for they are not the same for print text and for digital photographs and the particulars in the specifications reflect that.

This need for a level of flexibility, especially with regard to digital formats, is also apparent in the arrangement of the technical characteristics of a given type of work into two groups, preferred and acceptable. In many situations, there is a long list of file formats that could be or are included in the Recommended Format Specifications. Arranging them in a numbered order is visually useful and makes them more apparent to the user and therefore more easily accessible, but has the potential drawback of leading to unproductive debates over the placement of a given file format sixth in line as opposed to third. The Library is more concerned with whether a file format is "preferred" or "acceptable" and less whether it is number four or six in a list of file formats within those groupings. If a file format or a technical characteristic is listed as preferred, the Library has identified its use as promoting preservation and long-term access. If it is acceptable, then that file format or technical characteristic may or may not promote preservation, but at the very least is not an impediment to it. In dealing with digital content, it is important to avoid being too dogmatic and this is one attempt to keep a necessary flexibility within an equally necessary structure.

---

[3] Library of Congress. (2014). Collection policy statements and supplementary guidelines. Retrieved from http://www.loc.gov/acq/devpol/cpsstate.html

Recommended Format Specifications Goals and Uses

The Recommended Format Specifications seek to fill two key needs. One is to provide internal guidance within the Library to help inform acquisitions of collections materials (other than materials received through the Copyright Office). The Recommended Format Specifications do not allow Library of Congress staff to start recommending, selecting and acquiring any content that comes in a file format listed in the document. In some instances, there are digital acquisition workflows, tools and processes in place, and Library of Congress staff working with them should be able simply to integrate the specifications into their work. But in many cases, the necessary workflows and infrastructure have not yet been created to handle these formats. However, Library of Congress recommending officers and acquisitions librarians are often made aware of digital content that is available via gift, exchange or purchase. In all such cases where the intellectual content would be of benefit to the Library, the staff member must be cognizant of the technical characteristics of that content. By tracking the formats of digital material available for acquisition by the Library, Library staff can identify the range of content that is both intellectually suitable for the Library's collection and available in one of the preferred formats listed in the specifications. They can also gain insight into the types of format in use and provide feedback on this for use in future revisions of the Recommended Format Specifications.

It is also expected that Library of Congress staff will be able to inform potential acquisitions sources of the parameters within which the Library sees itself collecting in the future. This does not mean the Library will refuse to acquire any content that is not in one of the formats listed. The scope of the Library of Congress's acquisitions is broad and governed by the terms of its Collection Policy Statements. If the value of an item, for its intellectual content or for other reasons, is great enough, the Library will acquire the content even if it is not in one of the formats listed in the Recommended Format Specifications. However, these are expected to be exceptional

cases. For the Library to build the digital content in its collection on the scale it does with analog content, the Recommended Format Specifications will have to be used by staff as a guide to help identify content for acquisition into the collection.

The Recommended Format Specifications also fill a second, broader need. The work that the Library has undertaken in developing them has definitely been from its own particular perspective. Nonetheless, the fundamental purpose of the specifications, to identify the characteristics of creative works which best enable them to last and to be accessible in the long-term, is not one specific to the Library alone. The Library of Congress recognizes that the broader communities look to America's foremost library for guidance; and one of the Library's fundamental goals is to provide the benefit of its expertise and knowledge to support and assist those other communities and institutions. The Library intends to disseminate the Recommended Format Specifications as broadly as possible so that others might benefit from them and also that the specifications might benefit from the feedback the Library receives from those other stakeholders.

Future Work

The Library's commitment to the long-term survival of the creative output of the nation and the world means that this set of specifications must be a living document. The creative world by its very nature is a dynamic one and so the framework must live, adapt and grow alongside it. As such, the Library will be revisiting these specifications on an annual basis. It is not expected that this will result in root-and-branch changes in the course of any one of these revisions. It is in fact hoped that, by engaging with the specifications on an annual basis, revisions will be smaller and more manageable as there be less room for the Library's specifications to slip out of sync with developments in the creative world.

Over the months preceding the annual review, the Library will seek out and request input from stakeholders to ensure that all parties who could use and will benefit from this set of specifications are fully aware and engaged in any and all revisions. Not only will this provide for the best-informed decision-making when it comes to the revision of the Recommended Format Specifications, it also offers a chance to engage with other groups, organizations and institutions that have a vested interest in the goals of the specifications and, hopefully, move us all towards greater clarity and precision.

For example, with regard to the digital formats, there is a lot of fluidity and uncertainty in identifying the best way forward in meeting the needs of all concerned in encouraging and rewarding creativity, but also making it easy to share, preserve and access. This can be seen directly in the category dealing with datasets and databases (http://www.loc.gov/preservation /resources/rfs/data.html) in the Recommended Format Specifications. Instead of being able to identify precise file formats and technical specifications, the Library was forced to describe the desired attributes in more open-ended terms, for the simple reason that there is no clear consensus on any precise specifications with regard to them.

Conclusion

At a time of such great growth in the production of creative output, when not only are the frontiers expanding, but new ones seem to crop up faster than we can grasp them, there is a definite need for some expert guidance, so that this amazing creative content is not lost to us. The Library of Congress appreciates that it is uniquely positioned to provide that guidance and, in fact, that its position has given it that responsibility. The Library is the nation's premier institution instructed to further the progress of knowledge and creativity for the benefit of the American people. In producing and publishing the Recommended Format Specifications, it seeks to meet that charge, and to provide the benefit of its expertise for creators, vendors, and archivists, so that they might succeed in their goals to share and disseminate their creative output and benefit the nation generally.

Breaking It Down: Electronic Resource Workflow Documentation

Alexandra Hamlett, Baruch College, CUNY

Abstract

Managing electronic resources is a fairly complex process faced by librarians with ever more frequency in today's digital environment. In an effort to approach the possibility of purchasing an electronic resource manager (ERM), electronic resource workflow processes were investigated and documented. The life cycle of electronic resources takes a very different form than that of its print counterpart, and it can prove immensely useful to the library to examine these workflows. Such workflow documentation can offer the opportunity for analysis, exposure of problem areas, occurrences of overlap or duplication, and can lead to discussions amongst faculty and staff that are crucial to the smooth running of the institution. This talk will examine the methodology and framework used to document these workflows. It involves interviews with staff and faculty involved in these procedures, discussions with stakeholders at different levels of the electronic workflow, and clarification of the steps involved in these electronic workflows. Once the workflows have been documented, they will undergo analysis. This strategy can expose "gaps" in the procedure, indicate where the workflow can be streamlined, and encourage conversations within the library departments that can lead to new and more effective workflows.

This poster session presents an ongoing project documenting electronic resource workflows at the Newman Library at Baruch College, CUNY in New York City. The library embarked on this project with the purpose of evaluating the benefits of purchasing an electronic resource manager (ERM). After the workflows are documented, they will undergo analysis, which should help the library determine if an ERM will significantly streamline the processes involved in electronic resource management, and increase efficiency by presenting possibilities for staff and departmental reorganization. The methodology for the project was directly informed by the background research conducted, which illuminated the finite processes and work output involved in the lifecycle of different electronic resources. It became apparent after examining various resources that a majority of the libraries involved in similar projects underwent lengthy workflow documentation and analysis to take stock of intricate patterns of workflow that were in operation at their institutions. We performed a number of procedures before beginning the documentation. We consulted best practices and standards from NISO, the DLF ERMI, white papers, scholarly articles, and case studies. We conducted multiple interviews with that helped us accurately document the lifecycle of electronic resources. These interviews involved collection management,

acquisitions, serials, and the usability librarian. The workflows were published on an institutional wiki that will later be available for analysis. We have included images of two workflows created during this project. Figure 1 diagrams the database trial workflow and Figure 2 diagrams the licensing process, below.

The Newman Library anticipates this study will generate the following outcomes: a spec document to evaluate the purchase of an ERM, streamlined workflow, beneficial discussions amongst stakeholders, development of iterative assessment, ability to communicate our institutional needs with vendors, and development of a five-year strategic plan. We foresee that by documenting these workflows, we will get a better understanding of the work involved in managing electronic resources. We intend to analyze our findings as a means of streamlining processes, cut down on task duplication, and increase work efficiency.

There are a number of implications that result from documenting our electronic resource workflows including: a greater understanding of how staff and faculty are involved at different steps of the process, staff reorganization as an outcome of reorganizing workflows, platform consolidation, compliance with industry standards, access to more effective statistical reports, and the ability to assess our vendors' compliance with industry standards.

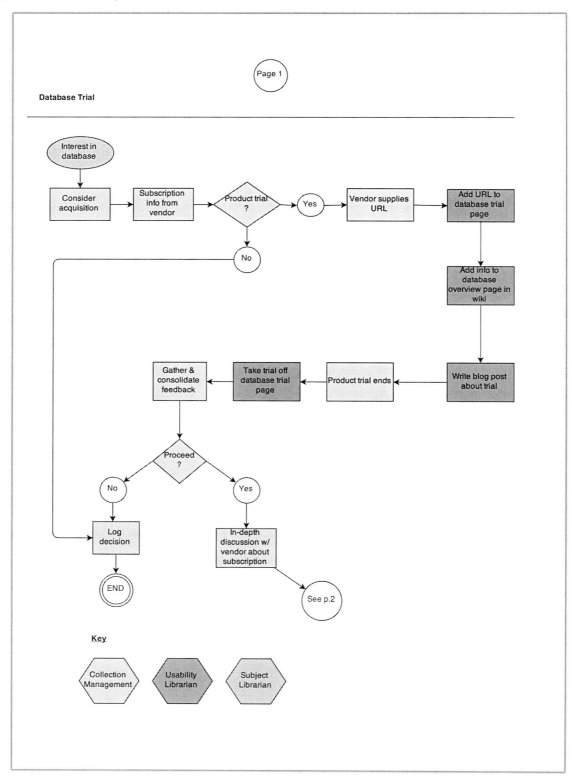

Figure 1. Database trial workflow.

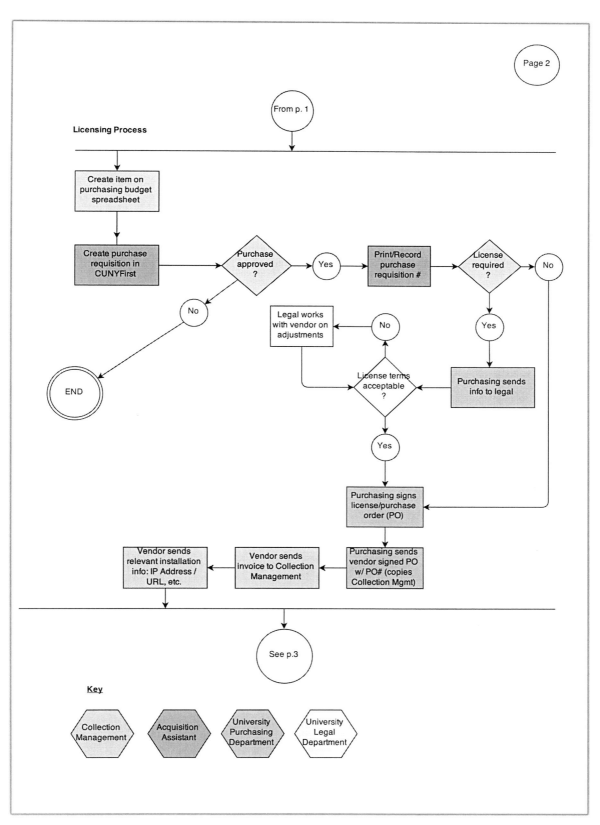

Figure 2. Licensing process.

Do Libraries' Needs Still Match Publisher Offerings?
"The Truth Is Rarely Pure and Never Simple" (Oscar Wilde)

John Banionis, Key Account Manager, Future Science Group
Nadia Lalla, Assistant Director of Collections & Information Services, Taubman Health Sciences Library,
University of Michigan
Don West, Sales Director, ACCUCOMS

Abstract

Given the continued state of strained library budgets and increasing content offerings from publishers, the authors set out to investigate this current environment from the perspectives of both library and publisher. After reviewing the array of publisher offerings as well as ongoing collection development issues faced by libraries, the authors moderated an open discussion with their peers to determine if any new models and solutions offered by publishers help to address these concerns, and if not, what the library community would like to see as an ideal acquisitions model.

What Do Libraries Need Today, and What Factors Shape This Need?

Libraries have emerged from the Great Recession with leaner funding and clearer missions. Most have become experts at doing more with less and recognize that the financial future will be a continuation of this practice. At the same time, the e-resource landscape has changed. This was helped by the explosion of mobile device use (primarily tables) , some significant changes in the type of e-resources offered by publishers (e.g., streaming media, data sets), legal decisions, and the open access movement. These changes present challenges to collection development. Acquisition decisions are essentially the same as before: they are driven by user demand or library priority. What has changed are the questions and issues surrounding access, discoverability, use, and retention as they pertain to e-resources.

A Brief History of E-Resources

From the birth of scholarly literature, publishers have offered journals in a print format with Issues set at regular intervals within each volume of publication. These print volumes were available for purchase on a title-by-title basis, or if a publisher carried multiple titles, these could be purchased by libraries in a single bundle if desired. However, when publishers began offering their journals electronically via the internet in the early 1990s, the types of content offerings grew substantially. With electronic journals, titles were still available individually, but publishers were now able to offer packages of titles with either perpetual or leased access, individual article purchases via Pay Per View (PPV), as well as digitized backfiles of their earlier print content available for subscription or outright purchase. Additionally, many large STM publishers began offering "Big Deal" packages to libraries, which typically allowed for leased access to the full body of that publisher's journal content for a fixed fee in exchange for a library's commitment to maintain their current subscription list with that publisher. The pros and cons of the Big Deal have been debated at length elsewhere, but the inherent inflexibility of limited cancellations has caused a strain on library budgets, which has in turn prompted some publishers to develop new, experimental models for content acquisition.

One such model includes the Journals Paid Trial, which was developed for the 2011 Subscription Year by John Banionis on behalf of Future Science Group. The Paid Trial is a patron-driven or data-driven acquisitions model for journals, in that it offers leased access to the publisher's full journal collection for 12 months at a deeply discounted rate, after which the library can review a year of usage data to make an informed collection development decision in the following years. For example, libraries might decide to convert one or more titles to perpetual access subscriptions while having the option continue the leased component depending on their evaluation of institutional usage trends. In this way, the Paid Trial is more flexible and customizable than the Big Deal. The University of Michigan was an early adopter of this model, and it continues to be a useful acquisitions model for the library.

Another model being considered by libraries and publishers is a PPV Ownership Model, or article-level acquisition. In this scenario, a library would prepurchase a package of article downloads from a customer, but instead of being single-use, the library would locally load the article on its network and catalog it for future use by its researchers, thereby eliminating the need to pay for an article more than once. When the library depletes their package of downloads, they can simply purchase another set to fulfill the ongoing need for the publisher's articles by their researchers.

Furthermore, aside from new models from individual publishers, smaller publishers have also banded together to create packages of content spanning multiple publishers offered at a discount, thus providing a greater value proposition for libraries. This has been successfully implemented in the ALJC Model, and is also being offered at the consortia level by publisher service companies such as ACCUCOMS.

Last, aside from direct offerings from publishers, third-party aggregators also offer journal databases to libraries. These databases provide access to most journal titles across each subject area at a fraction of the cost of a direct subscription to each title. However, the access is leased and includes an embargo of 12 months or more, which precludes the most current research articles from being included. Also, when subscribing to multiple databases, libraries will experience a great deal of overlap and duplication of many titles. Still, this is often a reasonable option for libraries trying to fill any gaps in specific areas of their collection.

Moving beyond journals, a vast body of e-books have been made available to libraries over the past decade. While publishers initially offered a limited number of "born digital" books while also digitizing older volumes, most current e-books are available as a fully searchable and dynamic product for the end user. Also, because e-books were a more recent offering of larger publishers who had received negative feedback about the Big Deal model for journals, most publishers make their e-books available via a more flexible patron-driven acquisition or demand-driven acquisition rather than offering a monolithic collection of their entire e-book portfolio. These PDA or DDA Models are often available through third-party e-book aggregators, but libraries can usually also opt to purchase e-books directly from the publisher as well.

Finally, there are a variety of multimedia resources that have been made available to libraries, such as music databases, video products, lectures, and other nontraditional materials. These resources provide important content for researchers not otherwise available in a text format, and more flexible licensing models similar to the Paid Trial have become available in recent years.

Ongoing Issues With E-Resources

Licensing language continues to be a primary issue for libraries. What trips librarians and vendors/publisher is not the standard legal language that's evolved about liability or ownership of vendor-developed content, it's all the "other stuff":

- Who is an "authorized user."

- Taxpayer-funded libraries that are required to provide walk-in access to the public.

- Confidentiality and nondisclosure clauses vs. Freedom of Information Act (FOIA) requests.

- Interlibrary loan use (who, what, when, how).

- Access by location (e.g., remote vs. building use only vs. dedicated workstation) or format (tablets only or tablet inaccessible).

- Fair use and digital rights management (DRM).

- Perpetual access rights.

In addition to the licensing language, there is a rising trend in academe away from library ownership of content and an increasing reliance on only leasing the same content. This is particularly problematic in some disciplines where the high-demand content is controlled by a few key publishers and locked into packages (e.g., health sciences and engineering). For many libraries, it is initially the most cost-effective means to provide the largest amount of content to their primary audiences. The flip side of that coin is that libraries do not retain any tangible property when the leasing is discontinued. How does a library justify the ongoing expenses?

If the answer to that question is usage stats, those same statistics come with their own problems. Libraries have been greatly aided by publisher acceptance and implementation of COUNTER-compliant statistical reporting. These reports give libraries tools to evaluate use of products and make some comparisons. But even in 2014, not everyone counts usage the same way. Some new disturbing trends/issues are the promotion of major new products without concurrent support for usage statistics and the tug of war that ensues when library-collected usage statistics differ from vendor-supplied usage statistics. Libraries are no longer accepting the numbers that are pushed out by publishers. Our inbred critical questioning is provoking some very difficult conversations about what should really be counted. The conversation is further complicated when one considers all of the different kinds of e-resources that libraries acquire: streaming video and audio, image databases, raw data. How do you count usage of this in a meaningful and consistent manner? The bigger publishers have figured this out; the smaller publishers are challenged to demonstrate the usefulness of their products.

Another issue is the definition of simultaneous or concurrent users. This is of particular interest to libraries that provide vast quantities of e-books in a course reserves capacity or have a DDA program in which purchases are triggered by use. When is

use counted? How is use counted? How should libraries interpret those usage statistics? What if usage is seasonal—can access be purchased or rented on a temporary basis?

Open access (OA) content is changing the conversation between libraries and publishers regarding the financing of scholarly communication. OA authors are approaching libraries for assistance in paying or subsidizing publication fees. Concurrently libraries and institutions are feeling pressure/responsibility to support OA initiatives via memberships that underwrite publishing costs. Where can libraries find this funding? Should collection monies previously allocated for traditional subscriptions or one-time purchases be channeled towards the OA efforts? How can libraries support both publishing options? How does OA change what a library collects?

A library has a responsibility to consider the overall end user experience. That experience raises its own set of issues for e-resources. Users continue to be frustrated by the myriad ways an e-resource behaves on a laptop versus a tablet versus a mobile phone. Users want to access content wherever and whenever is convenient for them with minimal changes from one platform to another. Mobile apps, mobile websites, and responsive web design are not equal methods of access. Our users want it all. Libraries are quick to inform publishers about the need to have those access methods now; we are less willing to pay for those expensive enhancements. Related issues include

- Discoverability—We all have cataloguing backlogs in e-resources. Not every resource comes with that perfect record that effortlessly uploads to an OPAC.

- Accessibility—For some libraries, a substantial amount of e-resources are unavailable to people with disabilities. This is not an insignificant problem and has legal implications.

- Privacy—Libraries continue to see a trend from publishers for personal customer accounts to manage individual profiles. Who sees that information? Should/can a publisher share details with the library that pays for access? Should libraries have access to that information?

- Security—How secure is patron information on nonlibrary supplied platforms?

The newest and potentially greatest issue is one of e-resource storage. What does a library do with the journal supplement of conference proceedings that arrives on CD but isn't included online in the paid journal subscription? If a library owns the streaming video content from database, how and where does it capture and store that content. These ongoing concerns surrounding storage are only going to increase as libraries grapple with "million dollar drawers" filled with content helpfully provided by publishers or harvested as part of an agreement. There is a plethora of preservation needs that requires strategy, human resources, expensive computer storage, and lots of money. At this time, there is no best practice.

Panel Discussion Results

After presenting this overview to our Lively Lunch audience at the Charleston Conference, some overarching themes arose out of our discussion. One area of agreement was that experimental models can indeed be helpful as an acquisitions tool, so long as they remain flexible enough to fit the needs of individual libraries. Also, while an article PPV ownership program would have substantial theoretical merits, the management of such a program may prove too cumbersome for large libraries, but may work at hospital or corporate libraries.

An ongoing issue for the librarians in our discussion was the reliability of usage data, particularly with regard to drilling down to subgroups of users. Knowing more about who is using what at an institution is helpful for collection analysis, but at the same time, individual privacy must be protected in any sort of data reporting.

Last, we posed the question as to whether there might be a way to integrate journals and e-books within in a single acquisitions model. Our initial suggestion was a single PDA model allowing for journal article acquisition and e-book title-by-title acquisition for each publisher. While there may come a time in which all content is treated equally, there are still significant challenges regarding library workflows and publisher revenue models that would prevent this unification across the industry in the near term.

Conclusions

Following from the robust discussion from our session, it is clear that there remains an ongoing need for flexibility and innovation in content acquisition models. Libraries and publishers will continue to be partners in delivering specialized research content to the end user, and as such, they must continue to operate in a way that is mutually sustainable. If the cyclical economic trends and technological advancements in recent years are any indication, each stakeholder must strive to be nimble if they are to thrive in their common mission.

No Crystal Ball: Planning for Certain Future Cuts When the Future Is Uncertain

Paoshan W. Yue, Head, Electronic Resources & Acquisitions Services, University of Nevada, Reno Libraries

Gail F. Stanton, Continuations Supervisor, University of Nevada, Reno Libraries

Karen S. Grigg, Science Liaison Librarian, University of North Carolina at Greensboro

Beth Bernhardt, Assistant Dean for Collection Management and Scholarly Communication, University of North Carolina at Greensboro

Abstract

This paper is a combined presentation from the University of Nevada, Reno Libraries and the University of North Carolina at Greensboro.

Many academic libraries have to make decisions about journal and database subscriptions before the university releases the upcoming budget. Often, it is necessary to not only make decisions for the following fiscal year without a final budget, but to plan ahead and forecast for an additional year. The University of Nevada, Reno Libraries approached it with a comprehensive collection review, covering print and electronic journals, journal packages, and databases. A wide range of data from various sources was brought together using Excel and Access. General assessment criteria were established. Communication, review, and the decision making process involving liaison librarians and faculty were managed with a combination of an online guide, SharePoint, Excel spreadsheets, and workshops. The goal was to correctly eliminate the journals with low demand to allow smart purchases of high-demand resources in the future. The presenters will address the methods used to plan for cuts in an uncertain future as well as present challenges to these methods and future efforts.

The Library at the University of North Carolina at Greensboro (UNCG) formed a Collection Development Team with members from several invested departments who could divide into subgroups, analyze data, and return quickly with proposed cuts. Different scenarios were identified, and a proposed plan for cuts was created for each potential scenario. This data-driven process provided CPU, circulation, and other data to assist the team in making decisions. Timelines were created to allow for ample input from liaisons and departments, including time for departments to react to the proposed cuts in their areas and to swap out items. To make better monograph purchasing decisions, the Library is moving to DDA for approval plan books, where three uses will trigger an order. To manage user needs to journal titles being cancelled, the Library is investigating use of pay-per-view options to allow "rental" of cancelled titles.

University of Nevada, Reno Libraries

In any fiscal year, the University of Nevada, Reno (UNR) Libraries often faces challenges of managing unpredictable materials budget to cover unpredictable material expenses. In July, the UNR Libraries typically receive information about the next fiscal year's library materials budget allocation amount and begins allocating to specific fund accounts. Right after the fall semester begins, student enrollment numbers are gathered and posted, which may mean additional funding from student tuition fees. In April, sometimes there could be end-of-year infusions of one-time monies from unspent university funding sources. Library material expenses are also unpredictable due to inflation rate, standing orders, demand-driven-acquisition expenditures and Interlibrary Loan's Copyright Clearance Center fees. Additionally, there are always some unexpected expenditures that crop up and need to be addressed. It is all a balancing act; some costs go down while others go up to offset the savings.

Collections Budgets

The University of Nevada, Reno is a medium-sized, state-funded public university offering over 145 degree programs including masters and doctoral degrees. It is a major research institution in the state of Nevada and has a student body of over 21,000. The University Libraries include the Mathewson-IGT Knowledge Center, serving as the main library on campus, as well as a number of branch libraries. Approximately 90% of the Libraries' $4 million annual collections budget is spent on digital resources.

Due to a marked decline in monetary support from the State of Nevada, the UNR Libraries' budget allocations from the University have been reduced or remained flat for the past seven years from 2007 to 2014, resulting in a $350,000.00 decline in the annual collections expenditures. In order to accommodate these shortages, the UNR Libraries have implemented subscription cancellation projects and relied more heavily on the student tuition fees and donor gift funds to help offset the shrinking funds.

Continuing this trend, the 2014–15 budgetary appropriation projections and expenditures, analyzed in mid-spring 2014, indicated a substantial library materials funding deficit of approximately $412,546.00. This required the UNR Libraries to make some major subscription cancellations in order to balance the budget for the coming fiscal year.

Collection Review Strategy at the UNR Libraries for Fiscal Year 2014–2015

In order to address the projected deficit, a three-phase collection review strategy was developed. The three-phase strategy included a comprehensive journal review, a journal package review, and a database review.

During the comprehensive journal review in Phase One, all of the UNR Libraries' active journal subscriptions were reviewed and assessed to uncover the most likely journal cancellation candidates, including individual titles, mini-journal packages, memberships, and combination subscriptions, which were handled primarily

through the UNR Libraries' two major subscription agents. In Phases Two and Three, large journal packages and databases subscribed to directly through publishers are looked at on a month-by-month basis by the Assistant Dean of Libraries for Collections as they come due.

Comprehensive Journal Review

The comprehensive journal review included all active individual journal subscriptions. The reason for looking at all journal subscriptions and not just database subscriptions is that the UNR Libraries have already focused on database cancellations and broken up the majority of the large journal packages during the last few years due to budget shortages. The goal was to incorporate into the review process all of the library resources with low demand to allow for smart purchases of high-demand resources in the future. Additionally, this all-encompassing cancellation push allowed liaisons to be made aware of all of the resources in their subject areas to better facilitate their outreach efforts with faculty on campus.

In an effort to provide an objective method for identifying the most likely candidates for cancellation by subject liaisons, the Assistant Dean for Collections established a set of criteria and key indicators. A title was flagged for liaison review if it met at least one of the following criteria:

- Greater than $5 per use.
- Used less than 50 times per year.
- Total cost greater than $400 for print journals; $1,000 for e-journals.
- Overlap with other resources.
- Monographic series to be cancelled.

In order to create a smooth review process and to encourage participation by liaisons and faculty, the Electronic Resources and Acquisition Services (ERAS) Department developed a seven-step process to manage the journal review project:

- Step 1: June 1–July 7 (~5 weeks)—ERAS prepared and compiled data for the upcoming journal review process. ERAS prepared two master lists for all active journal subscriptions, one for print and one for electronic. The master lists were posted on SharePoint for liaisons to access so that they could mark the journals in their subject areas for the first round of cancellations.

- Step 2: July 8–July 21 (~2 weeks)— Liaisons reviewed their own subjects and marked their decisions on SharePoint for first cut. During this period of time, the liaisons could seek additional information from ERAS staff to aid them in their decision-making process.

- Step 3: July 22–August 5 (~2 weeks)—The Assistant Dean for Collections reviewed the liaisons' decisions and talked with most of them about additional titles for possible cancellations in their subject areas. A final list of candidates for cancellation was developed.

- Step 4: Aug. 6–Aug. 12 (~1 week)—ERAS prepared two new "lists of journals to be cancelled" in SharePoint and a combined list for posting on a LibGuide, so that academic faculty and library liaisons could view them in order to dispute any titles on these lists.

- Step 5: August 13–Sept 5 (~4 weeks)— This was the dispute period for academic faculty to review all of the journals marked for cancellation and to register a dispute through library liaisons if they wanted to retain the journal(s).

- Step 6: Sept. 6–Sept. 14 (~1 week)—The Assistant Dean for Collections finalized the journal cancellation list, allowing some titles to be added back in.

- Step 7: Sept. 15—ERAS notified subscription agents and individual publishers of the journal cancellations for fiscal year 2014–15 and provided them with an Excel spreadsheet for inputting into their own systems. The due date to subscription agents for the annual renewals was graciously extended from the end of August to the middle of September 2014 this year.

Data Groups

In preparation for the two master journal lists, the ERAS staff compiled a list of data required by the established review criteria and other considerations. The staff gathered the needed data from various sources and presented them in a way that would allow liaisons to only focus on reviewing content. The goal was to present as much needed data as possible, organized logically in one spreadsheet, to facilitate the review and decision making process for liaisons. As a result, the two master journal lists included seven data groups as follows:

1. Review Indicator Group: This group included the predefined criteria as mentioned in the previous section of this article. A title was flagged for liaison review if it met at least one of those criteria.

2. Liaison Decision Group: This group allowed liaisons to register their review decisions and to make comments.

3. Basic Data Group: Cost amount, usage statistics, cost per use, subject, title, and publisher were in this group.

4. Title Relationship Group: A thorough individual order record review and data cleanup effort was made and all titles in relationships (such as memberships and separated order records for combined print and online subscriptions) were linked so that subject liaisons would see all of the included-in titles during their review and recommendation processes.

5. Title Links Group: Links were provided for liaisons to look up the title in the library online catalog and in the electronic journal portal for overlap checking.

6. Additional Data Group: Supplemental data in this group included bibliographic record number from the integrated library system, ISSN, and vendor code.

7. Administrative Data Group: This group of data was for ERAS staff use only.

Complete guidelines and instructions for each of the two master journal lists were provided for subject liaisons to follow when making their subscription renewal recommendations.

Project Management

There were four components in managing the comprehensive journal review project: data source, computing, workflow management, and communication.

Based on the identified data needed for the project, the ERAS staff determined the best sources for obtaining those data elements. The integrated library system served as the primary data source for most of the information collected. Subscription agents' journal renewal lists and local usage statistics system served as additional data sources. The computing applications deployed in the project included Microsoft Excel, Access, and SharePoint, which were used to manipulate the collected data into master journal lists. To manage the seven-step review process and workflows, the ERAS staff used SharePoint Lists, with its multiview functions, to centralize data input by all of the participants including subject liaisons and the Assistant Dean for Collections. To facilitate communication about the project, the Assistant Dean for Collections created a LibGuide on the library website containing all of the pertinent information needed by liaisons and separate links to two master journal lists on SharePoint. He also conducted two group meetings with liaisons explaining budgetary reasons for running a complete subscription review project and the steps for marking their decisions within these SharePoint Lists.

Overall liaison librarians were pleased with the journal review process. However, some of them expressed concerns about potentially losing a significant amount of content through journal cancellations. They wanted to know what journals would still be available in their subject areas after the cancellations. To address the concern, the ERAS staff provided, from the Libraries' journal knowledge base, a complete list of all the full-text e-journals available to library users, including back files and open access titles. A pivot table was further created from this list to display online journals by subject, allowing liaisons to filter journal titles across packages and platforms by subject.

In addition, since liaisons were instructed to focus on reviewing content only, they were not assigned a specific percentage to cut across subjects. To ensure cancellations were shared by all subjects, the ERAS staff monitored how much cancellation amount was proposed by each subject liaison in each of their subject areas.

Project Results

The review project was completed in about three-and-a-half months. It resulted in cancellations of 554 journal subscriptions, of which 340 were print and 214 were electronic, which represented 47% of the print journal subscriptions and 19% of the electronic journal subscriptions. It realized approximately $200,000 in savings and represented substantial progress toward covering half of the projected materials budget short fall for fiscal year 2014–2015.

Right after the journal review project was completed with significant savings in mid-September, the student enrollment number for the fall semester of 2014 was announced. It has increased by 9.5% from last year, meaning additional funding from student tuition fees for the University. As a result, the UNR Libraries would receive a 2.5% ongoing increase in the overall budget as well as a one-time additional amount to be used for library collections.

The news of additional funds came as a pleasant surprise as it reduced the pressure for the planned journal package and database reviews in the next phase of the collection review strategy. In response to the new budget changes, a new focus was placed on reconsidering liaisons' wish lists for high-demand materials purchases and on better filling users' needs for articles from unsubscribed journals. For the latter, the UNR Libraries started to use Get It Now from Copyright Clearance Center (CCC) to provide library users with speedy fulfillment of full-text articles from unsubscribed journals. In addition, the ERAS staff continued to work with Interlibrary Loan staff to monitor requests for cancelled journals in order to identify titles for possible reinstatement. Overall, this requires a balancing act between continuous reviews for cancellations and smart purchases of new resources.

Conclusion

The comprehensive journal review project did not proceed without challenges. For example, communication with liaisons and faculty required careful planning in terms of content, messages, communication venues, and timeliness. Data collection and presentation involved a huge amount of work and some advanced technical skills in the computing tools used. Since liaisons were not assigned a specific percentage to cut across subjects, whether the savings would cover budget shortage remained a question throughout the review process.

Looking into the future, conducting a cancellation project of this magnitude yearly or periodically

University of North Carolina at Greensboro Library

Planning for and responding to changes in library budgets is an integral part of every collection manager's responsibilities and skill sets. Too often, in the 21st-century academic library, the budget changes involve making cuts, rather than additions. When budget cuts are announced, collection managers are often asked to present their proposed cuts in short time. The task of making quick budget decisions is challenging enough, but, at times, the collection manager is informed that a budget cut is imminent, but that the amount of the shortfall is not yet known. How can collection managers and libraries accurately plan for the future when the future is uncertain?

Librarians at the University of North Carolina at Greensboro (UNCG) faced this very dilemma while planning for the 2014–2015 budget year. Universities across the state all initially informed that budget cuts were coming, but that amounts per school had not yet been decided. In September of 2013, UNCG learned that their share of the institutional budget cut would be 12.5 million dollars. However, the Libraries did not

does not appear to be a sustainable approach. Instead, incorporating collection review activities into regular workflows appears to be a better alternative. As such, a better collection review system is desired with future efforts in three areas: reporting collection usage and cost analysis, assessing impact of cancelled journals on ILL article borrowing requests, and managing wish lists for new purchases. Another lesson learned from the journal review project is that if there is a need to conduct cancellation projects outside of regular workflows, it would be most beneficial to start the projects early in the year.

Planning for certain future cuts when the future is uncertain has proved to be a moving target at the UNR Libraries. To meet the challenges of pursuing the moving target in the future, the UNR Libraries has found it essential to position itself well by establishing a sustainable collection review system while remaining flexible in response to unexpected budget fluctuations.

anticipate learning the amount of their share of the cut until the spring, upon which cancellations would need to be immediately made to meet fiscal year deadlines. So, decisions would need to quickly be made, even though the amount of our needed cuts was unknown. This article will address how UNCG Libraries rose to the challenge of making cuts with an uncertain future.

The University of North Carolina at Greensboro is one of 16 university campuses across the state. Its Carnegie Classification is Doctoral Intensive University 1, and as a research university with high research activity. The University's FTE is 18,500. Our collection consists of 2.8 million items (books, government documents, and microforms), 42,666 electronic journals, and over 250 electronic databases. The Libraries had survived several rounds of previous collections cuts. In 2009–2010, the budget was cut $300,000 for books, $240,000 for journals, and $130,000 for databases. In 2011–2012, the Libraries incurred an additional round of cuts: $296,000 for books, $260,000 for journals, and $130,000 for databases, or a total of $1,056,500 over a two-year period. In 2012–2013, there were no additional cuts, but nor were there any gains, as the Libraries were given a flat budget. Thankfully, one-time monies funded inflationary increases. The 2013–2014 budget was also flat, but there were no monies for inflation, thus essentially becoming a 4-5% cut. At this time, additional cuts to the collection were deemed too damaging, and the Libraries gave up four open positions to meet budget goals.

Needless to say, when the budget cuts to the University were announced, library staff were concerned. At this point, the "fat" had been well-trimmed, and cutting further resources would start to trim the bone. With time deadlines looming, a plan needed to be quickly proposed and implemented. The number of stakeholders with interests in collections was quite large, and involving all invested staff would not have allowed the nimbleness required. As there is already an existing Collection Management Team with members across departments, this team was a small but distributed group of librarians who were assigned with proposing a solution to the budget problem.

The timeline for the Collection Management Team was tight: the first meeting was scheduled for October, and cuts needed to be implemented by July 1. During most of the planning process, the team would not know the extent of the cuts. During the first meeting, the team agreed upon a plan of action. The Libraries were told that cuts could range from 15-25%. The team decided to create 15, 20, and 25% cut scenarios, so that librarians would be prepared in all cases. The team also created a timeline to ensure that cuts would be ready to implement by July 1. It was decided that the group could move at a greater speed if three small subgroups were created to work on proposals for the areas of books, databases, and journals. November was designated for creating the 15, 20, and 25% scenarios, and December would be allotted for these small groups to do their work, after which the big group would reconvene and refine the proposals. Though there was not sufficient time to involve all subject liaisons in initial scenario planning, it was crucial to include their input. The team decided that in January, the scenarios would be presented to the subject liaisons, who would provide their reactions and suggestions for modification, and would be given until February to give final feedback. In March, the finalized proposals would be sent out to campus at large, with faculty departments given a deadline of May 16 to provide their input. The Libraries expected that the final budget cut amount would be decided before the step of sending out proposed cuts to the faculty, so that adjustments could be made.

During the October meeting, the Collection Management Team began by deciding what percentage to cut the major areas of the collections budget. It was decided that books could take a larger hit than serials. The allocations were as follows:

		15%	20%	25%
Books	$ 693,340.00	$ 154,000.00	$ 205,333.33	$ 256,666.67
Serials	$ 1,723,597.00	$ 173,886.00	$ 231,848.00	$ 289,810.00
DBs	$ 869,204.00	$ 160,000.00	$ 213,333.33	$ 266,666.67
Other	$ 133,099.00	$ 25,000.00	$ 33,333.33	$ 41,666.67
	$ 3,419,240.00	$ 512,886.15	$ 683,848.20	$ 854,810.25

Table 1. Dollar amount of cuts by scenario.

	15.00%	20.00%	25.00%
Books	22.21%	29.62%	37.02%
Serials	10.09%	13.45%	16.81%
DBs	18.41%	24.54%	30.68%
Other	18.78%	25.04%	31.31%

Table 2. Percentage that each group was cut by.

During this same meeting, the group discussed what data was already available and what additional data was needed to make decisions on what to cut. This needed to be done between October and November, so as to adhere to the timeline. The group decided to pull cost for journals and COUNTER JR1 Statistics for 2011 and 2012 for all journals costing $100 or more. The amount of labor required to pull these statistics for titles under $100, as well as the time to analyze, was prohibitive. Additionally, the print journal and continuation usage statistics would be gathered, along with database statistics from the A-Z database and print journal/continuations usage statistics. The necessary statistics were distributed to each subgroup.

The journals group pulled together CPU statistics where they were available and began the process of creating cuts for each scenario. The initial scenarios were created:

	Cost	% cut at 15%	15%	20%	25%
Online plus P+E	$240,280.23	33.4%	$80,194.00	$96,500.00	$96,500.00
Print only	$46,249.30	64.9%	$30,000.00	$37,500.00	$37,500.00
Newspapers	$6,820.12	60.0%	$4,092.07	$4,092.07	$4,092.07
Continuations	$67,128.50	56.6%	$38,000.00	$47,500.00	$47,500.00
Memberships	$29,225.00	29.4%	$8,600.00	$10,750.00	$10,750.00
Microfilm	$22,893.49	43.7%	$10,000.00	$12,500.00	$12,500.00
Big Deals	$1,306,908.00	0.2%	$3,000.00	$23,000.00	$ 80,967.93
TOTAL	**$1,719,504.64**	**10.1%**	**$173,886.07**	**$231,842.07**	**$289,810.00**

Table 3. Cut scenarios.

Clearly, the cuts were not evenly distributed by percentage. At the 15% level, Big Deals would only be cut by $3,000, while these deals were cut by $23,000 at the 20% level, and $80,967.93 at the 25% level. The reason for this is that cutting Big Deals is always problematic. Key titles would have to be added back in, and the publishers often price these titles at a level where savings are minimal. So, the decision was made to make a minimal cut to Big Deals at the 15% level, while a couple of more expensive packages were identified as potential cuts if necessary.

The journals team looked at CPU for electronic titles and sorted by lowest CPU to highest with a running total column, that had markings at the 15, 20, and 25% cutoffs. The Print Only category was targeted for higher cuts, as users prefer electronic, and it is difficult to assess use with print titles. Continuations were also heavily targeted, after circulation data was presented for each title. Most of the continuations at the Libraries were not heavily used. Titles were sorted by use with a running total, with the least used continuations targeted for cancellation. The list of newspapers was small, so the entire group made title by title decisions. The group agreed that certain titles could be canceled regardless of the scenarios, so $4092.07 was immediately identified for cuts. Memberships required the input from the Dean of University Libraries, who identified the memberships that were strategically important. Cancellation targets were set at $8600 at 15% and $10,750 for 20 and 25%. Microfilm was also heavily hit, as users scantly use it.

The Databases subgroup also gathered CPU statistics and created a running total sorted by use. Canceling solely based on CPU was not necessarily an option for the group, however. Some subject disciplines had multiple core databases, while others had only one. Where multiple databases in a subject area were available, the decision to cut was based on CPU and coverage. When there were multiple similar databases, journal title coverage was considered. Some databases did not provide usage statistics, and the subgroup had to decide how important the availability of usage statistics were in making decisions on what to keep and what to cut.

The book subgroup met to decide their strategy for budget cuts. The decision was made to cut $90,000 right away from the approval plan, and to further cut all firm order accounts in disciplines that rely more on journals. Some departments have traditionally never spent all the allotted book monies available, so it was determined that cutting book budgets in those subject areas were not likely to be painful.

The larger group came back together to meet and put all the scenarios together. On January 17, the Collection Development Team presented the plan to all subject liaisons. Immediate feedback was that a few of the databases identified as potential cuts were essential. The liaisons proposed that the Team put $40,000 back into the databases budget line and take those funds from books and serials. So, the subgroups met again to adjust and work with the new figures. The Journals subgroup cut $3,000 more of print journals, cut an extra $11,000 in continuations, and $6,400 in Microfilm. The Databases subgroup went back to the original list and looked at statistics and other factors. The Book subgroup cut the approval plan again by $20,000.

The new plan was proposed, and the Subject Liaisons let the departments know that future cuts would be made in February. In order to present a more positive message, the emphasis was on what things the Libraries would be keeping, rather than on what would be cut. A budget web page was created for the faculty to consult, and at this point, the Team waited for the final budget cut news.

In March, the budget news for 2014–2015 was released. The Libraries would only have to take a 9% cut, or $362,000. This was a much better scenario than even our best-case proposed budget. The Collection Development Team reconvened and readjusted the plans, and then sent the budget website out to faculty to receive feedback. Faculty were able to keep proposed cut titles if they were able to offer up a cut elsewhere.

The departments were told that they could make adjustments, but would need to swap out similarly priced titles for others. After all the feedback was collected, and any adjustments made, the list was finalized, and the cuts were made.

In the end, though our cuts were smaller than expected, the Team's hard work was worth the time spent. The Libraries now has a basis for additional cuts, and much of the upfront work for cuts in the next few years has been done. This was an excellent exercise, too, to articulate the Libraries' collections priorities, as well as the priorities of faculty. The budget for the 15–16 fiscal year will probably be about 7%, and the work done for the 2014–2015 budget cut will assist with making decisions. It is more difficult to plan for budget cuts when the future is uncertain, but, with extra work and creation of scenarios, libraries can be prepared when the time comes.

The Challenge of Evaluating and Developing an Interdisciplinary Collection: The East Asian Collection at the Public College

Ewa Dzurak, College of Staten Island/CUNY

Kerry Falloon, College of Staten Island/CUNY

Jonathan Cope, College of Staten Island/CUNY

Abstract

When the faculty of the College of Staten Island, CUNY (CSI) introduced a new baccalaureate level program in East Asian Studies the library faced the challenge of evaluating the adequacy of its holdings to support the program and its future development. Multidisciplinary fields of study (e.g., East Asian Studies) that pertain to a specific geographical or cultural area present a unique set of evaluative issues because their subject content cannot be confined to set classification ranges, rendering the traditional methods of collection analysis inadequate . This poster will present the results of an evaluation of CSI's East Asian Studies collection, discuss some of the challenges the authors encounter when analyzing this collection, and it will propose ways that the collection can be strengthened in the future.

This analysis, as any analysis of a multidisciplinary field, must begin with clearly defining its span—in this case the scope of the East Asian Studies program at CSI. Then the authors will identify a few peer institutions with East Asian collections that can be used for purposes of comparison. Then the authors will examine how to best use the available tools (e.g., Aleph integrated library system, OCLC WorldShare Collection evaluation tool, and the CSI stacks).

The poster will then explore strategies for specific (call number, subject, and keyword) catalog searches and the types of searches available by the WorldShare Collection Evaluation tool which could render results relevant for the purpose of multidisciplinary content evaluation. The authors will share related subject headings lists and call number ranges that could be successfully used to cover the area of interest and the keywords crucial to successful searches.

Introduction

The faculty of the College of Staten Island, CUNY (CSI) introduced a proposal for a new baccalaureate level program in East Asian Studies to be initiated in the fall of 2015. Proposed program is truly interdisciplinary and its goal is to "introduce students to Asian cultures and societies through the study of translated literary and historical documents." It also proposes studying, through a variety of methods, the specifics of social structure and political systems of East Asian countries, as well as making available courses in major East Asian languages: Chinese, Japanese, and Korean. Additional spur came from the external evaluators invited to examine CSI Modern China program during the self-study process. In their report they encouraged the College to develop an East Asian program on the foundations of already strong Modern China program.

The timing of the introduction of a new program seems to be extremely adequate. The East Asian region, especially China, continues to play a major role on the world stage in the 21st century and its growing importance offers improved employment and advancement opportunities for students participating in the program. The Asian population in Staten Island borough increased 7.5% from 2000 to 2010 and it is expanding. The College of Staten Island is the only public institution of higher learning in the borough and the only one that offers an East Asian Studies programs. In this it follows other CUNY Colleges—Queens, Brooklyn, Hunter, and City College, which established similar programs some time ago. As interest in a program is expected to grow, the long-range plan to develop a Master of Arts in East Asian Studies in the next few years is being discussed.

The proposed courses concentrate on three major countries of the region: China, Japan, and Korea, and cover various periods of history as well as areas of culture, economy and politics.

With this proposal the College library faced the challenge of evaluating the adequacy of its holdings to support the program and its future development. Multidisciplinary fields of study (e.g., East Asian Studies) that pertain to a specific geographical or cultural area present a unique set of evaluative issues because their subject content cannot be confined to set classification ranges, rendering the traditional methods of collection analysis inadequate. Our presentation shares the results of an ongoing evaluation of the CSI's East Asian Studies collection, discusses some of the challenges the authors encounter when analyzing this collection, and it proposes ways that the collection can be strengthened in the future.

It must be stated that there is no perfect tool to conduct collection evaluation. To approximate collection depth and size a variety of methods and tools needs to be employed to guarantee adequate results. At this stage the most important tool of our analysis was OCLC's WorldShare Collection Evaluation, introduced by OCLC by the end of 2013. We also used our own online catalog (Aleph, version 21) as well as citation analysis of major East Asian journals. We also compared our electronic journals and database's holdings with the holdings of identified peer institutions. The process was and still is evaluated on the way. Evaluation adjustments and decisions about collection development are happening concurrently.

WorldShare Collection Evaluation Tool

WorldShare Collection Evaluation (CE) tool uses the Library's own holding data as reported to the OCLC Worldcat and provides an interface (still being developed, since the tool if fairly new) to help visualize them. The data can be represented in the table that enables us to look at the age, size, and format of the collection. It also allows for comparisons with other selected libraries, one on one, or with several libraries at once. The third function of analysis is the possibility of benchmarking against holdings of other libraries, as with comparisons—one on one or with a several libraries simultaneously. The data are presented on the screen in the form of a table or chart in a real time.

Comparisons and benchmarking are based on the subject list (conspectus) provided by WorldShare CE and founded on LC classification. The conspectus consists of 31 broad subject divisions, which are further subdivided into narrower categories and those into a third tier of more specific subjects. The corresponding LC classification ranges are assigned to every subject and subcategory.

The list of 31 subjects is as follows: Agriculture, Anthropology, Art & Architecture, Biological Sciences, Business & Economics, Chemistry, Communicable Diseases & Miscellaneous, Computer Science, Education, Engineering & Technology, Geography & Earth Sciences, Health Facilities, Nursing & History, Health Professions & Public Health, History & Auxiliary Sciences, Language, Linguistics & Literature, Law, Library Science, Generalities & Reference, Mathematics, Medicine, Medicine By Body System, Medicine By Discipline, Music, Performing Arts, Philosophy & Religion, Physical Education & Recreation, Physical Sciences, Political Science, Preclinical Sciences, Psychology, Sociology, Unknown Classification.

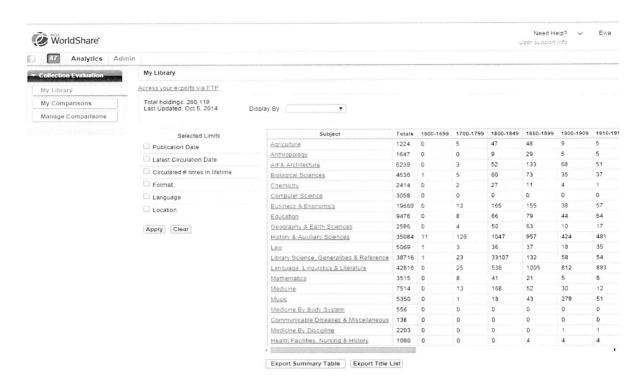

Figure 1. The screen shot of the Worldshare CE with subject and numbers of holdings in a table.

Each subject unfolds into a dropdown menu of narrower subjects (three tiers). An important feature of the Collection Evaluation is the possibility of obtaining list of holdings on the title level. Those came in the form of Excel files and can be generated for the whole library and on any specific narrow subject. It is worth keeping in mind that smaller lists of titles can be generated on more specific subjects and are easier to manage. Also the snapshot of the collection can be limited by the values visible on the right—publication date, circulation date, format, language, and location.

While analyzing the interdisciplinary collection one must keep in mind that the conspectus based on LC classification is discipline oriented and different aspects of the same topic are scattered throughout the classification scheme. Analyzing materials of different disciplines but limited to certain geographical area can be challenging. Only several subjects provided in WorldShare CE are subdivided geographically, at least on the current level of the of the tool development. Nevertheless some disciplines or divisions (as is the term in

WorldShare CE) are further divided into geographical areas on the second or third level of subdivisions. The easiest division to separate the East Asian area (understood by us according to our needs as China, Japan, Korea, Vietnam, Hong Kong, Shanghai) are History and Language, Linguistics, and Literature. Language, Linguistics, and Literature divisions naturally list in narrower subdivision languages and literatures of the world—East Asian languages and literatures included.

Here is a first glance at the numbers in Japanese, Korean, and Chinese literatures and languages. This short list immediately tells us that our holdings in Korean literature and language are very weak and this area needs immediate attention.

Japanese Language	13
Japanese Literature	94
Korean Language	1
Korean Literature	5
Chinese Language	35
Chinese Literature	152
Indo-Chinese, Karen, Tai, etc. Languages & Literat	10

Figure 2. Number of holdings in language and literature.

Each country's literature is further subdivided by either genre of literature or chronologically by literary period specific for this particular country and presented in the year of publication columns.

We also compared the numbers of our holdings as reported by OCLC with our local catalog holdings. According to OCLC holdings we have 152 titles in Chinese literature. The number of titles retrieved from our catalog with a subject = Chinese literature is—173—higher than holdings reported in OCLC. The difference is a result of our membership in a larger library system. We are part of the multilibrary CUNY system and our library shares a lot of electronic titles with other CUNY colleges—those are not listed in OCLC as the College of Staten Island library holdings, but as all CUNY holdings, which use different OCLC symbols. Being a part of a larger system widens

significantly our collections and it is truly advantageous to our users, who have access to holdings of all CUNY libraries.

Some of the divisions in WorldsShare CE, especially narrower subjects, are subdivided by geographical terms. Those are scattered through the subject spectrum. For example, the Art and Architecture division lists as follows: Architecture (China, Japan); Arts in General (Eastern and Southeastern Asia); Painting (China, Japan, and Southeastern Asia); Visual Arts in General (China, Japan, Korea, and Southeastern Asia). With these types of divisions it is easier to extract data about an art collection referring to East Asian countries. On the chart below our Visual Art holdings are reflected, divided by years of publication and color coded for three countries.

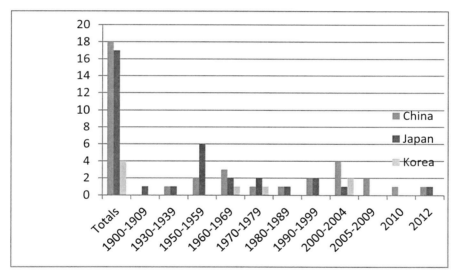

Figure 3. Visualization of our art holdings.

Other topics are subdivided "by region or country" only in a very general way. A good example is the division of Anthropology, which is subdivided into six narrower subjects: Anthropology, General, Ethnology, Social and Cultural Anthropology, Folklore, Proverbs, Manners and Customs, Social Usages, Etiquette. From those only one—Folklore—is further subdivided again into six narrower categories—Folklore, Philosophy Research General, Folk Literature by Form, Folk Literature by Race or Group, Folk Literature by Subject, and Folk Literature by Region or Country.

For the purpose of our evaluation we like to look only at those titles which refer to East Asia. In this case it is necessary to request a report of titles in this category. The report, as it was mentioned earlier, is prepared by the Worldshare CE in form of an Excel file and contains all the titles in category Folk Literature by Region or Country. One needs to establish the LC classification range for the appropriate area by consulting the LC classification scheme. In our case it is call number range: GR330—336 China, GR339-342—Japan, Korea.

The requested report is usually available the next day. The Excel file can be downloaded from the provided site and relevant titles can be extracted using the sort and filter option in Microsoft Excel. A word of warning—the downloaded file should not be too big—it might cause problems with download and manipulation, but the efficiency in extracting the data depends on familiarity with Excel.

As was mentioned before, WorldShare CE allows for comparison with and benchmarking against other libraries. Various institutions were chosen for comparison based on our faculty suggestions and the list of peer institutions provided by the Office of Institutional Research of the College of Staten Island. The library focused on the following East Asian programs as best-fitting comparisons: Queens College-CUNY, Hunter College—CUNY, Western Washington University, Union College, NY, and Wesleyan University. The main criteria used in selection were the level of the East Asian

program they already have established and the size of the student body.

As we noticed above, our weak holdings in Korean Literature needed immediate attention. We compared ourselves to the Union College Library and found out that while we have only six titles in this subject, they hold 62, with only one title shared. We also benchmarked ourselves against a few other libraries. In this case it was more than worthwhile to generate the title list to look at the titles we might add to extend our collection. Benchmarking is a useful tool in the collection development process—generated list of titles with different types of filters (like publication date) can be extremely useful in the future selection process. The list below is an excerpt of the list obtained from the Excel file from the report benchmarking our holdings on Korean Literature with three schools. Titles listed are not held by us, but are held at least by two other institutions and are definitely candidates for acquisitions.

1.	From Wonso Pond	PL991.38.K6	2	notHeld
2.	And So Flows History	PL992.26.M8	2	notHeld
3.	Modern Korean Fiction: An Anthology	PL984.E8	2	notHeld
4.	The Columbia Anthology of Modern Korean Poetry	PL984.E3	2	notHeld
5.	A History of Korean Literature	PL956	2	notHeld

Table 1. Korean Literature candidates for acquisitions.

Sociology is one of those general subjects that are subdivided by topic, not geographically. To find titles related to a specific geographical area one needs to consult the LC classification. For example in Social History, Social Problems, and Social Reforms subjects which are not subdivided by region, the call number range of HN50-995 is given as the range for other regions and countries. By consulting in more detail the LC classification tables one can establish that the range of call numbers HN720.5-HN755 refers to East Asian countries of interest. Titles with those call numbers can be generated and used for comparison and selection purposes.

WorldShare CE was our main tool to analyze our collection and the examples above show different

ways of using the tool. We also use the journal citation method. The analysis of 1,929 Citations in the *Journal of Asian Studies*, covering the period February 2012—February 2013 was undertaken as a pilot project. 29 monographs were cited more than once in a sample of 1,929 citations from five issues of the journal from February, 2012 (volume 71, issues 1, 2, 3, 4) and February, 2013 (volume 72, issue 1).

- 7 (24%) contained no geographical subject headings relevant to Asian Studies.

- 22 (76%) contained geographical subject heading relevant to Asian Studies.

This initial sample suggests that a small but substantial portion (in this sample 24%) of the monographs used in Asian Studies will not be identified based on LC subject heading analysis alone. We will continue our citation analysis in order to find patterns and identify titles essential to the East Asian Studies area.

Journal Evaluation

As our initial evaluation shows, our library subscribes to 23 journal titles related directly to the region of East Asia: 20 related to China, two to Japan, and one to Korea. During the evaluation 35 titles selected from the 140 most important journals in the field listed by Advisory Board of the Bibliography of Asian Studies were searched

across e-journal and database holdings at CSI. We discovered that CSI-CUNY held 70% of all titles (24), from which 50% were current, and 20% had a 1-4 year delay. CSI-CUNY did not hold 30% of all titles (11) from which ¼ were Korean related, ¼ Religious Studies, and ¼ Early Historical Studies. The rest were a mixture of cultural and language-related journals.

Database Evaluation

In an evaluation of the electronic resource holdings of 19 benchmark institutions with the College of Staten Island, the following databases were most prevalent. We will contact our faculty to solicit their opinion about our databases holdings and possible new acquisitions.

Core	CSI-CUNY Held/ Not Held
Bibliography of East Asian Studies	Not Held
Historical Abstracts with Full Text	CUNY Held
PAIS- Public Affairs Information Service	Not Held
MLA Bibliography	CUNY Held
JSTOR	CUNY Held
Project Muse	CUNY Held
Linguistics & Language Behavior Abstracts	Not Held

Table 2. Most prevalent electronic resources holdings.

Future Considerations

Our evaluation is ongoing. Currently we are continuing analysis of specific subjects holdings, our citation analysis, and electronic journals holdings. In the near future we would like to

- Generate monograph lists to enhance the strength of the existing collection East Asian collection.

- Determine the desired future collecting intensity or collection goal/acquisition commitment to East Asian Studies as seen below.

- Use vendor platforms (e.g., YBPs, GOBI) which utilize call number ranges to assist in future collecting in East Asian Studies.

LC Call Number Ranges	Subject Area	Collection Depth Levels Current | Future	
DS	History: Asia (General)	2 |	3c
DS 501-519	History: East Asia (General)	2 |	3c
DS 710-800	History: China	2 |	3c
DS 801-900	History: Japan	2 |	3b
DS 901-937	History: Korea	1 |	3b

Table 3. Current and future collection depth.

Don't Leave the Faculty at the Station:
Introducing Faculty to Collection Development Grants

Don J. Welsh, Head of Research, College of William and Mary, Williamsburg, Virginia

Martha E. Higgins, Research Librarian, College of William and Mary, Williamsburg, Virginia

Stephen D. Clark, Collections Strategist, College of William and Mary, Williamsburg, Virginia

Abstract

In 2012, a collection analysis report was published outlining the results of a year-long study of the College of William and Mary Library collections comparing it to those of other peer institutions using OCLC's collection analysis software. As a means to address some of the deficiencies brought out in the report as well as provide outreach and curricular support, the library began to offer collection development grants to college faculty. This has been a fruitful experience to build collaborative efforts with faculty; to fill gaps in the library collections; enhance curricular and faculty research support; and to provide outreach to the faculty community through library liaisons.

Introduction

In 2012, Swem Library performed a collection analysis using the OCLC collection management software in regard to monographic and database holdings. This analysis showed where we were lacking in certain call numbers—foreign languages materials, non-US history, music, and several other areas.

At William and Mary, monograph acquisitions are normally done by both liaisons and faculty members using YBP's GOBI. The ratio of faculty/liaison workload varies by academic department depending on the people involved, their interests and expertise, and so on.

Of course, faculty focus changes with the retirement of some faculty, the arrival of new faculty, and the expansion of new and interdisciplinary programs. Swem has an endowment fund to purchase materials for new faculty but this is not always enough. Every year brings new faculty, new courses, and new degree programs such as Middle Eastern Studies and Latin American Studies. The new faculty also bring new research interests to support.

How Did We Decide to Start the Collection Development Grants?

For approximately the last 10 years, Swem library has had a flat collections budget. Of course, with inflation and the increasing prices of monographs, this negatively affected our buying power. However, in the 2013-2014 budget, an additional influx of money was given to the library from the College as requested from the Dean, as it was still part of her "honeymoon period," that was to be used to address any deficits mentioned in the final collection analysis report. One staff member was familiar with the collection grant concept and we began brainstorming and came up with several positive reasons to introduce the program:

1. Public Relations: Faculty needed to know that we wanted their input, that we were listening, and that we were willing to spend money to address their needs.

2. Outreach: The collection grant process was an excellent outreach opportunity for our liaisons.

3. Attempt to fill in gaps in the collection analysis report.

4. Curricular support for new classes: Many new classes are being offered, new faculty, new minors, and shifting faculty interests.

5. Support for faculty research.

6. Build collaborative relationships for the future.

To start with, an amount of $50,000 was set aside with a maximum amount of $3,000 per grant to be used towards one time purchases. It was specified that these purchases were not to include journal subscriptions or databases with multiyear obligations.

Faculty and liaisons were to provide an itemized list of requested resources including prices, ISBN numbers when applicable, and ordering information. The faculty and liaisons were asked to write a brief proposal and answer the following questions:

1. What is the relationship between the materials you wish the library to purchase and the program, course or research for which they are intended?

2. How essential are these materials to your achieving the goals of the program, course, or research for which they are intended?

3. How will these materials strengthen the collection or address a recognized area of deficiency?

4. How often will courses be taught? How many students could benefit?

During the process, we got numerous questions from faculty about what these funds could be used for items other than collections. One wanted to buy equipment such as a 3D printer, one wanted to use the funds for travel, one wanted to buy some software for personal use, etc. We refused all requests which did not benefit our collection.

How Did the Liaisons Promote These Grants to Faculty?

- A letter from our Dean was sent to all faculty through the Provost's office.

- Personal emails.

- Visits to their offices or meeting faculty for coffee.

- Main library website featured it as a story.

- Our university daily news digest (which goes to all faculty and staff).

- We developed a LibGuide with guidelines, forms, and the 2012 collection analysis report.

Collaboration between the faculty and the liaisons was varied:

- Searching for new books on the topic.

- Going through title list to check if we already owned it.

- Checking title lists for pricing and availability.

- Going through extensive bibliographies to search for what we did not own.

- Collaborate with other groups/departments on campus to get more information.

Review of Collection Grant Proposals

The Collections Advisory Committee designed a basic rubric to grade the proposals. We received 29 applications from 38 faculty members representing all different areas of the college. Our rubric was very basic: giving 1-10 scores based on the materials relevancy to courses or research, interdisciplinary in nature, and would the materials strengthen Swem Library's collections or address a recognized area of deficiency that was indicated in our collection analysis.

In total, we awarded more than $70,000 in grants, with the average award being $2,400. The committee decided that for this year alone, we had enough money to fund them all—this will not be the case in the future! Some of the proposals were:

- Gifted education materials.

- South Asia and Indian Ocean history.

- Tudor and Stuart English history.

- Frederick Wiseman documentary films.

- Byzantine studies.

- Musical scores.

- Sustainability inspired design materials.

- Caribbean diaspora.

- Asian cinema films.

- Polynesian archaeology.
- Chinese art scrolls.

One librarian submitted a proposal to increase our holdings of local Williamsburg history, which will be greatly appreciated by our many local historians and genealogists.

Budgetary Aspect of Collection Grants

As has been stated previously, with a boost in the library's materials budget, we felt as though we had enough flexibility in our materials budget to offer small grants to faculty for the enhancement of their research and classroom support, with the added plus of filling in some gaps of our collection as reflected in our recent collection analysis. We initially started out with the goal of awarding $50,000 worth of grants with each grant totaling no more than $3,000. In the end, we granted nearly $70,000 in small grants to faculty. The grants which were awarded ranged from $340 to $4,000. The one grant which was over our "limit" of $3,000 was one that was very popular with our administration when they heard about it, so we felt that it would behoove us politically to award it.

The grants ranged in format from books to DVDs to CDs to a microfilm collection (we asked the distributor if this collection was in line for digitization, and were told that it was not) to reproduction Chinese art prints and scrolls to a materials library collection (samples of different types of materials in the areas of design, architecture, packaging, etc.).

There were some challenges in this venture. They related to timing, pricing, the types of materials requested, and some miscellaneous vendor problems.

Timing. Dealing with faculty at any time can be dicey, but it is best not to try to interact with them right at the beginning of the semester or around exam time. The announcement of the grants was made in late October and the proposals were due on December 2. Yes, this was a short turn-around time, and we received some blow back on it. Proposals were reviewed about a week later by the library's Collections Advisory Committee and awards were made the middle of the month. A

real timing kerfuffle was getting the proposals to the Acquisitions Department at the same time that folks in that area were under the gun to place a sizable amount of orders and in the throes of a myriad reorganization meetings. Adding all of this up, not all of the requests in the proposals—around $10,000 worth—were processed until the beginning of the new fiscal year. This year, all of the proposals which are given awards are going to the Acquisitions Department by the end of November for processing to begin.

There were also faculty who submitted grant proposals to support classes which they were teaching in the spring 2014 semester. Some material was able to be ordered and received in time for use in these classes.

Pricing. The pricing of items became problematic with some lists of items since the faculty members found much of their prices for their requests from Amazon.com. The library does a good deal of rush ordering from Amazon, but still is obligated to work with vendors with whom it has contracts. As a result of this, some of the grant ordering began to exceed the amount of funds which were awarded. In a few instances, where there was the possibility of over expending, it was minimal enough that it was allowed, but in other cases, there were negotiations between liaisons and faculty to cover the over expenditure with their departmental funds. As a result, we asked faculty to prioritize their requests so that once we reached their award, we would stop processing orders.

Materials. We ran into some interesting format obstacles. The first thing that we learned was that we needed to approve formats that were supported by the library. We had a situation with sound files which needed to be downloaded and then we were stuck with the question of how do curate and be able to distribute them. There was also the issue of licensing for these files, which needed to go through the College's Procurement Office. These two obstacles right then and there put a halt to the purchase of the sound files. As was mentioned earlier, we also approved the purchase of reproductions of Chinese art prints and scrolls. Arrangements were made ahead of time by the requesting faculty member and the liaison working with her to place these items in our Special Collections Research Center for the special handling and viewing needs that they presented. Then, there is the issue of formats which are becoming obsolete. We doubt that we will be awarding grants anymore which involve the purchase of microforms.

There were also issues involved in the types of materials which were applied for. We had queries as to whether the grant could pay the cost of digitizing material, whether we could purchase a 3-D printer, and even though one of our guidelines was that items would be for one-time purchases, there was a request for a subscription for a limited amount of time.

Miscellaneous vendor problems. Dealing with third-party vendors associated with Amazon or Alibris turned out to be a nightmare. Some proved to be difficult when there were issues of non-receipt, but our credit card was billed anyway. Some of these vendors just wouldn't deal with us. Another problem was with an order for a group of DVDs from a foreign country. The price which we were given on the website for the items was very good, but the vendor wanted more than twice the purchase price of the DVDs in shipping charges. As it turned out, the faculty member who wanted these DVDs was taking a group of students to this country for a study trip this past summer. He volunteered to purchase the DVDs that he wanted, bring them home to us, and we then reimbursed him for the cost of the items.

Dealing with used and out-of-print materials can be a problem. Several proposals included used or out-of-print titles in their requests and by the time the proposals were approved and the Acquisitions Department attempted to purchase them, they were either sold and no longer available, or in some instances, the prices had gone up dramatically.

The result of going through this process once is that we learned several things to do and not to do with successive collection grant projects.

- Stand firm with original grant funding guidelines. Even though we could afford to go over expend awards a little in the first year of the process, it can set a bad precedent, and we really needed to be more strict and tighter in applying the guidelines which we had set.

- Make sure to give all parties involved enough time to get their proposals together for submission and to process the requests to order and to pay for everything in the same fiscal cycle.

- Only award grants for materials that can be supported by the library. It can be very problematic purchasing material that cannot be technologically supported, curated, or handled in a manner that is appropriate for that material.

- Pricing for items requested needs to be accurate and not "Amazonized."

- Be ready to deal with proposals for material offered by vendors who use dubious pricing practices or those with whom it may be difficult to deal.

- Warn faculty ahead of time to schedule at least one semester ahead in making proposals to support specific classes in order to allow enough processing time to procure materials and have them ready for use.

Outcomes

This was a really positive collaborative experience for Swem Library. The liaisons received more faculty input from some departments than we had received in years. Faculty and liaisons were genuinely interested and excited about these new collections. Great relationships were formed between the librarians and the faculty, not only tied to the grants, but further partnerships in instruction and research as well as friendships.

Swem Library acquired some wonderful research materials that we may not have known about, or may not have known were wanted and needed. This was an excellent public relations program, and was definitely worth it. We just started our review process for our second year of collection development grants, and are looking forward to diversifying and building our collections.

Gift-Gaining: Ideas for Effective Gift Processing

Mark Henley, Contracts Librarian, Collection Development, University of North Texas Libraries

Abstract

Personnel turnover and other factors led the University of North Texas Libraries to repurpose staffing to process gift items in 2014. None of the new personnel had experience in evaluating gifts. As the reassigned personnel began its work, it became clear that intensive training and a reevaluation of procedures was necessary for effective processing of these materials. This presentation looked at the issues that arose and the solutions that emerged from the reevaluation. Told from the perspective of the new gifts coordinator, the session sought to present a case study that provided attendees with examples of tools they can implement and pitfalls to avoid as they evaluate their own gift policies. Attendees also shared some of their own experiences in dealing with gift processing in their libraries.

Introduction

In 2014, the intake of and processing of gift materials by the UNT Libraries shifted significantly to staff who were previously uninvolved in the process. With the change in the number and positions of the staff, the gift procedures needed to be evaluated and updated. This presentation walked through those procedures, exposing the issues that the staff faced as they grappled with their new responsibilities. The presentation concluded with reflections on the process, some of the lessons learned, and ideas for future success.

Setting

The University of North Texas Libraries received 3,045 book gift donations in 2014, up from 2,675 in 2013. 1,169 or 38% of those donations were added to the Libraries' holdings, going into the current collections, added as second copies, or sent to remote storage. 1,379 or 52% were added to the holdings in 2013.

The Coordinator of Collection Development announced her imminent retirement at the end of 2013. One of her duties was coordinating gift intake and evaluation. The Contracts Librarian absorbed those duties fully at the onset of her retirement in April 2014. The Contracts Librarian had no experience with gift processing prior to assuming these duties.

Gift evaluation prior to the departure was done by the Coordinator of Collection Development and one graduate assistant. Since the departure, gift evaluation has been done by the Contracts Librarian, a graduate assistant, a student assistant, and two ordering staff. Gift processing is not the primary duty of any of these staff members.

Gifts are governed by the UNT Libraries' Collection Development Policy (http://www.library.unt .edu/policies/collection-development/collection-development-policy) and the UNT Libraries Gift Policy (http://www.library.unt.edu/policies /gifts/unt-libraries-gift-policy). The gifts coordinator performs a triage of donations. There are five item types that are not evaluated by the gifts coordinator: those of interest to the Special Collections department, government documents, music, media, and periodicals. These types of items are sent to their respective departments. For various purposes, the extent of each donation must be forwarded by the gifts coordinator to the Libraries' Assistant Dean for External Relations. The gifts coordinator also determines if a bookplate is necessary for the donated items and maintains a spreadsheet of the names of donors and the types of items included in the donation.

Items are then evaluated for condition and retention. Books that are mildewed, have missing parts, or for some other reason are unacceptable for the collection are disposed of in the most effective way, usually discarding or recycling. Items that are physically suitable are then evaluated for addition to the collection. Some uncommon items have special rules. These include UNT dissertations, art catalogs, art books, popular works, graphic novels, UNT yearbooks, computer books, older science books, cookbooks, and kits.

Evaluating staff first check the online catalog to determine if the Libraries already own a copy of the item. If not, the item it is added to the collection if it supports curriculum or research initiatives. If the Libraries own a copy then it is added to the collections as a second copy or second volume. Items with older publication dates (older than five years) and earlier editions of things already in the collection (that have 10 or more circulation instances within the last two years) are sent to remote storage. Items with publication dates within the last five years and the most current editions of items that circulate heavily (10 or more circulation instances in the past year) are added to the current collections. High circulation is defined as circulation of 10 instances in one year. The print version of a library-owned e book is kept, as well as books that are included in the Libraries' McNaughton book rental plan. Books with CDs, disk, etc., are given to the gifts coordinator, as well as problem books such as discs where the book cannot be located and instructor's manuals where the accompanying book has not been located. If necessary, bookplate information is added and the statistics worksheet is updated. This spreadsheet indicates who processed items for a certain day and the number of items that were added to the current collections, sent to remote storage, marked as an added copy or volume, recycled, marked for surplus, or sent to another department.

Issues/Solutions

As the new gifts coordinator assumed his duties, several issues arose that hindered effective gift processing. First, effective training was difficult. The two ordering personnel had been briefly trained six months prior to the retirement of the Collection Development Coordinator. With no additional practice supplemental training was necessary. Two training sessions took place in May and July. The inexperience of the gifts coordinator, the nature of the procedures document, and looming end-of-year ordering deadlines stalled the effectiveness of the training.

Bookplates presented a problem. Directions for bookplates were not in the procedures documentation. There was some recollection that bookplates were necessary for any item where the identity of the donor was known. This was putting a tremendous strain on the evaluating and cataloging personnel due to the massive amount of donations coming in during the summer break (around 10 boxes each week). In addition to the volume of donations coming in the task of keeping track of individual donations in the sorting area became problematic. After consulting with the Libraries External Relations department it was determined that bookplates would only be created only in those cases where the donor explicitly asks for one to be included.

No instruction as to what was appropriate to the curriculum was present in the procedure materials. The previous gifts coordinator was heavily involved with the collection and with the faculty of many University departments. The new gifts coordinator was strictly involved in acquisitions for the majority of his career. The new Collection Development Coordinator created a list of Library of Congress subjects that were included in the Libraries' approval plan so that staff evaluators could more easily determine if the donated item supports curriculum and research initiatives.

During the intake of materials, many items in foreign languages, particularly Chinese and Russian, were being evaluated. Since the university does not offer degrees in those languages, some of the staff suggested that those materials not be added to the collection. Similarly, the Special Collections department clarified their policies and significantly narrowed their scope of desired materials. The wording in the procedures document for Special Collections evaluation now reflects their policies. In both instances, previously evaluated materials required reevaluation.

The revisions to the bookplate policy, the foreign language policy, and the special collections policies, as well as the creation of the curriculum aid led to a revision and reorganization of the procedures document. The original procedures document was oriented toward the individual coordinating gifts, but was difficult to follow by those not familiar with the procedures or evaluating materials. The new gifts coordinator revised the document to include an overview of the entire process at the beginning of the document and sought to make it usable by any personnel if the gift coordinator were to leave or be absent. For example, the instructions for intake, originally at the beginning of the procedures document, were moved to the end as an appendix since the majority of the staff members using the document do not need that process to complete their evaluation of materials.

Assessment and Next Steps

In reflecting on the change in personnel, there are a couple of lessons learned. Although the outgoing gifts coordinator helped train some of the staff, it was only after her departure that the workflow became clearer. For any future changes of this magnitude, it would be wise to plan for considerable time after the staff change to assess workflow and make adjustments.

After the changes in specifications for foreign language and special collections materials, many items were reevaluated. In retrospect, there could have been better negotiation with other departments, and the changes could have been applied to future gifts only. Since new gifts are being taken in continually, having to reevaluate older material is possibly an inefficient use of time and resources.

Moving forward, there are several concrete steps to ensure future success.

1. Create an issues log as part of the procedures document. This will allow issues to be captured in the moment, and addressed during procedure revisions.

2. Create a working list of interest areas. This will allow the staff to quickly determine if gifts are useful to the collection, or will most likely be discarded. Positively, this could include new University programs where a collection has not been established. Or, a list of commonly donated items that the Libraries already have in the collection and that are commonly discarded or sent

to surplus could be compiled to influence the types of materials gifted.

3. Update procedures regularly. This keeps the process fresh in the coordinator's mind.

4. Provide refresher training regularly that includes hands-on instruction. Because this activity is no one's primary assignment, it is easy to forget the process and get confused when evaluating items. It might prove wise to conduct training whenever significant updates to the procedures occur.

5. Run an assessment of the efficiency of the gift processing procedure. This can be helpful to streamline workflows and direct staff resources. One potential investigation would be to evaluate the percentage of items added from donations to determine the priority of gift addition. Another area of investigation would be to see if items should be evaluated for addition to the general collections before triaging the items to specialized departments.

Conclusion

Staff turnover in 2014 led to the reassigning of various roles in the University of North Texas Libraries Collection Development department. One such reassignment was the Contracts Librarian assuming the role of gifts coordinator. Very quickly, the new gifts coordinator saw the need for additional training. Training sessions allowed staff to gain gift evaluation experience and express points of confusion and clarification with the evaluation procedures. Staff comments based on their evaluating experiences led to gift workflow reassessment which, in turn, provided the impetus for the new gifts coordinator to create a new procedures document to capture information and establish consistent methods for all of the staff working on this project. With necessary maintenance and updating, these new procedures will help ensure effective gift processing in the future.

End Users

Share Those Stats! Collaborating With Faculty to Make Evidence-Based Serials Collection Development Decisions

Alana Verminski, St. Mary's College of Maryland Library

Abstract

During the 2014 fiscal year, the St. Mary's College of Maryland Library faced a temporary budget reduction, and library administration anticipated much larger and permanent cuts in the coming fiscal years. This budget reduction prompted a need to critically evaluate the library's journal subscriptions and as a consequence, the author developed a new collaborative review process. In this new process, librarians leveraged usage statistics, collection development experience and the subject expertise of faculty to make more informed collection development decisions. Although many libraries have involved faculty in journal cancellation projects, the St. Mary's College of Maryland librarians took a proactive approach by implementing a unique collaborative review process before experiencing their severest budget cuts. By starting conversations with faculty early, the librarians were able to make evidence-based collection development decisions that emphasized usage statistics, increased transparency, and built faculty trust. Librarians used a variety of methods to facilitate faculty-librarian collaboration, the most important of which was the sharing of usage statistics with academic departments. This presentation explored the strategies implemented by the St. Mary's College of Maryland Library to increase transparency and encourage faculty involvement in journal renewal decision making.

Journal Reviews and Renewals at the St. Mary's College of Maryland Library

With the start of the 2014 fiscal year, the St. Mary's Library faced a budget reduction, which was described as temporary, but forecasts indicated the cuts would become permanent. The librarians decided to proactively address the budget reduction's impact on serials collection development ahead of larger cuts. Additionally, the Library had been operating under a flat budget for several years with a policy of "add one, cancel one," which was no longer fiscally possible and further emphasized the need for a collaborative and comprehensive assessment of the entire journal collection. In response, the author developed an entirely new review and renewal process for journals and revised the serials collection development policy accordingly. The new process factored usage statistics into renewal decisions and invited faculty to share their subject area expertise and recommendations in departmental journal reviews. By engaging faculty early, before journal subscriptions reached a crisis point, the librarians hoped to maintain positive relationships with their faculty colleagues and gain buy-in and support.

The primary goals of the journal reviews were to improve collection development decision-making, streamline the collection, and better align journal holdings with campus teaching and research needs. Transparency and faculty-librarian collaboration were essential themes that drove the new renewal process. The St. Mary's Library had not assessed its serials collection comprehensively since the 2004 fiscal year, during a large-scale cancellation projected targeted at the print collection. Unfortunately, this past project generated an excess of ill will towards the Library. The cancellations came as a shock to faculty who were not consulted or notified of the project until after cancellations were made. Although librarians involved in this current project were not part of the earlier cancellations, they were especially sensitive to this particular piece of institutional memory. Additionally, the St. Mary's community is small and close-knit. The College employs approximately 143 full-time tenure and tenure-track faculty. The Library currently enjoys a positive reputation on campus and the librarians have successfully built partnerships with both academic and administrative departments. Transparency and openness seemed to be the best strategies to keep and improve those valuable relationships.

Literature Review

Journal reviews and high-impact cancellations have become the norm in academic libraries. As Sinha and Tucker (2005) note, most libraries tackle reviews at point of crisis, when librarians are forced to make difficult decisions and are often put in the uncomfortable position of balancing the demands of a reduced budget while maintaining positive relationships with faculty. Multiple authors describe methods of gathering and incorporating faculty feedback into journal cancellation projects for the purpose of improved decision making and protecting working relationships (Murphy, 2012; Carey, Elfstrand, & Hijleh, 2008; Sinha & Tucker, 2005). The North Carolina State University and University of Nevada Las Vegas Libraries in particular created a dedicated website to inform faculty of the changes and provide another avenue to share feedback (Day & Davis, 2009; Sinha & Tucker, 2005). Most case studies that describe journal reviews, which incorporate faculty input, focus on a single cancellation project triggered by a budget reduction and completed once a target budget was reached and not an ongoing effort to refine the journal collection.

Project Strategies

The themes of transparency and faculty-librarian collaboration weaved together to influence many aspects of the project. Faculty were first notified of future journal reviews and changes to the renewal process at a department chair retreat, during which the interim library director introduced the project. The announcement was made a semester in advance of journal reviews and both department chairs and departmental faculty were encouraged to seek further information and clarification during the initial meeting's Q&A session and later as concerns arose. To further distribute information and address faculty question and concerns, web pages were designed and added to the library website to explain the details of the project, point faculty to the revised serials collection development policy, outline the steps of a typical departmental journal review, and illustrate how usage statistics are gathered and measured as part of the review. This

dedicated portion of the library website will also serve as a platform for faculty feedback. Before final decisions are made, all journals recommended for cancellation will be posted to the library website with an open comment period.

Most significantly, usage statistics for current journal subscriptions were shared with academic departments undergoing review. Statistics were distributed via e-mail far enough in advance so department members could review the data and ask questions. After usage statistics were shared, liaisons scheduled in-person meetings with academic departments to answer remaining questions about the usage data and communicate their recommendations for subscription changes. In discussions with faculty, librarians were honest about the intent of the reviews and outlook of the library's journal collection. Throughout the entire process, faculty were encouraged to send questions and concerns to their liaison and the interim library director, or schedule additional in-person meetings with their liaison.

Biology Journal Review

The journal reviews and new renewal process were recently implemented and at the point of presentation, only one academic department had undergone a review. The Biology Department, one of the largest departments on campus, participated in a review during the spring 2014 semester. (The liaison librarian for the department and author are one and the same). The newness of the project prevents any in-depth analysis, but the following observations were made about the initial review.

During the first meeting, conversations between the author and departmental faculty were candid and faculty were receptive to participating in the review, although, talks did not lead directly to productive next steps. Faculty were eager to share their recommendations for new subscriptions, but hesitant to recommend any single title for cancellation. The author recommended a small number of journals as candidates for cancellation, but faculty immediately opposed the recommendations, despite recoded low usage. The author and department faculty did agree to revisit the recommendations again the following spring semester with another year's usage data to determine if continued subscription was the most effective means of access.

Sharing the usage statistics served two unexpected purposes. First, it indicated to faculty that librarians were genuinely interested in involving faculty in the process and signaled the level of participation expected. Second, usage statistics became a comfortable starting point for conversation. For the biologists especially, seeing the usage statistics and cost per use analysis provided evidence that direct subscription was not necessary for all journals and for some titles, interlibrary loan was the more fiscally advantageous mode of access. Focusing on the data at least initially seemed to reduce an automatic opposition to the process.

Future Work

The Library plans to conduct similar journal reviews will all academic departments, while refining the process further. One lesson learned from the biology review is liaison librarians will have to be more assertive in recommending

journals for cancellation. Without the policy of "add one, cancel one" as an option, faculty are far less willing to let go of current subscriptions. The Library is open to starting new subscriptions, but only with sufficient cost savings from cancellations. If faculty continue to be closed to the idea of cancellations, the Library will be hard-pressed to make any changes to the journal collection without making cancellations a requirement.

The journal reviews are meant to be ongoing and reoccurring. The goal of the project is not to reach a budget target or cancel a certain number of journals, but rather ensure relevance and develop a streamlined collection. The author could track the budget percentage spent on journals over time, or average the cost per use of the collection before and after reviews for some indication of effectiveness. To take a more evidence-based approach, librarians could survey faculty to rate the perceived relevance of existing journal subscriptions. Librarians could also ask faculty to evaluate how well each subscribed journal met program needs, and quantify those evaluations for renewal decisions.

References

Carey, R., Elfstrand, S., & Hijleh, R. (2006). An evidence-based approach for gaining faculty acceptance in a serials cancellation project. *Collection Management, 30*(2), 59-72. http://dx.doi.org/10.1300/J105v30n02_05

Day, A. & Davis, H. (2009). A look at librarianship through the lens of an academic library serials review. *In the library with the leadpipe*. Retrieved from http://www.inthelibrarywiththeleadpipe.org/2009/a-look-at-librarianship-through-the-lens-of-an-academic-library-serials-review/

Murphy, A. (2012). An evidence-based approach to engaging healthcare users in a journal review project. *Insights, 25*(1), 44-50. http://dx.doi.org/10.1629/2048-7754.25.1.44

Sinha, R. & Tucker, C. (2005). Finding the delicate balance: Serials assessment at the University of Nevada, Las Vegas. *Serials Review, 31*(2), 120-124. http://dx.doi.org/10.1080/00987913.2005.10764968

Return on Investment: New Strategies for Marketing Digital Resources to Academic Faculty and Students From Three Perspectives: Publisher, Collection Development, and Research Services

Elyse Profera, Regional Sales Manager, Central U.S. Taylor & Francis Group

Michael A. Arthur, Head of Acquisitions and Collection Services, University of Central Florida Libraries

Barbara G. Tierney, Head of Research and Information Services, University of Central Florida Libraries

Abstract

Game-changing strategies for marketing digital resources to end users are crucial for establishing return on investment in this period of reduced library collection budgets and challenging resource prices. When expensive digital resources are purchased by academic libraries, there needs to be a marketing plan in place for getting these resources into the hands of end users as quickly as possible.

One strategy for success is a marketing collaboration between the publisher and the academic library. The Profera, Arthur, Tierney 2014 Charleston Conference presentation on this topic focused on the success achieved at the University of Central Florida Libraries where such a collaboration included experts from Taylor & Francis working closely with the Head of Acquisitions & Collection Services and the Head of Research Services. Together they sponsored a digital resources educational workshop that included presentations by faculty, librarians, and Taylor & Francis representatives and reached out to end users as well as librarians from several Florida institutions. The UCF Libraries has also partnered with publishers to promote resources through various events sponsored by publishers and aimed at librarians and faculty from UCF and surrounding institutions.

The presenters covered innovative strategies for marketing digital resources including hosting vendor presentations and trainings in library classrooms or at academic faculty workshops and hosting webinars and presentations. With the focus on marketing to end users, the presenters concentrated on ways that academic faculty and librarians have been included in training and outreach related to new products or major enhancements to existing library resources.

Taylor & Francis Perspective

Taylor & Francis (T&F) rolled out a new initiative in 2014 to host collaborative library-publisher-academic workshops in key areas across the Americas with the intent of fostering relationships and goodwill in the library and academic community. Recent primary research conducted by T&F to the library community cites that 77% of librarians agree that interactive workshops are the number one activity publishers can do to raise awareness of their content.

Taylor & Francis and the University of Central Florida (UCF) collaborated on one of these workshops that was held in February 2014. The workshop raised the profile of both Taylor & Francis and the University of Central Florida across the state and this workshop was the foundation of a partnership that continued throughout 2014. UCF is a partner with one of the largest commercial publishers in the world. The success of this workshop emphasizes the importance of human-to-human communication and the impact it can have with publisher-library relations and marketing outreach to end users.

Facilitating Relationships

In 2014, Taylor & Francis conducted research on how to personalize library service to improve scholarly communication; the results were then presented at the 2014 NASIG conference. When asked what publishers can do to work with institutions to raise awareness about their content, survey respondents provided the following top five tactics:

1. Publisher-library workshops (77%).
2. Quarterly newsletters by subject (73%).
3. Free access months (65%).
4. Print and e-promotional items for library distribution (61%).
5. Email campaigns to end users at (45%).

Human-to-human communication has been a highly effective way to nurture existing relationships and cultivate new partnerships, and that has been the focus of T&F outreach in 2014. T&F has been engaging nonstop with customers, and working alongside regional sales teams to help drive results and return on investment for libraries. Successful initiatives included the hosting of workshops in the US, roadshows in India, author talks in China, one-on-one visits to customers in the US, and conducting country tours in South America to roll out Taylor & Francis Online (TFO) platform training. Throughout this work, people began to associate T&F with the humans that represent the company, and the excellent outreach fostered a sense that professional and personal connections have a profound impact on engaging with the market. Human-to-human communication reinforces the notion of developing your own personal brand. Because of the outreach efforts of Ms. Profera and others at T&F, librarians at UCF now automatically associate her as the representative and face of the company and this establishes a strong bond. This bond and name recognition is important for the publisher and the library because with it comes trust and reliance as each of the partners invests in the other with the overall goal being to provide users with the best content and experience while also focusing on return on investment.

Raising the Bar

During her time as Library Communications Manager, Ms. Profera has continually sought new ways to help T&F stand out in the marketplace and differentiate itself from the competition. She advocates for the T&F brand and communicates

to the library community that T&F wants to hear what librarians have to say. T&F wants to be part of the conversation with a focus on brand loyalty and a lasting positive impression. Toward this aim, Ms. Profera decided to implement a plan for library-publisher workshops across the US and Latin America to help raise the profile of the company, and to establish a presence with information professionals that did not previously exist. The UCF workshop set the tone for how T&F would make their mark with future library workshops. Ms. Profera hosted four workshops in 2014 before transitioning to a new role with T&F.

Planning a Workshop from Start to Finish

Ms. Profera outlined nine key steps to rolling out and hosting a successful workshop event: research/concept; planning, budget, and control; resources and allies; production of collaterals; marketing and promotions; sales and registrations; logistics/administration; on-site management; and post-event review. She described the process of planning the successful two-day UCF workshop event in a case study.

Prior to the event, Michael Arthur, Elyse Profera, and the US sales team for T&F worked diligently to pull together a list of invitees that they wanted to attend the workshop. At the time, T&F was in the process of finalizing a sales deal with the Florida Virtual Library Campus and 19 of its institutions. Mr. Arthur extended T&F's efforts by sending invitations to various statewide groups that included members from the state universities, state colleges, and independent colleges and universities of Florida. Mr. Arthur and T&F worked together to establish a compelling two-day agenda. Ms. Profera developed a business plan for the event, set a budget, secured UCF as a key location, and leveraged relationships both externally and internally across T&F's editorial and sales departments. Additionally, she developed presentations, event kits, name tags, a registration list, thank you gifts, and reports.

T&F/UCF Workshop: Panels, Presentations, and Usage

It is important to note that the T&F/UCF workshop was not a sales pitch; rather, this was a two-way dialogue where publishers and librarians came together to discuss and listen to library-centric topics.

The first day of events consisted of partnering with an academic, Dr. Rosalind Beiler (Director of Public History and Associate Professor of History, University of Central Florida) to present on classroom teaching with a digital primary source archive and how the resource was integrated into her curriculum and syllabus; an eight-person Subject Librarian panel discussion in which UCF Subject Librarians discussed how they conducted their own marketing efforts to reach academic faculty and end users; and a panel on open access in which topics like discoverability of free content and its permanence were discussed.

The second day of events included an in-depth look at usage for not only UCF but also the state of Florida, as well as a workshop conducted by T&F's new Library Communications Manager, Stacy Sieck, regarding "Tips on How to Get Published and the Peer Review Process." The in-depth usage analysis for UCF led T&F's research and business intelligence team to develop a global tool to streamline ways for future reporting and analytics to be developed for future events and customer visits.

This workshop was the start of a mutually beneficial relationship for the UCF Libraries and Taylor & Francis. In July, Mr. Arthur visited the T&F office for a tour and to cohost a focus group on T&F's newest white paper, "Social Media in the Use of Libraries." In addition, T&F and UCF worked together to present "Return on Investment: New Strategies for Marketing Digital Resources" for the 2014 Charleston Conference. Most recently, T&F representatives, including Ms. Profera, visited the UCF campus to speak on T&F's research in the open access marketplace. This workshop allowed Ms. Profera to benchmark other workshops that T&F hosted at Loyola Marymount University (LMU) and the International Spy Museum, as well as a different approach in Santiago, Chile, where the company explored the concept of delivering the workshop to the customer in April 2014. At the LMU workshop, Jeffra Bussmann (STEM/Web Librarian at CSU East Bay) spoke on transforming

knowledge with research justice. Most recently, at the International Spy Museum event, Syracuse University's Annie Rauh (Engineering Librarian) spoke on an OA research project that Cornell and Syracuse Libraries embarked on together.

The aforementioned initiatives speak to the value and success T&F has achieved from working together with the library community to build trust and camaraderie. These efforts have helped set T&F apart from other large commercial publishing organizations by taking a friendly, yet professional, approach to engaging with the library market.

The UCF Perspective

The expectations for marketing to end users and improving usage through active partnership with publishers increased dramatically in 2014 as a result of the collaborative efforts with T&F and other major publishers. Subject Librarians and Acquisitions and Collection Services have always been focused on alerting users to new resources and training end users. However, the start of a new Subject Librarian model in 2013 resulted in a new emphasis on the public face of the library and greater expectations for librarians to be actively engaged in the disciplines they represent.

The Head of Acquisitions & Collection Development has now established a high priority for marketing new and existing products and has focused heavily on arranging training for Subject Lbrarians. Building on existing relationships with publishers and vendors has proven advantageous for UCF and several publishers have been eager to provide training and marketing assistance. The initial workshop jointly hosted by T&F and UCF definitely raised the bar for future events and at the time of the 2014 Charleston Conference presentation more plans are in place for UCF to host similar events.

The Head of Acquisitions and Collection Services hired a new assistant with an academic background and interest in marketing. Her assistance and collaboration throughout the early part of 2014 helped in the development of new goals in the area of marketing library resources. Librarians working in Acquisitions and Collections

Services are encouraged to seek out partnerships with public services librarians, teaching faculty and interested units on campus as a way of marketing library resources and gaining valuable insight into the needs of faculty and students.

Efforts at UCF to increase awareness of new library resources and improvements or updates to existing resources include:

- Refinement of the Collection Development website.

- Collaboration with the UCF Faculty Center for Teaching and Learning, resulting in weekly email blasts to all UCF faculty, and regular articles in *Faculty Focus,* the quarterly newsletter for UCF.

- Regular marketing of digital resources on the mastheads of the library home page and Scholarly Communication web page, as well as through digital signage in the library.

- Hosting webinars and presentations (for both academic faculty and librarians) that focus on exciting new products or major enhancements to existing library resources.

- Hosting vendor presentations and trainings in library classrooms or at academic faculty workshops.

The Role of Subject Librarians in Marketing to End Users

The University of Central Florida Libraries has 15 Subject Librarians (http://library.ucf.edu /SubjectLibrarians/) who are encouraged to engage in proactive outreach to their assigned academic programs, faculty and students. UCF Libraries believes that the Subject Librarians are excellent conduits for connecting end users with library resources.

The Subject Librarians market UCF Libraries' resources via e-newsletters, customized web-based research guides, library instruction sessions, and presentations at academic department and university-wide meetings and workshops. For example, when T&F sponsored the workshop on

digital resources that was attended by both academic librarians and faculty at the main UCF Orlando campus in spring 2014, the UCF Subject Librarians presented a panel program which focused on innovative outreach strategies for marketing library resources to UCF constituencies.

UCF Subject Librarians reach out to their assigned academic departments and faculty through regular librarian-authored e-newsletters that are sent out at the beginning of each semester.What messages are the Subject Librarians sending to their academic departments and faculty? Often the Subject Librarians are updating faculty regarding major library purchases of new digital resources. These messages are developed and disseminated after collaboration between public and technical services librarians in a positive partnership that continues to benefit the UCF community. Below is a sample of articles which UCF Subject Librarians used in their Fall 2014 Newsletters:

Streaming Videos

"We currently have three streaming video services available. Here's an overview:

Alexander Street Press includes thousands of titles in 12 subject collections; FMG Films on Demand mostly provides films for the Humanities and Sciences and offers more than 130 titles; Swank's Digital Campus provides a collection of over 19,000 theatrical films and television programs available to embed in webcourses."

Springer eBooks

"Springer is a major publisher of academic and professional books and book series. Their eBooks are suitable for research, study, and course projects, and can be assigned as textbooks. The UCF Library has perpetual rights and online access to Springer books published in English between 2005 and 2014, comprising over 16,000 volumes. In addition, UCF users have access to all of Springer's major book series (from 1997 to 2014) including the well-known Lecture Notes Series. Springer eBooks are available to all UCF students, faculty and staff anywhere, anytime. Because Springer eBooks are in PDF format, students can print, e-mail, and download entire chapters and books to read off-line on a cell phone, eBook reader (such as Kindle), laptop, or any computer."

The Important Role LibGuides Play in Marketing Library Resources

LibGuides are an important tool for providing basic instruction and serve as a platform for research instruction. However, at UCF Subject Librarians also are using them as an innovative way to market new resources and services and to assist users in finding alternative sources when the library is not able to provide the exact content being requested. Frequently the Subject Librarians create LibGuides that serve as step-by-step instructions for using particular databases or digital collections. They publicize the URLs for these guides on bookmarks, instruction handouts, newsletters, or in web-based course syllabi.

One of UCF Libraries' most heavily used LibGuides is entitled: "Textbooks, Textbook Alternatives & Course Readings from Library Resources" (http://guides.ucf.edu/textbooks).

This particular LibGuide encourages academic faculty to utilize library owned e-book content for their assigned class readings as an alternative to expensive print textbooks. The introduction of this Lib Guide states: "UCF Libraries offers thousands of full text online books that can be used in the classroom or by individual students to supplement class readings. Please contact your Subject Librarian for help with incorporating the books into your syllabi."

This LibGuide goes on to list each of the online book databases to which UCF Libraries subscribes, with a listing of each subject area covered by the database and the number of titles included for each subject area. For example:"the Sage e-books digital collection offers a total of 16 disciplines, with 604 e-books in the Business and Management section, 999 e-books in the Sociology section" and so on. LibGuides such as this are very helpful to faculty who are interested in using digital collections for their class readings because they provide specific information about the resource and are ideal for marketing library resources. Links to general and subject specific

LibGuides can easily be placed in regular Subject Librarian-authored newsletters to faculty.

Subject Librarian Engagement in the Academic Community

At UCF Libraries there is a new emphasis on Subject Librarians becoming more mobile. Subject Librarians are getting out of the library building and spending quality time visiting their assigned academic departments and individual faculty members. They are meeting with student clubs and associations throughout campus. The Subject Librarians use these opportunities to introduce their faculty and students to new and under-used digital resources and to demonstrate how these resources can be used to assist with their teaching and research. Publisher sponsored events including the one with T&F attract faculty members who may have little previous interaction with the library thus setting up new opportunities for librarians to later meet them in their offices to discuss ways the library can contribute to teaching and research.

Subject Librarian Training

The Research and Information Services and Acquisitions and Collection Services Departments are working together to provide training for the Subject Librarians to support them in their digital resource marketing role. The Research and Information Services Department coordinates annual all-day reference retreats, monthly reference meetings, and an online "Subject Librarian Toolkit" Lib Guide http://guides.ucf.edu /subject-librarian-toolkit to support the Subject Librarians in marketing digital resources.

The Acquisitions and Collection Services Department works closely with UCF Libraries' many vendors to coordinate frequent publisher training workshops for librarians and academic faculty that focus on new or under-utilized resources. Having close relationships with publishers and the academic community helps to improve the success of marketing library resources.

Measuring the Success of Subject Librarian Marketing of Digital Resources

Success is measured by evaluating the overall impact of the Subject Librarian model on resource utilization. Does the Subject Librarian marketing role promote the desired return on investment for expensive library digital collections? Do librarians feel more engaged with academic faculty? Are Subject Librarians given time to speak at university and academic department meetings and to distribute information about the Libraries' new resources and services?

The important interaction between dedicated Subject Librarians and appointed academic department representatives remains at the heart of this new resource marketing initiative. The development of positive, trusted relationships with academic departments, faculty, and students is the foundation for all marketing initiatives.

Looking ahead to the future, the success of this new Subject Librarian digital resource marketing model will be measured by:

- An increase in Subject Librarian outreach to academic departments, faculty and students.

- An increase in academic faculty participation in collection development.

- An increase in faculty-student-librarian use of the libraries' digital resources (as shown by the number of hits and downloads each resource receives).

- More informed collection development that will lead to even stronger collections and more effective use of UCF Libraries' limited materials budget.

The new emphasis on marketing has provided UCF Libraries with an opportunity to succeed in new ways and to develop stronger ties with UCF academic programs, departments, faculty and students. The aforementioned efforts to collaborate with T&F resulted in increased efforts to reach out to other publishers to provide more training to librarians, and to raise awareness of new resources with librarians and faculty. Finally, the emphasis on collaboration with publishers and faculty has also inspired a stronger sense of cooperation between two departments at UCF, Acquisitions and Collection Services and Research and Information Services. Together these departments are finding new ways to work together to improve library resources and make a positive impact on the teaching and research mission of the University of Central Florida.

How Users' Perceptions of E-Books Have Changed—Or Not: Comparing Parallel Survey Responses

Tara T. Cataldo, Biological Sciences Librarian, University of Florida

Trey Shelton, E-Resources Librarian, University of Florida

Steven Carrico, Acquisitions Librarian, University of Florida

Cecilia Botero, Director of Health Science Center Libraries, University of Florida

Abstract

This project focuses on comparing the results of two surveys conducted on e-book usability at college and university libraries across the state of Florida. The first survey was carried out by librarians from the University of Florida in 2009 and provided benchmark responses for similar questions asked in a follow-up survey completed in 2014. Results of the two surveys conducted five years apart are an enlightening snapshot of user feedback on e-book usability, while providing insight on key issues and trends in e-book use. In addition to measuring side-by-side results of the two Florida surveys, the paper frames this comparison in a broader context by drawing upon data taken from other surveys published on e-book use in academic libraries.

Introduction

The study of e-books and how they are accessed, perceived, and used has been a popular area of research for many years. The idea of conducting a survey in Florida academic libraries on e-book usability blossomed at a summit preconference and library conference held in Tallahassee, FL in 2009 (FSU/PLAN, 2009). It was evident at the e-books summit preconference and subsequent conference discussion forums that many librarians and publishers in attendance had preconceived ideas about how e-books were used by library users. Missing from these discussions were perspectives from the users themselves on the extent and nature of how they accessed and used e-books. To that end, a team of librarians from the University of Florida George A. Smathers Libraries (UF), working with partner librarians from the state's largest library consortium, developed a survey on e-book use in 2009. (CSUL, 2012) The survey was designed to elicit information on who was using e-books, why they were using them, and how they were being used. The survey was distributed to college, university, and health science center library users in the state of Florida in the hopes to acquire feedback and data that might spur libraries to make improvements for e-book access and navigation.

The 2009 survey data was shared with librarians in the state's largest academic consortia, but only used internally and never officially published. In 2014, with e-book acquisitions on the rise in most academic libraries in Florida, a second team of librarians from UF decided to slightly update the survey to better reflect the expanded e-book environment and run the survey again to see what had changed in users' perceptions and behaviors over time. In addition to comparing the two Florida surveys, the team also matched response data from surveys with related questions and data published in several other large e-book user studies. Comparing data from a variety of e-book user surveys identified fascinating trends and legitimized the findings. Results from the following studies were referenced for direct comparisons to a select number of Florida survey questions: a University of Illinois multi-institutional project in 2008 (Shelbourne, 2009); findings from two publications based on a JISC's UK National E-books Observatory study conducted in 2008 (Nicholas, Rowlands, Clark, Huntington, Jamali, & Olle, 2008; Jamali, Nicholas, and Rowlands, 2009); Primary Research Group's survey of American college students (Primary Research Group, 2009); and ebrary's 2008 and 2011 surveys (McKeil, 2012).

Methodology

In 2009, a survey consisting of numerous but straightforward questions regarding e-book use was designed and loaded into Survey Monkey and routed to libraries interested in participating. The survey were centrally hosted and administered by a librarian team from the University of Florida. Almost all the survey responses were derived from users representing two library consortia in Florida: the Council of State University Libraries (CSUL), comprised of eleven of the largest public academic universities and includes their Law, Health, and Medical Libraries; and the Independent Colleges and Universities of Florida (ICUF), which encompasses many private universities and colleges in the state. Due to conflicting surveys and crowded websites, very few college and university libraries elected to publicize or link the Florida e-books survey on their library's home pages; instead librarians at these institutions most often routed through e-mail the announcement of the survey with a link to Survey Monkey to their faculty, students, and other library users individually.

In 2014, the UF team modified the survey, primarily to reduce the number of questions and to update the survey to reflect the current e-book environment. For the best possible comparison of results from the 2009 and 2014 surveys, the wording for most questions was kept identical. The 2014 survey was loaded into the software, Qualtrics, and an e-mail announcement with a link to the survey was distributed to appropriate listserves and consortia members in Florida. As in 2009, few college or university libraries chose to publicize or provide a link to the e-books survey on their websites, but many librarians did respond to the survey themselves and frequently routed the announcement to library users and faculty at their institutions. In addition, for a two-week period in the fall semester the survey was placed as a Web pop-up on approximately four-hundred pubic computers located in the University of Florida's libraries. The pop-up worked this way: when a library patron logged on to the computer, a browser window to the survey automatically opened; for patrons unwilling to participate, users could close the browser, hit the home button, or type in a new URL and skip the survey. Results were analyzed in Microsoft Excel.

Results and Discussion

Respondent Demographics

Results from the 2009 and 2014 e-books surveys are revealing. In 2009, 895 users started the survey and 536 users completed it. In 2014, 1,245 users started the survey with 592 completions. E-book users from twenty-eight academic libraries took part in the survey in 2009; in 2014 users from thirty academic libraries in Florida participated in the survey. A slight decrease in user responses from the state universities (97.3% in 2009 to 83.5% in 2014), was countered by increases in user responses from the colleges (1.9% in 2009 to 8.3% in 2014). The vast majority of responses in both surveys were from the University of Florida, 80% in 2009 and 72% in 2014.

The status of the respondents was significantly different between the two surveys. The 2014 survey had significantly fewer professional degree (MD, DVM, JD, etc.) and faculty respondents compared to the 2009 respondent pool. In 2009 only 21% of those taking the survey were undergraduates, while the percentage of undergraduates taking the survey rose to 61% in 2014. The dramatic rise in undergraduates responding to the second survey as compared the first survey is mainly attributed to the pop-up web tools used at UF in 2014, as undergraduates are more likely to use the library's general computers.

The status of the respondents was significantly different between the two surveys. The 2014 survey had significantly fewer professional degree (MD, DVM, JD, etc.) and faculty respondents compared to the 2009 respondent pool. In 2009 only 21% of those taking the survey were undergraduates, while the percentage of undergraduates taking the survey rose to 61% in 2014. The dramatic rise in undergraduates responding to the second survey as compared the first survey is mainly attributed to the pop-up web tools used at UF in 2014, as undergraduates are more likely to use the library's general computers.

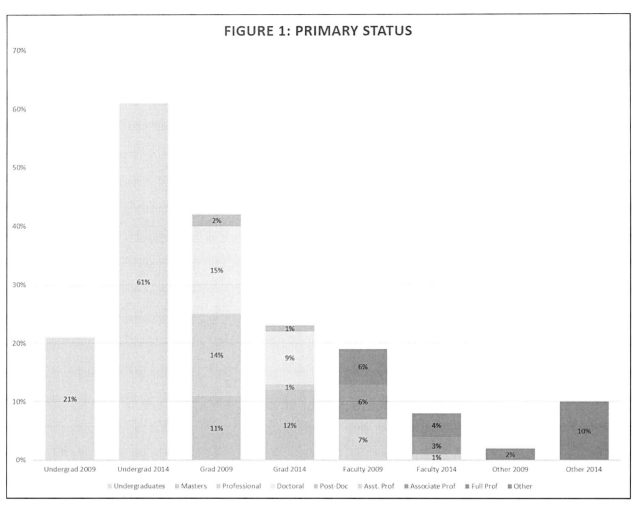

FIGURE 1: PRIMARY STATUS

Legend: Undergraduates · Masters · Professional · Doctoral · Post-Doc · Asst. Prof · Associate Prof · Full Prof · Other

Figure 1. Primary status.

E-book Usage

In both the 2009 and 2014 Florida surveys an essential question was asked, "Have you ever used an e-book?" 77% of respondents in 2009 said they had used an e-book, while the 2014 survey showed almost the exact figure, 76%. Yet, when compared to data from national surveys these figures are far higher, as only 57% of the 2008 University of Illinois respondents and 60% of the 2008 JISC respondents stated that they had used e-books. The comparisons between the Florida and national surveys showed Florida users had a higher percentage respond in the affirmative, but it is unclear why this is the case.

Another question from the two Florida surveys asked users, "Did you know that you have access to e-books through your college or university libraries?" The percentage of respondents stating in the affirmative was similar, 73% in 2009 and 70% in 2014. The almost flat line is somewhat puzzling, as it shows no real progress has been made at Florida academic libraries to market acquired e-books. Comparing these figures to the national surveys is interesting. The 2008 University of Illinois survey had only 55% of respondents reply they were aware they had access to e-books through their library. The 2009 Primary Research Group (PRG) Survey of American College Students asked a similar question, "What do you think of your college library's e-book collection?" Responses showed only 58% indicated they knew their library had e-books. These figures may indicate that the promotion and marketing of e-books has been largely ignored or is not getting through. Although it must be pointed out in the ebrary's 2011 global student survey, students were asked the straightforward question, "Does your library have e-books?" Results revealed that 65% of respondents said "yes."

A third basic question asked in all the surveys was, "Have you ever used e-books provided by your library?" Results from the two Florida surveys show that 66% of respondents in 2009 and 56% of respondents in 2014 said "yes." The JISC user survey from 2008 also asked this question with 47% respectively stating yes. What is particularly frustrating about survey responses showing a drop in the reported use of library e-books is the

abundance of usage statistics at UF to prove users are finding and accessing the e-books. Figure 2 shows the University of Florida Libraries' use of the Springer e-books (the 2008 front list) between 2009 and 2013 and reveals usage more than doubled in the Social Sciences and Humanities, almost tripled in the STEM disciplines, and more than tripled in the Health Sciences areas. This is but one example of e-book use on the rise at UF. What this disparity between survey responses and usage statistics tells us is that library users often fail to recognize the library as the source for many of the e-books they access. It stresses once more that libraries are poor at marketing and branding the resources they make available.

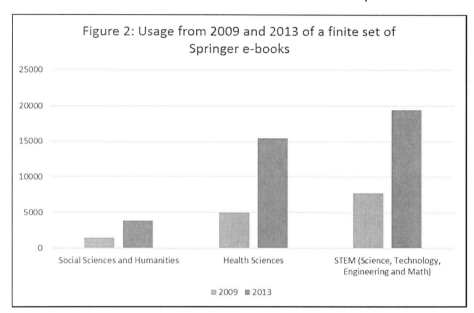

Figure 2. Springer e-book usage.

Print Books versus E-Books

The various surveys cited in this project all attempted to discern user preferences in the important issue of print books versus e-books. In the two Florida surveys the same question was asked, "When you have the choice of using an e-book or a print book, how often do you choose the e-book option?" The answer choices offered a five-point range from "always" to "never." In the 2009 UF survey, 48% of respondents said they chose the e-book "always" or "most of the time" but in the 2014 Florida survey the responses to the two ranges dropped to 25%. The 2008 ebrary survey indicated that 51% of the respondents

used e-books "almost" or "most of the "time" while the 2011 Ebrary survey showed the two ranges at 48%. The two ebrary surveys showed user respondents are fairly similar between the three-year period, while a more dramatic drop in respondents preferring e-books over print books occurred in Florida. This shift in preference from using e-books may be a statistical anomaly when compared to the ebrary surveys, but at the very least it does indicate that print has become the preferred format for Florida. This shift in large part could also be explained by the increased number of undergraduates responding to the 2014 survey.

When library users were asked what they dislike about e-books, the responses from the 2009 and 2014 Florida Surveys present a revealing picture of what has changed and not changed during the five years between surveys. Issues related to a general preference for print, aversion to reading on a screen, and navigation problems ("I can't flip the pages") have only increased over the years. Complaints about Digital Rights Management (DRM) and a lack of available titles have decreased. Virtually unchanged are frustrations about annotating e-books. Some revealing comments from the 2014 Florida survey included:

- "I personally like the feel of paper books as it is easier for me to read and take notes. However e-books are more convenient"

- "I have difficulty finding things in some platforms. I have difficulty remembering where in a book something is—or which book, when all look and feel alike."

- "E-books are too tied to their platforms. Public libraries have e-books that can be downloaded onto a personal reader for offline reading, but this is uncommon in academia. This should change."

- "I don't like reading from a screen."

- "No paper, no soul."

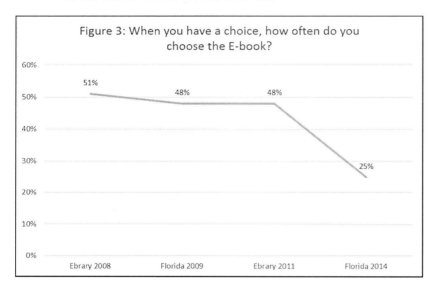

Figure 3. When you have a choice, how often do you choose the e-book?

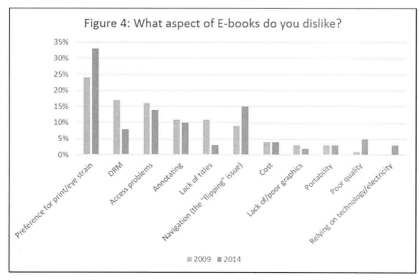

Figure 4. What aspect of e-books do you dislike?

User Behavior and Attitudes

A large percentage (74%) of respondents in the 2009 Florida survey stated they used e-books primarily for research as compared to the 2014 Florida survey where users indicated their primary reason for using e-books was "for study." This switch in the primary reason the users access e-books seems consistent with the increase in the number of undergraduate students that completed the survey in 2014 as compared to 2009. Another change in user attitudes between the 2009 and 2014 Florida surveys is displayed in responses to the question, "Will you be using e-books more in the future?" In the 2009 Florida surveys a vast majority of the respondents indicated they would use e-books increasingly in the future (81%) but this outlook changed dramatically (64%) in results from the 2014 Florida study.

Almost all the surveys cited in this project indicated that instant access and navigability are the top perceived advantages to e-books for users. Fairly universal in all survey results are users' preference for the print format when reading a book cover to cover. Users also want to see more e-books available in their research areas. A comparison that held little surprise were answers received to the question on where users start their searches for e-books. In the 2009 Florida survey the library website as a starter place was the most popular answer; but by the 2014 Florida survey, a large percentage of users indicated they started their e-book searches with Google. The fact that most users in 2014 responded their web searches start in Google or another search engine is hardly news, but it now seems rather remarkable that five years earlier the majority of survey respondents started a search at the library website. The ebrary surveys saw a similar trend when they asked respondents where their starting point was. In 2008 74% stated the library website but this dropped to 65% in 2011 while Google, and particularly Google Scholar, rose over that time period.

Textbooks

The rise in the use of and debate surrounding e-textbooks prompted the project team to add a couple of questions to the 2014 Florida survey, particularly as this was not an issue explored in 2009. In the 2014 Florida survey a question asked faculty and instructors if they had assigned e-books as either course textbooks or readings, and the majority (61%) indicated they did not. When students were asked if they preferred their course texts and readings to be in print or electronic format, 40% selected the answer "both"; 30% selected print; and only 14% chose electronic. Another 16% chose the response "it depends" and provided comments. It is somewhat contrary to prevailing policy at UF to add e-textbooks and e-books whenever available to course reserves, particularly as e-books better support distance learning initiatives, creating a dilemma for the libraries.

Conclusion

After comparing user responses from the 2009 and 2014 Florida surveys, the project revealed insights and observations of note that are best summarized by a few take-aways:

- The increased number/percentage of undergraduates that took the survey in 2014 versus 2009 can be explained by the pop-up application placed on general use computers at UF.

- Many users are still unaware that e-books are available in their own libraries or that they are using e-books that are provided by their libraries, which may reveal a failure in marketing and branding.

- Many users are frustrated that they cannot access e-books the way they want (e.g., device and platform neutral) and e-books are often difficult to navigate and annotate; many users also profess frustration that so often academic titles are not available as e-books or, if available as e-books, not offered through their library.

- A large percentage of library users (many from the digital native generation) responded they prefer using print books. This preference for print books is so strong that many users state they intend to use e-books less in the future.

Surveys like the two survey projects for Florida, along with the five other surveys conducted nationally as cited, provide important feedback on library users' behaviors, attitudes, and preferences on e-books. Survey results are far from scientific but are extremely helpful to librarians and staff hoping to determine better ways to improve methods of access and navigation to their users. Yet, survey instruments have limitations so focus groups and live interactions with think-aloud protocols would be excellent next steps. Going forward e-book use needs to be consistently studied if academic libraries wish to improve upon the user experience.

The 2014 Florida survey and data can be found in the University of Florida's Institutional Repository at http://ufdc.ufl.edu/IR00004919/00001.

References

CSUL. Council of State University Libraries. (2012). State University System of Florida: University and Library websites. Retrieved from http://csul.net/content/state-university-system-florida-university-and-library-websites

Florida State University Library/Panhandle Library Access Network. (FSU/PLAN). (2009, March). Collection Development/Resource Sharing Conference. Tallahassee, FL.

Jamali, H. R., Nicholas, D., & Rowlands, I. (2009). Scholarly e-books: The views of 16,000 academics: Results from the JISC national e-book observatory. *Aslib Proceedings, 61*(1), 33-47. http://dx.doi.org/10.1108/00012530910932276

McKiel, A. W. (2012). *2011 global student e-book survey.* Ebrary. Retrieved from http://site.ebrary.com/lib/surveys/docDetail.action?docID=80076107&ppg=1

Nicholas, D., Rowlands, I., Clark, D., Huntington, P., Jamali, H. R., & Olle, C. (2008). UK scholarly e-book usage: A landmark survey. *Aslib Proceedings, 60*(4), 311-334.

Primary Research Group. (2009). *The survey of American college students : Student use of library e-book collection*s. New York: Primary Research Group.

Shelburne, W. A. (2009). E-book usage in an academic library: User attitudes and behaviors. *Library Collections, Acquisitions, and Technical Services, 33*(2/3), 59-72. http://dx.doi.org/10.1016/j.lcats.2009.04.002

Implications of Online Media on Academic Library Collections

Kirstin M. Dougan, Music and Performing Arts Librarian, University of Illinois at Urbana-Champaign

Abstract

Libraries' market share of discovery has been declining rapidly, and in some cases this is directly related to where the content users need and want resides. Music recording delivery models have changed dramatically in the last several years, with more performers and labels offering content directly to consumers via downloads only. Unfortunately, this model is one in which libraries cannot usually legally participate due to licensing agreements. Another issue at play is the growing presence of quality content on sites like YouTube, which users are already very familiar and comfortable with. In light of this, user behavior has been evolving to incorporate more and more nonlibrary sources of music discovery and acquisition. Patrons no longer see the library as the sole source for music content (if they ever did). This is due in part to the convenience of online sources and the fact that, while libraries may still need to buy CDs, users would rather have recordings they can listen to anywhere and anytime. So how can academic libraries address these challenges to continue to meet our mission of building collections and serving our patrons? This paper will discuss current music delivery models, collections and acquisitions pressures involved with online media (primarily audio), the current music discovery and access environment, and information seeking behaviors of music faculty and students. We will offer some suggestions for librarians wishing to address these issues.

Introduction

This paper offers some suggestions for librarians facing the changing nature of music recording delivery models and will address issues around current music delivery models, collections and acquisitions pressures involved with online media (primarily audio), the current music discovery and access environment, and information-seeking behaviors of music faculty and students. While the title of this paper uses the term "media" and this talk is relevant to audio and video, the author is writing from the perspective of a librarian who works most closely with audio collections primarily and video collections secondarily.

Music and Mediation (Formats and Delivery)

Unlike text, music, either in print or recorded form, can never be disintermediated from the voices, instruments, or machines with which to play it back in order for it to be reproduced or consumed as intended by the composer. Online audio comes closest to being a universal format (for lack of a better term), in that a digital file, depending on the format, can often be played on a smartphone or any computer, but those devices are still necessary. The understanding that music

must be mediated is an important thought to hold on to, because this has presented many challenges ranging from acquisition considerations to the maintenance of playback for audio and video materials in libraries and classrooms.

There are several models of music delivery and access in active use, such as compact discs, downloadable files such as MP3s, and streaming audio (and/or video) files. Older formats, including LPs and magnetic cassettes, are still in use as well (the former more so than the latter). Streaming media can be viewed as having several subforms. On one end of the spectrum are licensed subscription tools provided to patrons by libraries and obtained from vendors such as Alexander Street, whose Classical Music Library was released in 2003, and Naxos, whose Music Library launched in 2004. On the other end are free sources such as YouTube (launched in 2005), which offers a combination of creator-uploaded and third-party uploaded content, and Spotify (available in the US in 2011), which offers licensed content only, and many others. It is clear that the library is not now, and perhaps has not been for a long time, the sole source of discovery or access for media content. Tools from outside of the library are prominent and pervasive, easy to use, and always available.

Many students have used them for years before arriving at college.

Music in libraries then is doubly mediated, both in discovery and in access. In many, if not all, cases patrons need to not only come to the library but need consult with staff to obtain physical media, either for in-house use or to take home. And even subscription streaming tools frequently require that the patron sign in to use them, especially if they are off-campus.

Music Collections and Acquisition Pressures

A core goal of music libraries, especially academic ones, is to collect and curate materials regardless of format as a record of scholarship and creation in music. Music libraries frequently need to collect deeply and broadly. Deeply, because every performance is different and each interpretation is unique. Therefore musicians and scholars (and also libraries) often want access to recordings of more than one performance or production of the same work. Broadly, because over time libraries' collecting scope has expanded as music curricula and scholars' research areas have broadened to include popular and non-Western musics and materials in interdisciplinary areas.

However, there have always been materials that music libraries have not been able to obtain either because of their format or because of how or where they were produced. For example, session recordings and ethnographic field recordings are rarely commercially available. There are also frequently music scores that can only be obtained on a rental basis (e.g., film scores). Materials from certain parts of the world have also been historically difficult for US libraries to obtain. Now this issue is presenting itself in a new variation, as musicians explore making materials directly available to consumers via download-only MP3s (Hoek, 2009). In these cases, music libraries are not able to purchase, download, and circulate these recordings due to end-user license agreements (EULAs) that prohibit redistribution. Nevertheless, this direct-to-consumer distribution model is not always something students can afford, even though personal collections of scores

and recordings have always been important to musicians.

Budget trends over the last few decades have reinforced the idea that no one library can collect all material in a subject (unless very narrowly defined). Media materials continue to be among the least-loaned formats on ILL (Conor and Duffy, 2012), so libraries and patrons cannot rely on this method to greatly increase their access to media. While CD buying has declined drastically among the general public (Friedlander, 2013), libraries often find that for various reasons they still need to acquire CDs. This includes issues of campus wireless loads, classrooms not universally equipped with reliable network connections, and patrons who do not all have access to technology or connectivity to access online media. Those managing media collections have long had to contend with the issue of format obsolescence. Library collections continue to be comprised of formats spanning many decades, from wax cylinders to streaming files, and this will not change any time in the near future given lack of resources for large-scale digitization projects and the restrictions copyright places on reformatting and delivery. Added to this, new laptops do not all come with CD or DVD playback capability.

Libraries that maintain music media collections struggle with the balance between licensing (or purchasing) online streaming tools and continuing to build physical collections of owned materials. As Theil (2003) points out, if physical or licensed recordings no longer exist leading to a "potential loss of long-term ownership of digital music formats," this is problematic for libraries as it disrupts libraries' goal of preservation, let alone the one of access. And even licensing doesn't directly meet our core mission of building permanent collections. Do research libraries especially need to reassess that part of their mission, or can we gain any control over this situation?

Another consideration is the fact that for several years libraries have been transitioning from building collections "just in case" to a "just in time" patron demand-driven model. While this can be a good way for librarians to adjust to constantly shifting patron needs, it can at times be problematic because of the rate at which CDs and DVDs go out of print compared to books. In addition, this author has not found a vendor who is able to set up a PDA program for physical audiovisual media. This model also potentially creates tension between patrons and library collections, as when faced with library collections that may lack what they want or that they can't find in library tools that make it difficult to search for music, many library patrons turn to easy and accessible tools like YouTube. Students (and faculty) no longer see the library as the only source for music (if they ever did). Faculty and students are as accustomed to finding music online outside of library tools as they are to using library collections (physical and virtual) (Dougan, 2013, 2014).

Music Discovery/Access Environment

Music librarians have long known that those searching for music scores and media materials face information retrieval challenges that go beyond those faced when looking for books because they are dictated by the specialized nature of music materials. The variety of foreign languages and nicknames used in music work titles, the plethora of titles with generic terms such as "symphony" and "sonata," as well as minute but essential levels of metadata such as key and opus numbers that can be difficult, if not impossible, to focus a search on given that they are but one letter or number in a sea of data, all create searching challenges.

The fact that those searching for music materials frequently need items in multiple formats such as books, scores, and recordings, not to mention the various formats scores and recordings come in, means that any search system is challenged to find all of these things given that they are necessarily described differently. The searcher is also reliant on the cataloger and how much information she or he decided to include in the catalog record (which varies not only due to any cataloging rules in force at the time but also to the cataloger's discretion). Full contents notes and added entries for composers and works are helpful but unfortunately not included in every record. Uniform titles help when the record in question has them, but if there are multiple works

on the recording or in the score anthology, then there is no uniform title (and many searchers do not know how to make use of one to their advantage when it does exist).

Traditional library systems have made some improvements over the years with keyword searching, automatic truncation that means a search for "symphony" retrieves "symphony" and "symphonies" (but not Sinfonien), postsearch facets, and now the use of FRBR in some catalogs and web scale discovery systems, which attempts to collocate the many versions and editions of works. Yet for all of that, traditional catalogs still cannot tie composer to piece, so that when one searches for Beethoven symphonies one does not retrieve a recording with a Beethoven overture and a Mozart symphony. This consistent problem of many works to a single object, often with a title different than that of any of the works contained therein (in the case of many songs in a score anthology or many sonatas on a CD, for example), means that library catalogs have always been challenged in retrieving and displaying information in a way that is helpful to searchers whether they be musicologists or performers.

In addition, when faced with a list of search results that includes titles such as "200 Songs in Three Volumes for Voice and Piano," "21 Schubert Lieder," or multiple versions simply titled "Schubert Lieder," the average searcher will be frustrated and unlikely to click through these to find the version they need. One could argue that this is a problem of poor interface design and not one of metadata or infrastructure, and yet no widespread practical solutions have been created for these problems.

Separate silos of content, which some see as a problem for discovery, continue to exist for media materials. While one approach to this is to employ a web scale discovery layer or similar tool, they are not ideal for music given the issues named above. In this case separate media-specific silos may actually be a good idea. Another approach is to load vendor-created MARC records (or MARC-XML records) for individual recordings in library streaming resources into library catalogs. However, these records are often of inferior quality and rarely can the vendor keep up with the demand, so not all works have records available. If all of the records aren't in one place, patrons still need to search in multiple places.

Information-Seeking Behavior

There is not an easy way to see the entire picture of student and faculty media consumption and determine where exactly the library fits into the equation. We don't know if the library is used for 30% of discovery and 80% of access, or 10% discovery and 10% access, or some other balance. Studies show (Dougan, 2013) that students use multiple tools and there are many variables: where they are at the time, what technology they have access to, what they are looking for, and what the eventual end use of the item will be. In an informal conversation with a music faculty member that spanned CDs, DVDs, library streaming tools, YouTube, and Spotify, it was clear that there are nuances involved that take into account the variables listed above as well as whether the faculty member needs audio, video, or both. The quality, legality, and scope of content available are also factors. He also revealed that for him interfaces do play huge part in the decision to use or not use a tool. Useful features don't even have a chance to get discovered if a user can't get past the interface.

As Schonfeld (2014) said, we need to understand the reasons users don't always start with the library. However, I'd argue where patrons start is somewhat irrelevant. Where does the library fit anywhere in the process? Research projects rarely have one point of origin and by nature are iterative, so does it really matter if the library is the very first point? What is influencing what most? Are libraries' tools and collections having an effect on user behavior, or vice versa? Which should be the driving the cause? Do patrons go to YouTube because they don't like library-based tools and/or because library collections don't have what they want? Or is it because patrons already use YouTube that patrons don't bother to come to investigate library collections and tools? The answers to these questions are crucial in aiding libraries in building collections and tools.

Suggestions for Solutions

It's clear that there is no one solution to address the effect that online media, both free and licensed, have on library collections and user behavior. Librarians should make every effort to understand their patrons' needs and information-seeking behaviors. It may become clear that patrons do not use library resources because they are unaware of them, or perhaps because they do not meet their needs. Depending on the issues discovered, some approaches to addressing them may be found in the following: 1) target marketing of library physical and online media collections to specific classes and studios, 2) weave mention of the tools and collections into tours and classes and well as into class and subject guides, 3) consider making one guide just for faculty about the library's online media collections with suggested uses and links to tutorials, 4) consider circulating media and loaning it via ILL (if you don't already), 5) in instruction sessions highlight the significant difference that can be found in sound quality in different media formats, and 6) work with vendors to develop PDA programs for media materials. On a larger scale, librarians should continue to advocate for music and or media specific search tools or improvements to broader tools. Finally, priority should be given to digitizing and/or preserving unique media collections at institutions, as these materials are deteriorating far more quickly than print in many cases.

Conclusion

Librarians must carefully consider the collection development equation from many angles, including choice of vendors, cost, subject area, and formats. As libraries and librarians we often talk about whether we can afford particular products from vendors in a monetary sense. But we also need to think about the parallel question of whether library patrons can afford to use the library, not in a monetary sense, but in a time, convenience, and outcome sense. Our initial reaction is that surely they can't afford not to, but they may prove us wrong if we aren't more proactive than reactive.

References

Conor, E., Hansen, L., & Duffy, Michael J. (2012). Interlibrary loan and music collections: A survey of current practices. *Music Reference Services Quarterly*, *15*(1), 2–21. http://dx.doi.org/1080/10588167.2012 .647599

Dougan, Kirstin. (2014). Finding the right notes: An observational study of score and recording seeking behaviors of music students. *The Journal of Academic Librarianship*. Forthcoming. http://www.sciencedirect.com/science/article/pii/S0099133314001888

Dougan, Kirstin. (2014). "YouTube has changed everything"?: Music faculty, librarians, and their use and perception of YouTube. *College & Research Libraries*, *75*(4), 575–589. http://dx.doi.org/10.5860 /crl.75.4.575

Friedlander, Joshua P. (2013). News and notes on 2013 RIAA music industry shipment and revenue statistics. Retrieved from http://76.74.24.142/2463566A-FF96-E0CA-2766-72779A364D01.pdf

Hoek, D.J. (2009, July 27). The download dilemma. *American Libraries.* Retrieved from http://www.americanlibrariesmagazine.org/article/download-dilemma

Schonfeld, Roger. (2014). Does discovery still happen in the library? Roles and strategies for a rhifting reality. Ithaka S+R. Retrieved from http://www.sr.ithaka.org/blog-individual/does-discovery-still-happen -library-roles-and-strategies-shifting-reality

Theil, Gordon. (2003). The challenge of supporting current music research and instruction. *Fontes Artis Musicae, 50*(2–4), 106–113.

"Punctuality Is the Thief of Time":
The Earnest Pursuit of Social Media in the Library

Elyse L. Profera, Regional Sales Manager, Central US Region, Taylor & Francis Group

Maria Atilano, Marketing Outreach Librarian, Thomas G. Carpenter Library at University of North Florida

Abstract

The way social media tools are selected and used in the library changes regularly in an evolving digital and social climate. The opportunities social media presents to the library community includes, but is not restricted to, user engagement, professional networking, informational exchange, and increasing the discoverability of existing online resources at the library.

Taylor & Francis recently released its white paper entitled "Use of Social Media by the Library: Current Practices and Future Opportunities." The white paper has been researched and compiled by Taylor & Francis to provide an overview of current practices relating to the use of social media in the library from a world-wide perspective. This presentation shares results of the white paper, as well as a case study on creating a social media strategy that includes scheduling updates ahead of time to appeal to students throughout the semester, creating relationships with other on-campus clubs and organizations via social media.

Introduction

Social media has the potential to facilitate much closer relationships between libraries and their customers. In general, according to Taylor & Francis's research findings, many librarians agree that it is difficult to predict how social media and its use will evolve, and the priority for most of the librarians who participated in the research is to remain experimental and flexible.

There is little doubt that use of social media is well on its way to becoming an integral part of how people communicate with each other—not surprisingly, an overwhelming 88% of respondents to the online survey felt that social media would become more important to the library in the future. A more integrated future is imagined, and some librarians see their role becoming one of helping users find paths through complex content, and directing them towards making useful connections as efficiently as possible through the use of social media.

Research Objectives and Demographics

Taylor & Francis Group wanted to create an open forum for the library community to share their thoughts in formal and informal settings. The specific research objectives of the primary research were to further understand how libraries are using social media in the library, to further understand for what purposes librarians are using social media in the library, and to further understand the opportunities and challenges libraries see when using social media in the library.

The research was international in scope and was conducted through a number of channels:

- Three focus groups with librarians (one held in the UK, one in the USA, and one in India).

- Ten individual phone interviews with thought leaders from the library community.

- A Twitter party, with participants from the UK, USA, Australia, Canada, and South Africa.

- Follow-up desk research to identify relevant studies and commentary articles.

- An online survey, which was distributed in July 2014 to librarians around the globe, including Indonesia, Singapore, Japan, India, and Pakistan.

Of the 497 survey respondents, the majority (56.0%) came from the United States; 15.4% from the United Kingdom, 3.7% from India, and 3.7% from Australia. The majority of respondents also came from librarians working in academic libraries (78%), with small representation from librarians in other sectors, including public and professional libraries.

How are Libraries Currently Using Social Media?

The results of this research highlight the growing role of social media in the library, with 72% of survey respondents noting that social media in the library is important. Survey data also revealed a general profile of the current use of social media in the library. More than 60% of libraries have been using social media for three years or longer, and 67% of libraries manage between one and four social media accounts, with 23% managing more than five accounts. Facebook and Twitter are the most popular social media channels, followed closely by blogs, and 30% percent post to social media on at least a daily basis.

Approaches to social media policy implementation in terms of managing the output of social media channels is split, with 29% having a social media policy in place, and 28% are planning to implement one. However, 43% of survey respondents had no plans to introduce a policy—perhaps indicative of the early stage libraries are in when it comes to experimenting with social media.

Reasons for using social media covered a wide range of objectives, including seeking the opinion of library users; reaching users in their homes or virtual spaces; promotional purposes, such as publicizing events, services, or new content; connecting with specific user groups and network with other librarians; and building a sense of community.

The survey also suggested attitudes towards social media assessment are changing. While 72% felt there was currently no or little value to tracking social media results, a similar number (70%) envisaged spending more time in the future with measuring the impact their social media activity had.

Conversations held during focus groups and phone interviews found similar results as the survey. For one, the social media channels most frequently mentioned by focus groups and in phone interviews were Twitter and Facebook, with the latter particularly key for engaging with students. Twitter is felt to be more effective for communicating with researchers and other institutions, and blogs are used for sharing information and news.

Librarians also reported an accelerating uptake of visual channels, such as Slideshare, YouTube, Pinterest, Flickr, and Instagram. YouTube is being used for educational purposes, such as providing instructional information and for collection management; while Pinterest is used for showcasing new acquisitions, and Flickr for posting photos of library activities such as a refurbishment.

Part of the rise of the usage of more visual channels seemed to be reflecting changes in the way in which people are responding to visual over verbal messages. Multiple sources report that in social media marketing, visual postings attract higher levels of engagement. We're able to process images 60,000 times faster than text, so part of this preference may be reflective of a growing preference as the volume of information that we're exposed to every day continues to grow.

In the Taylor & Francis survey, when asked whether they agreed that visual communication was becoming more important in social media, 81% of librarians agreed. With information overload continuing to be a problem, a continued move towards greater use of image-based social media channels by librarians is likely.

The survey also asked librarians to rate how important social media is to achieve a set of objectives in their library. The results indicate that social media is primarily being used by libraries currently to fulfil marketing and promotional objectives, whether that be the promotion of events, collections or services. However, engagement with faculty and students is not far behind in terms of priorities, and the top five uses for social media include:

1. Events promotion.

2. Library services promotion.

3. Collections promotion.

4. Library refurbishment updates.

5. Promotion of new acquisitions.

At the other end of the spectrum, using social media in a teaching or learning capacity is a much lower priority; the five least popular objectives were:

1. Highlighting subject specific information.

2. Connecting with potential students.

3. As a teaching tool to promote information literacy.

4. To promote courses.

5. As a research tool to locate official documents.

Opportunities and Challenges

The most popular opportunity relating to the use of social media was the chance to raise the professional profile of the library, with 72% of survey respondents feeling this was an opportunity.

Other opportunities cited included the freedom to connect regularly with users and collaboration with other departments within the organization, indicating perhaps that social media is seen as a freer, alternative communication channel which can be used in a more informal way to reach key audiences.

Advantages and benefits of using social media in the library include the perceived low cost of using social media, and the fact that there is generally little training required to use the different channels. The speed at which news and promotional messages can be disseminated through Facebook and Twitter, among others, is also one of the major benefits of adopting social media policies. Increasing engagement and

interaction with library users (and thus increasing usage of content) is also an important opportunity libraries seek to take advantage of with their social media policies. Social media can also provide a new and different channel through which the library can get feedback from end users. They can then use the feedback to enhance services. Library staff can also share information on outreach activities beyond the library itself; consequently, social media is an opportunity to reach the community and people who do not normally get library messages through the university.

Despite the many opportunities of social media, there are several notable challenges to implementing social media policies in a library. The most significant challenge to the survey respondents was seen to be time and resources, with 67% stating this was a challenging issue. This was followed by judging an appropriate tone for communications (formal vs. informal, with 64% citing this as a challenge), and making sure others were aware of the library's social media activities (61%).

Other challenges which were seen to be a significant issue included:

- Levels of interest in and skills with using social media varying across library staff.

- Limited funds to support more advanced social media usage/features and training.

- Maintaining engagement with library users and attracting popularity (followers, likes and so on).

- Difficulty maintaining library branding for content/resources made accessible via social media.

- Potential copyright issues when using social media such as YouTube to build collections.

- External factors such as Internet connectivity, technological infrastructure, and government restrictions on the use of social media.

These common themes which reemerged from respondents indicated that they were concerned about the amount of time and level of skillset needed in order to adequately maintain a social media channel and benefit from a good level of returned success.

Channel Applications

This research on social media in the library also looked at how libraries were using social media for specific tasks, and which channels they felt best served a specific purpose. These can be loosely grouped into a number of key areas, including customer service, engaging with users, and collection development and outreach.

Customer Service

Using social media as a customer service tool was frequently cited across the research. During the Twitter party, participants heard about some specific examples of how librarians are using the channel in a customer service capacity, from simple information broadcasting through to more detailed feedback. One participant in the Twitter party noted that, "Students use [Twitter] to tell us if they're too hot, there's noise in the quiet area; if they're in a long queue." Real-time feedback was also cited as a valuable return on social media messages.

Although social media challenges provide opportunities for engaging with patrons, a key challenge relating to customer service provision via social media is responding in a timely fashion, as users expect quick answers to their questions, whatever the time or day of the week.

Institutions in the focus groups reported declining usage of websites for accessing library service information, with some suggesting that these pages were now used primarily by external audiences. However, librarians were still putting effort into maintaining current information on them. It was felt that, because of its immediacy and transient nature, social media was a better way to provide ongoing updates of information that was changing with any degree of frequency. Emails are still used for important reminders.

Several key take-away points emerged from the research when looking specifically at applying social media channels as a customer service tool.

For one, a quick response to a customer query is essential. If users feel they will not get the response they need, they will quickly move away from the social media channel, use other means to voice their views, or won't bother to provide the feedback at all. While an immediate response is generally unrealistic, aiming for a minimum response time will help ensure that users continue to provide feedback and return to the channel in the future.

Making the most of staff time is also imperative, with focus group discussions focusing on the importance of assigning a role to different individuals so that monitoring of social media channels for responses doesn't just fall to one individual.

Driving User Engagement

User engagement also proved to be an important use of social media. Over time, social media can help create central communities which are strongly linked and have an influential voice.

According to one survey respondent, "One of the opportunities with social media is listening to your community . . . I think that's primarily why we have a Twitter account, and we have also claimed our foursquare location, so we kind of can listen and monitor and do that kind of work, so that's yielded some pretty positive reviews and results."

For example, an image can be used to convey a message far more effectively than text and will grab the attention of the user base with more immediacy. Through telephone interviews, librarians shared their experiences with visual social media. One US library posted pictures of library buildings along with corresponding interesting facts, and found that students were highly receptive to this, being motivated to comment on the original post and go on to share their own pictures. In turn, they found that the number of likes to their channel dramatically increased.

It's also imperative that librarians engage with users on topics that matter to them. One librarian commented how they liked to look out for events which were important to their students, such as exam week, and enter the conversation to offer their support. This type of initiative adds a more human element to the social media channel, and demonstrates an open and receptive approach.

Variety is key when it comes to keeping users interested—maintain a mix of more informative messages with informal observations, opinion pieces, or questions.

Collection and Promotion

Social media is also regularly used to promote collections, particularly core databases, but current activities are diverse and ad hoc. From the results of the survey Taylor & Francis undertook, promoting the library's collection was within the top three objectives for using social media.

A key challenge, however, was found to be the niche interest of library users, which made it difficult to serve up tailored communications. One suggestion was to work more closely with subject experts in using social media to engage with users with relevant content.

Social media was recognized as having potential to encourage dialogue with users, providing opportunities for collection development. Listening was felt to be as important as broadcasting. Social media was frequently cited as a powerful collection management tool, both for hosting resources and transforming digital cataloging.

One of the librarians interviewed via telephone detailed how YouTube was a valuable collection management tool for the University of British Columbia. The library uses webcasting services as a way to deliver broadcasts through the internet. These broadcasts are delivered via YouTube so that end users are able to easily view content from the comfort of their own desktops.

It was apparent from much of the feedback from focus groups that approaches to collection development and management are ad hoc, and many felt that social media channels were restricted to promotional activity only. Research suggests that playing to each channel's strength is imperative for success.

Creating a structured approach so that collection development becomes a regular part of a social media plan is also important. Some libraries cited regular initiatives such as "Information Literacy Friday," when regular posts would be made about an aspect of the library's collection.

Posts that focus on a human interest element may also create buzz and encourage users to comment or repost to their followers. For example, a UK library posted pictures of an old phrenology map to represent content they held in their History of Psychiatry Section.

Policy and Management

The research also explored library experiences in managing the output of their social media channels and whether they had any metrics in place for measuring impact. Interestingly, only a small minority of libraries are scheduling their posts in advance, with a majority of 75% of librarians approaching the output of their channels on a more ad hoc basis.

Of those who do manage the output of their accounts using online tools, there are a range of sites currently being used. These social media management tools can be helpful when managing multiple channels, or multiple accounts on the same channel, and can cut down on time spent planning posts considerably. Hootsuite was used by the majority of respondents, with 44% choosing to plan posts in advance using this service.

The research found that measurement of impact is generally ad hoc, but some institutions were beginning to analyze results more closely, indicating that perhaps social media account management is still at a relatively early and experimental stage.

Comments from the focus group suggest several tips for managing social media channels:

- Implement an easy-to-follow social media plan to maintain appropriate and engaging output for a social network. Introducing complicated style guidelines and rules may stifle creativity.

- Track results to ensure the library is not running a social media channel that no one is using. Basic tracking of followers, likes, mentions and sharing of posts is essential to ascertain the success of a social media channel.

- Correlate results with real-time data of the launch of key promotions to help evaluate posts and inform social media activity.

- Incorporate observations into ongoing social media plans—are certain topics more popular than others? Does the timing of posts influence their success?

The Future of Social Media

Across the survey, focus groups, and phone interviews, there was much common ground. Many librarians were particularly interested in the future of social media, and the majority of librarians see it having an important place in the library going forward and expect to see dedicated social media roles appear. How and what that future might look like was harder for some to articulate, as the digital world is constantly changing.

One librarian commented on the growing need and demand for social media based on the next generation of students coming through the library, no matter what that may look like.

"It is crucial to note that our upcoming wave of library patrons—students, colleagues, and staff—will be from this generation of technologically sophisticated, well-connected on the social web, entrepreneurial, and oftentimes impatient," the survey respondent said.

Other suggestions included a need for the library to be more strategic, integrating social media more closely with their other existing systems. While some feel that social media is a transient communication method, many believe that social media will form an increasingly central part of the librarian's role and become an everyday part of communication with end users.

Thinking the Unthinkable: A Library Without a Public Catalog

Coen Wilders, Subject Librarian History, Utrecht University Library

Abstract

Two years ago Utrecht University Library (UUL) in the Netherlands decided to focus on delivery instead of discovery. Based on international studies, users statistics, and surveys, UUL concluded that library discovery tools have become less relevant because users find their research and teaching material increasingly outside the framework of the library. This conclusion had major implications for both UUL and its users. In 2012 UUL decided to shut down the discovery system Omega, custom-made for finding electronic material owned by its library, and—more important—not to implement another library discovery service. After nine months of preparation, on September 1, 2013, Omega closed. Recently UUL decided to close its own public library catalog too. Instead, the library advises users to find their material via alternative general or subject specific discovery tools.

This paper hopes to encourage libraries to rethink and evaluate their efforts on discovery and delivery. The principle idea while doing this should be that it does not matter where users find their material. What matters is that they can use the relevant material they find.

Where Do Users Search for Literature?

International studies and user statistics show that students and academic staff are moving away from the library website and the online library catalogs. Figure 1, which contains charts based on international surveys, shows that in 2010, 83% of the students started their search in a general search engine on the Web. None of the students used the library website as a starting point for their search for literature. And as for scholars, 47% used a specific research database and only 18% used the library catalog.

These numbers were the reason for UUL to have a look at its own users statistics too. Like any other library, UUL has always offered users a public catalog. The library was founded in 1584 and around the year 1600 a list of books was produced, which helped visitors to find the available books. In those days the library was located in an empty former Catholic church and housed only a few hundred books. But as years, decades, and even centuries passed by, the library grew larger, moved to other locations, and now contains millions of books. How to find anything in these large numbers of books without using a catalog?

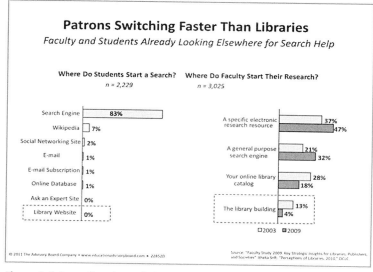

Figure 1. International trends in search behavior (2010).

http://dx.doi.org/10.5703/1288284315584

However, as in the last two decades digital material became more dominant, the traditional catalog became less sufficient, especially for finding scientific electronic articles. For that reason in 2002 UUL built, only slightly more than a decade ago, its own discovery tool, Omega. At that time UUL told users that if they were looking for print material they should use the catalog. And if they were looking for electronic journal articles they should use Omega.

But since 2002 things have changed dramatically. New commercial discovery tools such as Primo and Summon entered the library market. While during the first years Omega was top of the bill and heavily used, in the following years it became rapidly outdated, to the point where it was not even able to access all the digital material of UUL. This made UUL think very hard about possible alternatives.

Meanwhile more and more users were finding their way to licensed journals through larger and stronger web-based search engines, like Google Scholar, and made increasing use of paid databases like Web of Science and Scopus in their search for literature.

Figure 2 shows the trends in search behavior of Utrecht users in the years 2006-2012. During this period the number of searches in the UUL catalog and Omega—the two bottom lines, light brown and red—stayed equal over the years while simultaneously the number of searches in particularly Google Scholar and Scopus increased relatively. This does not mean that Omega had lost its relevance—the user statistics still showed 1.2 million searches per year—but the trend that other discovery tools were becoming more dominant was inevitable.

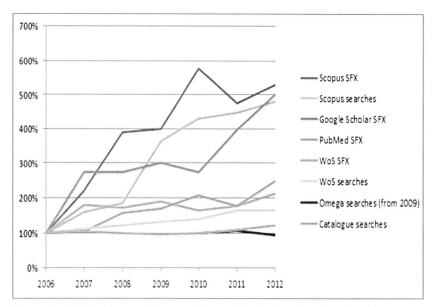

Figure 2. Relative increase/decrease in search behavior, Utrecht University Library, 2006-2012.

Given all these facts, what is the relevance for libraries of investing in their own, expensive discovery tool? And as we at UUL asked ourselves that question, we also started to wonder about a question which had previously been unthinkable: what is the relevance for libraries to have their own public catalog?

To see whether the UUL user statistics were in line with the opinion of our users, UUL conducted a

survey under 12 researchers and 18 students, as representatives from all main disciplines. During these interviews it became clear that by far the most of them searched for full text articles, and most searches started in Google Scholar. Of course, this is the general image and there are huge differences between disciplines. For instance, within the field of Humanities, Google Scholar is less popular than in other disciplines. And of course the preference for search engines depends on what type of information or publication is needed. But the overall image is clear.

Based on the user statistics and the general findings of the survey, UUL concluded that there was no need to invest any further in updating the custom-made discovery tool Omega for scientific journals, and, more important, there is no need to buy and implement another discovery tool. Second, because most of the users are capable of finding information without the help of the library, UUL decided to focus predominantly on delivery.

Besides these rather radical conclusions, we also concluded that for the time being, we would continue our public catalog. For two important reasons, basically. First, at an international level there was no good alternative for the discovery of special collections, especially for nondigital information like old books, maps, pamphlets, and manuscripts. Many search engines give access to only a small part of these collections, there are problems with the metadata, and so on. The rather large and important special collection of UUL would not be easily accessible for users without the public catalog.

Second, in most search engines it is not possible to filter sufficiently on what is available in your own library, or not in a very easy way for users. Especially for students, it is very helpful to know what their library owns or has access to, to have quick access to material they can use to write their papers, for instance. For this type of what you might call "local discovery" a public catalog is still indispensable.

How to Focus on Delivery Instead of Discovery?

Since 2012 UUL focused on shutting down Omega and on improving delivery. But how do you do that? The strategy of UUL was based on three pillars: communication, changing the library website, and improving online support.

Communication is of course always very important in these kinds of transition processes. Despite the fact that other search engines had

become increasingly popular over the years, UUL also had to take into account that many users still used Omega as a discovery tool. To them UUL had to explain the decision to shut down Omega and to offer good alternatives or even better ways of finding material. To do so, UUL made an extensive communication plan which was optimistically named "Better Ways of Finding" UUL discussed plans with users, for instance, while supporting them to find literature, and used social media like Facebook and Twitter to inform students and academic staff. And as a visual reminder of the impending changes, UUL added a counter to its website, counting down the days until Omega would be switched off.

Moreover, UUL redesigned the library website. The goal was to implement a website structured on the various needs of users. Users not only come to the library website to find literature, but also for help on managing data and literature and for support on publishing. These library services are now prominently featured on the homepage of the UUL website.

But probably the most important changes, at least for users, were related to online support. UUL redeveloped a list of available search engines on the website. UUL advises users to use various discovery tools based on their needs and make users aware of possible biases in whatever search engine they are using. The choice of, for instance, a combination of more general and subject specific discovery tools has to depend on the type of information or publications users need. The library website facilitates this.

Besides, UUL kept in mind that most students and staff members do not visit the library website at all, or at least not very often. UUL wants to support this group, too. For them we offer a simple Javascript bookmarklet users can add to their internet browser. This enables them to log in with their Utrecht ID and password while searching off-campus and get all the access to material they would have had if they were searching via the library website.

And UUL offered its SFX knowledge base to Google Scholar and Scopus so these engines know which journals the Utrecht users have access to.

As a result, when students or staff members are searching for information in, for instance, Google Scholar, they will see whether the articles can be accessed by them; and, via the so-called UBU link, get access to the full text if possible.

Of course, these actions were not new, not to UUL and not within the library world. But because of our focus on delivery we see and realize how often things go dramatically wrong. Links that don't work well, material that is not findable, users who don't know how to get access to licensed materials, and so on.

What Happened When UUL Had Shut Down Its Library Discovery Tool?

After almost a year of intensive preparation, the big day came. On Sunday September 1, 2013, Omega was switched off as planned. Despite all our efforts, UUL expected to receive complaints, face problems we had not foreseen. But almost

nothing happened. No major complaints, a lot of hits on the "searching for literature" webpage on the library website. And on September 2, there was an enormous increase of visits to Google Scholar and Scopus via the proxy server, a trend that especially for Google is still continuing (see Figure 3). In fact, the sudden increase of Google searches via the library server was so immense that Google thought they were searched by a robot and replied with a captcha, until they realized that humans were using Scholar.

More than a year later UUL has embedded its focus on delivery in the entire organization and work processes. We keep track of where our users are, by means of trend watching, international studies, user surveys and statistics. UUL cooperates with other libraries or groups of libraries to be more able to influence suppliers, vendors, and publishers, to use international standards, to improve linking mechanisms, and to offer smooth access to licensed users.

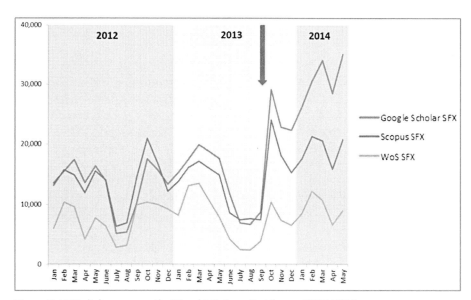

Figure 3. SFX-clicks per month, Utrecht University Library, 2012-2014.

But has UUL received no complaints at all? Yes, mainly from students and academic staff with a Humanities background. Their complaints were twofold: for some of them, shutting down Omega came as a surprise. With hindsight we had to conclude that our communication was not custom-made enough, at least not for all users, maybe relying too much on social media for

instance. It also confirms that when major changes occur libraries have to involve their users as early as possible, in this case certainly those disciplines which are less digitally oriented. As said before, we did our best to inform users, but for some it was not enough.

Besides the communication aspect, there is also a deeper reason why shutting down Omega was not welcomed within the Humanities as warmly as in other disciplines. Many paid databases like Scopus and Web of Science are no good alternatives for Humanities scholars because they contain not enough relevant material for them. In that respect, Google Scholar might be a better alternative, but in another sense more problematic because in this database it is very hard to filter on relevant material which you have access to. And, especially for students, it is often difficult to assess the quality and relevance of the (many) Google search results. So far, the best alternatives for Humanities scholars are probably those databases with bibliographical information on specific disciplines or subjects. In instructions and on the website UUL guides users to all these alternatives.

So, although shutting down Omega was for the most part a success story, UUL also faced problems.

Will UUL Shut Down Its Public Catalog Too?

And what about thinking the unthinkable? Will UUL close its public catalog too because most users don't need it anymore? Yes, we probably will. Up to this day the special collections of UUL are only accessible in a satisfactory manner via the public catalog. But we think that in the near future it will be possible to make our centuries-old books, pamphlets, writings, maps, and so on accessible via general search engines. In fact, we thinks this is a necessity in order to make this kind of extremely valuable, unique material better known and as a result more used. Moreover, until now even many contemporary (e-)books are not adequately accessible via general or subject specific search engines. A lot has to improve related to the discovery and delivery of publications, especially those who are not electronic journal articles. But we are convinced this is all a matter of time (and hard work of course).

And what about what you might call "local discovery"? Will it stay relevant for users to have a discovery tool for knowing what their library owns or has access to? For bachelor students who want

quick access to material this will be the case, maybe. But is any serious scholar not primarily interested in having access to literature most relevant for research or study, instead of wanting to use material his or her library happens to have access to? Libraries should facilitate this.

UUL realizes that the focus on delivery instead of discovery is up to this moment, in some respect, more a mindset than a reality. Of course, discovery is still important to us. UUL supports users in finding their material in the best way possible, but just does not think that library discovery tools are the best way to do so. And, given user statistics and surveys, most users agree with that. Simultaneously, UUL thinks that, related to discovery, our primary responsibility will be more and more to make both the publications of academic staff and the unique material we own findable worldwide, via as many relevant search engines as possible.

And what about delivery? In addition to developing technological facilities, UUL believes in a stronger cooperation between libraries. The Utrecht holdings are part of the Dutch national catalog and of WorldCat as well. We are looking in this direction to see if we can give users a sufficient alternative. For instance, it would be a major step forward if it were possible to filter sufficiently in general search engines on material that is owned by or accessible via one's own library. And to see whether material is currently available and in what way. Or, to give another example, that Humanities related material is better harvested and on a larger scale by Google Scholar and Scopus, so that both scientists and scholars can use these search engines. Through a stronger cooperation between libraries it is possible to build pressure on companies who develop discovery tools to make these kind of developments obvious.

To conclude, not so long ago we at UUL were convinced we needed our own discovery tool. However, when it comes to discovery we had to admit that others apparently do a better job than we do, or at least a job more users prefer. And we think this applies to most libraries. Libraries should stop spending so much time and money on discovery and focus more on delivery. After all, it does not matter where users find their material. What matters is that they can use the relevant material they find.

References

Redesigning the academic library. Managing the migration to digital information sciences (2011). *The Advisory Board Company*. Retrieved from http://www.educationadvisoryboard.com, 22852D.

Kortekaas, S., & Kramer, B. (2014). Thinking the unthinkable—Doing away with the library catalog. http://dx.doi.org/10.1629/2048-7754.174

Schonfeld, R. C., Housewright, R. (2010). Faculty survey 2009: Key strategic insights for libraries, publishers, and societies. New York: Ithaka.

Discovery, a New Way of Searching (Thinking): The Challenges, Trials, and Tribulations

Margaret M. Kain, Electronic Resources Librarian, University of Alabama at Birmingham

Abstract

Google and like search engines have changed the way library users search and retrieve information. The typical library user has come to expect discovery or other search tools to provide one-stop (one-box) searching with seamless and immediate results. While our students and faculty are traveling on this new discovery highway, not all of our library faculty and staff have made it to the on-ramp for this new approach of searching (Thinking).

Introduction

Libraries are moving forward from silos to a more fluid, single interface. The Integrated Library System is no longer the end-all when it comes to the type of searching library users have come to expect. Library users walk around with computers and Internet browsing capabilities in their pockets; they have come to expect a one-stop search shop. As librarians, we balance the need to provide research our users need using search tools that are easy to operate, and are applicable for all types or levels of research. Discovery layers provide a starting point for users that return a variety of resources. These new discovery tools provide rich and diverse opportunities for library users and research (Fyn, Lux, & Snyder, 2013).

Jody Condit Fagan has noted that a single search box or tool is not the ultimate goal of the library (Fagan, 2012). It is important to keep in mind that a discovery layer is just one more tool in the librarian's toolbox; it is not the only tool. Library users should be mindful that entering terms into a search box is simple and easy. Searching, however, is not a simple task; it is a complex task that requires skill and specialized focus (Badke, 2014).

In general, libraries began the discovery journey years ago with the implementation of the federated search. Due to the large amount of data returned in search results and other factors, this tool for many libraries was found unreliable. At times it did not provide results users needed, provided too many results to evaluate, or took too long to return the search results. Through innovation, new tools Marshall Breeding labeled

"discovery interfaces" began to emerge in the 21st century. These discovery interfaces would help library users discover content in all formats, whether it is physically in the library or available through an electronic content database provider (Breeding, 2010).

These discovery interfaces are inevitable next steps as libraries break down the silos of library resources. As such, it is important that public services librarians be familiar with and take a proactive role in the utilization of the discovery interface, so they can readily address users' questions and concerns (Kornblau, Strudwick, & Miller, 2012).

The UAB Sterne Library Experience

The University of Alabama at Birmingham (UAB) is a fairly young academic institution with a long rich history as a medical institution; established in the 19th century as the medical school of the University of Alabama. UAB began as an academic extension school in the mid-20th century through 1969 when the University of Alabama system was established, and three autonomous campuses were named. UAB is an urban campus, with an FTE of approximately 14,500 and a diverse user population. The University is home to three libraries: Mervyn H. Sterne Library, the academic library; Lister Hill Library of the Health Sciences; and Reynolds Historical Library. As the academic library, Sterne serves all of UAB and must be ready to meet the research needs of our users.

For several years, it has been the goal of the UAB libraries to provide access to all library resources from one interface. Currently, Sterne Library and Lister Hill Library maintain two separate legacy integrated library systems. Sterne Library migrated in the late 1990s to self-hosted Ex Libris Voyager and Lister Hill to SirsiDynix Horizon. The question we face is how can UAB libraries move from silos of information to a tool that would appear to seamlessly provide search results from multiple sources.

Early in 2009, when discovery implementations were just beginning to develop, we received information about an offer from OCLC providing the opportunity to implement WorldCat Local "quick start" ("WCL-QS"). This abbreviated discovery implementation was provided at no additional charge with a WorldCat on FirstSearch subscription. At the time of this release, Sterne Library had experienced a significant reduction in our annual budget; and in that same year, the Alabama Governor declared two separate instances of proration. As a result, we were charged with providing innovative tools without incurring additional cost. The OCLC release of WCL-QS provided Sterne Library with a multifold opportunity; through it we would be able to provide a new tool for UAB users to search library resources, as well as provide an opportunity for us to learn how to implement and work with the "new" discovery technology. Most significantly, it was a way to begin building information bridges.

Like many academic libraries, Sterne had implemented one of the older federated search engines. Our federated search, however, never seemed to work as it had been intended. As such, we had considerable concerns about the new discovery technology and anticipated that the technology would present several challenges. We were unaware; however, the extent to which this would be a challenge to some of our users.

With a contract for WCL-QS signed and in place in the summer of 2009, we began our discovery journey. A soft roll-out of Sterne Library's WCL-QS took place in the fall of 2009 with an "official" announcement released early 2010 in conjunction with the rollout of the library's new webpage, and a major Voyager upgrade. Library users were encouraged to use the single "Google-like" search tool to explore UAB Sterne Library and libraries of

the World (Kain, 2010). Not only were we introducing a new tool, we were also introducing a new way to search library resources. In conjunction, we began to look at cataloging functions and other traditional work flows; realizing we would need to rethink and reevaluate some of these functions. We opened the door to change, moving away from our library silos to a shared library research environment.

One of the greatest challenges we faced as we began to work with and introduce this new library tool was gaining acceptance of library staff. Unfortunately, in many cases there is more emphasis on the technical journey than promoting staff acceptance and understanding, and our journey was no exception. Working with the one-search box, we discovered hiccups in our local catalog; some were ghosts from systems past, while others revealed the differing philosophies among Sterne catalogers in the creation of catalog entries. The technical issues seemed to build up the walls of staff resistance; when the discovery interface produced more errors than successful searches, users were unwilling to use it.

We determined the biggest technology challenge we faced centered on the format of the OCLC numbers; some OCLC numbers in the catalog record contained a prefix of "ocn/ocm" while others did not. WCL-QS provided us only two options when searching the local catalog; both options were left anchored searches one with the prefix and one without. As our records were evenly mixed, either setting produced a fairly high error rate; this became our major stumbling block for success. At that time after several long discussions with systems and cataloging representatives, it was decided we would handle standardizing the OCLC number format in the local catalog for the approximate 1.2 million records ourselves; so we set out on a journey to create a way to tackle the problem. Not resolving this issue quickly created more strain between the systems staff and the public services staff. After some failed attempts we finally developed a systemic strategy that worked within the code parameters of our integrated library system that would successfully add the "ocn/ocm" prefix to the 035 field in each record. While this did not completely resolve the issue it did correct a significant portion of the catalog records and standardize the OCLC number entries.

With most of the challenges resolved, we moved more to one-on-one conversations with library staff. We spent days with individual subject librarians walking through endless searches, answering questions, etc. Some of these conversations were at times rather heated as librarians were frustrated working with the new technology, especially when this new technology did not operate the way it was expected to work.

Significant progress had been made in the manual cleanup of our catalog records, so a decision was made to migrate to the paid version of WorldCat Local with the additional features. Migration to the full resource was rather uneventful.

While our local catalog cleanup was not complete, it was agreed that a full batchload project would be the next course of action. Before submitting our records for a batchload project additional internal decisions and evaluation was necessary. An item count was pulled by location code. A cataloging decision was made many years ago by Sterne cataloguers to use the location code to provide granularity regarding the item type. As such, our location codes are a mix of item types and physical shelf locations. Some location codes in the local catalog are vendor designations for electronic resources, some are temporary shelving locations (e.g., "Course Reserves"), and some are a mix of the physical description as well as the physical location (e.g., "Rare Book Oversize – Horizontal").

An additional piece of the puzzle related to electronic resources. For some of our electronic resources we have purchased vendor MARC records and per the license agreements are restricted as to what we can do with the records. Depending on the restrictions, those records and record locations were eliminated from the batchload submission. As we worked through the location code process, we continued to identify more issues we could easily resolve by hand; thereby completing additional presubmission clean-up of the records. All in all, this was a

tedious technical process that actually worked to our advantage.

In early 2013, we submitted approximately 1.2 million records to OCLC for our full batchload project. The initial run of our records, matched first using the OCLC number and additional filters of authors and/or title. Out of the approximate 1.2 million records approximately 5,200 were reprocessed; matching only on the OCLC number without the additional filter of author and/or title. Of those records that were reprocessed, we received two files totaling 560 records which had to be addressed by the catalogers. While waiting for this process to be completed and the records overlayed in the local catalog, work on the knowledgebase began. In anticipation of the migration to a paid discovery product, we had already identified the electronic resources that UAB had access to, based on license agreements. Thus, building the knowledgebase that would support the discovery implementation was a fairly easy though a time consuming process.

With the standardization of the OCLC numbers and the cleanup of catalog records completed, we moved forward to our next step to setup question driven vendor training sessions. It appeared that we had at long last moved forward beyond just addressing the broken parts and could now focus on building search techniques. We setup multiple times/days/sessions for the live training ("WebEx"). All library staff were encouraged to attend; the content of each session while providing some standard information was driven by the library staff in attendance. Prior to each training session, an email was sent to all library staff encouraging them to send in comments, questions and/or concerns they wished to have addressed in each session. The vendor/trainer specifically addressed the questions and answered others that came up during the session. All sessions were recorded and links to the recorded sessions were distributed to all library staff. Our discussions did not end with these training sessions as one-on-one conversations to address staff questions and concerns continue to this day.

Search results became a major point of contention for some of the library staff; some staff felt it was imperative that users had the ability to search the same way they searched the local catalog. Fortunately, staff members from the cataloging department were able to provide valuable insight regarding specific search parameters. Using Connexion and comparing results in the discovery layer, provided library staff with a better understanding of the index in place, how the subject headings were being indexed and resolved. Through these discussions, we were able to determine that this new resource was actually employing modified search algorithm. Understanding the how and why seemed to help some library staff users as they moved forward from the traditional way of searching to this new way of thinking. By relating this new technology to the more customary library tools, library staff appear to be more willing to try this "new" way to search. It is no longer "broken" but just a new twist on something they are familiar with using.

Conclusion: Moving Forward

As we continue to work with a discovery interface, our current technical challenge is setting local holdings information for serial records. In the early years, Sterne Library was a part of a Union List of Serials project and local holdings were added for participating Alabama libraries to OCLC through SOLINET (n.k.a., Lyrasis); SOLINET was at the time the OCLC regional provider. When the project was discontinued, Sterne made the decision not to continue contributing local holdings to OCLC. Unfortunately, this means that we have not provided serials holdings in our catalog records that can be seen through a discovery interface; as such, the user cannot tell what specific volumes are actually held. To correct this going forward, for new serials records, we have begun to add local holdings. For those serial records already in the local catalog, we are still in the process of formulating a plan of action. Our goal is to submit catalog records for an OCLC local holdings batchload project within the next twelve months. Completion of a local holding maintenance batchload will improve discoverability and allow additional granularity for ancillary services such as Interlibrary Loan.

Conversations among library staff members are continuing; and there appears to be more understanding and acceptance about moving to this new way of searching and thinking. That being said, like all libraries, there are still a few library staff that will not go willingly into this new discovery environment.

Sterne and Lister Hill are currently undergoing several administrative changes which will have a significant impact on the technology the libraries implement in the future. We are in the process of merging into the UAB Libraries and the first Inaugural Dean of UAB Libraries has been appointed. We have just begun the process and do not know where it will lead. Eventually, one integrated library system will take the place of the two. Once that happens, the choice of the integrated library system vendor may determine what discovery tool, if any, is selected and implemented.

We have had the experience and gained expertise in having built a knowledgebase and implemented a discovery tool. We have identified issues; some have been solved and we continue to work through others. The records in our local catalog have been cleaned up; we have procedures in place to prevent inconsistencies with ongoing cataloging. This has also provided additional opportunities for ongoing discussions among library staff.

This has been a worthwhile learning experience for everyone and our migration to a new integrated library system and other library tools will be much easier as a result of our work and this experience.

References

Badke, W. (2014). Mythbusting—Seven Google myths that complicate our lives. *Online Searcher, May/June,* 22-26.

Breeding, M. (2010). State of the art in library discovery 2010. *Computers in Libraries, 30*(1), 31-35.

Fagan, J. C. (2012). Top 10 discovery tool myths. (Editorial). *Journal of Web Librarianship,* pp. 1-4. Retrieved from http://search.ebscohost.com/login.aspx?direct=true&db=lxh&AN=73540978&site=ehost-live

Fyn, A. F., Lux, V., & Snyder, R. J. (2013). Reflections on teaching and tweaking a discovery layer. *Reference Services Review, 41*(1), 113-124.

Kain, P. (2010). Libraries of the world come to UAB. *Mervyn H. Sterne Library Directions, 26*(1), 5.

Kornblau, A. I., Strudwick, J., & Miller, W. (2012). How web-scale discovery changes the conversation: The questions librarians should ask themselves. *College & Undergraduate Libraries, 19*(2-4), 144-162.

Evolution of Mobile Device Use in Clinical Settings

Robert Brooks, Senior Director Business Development, Wolters Kluwer, Medical Research
Jeannine Creazzo, MLIS, AHIP, Manager, Library Services, Saint Peter's University Hospital

Abstract

In September 2014, Wolters Kluwer, Medical Research completed its second annual survey of end user search and access behavior with professional health information. The questionnaire addressed changes in clinical workflows resulting from the increased use of mobile devices in clinical settings. Through comparison with prior year's data, we contemplate changes in how specific use cases fit with specific devices, the effect of multiple screens on usage behavior, and how users value different content types in the mobile environment. With responses from over 12,000 users (approximately 4,000 physicians, 3,400 nurses, and the remainder medical students, faculty, and other provider groups), we identified a drastic 20% year-over-year increase in the number of professionals that routinely access "three screens" (tablet, smartphone, and desktop) for professional purposes. Significantly, the findings strongly support the notion that "more screens = more access," as both smartphones and tablets are becoming increasingly embedded, for a wider range of activities, in the clinical workflow.

Concurrently, increased demand for mobile access to healthcare information is creating new challenges for medical librarians. Faced with budget constraints and intensified scrutiny over spending decisions, librarians must balance demands for electronic and print resources while collaborating with IT departments to ensure mobile device access, support, and privacy adherence. Based on survey data, we conclude with "win-win" opportunities for librarians and vendors to work more closely together to increase the effectiveness of mobile initiatives, including the need for more comprehensive usage statistics and more flexible licensing models.

Mobile Usage Trends

Undoubtedly, the increased use of mobile devices by clinicians is changing both workflows and information consumption habits of healthcare professionals. Wolters Kluwer's 2014 end-user survey intended to identify market trends, better understand the impact of mobile device on information "use cases," and discover any emergent customer product or service demands arising from their changing preferences and behaviors with respect to mobile access.

According to our survey, 72% of physicians use tablets in their daily practice (up from 60% in 2013), and across all healthcare professionals, two-thirds reported to be "three screen users," routinely accessing tablets, smartphones, and desktops in their clinical workflows. This represents a 20% increase from 2013. As a result, while the average overall time spent accessing digital resources during the workday continues to increase (reaching 2.9 hours per day for physicians and 3.5 hours per day for nurses), the percentage of this time spent on a desktop continues to decline. The desktop's "share" (based on time utilized) has fallen to 50%, while the smartphone represents 29% of usage time, and the tablet's share has risen considerably to 21%.

Additionally, our data confirms the popular belief that "more screens = more access." "Three screen users" report a 28% higher average number of daily "digital sessions," accessing digital resources an average of 37 times per day (vs. 29 times per day for other users). Significantly, our data also reinforces the idea that tablet access does not notably cannibalize other access mediums. In fact, four out of five heavy tablet users reported no decrease in their use of other digital access points, and 25% of this group even indicated that their tablet usage actually led directly to increased usage of other digital mediums.

Changing User Behaviors

Survey data also led to new insights in terms of the evolution of device use cases. For instance, while clinicians have historically lagged behind students and residents in terms of using mobile devices for reading journal articles, our new data suggests that this gap is closing. According to a recent article in the *Journal of the Medical Library Association*, 50% of students and residents read journal articles on mobile devices.[1] Our survey found an increase in physician use of both tablets and smartphones for reading articles, reaching 33% for tablets and 21% for smartphones. Nurses reported slightly lower levels of journal reading on mobile devices, with 24% using tablets and 17% using smartphones.

Increased tablet ownership is also changing clinician behavior at the point of care in two distinct ways. First, the tablet continues to transition from being purely a desktop alternative for research ("lookup") to being increasingly used for direct patient management. More than one in eight physicians now use tablets in the clinical workflow, and this will only increase as more applications allow for integration with clinical notes and electronic medical records. Additionally, while smartphones remain the predominant source for access to drug information, tablets have now surpassed smartphones as the preferred source for access to evidence based tools at the point of care. This is indicative of a growing interchangeability between phones and tablets, with tablets now being accessed almost as often per day by physicians as smartphones (3.5 times for tablets vs. 4.3 time for smartphones).

Surprisingly, the greatest insight from our data may be about what is not changing—the resiliency of the desire to access print versions of journals. Even as online and mobile journal access continues to grow, now at 86% for physicians and 80% for nurses, there was not a corresponding drop in access to print journal content, which remained flat at around 65% of all end users. However, there was a 10% drop in physician respondents that stated they "typically" access print journals, so this may indicate an underlying decline in the actual number of times print journals are accessed.

Finally, our data provides detail into specific online journal access and search behaviors. 52% of physicians indicated that their primary method to access online journal content was through institutional resources, while 48% relied predominantly on personal subscriptions. In terms of search preferences, respondents overwhelmingly favored public sources such as PubMed (60%). Less than half of respondents initiate a search by visiting a journal-specific website. This growing preference for journal-agnostic search is also evident from a substantial 25% decrease in the number of respondents who rated search within a specific journal as "an important way to search for journal content."

Implications for Content Providers

In today's clinical environment, where 63% of physicians access medical research on tablets, and 43% via smartphones, publishers must adapt to this new norm of "three-screen access." With all three devices now being used (to varying degrees) across the use cases of search, reading, and point-of-care reference, successful content providers will be the ones that can meet rising customer expectations for a *single user experience* across device types. Given that users generally do not have the time read full-text during search, a majority (67%) save an article (in print or online) for reading when convenient, with increased desire to seamlessly share documents across all their mobile devices for anywhere, any time access.

Another opportunity from increased mobile usage is the enhanced ability for providers to better understand their users at the individual level, catalyzing the development of new products, services and business models. Our survey data reveals that, at minimum, publishers should look to redesign content for deeper integration with professional workflows, including services such as headlines, synoptic content, and alerts customized to the end user. Finally, publishers should

---

[1] Boruff J., Storie, D., "Mobile devices in medicine: A survey of how medical students residents and faculty use smartphones and other mobile devices to find

information." *Journal of the Medical Library Association,* *102*(1), 22–30.

continue to monitor the use of social media and networking sites. Our data found that over seven in ten physicians and eight in ten nurses utilize social networking as a source for professional information. This is consistent with an earlier study that found that on a weekly basis, 61% of physicians scan social media and 46% actively contribute to online postings and discussions.[2] Presumably, increased use of mobile devices will also lead to increased time spent by professionals on social media. Publishers should both stay abreast of social media trends, such as the popular platforms and destinations beyond mainstream sites like Facebook, as well as find ways to engage users through targeted content or better collaboration tools.

Implications for Medical Librarians

Medical libraries play a fundamental role in providing awareness and access to informational resources for a range of patron groups, including physicians, nurses, nurse practitioners, residents, fellows, medical and nursing students, nonclinical staff, patients, and visitors. Through strategic acquisition of print and electronic resources, medical librarians and their colleagues contribute to reducing the length of hospital stay, promoting patient safety, and reducing medical errors. However, in today's cost-conscious environment, libraries are increasingly forced to justify their budgets and purchase decisions, while facing increasing patron demand for increased mobile access options. While these conflicting forces are adding complexity to collection management strategies, there are also emerging technological barriers that can impact usage levels for mobile resources. Medical librarians must partner with internal IT departments in order to ensure data privacy and security, IT support for certain mobile devices, and bandwidth availability. Also, patrons needing to visit multiple access points (virtual private network [VPN], proxy server) in order to log in to the resources can be discouraging and cumbersome.

Given both the rapid changes in end-user mobile data consumption habits as well as technical uncertainties in implementing mobile initiatives, libraries are understandably encouraged to remain cautious and focus on providing access to a smaller number of highly used mobile resources instead of a huge collection until library-licensed mobile resources have streamlined processes.[3] However, based on our customer survey, there are a number of low-risk opportunities for librarians and content vendors to work together to increase the value of mobile resources. Specifically, librarians should utilize multiple communication methods (instruction, orientation, library's website, and social media posts) to educate patrons on off-site access, embargo dates and license restrictions, and attempt to redirect patrons away from search engines by communicating to them on an ongoing basis all the resources (both licensed and free products) that are available to them and how to access them. It is also critical to use multiple tools and surveys to collect substantial feedback from patrons to determine what types of mobile devices patrons use and which formats they prefer their resources to be in.

Librarians should collaborate with content providers around mobile product development, quality, and creating a simplified login process. Both parties should also work together to collect comprehensive usage statistics, allowing them each to see who is using the database, what access points they are using to gain entry to the database, and what resources within the database they are using and not using. This data can lead to the development of new, more flexible licensing models, which will ultimately yield benefit to both parties. Finally, given the constant evolution of mobile products and clinical uses, it is essential to continually monitor user preferences to be able to meet their changing information needs.

[2] McGowan, B. S., Wasko, M., Vartabedian, B. S., Miller, R. S., Freiherr, D. D., Abdolrasulnia, M. (2012), "Understanding the factors that influence the adoption and meaningful use of social media by physicians to share medical information." *J Med Internet Res*, *14*(5): e117.

[3] Boruff, J., Storie, D. (2014), "Mobile devices in medicine: A survey of how medical students residents and faculty use smartphones and other mobile devices to find information." *Journal of the Medical Library Association*, *102*(1), 22–30.

The Ethereal Library: Thinking Creatively When You Have No Space to Think

Corey Seeman, Kresge Library Services, Ross School of Business, University of Michigan, Ann Arbor

Abstract

Today's library operates in two distinct spaces. First, there is the physical space, where we provide our community a place to work, where we provide access to print materials, and where we can provide a place to provide service. Second, there is the ethereal space, where we connect with users, provide outreach, and where our value is revealed. And in the best case scenario, a library has these two spaces to operate from. However, over the past few years, many academic libraries have seen their footprint errode. This is especially true from the vantage point of the academic departmental library which has been seeing its footprint erode.

Starting in 2014, the Kresge Business Administration Library at the Ross School of Business will cease being a full-service library as has been traditionally the case. Instead, our footprints will be reduced to little more than is needed to house the librarians and staff. Using these challenges, as well as those being faced by other academic departmental libraries, the presenter will share accounts of how the reduction and elimination of library space did not also lead to the elimination of core library services coming from that group. Among the topics to be discussed are expanded reference, embedded librarian programs, and the adoption of new services that were possible and desired by the school. The presenter will showcase how you can move from a physical library to an ethereal one, while retaining services, people and your connection to the school.

The Two Spaces of the Library

In 2013, I was given an opportunity to think about the Library as Place for a program sponsored by the Michigan Library Association. In that program, I shared the notion that the Library had two spaces: a physical space and an ethereal space.[1] While both places are critical for members of the library community, each space provided a distinct function and benefit.

The physical space is used for a variety of functions, including the storage and retrieval of print materials and other physical objects; computer terminals for walk-in access to licensed resources; staff workspace; public desks or interaction spaces; individual student study; and group study. For some of these spaces, especially student individual and group study spaces, the physical space may be managed just as well by others. While librarians had historically done a good job managing student space in a library, that work did not necessarily constitute the full notion of what a library is on campus.

We have heard many things about the future of the library and what that might entail. While print collections might be 2% of the usage, it represents at least 50% of the perception of the library, maybe more. These numbers are drawn from our experiences in the business space, naturally, with social sciences and humanities, the use of print is considerably higher.

When given the task of coming up with a characteristic for the other space of the library, I was drawn to the notion of the "Ethereal Space" or the "Ethereal Library." Instead of a physical place that might be managed by just about any office on campus, I wanted to think about the library that is a true value add to the campus community. And while we see print books, reference works, and journals morph into electronic resources, the ethereal space is exactly where we would like to be in the library community. That was the true "value add" of the library and what we provide to the campus.

The ethereal space was where the higher level work of the library took place. This is the place where we connect with our community. This is where we provide clarity to a complicated information universe. This is where we SHINE! And since (especially in the business library

---

[1] See http://hdl.handle.net/2027.42/97763

environment), we have nearly 98% of our usage from electronic resources—librarians and library staff can operate from almost anywhere. And with ethereal space, we actually have real estate (so to speak) that our administrators and governing bodies cannot take away from us.

So that leads me to think about the academic business library and what does their future hold. Furthermore, what if we could only have one of these two types of spaces—what might we choose? Would you elect to preserve your physical space (for student study and physical library materials) or would you elect to preserve the ethereal space (symbolized by the services that we provide). And while it would be great to think that we can chart our own course here, it is very clear to me that there are space constraints on academic campuses that have mostly spared the library. That might not be the case moving forward. Space is a luxury on academic campuses and provosts are asking the questions about whether we need to retain large academic libraries in order to provide the campus with the resources that it needs. And in many cases, including ours, the decision was made for us. Our path forward was one of our own making, but with the restrictions and limitations established by others.

Kresge Business Administration Library

The Kresge Business Administration Library[2] serves the research, instruction, and curriculum needs of the faculty, students, and staff of the Ross School of Business. The Kresge Business Administration Library is a charter member of the Academic Business Library Directors group and is one of the leading business libraries in the country. The Library is independent of the main University Libraries, receiving our funding from the Ross School of Business. This allows us to focus on the specific information resource needs of the Ross Community, especially in support of faculty research and action-based learning programs (such as MAP). While independent, we

work closely with the University Libraries at Michigan on collaborative purchases and services.

If this presentation were given in 2012, the presenter would have made the following points:

- The Library was built in mid-1980s to serve the research and curricular needs of the Ross School of Business.

- Kresge Library is open 108 hours during the fall and winter terms and fundamentally closes the same time as the Ross Campus closes.

- Kresge Library provides seating for nearly 700 students.

- The Library was very visible and centrally located in the center of the Ross Complex.

- While the library originally occupied around 45,000 square feet of the Kresge building, the library controlled space was around 27,000 square feet. This does not include around 7,000 square feet of group study rooms that double as interview suites.

- Kresge had a print collection of over 140,000 volumes in Ann Arbor and Flint (where they are stored at the University of Michigan-Flint).

One additional point to be made was that the library had found itself in a constant state of erosion when it came to space. Kresge Library was being viewed when new offices needed space. So it came as little surprise that we would find ourselves with less space when we learned about a large construction project at the Ross School of Business. The bigger surprise was that we found ourselves with much less space.[3]

In September 2013, Stephen Ross (for whom the school is named) gave an additional $200 million to the University of Michigan, to be split between

---

[2] http://www.bus.umich.edu/kresgelibrary/
[3] See Dividend Fall 2014,
http://michiganross.umich.edu/our

-community/alumni/dividend/fall2014/completing-the-vision

the Ross School of Business and Athletics.[4] The $100 million going to the Ross School of Business was to renovate the buildings (including Kresge Library) that were attached to the new Ross building that opened in early 2009, the result of his initial $100 million dollar gift to the University. As the plans developed with architects, it became apparent that we would not have as much space as we would have liked. In a scenario where no one department received all that they asked for in the planning stages, the Kresge Library was left with getting less than what they had in the old building. Sadly for the Library, they were unique in this scenario. The space afforded to Kresge during construction and in the future essentially translated into staff areas with very modest room for print materials. We currently have 200 books and are at about capacity.

By February 2014, it became apparent that there was no room for a print collection of any kind. There were around 70,000 volumes in Kresge at the beginning of the year. When news first broke about this project and the likelihood that we would lose collection space, I started a dialogue with the University Library at Michigan to see if they could take on any of the print material. In the end, they agreed to take on the print and microfilm collection that was not otherwise replicated in their existing collection. Second copies and duplicates between the libraries would not be retained. In all, around 37,000 volumes and items went to the University Library. The remaining items were given to Better World Books, where the University had a contract. This is in addition to nearly 50,000 volumes given to Better World when Kresge was asked to vacate the collection space at Flint where we had low-use books since 2006.

Since the Kresge Library building was to be completely renovated, the staff were located into temporary quarters. These quarters are tight and do not afford us a good service point, so we had to give up course reserves and change the way that we work with course materials (cases, etc.).

For Kresge, losing the physical space forced the staff to come to grips in a short amount of time with major changes to the library and their value proposition on campus. Gone are the days that Kresge was a student destination for individual or group study. Gone are the days that Kresge could be format agnostic when it came to collection. But not gone were the reference services that we provided, support for action-based learning and management of the curriclum materials. That is a key to the rebirth of the Kresge Library.

In planning for these changes, we established the priorities as follows: staff, services, stuff, and space. In the end, we managed to hold onto the staff and services while losing our stuff and our space. In planning, we had to focus very closely on building a new library based on what we have, not on what we had. We had no choice but to build an Ethereal Library! In building the parameters of the Ethereal Library, I used some guiding principles that I am calling the 6P Approach: philosophical, patient, positive, proactive, perform, and follow Ms. Pirkola's rules.

Be Philosophical

As difficult as this transition was, we were afforded an opportunity to also be freed from what worked and did not work from the past. With significantly less space, we had to be careful to not try and recapture everything we did before the construction project. If we did, we would be bound to failure. In many ways, this is territory that I had been in before, when I talked about decisions made by staff when undergoing migrations of library systems. Staff often wanted to replicate systems and procedures from their old systems into their new ones.[5] That approach helped with the comfort from the move, but it did not enable the libraries to fully take advantage of the new system.

Being separated from the space that the library occupied enabled me to think about what our value is and how to continue with the new

---

[4] http://michiganross.umich.edu/news/u-michigan -receive-200-million-prominent-real-estate-developer -stephen-m-ross

[5] Seeman, C. (2002). Invisible fences: A shocking theory for re-examining work flow. *Computers in Libraries, 22*(7), 24– 30.

constraints. As a group, we brainstormed about service points, both real and virtual. And with any type of entrepreneurial exercise, failure is an option. It enabled us to try things that we might not have tried in the past. It enabled us to move our reference service point during the first term and find something that provided the staff with stability and visibility needed to serve our community.

Be Patient

Making this type of dramatic change in a relatively short amount of time is not easy for anyone within the library. In many ways, each staff member goes through Elisabeth Kübler-Ross's Five Stages of Death in the process: denial, anger, bargaining, depression, and acceptance.[6] Even more important is that everyone moves through these changes at their own pace and related to their own job responsibilities. For reference librarians, the fundamental changes are relatively minor, as most of the resources we would regularly use are electronic anywhere. At Kresge, we had long encouraged flexible scheduling and work environments, which allowed people to do work remotely. Besides being a good benefit for librarians, this actually helped prepare us for this eventuality. For staff, especially those in positions where managing and processing physical objects was important, the transition was more uncertain and nerve-wracking. So it became clear that everyone was moving through the challenges at their own pace.

While we needed to be patient with staff as they move through the process of the transformation of the Library, I also asked the staff to be patient with me as we moved through these changes. The changes made it very clear that becoming a digital library is much more difficult than being born that way. The two most well known "born digital" libraries (BiblioTech in San Antonio[7] and Florida Polytechnic University in Lakeland[8]) come to mind. There are tremendous difficulties and culture changes that take place when converting a full-service library to one that is digital.

Be Positive

When going through this type of challenging process, it is very easy to be mired in self-doubt. The image of loss cannot be your brand or how you are seen by others in the community. To this end, it is important not to dwell on the decisions that had been made and look towards the new future. Quite honestly, it is difficult to do this, but the choices we have as individuals (to stay or leave) will enable us to make the decisions that work the best.

In thinking about the upside of losing our study space, there are actually a few silver linings that appear. First, we will not have to worry about expanded hours for exams. Additionally, we were open until 1am four days a week. That put student temporary staff on campus walking home at 1:15 am (not a great situation from an employer POV) Second, being in Michigan, winter weather can be problematic. So not having to worry about opening the library on challenging weather days is a plus. Third, being a public university, we provided walk-in access to people who appeared to use the computers as their personal office. With losing space for these computers, the associated problems go away.

The process of creating a positive approach to this situation is about making the best of what we have. It is a process of trying to determine how we can continue to meet the needs of the school and the number of communities we serve. It is a process that takes time and reflection. And despite everything—we'd rather be happy than angry.

Be Proactive

During the transition from a centrally located library to one that will be more of a service unit, the biggest issue that we face is that we will be out of sight at the school. The lack of visibility is the biggest challenge moving forward. This situation forced the library to be more proactive with outreach and connecting with the school's faculty and students than we had been. While we

---

[6] http://www.ekrfoundation.org/five-stages-of-grief/

[7] http://bexarbibliotech.org/
[8] https://floridapolytechnic.org/library-search/

have uses all virtual reference systems (chat and e-mail), we needed to push them more with the community in order to remain visible to the campus community.

In building the library services prior to this change, I have been a strong proponent of the reference desk—even as many libraries are moving away from that model. Having a central place where people could come for help allowed students and community members to easily approach us with questions. In many ways, the reference and the circulation desks are the face of the library. In looking at where we might have a dedicated reference service point, we explored a number of options. The one with started with was in the School's Tozzi Center (trading floor) where we had a table and librarians on duty would bring a laptop. The service ran from 1pm to 5pm. While we were appreciative of the space, it was not ideal. It felt like we were crashing on a friend's sofa. With this realization, something that can only be learned by trying it out, we looked for alternatives. We were able to repurpose the desk that is at the entrance to the Ross Modular Offices where the library staff is located. We originally conceived this as a welcome desk with more of a reception role, but that turned out to not be fully needed. So we repurposed the desk as the new reference desk. We expanded our hours to start at 10am and end at 5pm. What became very beneficial is that replacing someone's shift time became easy because they librarians are all in the building. We are working on creating some light-up signs that we can use to let people know in the main Ross building when the library services are open.

Be Performers

In this change to the space and collection of the Kresge Library, there was never an issue about Kresge Library as a service point. That is the entity that truly kept the library moving forward and going as a unit amid these changes, and it would be the entity that would propel us into the future. Drawing from data from the Ross School of Business exit surveys of MBA and BBA students, Kresge Library had been one of the best-reviewed service units at the school. It had always been a great source of internal pride and motivation.

Since Kresge lost our space, we were going to be less about a place to study than a place where to get help. We needed to be creative in how we deliver services to our community. If we failed in our attempts to deliver the information services to the school, there would likely be a reconsideration of the library as on ongoing entity. In many regards, we wanted to simply continue the great work that we were doing at the library and rebuild with that success in mind.

Be Like Ms. Pirkola

Ms. Pirkola was my older son's third-grade teacher in the 1990s. While it has been many years that he has been in her classroom, hardly a month goes by when we do not call her out by name. Besides being a great teacher, she preached flexibility. This was a great lesson for my son and it is a great lesson for me. If the Kresge Library needed anything during this transformation, it was a continued appreciation and understanding about being flexible. For this to work, we needed to be flexible in all directions. We need to be flexible with staff as they to work with these new confines. We asked the staff to be flexible with the leadership as we worked through our situations.

Equally important to flexibility is balance and empathy. With empathy, greater preference for one group can have a direct impact on another. With libraries or other service units, the needs of patrons and the work that staff do need to be balanced against each other. In the library, the more we provide for patrons, the greater we lean on staff. Conversely, the more we provide for the staff, potentially the less we provide for patrons. Keeping the needs of both the library staff and the library community in balance is a great need here.

Putting It All Together— The Big Changes at Kresge

In thinking about the big changes that are taking place at Kresge Library with this transformation, it is clear that there are services that will continue, as well as new opportunities that will be possible. The additional services are possible in large part because of the loss of work that is associated with the removal of the print collection from the library.

There are many existing programs that will not change that much in this new situation. Kresge Library's embedded librarian program to support Multidisciplinary Action Projects (MAP) will continue at Ross.[9] In these programs, each student team working on a "real-world" problem for a sponsor will be assigned a team of faculty and staff (which includes a librarian) to help them find the information that they need to assess and solve the project. MAP for MBA students (as well as Weekend MBA and Executive MAP) is a required core class. While finding space to meet will be a challenge during the construction, the fundamental work does not change. Additionally, starting in fall 2014, the librarians supported a new core class for undergraduate students. BA 200 is the first class taken by business majors (BBAs) in the fall term of their sophomore year. They set out to explore two companies and their response to a social issue. The librarians are assigned to each section of 35 students to provide research support and guidance as the students work on the project. In addition, the Kresge librarians are supporting the faculty through the Faculty Research Service, which provides detailed assistance to more rigorous research projects. Finally, we continue to support other student information needs for any reason they might have (we often classify this as the 5 Cs: coursework, clubs, careers, case competitions, and curiosity).

A very important element to Kresge Library is our management of coursepacks used at Ross for cases and other licensed material that are required readings for classes. The faculty work with Kresge staff to identify cases, articles, book chapters, and simulations that will be required for students. Previously, this was a print solution, but the space constraints with the construction project made continuing in this system difficult if not impossible. We moved to online course materials with a commercial vendor, study.net, since they have a strong relationship with Harvard Business Publishing. While the costs will increase

with a commercial vendor, many students are happy with the added ability of having electronic course materials. We have an optional print version of the cases that may be purchased by students.

With this change, we were also to look at our services and explore possible additions to our offerings. Rather than try to brainstorm about what might be useful, and then try to find the market to adopt it, we looked at programs that were already being tested by other groups. One program that was taken in by Kresge was the exam and assignment program, formerly run as a pilot by the school's Faculty Support Group. The premise of the exam program is that many faculty do not want to use class time to hand back assignments and exams. Additionally, many faculty do not let students keep completed exams, but instead, they can review them, but must hand them back to the faculty member. This service ran as a pilot in winter term and went into full service with the Library in fall 2014. With the attention to detail and good customer service focus with the students, the Kresge Library team was well suited to take on this project and service. Additionally, the workload for the exam program balances very nicely with the existing work to support the curriculum materials. For the most part, the peak work for these two services are at different times of the term, which makes it easy to marry to two together.

Other new programs that we are implementing include serving as a pickup location for the Ross School of Business requests for books delivered from the main library and ILL. We are also exploring the opportunities to support other programs in the management of course materials (such as the Global MBA Program which had been run independently). We are also shifting evening reference from in person work done by the Kresge Library supervisors (typically School of Information students) to having evening and weekend reference done electronically only. The benefit is that the people doing evening and weekend reference may do so from the comfort

---

[9] Berdish, L., and Seeman, C. (2010). A reference-intensive embedded librarian program: Kresge Business Administration Library's program to support action-based learning at the Ross School of Business. *Public Services Quarterly, 6*(2-3), 208–224.

of their own home or anywhere else where they can connect to the Internet.

Providing Value With New Constraints

While there has been a great deal of discussion about the "value" of the academic library, we need to explore what it means to live with constraints that are not temporary, but permanent. I believe what happened at Kresge very well could happen at other libraries. It is an indication that we are not going to be able to operate as we have done in the past. The same would be true of many other industries (automotives, pharmaceuticals, journalism, and publishing just to name a few). Our task is very simple—we must provide great value to our community with new constraints. This alters our value proposition for what we can provide to our campuses.

At Kresge Library, we no longer can provide space for students to study or space for collections (in any physical formats). Instead, we need to focus on what our new value proposition will be for the campus. This means that we will need to shift our entire thinking:

- Live within the restrictions of virtually no collection space.

- Figure out new collaboration mechanisms to serve our community.

- Move away from the model where we provided student study space.

- Focus on what we can do versus what we have done in the past.

We are currently working on refining the Kresge Library Value Proposition and what roles we can play at the school. This will involve reaching out to the different stakeholders at the school (undergraduate students, graduate students, PhD students, part-time students, faculty, and staff) and find out specifically what their information needs are and how we can support them. Hopefully, this project will be done by the middle of 2015.

Closing Thoughts

Despite this dramatic change, there are some things to be positive about. One of the most important is that we had a very large win in that we were able to retain our staffing. There were some University priorities that caused two Kresge staff members to be redeployed at the school. However, we were able to proceed with 19 staff members (including librarians) that we had before the change. We are assessing right now if this is the right number and are working with the schools HR office to ensure that we have the correct amount of work for the people here. The premise with this reduction has been space and space alone. However, we needed to be realistic about the work that remained in the Library and the new services that we brought on. While we had no full-time staff losses related to this move, our temporary staff counts are reduced from around 4.5 FTE to 0.5 FTE. This was the result of dramatically reducing service hours.

In addition, it seems that we have been in this cycle of greater uncertainty for space dedicated to academic libraries. Space is at a premium on campus and where it is for labs, study space, or staff/faculty offices, the libraries might lose. The future appears to me that academic libraries will continue to lose space until it is mostly gone. This time horizon is 20 years, but for smaller schools, it might take place quicker. For academic libraries to succeed, we need to be nimble and flexible to meet the needs of the school.

One of the difficulties in moving from a multiformat collection to one that is just electronic is the long-term collection management. Kresge Library managed a print collection the way that many academic libraries are managed. The collection is built on the needs in the current time period and down the road. There have been many studies that have shown that the majority of works will be used within 10 years of their acquisitions. But in an electronic environment, there is not the long-term stability that you have with materials on your shelf, especially with resources that are licensed year in and year out. It seems there will be a growing print divide in the coming years, separating libraries with a historical collection and those with only commercially available electronic resources.

Finally, we have decided to change our name from the Kresge Business Administration Library to Kresge Library Services. The rationale about making this change is to reflect that we will no longer be a "destination" or a library in the traditional sense. We have moved from being a place you visit to being a service that one can utilize. The name "Kresge Library Services" enables us to keep the Kresge name, which has great brand recognition both on campus and at the school, and identify us as a library service unit. We opted to do that so we did not get confused with existing units at the school (Information Technology or Research). This name reflects a good part of the value proposition that we are hoping to provide to the school.

All across academic libraries, especially departmental and branch libraries, decisions are being made to contract and centralize library operations. Departmental libraries have been closing and shrinking for many years. So for those types of libraries, does this activity serve as the "canary in the coal mine?" Our space contraction appears to be the future of libraries everywhere— we just had it happen all at once. However, what saved the Kresge Library operation at Michigan was the focus on service and the ability to move from a traditional library to one from the future.

How Do Librarians Prefer to Access Collections?

Julie Petr, University of Kansas Main Campus
Lea Currie, University of Kansas Main Campus

Abstract

The University of Kansas (KU) Libraries first made the discovery tool, Primo (Ex Libris), available to their users in the fall of 2013. Since that time, in spite of many improvements and updates, librarians still prefer to use other resources. In an effort to facilitate open and honest discussion about the Primo discovery tool and to make recommendations to improve the functionality of the instrument, librarians at KU were asked to complete a survey that helped them compare Primo to their favorite database and to Google Scholar. The survey included a known item search, a prescribed topic search, and the opportunity for them to search for a topic in their subject expertise specialty. The librarians were asked the following questions about each resource they used:

- Looking at the first ten results, how many of them are relevant?

- Did you change your search strategy or use the facets in Primo or other methods of narrowing in on a topic to find more relevant results?

- What was your reaction to the results in each resource?

- Was it obvious the results included books, articles, or other resources?

- Were the results easily accessible?

In this session, KU librarians will share their survey instrument. They will discuss, in detail, the results of the survey and the comments made by librarians while completing the survey. They will also share the recommendations for improvements they made to IT staff who administer Primo. Audience members will be asked to share their experiences with discovery tools at their libraries.

Background

The University of Kansas (KU) Libraries has a long history of developing and making discovery tools available to their users. In 2002, as part of the KU Digital Library Initiative, the KU Libraries reached an agreement with Endeavor Information Systems to implement the ENCompass system for managing, organizing, and linking KU's digital library collections and providing a search for all of these resources using a single search box.

The expectation that ENCompass would become the primary search mechanism on the Libraries' web site quickly faded. Not only was the ENCompass search extremely slow, often the searches in some of the databases would time out before they were completed. Once the results were retrieved, KU users had to figure out what to do with them. Some of the results would link directly to full-text, but most of the results would only display the record for the article or book. KU librarians soon realized that it was essential to teach ENCompass searching in all of their library instruction sessions, since students were drawn to the search box, whether they were successful in using it or not.

A great deal of planning and thought went into the subsequent discovery tool. A large group of library staff, representing all areas of the library, was formed to make recommendations on how to design the new "Information Gateway." The large group was split into several small groups, each of which was assigned a persona who represented a typical KU Libraries' user, including faculty, undergraduates, and graduate students in the sciences, social sciences, and humanities. Each small group was asked to brainstorm together to form a list of the resources that their individual persona would want to see on the library web site. Every group reported that their persona wanted a single search box that was similar to Google, which would search all of the resources in their subject area.

The next-generation federated search tool that KU developed was Serial Solutions' 360 Search. 360 Search was highly customizable, so IT staff, with the aid of an advisory group of librarians, spent several months in 2007 and 2008 preparing the search for a soft rollout in the summer of 2008. The advisory group felt that it was very important to get the support of the Libraries' staff, so they attended many meetings and gatherings to get feedback about the resource, with the hopes that IT could customize 360 Search to be a much more functional resource than ENCompass had been and more popular with staff. KU's customized version did permit the user to choose databases other than the three default general databases, allowing users to search across almost all the databases that KU users could access through the Libraries' web site. The results when users did this mimicked Google, in the respect that it brought back thousands of results.

Over time, Libraries' staff became increasingly disenchanted with 360 Search. Librarians were not impressed with the results students were getting with this tool and sentiments began to suggest that a resource that could search Libraries databases as well as local collections was needed. In the fall of 2011, a task force was formed to research and review the many new discovery tools that had become available on the market, both commercial and open source products. After talking to colleagues at other schools and inviting vendors to demonstrate their products, KU librarians chose Ex Libris' Primo because of the ability to customize the look and feel and functionality.

It took IT and cataloging staff almost a year to get Primo up and running. All of the catalog records in the Voyager local catalog had to be loaded into Primo as well as digitized local collections. A second small task force of collections librarians had to decide what collections to turn on in the expansive Primo Central index provided by Ex Libris. The Primo development group worked to customize the search tool to the specifications

identified by the task force who had earlier reviewed all of the discovery products.

The Primo development group, with the help of instructional services librarians, conducted a series of workshops during the summer of 2012 to introduce Primo to the rest of the Libraries' staff. During these sessions, librarians were asked to search Primo for specific topics and provide feedback on their results and ask questions. The development group took copious notes and made changes based on the feedback they heard from Libraries' staff who attended the workshops. Finally, Primo went public at the start of the fall semester 2013.

The promise of Primo was that it would allow users to search a Google-like search box and then provide facets that would help users narrow their search by peer-reviewed journal articles, format, date ranges, and more. Primo offers suggested new searches and the ability to access full-text and images. If an item is available in Voyager, users can check the availability and location, recall the item if it is checked out, and use the retrieval system to have the book pulled from the shelf and put on hold for them at a circulation desk.

Much to the chagrin of the development group, many librarians complained bitterly that the resource was not what they had anticipated. Librarians did not understand that Primo is not a federated search tool like ENCompass or 360 Search, but it is actually searching the large Primo Central index. Usability testing was conducted with students and Libraries staff. Students were mostly satisfied with the results they received when searching Primo, but Libraries staff were not as accepting. The negative sentiments kept some librarians from promoting Primo in the classroom and to individual users.

In the meantime, the development group continued to seek out input from collections, instruction, and reference staff to make improvements to Primo. Content was added to Primo Central on a regular basis and Ex Libris scheduled multiple upgrades. Upgrades included a browse search, which greatly improved known item searching and title searching, and the ability to search by ISBN, ISSN, OCLC code, and publisher, which were not included in the original version of Primo. Users can now "shelf browse," which enables them to view the books in call number order that surround a book they discovered using Primo. The capabilities of Primo have improved greatly since it was made public a year ago, but the development group continues to encounter problems and bugs that must be fixed.

The development group also monitors the usage of Primo and has watched this usage gradually increase over time. By monitoring Google Analytics in Primo, they have been able to make improvements based on what links and facets are being used most. One of the most recent improvements to Primo is the ability to search for database titles in the Articles and Databases tab. Previously, this search limited the user to searching for articles only, but after the developers exported the Databases A-Z list into this search, users can now search for database titles and get a link to the database in the results.

The Survey Instrument

In order to gain even more information to make improvements, the authors of this paper decided to design a survey that would provide feedback from their librarian colleagues. The survey was designed as a comparison of searching in Primo to searching in Google Scholar and favorite subject databases. Librarians were given a known item search and a topic search and were asked to compare their results, provide positive feedback, and provide suggestions for improvement to Primo. Then they were asked to search their favorite subject database for a typical topic in their subject area and compare their results to their experiences with the other resources. The results that follow identified more ideas for improving Primo.

Results

Known Item Search

Librarians were asked to compare the results of Primo and Google Scholar when conducting a search for "Tennessee Williams—A Streetcar Named Desire." Four of the searchers expressed a preference for Primo, citing the better

facets/delimiters available in Primo. For this known item search, one participant preferred Google Scholar. Two of the librarians expressed no preference. Three of the searchers indicated that they typically would not have used Primo or Google Scholar for such a search, but would have selected either the online catalog or Google Books.

The authors crafted this known item search to be deliberately vague. They did not specify whether participants were meant to find a copy of the play itself or criticisms of the play. The intention behind this was to allow for the greatest flexibility in the search. Many of the librarians reported that they were surprised by the range found in the results. Indeed, one searcher reported a number of results that were related to musical versions, leading to the concern that this might mislead a novice student into thinking that the play was a musical. Another searcher noted that none of the first ten results linked to the actual play, but rather literary criticisms and scholarly articles about the play. These ranges of results were reported when using both Primo and Google Scholar, and may have contributed to the preference for Primo's results, since Primo offers superior facets and delimiters to further narrow the search. Several of the searchers reported using the facets to narrow down the results and ultimately find a copy of the play.

> "My first reaction to these results is that they are probably less useful to most undergraduates who might be doing a search on both Primo and Google Scholar. The Primo results look to be a) almost immediately useful, and b) less scholarly. I would add that Primo allows more options along the left side for refining the search."

And

> "In comparing the two searches, I would feel somewhat frustrated that I did not locate the play 'A Streetcar Named Desire' easily in either search interface. However, in the Primo search, I did eventually get a call number and location after narrowing by format, then by author. In the Google Scholar, I never did find a digitized version."

Prescribed Search

Using Primo and Google Scholar, librarians were asked to compare and rank the first ten results for the topic: treatment for attention deficit disorder. The searchers were asked to rank the first ten results of both searches, with a ranking of 1 being the most relevant and a ranking of 5 being not relevant at all. For overall averages, Google Scholar scored 2.13 and Primo 2.69.

Seven of the searchers of the prescribed search preferred the results found in Google Scholar, although often this appeared to be a slight preference, which is reflected in the rankings. One searcher wrote:

> "With respect to ADD, both were relevant and useful in their own ways. The top ten Primo results were more recent, but the top Google Scholar results perhaps got at the topic better."

Two of the participants preferred the results found in Primo, with one searcher noting that the facets/delimiters in Primo made the results similar to those found in Google Scholar.

> "I believe that Google Scholar gave a better concentration of relevant items. I did not use the facets to improve the results until I read this question [Please describe any changes you made to get better results]. When I eliminated reviews, newspaper articles, AV, etc., the results were more on a par with Google Scholar."

Some of the searchers created more advanced searches for this prescribed search. One searcher, searching Primo, did a subject search for "attention deficit disorder" coupled with a keyword search of "treatment," and limited the results to the last 20 years. In Google Scholar, the searcher did "attention deficit disorder" as an exact phrase search in the advanced search feature, combined with "therapy, treatment" in the "with at least one of the words" field, and also limited the results to the last 20 years. The searcher reported a slight preference for the results found in Google Scholar.

Several of the searchers expressed frustration with the high number of duplications found in the Primo results.

Searchers were also asked to share three positive comments and three suggestions for improvement in Primo. A number of the positive comments remarked upon the benefits of the facets and filtering options. A typical comment was: "I like the filtering options for Primo and that you get different types of media. I also like that you can use the browse-the-shelf feature."

Primo searches over 110,000 journals, KU Libraries' catalog, digital images, and open access research from KU ScholarWorks. One searcher noted:

> "I am always surprised at what Primo produces. I would NOT rely on it as a primary search tool but it can be useful in coming up with information resources one might not have actually thought to seek, or added resources of potentially tangential interest."

One of the more common concerns voiced by librarians has to do with an uncertainty about what information is being indexed in Primo, particularly regarding wanting to know which databases are searched in a Primo search. This concern was addressed in one of the comments:

> "I'm never certain what universe I'm looking at in Primo . . . Also, as a commercial database, it is subject to market influences. What's in there today is not necessarily going to be there tomorrow, depending on what info has been licensed for inclusion."

Suggested improvements were more varied, with comments about relevancy ranking and duplication elimination. Others noted more specific areas for improvement, such as:

> "When a result points to multiple 'versions' of something, they're often completely different things (movie vs. book vs. translation), so I'm not sure that collapsing them into one result makes sense since a user might glance at the first 'version' presented in the results list and think that all the 'versions' would be movies, etc."

Subject-Specific Database Search

Participants were asked to search for resources in their favorite subject-specific database using a typical research question in their subject areas. They were then asked to rank each for relevance on a 1-5 scale, with 1 being most relevant and 5 not being relevant at all. One searcher gave the subject-specific database an overall rank in the 3 range. Two of the librarians' overall ranking for the subject-specific database was in the 2 range. The remaining participants all ranked their favorite subject-specific database results in the 1 range. They were then asked to discuss their reactions to the results from each resource: Primo, Google Scholar, and favorite subject-specific database. They were further asked to identify which resource gave the best results. And finally, the participants were asked whether there was anything outstanding about the resources to note.

Six of the searchers preferred the subject-specific database results over any they had found in Primo or Google Scholar. One of the participants noted:

> "I think it is clear that using the proper subject database is much more effective IF you have an idea of what you need to retrieve AND realize that kind of question needs a sophisticated, built-over-time tool."

Several of the searchers clarified that they did not find useful results in any of the databases, indicating that an online catalog would have been the resource most appropriate for the research need.

> "I wasn't happy with the results with any of these three sources—[humanities database], Primo, and Google Scholar. There are obviously very little contemporary articles on this subject, so it would be necessary to go to other sources, including the online catalog."

One participant expressed surprise at the quality of the results in Primo.

> "I was surprised that Primo compared more favorably than Google Scholar for the prescribed searches in 1 & 2. I still got the best search results by going to my subject-

specific database to search for materials on a typical topic for [the discipline]."

Another searcher had the opposite experience:

> "I found Primo to be frustrating to use. There were many duplicates which decreased efficiency and the results were less relevant and less scholarly when compared to using Google Scholar."

Recommendations and Conclusions

One of the most common complaints among the librarians who took the survey was too many duplicated results. This is an issue that Ex Libris continues to work on and hopefully, a future upgrade will take care of this problem. Collection librarians may be able to alleviate this problem to some degree by turning off some of the duplicative content available in Primo Central.

The librarians are still not satisfied with the relevancy ranking of Primo results, even though there has been much improvement since Primo was first introduced and Ex Libris and the KU development team continue to make tweaks that will improve results in the future.

The survey will be most beneficial to the development group by serving as a benchmark. Developers can use the search terms from the survey in Primo after upgrades and compare their results to those in the surveys to find out if the upgrade improved the results.

Finally, the results from the surveys drove home the need to educate the librarians and engage them in using Primo on a regular basis. After becoming so accustomed to federated search tools, KU librarians are having a hard time understanding that Primo does not provide a federated search. Librarians continually ask for a list of what Primo is searching, expecting to get list of databases, but databases are the smallest number of resources that Primo is searching. The Primo Central index provides content from individual publishers, scholarly societies, institutional repositories, and local collections. A better understanding of what Primo is searching will help librarians understand their search results. Primo is a good resource for discovering local collections, so educating librarians to use Primo for searching special collections, digitized local collections, archives, and image collections should improve overall support of Primo.

Mobile Access—What the Library Wants: Mobiles as Discovery Enhancers

Laura Horton, Global Library Communications Manager, Taylor & Francis Group
Presented by Stacy Sieck, Library Communications Manager, Americas Region at Taylor & Francis Group

Abstract

Library users now expect to be able to access academic content at any time from any location—not just in the library on a computer, but on their mobile phones, tablets, e-readers, and other mobile devices. Taylor & Francis surveyed 139 individuals to discover how use mobiles are used in a library setting, how publishers can help with content discovery in the library and which mobile functionalities are considered important. Taylor & Francis found that 78% of respondents rated mobile integration to find resources as important.

Publishing has changed dramatically over the last decade, making the shift from print to electronic. From online publishing, publishers moved to the need for digitizing archival content and finally to the phenomena of open content, enhancing discoverability of our platforms, making content accessible via mobile, and the use of social media to promote content, all of which suddenly became top priority for both publishers and librarians.

The following case study from Temple University explores the end-user approach to what professors and researchers need and want from the library. Laura Katz Rizzo, Director of the Dance BFA Program in the Esther Boyer College of Music and Dance at Temple University, has noticed a significant increase in student use of digital and mobile documents and applications in accessing material from the library and other research databases for both scholarly and research work in class and in performance.

Various strategies in use by publishers include creating a contained application native to a specific operating system (native app), developing an alternate web site that automatically launches when any mobile device is detected (mobile site), and developing journal web sites that resize when a mobile device is detected (responsive design). To determine the prevalence and functionality of these various strategies, top Library and Information Science journals were examined. It was discovered that responsive web design is the most popular strategy. Advantages and disadvantages of each strategy is described, and each strategy's impact on the user experience is explored.

Survey Research Objectives and Demographics

The specific research objectives of the Taylor & Francis Mobile survey were:

- To understand how individuals are using mobiles in an academic and library setting.

- To determine how publishers can help with discovery in the library through mobile use.

- To know which mobile functionalities are considered important and which features add value to the library.

Of 139 survey respondents, 49% were students, 38% were academics, 7% were practitioners, and 6% were librarians.

Survey Results

The survey results show the overwhelming use of mobile for accessing content, with 85% of respondents using their mobile devices at least once a week. This highlights the importance for publishers and librarians to make their content accessible by this avenue.

The popularity of mobile use may be linked to the fact that mobiles allow constant access to content. 78% of survey respondents stated how important it is that they have access to library content off site. Only 6% of individuals felt that it was either "not at all important" or of "low importance."

One respondent shared, "Having access to content in locations when you have time to spare creates more time for looking at content, and finding relevant information for research and teaching." Another respondent stated, "I can read while I am on public transportation or in bed, right before I sleep. Therefore, I gain in matter of time and comfort."

The survey results reveal that mobiles are used for multiple purposes in the library. Over 76% of respondents stated that they use mobile for searching and reading online content. 65% of respondents download content to read later and 31% use mobiles to view reading lists.

Search functionality was revealed as the most important feature of mobiles, with only 1% of respondents feeling it was "not at all important." 92% of people thought it was of high or extreme importance to a mobile, showcasing how mobile is very much a discovery enhancer tool.

Other uses of mobile voted of high importance were "journal browsing," which 63% of respondents chose as "extremely important" or of "high importance" and "saving to favorites," voted as "extremely important" or of "high importance" by 55% of respondents. Functionalities such as "also read" and "sharing of articles via email and social media" were deemed less important, with just 40% of respondents voting "also read" as "extremely important" or of "high importance" and 26% viewing "sharing articles via social media" as "extremely important" or of "high importance."

The survey results show the importance of mobile technology for end users globally in discovering content, and the importance of having a mobile policy in libraries which enables users to gain access to academic content when they need it.

Conclusion

The Taylor & Francis Mobile survey shows that library users utilize mobile devices to view reading lists, download content to read later, and search

for and read online content. These results highlight the fact that people use mobiles to fulfil more than one need. The mobile functionalities deemed most important are search functionality, journal browse and saving to favorites.

With the discovery that 85% of survey respondents use their mobile devices at least once a week, it is clear that publishers and librarians must make their content accessible through mobile.

The End User: Temple University Case Study

Laura Katz Rizzo, Assistant Professor and BFA Program Coordinator, Esther Boyer College of Music and Dance, Temple University

Dr. Katz Rizzo states, "In order to reach out to the student populations that I teach as well as the increasingly online world of scholarly and creative research communities, I have had to learn how to incorporate these mobile access points into my teaching and into my own research processes and portfolio building activities . . . I have found I must utilize mobile apps and online material to engage dance majors, facilitating the completion of their research assignments in required courses."

Temple University has a nationally significant Dance Collection housing the documents of major dance companies in Philadelphia. The Temple Collection is searchable through mobile apps and devices, and students use it for research projects required for their dance history class. The institution's special librarian devoted to Music and Dance has created guides for each department in the College and visits classes to teach students how to use digital processes to search, save, and cite digitized materials in the library's collections.

Senior Seminar is a senior capstone writing class in which students articulate their comprehensive knowledge (summarizing the majority of their curricular work over the past three and a half years) and use this knowledge to develop a sense of where they want to go after graduation and how to create digital portfolios housed on websites that they can use in marketing themselves in the wider dance field. They must build a digital portfolio that includes an artistic vision/mission statement, teaching philosophy, video reel, photographs, CV, business cards, logo, and a website that houses all of this information.

Temple University's General Education Program has stringent requirements for course proposals that ensure that all approved courses in a specific area address not only the larger general education learning goals, but also the learning goals for each area, whether it be Quantitative Literacy, Race and Diversity, World Society, or Science and Technology. The course encourages both information literacy and critical thinking in engagement with mobile resources on the part of students. Students research the companies they will see through their online profiles on Facebook and Twitter, as well as library resources including video databases, the online dance encyclopedia, and other online research guides. Part of the course involves deciphering differences in how an artist is represented on their website, on Facebook, in newspaper reviews and in scholarly dance research.

In writing her latest book, *Dancing the Fairy Tale*, Dr. Katz Rizzo used mobile applications to research the specific details of dance and other cultural productions as well as other important events affecting the context in which these productions took place (Philadelphia). This included online research guides and catalogs as well as social media groups and the websites of performance venues and other important landmarks and cultural institutions.

The Society of Dance History Scholars, Congress on Research in Dance, Popular Culture Association, CORPS de Ballet, International, National Dance Education Organization, American Ballet Theatre, National Choreographic Competition, and Jacobs Pillow all have online presences including archival material, blogs, Facebook and Twitter pages, blog feeds, and relationships with libraries housing special collections of content important to these organizations and their specific missions. Temple's Library directs users to different blogs and archives, as well as research grants in special areas.

Conclusion

The survey results and the case study from Temple University showcase that due to the nature of mobile, the library is also becoming mobile in nature. The library is no longer one physical location, and mobile devices are popular discovery enhancement tools that enable users to access library content from any location, at any time.

Should There Be an App for That? Scholarly Journals on Mobile Devices

Linda Wobbe, MLIS, Head, Collection Management, Saint Mary's College of California

Background

Academic library users want library resources on their mobile devices. Surveys show 80% of college students own smart phones. A Ball State University survey finds 89% of their students own smart phones (Ransford, 2014). The Pew Research Internet Project Mobile Technology Fact Sheet (2014) reports 83% of the 18-29 age group owns smart phones. An annual survey conducted for Pearson (2014) by the Harris Poll concludes that 75% of high school students have smart phones and 42% use tablets. Pew (2014) reports tablets are owned by 42% of adults.

Students report interest in using their mobile devices for conducting library research (Barnett-Ellis & Vann, 2014; Caniano & Catalano, 2014). Libraries have implemented mobile sites and developed or purchased mobile catalogs. But libraries don't control the mobile sites of scholarly content. Schmidt (2013) offers a critique of carefully designed mobile library sites connecting to the widely varied mobile publishing strategies offered by publishers.

Options for delivery of mobile content. In 2011, mobile apps for databases and journals were released (Burns & Rofofsky, 2011; Hawkins, 2011; Kaser, 2011, Krishnan, 2011). While thousands of individual journal apps exist, dedicated apps must be designed for every operating system, which would be an enormous undertaking (Clark, 2012).

Alternatives to native apps include mobile sites and responsive design.

Study

This investigation used library and information technology journals to identify the omobile options in use by publishers. To determine a list of journals to test, highly regarded journals (Manzari, 2013; Nixon, 2014), and highly cited journals (Nixon, 2014; Xia, 2012) were reviewed. Widely distributed journals were determined using *Gale Directory of Publications and Broadcast Media* (2014). The top 25 journals from these studies were investigated to determine the availability of mobile apps, mobile sites, or responsive design. Testing devices were an iPhone 4S, and and iPad mini.

Journals Investigated and Results

1. *American Libraries*—American Library Association—0002-9769 **(c)**

2. *Annual Review of Information Science and Technology*—Information today/Wiley– 0066-4200 **(c)**

3. *Aslib Journal of Information Management*—Emerald—2050-3806 **(b)**

4. *Chronicle of Higher Education*—Chronicle of Higher Education—0009-5982 **(a)**

5. *College & Research Libraries*—Association of College and Research Libraries—0010-0870 **(a-BrowZine open access content)**

6. *College & Research Libraries News*—Association of College and Research Libraries/Highwire—0099-0086 **(b)**

7. *Collection Management*—Routledge/Taylor & Francis—0146-2679 **(b)**

8. *D—Lib Magazine: The Magazine of Digital Library Research*—1082-9873 **(c)**

9. *Government Information Quarterly*—Elsevier—0740-624X **(c)**

10. *Information Processing and Management*—Elsevier—0306-4573 **(c)**

11. *The Journal of Academic Librarianship*—Pergamon—0099-1333 **(c)**

12. *Journal of Computer-Mediated Communication*—Wiley—1083-6101 **(c)**

13. *Journal of Documentation*—Emerald—0022-0418 **(b)**

14. *Journal of Information Science*—SAGE—0165-5515 **(b)**

15. *Journal of Medical Internet Research*—1438-8871 **(b)**

16. *Journal of the Association for Information Science and Technology (JASIST)*– John Wiley—2330-1635 **(a)**

17. *Journal of the Medical Library Association*—Medical Library Association/PubMed—1536-5050 **(b)**

18. *Library Collections, Acquisitions, and Technical Services*—Taylor & Francis—1464-9055 **(b)**

19. *Library & Information Science Research*—Pergamon/Elsevier—0740-8188 **(c)**

20. *Library Journal*—Library Journals—0363-0277 **(a)**

21. *Library Quarterly*—University of Chicago Press/JSTOR- 0024-2519 **(b)**

22. *Library Resources & Technical Services*—American Library Association—0024-2527 **(c)**

23. *Library Trends*—Johns Hopkins/Project MUSE– 0024-2594 **(c)**

24. *Libri: International Journal of Libraries and Information Services*—De Gruyter Saur—0024-2667 **(c)**

25. *Reference & User Services Quarterly*—American Library Association—2163-5242 **(c)**

Native Apps—16% (a). Four of the 25 journals investigated provide native apps. Two of the four apps are not available for iPhone, only iPads. BrowZine, a subscription app, is available for 76% of the journals studies. Android apps were not tested. ITunes apps allow for a sleek reading and browsing experience, although authentication can require a visit to the standard site. Sharing options that are standard on iPad's include printing, emailing, texting, or social media.

BrowZine: Available by subscription, or use the free app to access open-access content. Provides access to all but four of the top 25 titles; limited to scholarly journals. Exceptions are *American Libraries*, *Chronicle of Higher Education*, *College & Research Libraries News*, and *Library Journal.* BrowZine does not currently offer search.

Mobile Sites and Web Apps—36% (b). Nine of the 25 journals studied offer mobile sites. Most journals have both html and pdf article options. Pdf articles on iPads or iPhones are easy to read, or save to iBooks or Google Drive for other saving or sharing options, including print and email. HTML is more variable. On an iPad, HTML usually allows for social media sharing, as well as printing and email. Authentication can be achieved using standard authentication although vendor instructions describe a complicated pairing system requiring users to access the site on campus first to register. Pairing expires. Most versions are not optimized for the iPad mini. JSTOR's web app offers a link to "Get Access" using standard authentication for registered institutions.

Responsive Design—48% (c). Twelve of the 25 journals offer responsive design. You navigate to the regular site using standard authentication, and the site is altered depending on the device. Similar to the web apps, some sites have three sizes, one for each a smartphone, tablet, and computer. Small laptop screens, like a MacBook, are sometimes detected as tablets. A small tablet, such as an iPad mini, is sometimes detected as a smartphone. This results in some silly experiences, such as search results limited to 1/3 of the screen, which is unreadable on a mobile phone. Most are very difficult to read on an iPhone; exceptions are noted below.

American Library Association, MetaPress. Responsive design. Complicated registration process.

De Gruyter Saur. Responsive design renders reasonably well on both iPhone and iPad.

Mobile Problems

Authentication. With native apps and some mobile sites, authentication can involve a complicated pairing system that expires in a few months.

Device recognition. Mobile-recognition strategies are unable to meet the needs of the wide variety of devices available.

Full site. W3C's basic guidelines (2008) state that a link back to the full site should be utilized on all mobile apps and optimized sites. Unfortunately, the link back to the full site is often difficult to locate or not available on scholarly publisher sites.

Accessibility. A website designed according to standards for a mobile device can serve as a way to improving accessibility for all users. W3C (2009) provides a cross-walk between the two standards to highlight what needs to be done whether you already have an accessible site, or you already have a mobile site. iPads and iPhones have an array of built-in accessibility features (Baga, 2012).

Sharing. Both iPhones and iPads have sharing options built in, and every mobile site can be bookmarked, every pdf article can be shared through many social media options, emailed, printed, or saved to iBooks.

Communicating to users. There is no systematic approach to informing users of mobile options. Trott & Jackson (2013) found that 87% of 99 ARL Libraries' lists of databases had no information about mobile database apps or interfaces. Some creative approaches to this problem exist. Watkins, Battles, & Vacek (2013) report the development of a Drupal system to display an identifier for databases that are most suitable for mobile devices. The University of California California Digital Library support policy (2010) abdicates responsibility for providing assistance, and says "the user expectation must be set that use of non-mobile-optimized interfaces is unknown territory, and . . . these sites may have problems with access, display, and performance."

However, CDL notes that the greatest difficulty with mobile sites is authentication.

Conclusion

Each solution presents suboptimal user experience. Native apps provide authentication challenges. BrowZine, an app that provides access to almost all the journals investigated is subscription-based and does not offer search. Mobile sites do not render well on all devices, and present authentication challenges. Responsive design, the most frequently used strategy, uses standard authentication, but is not optimized for all devices.

References

Baga, J. (2012). E-resource round up: Emerging technology as assistive technology: Conference report. *Journal Of Electronic Resources Librarianship*, *24*(1), 46-48. http://dx.doi.org/10.1080/1941126X.2012.657108

Barnett-Ellis, P., & Vann, C. (2014). The library right there in my hand: Determining user needs for mobile services at a medium-sized regional university. *Southeastern Librarian*, *62*(2), 10-15. Retrieved from OmniFile Full Text Mega database.

Burns, R., & Rofofsky Marcus, S. (2011). EBSCOhost mobile. *Reference Librarian*, *52*(1/2), 190-196. http://dx.doi.org/10.1080/02763877.2011.527813

Caniano, W., & Catalano, A. (2014). Academic libraries and mobile devices: User and reader preferences. *Reference Librarian*, *55*(4), 298-317. http://dx.doi.org/10.1080/02763877.2014.929910

CDL mobile support policy for CDL licensed resources (2010). Retrieved October 3 from http://www.cdlib.org/services/collections/mobile.html

Clark, J. A. (2012). *Building mobile library applications*. New York: Neal-Schuman. Retrieved from ebrary database.

Gale directory of publications and broadcast media (2014). (150th ed.). Detroit: Gale. Retrieved from Gale Directory Library database.

Hawkins, L. (2011). New product news. *Public Libraries*, *50*(5), 52-55. Retrieved from Education Full Text database.

Kaser, D. (2011). Behind the lens: Show us your app. *Information Today*, *28*(5), 3. Retrieved from Business Source Complete database.

Krishnan, Y. (2011). Libraries and the mobile rev. *Computers In Libraries*, *31*(3), 6-40. Retrieved from Business Source Complete database.

Manzari, L. (2013). Library and information science journal prestige as assessed by library and information science faculty. *The Library Quarterly: Information, Community, Policy*, *83*, (1), 42-60. http://dx.doi.org/10.1086/668574

Nixon, J. M. (2014). Core journals in library and information science: Developing a methodology for ranking LIS journals. *College & Research Libraries*, *75*(1), 66-90. http://dx.doi.org/10.5860/crl12-387

Pearson (2014). *Pearson student mobile device survey, 2014*. Retrieved November 28, 2014, from http://Pearson-K12-Student-Mobile-Device-Survey-050914-PUBLIC-Report.pdf

Pew research internet project. (2014). *Mobile technology fact sheet*. Retrieved October 29, 2014, from http://www.pewinternet.org/fact-sheets/mobile-technology-fact-sheet/

Ransford, M. (2014). *Study: College students not embracing tablets as originally predicted*. Retrieved October 3, 2014 from http://cms.bsu.edu/news/articles/2014/4/students-can-live-without-tablets-but-not -smartphones

Schmidt, A. (2013). The mobile challenge. *Library Journal*, *138*(8), 19. Retrieved from Literature Resource Center database.

Trott, B., & Jackson, R. (2013). Mobile academic libraries. *Reference & User Services Quarterly*, *52*(3), 174-178. Retrieved from Academic Source Complete database.

Watkins, S., Battles, J., & Vacek, R. (2013). Streamlining data for cross-platform web delivery. *Journal Of Web Librarianship*, *7*(1), 95-108. http://dx.doi.org/10.1080/19322909.2013.748393

W3C (2008). *Mobile web best practices: Basic guidelines.* Retrieved October 3, 2014 from http://www.w3.org/TR/mobile-bp/

W3C (2009). From WCAG 2.0 to MWBP: Making content that meets web content accessibility guidelines 2.0 also meet mobile web best practices. Retrieved October 3, 2014 from http://www.w3.org/TR/mwbp -wcag/wcag20-mwbp.html

W3C (2010). *MobileOK checker, version 1.4.2.* Retrieved October 3, 2014 from http://validator.w3.org /mobile/

W3C (2104). *Standards for web applications on mobile: Current state and roadmap.* Retrieved October 29, 2014 from http://www.w3.org/Mobile/mobile-web-app-state/

Xia, J. (2012). Positioning open access journals in a LIS journal ranking. *College & Research Libraries*, *73*(2), 134-145. http://dx.doi.org/10.5860/crl-234

Management and Administration

Cost Impact in Managing the Transition to an Open Access Model

Gayle R. Chan, Head of Collections, University of Hong Kong

Abstract

Open access to scholarly resources is a growing dimension in the universe of scholarly communication. The impact of open access on the traditional model of acquisition and access is just beginning to surface. In managing the transitioning toward open access, libraries will benefit from the model of use analytics developed by the collection development team at HKU to rationalize the value of library investment and to refine collection priorities for the future development of the collections and budget. This paper will discuss the collection building strategies of my university to tackle the major challenges in managing the transition to open access model. In particular, I will focus on the analytics employed to evaluate the use and cost impact of e-journal big deals within an open access environment. The shift to open access of scholarly contents, which is a critical component in the research process, must be prudently managed in keeping down the total costs of ownership. The cost impact of open access must be factored into the big picture in developing new pricing models for greater optimization of resources and budget.

Addressing the Challenges

Today we face a big challenge of sustainability in a world of open knowledge. Decisions on what contents to buy and retain have become highly complex under the constraint of a flat recurrent base budget. The impact of the mass digitized environment and the shift to the open access movement in scholarly communication further exacerbate the complexities in the way libraries develop and acquire collections and knowledge resources. Moreover, there is huge cost impact on scholarly contents and for all stakeholders, researchers, libraries, and publishers, in managing the transition to open access.

From the library's perspective, the larger initiatives undertaken at the University of Hong Kong (HKU) include partnering with publishers to further explore and develop new models of access and acquisitions to support broader research needs. Our libraries have gradually moved from a "just in case" strategy to a "just in time" approach in recent years, toward increasing on-demand purchasing and investments in evidence based model access in order to broaden access limited by ownership and making more effective use of library funds. Aggregated models that incorporate on-demand content licensing and purchasing contents in multiple formats for mobile access to increase use and value are being implemented. Recognizing the limits of ownership, strategies include support to strengthen and enrich the knowledge base of born digital materials such as open access repositories, both institution and discipline based. On a collaborative front, we work with local and international consortiums in purchasing digital resources to leverage our expertise and use of funds. No library can afford to be comprehensive but to embrace a model that ensures broadened access to complement ownership of scholarly materials.

In addressing the challenge to bring the broadest and most current print, digital, and media contents to our users under the constraints of a flat recurrent budget and cost increases that outstrip funding, library decisions on what to buy and retain have begun to shift toward evidence-based model. Libraries and institutions face additional challenge when the tipping point was reached in open access with over 50% of new research published in 2011 made freely available, either in green or gold (European Commission 2013). Morrison emphasized that "prudent transition of academic library budgets from support for subscriptions journals to support for open access publishing will be key to a successful transition to open access" (Morrison, 2013). Libraries as well as stakeholders including funders, universities, researchers, and publishers need to understand the concerns with issues in investment and budget to manage this transition. This paper will discuss the collection building strategies of The University of Hong Kong (HKU) to tackle the major challenges in managing the transition to open access. In particular, I will focus on the analytics employed to evaluate the use and cost impact of e-journal big deals within an open access environment.

An Open Access (OA) Research Environment

The European Commission issued a press release in August 2013 announcing that half of the research published worldwide in 2011 was now available for free after an embargo of a year. The tipping point signifies a point of no return in open access of published research. The study reported that several countries and research areas in the general science and technology, biomedical research, biology, and math and statistics have reached the tipping point, that is, "more than 50% of the papers published 2011 are available for free" (Archambault et al., 2013). The new research published made available free online is a diversified mix of green or self-archiving, and gold and hybrid (pay per article for OA release), subject to publishers' open access policies. Laakso used the SHERPA RoMEO database to inform that 80% of accepted articles indexed in Scopus are green OA, that is, allowed to be uploaded in an institutional repository within 12 months of publication (Laakso, 2014). The OA policies of "the majority of 48 major science funders considered both key forms of OA acceptable, and more than 75% accepted embargo periods of 6 to 12 months." The European Commission mandates all research supported by funding from Horizon 2020 to be made open access from 2014 (European Commission, 2013).

Lewis's prediction that open access is a disruptive innovation which will replace the established subscription-based journals is informed by the S-curve pattern of growth (Lewis, 2012). He projected that the pace of substitution of gold OA for traditional subscription models will accelerate to "50% by 2017-21 and 90% by 2020-25," thereby suggesting a radical shift in the scholarly publishing in the next decade (Lewis, 2013). This development is attributed to the dramatic growth in mega-journals which began with PLOS ONE in

2006. Binfield extrapolated the growth of megajournals to reach 75,000 articles in 2013, which is approximately 8% of all STM article output (Binfield, 2013). The Open Access Scholarly Publishers Association (OASPA) concurrently reported that almost 400,000 articles have been published since 2000, and 120,972 of these were published in 2013 (OASPA, 2013). It is clear that by 2013 the transition from the journal subscription model to open access model was well underway, with progressively new funding model successfully implemented, such as SCOAP3 and arXiv, which are both supported by crowd funding directly from leading research institutions.

The impact of open access is significant when you consider the lowering cost model of open access. The subscription cost model is challenged by the Open Journal Systems ranging from US$188 up to US$5000 for hybrid journal article (Morrison, 2013). Sutton argues that the "costs associated with online distribution of articles have and will continue to fall to the point that the marginal cost of adding additional users is practical zero . . . zero is inevitable" (Sutton, 2011). In spite of the lower production and marketing costs, major funders spend significant amounts to support various open access models. In 2012/13 Wellcome Trust spent 6.5M on author publication charges, covering 2127 articles at an average cost of $3055 per article, in both hybrid and open access journals. The top scholarly publishers benefitting from APC spending were Elsevier, Wiley, Springer, and Oxford University Press. What Wellcome bought include many hybrid articles with 12-month embargoes to make them free early. Funders support no doubt boosted the income of publishers of hybrid journals.

Rationalizing Budgets and Resources

The developments in open access, government mandates, lower cost, new cost models, and increased access by research communities raise questions of value for libraries seeking to optimize scholarly resources and budgets. Within an emerging open access environment, it is crucial to examine and recognize the impact on library subscriptions to rationalize investment. Cost and use data of a core publisher's big deal are analyzed to inform the distribution of use, cost effectiveness, and collection priorities to enable our library to justify and optimize the value of our subscriptions. Data analyzed include the contents of a core publisher's big deal license, aggregated use, license fee, cost per article download, and the distribution of use. The findings are considered in the context of the changing research environment and the universe of publication to illustrate the ongoing transition toward open access of scholarly resources.

Our study findings show significant increase in the cost of scholarly articles resulting from a marked decline in "bundled" contents and aggregated use of a typical big deal e-journal licensed package. There is evidence to suggest that the decline in use of subscribed e-journal contents may be due to gravitation toward use of similar contents in open access journals. The development of a framework to evaluate the cost impact in an open access environment has enabled our library to rationalize our investment and to make budget decisions in an informed way.

The typical bundle has become something less than the publisher's complete list. As much as 16% of the titles are excluded, which suggests some inadequacy in our contents acquisition over time (Figure 1). Publisher's explanation is that certain society or proprietary titles do not grant the rights for inclusion in a big deal. Incidentally, it is found that this publisher now publishes 9% of its journal output in open access under the APC model. Moreover, the majority of subscription titles are hybrid that charge an optional author fees for immediate open access. It is observed that "big deal" is not everything, excluding niche areas, subject series, proceedings, and emerging research that are not covered, but which compete for funding support.

Our review of aggregated use data reveals a falling trend in 2013 usage compared with 2012. Overall use declined by as much as 19% and 23% respectively according to the latest COUNTER JR1 and JR5 reports for the latest two years (Figure 2). Whereas JR1 informs total full-text article

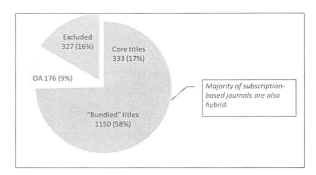

Figure 1. A "Big Deal" as a percent of publisher's journal output.

requests by use period at the journal level, JR5 reporting by year-of-publication reflects the use of current contents being subscribed that year, and serves better justification for return on investment. The cost per article download derived from JR5 use report against the annual license fee reflects a more realistic costing. For 2013 the cost per use represented 38% increase at the cost of US$22 per article cost, which is very substantial, despite broader and more diverse access to e-journal contents in the big deal (Figure 3).

To put value into perspective, the publisher has not exactly fulfilled the big deal cost model of the big deal by providing access to all of its contents. As we know the big deal is subject to an annual increase locked in by a multiyear license that guarantees the % of increase in the price model. Continued rising license fee, per article download at US$22, and overall lesser contents are causes to raise concerns and questions in the value of big deals. Furthermore, COUNTER JR1 GOA reveals that 4.5% of the aggregated usage comes from gold OA articles for which publication charges have been paid and by authors, funders or institutions.

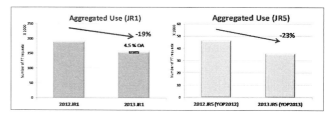

Figure 2. Aggregated use—JR1 & JR5.

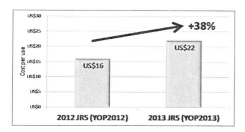

Figure 3. Increase of cost per use.

Changes in academic direction reflect changing needs and collection priorities. Acquisition models should enable the library to develop a robust collection with the opportunity to opt out of marginal titles as necessary in times of retrenchment. A distribution curve is useful to measure the level of overall use as well as to identify the high demand areas versus the marginal contents. The core collection no doubt attracts higher average per title than the bundled titles as suggested by the bell shape curve. The majority of core titles attracted medium range use. In contrast, the bundled collection use results in a sliding curve, with a vast majority of titles in the low use range attracting zero or marginal (Figure 4). The long-tail analysis shows the marginal value of niche areas, which the publisher sells more of less (expected use). Study findings show 66% of the core collection titles attracted marginal use at less than once per week or less than 42 uses in a year (Figure 5). To optimize value, a library in consultation with the faculty may target cancellation to channel resources to collection priorities identified. When our library was faced with a flat budget base, the library used the analytics to inform how we might target a reduction of 15% over a three-year period with annual inflation of 5% to keep the budget flat.

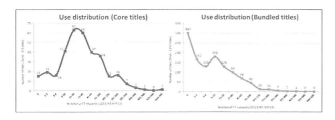

Figure 4. Use distribution—core and bundled.

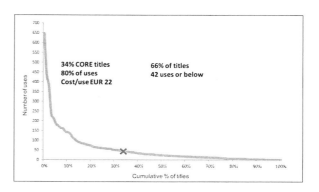

Figure 5. The long-tail analysis shows the marginal value of niche areas.

Open Access Impacts Use and Cost

Open access is a growing dimension in the universe of scholarly communication. The impact of open access in the use and cost of traditional model of acquisition and access is just beginning to surface. In managing the transitioning toward open access, libraries will benefit from the model of use analytics developed by the Collection Development team at HKU to rationalize the value of library investment and to refine collection priorities for the future development of the collections and budget. The analytics enable the library to see beyond the aggregated use of subscribed journal contents to recognize the impact of open access.

The most significant finding of the recent study is the evidence of decline in the use of core journal titles resulting in a substantial increase in cost per article download. This may be evidence that journal usage is gravitating toward high growth open contents that are free and accessible in the research arena. Another significant finding is the use of open access articles within a licensed big deal. Though the total download of open access articles at 4.5% of the total publisher bundled contents is still quite low considering the number of hybrid journals available, publishers are expected to apply appropriate reductions from journal subscriptions in sync with author, funder, or institution contributions to avoid "double dipping". Publisher has yet to rationalize the hybrid income to lower subscription costs. The big deal based on historical print expenditures of past decades is not sustainable or justifiable when use decline and cost per article rises substantially.

Unbundling of big deals may not materialize soon due to complex logistics and politics. Libraries and publishers have to work in partnership to find sustainable pricing models that help libraries rationalize the impact of open access.

Libraries and their institutions must recognize that rechanneling of current budgets toward open access APC support is inevitable. HKU currently contributes to several OA programs to support authors who choose the OA route in their field. An overarching aim for academic research library is to strengthen ownership through deeper collaboration while addressing the limits of ownership. The shift to open access of scholarly contents, which is a critical component in the research process, must be prudently managed in keeping down the total costs of ownership and access. The cost impact of open access must be factored into the big picture in developing new pricing models for greater optimization of resources and budget.

References

Archambault, E., et al. (2013). *Proportion of open access peer-reviewed papers at the European and World Levels—2004–2011*. Retrieved from http://www.science-metrix.com/pdf/SM_EC_OA _Availability_2004-2011.pdf

Anderson, K. (2014). *Wellcome money—In this example of open access funding, the Matthew Effect dominates*. Retrieved from http://scholarlykitchen.sspnet.org/2014/03/21/wellcome-money-in-this -example-of-open-access-funding-the-matthew-effect-dominates/

Binfield, P. (2013). *Open access megajournals—Have they changed everything?* Retrieved from http://creativecommons.org.nz/2013/10/open-access-megajournals-have-they-changed-everything/

European Commission (2013). *Open access to research publications reaching 'tipping point'* (Press release). Retrieved from http://europa.eu/rapid/press-release_IP-13-786_en.htm

Laakso, M. (2014). Green open access policies of scholarly journal publishers: A study of what, when, and where self-archiving is allowed. *Scientometrics*. http://dx.doi.org/10.1007/s11192-013-1205-3

Lewis, D. W. (2012). The Inevitability of open access. *College & Research Libraries*, *73*(5), 493-506. Retrieved from http://hdl.handle.net/1805/2929

Lewis, D. W. (2013). *The inevitability of open access: Update one. Scholar works*. Retrieved from http://hdl.handle.net/1805/3471

Morrison, H. (2013). Economics of scholarly communication in transition. *First Monday*, *18*(6). Retrieved from http://firstmonday.org/ojs/index.php/fm/article/view/4370/3685

OASPA (2014). *Growth of fully OA journals using a CC-BY license*. Retrieved from http://oaspa.org/growth-of -fully-oa-journals-using-a-cc-by-license/

Research Europe (2013). *The tipping point? Half of all research results available publicly a year after publication is paralysis, not progress*. Retrieved from http://www.researchresearch.com/index.php ?articleId=1338072&option=com_news&template=rr_2col&view=article

Sutton, C. (2011). Is free inevitable in scholarly communication? The economics of open access. *College & Research Libraries News*, *72*(11), 642-645. Retrieved from http://crln.acrl.org/content/72/11/642.full

Serious Savings With Short-Term Loans

Erin L. Crane, E-Books Librarian, Jerry Falwell Library, Liberty University

Abstract

The Liberty University Jerry Falwell Library serves a student body of over 100,000 students, most of whom are enrolled in online programs. By necessity the library prioritizes electronic resources, and in recent years, it has begun to invest more heavily into e-books. In spring 2010 the library adopted a patron-driven acquisition (PDA) program with ebrary in an effort to better support the needs of the online students. The program was very successful, but as patrons became more comfortable with e-books and the online student population increased, costs also rose dramatically. In addition, the library had implemented an evidence-based method for additions to the patron-driven acquisition selection pool in fall 2012. This strategy added to the higher costs involved in running the program. In order to control the expenses in light of limited funds, the library decided to pilot short-term loans (STLs) in fall 2013. The pilot was very successful and resulted in significant cost avoidance. In fall 2014 the library included STLs as a standard fund in the budget. In the summer of 2014, however, STL prices were raised by some publishers, so the cost-effectiveness will need to be monitored.

Background

Liberty University, founded in 1971, began pioneering distance education in 1985. It is now the nation's largest private, nonprofit online educator. Of the University's over 100,000 students, more than 90,000 receive online instruction. These students are usually enrolled in one of the 187 degree programs Liberty University Online offers at the undergraduate, graduate, and doctoral levels. The demand for online resources for these students is enormous. The Jerry Falwell Library provides those resources, focusing more on e-books in recent years. The library also provides access to the physical collection through interlibrary loan, but the fast pace of many online classes (eight weeks) often does not allow for the shipping time. Online students are also mostly middle-aged, working full-time or have a family. These other demands on the students mean that many of them are working on assignments at the last minute, so interlibrary loaning physical books is not an option.

To respond to the need for scholarly books available online, the library began a pilot e-book patron-driven acquisitions (PDA) program through ebrary in 2010. While many libraries choose to pilot the program with a very small collection, the Jerry Falwell Library decided to immediately create a large collection of over 40,000 titles. To

better manage the e-book collections the library also hired an E-Books Librarian, Erin Crane, in the spring of 2011.

The library's philosophy of collection development, especially in terms of the PDA program, is to provide access to what is needed when it is needed. The priority is to provide access "just-in-time" rather than "just-in-case." The library does not intend to be a storehouse for scholarship in general like other larger research institutions might be. This philosophy is part of why the library emphasizes the patron-driven acquisition program in funding.

The library has also never limited the profiles to a small pool of publishers or subject areas. Some publishers have been excluded based on whether or not the content provided is academic, but otherwise many smaller publishers have been included. However, the Head of Collection Management at the time, Carl Merat, did determine that the scope of the profile should be limited in other ways. In the summer of 2011, a major weed of the profile was conducted which removed e-books with prices over $200 and publication dates earlier than the past 5 years. The first criterion was introduced to start controlling costs. The second was introduced to provide focus to the PDA program. Only the most recent publications would be added. This weed reduced the profile to approximately 15,000 e-books. To further narrow the scope, in the fall of 2012 a formula was created which would help predict potential usage of titles added to the PDA pool. This formula became the main method for selecting e-books to add to the profiles.

Goals

The library has multiple goals for the PDA program broadly and the STL program specifically. One of the goals is, of course, cost savings. However, "savings" is a misleading term which can frighten publishers. The library has a budget for e-books that it will spend one way or another. The hope is that the PDA program helps spend the library funds more effectively. The library would never purchase everything which it includes in the PDA profile. If PDA were no longer an option, the library would not purchase more than it had with the PDA program. The same amount of funds would simply be spent in a different way. Thus, while many librarians who discuss PDA programs and STLs use the term "savings," anything that is "saved" is spent on more e-books.

The goals of the PDA program are to:

1. Meet the information resource needs of the ever-increasing number of online programs and students.

2. Increase ROI by only purchasing titles with the most use.

3. Satisfy an institutional priority to create comparability between residential and online student experiences.

4. Fulfill institutional strategic plan objectives (the library's PDA program is actually delineated in the institution's strategic plan).

The goals of the STL program are to:

1. Decrease the overall cost the PDA program.

2. Further increase ROI by only purchasing titles which have received multiple triggers.

Context

Why Short-Term Loans?

As mentioned, in the fall of 2012 the E-Books Librarian and a colleague created a formula to predict the use of a potential batch of e-books for the PDA profile. Historical e-book use based on Library of Congress (LC) Classification was used to create a percentile rank for LC classes by the hundreds (BS300, BS400, etc.). The percentile rank indicates the likelihood that, given its LC class, the title will receive high use. When potential additions to the PDA profile are run through the formula, they are assigned the appropriate rank based on classification. Thousands of records were added in fall 2012 and spring 2013 based on this formula, though the E-Books Librarian also included e-books from YBP recommended lists. The predictions proved accurate, and the cost for the program grew to outpace the PDA program's first year, despite the fact that the pool of titles was now much smaller than the original pool. The program expenses increased beyond the limits of the budget. While in FY12 the cost for the program was $121,968, in FY13 it increased incredibly, by 138%, to $290,769. A correspondingly high increase in use occurred, with section requests (COUNTER Book Report 2) on ebrary rising by 182% from FY12 to FY13. Twice the library staff had to transfer a large amount of funds from the print book allocation to the e-book allocation in order to maintain the PDA program until the end of FY13.

Since the program effectively helped meet the needs of online students, the E-Books Librarian and the Head of Collection Management, now Rusty Tryon, did not consider ending the program even though the costs were high. As a large budget increase was unlikely, they assessed whether STLs could provide the cost savings necessary to continue the PDA program without decreasing the size of the profile. In fall 2013, the library began a pilot STL program with $25,000 allocated.

Implementation

Implementing an STL program with ebrary involves making a few decisions about the setup.

Libraries can choose to mediate PDA or STL programs, but the Jerry Falwell Library librarians have always left the PDA program unmediated. The STL program would also be unmediated. Ebrary also allows libraries to determine how many STLs to trigger before a purchase and whether each STL is for one day or one week. STLs cost a percentage of the list price of the e-book (determined by the publisher), with one-week loans at a higher percentage. The library chose to implement STLs as follows:

- Loan in one-day increments.

- Loan three times and on the fourth trigger purchase the e-book.

The fast pace of the online courses informed the decision to choose one-day loans. As mentioned, students often conduct their research at the last minute or over a weekend and do not need a week's worth of access. The E-Books Librarian also analyzed past usage patterns, especially the number of sessions per e-book, and determined that allowing three STLs before purchase would be cost-effective.

With ebrary librarians have the capability to create and manage fund codes. The E-Books Librarian added a Short Term Loans fund code with $25,000. Ebrary can then alert the library when the fund code is reaching a low balance.

STLs were activated starting in September 2013. July and August 2013 both operated under regular PDA conditions without STLs. Costs were therefore higher than they would have been if STLs were used the entire fiscal year.

Results

STLs have proven wildly successful in maintaining costs and improving ROI, as only those titles with demonstrated significant use are actually purchased. Costs from FY13 to FY14 decreased 50%, dropping $144,562 (see Figure 1). Ebrary use continued to increase during this time, making it clear that the cost control was necessary. From FY13 to FY14 section requests increased 63% (see Figure 2).

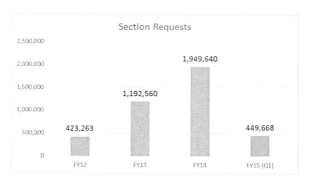

Figure 1. Ebrary PDA and STL costs by fiscal year.

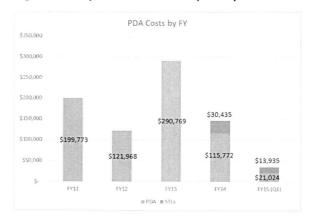

Figure 2. COUNTER Book Report 2 for ebrary section requests by fiscal year.

The original $25,000 allocated almost covered the entire cost of STLs for the fiscal year. Two transfers were made to boost the funding so that it would last until the end of the FY. One week in April 2014 the STLs had to be shut down for lack of funds, so for one week in April all triggers created purchases rather than STLs. At the end of FY13, the total STL cost was $30,435 for 2,929 STLs. The average cost for an STL in FY13 was $10.39.

In order to reveal the cost savings, the E-Books Librarian determined what purchasing all of the triggered content would have cost compared to the actual cost using STLs (see Figure 3). The cost savings totaled $131,694, reducing the potential cost by 47%. The library also analyzed whether choosing the one day STL was effective. The E-Books Librarian tracked the number of times STLs occurred within the same week. At the end of FY14 that percentage was 27%, so the majority of the STLs occurred more than a week apart. This result confirmed that the decision to use one day STLs was cost-effective.

STL Savings, FY14	
Potential All PDA Cost:	$ 277,900
Actual STL and PDA Cost:	$ 146,206
Cost Savings:	$ 131,694

Figure 3. Potential cost if all triggered titles were purchased vs. actual cost with STLs activated.

Future Considerations

Though the STL program produced significant, there are options to consider for the further enhancement and effectiveness of the program.

First, as mentioned, the cost-effectiveness of the program must be monitored because of the publisher STL pricing changes begun in summer 2014. The library found that some publishers were not included in the current profile, but many were. These cost increases have upped the average STL costs for FY15 by 55%.

- FY14 Average STL Cost: $10.39.

- FY15 (Q1) Average STL Cost: $16.09.

Soon after the library received the notification of the change in STL costs, publishers whose one-day loan percentage cost was increased to over 35% were removed from the profiles. If costs become unmanageable, the cutoff for loan percentage cost will be lowered. The content from these publishers will either be removed from the profiles altogether or moved to a profile which does not use STLs. The titles would instead trigger a purchase upon the first use.

Second, the library will investigate a combination approach of STLs with Extended Access enabled to provide better "just-in-time" service. Ebrary's Extended Access option allows another user to view an e-book that is already in use. If the second user reaches the trigger point, either an STL or a purchase is triggered. From November 2012 to February 2013 the library piloted Extended Access with triggers creating purchases. $25,000 was allocated, but because of the popularity of online resources, the funds were spent quickly. If Extended Access were used in combination with STLs instead, costs would be more manageable.

By providing Extended Access, the library reduces the number of turnaways and allows unmediated access to more users where there is demand.

Last, the E-Books Librarian and Head of Collection Management are attempting to acquire more funding for e-books. The library administration recently collaborated with a consultant to create a plan for funding print books into the next several years. The original plan was to aggressively purchase print for the next few years. However, with the increasingly large online population, it may become necessary to shift print book funds to electronic book funds sooner. The collection management team at the library believes that print and electronic will both be valuable in the near future, but the focus is shifting to electronic sooner at the Jerry Falwell Library because of the large online population. Many of the students most likely prefer print books, but the fast pace of the online classes does not allow them to easily access the print books at the library. Our electronic e-book use likely outpaces other institutions because of this scenario. As the use of e-books continues to grow, the costs will creep back up even though STLs have been implemented.

Conclusion

The Jerry Falwell Library's STL pilot program was a success. STLs effectively provided cost savings and allowed the library's funds to stretch into more access to more content. The price increases that publishers have introduced, however, will require the E-Books Librarian and the Head of Collection Management to continue monitoring the cost-effectiveness. As of Q1 of FY15, the program is still providing cost savings and there have been no more announcements of price increases. Publishers and vendors question the sustainability of STLs, and some doubt that STLs will remain an option. If STLs were to be removed, however, the E-Books Librarian would have to further limit the profile with more selective criteria. Removing STLs would not mean that the library would spend more funds on purchasing e-books. Instead, the scope of the program would shrink to accommodate the costs and the library would have to offer faculty and students a smaller selection. Hopefully STLs will remain an option with most publishers and the library can maintain the e-book development strategy it currently has.

Earnestly Finding the Fun in Fund Codes

Leslie O'Brien, Virginia Tech
Tracy Gilmore, Virginia Tech
Connie Stovall, University of Alabama

Abstract

Collections and acquisitions staff at Virginia Tech and The University of Alabama presented two very different models for structuring fund codes and discussed the benefits and difficulties inherent to each method. Both groups share their philosophy and approach for allocating appropriate fund codes for budgeting, reporting, and analytical purposes, and highlight important considerations to be made when creating a fund code structure.

Where Is the Fun in Fund Codes?

At the heart of it, fund codes are a financial reporting and collection development tool used to align appropriations with expenditures and encumbrances. Creating them may seem like basic stuff with little need for consideration or creativity. However, the way fund codes are structured can have major consequences and it is extremely important to put much thought into their configuration before implementing new fund codes. The creative aspect of budget allocation lies in the diversity of options in structuring fund codes. How a library chooses to structure its fund codes is determined as much by accounting and budgetary obligations as it is by the ILS, staff, and workflow processes, and the libraries preference and philosophies for meeting these challenges.

Libraries of all types are constrained by budget shortfalls that make robust fiscal management an ever more important aspect of collection management and acquisitions. Fund codes are in essence a financial tracking mechanism for acquisitions, connecting purchases with the appropriate account. They provide an accounting outline and schema for aligning appropriations with expenditures and encumbrances and thus can provide details about a library's material budget spending with more specificity. Depending on how fund code allocations are constructed, internal library operations can be streamlined to improve accounting and to better anticipate spending obligations for all resources.

Different Fund Code Structures

The degree of complexity built into a fund code structure depends on the scale of manual versus automated processes built into the workflow, the type of reports required, and the level of reporting granularity desired by the library. As with other Association for Research Libraries (ARL), reporting drives fund code structure at The University of Alabama and Virginia Tech. ARL requires its members to compile and report each year on various metrics, such as the number of volumes added to the library, the number of journal and database subscriptions, and the number of e-books. Additionally, both schools report each year to publications like the *US News & World Report Best Colleges* edition, and to regional and academic program accrediting bodies. These reports typically need library resource data at the subject level.

Internally, carefully crafting fund codes can help with better financial management. An opportunity exists for institutions to consider various ILS acquisition fund designations and to align their funding structures in meaningful ways and facilitate easier analysis. With this in mind, Virginia Tech and The University of Alabama compare their various style and approach to structuring fund codes.

The differences between the two universities' structures are quite evident when comparing fund codes for the academic subject/discipline of History. These differences are significant as they affect workflow processes at the beginning and end of the acquisition process.

Virginia Tech utilizes the Sierra ILS platform and has a relatively flat fund structure with very broad subject categories. This type of structure facilitates ease of use for selector and greater flexibility. To elicit granular details, queries must be written within the ILS to obtain information from the order record fixed fields. However, III Sierra's "Create Lists" function within each ILS module makes for relatively easy access to those details in a user-friendly interface. Collections, acquisitions, and technical services staff with even the most basic understanding of ILS record relationships can create lists on the fly.

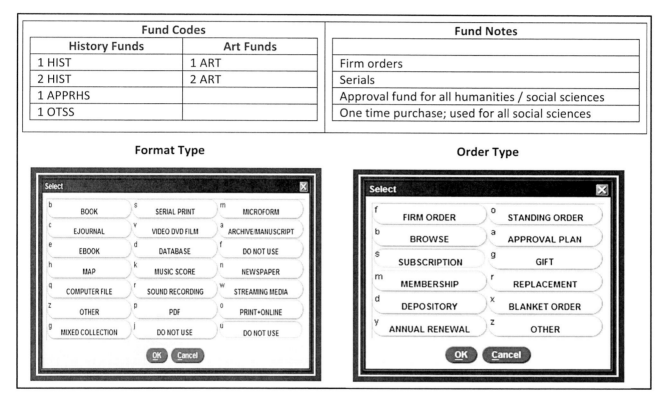

Figure 1.

In contrast, the University of Alabama uses the Ex Libris Voyager ILS platform, version 8.2. With Voyager, there is no equivalent to "Create Lists" within each individual module. Instead, data must be retrieved through Voyager Access Reports, a module of its own which works in conjunction with Microsoft Access, complete with several hundred canned Voyager tables. Running queries to find precise data among the tables requires the knowledge and use of a 48-page data dictionary.

As such, the University of Alabama employs a report writer with high level MS Access skills to run these queries. Given the learning curve associated with learning MS Access and the tables

specific to Voyager, very few people besides the report writer routinely retrieve financials on their own, so requests must be put in and some wait for data may be necessary. To speed up reporting, The University of Alabama structured fund codes so that minimal queries are required within the ILS; the fund code itself is used to identify details such as format. In fact, just a glance at the materials ledger provides dollar amounts spent on history with one-time funds.

The summary fund is the top level where the money is actually allocated. The reporting funds allow for additional granularity. This approach does mean, however, that selectors must keep up with many more fund codes and allows for more errors in acquisitions processing when so many funds are available.

Fund code allocations and accounting schemas may not be fun, but they are fundamental to managing a library's bottom line. Exploring various approaches to managing allocations and budgeting can improve every aspect of the acquisition process.

FUND CODES		FUND NOTES
History Funds	**Art Funds**	
AS/HY	AS/ART	Summary Fund
AS/HY/ER/1X	AS/ART/ER/1X	Electronic resources 1x spending
AS/HY/ER/AI	AS/ART/ER/AI	Electronic resources abstract & indexes
AS/HY/ER/FT	AS/ART/ER/FT	Electronic resources full text
AS/HY/ER/SAV	AS/ART/ER/SAV	Electronic resources streaming audio visual
AS/HY/FF/EBK	AS/ART/FF/EBK	Firm form eBook
AS/HY/FF/MF	AS/ART/FF/MF	Firm form microfilm
AS/HY/FF/PRT	AS/ART/FF/PRT	Firm form print
AS/HY/FF/VR	AS/ART/FF/VR	Firm form video
AS/HY/SER/JNL	AS/ART/SER/JNL	Serials journal
AS/HY/SER/MF	AS/ART/SER/MF	Serials microfilm
AS/HY/SER/PRT	AS/ART/SER/PRT	Serials print
AS/HY/YBP/AO/EBK	AS/ART/YBP/AO/EBK	Approval eBook
AS/HY/YBP/AO/PRT	AS/ART/YBP/AO/PRT	Approval print

Figure 2.

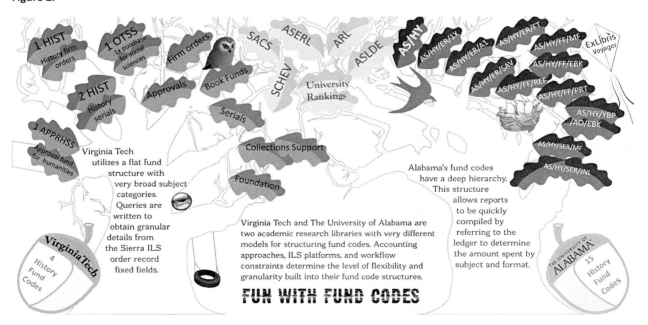

Figure 3.

I'll Be Back: Post-Purchase Activities and ROI

Michael Arthur, Head of Acquisitions and Collection Development, University of Central Florida
Tim Bucknall, Assistant Dean of University Libraries and Founder/Chief Negotiator for the Carolina Consortium, University of North Carolina at Greensboro and Carolina Consortium
Stephanie Kaelin, Library Sales Manager, Cambridge University Press
Sarah Schulman, Account Development Specialist, Springer
Moderator: Kristi Showers, Library Marketing Specialist, Springer

Abstract

What kinds of services and support should be expected after the sale? Vendors are increasingly providing postsale services to their customers, typically in the form of account development. This panel discussion examined experiences that vendors, libraries, and consortia have had with one another, including which services have been beneficial, and explored future enhancements that will benefit libraries and users. The panelists provided specific examples of past collaborations, including customized trainings, usage analysis, and professional development events. Panelists discussed topics of interest to librarians and vendors with a focus on ways to get the best ROI out of library resources. Librarians and publishers on the panel highlighted the important role that each side has in improving ROI and marketing the resources to the library community.

Q: Michael, can you tell us a little about your role at the University of Central Florida and a few ways you recommend your staff interact with vendors?

Michael: I am Head of Acquisitions and Collection Development. I manage the Subject Librarian-Faculty Liaison collection development program and the library materials budget. I also work with library and publisher partners to leverage purchasing and share in collaborative ventures. I encourage my staff to build positive, mutually beneficial relationships with publishers and vendors. Our E-Resources Librarian and Acquisitions Librarian are both active in committee work and publisher relations. We feel there is mutual benefit to working closely with vendors.

Q: Tim, can you share with us a bit about your role as Founder/Chief Negotiator for the Carolina Consortium and how you facilitate communication with vendors among the members? What are the benefits of working within a group?

Tim: I coordinate 180 public and private libraries and community colleges in a buying club. We have a cost avoidance of $250 million a year. This is an informal, buyer's club group (rather than a more traditional consortium). Communications are not so easy. Negotiators do the work and then distribute the offers to members of the buying club.

As for advantages of working in a group, there are several. The entire group benefits from a collective wisdom. They share (stories of) benefits and problems with products, vendors, support, functions, pricing. Each library has its own expertise. We meet once a year. Some library experiences may not be valid. For example, someone may have had a bad experience with a particular sales rep, while others have had positive experiences with a different rep from the same company. The bad rep experience does not inform total company experience.

Q: Sarah, can you give us some insight into Account Development at Springer a few of the tools your team use in their work with libraries?

Sarah: My team, Account Development, helps customers achieve the best possible value or ROI from their purchases. We provide assistance with end-user marketing, including offering on-site presence for library or campus-wide promotions and events (such as library days, vendor exhibits).

We also provide regular usage and statistical analysis, for our own purposes and upon request. This helps us to keep track of customers and usage trends. A newish tool in our repertoire is a sophisticated web analytics program called WebTrekk. This helps to gauge end-user behavior .

Additionally, I offer implementation and discovery assistance to customers as needed.

Stephanie, you have worked in account development at both an STM publisher and a university press. How does account development differ between the two types of companies?

Q: Stephanie: It's the difference in working with larger vs smaller publishers. Access to resources is obviously a big difference. My role at Cambridge is hybrid, in that I have traditional sales responsibilities in addition to managing the account development program. However, having my fingers in lots of pies and wearing many different hats has its benefits. This provides more opportunities to meaningfully interact with different departments within the Press and communicate the needs of our library customers internally. Also, unlike an STM publisher, the diversity of content published by a university press can prove challenging. For example, how do you compare your STM content with the humanities content when it comes to expected usage?

Communication and Philosophies: Digging Deeper

Q: Tim and Michael, could you describe a few of your philosophies and techniques for interacting with publishers and vendors? What are some obstacles to communication you have experienced?

Michael: When working with publishers and vendors, my policy is "open door, open dialogue." This allows for collaboration and leverage of relationships. We appreciate the opportunity to assist with development and refinement of products and to act as beta sites. We often share experiences with other libraries through our involvement on library advisory boards and participation in various publisher and library forums. It is important to bring the wisdom of the various publisher representatives into the library environment. They visit with numerous libraries

each year and are willing to share these ideas. They are a good resource.

Typically, subject librarians only get to see publisher representatives during on-campus events. More interaction is better, because it is possible to learn a lot from publisher representatives. We don't want publishers and vendors to fear contact with the library and rather we encourage collaboration including working together on presentations and articles.

Tim: Don't start off with antagonistic relationships from consortium to vendor. When more schools are involved, the price point is lower. Both sides are looking for positive outcomes. However, as a consortium you must be willing to walk away. No negotiation is legitimate without that willingness to walk away. Why talk to a rep who is unwilling to negotiate any concessions with me? When there is one deal for schools in more than one state, there can be problems. The more obstacles with permissions on the library purchaser side, the tougher it is to coordinate.

Q: Sarah and Stephanie, what are some of the ways you interact with the library community in a given year?

Sarah: Throughout the year, I visit customers to present usage and end-user behavior analyses. Conferences provide many opportunities for interactions—not only with scheduled meetings, but also via impromptu conversations at the booth and between sessions.

I also work with librarians to plan events of various types: training, end-user-focused, professional development, to name a few. For example, my colleague hosted a Big Marketing workshop where area librarians traded ideas and shared experiences in marketing their libraries. It was so highly rated, we repeated it at ALA Annual in Las Vegas.

Another way is reaching out through social media (see Springer's LibraryZone on Facebook), whether it's to share library news stories or for larger marketing campaigns like one we did for International Open Access Week.

Stephanie: We do less travel at Cambridge as a smaller publisher, but the methods are similar. I share usage analysis and tracking with clients and other sales staff at Cambridge. Additionally, we provide customers with promotional and instructional documentation for new purchases. And most recently, we undertook a benchmarking project to identify what "good" usage looks like at different levels of research intensity.

Audience Question: Sarah, how would you prove the ROI of the Account Development program to Springer if asked?

Sarah: To give a glimpse "behind the curtain" at Springer, we have a combination of monetary and customer engagement-related goals each year. We have reasons behind each bit of customer engagement. Feedback from librarians is a big part of our ROI. We are here to listen and bring your feedback to upper management. When Springer's reputation is enhanced after a successful event (whether it's a customer visit or larger event), that is also ROI.

Michael: Events involving faculty, staff, and other libraries are also ROI.

Audience Question (Charlie Remy, UTC): You mentioned that you do platform trainings. How would you respond to the comment Rick Anderson made that platforms should be intuitive, and that a platform which requires training is a bad platform?

Sarah: Our platform does not necessarily need training as such, but certain features and quirks that librarians need to know are important in the face of so many vendor platforms they deal with on a regular basis.

Michael: I see it not so much as staff training, but as a chance for all to see the product in the collective and give feedback to the vendor. Even with a very intuitive platform, it is beneficial to have someone point out the highlights.

Collaboration: Marketing and Usage

Q: All panelists, now that we have some background info, please tell the audience about a past example of collaborations. This can include

onsite events or "behind the scenes" projects (such as statistical analysis).

Tim: For the first 10 years of the Carolina Consortium, each of our 170 libraries decided on their own whether or not to participate in each of the consortium deals. And that makes sense because no one knows a campus's information needs better than that campus's librarians. On the other hand, that meant each school was making decisions in a vacuum. We were losing collective benchmarking. I got in touch with our seven biggest publishers and asked them for usage and cost data, including cost per use for all schools and all deals. I made all the data available to schools in the consortium via a password-protected document on the website. Different schools can see how their cost per use compares to similar schools. It was easy to get the data from the publishers, and I'm glad they cooperated. This is an ongoing project, currently with five years of data. The data is assessed at three levels. I can compare which deals are best and worst for the consortium as a whole, which is great information for both the consortium and the publishers when it is time to renegotiate.

Within a given publisher deal, each library can see how much they are paying relative to other schools (both in total dollars and in cost per use). Each year I alert schools that have high cost per use. But I also emphasize that poor cost per use should not automatically trigger cancellation; there are many other factors to consider.

If a school is considering canceling a big deal, I can use their usage data to build a model that predicts what would happen to number of available titles, total usage, total cost, and cost per use, if they were to substitute direct subscriptions for the big deal.

But the schools in the Carolina Consortium don't use usage data to trigger automatic decisions. We use it more as a "warning flag" to alert us to gather more data, consider more factors, and look a little more closely at particular deals.

Stephanie: Cost per use is one measure—and certainly an important one—but not the only measure. I've done deeper usage analyses where I provide usage by subject. For instance—how does each subject perform compared to the number of titles in the collection? Which subjects are pulling their weight? Which are falling short? When we share this data with libraries, they can tell us if the results are surprising or expected. And looking at this helps us determine how we can best collaborate and which subject areas might need additional promotion or attention.

Michael: At the University of Central Florida, we had a University-wide event for Open Access Week with activities and speakers, including a publisher panel with representatives from Springer, Taylor & Francis, IEEE, and Gale. This was a great success and was only possible because of past, ongoing collaboration. If you keep a positive relationship with publishers and vendors it opens the door for these types of events that benefit faculty and librarians.

Sarah: This year, I held a professional development event at a large university where the goal was to facilitate communication between librarians, faculty, and publishers. When asked how the subject librarians collaborate with faculty at this school, the answer was "we don't hear from them unless they need something."

We held a mini-summit with publisher, faculty, author, and librarian speakers providing different viewpoints on a variety of topics in scholarly communication, such as Open Access and how faculty selects teaching resources.

Audience comment (Krystie Klahn, Columbia): At Columbia, sometimes students request publishing-related workshops (i.e., how to get published). Sometimes they are created by the library based on our ideas.

Audience comment (Richard Gedeye, Oxford): Graduate students in particular are seeking assistance on things like how to be an author and how to do peer review.

Q : Michael/Tim, how do your libraries communicate new purchases to end users?

Michael: We have a newsletter in the bathroom stalls about new purchases or enhancements to existing products. The library website with a push

to our social media pages is also a way to communicate with end users. Our subject liaisons do a quarterly update and we send out weekly blurbs via the news blast from the Faculty Center for Teaching and Learning.

Tim: Make sure all your resources are very thoroughly covered by your discovery services. Advertising is less important than technical access and clear paths to the content needed at the time that it is needed. We use social media primarily to promote events at or by the library.

Q : Tim, how would you advise an institution in your consortium requesting marketing assistance?

I would point the librarians to vendors and publishers for assistance. We also have a white paper within the consortium on marketing ideas in the Carolinas.

Q: (Sarah & Stephanie), you have both mentioned usage as a priority in your Account Development teams. What metrics do you use to determine if usage is "good," and how would you work with an account whose usage stats are not where you want them to be?

Stephanie: We could spend all day trying to define "good" usage. Defining usage metrics is difficult, as usage is relative. We know that STM content is used very differently than HSS content, and different universities have unique programs with unique needs. Of course, peer-to-peer usage comparison and benchmarking can be helpful here. But ultimately the value of the content and how value is measured is the library's prerogative. Rather than making value judgments, it's our job as publishers to supply this data, do analysis, and show trends to relieve some of the burden on libraries who already do a lot of analysis on their end.

Sarah: (as was mentioned earlier), "Good" usage does not necessarily equal costs per use. At Springer, my team keeps data sheets where we look at cost per year and compare it against previous years. We want to see positive trends. We do look at cost per use, as we do not want it to be too high. Our journals package is a more consistent "big deal" package where we have clearer benchmarks for seeing positive trends. E-books are an ownership project. We examine usage four times per year, and look at things like date of purchase, allowing time for content to get added to the discovery layer.

The intervention process generally looks like this: we check to ensure access is up on the platform, then we look at the purchase timeline. Next, we perform a "discovery review" where we look at the library website. How easy is it to find Springer content? The last step is to contact the library and talk about the situation.

Stephanie: At Cambridge, we also have differences in usage between journals and books, but there is also the difference between science and humanities content to look at as well. We have to take inherent differences between subjects into account.

Audience comment (Richard Gedeye): Take into account the numbers of students and faculty in each department. Bigger and smaller departments should mean more and less usage. Some journals have less content than others. More articles per year should get more use. More users should yield more usage. Aggressiveness in some disciplines with research and assignment of more use of content.

Tim: Single most effective starting point in a conversation when demonstrating data is to sort by cost per use. The most expensive publisher in the Carolinas Consortium is three times more than the cheapest cost per use. Is the value of the most expensive content at least three times that of the least expensive? Alert schools of value based on cost per use.

Michael: Agree with other panelists. We want to focus on downloads, not sessions. Cost per use is important and the annual report has this data. We also look at environmental issues, such as changes in programs or changes in faculty acceptance of a product.

We pay attention to resources that are critical to certain areas even if the usage is low. It could be that the resource supports a unit that receives a large amounts of grants, or produces a lot of

research with few faculty or students so usage is low. What is important is the final outcome of the usage, not necessarily the amount of usage. Put products in the context of curriculum mapping. Map your resources to our research activities. Make it easier for faculty. Faculty are so overwhelmed with teaching, so they need help with mapping of resources and assessment to bring in relevant content.

Looking Forward

Q: (Tim & Michael) In a perfect world, what sort of services would all vendors provide that is currently not offered?

Michael: Publishers need to be able to relate how effectively the library is using the publisher's offerings. More collaboration with libraries in development of business models. There needs to be acceptable variations from all or none regarding big deals. If the offer is the big deal or nothing then the publisher may find that during difficult financial times that the decision will be to cancel the entire package. Sometimes we have to sign an unbelievable number of license agreements with the same publisher. There are far too many licenses per publisher. Having so many contracts to work through delays ordering and payment processes. I would like to see a limit on the need for license agreements for every product.

Q: Stephanie, what are some challenges you've faced in building a nascent account development program? What do you hope for your team to look like in 2015?

Stephanie: Luckily, building the account development team at Cambridge has provided more opportunities than challenges. As we grow, we seek more engagement from libraries. We'll do more outreach going forward to learn how we can be more creative and what kinds of additional support libraries would like to see from us.

Q: Sarah, You have been with Springer for four years, and in the Account Development position for three. How has the position changed over the years, and what do you predict for the future?

Sarah: The position is always evolving to keep up with the changing library world. We look different now than before. In the past, the services we offered were more sparse and less developed, especially when it comes to end user marketing and communication. For the future, I predict we will continue to delve more into end user and author outreach and services.

Employing a Use Factor to Distribute Monographic Funds

Cindy D. Shirkey, Collection Development Librarian for the Humanities, Joyner Library,
East Carolina University
Lisa Sheets Barricella, Head, Monographic Acquisitions and Preservation and Conservation,
Joyner Library, East Carolina University

Abstract

In the fall of 2012 East Carolina University's Joyner Library was looking to create a new fund allocation formula. The current one at that time had been in use since 1982, and we felt there might be a better way of distributing money—a way that took into account current needs. To create the new fund allocation formula, we took a collection evaluation concept and married it with knowledge gained about fund allocation formulas through research of the literature and investigation into our own past. We ended up with a fund allocation formula that employs Bonn's use factor and the average price paid per title per fund to achieve a more equitable distribution of funds.

History

In 1982 the Faculty Senate at East Carolina was concerned with creating a fund allocation formula that accurately portrayed a measure of faculty productivity. They had tried for several years to come up with a factor that could in some way account for creative and scholarly output of faculty, but had ultimately failed in this attempt. Instead, they came up with a very large weighted variable formula that made extensive use of proxies of utilization. (For more on different types of formulas, please read Catalano and Caniano's "Book Allocations in a University Library: An Evaluation of Multiple Formulas" in *Collection Management*. The authors provide a very good explanation of what a weighted variable formula is.) For example, instead of actual usage of the collection, factors thought to be predictive of use, such as faculty FTE and number of credit hours, were part of the formula. Some factors, such as average price per item and faculty FTE were weighted, while others, such as undergraduate credit hours, were not. The result was a beastly formula that was unwieldy to use and for which it was difficult to gather all the necessary statistics.

New Formula

In going forward with the investigation of a new fund allocation formula we had a few requirements. First all of the data necessary for calculating the formula must be readily available

to us. Second, all of the data must be from the same reporting cycle. We had also been heavily researching collection evaluation methods and felt there might be a way to employ Bonn's use factor as representative of actual use, rather than rely of proxies of use, as had been done previously. Bonn's use factor is the percentage of circulations divided by the percentage of holdings. (Aguilar, 1986; Bonn, 1974) Using percentages like that avoids the problem of a small collection always having less use than a large collection simply because of its size.

One of the things we had to do in order to make this work was to break up every bit of the LC classification scheme into a subject fund. We have 42 subject funds, of which three are completely interdisciplinary and cannot be covered by LC class numbers. That means that every part of the LC class system had to be assigned one of 39 fund codes. Some subjects are quite easy: psychology is all of the BFs. History is the Ds, Es and Fs. Some others get into rather tedious breakdowns: biology is comprised of 14 different call number spans and English is comprised of 11. In the end, we relied heavily on a document that was used years before to pass out yellow slips from book vendors to the correct selectors.

Another piece of our equation was the number for average price paid per title per fund. This was easy to find as our Symphony ILS has a function that keeps track of this information. For FY 2014 we used data from FY 2013 as that was the most complete year, and then for FY 2015 we used data for FY 2014. Although Bowkers and YBP can provide industry normative figures, we found our ILS's statistics to be a truer representation of what we actually spend in each fund, especially since we prefer paper bindings and both Bowkers and YBP's figures are based on hardcover costs.

In the end, in 2013 we found Bonn's use factor for four years: books added in 2008–09, 2009–10, 2010–11, 2011–12. We stopped at 2011–12 because we felt books added later to the collection might not have had time to circulate much. Then, we took an average of those four years and added it to the average price paid per title number for each fund. The resulting figure was expressed as a percentage of the whole each fund was entitled to.

Results

Some funds, such as education and business, showed steep declines in funding. Both of these subjects were heavily funded under the old weighted variable formula because they have such large programs. What we found when we ran our formula, however, is that neither see the kind of use that would bear out such funding. Other funds, such as nutrition sciences and interior design and marketing, showed steep increases in funding. These are relatively small programs that cover very small ranges of the LC call number scheme. Even though these programs are relatively small, usage in these areas is heavy; therefore they were entitled to larger amounts of funding.

After we developed the formula in early 2013 we had two main objectives for the upcoming fiscal year. We wanted to trial the funding allocations suggested by the new formula for a year to see what selectors thought of them. We also wanted to present our findings to the Senate Libraries Committee and have them vote on whether to adopt the new formula, go back to the old formula or start over on the search for a more equitable means of distributing funds. The selectors were mostly pleased with the new allocation amounts, especially when we explained that use was the deciding factor in most cases.

The selector for chemistry and nutrition sciences, however, mentioned that she had a hard time spending out her funds that year because they were larger for those two subject areas. The Senate Libraries Committee unanimously voted to adopt the new use factor-based formula going forward.

When it came time to do the allocations for FY 2015 we collected data and ran the formula again, this time for 2009–10, 2010–11, 2011–12 and 2012–13. We also included two new figures in our calculations: in-house use and e-book use. Getting in-house use statistics was much easier than we thought; it was only a matter of pulling the report in the correct way. E-book statistics, however, were challenging because of the question of how to accurately measure use.

How We Incorporated E-Book Statistics

The vast majority of our e-books purchased as firm orders with subject allocation money come from ebrary. As well, beginning in October 2011, we implemented an e-book DDA plan with ebrary. We pulled usage statistics by running reports from the administrative module of the ebrary interface. Like we did with print books, we gathered usage for titles bought in 2009–10, 2010–11, 2011–12, and 2012–13 and assigned each title a subject fund based upon LC call number. For DDA titles we only included statistics for titles that triggered a purchase; however we are investigating whether to include DDA untriggered to the allocation formula in the future.

The ebrary report provided a variety of usage figures such as pages viewed, pages copied, pages printed, number of user sessions, and chapter or book downloads. We decided to have the number of user sessions be our count of usage. We believe that for the purposes of our allocation formula that the number of ebrary user sessions is equivalent to the check-out and in-house usage we gathered for printed books. Generally speaking, the number of ebrary user sessions equals the number of "circulations" with the caveat that we subtracted one user session from all titles because cataloging and activation in our ILS means that Joyner staff are verifying access to the title by viewing it from their workstation. We would have artificial use of each book if we did not take this library workflow into account. In the end, we did not count titles which only had a single user session of only a few pages viewed. We equated that to be comparable to a printed book only being opened and read by a staff member in order to catalog the book, apply a label or barcode and then the title never having any checkouts after being placed in the library stacks.

How E-Book Statistics Impacted the Use Factor When Included in Year Two

With the addition of e-book statistics, we tried to analyze the changes it made on each subject's use factor percentage. It is a bit hard to draw a firm conclusion this first year. There is uneven adoption of e-books as a substitution for paper and for many subjects the inclusion of e-book data did not significantly alter the use factor percentage. However, for a few subjects, where there is high e-book adoption and also a high number of user sessions then adding e-books did improve the use factor, perhaps due to the very fact that an e-book can "circulate" many more times in a year than a print book.

Music Fund

Over the course of two years, our music fund is an interesting case study. Traditionally our music library has been very well-funded because it is a stand-alone library serving a large and active department. When we first ran the formula for fiscal year 2014 we did not include in-house use statistics because we did not know we kept them. The funding projected for music that year was much lower than it had previously been. After talking with employees of the music library, we realized that in-house use statistics were a valuable source of data for them, as a good portion of their collection is in-house use only. The music librarians assured us they were very diligent about keeping in-house use statistics in our integrated library system. We revised the music allotment upwards thinking that we were missing a vital piece of the picture. Then, for FY 2015 we ran the formula again, this time with in-house use statistics and e-book usage included. Music still was allotted a rather small number:

approximately half of what it had been allotted under the old formula. We delved deeper because that seemed counter-intuitive to us. It is, however, correct. One of the things that brings the amount allotted for music down is that its average price per title is under $30, which is quite low compared to the overall average price paid for title of approximately $65. Music also received a large gift in 2012–2013. Although the usage for that year is close to what it was in other years, the number of items that it was counted against was much higher because of that gift. And finally, a third factor which artificially drove up the amount music was allotted to under the old formula was that we were counting number of classes as part of the previous equation. Music, as a discipline, has a large number of small classes, many of them graduate level classes that were weighted twice what undergraduate classes were. In short, we found that music is entitled to a much smaller percentage of the whole than previously thought. It should be noted that when the director of the library agreed to let us develop a revised formula, she placed a monetary cap on drastic changes to a subject allocation as a result of our work. What this means is that if the use factor allocation formula indicated a significantly increased or decreased subject allocation from the amount they were entitled to under the old formula we would implement the changes by no more than $2000 per year.

Things We Would Add or Do Differently

Eventually we'd like to add in ILL data to our formula to represent that amount of borrowing we do for certain funds. There is another use factor: ratio of borrowings to holdings that can be used to express this concept as a number. (Aguilar, 1986). We believe adding this number would give us an accurate description not just of the funds that are heavily used, but also those for which there is heavy borrowing, indicating a higher percentage of the pot should be devoted to them. We tried doing this for fiscal year 2014, but were stymied by a query that returned incomplete data. We have asked our Interlibrary Loan Librarian to look into this problem to see if it can be fixed.

Another thing we might do differently next year is to use a respectively later four-year average of the use factor. By this we mean instead of using 2010–11, 2011–12, 2012–13 and 2013–14 for fiscal year 2016, we might continue to use instead our previous years of 2009–10, 2010–11, 2011–12 and 2012–2013. The reason for this is that we have noticed that the most recent year's worth of circulation statistics is much lower than the previous years. We plan to investigate this and see if there is such a sharp circulation drop-off if all the books in the study have had more time to circulate. We are loath to do this, however, because it means our data is one year older.

We could also add additional e-book vendors next year. This year, we only added ebrary. We chose to add it because it is our primary vendor for demand driven acquisitions (DDA) and it has been our preferred vendor for firm order e-books. We have recently added both EBL and JSTOR and so we could count them as well next year. And finally, we do have a few e-books from EBSCOhost, so we could factor those in, too.

Conclusion

Overall, we are pleased with this new use factor-based allocation formula. We feel that it provides a more accurate representation of usage in monetary terms than our previous weighted variable formula gave us.

References

Aguilar, W. (1986). The application of relative use and interlibrary demand in collection development. *Collection Management, 8*, 15–24. http://dx.doi.org/10.1300/J105v08n01_02

Bonn, G. S. (1974). Evaluation of the collection. *Library Trends, 22*, 265–304. Retrieved from http://search.ebscohost.com/login.aspx?direct=true&db=llr&AN=521800407&site=ehost-live

Canepi, K. (2007). Fund allocation formula analysis: Determining elements for best practices in libraries. *Library Collections, Acquisitions, & Technical Services, 31*(1), 12–24. http://dx.doi.org/10.1016/j.lcats.2007.03.002

Catalano, A and Caniano, W. (2013). Book allocations in a university library: An evaluation of multiple formulas. *Collection Managemen*t, 38(3), 192–212. http://dx.doi.org/10.1080/01462679.2013.792306

Developing a Weighted Collection Development Allocation Formula

Jeff Bailey, Library Director, Dean B. Ellis Library, Arkansas State University

Linda Creibaum, Acquisitions and Serials Librarian, Dean B. Ellis Library, Arkansas State University

Abstract

In this session the presenters demonstrated and discussed how to create a spreadsheet-based library collection development allocation formula to help acquisitions personnel better manage their library's limited collection development resources. The presenters demonstrated and led participants through Arkansas State University's process of creating an Excel-based formula that utilizes criteria relevant to their specific library and institution. Key to the success of this formula is the use of a separate weight applied to each factor used in the formula. Factors selected include the number of students graduating from each degree program, courses offered by each academic department, departmental credit hour production, the number of faculty in each department, and the average costs of books and journals in a discipline. By carefully assigning weights to each factor, the output of the formula results in a more equitable allocation of funds to each subject area.

Introduction

After introducing themselves and welcoming attendees, Bailey and Creibaum briefly discussed the history, development, and use of an allocation formula at the main campus of Arkansas State University. This was followed by a short discussion of how the basic formula has been modified over time at Arkansas State and examples of ways the formula could be individualized for use in a variety of library settings and types.

Discussion included the methods by which the formula can be modified as conditions warrant and campus circumstances change.

Developing a Weighted Collection Development Allocation Formula

Background

In 1997 Arkansas State University's Dean B. Ellis Library had no equitable means of providing the university's various departments with financial allocations of collection development funds to the for selection of library materials. Departmental allocations had become unbalanced to the point that one department accounted for almost 20% of all collection development expenditures. Funds had not been reallocated or redistributed in many years, and as a result the library had no means to purchase materials in support of new programs.

Arkansas State librarians searched professional literature to discover methods of making allocations, including the use of a formula, and ultimately decided to develop a formula for their institution that was based on one used by Colorado State University and described in SPEC Kit #36 (September 1977).

Gathering Data

Before selecting formula factors, it was necessary to gather the relevant data needed to make informed decisions. A brainstorming session regarding possible formula factors was conducted and several potential factors received serious consideration, including:

- Accreditation requirements.
- Average cost of materials by academic discipline.
- Circulation of materials by subject area.
- Consortial arrangements.
- Credit hours per discipline.
- Degree levels.
- External funding received by each department.
- Faculty publications.
- Graduation data.

- Interlibrary loan requests.

- Number of faculty.

- Number of majors.

- Number of students in each major.

- Prices of books and journals.

Bailey and Creibaum discussed how to evaluate and refine the list of possibilities until the final choices for formula factors have been made. Duplicates, such as cost of materials and prices of books and journals, were consolidated, and nonviable suggestions, such as identifying the users of books and journals by major, were eliminated. It was noted that some potential factors may be viable at one institution but not at another due to the varying methods of collecting data, and that some suggestions might not be appropriate to the formula at all. Additionally, when determining what data is available, participants were reminded that some data may be obtainable at some institutions but not at others. When building a formula, a library should gather samples of available data and eliminate from consideration all factors for which complete data cannot be obtained.

Factor Selection

Selection of formula factors should be completed only after each possibility is examined for completeness of data and relevance to the institution's collection development goals. It is at this point that the endorsement of advisory boards, faculty committees, or administrative personnel should be sought according to the structure and culture of each institution. Documentation should be retained for all factors considered for inclusion in the formula, whether they were selected or not, including the specific reasons for those not included in the allocation formula. There is a strong possibility that at least some of this information will be needed when rerunning and/or making changes to the formula in the future.

Weights

Weighting is the assigning of values to indicate the importance or impact of each factor in the formula relative to the other formula factors.

When building an allocation formula there are various considerations involved in determining what weight to give to each formula factor. These considerations are particular to each individual institution and may include additional input from a library committee, faculty senate, or other constituency. Factors may be subdivided before assigning weights. An example of this would be subdividing undergraduate and graduate semester credit hour production. This would allow assigning a different weighting factor to each, with a higher weight being assigned to graduate credit hour production due to the degree of intensive research involved at that level. Doing test formula runs throughout the process is highly recommended, as minor changes in weights or the data collected for factors can sometimes yield unexpected (and unbalanced) results! Be prepared to make changes.

Options

Formulas may be run to allocate financial resources for books, journals, print materials, online resources, or any other budgets your library may have, either separately or in combination. Libraries may choose to allocate all available funding or retain some for in-house use in accordance with local campus culture and practices. There may be reasons to make adjustments to individual allocation amounts after running the formula, including not wanting to reduce any department's existing allocation, choosing to reduce/not increase an allocation amount because a department had a history of not spending a satisfactory portion of previous allocations, the presence of endowed funds for some disciplines, or adding an amount to help cover start-up costs for new programs. Additionally there might be special entities, accreditation demands, or campus political issues to consider.

Running the Formula

Attendees were then led through a discussion of a how the Excel-based spreadsheet formula works, including a quick look at a working version of an allocation formula. During this discussion, Bailey and Creibaum explained various aspects of running the formula, mentioning how the spreadsheet looks and the actual math contained within the spreadsheet itself, and the relationship of the weighting to the final output.

Comments

If a decision is made to develop and use an allocation formula, it is vitally important to thoroughly document the factors you used and how the formula data were gathered. Comparable information will be needed in future runs of the formula, whether a library is rerunning an unchanged formula with updated information or has decided to modify a previous formula to incorporate different factors. In recent years the formula used at Arkansas State University has been revised to include additional factors, such as external research funding received, as the campus and campus culture have changed, and other libraries' formulas will almost certainly need to be modified in the future because of changes in the library or in the institution's makeup or needs.

PowerPoint slides for the presentation and a downloadable interactive basic version of the formula spreadsheet may be accessed at: www.astate.edu/a/library/charleston.

References

Association of Research Libraries. (1977). *The allocation of materials funds in academic libraries,* SPEC Kit 36. Washington, DC: Association of Research Libraries.

How Is That Going to Work?

Part II—Acquisitions Challenges and Opportunities in a Shared ILS

Kathleen Spring, Linfield College

Damon Campbell, University of Oregon

Carol Drost, Willamette University

Siôn Romaine, University of Washington

Abstract

Building on a presentation given at the 2013 Charleston Conference, this article continues the discussion about acquisitions policies, workflows, and consortial collaboration in a next-generation shared ILS. The Orbis Cascade Alliance is a consortium of 37 public and private academic institutions in Oregon, Washington, and Idaho. In January 2013, the Alliance began a two-year process of migrating all 37 institutions (in 4 cohorts, with a new cohort going live every 6 months) to Ex Libris's Alma and Primo in order to realize efficiencies and increase collaboration within the consortium. The authors, who represent institutions in the first and third cohorts, offer perspectives on new consortial structures stemming from changing workflows, policy issues to consider from a consortial viewpoint, challenges and opportunities for the new system, partnering with vendors, and ongoing considerations for large-scale cooperative collection development and assessment.

Introduction

How much difference can a year really make? At the 2013 Charleston Conference, three librarians from the Orbis Cascade Alliance (the Alliance) discussed the initial phase of migration to a shared, next-generation Integrated Library System (ILS) (Spring, Drake, & Romaine, 2013). At that time, only six Alliance institutions had gone live with Ex Libris's Alma, a product still very much in development. Just one year later, 30 Alliance institutions have migrated, with the final cohort completing migration in January 2015 (Orbis Cascade Alliance, 2014d). Although significant improvements have been made to Alma, challenges continue to exist, particularly for consortia like the Alliance with a strong focus on collaboration.

What policies and procedures are needed before all participants have migrated? What decisions must wait until migration is complete for all institutions, and what can or should be addressed while migration is still occurring? As the end of migration nears, does the shared ILS still hold the promise of greater efficiency and better collaboration for the Alliance? By drawing on experiences from institutions in two different cohorts and the opportunities and challenges

they have faced, the authors offer practical guidance for institutions considering similar collaborative efforts.

Background: The Alliance

The Alliance is a consortium of 37 public and private academic institutions in Oregon, Washington, and Idaho. Collaboration dates back to 1993, when five public academic libraries in Oregon formed the Orbis Union Catalog. By 2011, collaboration had come to include other shared services: a courier and resource sharing program, an archives program, joint electronic resources negotiation and licensing, a distributed print repository, a preferred monograph vendor, and a demand-driven acquisitions (DDA) e-book program (Orbis Cascade Alliance, 2014a; Orbis Cascade Alliance, 2014e). Realizing cooperative collection development and shared technical services would require some form of shared ILS, the Alliance issued an RFP for a consortial ILS in 2012, ultimately selecting Ex Libris's Alma and Primo products. Ex Libris's concept of the Network Zone, which allows member institutions to share resources and bibliographic records and see holdings from other institutions at the point of order, held particular appeal for a consortium interested in taking collaborative efforts to the next level.

Alliance and Alma Structures

Alliance-wide committees and groups guide decision-making and policy development for the shared ILS. To date, work largely has been coordinated by a Shared ILS Team (SILS), with support from a Collaborative Technical Services Team (CTST). With migration nearly complete, the Alliance is transitioning to a new team structure to guide work moving forward (Orbis Cascade Alliance, 2014i); this structure aligns with the Alliance's five program areas and Strategic Agenda initiatives to "work smart," "design for engagement," and "innovate to transform" (Orbis Cascade Alliance, 2014j).

The Ex Libris consortial ILS model consists of an Institution Zone (IZ), a Network Zone (NZ), and a Community Zone (CZ). The IZ contains local inventory, ordering/licensing/vendor information, patron data, and a handful of bibliographic records that cannot be shared across institutions. The NZ contains the vast majority of bibliographic records shared by all Alliance libraries, allowing staff at any institution to see which resources are held by other institutions. The CZ is available to all Alma customers and utilizes Alma's Central Knowledge Base; it primarily contains bibliographic records for electronic resources.

In Alma, acquisitions and cataloging workflows generally begin with a purchase order line (POL) and inventory in the IZ, attached to either a bibliographic record in the NZ or to a bibliographic or collection record in the CZ. Because of the need to use and share bibliographic data in the NZ, acquisitions staff must pay close attention to Alliance policies and standards for bibliographic records.

Sharing the Work

To ensure all institutions would benefit from a shared ILS, the Alliance initiated discussions about shared standards and policies early in the process. Seven bibliographic shared best practices mandates emerged from these discussions. Alma workflows blur the lines between acquisitions and cataloging, so it is essential for all technical services staff at member libraries to be familiar with and follow the mandates. The mandates require the following:

1. Institutions must use OCLC as their bibliographic utility and attach their holdings in OCLC.

2. Institutions must abide by a floor bibliographic standard, which sets minimum levels for completeness and mandatory elements (some exceptions allowed).

3. Institutions must use separate records for each format of a title.

4. Institutions must use provider-neutral records.

5. Institutions must catalog at the WorldCat level.

6. Institutions must maintain at least their current level of contribution to the Program for Cooperative Cataloging.

7. Institutions must, whenever possible, use vendor records that meet Alliance bib standards and best practices (Orbis Cascade Alliance Shared ILS Preparation Team, 2012).

At go-live, the first cohort immediately realized policies were needed specifically to address working in Alma. Since that time, the relevant SILS working groups have collaborated with CTST and its internal working groups to identify issues and draft policy, gathering feedback from all relevant constituencies and incorporating changes as needed. Generally, policies are approved by CTST and, if necessary, are sent to the SILS Implementation Team for final approval before they go into effect for the entire Alliance. Alma-specific policies pertaining to acquisitions cover in-process brief bibliographic records, minimum acquisitions data, overlay of records, and best practices for non-serial electronic resource management (ERM) (Orbis Cascade Alliance, 2014b).

In-process brief bibliographic records need to be imported into the NZ or shared with the NZ so that other Alliance institutions can see what materials are on order across the consortium and avoid unnecessary duplication (of both bibliographic records and the materials themselves). This policy also sets a floor standard for the information required in a brief bibliographic record (Orbis Cascade Alliance, 2013).

The minimum acquisitions data policy requires all institutions to create POLs at the point of order. It also requires that gift materials be added to the NZ as quickly as possible (Orbis Cascade Alliance, 2014f).

The overlay policy deals with replacing records in the NZ via manual export from Connexion or via daily OCLC loads (which add, update, and delete records where Alliance institutions have holdings). The policy's purpose is to make it clear when overlay is and is not appropriate, and to avoid adding duplicate records to the NZ that will need to be removed once the final cohort has completed migration (Orbis Cascade Alliance, 2014h).

The best practices for non-serial ERM document provides a set of guidelines for libraries to use when making decisions about how to handle non-serial electronic resources in Alma. A decision tree assists staff as they try to balance the need for Alliance-level coordination with local conditions that may influence workflow decisions (Orbis Cascade Alliance, 2014g). This tension is at the heart of many of the policy discussions the Alliance has had since the start of migration.

Beyond policy, the CTST Acquisitions Working Group has created Alliance-wide brief bibliographic record templates. These templates live in the NZ in Alma and are accessible to staff at all Alliance institutions who have permissions to create bibliographic records. This is one example of a coordinated effort to "work smart"—by creating a set of shared templates intended for use at all institutions, there is no need for all 37 institutions to create their own templates. To the greatest extent possible, shared templates also ensure consistency in coding for fixed fields and in

the fields and subfields used. Similar to the best practices mandates, the shared templates demonstrate the blurred lines between acquisitions and cataloging in Alma; while bibliographic records traditionally have been the domain of catalogers, acquisitions staff are more likely to use shared templates, given the workflows in Alma.

Sharing the Pain

Although sharing work remains a central goal for the Alliance, the reality is that many pain points are also shared since Alma is still being developed. Two examples of shared pain points are record loading and import profiles. With migration for all cohorts almost complete, the Alliance is exploring how the potentially time-consuming burden of record loading might be addressed by leveraging the architecture of the NZ, where records for shared packages need only be loaded once. For electronic resources, bibliographic records may be centrally loaded into the NZ (or activated in the CZ) and then made available for all institutions or a select subset. Task groups have been formed to pilot and document shared record loading for electronic Marcive documents, for multi-institution packages like Alexander Street Press, and for streamlining vendor record match points across Alliance institutions.

Import profiles, which dictate how new bibliographic records are loaded into Alma, have been another pain point. Many Alliance institutions use YBP's Electronic Order Confirmation Record (EOCR) service to create bibliographic and order records in their ILS. In order to use the EOCR service, institutions had to set up import profiles once they were live in Alma. Earlier cohorts did much of the initial setup and testing work, documenting their successes and unresolved issues, thereby lessening this pain point for later cohorts. A weekly acquisitions call open to staff from all Alliance institutions allowed participants to share other pain points, ask questions about Alma acquisitions workflows, and suggest Alma enhancement requests that could benefit all institutions.

Basic Functionality to Better Usability: Collaborating to Improve Alma

Throughout migration, Alliance institutions have utilized two primary tools to communicate problems to Ex Libris and to suggest changes to Alma and Primo: support cases and enhancement requests. Ex Libris uses Salesforce to track support cases and enhancement requests for both Alma and Primo. Select personnel at individual institutions can file cases, as can SILS working group chairs in order to document Alliance-wide problems or requests.

The Alliance selected Alma as its shared ILS with the understanding that it would need continued development to build out missing functionality. Enhancement requests are designed to address that missing functionality, as well as to address existing functionality that could be improved. Requests usually come from staff within functional areas, who relay their ideas to members of the relevant working groups. If the working group supports the request, an Alliance-level case is filed with Ex Libris. Enhancement requests often, but not always, make it into Ex Libris's roadmap for Alma and appear in future releases. (Ex Libris has a monthly release cycle for Alma, which requires diligence on the part of staff since the new features sometimes have unintended and adverse impacts on other parts of the system, particularly the NZ.)

Beyond support cases and enhancement requests, the Alliance and Ex Libris have instituted a Center of Excellence (COE) to "focus on the development and continual enhancement of Alma, Primo, and best practices for consortia" (Orbis Cascade Alliance, 2014c). One proposed initiative that may be addressed through the COE deals with improvements for usability, accessibility, and ergonomics in Alma. This proposal addresses a broad swath of issues to improve efficiency, streamline processes, and reduce the need for workarounds using external systems.

Third-Party Vendor Collaboration: Real-Time Acquisitions in Alma

In addition to collaborating with Ex Libris through their established channels in order to improve Alma, opportunities have arisen for collaboration with third-party vendors. At the Ex Libris Users of North America (ELUNA) annual meeting in May of 2014, staff from Willamette University Library and the University of Minnesota Libraries met with staff from Ex Libris and YBP to discuss partnering to develop an API that would streamline the YBP ordering process and enhance workflow efficiencies in Alma. This new API would replace existing ordering processes that required waiting overnight to retrieve order files via FTP before loading them into Alma the next day. Ex Libris and YBP needed libraries of different sizes—one small, and one large—in order to cover the spectrum of issues found at each type. Willamette's consortial ILS setting presented the additional challenge of multiple zones, since all orders must have inventory represented in both the NZ and the IZ. Ultimately, all parties agreed to move forward with the collaboration, with a projected implementation date of fall 2014.

After several weeks of testing and debugging, the first version of the API was released in September 2014. Using this new service, acquisitions staff can place orders in YBP's online bibliographic platform, GOBI[3], and see the corresponding order data updated automatically in real time in both Alma (in both the NZ and IZ) and GOBI[3]. Future releases of the API will include the ability to match on different control numbers (matching currently occurs only on ISBNs), allow for manual handling when an ISBN matches multiple records, and integrate duplication control. This collaborative effort is a promising example of relatively quick product development that benefits not only Alliance institutions but also other Alma customers worldwide.

Challenges and Opportunities for Collaboration

Much policy work and decision-making across all functional areas still needs to be done before the shared ILS will enable the Alliance to fully realize its "work smart" strategic objective. While migrating to a shared ILS has allowed us to construct the foundation on which we will build a house together, the final placement of the walls, windows, and doors—and who will place them—is uncertain. For example:

- In a shared system where one institution may do work on behalf of several or all institutions, how is that institution compensated? How is shared work coordinated and distributed? With 37 institutions, is it practical to expect that shared work can be evenly distributed?

- As Alliance-wide policies and procedures are developed, how do we strike a balance between institutional autonomy/local practice and consistency across the consortium in such a way that maintains flexibility and efficiency while minimizing confusion for staff and patrons?

- With migration nearly complete, how should future training be done, and who should coordinate it?

- How can participation in Alliance-wide committees and groups be increased to guard against burnout and widen the existing pool of expertise?

- Should everyone be able to manage bibliographic records in the NZ, or should that access be restricted?

- Some institutions use CZ records with minimal metadata to describe electronic resources; others only use fully cataloged NZ records. In a shared environment, is there a right way to describe and manage electronic resources, or is a mixed approach acceptable?

- Although Alma allows institutions to see others' inventory, it does not (yet) allow institutions to see one anothers' order data. Is shared order information critical to building a more collaborative purchasing model or to sharing technical services work? How will the Alliance do consortial assessment given existing limitations in Alma's reporting tools?

Moving from How Is *That* Going to Work to How Are *We* Going to Work?

Eighteen months after the first six institutions migrated, the Alliance has a much better sense of how a shared ILS can work, what Ex Libris can provide, and what Alliance institutions can expect from each other. We are developing workflows that will allow us to maximize efficiencies and minimize pain points so that we "do things once, do things the same, do things together" (Orbis Cascade Alliance, 2014j). The Alliance is actively working with third-party vendors to integrate workflows into Alma and improve discovery in Primo. We agree that being able to share and manage license records, serial publication patterns, and DDA subscription information at the network level are all desirable features; as such, we are collaborating with Ex Libris to incorporate these features into Alma. Despite the incredibly diverse nature of the 37 member institutions, it appears clear we are better off working with Ex Libris collectively to resolve workflow blockers and cross-institutional issues than going it alone. We know the Alliance will continue to encounter both technical and philosophical challenges in the post-migration era, but we are optimistic the solid foundation we have laid will support us in our future collaborative work.

References

Orbis Cascade Alliance. (2013). *In-process brief bibliographic records*. Retrieved from https://orbiscascade.org/file_viewer.php?id=451

Orbis Cascade Alliance. (2014a). *About the Alliance*. Retrieved from https://www.orbiscascade.org/about/

Orbis Cascade Alliance. (2014b). *Alma operational policies*. Retrieved from https://www.orbiscascade.org/alma-policies/

Orbis Cascade Alliance. (2014c). *Center of excellence.* Retrieved from https://www.orbiscascade.org/center -excellence

Orbis Cascade Alliance. (2014d). *Cohort plan for the shared ILS implementation.* Retrieved from https://www.orbiscascade.org/cohort-plan-for-shared-ils

Orbis Cascade Alliance. (2014e). *Collections.* Retrieved from https://www.orbiscascade.org/collections

Orbis Cascade Alliance. (2014f). *Minimum acquisitions data policy*. Retrieved from https://www .orbiscascade.org/file_viewer.php?id=1175

Orbis Cascade Alliance. (2014g). *Non-serial electronic resource management best practices*. Retrieved from https://www.orbiscascade.org/file_viewer.php?id=1705

Orbis Cascade Alliance. (2014h). *Overlay*. Retrieved from https://www.orbiscascade.org/file _viewer.php?id=2181

Orbis Cascade Alliance. (2014i). *Program structure*. Retrieved from https://www.orbiscascade.org/file_viewer.php?id=1525

Orbis Cascade Alliance. (2014j). *Strategic Agenda.* Retrieved from https://orbiscascade.org/strategic-agenda/

Orbis Cascade Alliance Shared ILS Preparation Team. (2012). *Summary of seven bibliographic shared best practices mandates*. Retrieved from https://www.orbiscascade.org/file_viewer.php?id=453

Spring, K., Drake, M., & Romaine, S. (2013). How is that going to work? Rethinking acquisitions in a next-generation ILS. In B. R. Bernhardt, L. H. Hinds, & K. P. Stauch (Eds.), *Charleston Conference proceedings 2013* (pp. 372-377). West Lafayette, IN: Purdue University Press. Retrieved from http://docs.lib.purdue.edu/charleston/2013/Management/12/

Doing Things Differently in the Cloud:
Streamlining Library Workflows to Maximize Efficiency

Vanessa A. Garofalo, Technical Services Librarian/Associate Professor of Library Services, Southeastern University-Steelman Library

Abstract

Libraries share many common challenges, including ever more complex collections, systems, and workflows, as well as increased user demand. To help manage these challenges, today's cloud-based library management services are offering workflows that save library staff time and discovery solutions that meet users' needs. Libraries using these services are seeing drastic reductions in the time it takes to perform routine tasks because of the integration between libraries, applications, partners, and data.

As a result of doing things differently, libraries save staff time and money while streamlining workflows and improving efficiency. In short, cloud-based library management services like OCLC's WorldShare Management Services allow you to manage your library's back office tasks differently—from acquisitions to cataloging to collection development. This paper gives a synopsis of the efforts of Southeastern University's Steelman Library to streamline technical services workflows after going live on WorldShare Management Services (WMS) in July 2013. The impact that WMS has had on the library workflows at Clearwater Christian College will also be discussed briefly.

A Changing Climate

The library realm has experienced great change in the last several decades due to an ever-evolving technological climate. As a result, libraries share many common challenges, including ever more complex collections, systems, and workflows, as well as increased user demand. Academic libraries in particular have greatly changed the methods by which they offer services and resources to their patrons. This transformation goes hand-in-hand with the changes that have been taking place in higher education. The traditional face-to-face classroom experience now coexists with blended and online education and extension sites. Patrons can be anywhere, at any time, and they expect to be able to access the resources and information they need in the same fashion.

As these changes have occurred, libraries near and far have experienced (and continue to experience) budget reductions, often resulting in the reduction of staff. Though our budgets may be shrinking, the demand for more and more resources, especially electronic and digital resources, seems to be ever increasing. Furthermore, libraries are feeling the pressure to reimagine spaces and services in order to remain relevant in a climate that is constantly in a state of flux. As a result, many libraries are exploring ways in which they might address these changing needs, but with less money and staff.

One area in which libraries have been making changes is automation. Marshall Breeding describes library automation as "moving forward through an ongoing series of cycles, consistent with the epochs defined by the broader realm of information technology" (2012b, p. 23). I would take that illustration a step further and say that libraries in general are moving through these cycles. As user needs change, the goals of libraries must change to meet the demand.

Libraries in the Cloud

One of the ways libraries have endeavored to reduce costs and investment of staff time is to explore cloud-based systems. Cloud computing, a concept that didn't really begin to take shape until the late 1990s, now offers libraries a way to do this. A primary example is the adoption of the cloud-based integrated library system (ILS). Outside of the cloud, the traditional ILS relies on a local server that must be maintained. The need for necessary hardware, software, and IT expertise to maintain such an infrastructure is very costly. The traditional ILS also requires that software be installed and continually updated on a number of individual computers. This requires an additional investment of staff time.

Another downside of the traditional ILS is that it is not designed to keep up with the changing demands of our profession. It has been noted that the traditional ILS "does not have sufficient capacity" to meet these changing needs, "such as managing a wide variety of licensed electronic resources" (Fu and Fitzgerald, 2013, p. 47). In a climate where electronic and digital resources are quickly outpacing print materials, this is a problem.

In contrast, the cloud-based ILS is more flexible and mobile. It is accessible anywhere and at any time because it can be accessed via the Internet, rather than locally installed software. This makes it easier to add new services and resources while providing ease-of-access to users. This new model has greatly changed the way that library staff function, systems staff in particular. When an ILS is updated, it happens universally and simultaneously; individual software updates are no longer necessary. The cloud-based ILS can be accessed from different types of devices, including desktop computers, laptops, tablets, and smartphones. As cloud-based systems are becoming more common, a new type of cloud-based ILS has been emerging, the "next-generation ILS" also referred to as the "second generation ILS."

The Next-Generation Integrated Library System

What sets the next-generation ILS apart from traditional systems is that it is a unified system in a cloud-based environment. Not only is the next-generation ILS fully integrated, but it is often designed following service-oriented architecture (SOA). By definition, "a service-oriented architecture (SOA) is an architecture for building business applications as a set of loosely coupled distributed components linked together to deliver a well-defined level of service" (Yongming and Dawes, 2012, p. 79). This is as opposed to the

client-server computing model that is typical of the traditional ILS (Fu and Fitzgerald, 2013, p. 50).

In July 2013, Southeastern University's Steelman Library went live on OCLC's WorldShare Management Services (WMS) after migrating from the cloud-based open source ILS, Koha, hosted by LibLime. WorldShare Management Services is a next-generation ILS that includes the typical circulation and acquisitions functions expected of an ILS, but also integrates resource sharing (interlibrary loan), analytics, WorldShare Metadata collection management, OpenURL resolution, an A to Z journal list, and a discover layer in one unified system. For its OPAC, WMS uses WorldCat Local, though a new discovery interface is currently under development and is available in beta. Such integration removes the need for the investment in additional ILS add-ons such as SFX and MetaLib. Additionally, OCLC offers License Manager for an additional cost, though Steelman Library does not currently use this feature.

Before taking the position of Technical Services Librarian at Steelman, I had just completed the migration from Koha to WMS as director of Easter Library at Clearwater Christian College. At the time, the staff at Easter Library consisted of two full-time faculty librarians and one part-time paraprofessional, with the size of the College being somewhere around 420 FTE. Upon going live on WMS in May 2014, I found that we were able to greatly increase our efficiency in the area of cataloging which was a significant advantage for such a small staff.

At Steelman Library, we have six full-time faculty librarians, four full-time and two part-time paraprofessionals. With a university FTE around 3,200, the library supports 69 academic programs that include traditional, online, and extension site students. Southeastern University currently has 20 extension sites located around the United States. While Steelman is the larger of the two, both libraries are relatively small in comparison to the surrounding state university libraries and public library systems.

While different in size, both libraries dealt with the same challenges that are common for a system migration: change management, extraction and migration of data, configuring and learning to use a new system, and addressing the need to update workflows. For the purpose of this paper, I will be focusing on the impact that WMS has had on technical services workflows at Steelman Library.

Streamlining Workflows at Steelman Library

While the traditional ILS is designed to facilitate traditional library workflows, the next-generation ILS allows libraries to take a fresh look at their existing workflows and tailor them with relative ease. One of the significant differences is that various procedures are far less compartmentalized than is typical in traditional systems. This can offer both advantages and disadvantages.

As the new Technical Services Librarian at Steelman Library, one of the first things I focused on is the analysis of existing technical services workflows. While workflow analysis allows one to identify problems that might not be noticed otherwise, it also provides the opportunity to pinpoint tasks that don't need to be completed anymore as well as gaps in communication or staff training (Anderson, 2014, p. 23). Perhaps most greatly affected from my analysis was our cataloging workflow. It is important to note that as Technical Services Librarian, I am the only cataloger. I also serve as the liaison librarian to Southeastern's College of Behavioral and Social Sciences and spend part of my time doing reference and instruction. Because of how WMS has affected our technical services workflows, my hybrid position in both technical and public services is a new one.

When I began my position, I sat down with several different staff members and librarians to discuss various technical services workflows, including acquisitions and cataloging of print and electronic materials, serials acquisitions and check-in, and our newest endeavor, patron-driven acquisitions (PDA). We discussed what was working and what wasn't and what could be pared down in order to free up time for higher-level projects, keeping in mind that our overall goal is to grow the library

and not just sustain it. We also examined problematic areas within various workflows: tasks that need to be completed by different people simultaneously, issues with communication, and so on. What I began to discover was that different staff were using WMS as if it were a traditional ILS. Many features and functions were either being underutilized or not used at all.

One of the questions I kept asking was, if you are no longer using a traditional ILS, why remain tied to the traditional workflows? This was part of the postmigration change management process with some of the staff. The ability to streamline various procedures is greatly beneficial for a small or understaffed library. Often, you can ease the burden of overload for some staff, while freeing up time for more specialized projects for others. The key is to develop workflows that work for your library and the size of your staff and resources, as no two libraries are identical. What works for one library, may not work for another.

Cataloging of Print and Electronic Resources in WMS

As mentioned before, our cataloging workflow was greatly affected by the new ILS. Previously, Steelman staff had been using OCLC's Connexion for both original and copy cataloging. The cataloging librarian would identify or create the appropriate bibliographic record for an item and then import it into Koha before forwarding the item to the cataloging clerk. Once the record was available, the cataloging clerk would then add the item record into Koha and then forward the item on for physical processing. Though effective, the process was often clunky and time-consuming if there was a large volume of print materials waiting to be cataloged. Furthermore, the same procedure was being used for e-books.

As I delved further into my analysis of the cataloging workflows using WorldShare Management Services (WMS), I was struck with the realization that the staff had been following the same cataloging procedures in WMS as they had in Koha for both print and online resources. Instead of using the cataloging features that are integrated into WMS, staff was still using Connexion to manage records and update holdings. The extra steps involved were time-consuming and unnecessary.

After the workflow was changed to fit the functionality of our new ILS, we no longer import and export MARC records or add item information outside of WMS like we did with our previous system. The new print cataloging workflow involves the copy cataloging of materials in WMS by the cataloging clerk. The clerk identifies the bibliographic records for items with Library of Congress MARC records and adds a local item record within WMS, which automatically attaches the library's holdings. The cataloging librarian reviews anything without a Library of Congress record in order to identify the best MARC record and then the cataloging clerk adds the local item information in WMS. All original cataloging still goes through the cataloging librarian for a MARC record to be created before the clerk adds the item record. The new workflow has greatly reduced the amount of time it takes to catalog items, as everything is integrated into one interface.

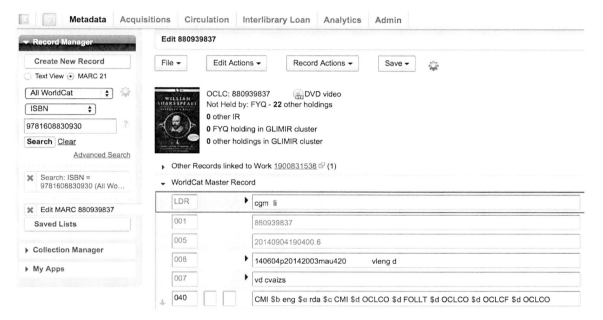

Figure 1. Viewing master bibliographic records in the WorldShare Record Manager.

As far as the cataloging of electronic resources is concerned, one key difference between the two ILSs is that WMS has a knowledge base that can be used to provide access to electronic and digital content such as e-books and databases. Instead of cataloging an e-book, importing the MARC record, and adding a local holding record with a URL in the 856 MARC field, a title is simply selected in the WMS knowledge base and becomes immediately discoverable in the public catalog. This feature of WMS was not being used before my arrival and was one of the first things we changed with our workflows. The new workflow using WMS has reduced the amount of time spent cataloging e-resources by about 50%.

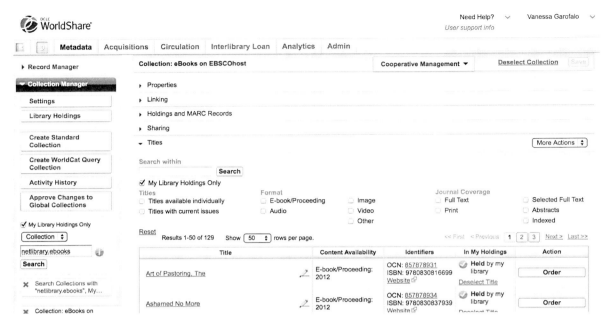

Figure 2. Viewing eBook collections in the WorldShare knowledge base.

The WorldShare knowledge base is cooperatively managed. Vendors can share their data with OCLC so that titles and collections remain up to date, removing the need to maintain resource URLs. Additionally, member libraries can add titles to global knowledge base collections as well as review and approve changes made by other member libraries. If a collection does not exist in the knowledge base, the library can create their own private collections that they manage locally. This is particularly useful for specialized collections that are specific to a library.

For patron-driven acquisitions (PDA)/demand-driven acquisitions (DDA), OCLC is working to partner with e-book vendors such as ebrary and JSTOR in order to provide automatic updates to PDA e-book collections in the WorldShare knowledge base. Once a title is triggered for purchase, it automatically moves from the PDA collection into the library's owned titles collection, making it much easier to manage PDA collections. The WMS knowledge base also pulls article-level holdings into the catalog, positioning print and electronic materials side-by-side. The built-in link

resolver then generates a "View Now" link that takes the user directly to the resource. With a mobile-ready discovery interface, users can access these resources from a variety of mobile devices. All of these features have greatly reduced the time it takes to manage these workflows and provide seamless access to our patrons.

Print Serials Check-In in WMS

As mentioned previously, when doing workflow analysis and revision, it is important to tailor workflows to your library's staff model. However, you should also keep in mind your users and how certain workflows might affect how things display on the user end, as in your online catalog. After a year of using WMS for print serials check-in, we have noticed that checking in individual issues of periodicals into WMS results in a long scrolling list of issues in the OPAC. The list can become very long and ultimately buries the other information in the record at the bottom, such as the hyperlinked subject headings. This can be difficult for patrons to look at and determine a library's serials holdings, especially for titles that are published on a weekly or biweekly basis.

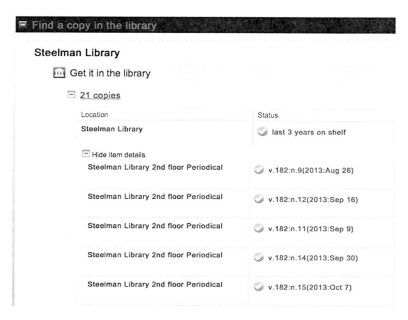

Figure 3. Print serials holdings in the WorldCat Local catalog.

As a result, we have revised our serials workflow and have done away with serials check-in in our ILS all together. Instead of listing individual issues of periodicals, we put a range in the item record in WMS that represents the starting and ending volume, issue and year of a title's holdings. In addition, we provided constructive feedback to OCLC, letting them know about what we considered to be a design flaw. Serials check-in is done online through our main subscription agent, EBSCO and claiming is done as needed. The new workflow has cut the time it takes to check in serials in half, slightly easing the burden of a staff member who multitasks in several different areas.

Managing Projects and Workflows

Before I began revising our technical services workflows, our library director suggested that we experiment using a free, web-based project management program called Trello to manage some of our projects we have been working on. Similar products exist such as Basecamp or ProWorkflow, but due to a limited budget, our director chose the free version of Trello. Project management software is beneficial in that it helps keep track of various elements associated with a project such as due dates, assignment of tasks, and keeping communication open among project members.

While we have been using Trello for special projects like setting up our new institutional repository, I have found an application for it with our new e-book cataloging workflow. While our print workflow is straightforward, we found that communication was breaking down with our e-book acquisitions. With six different librarians doing purchasing, we needed a way to keep track of different e-book collections and title lists that are purchased. When a librarian initiates a purchase, they notify me and then the titles or collection is entered into Trello in order to track payment of the invoice, selection of the resource in the WMS knowledge base, verifying access, and any other related tasks involving various staff.

The Impact of WMS on Easter Library

Prior to taking the position of Technical Services Librarian at Steelman Library, I served as the library director of Clearwater Christian College's Easter Library until June 2014. As the director, I led the ILS migration process that included around 90,000 bibliographic records extracted from Koha and migrated to our new instance of WMS. With only two librarians and one part-time paraprofessional, the change management process involved our users and campus community more than the library staff itself. Our very small staff was in agreement that we needed a more efficient solution for our workflows and WMS appeared to offer that.

While challenging, the migration process itself was not impossible. OCLC migrates libraries to WMS in small cohorts with an assigned OCLC migration manager. The migration included regular training webinars attended by all cohort member libraries, virtual office hours with the migration manager, and an online support center website with tutorials and documentation. With little to no IT support from the college throughout the process, various tasks surrounding the migration of data and configuration of the new system were often difficult, even for a librarian who is no stranger to technology.

Our main focus in letting our users and campus community know about the upcoming change to our system was to market the new public interface as more user friendly, with enhanced discovery of print and electronic materials. To convince college administrators, it was explained how the back-office system would allow the library staff to work more efficiently, freeing up time to work on more specialized projects. Today, the new director of Easter Library is working to develop an Undergraduate Research Symposium,

with additional plans for creative programs and services. They have also experienced increased efficiency in the area of cataloging in WMS

Looking Forward

As we look forward, it will be intriguing to see how OCLC's WorldShare Management Services will continue to develop as other next-generation ILSs continue to emerge and become more prominent. How long before the traditional ILS fades from our professional landscape? While the next-generation ILS such as WorldShare Management Services is far more integrated than the traditional ILS, it is certain that there is more room for development for added features and functionality that will streamline workflows even more.

As Marshall Breeding has noted in his article about the transition occurring in the automation marketplace, the change that is occurring is a delicate business and libraries usually don't respond well to such abrupt transitions (2012a, p. 30). Unfortunately, that is the nature of our business as librarians. Libraries have been evolving since their inception and should continue to evolve to adapt to ever-changing user needs. Our profession should look for and embrace opportunities that will allow us to better serve our patrons. For academic libraries, further changes in the areas of technology and its certain impact on higher education are sure to keep us on our toes!

References

Anderson, E. K. (2014). Workflow analysis. *Library Technology Reports, 50*(3), 23-29. Retrieved from http://search.proquest.com/docview/1539271410?accountid=43912

Breeding, M. (2012a). Agents of change. *Library Journal, 137(6)*. 30-36. Retrieved from http://search.proquest.com/docview/940870394?accountid=43912

Breeding, M. (2012b). New library collections, new technologies: New workflows. *Computers In Libraries*, *32*(5), 23-25. Retrieved from http://search.ebscohost.com/login.aspx?direct=true&db=ofm&AN= 76378222&site=ehost-live&scope=site

Mavodza, J. (2013). The impact of cloud computing on the future of academic library practices and services. *New Library World, 114*(3), 132-141. Retrieved from http://dx.doi.org/10.1108/03074801311304041

Ping F., & Fitzgerald, M. (2013). A comparative analysis of the effect of the integrated library system on staffing models in academic libraries. *Information Technology & Libraries, 32*(3), 47-58. Retrieved

from http://search.ebscohost.com/login.aspx?direct=true&db=ofm&AN=90292067&site=ehost
-live&scope=site

Yongming, W., & Dawes, T. A. (2012). The next generation integrated library system: A promise fulfilled. *Information Technology and Libraries, 31*(3), 76-84. Retrieved from http://search.proquest
.com/docview/1080966990?accountid=43912

The Devil Is in the Details:
Managing the Growth of Streaming Media in Library Collections

Jesse Koennecke, Director, Acquisitions and E-Resource Licensing Services, Cornell University Library
Susan Marcin, Head of Electronic Resources Management, Technologies and User Experience, Columbia University Libraries
Matthew Pavlick, Head, Monographs Acquisitions Services, Columbia University Libraries

Abstract

With the advent of streaming music and video services, patrons have grown accustomed to accessing media on their computers and mobile devices. This method of consuming media has spread into the realm of libraries and includes less-than-mainstream content not available through Netflix, Amazon, or Hulu. Some vendors have addressed this growing demand by making their video content available for streaming through subscription databases or by renting and purchasing individual titles to be hosted on a server. Streaming video content not available through databases or purchasing and renting individual titles, usually involves acquiring the DVD, encoding it and hosting the file on a local server—a very labor-intensive means to provide access. This paper examines current trends in streaming video, a detailed look at the locally encoded and hosted workflow at Columbia University Libraries, and best practices going forward.

Libraries have been recently begun exploring and expanding streaming video content for their collections. Motivations for this range from course content and training support, to entertainment and academic collection building. Streaming video allows for viewing by multiple users over a computer network, breaking away from the traditional library model of providing physical media for video content such as VHS tapes or DVDs. Library staff seeking to work with streaming video will encounter some new licensing and purchase models and will have to consider a number of workflow questions as they begin to grapple with this new content format.

Licensing Models

Streaming video is available to libraries through a wide range of licensing models. Many of these models are familiar to the library acquisitions and collection development world, though there are some aspects that may seem unique to the video streaming market. Furthermore, new acquisition models are being offered frequently by existing and emerging vendors in the market. Among the more familiar patterns are database subscriptions, collection licensing and title-by-title firm ordering. Features of streaming video that are less common to other types library resource acquisition are

local hosting of content and limited term licensing where previously libraries could purchase the content outright. Three common models help to illustrate many of the factors libraries will encounter when licensing streaming video: database subscription, third-party hosted, and locally encoded and hosted.

Subscription databases from vendors such as Alexander Street Press, Naxos, and Ambrose Video provide access to large collections of streaming video content at a relatively low cost per title. These are relatively easy for libraries to implement, with sources for title level MARC records, IP authentication, remote access, and many other features that libraries have been accustomed to dealing with in database, journal, and e-book collection subscriptions for years.

Third-party hosted streaming video consists of rental licenses with the streaming files managed on a vendor site. This model offers a wide range of options with vendors such as Kanopy, Alexander Street Press (Academic Video Store), and Swank Motion Pictures exploring and offering flexible access and purchasing models such as single title and collection licensing, demand and evidence-driven options, and volume discounts. Vendors are frequently developing new licensing options, making this third-party hosting model seem somewhat like the wild west of library acquisitions. This model allows libraries to build very specific targeted collections, though at a higher cost per title than the subscription databases. The workflow for licensing these is much like purchasing a single e-book title or collection.

A third licensing model, *locally encoded and hosted streaming content*. This is often licensed directly with the producer or distributor whose content is not available from a hosting vendor or for which the library might be seeking special terms. Licensing these titles involves obtaining permission to encode a digital file for streaming (typically ripped from a DVD or supplied as a digital file) and to host it on a locally managed or hosted secure server to the appropriate audiences. This process is considerably more time consuming than the previously discussed acquisition models and raises a number of issues that are not typically encountered with other licenses resources. Many of these are addressed below as this model is explored in greater depth.

Locally Encoded and Hosted: Columbia University Libraries

Specific requests from faculty for streaming video content to be held in course reserves at Columbia University created a new demand that could not be addressed through subscription databases or remote hosting. To provide access to streaming content not available through databases or remote vendor hosting eventually led the Libraries to the realization that the DVD would have to be purchased, ripped, and hosted on a local server. Meetings were held in the fall of 2012 to determine policy and procedure on acquiring and processing DVD + streaming course reserve requests. Participants in the meetings included representatives from access services, collection development, subject specialists, library systems and acquisitions departments. These meetings resulted in initial draft processes and workflows. In the spring of 2013, streaming for course reserve requests was launched as a service at Columbia University Libraries.

Similar to book orders for course reserves, streaming requests for reserves are extremely time sensitive. However, unlike ordering a book to be placed on reserves, processing requests for streaming can be a complicated and drawn-out procedure. First, the Libraries have to determine ownership. Second, the streaming license must be requested, sometimes negotiated, and agreed upon. Third, the DVD must be acquired. Fourth, the DVD needs to be encoded and hosted on a secured server. The steps in this process, which involve several departments, can take a matter of minutes, or drag on for several weeks before they are resolved and the DVD is ripped and hosted. Meanwhile, faculty members and students expect the streaming content to be available for the course being taught the same semester.

At Columbia University Libraries, the course reserve streaming workflow resembles the following flowchart:

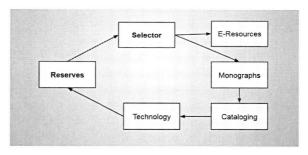

Figure 1. Streaming workflow, fall 2012.

The streaming request is submitted to the Reserves Unit by a faculty member. The Reserves Unit goes through a checklist to determine ownership and license with streaming rights:

- Check subscription databases, such as Swank and Alexander Street Press to determine if title is available.

- If the title is available through a subscription streaming database, Reserves processes the order and adds the link to the streamable content in the course reserves system.

- If the requested title is not available through one of the subscription databases, Reserves determines if the Libraries own the DVD.

- If the Libraries own the DVD, Reserves checks the Electronic Resources Management (ERM) system to determine if we have the rights to stream.

- If streaming rights are not held, Reserves submits a request to obtain streaming license to Electronic Resources acquisitions.

- If the DVD is not held in the collection, Reserves forwards the streaming request to the appropriate subject specialist along with the course information.

- Selector determines license terms and cost of DVD + streaming and submits order to E-Resources via the online E-Resources Order Form.

- E-Resources forwards DVD order to Monographs Acquisitions Services (MAS).

- MAS places order for DVD + streaming while E-Resources requests and negotiates license.

- DVD is received in MAS and routed to Cataloging with a paper "Streaming" rider attached.

- DVD is rush cataloged and routed to Technology for encoding.

- Technology routes DVD to Reserves and waits for notification that the streaming license has been signed by Collection Development.

- Reserves posts link to streaming content on course reserves server which requires authorization to access.

As it was originally constructed, the DVD + streaming workflow at Columbia Libraries was very work intensive, stretching across several departments and with many hands involved in the process. In addition to being very time-consuming, the workflow was confusing for selectors and staff. Selectors were unsure if the workflow applied to all requests for streaming media, not just course reserve requests, and the extent to which they were responsible for locating the DVD and determining if a streaming license was available. Certain selectors were also concerned that their budgets would be used to pay for the all of the costly DVD + streaming course reserve requests, which would quickly deplete their accounts. A series of meetings with selectors, Collection Development and Technical Services resolved these issues and allayed selectors' concerns. Streaming requests were only for course reserves; selectors were expected to research the streaming request before forwarding it to E-Resources; and a separate Reserves Streaming Video fund was created and allocated to pay for streaming requests.

The DVD + streaming workflow also created confusion for staff who handled the orders in E-Resources and MAS. Since the requests includes both electronic (streaming) and physical (DVD) components, it crossed two different departments within two different divisions. The E-Resources staff, who were not used to placing orders for physical objects, were unsure if they were responsible for ordering the DVD and the streaming component, while MAS staff were confused about ordering the DVD and paying for the streaming component, which was usually handled in E-Resources. Not unlike selectors, staff in MAS were also confused as to which fund to use for payment of the DVD + streaming as electronic resources were normally paid on funds not used for books or audio-visual objects. The issue of ingesting and processing the order in two different departments was addressed by redesigning the E-Resources Order Form to automatically email the order to the two departments. This eliminated the added step of forwarding the order between departments and allowed E-Resources to begin processing the streaming license while MAS ordered and paid for the DVD + streaming. The confusion surrounding which budgetary fund to use to pay for the DVD + streaming in MAS was addressed by the creation of the Reserves Streaming Video fund by Collection Development.

The initial DVD + streaming workflow benefited greatly from streamlining aspects of it and eliminating confusion of selectors and staff in the ordering process. Acquisitions librarians in their respective departments documented the changing policy and procedure on their wiki pages and shared with staff across various divisions within technical services. To keep selectors informed and updated on the locally encoded and hosted process at Columbia Libraries, a document describing what type of requests were appropriate for DVD + streaming orders, how to submit such an order, and what fund to use was created and posted on the Information for Selectors wiki. The steps taken to streamline the new DVD + streamlining workflow, eliminate confusion, and document and share the process at Columbia Libraries has allowed technical services librarians and staff to handle these orders with the possibility of expanding it to campus-wide requests.

Planning for Streaming

Though it all falls under the label of "streaming," streaming materials can be of several types, and each of these types of materials will likely be handled differently by a library and present different challenges. With subscription streaming collections, collections of streaming titles are available for subscription or purchase for access on the provider's Web site, and the vendor shares in the management of the streaming collection. Third-party hosted titles can add a layer of complexity in that these titles are generally purchased or rented/subscribed to on a title by title basis. The same or similar amounts of processing time is involved with each title, including licensing, invoicing, payment, and cataloging. Library encoded and hosted titles can add yet another layer of complexity to the management and access of streaming materials. The library will be involved in controlling access to the content on a server and in monitoring the terms of the license to remove the content when the access period has expired.

Given that there are different types of items that fall under the broad category of streaming, it can be a good idea for a library to develop a plan for streaming. If new to streaming, one good place to begin is by researching distributors and their streaming rights to get a sense of the different models that certain providers offer. There are several guides and places that such information can be found, including National Media Market's vendor grid and resources at

http://www.nmm.net/market-resources (National Media Market, n.d.).

As part of a plan for streaming, a library might decide to begin by acquiring or licensing streaming materials of one type—subscription databases, hosted rental/purchase titles, locally encoded/hosted titles—then expanding into other types as budgets, staffing, and systems allow.

The following chart attempts to convey some of the variant streaming options that a library might come across and need to develop a plan for, should they choose to license such streaming titles. A vendor might host the content. A library might be expected to host the content. The access might be perpetual. The access might be for a limited term. And each of these intersects so that, for example, a library might be expected to host content for a limited or unlimited time and a vendor might do the same.

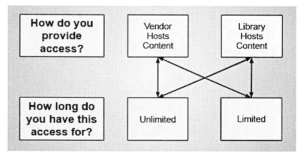

Figure 2. Streaming access options: hosting content, duration of licensed access.

Streaming Servers for Locally Encoded and Hosted Titles

If a library opts for locally encoded and hosted titles, this will require a place to put the files for users to access them. Several products and platforms are available for hosting library streaming collections, including Kaltura, ShareStream, Kanopy, Ensemble Video, Helix, Wowza, Media Amp, Avalon, and Video47. This list of hosting servers was generated from an ALCTS E-Forum titled "Streaming Media: Acquisition, Discovery, and Usage Data" (Gibson & Marcin, 2013).

An obvious criterion to look for in a streaming server is the ability to upload and store streaming video files. Beyond this, some added features to look for in a streaming media server might include:

- The ability to track access and rights management of streaming titles so that the library can secure and control access to content.

- The ability to track titles and manage access when licenses terms expire, so the library knows to take down content with expired licenses or to relicense.

- Stable URLs to include in a library catalog or course management system.

- The ability to preserve master files that can be converted to future standard formats.

- Reporting and assessment tools to show how the content is being used, including title level usage statistics.

Tracking Locally Encoded and Hosted Streaming Titles

Tracking the renewal of multiyear licenses when access rights expire will likely be a concern, particularly with a library's locally hosted titles. With vendor-hosted titles, the information provider often provides proactive assistance in monitoring when subscriptions and access terms expire so that the library can renew titles. With library/locally-hosted titles, this burden is shifted to the library to monitor. When opting to pursue locally encoding and hosting streaming licenses, how do libraries account for the varying terms of access by title-by-title and can the media server itself or an electronic resources management system assist with this? What other practices can assist with tracking streaming titles with limited duration licenses?

Locally hosted streaming titles are often part of one-time purchases of streaming rights with a DVD (streaming + DVD), and many providers are not proactive in notifying libraries when the streaming license term has expired. Even though the DVD is a purchased item which the library then owns, the accompanying streaming rights may be of a limited duration. Common streaming

license durations can be for one year, three years, five years, or for the life of file. It is then the responsibility of the library to monitor the length of the streaming license terms and make sure that content used within the parameters of the agreement, including removing expired content from local servers or relicensing as needed. It is this added responsibility of the library to monitor the length of the streaming license terms to control access which can pose challenges.

One manual process that Columbia University Libraries has experimented with to record license duration is to include this information within bibliographic records for streaming titles in the form of suppressed notes. For example, a note might be listed as such:

- Five-years streaming; 2/22/2013 - 2/22/2018; IP access.

- Streaming for life of file; 2/26/2013 onward; encoded by Libraries.

This indicates: 1) license duration, 2) the specific dates of licensed access, 3) whether the title is IP-accessible on the provider's site or locally encoded and hosted by the libraries. This way, relevant information can be easier for various departments to locate. This is a very manual process though that is not particularly scalable to large collections and easy to lose track of as licenses are renegotiated with different terms of access.

Another process that Columbia University Libraries has experimented with to record license duration is to put access dates in an ERM along with the license. If properly set up and continually maintained when new licenses are added, and depending on what ERM a library uses, inputting license dates can trigger license alerts to email you in advance of your license expiring.

Beyond notes in an ILS and dates entered into an ERM, both of which list the useful information of access dates in a separate location from the streaming file itself, a more elegant and useful solution might be to choose a streaming server that allows access dates to be input with the title and controls user access to the content based upon the dates entered into the administrative portion of the streaming server. This way the dates of licensed access are available at a point of need with the encoded content and cannot be overlooked as easily.

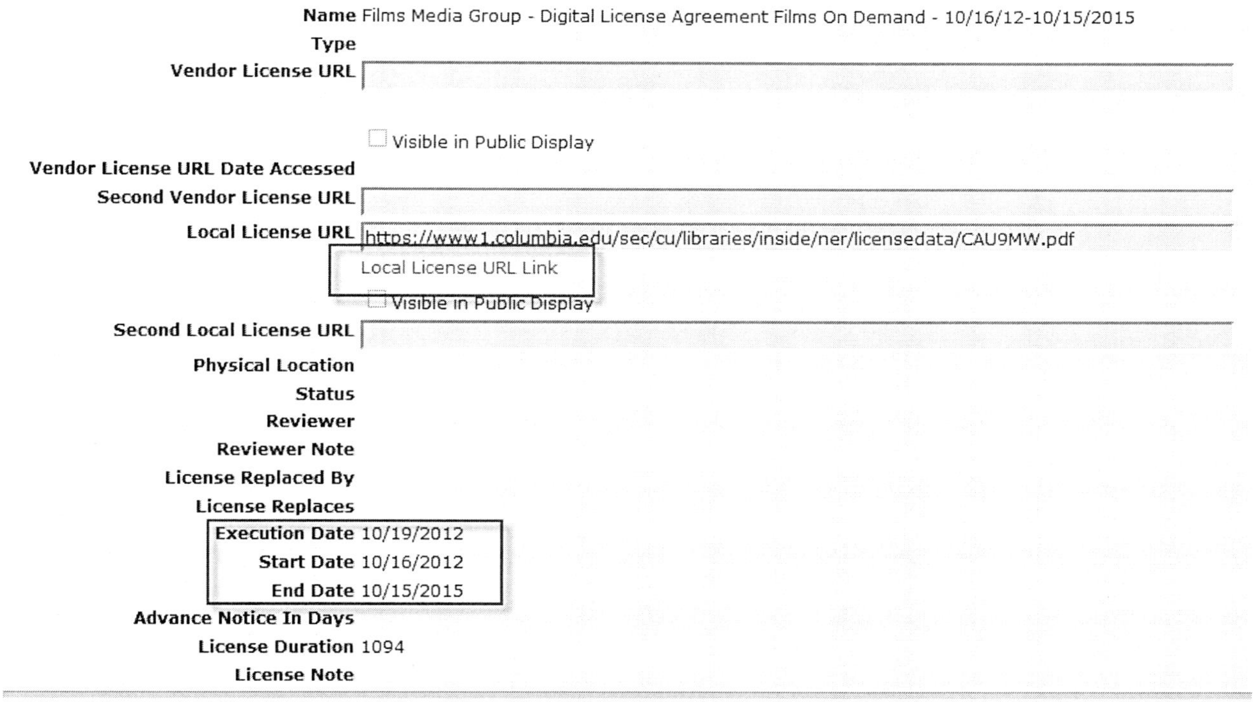

Name Films Media Group - Digital License Agreement Films On Demand - 10/16/12-10/15/2015
Type
Vendor License URL

☐ Visible in Public Display
Vendor License URL Date Accessed
Second Vendor License URL
Local License URL https://www1.columbia.edu/sec/cu/libraries/inside/ner/licensedata/CAU9MW.pdf
Local License URL Link
☐ Visible in Public Display
Second Local License URL
Physical Location
Status
Reviewer
Reviewer Note
License Replaced By
License Replaces
Execution Date 10/19/2012
Start Date 10/16/2012
End Date 10/15/2015
Advance Notice In Days
License Duration 1094
License Note

Figure 3. Example license page in electronic resources management system.

MARC Records and Streaming Collections

The variant types of streaming materials, in combination with license requirements, can each present challenges in adding items into the catalog and in records management.

- Subscription databases: some vendors supply MARC records, though there can be an inconsistency in the quality of these MARC records, based on the vendor supplying them. Not all vendors supply records, which may then entail the need for local copy or original cataloging of items. Some subscription collections exist in ERMs for ease of management.

- Third-party hosted: providers may offer MARC records, but Library may have to monitor removing records when access rights expire.

- Locally encoded/hosted: it is highly unlikely that providers will offer MARC records. Library may have to monitor removing records when access rights expire.

In terms of some of the considerations for adding title-level records for discovery, licenses should also be reviewed to see if there are any terms restricting this. For example, is the content restricted to one course or open to all authorized users? How long can the library stream the content: 1 year, 5 years, 1 semester, perpetually? If streaming duration is limited, records management should be part of the planning.

References

Gibson, S., & Marcin, S. (2013, October 13). *Streaming media: Acquisition, discovery, and usage data*. Retrieved from http://www.ala.org/alctsnews/features/streaming-media-e-forum

National Media Market (n.d.). *Resources*. Retrieved from http://www.nmm.net/market-resources

Streamlined Licensing Through Institutional Master Agreements: A Success Story

Corey S. Halaychik, Assistant Professor and Electronic Resources Specialist, University of Tennessee Knoxville

Abstract

The University of Tennessee implemented a master agreement initiative in fall 2012 as an effort to create a more effective and efficient contract review and approval process. The initiative, a joint venture between the campus libraries, the University's System Office of Contracts Administration, and the Purchasing Department, started with one basic master agreement and quickly expanded to over 115 signed documents. The agreements cover the vast majority of library electronic and media resource vendors and have reduced contract volume by more than half. When master agreements are in place, terms and conditions no longer sit awaiting review and approval for multiple weeks or months, which virtually eliminates the danger of access to library resources being shut off. Additionally, master agreements have removed obstacles which had previously impeded the University's various campus libraries from working together to save money and broaden access through joint purchases.

Landscape

The University of Tennessee is a multicampus state university system with campuses and institutes in the cities of Knoxville, Memphis, Chattanooga, Martin, and Tullahoma. These organizational components spend several million dollars per year on resources that support teaching, research, and learning with many expenses requiring contracts to be signed. System-wide, the University processes more than 5,000 contracts annually. Generally, the various contract offices have a small number of staff dedicated to reviewing contracts. With continued interest in acquiring electronic resources, library contract volume has seen a steady increase in volume.

Because the system is an instrumentality of the state of Tennessee, all contracts are required to comply with a multitude of state laws and fiscal policies, including policies that strictly restrict the number of individuals authorized to sign contracts on behalf of the system. Certain contracts are required to go through the campus-level contract office, the system-level contract, and the University's office of general counsel. Many vendors are very slow to respond to changes requested by the University, sometimes delaying the process by months.

The Challenge

These factors created a setting in which the review and approval process for library contracts and amendments was extremely slow to complete. This frustrated library staff as these delays could result in existing resources being shut off while contracts were processed. Purchasing new products also proved to be problematic for librarians as new contracts needed to be signed or existing agreements amended.

Office of Contracts Administration personnel were equally frustrated as the number of redundant library contracts—that is, contracts for the same products that multiple campus libraries subscribed to—required separate reviews and approvals to account for slight differences in content such as technical contacts, prices, or full-time equivalent totals. This, coupled with the vast number of library resources requiring contracts, resulted in a disproportionate amount of time being spent by staff on reviewing library contracts, resulting in a general backlog for all contracts across the system.

Vendors found the system's policies confusing and challenging as the need for multiple contracts and yearly amendments distracted from their sales efforts or increased their own contract review costs. New vendors in particular often struggled to understand which system department handled what and whom to contact to inquire about delays or negotiate license terms. Payment delays were a frequent issue that caused concern for all vendors as minute differences between a contract and invoice content (for instance, a title being spelled out in a contract but abbreviated on an invoice) could prevent a payment from being made.

By early 2012, librarians involved with electronic resources management recognized that the current policies and procedures were encumbering them from performing their mission. Additionally, stakeholders agreed that the current environment strained relationships and created extra work across the board. In an effort to address these challenges, personnel from the libraries, the University's System Office of Contracts Administration and Purchasing Department collaborated to examine existing procedures and identify a solution that would streamline existing processes while ensuring that existing fiscal policies and state laws were followed.

Proposed Solution

The System Office of Contracts Administration, responsible for the bulk of the license review and approval work, took the lead in investigating possible solutions to address the timely and redundant contract review process. After exploring available options, stakeholders determined that a master agreement would address the issues encountered by the campus libraries, Office of Contracts Administration, and Purchasing Department. While not an entirely new concept—many vendors use master service agreements for their products—the idea of creating an institutional master agreement issued by a university that covered library resources was new.

The institutional master agreements, as proposed, would depart from typical vendor supplied agreements by removing library specific business terms (price, title lists, FTE numbers, etc.) from the contract. Instead, they would include standardized language applicable across the system addressing governing law, termination,

severability, indemnity, notification, online terms and conditions, and other language not prone to frequent changes. Library business terms would be covered on system-issued purchase orders. University of Tennessee policies dictate that purchase orders are requested by campus departments and issued by the Purchasing Department. This combination—having the standard terms and conditions covered in the institutional master agreement and moving business terms to a system-issued purchase order—would allow the contract review and approval process to be bypassed for future renewals or new purchases with vendors that had master agreements in place.

In order to lessen the burden on Office of Contracts Administration personnel, it was suggested by the campus libraries that they be responsible for contacting vendors about switching to institutional master agreements. The libraries were amenable to this switch since they had existing relationships in place with vendor representatives and it was believed these relationships could be leveraged to expedite the transition to institutional master agreements. To cut down on duplicative efforts and take advantage of the close proximity to the Office of Contracts Administration, it was decided that Knoxville campus libraries' Licensing, Electronic Resources, and Serials Department would coordinate overall efforts and serve as the main point of contact for all vendors setting up institutional master agreements.

Process

As a collaborative effort between the campus libraries, Office of Contracts Administration, and Purchasing Department, the institutional master agreement negotiation, creation, and approval process had the potential to fall victim to the same bureaucratic red tape that plagued the pre-existing process. It therefore became a priority to keep the process as streamlined as possible; limiting the number of University of Tennessee individuals involved in facilitating institutional master agreement implementation is paramount. Master agreements are currently coordinated by a single librarian at the Knoxville campus and an attorney with The Office of Contracts

Administration. Each of these individuals serves as a liaison to counterparts at other campuses or system offices as needed.

Another way that the process remains streamlined is through the use of an agreement template. As a matter of convenience and to create a uniform appearance, an institutional master agreement template was created that contained all of the legal language required by the system. Vendor licenses are attached to the template. This allows parties to easily merge contract documents instead of rearranging or negotiating where specific clauses should be placed.

The process of setting up a master agreement begins when a campus library suggests one be pursued with a specific vendor. The vendor is contacted by the Electronic Resources Specialist at the Knoxville campus Libraries who provides information about master agreements and requests an editable version of the vendor's existing agreement. Once the agreement is received, it is edited to ensure compliance with University of Tennessee policies, state law, and library business practices. The edited agreement is returned to the vendor and negotiations take place as each side works together to settle on language that is agreeable to both sides. When negotiations have ended, a clean copy is prepared and submitted for signature and then a fully executed copy is filed with system. The fully executed copy allows all future renewals and purchases to be handled with system purchase orders which contain individual campus library subscription and business terms such as date ranges, title lists, and costs.

Results

The first library institutional master agreement became effective on August 15, 2012 and as of October 21, 2014, 118 have been completed. The agreements have been widely successful in streamlining purchases and renewals of databases, e-books, journal packages, and streaming media. The work time being spent reviewing, negotiating, routing, and tracking library contracts has been reduced 55% and has resulted in a savings of approximately $62,000.

Feedback from all stakeholders has been overwhelmingly positive. Librarians and library administrators feel empowered by the agreements as they have restored a level of autonomy in the negotiation of library business terms. The streamlining enabled by the agreements has also solved most of the issues with resources being shut off due to delays caused by licenses bogged down in the contract review and approval process. Office of Contracts Administration personnel spend less time reviewing redundant library contracts and amendments. Vendor sales representatives and accounts payable staff appreciate the bypassing of bureaucratic red tape when it comes to closing sales or receiving payment.

Lessons Learned

The University of Tennessee has had to remain flexible in its approach to getting institutional master agreements signed by vendors. The libraries have had to remain focused on the purpose of the agreements—to streamline the renewal and purchase process—and as a result, have had to forego lobbying for major changes to language addressing topics such as open access, confidentially, and data mining rights. The Office of Contracts Administration has had to occasionally make compromises concerning the preferred template and attachment format. Instead, some institutional master agreements have been created by inserting the system's required language into a vendor's existing agreements.

Timing and persistence have also played key roles in successfully negotiating institutional master agreements. It should come as no surprise that vendors are more open to the idea of renegotiating an agreement when subscriptions are up for renewal. Coinciding attempts at obtaining an institutional master agreement with renewal dates is a tactic that has been used successfully multiple times. Additionally, tying the purchase of a new product or subscription has also helped convince vendors to sign institutional master agreements when they have otherwise been hesitant to do so. Persistence and not taking "no" for an answer has had a positive impact in reaching the number of institutional master agreements that have been signed. Several vendors initially declined to enter into the agreements but repeated emails, phone calls, and face-to-face meetings paid off in the majority of cases. Generally, it is a matter of identifying the right individual who can make the decision to enter into the master agreement and setting up a time to discuss.

Going Forward

In a perfect world, all of the libraries' renewals and purchases would be covered by institutional master agreements. Realistically though, this is a difficult goal to achieve as there continues to be a small number of vendors who refuse to make the change due to their own fiscal policies and procedures. Despite that limitation, the majority of library vendors working with the University of Tennessee have now signed institutional master agreements and efforts will continue to be made to reach the 100% mark.

The success of the agreements has also caught the attention of other institutions. Most notably, The Tennessee Board of Regents college and university libraries have asked for assistance in setting up their own master agreements. Several

meetings have been taken place between University of Tennessee and Tennessee Board of Regents personnel; and a working group comprised of librarians, contract officers, and purchasing agents, was recently formed to help speed the process along.

Summary

In an effort to create a more effective and efficient library contract review and approval process, the University of Tennessee decided to implement institutional master agreements. A collaborative effort between the system's libraries, Office of Contracts Administration, and Purchasing Department, the agreements were launched in August 2012 and there are now over 115 in place. Institutional master agreements have been extremely successful at streamlining renewals for existing subscriptions and acquiring new products and have reduced overall library contract volume by 55%. Emphasis continues to be placed on entering into additional institutional master agreements with vendors, and the system is working with other colleges and universities who are interested in duplicating the success that The University of Tennessee has had.

Relax, Be Earnest: Marketing a Serials Deselection Project

Stephanie J. Spratt, University of Colorado – Colorado Springs

Abstract

Many libraries use the fear of public outcry as a reason to limit interaction with their communities while in the process of deselecting materials. This paper proposes that well-written policies, process transparency, and a properly managed promotional plan are the best approaches to building goodwill and support among concerned constituents. "Throwing away books" does not have to be done in secret. A process for transforming internal goals into external communications and marketing events is provided along with a discussion of the partnerships and resources needed to accomplish that transformation. Outcomes of the project, including reutilization of space, updated library policies, and reactions from the community are also presented.

Introduction

Let's face it—deselecting materials is a necessary evil. Librarians have been aware of the benefits of a well-weeded collection for years and yet the process continues to fill us with dread. Especially the thought of our users discovering that we are doing it. As one librarian states, "don your black clothes and come to the school [or library] in the dead of night to haul your double bagged discarded books to the dumpster" (Allen, 2010, p. 33). We have heard horror stories of library users arguing with libraries for removing materials. Some deselection projects have stopped dead in their tracks after powerful users made their disagreements with the project known to higher levels of administration.

Despite those obstacles, the need to move out undesired books and journals to provide for more appropriate use of library space is ever present. So, while some libraries may take the secretive path to deselection, this paper advocates for more, rather than less, communication with users about these projects. As the experts in the field, librarians have the best ability to decide when it is time for some materials to go, and librarians involved in these projects should prepare themselves for those difficult conversations about why they are removing materials to the users who have concerns.

While the subtitle of this paper is "Marketing a Serials Deselection Project," the term marketing is used very broadly. According to Kennedy (as cited in Richardson, 2014), "marketing [is] 'a strategic communication with your library patrons. It's an intentional conversation'" (p. 43). Any form of communication with library users or stakeholders is, in a sense, marketing.

Project Need, Goals, and Methods

As many academic libraries have discovered, space is at a premium. Student study space, computer labs, and dedicated service spaces (i.e. meditation space or athletic department tutoring spaces) are becoming more desirable than collection space. The Kraemer Family Library (KFL) at the University of Colorado-Colorado Springs (UCCS) performed a bound serials weeding project during early 2014, when staff members were asked to reduce the library's serials collection by over 50%. The work needed to be completed in approximately six months and was further constrained by limited tools, personnel, and budget.

UCCS is a medium-sized institution with full-time enrollment around 8,500. The library is centrally located and shares its building with the campus Information Technology Department and the University Student Center. The main doors in and out of the library lead to the outdoors and the west side of campus and open up to the main circulation desk and reference desk. The rear doors lead to the student center and open up to a smaller circulation desk and the bound periodicals shelving. User traffic is heavy with some visitors using the aisles nearest the bound periodicals solely as a walkway between the outdoors and the student center.

The project had formed largely due to the need for more student collaboration space and seating. It began slowly in early 2014, just before a new Electronic Resources and Serials Librarian was hired, through the examination of JSTOR archive collection holdings. These electronic holdings were compared to print holdings, and thus the project was born.

There was very little in the way of documentation to follow to implement the project. The Collection Development Policy was from 1992 and had not been reviewed or fully practiced for many years. The task of deciding how to meet the project goals and manage its implementation fell almost solely on the Electronic Resources and Serials Librarian beginning in late March 2014. The deadline for completion was the beginning of the fall 2014 semester. No commercial collection analysis tools were available, therefore entitlement lists from vendors compared to holdings reports from the integrated library system using Excel was largely the method implemented to determine which materials could be withdrawn.

Over the course of the project, 1,620 print serial titles were reviewed. Of those, the subject librarians chose to completely remove 1,031. During the months of June, July, and August 2014, 37,225 serial volumes were either donated or recycled from an original count of 74,551. Although KFL did not quite reach its goal of removing over 50% of the bound serials volumes, the volumes and shelving were removed and new furniture was placed in time for the first day of fall classes.

Prior to the removal of deselected serials, the UCCS student newspaper printed an article calling for the "spring cleaning" of the "dusty old tomes" held in the library due to lack of use (Wefler, 2014, p. 9). During the project, the library kept a recycling dumpster at the library loading dock for holding and hauling away the withdrawn serials. This prompted a few students to voice their concerns to the local television news station. An investigative reporter visited the library and spoke to the Dean of the Library. A few days later, the station aired a brief news clip containing the Dean's interview and video of volumes being tossed into the dumpster. After the completion of the project and the rearrangement of library shelving and furnishings, another article was printed in the student newspaper, this one providing simple quotes such as, "I like it, it's roomier" (Deveyra, qtd. in Skelton, 2014, p. 1). The lack of further concerns after the airing of the news clip and the change in layout at the library meant the communication efforts of KFL were effective.

Transform Internal Goals into External Communication

When planning for this project, the library focused on what was best for the students. The project's goals were based on information KFL had received from student surveys, from an article in the student-run newspaper calling for removal of outdated journals, and from other libraries' weeding projects. Having goals that stem from user needs helps build a foundation for communicating the necessity and benefits of a deselection project.

Once goals for the project are defined, the formation of a chart to document marketing messages which can be used to support and describe the goals is a method which helps prepare library staff for any communications that may be needed throughout the project lifecycle. Documenting in the chart the goals, messages, and message delivery methods provides a source of information for future communications. Planning ahead will ensure that libraries are responding to concerns with confidence and authority.

The chart can be used for both internal (among library staff) and external communication efforts. An example chart that comprises some of the goals that KFL had for their deselection project and the messages and delivery methods that were used is offered here as a starting point for other libraries.

Goal	Internal Message and Delivery Method	External Message and Delivery Method
Identify bound serials to deselect.	Provide spreadsheets of data to aid in decision-making via emails to those involved.	If gathering faculty or others' input on which materials can be deselected, utilize email or web forms.
Move deselected materials out of the building.	Provide the project deadline and other expectations in face-to-face conversations with all staff members who are affected.	Provide faculty members, university departments, and nonprofit groups the ability to request deselected materials via the library's website or an email message. Set up flyers in the affected area briefly describing the project and warning users that it may be noisy at times.
Respond promptly to concerns from library users.	Keep all staff members informed of specific concerns and how they were addressed via email or in meetings. Provide them with the proper person to contact if further concerns are brought to their attention via email.	Create, maintain, and provide public access to a collection development policy which addresses deselection. Provide details of the project via the local television news outlet.
Keep staff members tasked with the labor-intensive job of materials management motivated.	Post pictures and supportive comments on social media sites.	
Increase the amount of student collaborative space that is available in the library.		Announce the changes in a library newsletter and on the library's website.
Complete the project on schedule.	Hold an internal project completion party. Provide gift bags to those people whose work was instrumental in the project's completion.	Invite the public to an open house to celebrate the completion of the project and to show off the results. Provide fun without hiding the fact that materials were recycled, e.g., using weeded volumes as art.

Table 1. Transforming goals into marketing messages.

Use Communication to Build Trust with Constituents

One of the most powerful communication tools to have at the ready in cases of deselection projects is an up-to-date collection development policy which addresses deselection. Allen (2010) remarks, "While weeding can be controversial, a carefully prepared and fully documented policy on weeding (or deselection) can lessen or alleviate misunderstandings" (p. 32). Always have your policy at the ready should anyone challenge the library's authority to deselect and remove materials.

Another useful communication tool, as suggested by Jett (2014), is to sandwich negative statements inside positive statements. For KFL, a fitting example could be, "The amount of seating/group study space available to students has increased significantly. Yes, because of a looming deadline we had to recycle instead of donate much of our serial collection to make that space. And, through our partnership with the Sustainability Office on campus for that project, we've identified four new classes of materials that we can recycle instead of put in the trash."

Trust is a two-way street. Librarians should trust that their users are able to listen to and understand the reasoning behind materials deselection processes. By acknowledging concerns, and responding to them with a calm, practiced approach, library staff can better provide transparency and communication which are trust-building activities. Ease the fears of library users by explaining the ethical methods used during deselection. Sometimes the content of the materials are not being recycled in the way that users hope (i.e., donated to other libraries or organizations instead of becoming recycled paper). However, libraries use exchanges and charities such as Better World Books as often as they can. When those options are unavailable, the next best option is used. Due to the strict deadline with which KFL was working, donation was not always a viable option, but no materials were ever thrown in the trash. A partnership with a recycling company assured ethical measures were taken to discard the materials.

Create Partnerships for the Long Term

Not only is the creation and retention of mutually beneficial partnerships already an important goal of libraries, it is essential in maintaining good will with campus administration and library users. Some of the partnerships that KFL relied upon for the proper management of the deselection project included the UCCS Office of Sustainability, the provost and upper university administration, the local recycling company, and other local libraries and nonprofits.

Sandler (2014) states:

> Leverage partnerships. Publishers, authors, and libraries share a common interest in promoting the use of scholarly content and,

to a lesser extent, library services that promote discovery and reading . . . Marketing is a two-way street: it's about telling the library story, but also learning anything and everything about a targeted user community—who they are, what they do, what they need, and how well they think the library is addressing their needs . . . Market to the insecurities of the campus. Attack the gap between what users want . . . and the limitations of their own abilities. Libraries should be promoted as the difference between academic success and failure. (p. 196)

Building these partnerships helps provide another positive outcome when undertaking deselection processes. As stated in the example positive-negative-positive statement in the section above, the connection that this project secured with the Office of Sustainability provided a beneficial growth of the library's recycling efforts that will last long into the future.

Conclusion

The marketing messages and programs presented here are only examples of what libraries can do and say to promote deselection projects. Many others can be used to match the expectations of individual library communities. For example, Røgler (2014) states:

> Discarding is usually something that takes place in silence, without the user's knowledge. The idea of throwing away books is uncomfortable for both librarians and the public. However, this attitude stands in the way of the library's development. When the discarded books were transformed into art, we lifted them out in the public space. We dared to highlight weeding as part of professional practice. (p. 390)

The most important messages to convey are the library's expertise in effectively managing the print collection, and that the library is willing to enter into a discussion with anyone who may be concerned. Librarians should overcome their fear of public outcry, and let their adeptness at providing the best selection of print materials as possible be known to their users. "The aim of the various measures is to enter into dialogue with sceptics and work as a team with those who are positive" (Røgler, 2014, p. 395).

Deselecting print resources has long been a regular practice of public libraries and has evolved to be a regular practice of research libraries as well. As such, it is a practice that deserves commitment from the libraries and librarians who utilize it. Sharing the benefits of the process with library users is part of that commitment. Start "throwing away books" out in the open and see where it takes you.

References

Allen, M. (2010). Weed 'em and reap: The art of weeding to avoid criticism. *Library Media Connection, 28*(6), 32-33.

Jett, H. (2014). Leading the way to yes: Building good will through circulation policy and practice. *Back in circulation again 2014*. Presentation conducted from University of Wisconsin-Madison School of Library & Information Studies, Madison.

Richardson, H. & Kennedy, M. (2014). How to market your library's electronic resources. *The Serials Librarian: From the Printed Page to the Digital Age, 67*(1), 42-47. http://dx.doi.org/10.1080/0361526X.2014.899289

Røgler, J. (2014). The case for weeding: The Buskerud Bandits' contribution to a knowledge-based discarding practice in Norwegian public libraries. *Journal of Library Administration, 54*(5), 382-402. http://dx.doi.org/10.1080/01930826.2014.946752

Sandler, M. (2014). Coffee's for closers. *Choice, 52*(2), 194-197.

Skelton, E. (2014, September 22). Summer remodel changes arrangement of library. *The Scribe, 39*(4), 1.

Wefler, A. (2014, April 7). Library due for spring cleaning, not elimination. *The Scribe, 38*(24), 9.

From Collection Development to Content Development: Organization and Staffing for the 21st Century

Sara E. Morris, Associate Content Development Librarian, University of Kansas
Lea Currie, Head of Content Development, University of Kansas

Abstract

The University of Kansas (KU) Libraries has a new organizational structure that resulted in the creation of the Content Development Department, with fewer librarians dedicated to stewardship of the Libraries' collections. The impending retirement of three long-standing and knowledgeable librarians prompted a review of the responsibilities of the new department and identification of the human resources needed to meet the collection demands of a user-centered library. In an effort to determine how the Libraries can proceed, we completed an environmental scan of current activities and identified, through the literature and contacts with academic colleagues, how collecting practices and formats will develop. Based on evidence gained through a survey of faculty and graduates students at KU, there is a strong sentiment that library resources need to be carefully managed to support the teaching and research needs of the university. This paper will discuss efforts to make a case to continue to support deep subject expertise for collection development, particularly in the arts and humanities. By clearly identifying collection development responsibilities (it's not just buying books!), KU librarians were successful in transitioning into the new organizational structure with the staffing needed to make knowledgeable collection development decisions.

KU Campus Environment

Analyzing existing structures and making adjustments to make KU a stronger institution of higher learning have become the new normal. In 2009, a new chancellor arrived on campus, replacing her predecessor, who had served in this capacity for fourteen years. The next year, a new provost joined the leadership team. Together, these new administrators established lofty goals to raise KU's research output and reputation and streamline operations to improve stewardship of KU's precious dollars. The two most consequential of these efforts were "Changing for Excellence" and "Bold Aspirations." In the summer of 2010 "Changing for Excellence" began evaluating business practices to increase institutional efficiencies and decreasing expenditures (University of Kansas, 2013). KU's strategic planning efforts, which started in the fall of 2010 resulted in the plan "Bold Aspirations" which framed KU's short-term goals into six areas (University of Kansas, 2012):

- Energizing the educational environment.

- Elevating doctoral education.

- Driving discovery and innovation.

- Engaging scholarship for public impact.

- Developing infrastructure and resources.

- Developing infrastructure and resources.

Since KU adopted these two programs, they have become the foundation for decisions of all types on campus, and the KU transformation began with the Libraries leading the way.

KU Libraries' Strategic Planning

The campus strategic plan, "Bold Aspirations," was released in October 2011. By November, the KU Libraries had not only pledged to be the first campus unit to undergo a strategic planning process based on KU's plan, but had already established a steering committee for strategic planning. This group of appointed individuals worked quickly to identify and determine the goals for the strategic plan. By the spring various working groups were establishing outcomes and strategies for each goal. When the final plan was released, the libraries "Strategic Directions" put forth the following goals (University of Kansas Libraries, 2012):

- Integrate information literacy, research skills, and information resources into the curriculum to enhance critical thinking, academic success, and lifelong learning.

- Advance scholarship through proactive engagement in research and scholarly communication.

- Strengthen KU Libraries' position as an agile responsive organization capable of continual improvement and change.

- Stabilize and grow existing funding sources, secure new funding opportunities, and enhance public accountability.

Shortly after the release of the KU Libraries' strategic plan, the dean of libraries created the Organizational Review Team (ORT). The dean charged ORT to review all aspects of the organization and to make recommendations for a library structure that embraced the objectives put forth in "Bold Aspirations" and "Strategic Directions." ORT's report went directly to the dean of libraries who utilized their findings, along with her own knowledge of trends in research libraries, to create the new structure. She proclaimed the new organization a "User-Focused Organizational Structure."

Reorganization

KU Libraries' new organizational structure began in May 2013. Most of the library staff now report within one of five divisions (University of Kansas Libraries, 2013):

- The Division of Innovation and Strategy, comprised of Assessment Services.

- The Division of Information Technology and Discovery Services, comprised of Metadata and Data Discovery Services and Cataloging, Archival Processing, and Digitization Services.

- The Division of Distinctive Collections, comprised of Special Collections, University Archives, Kansas Collection, International Area Studies, Conservation Services, and Digital Collections.

- The Research and Learning Division, comprised of the Center for Faculty and Staff Initiatives and Engagement, the Center for Graduate Initiatives and Engagement, the Center for Undergraduate Initiatives and Engagement, and the Center for Community and Affiliates Initiatives and Engagement.

- The Content and Access Services Division, comprised of Access and Reference Services, Acquisitions, Resource Sharing, the Annex (collections storage facility), and Content Development. Collection development's name changed to "content" to reflect the idea that research libraries had moved away from developing warehouses of owned materials.

The new Content Development Department has six content development librarians and one departmental head. Before the reorganization, more than thirty subject librarians participated in collection development activities. Many of these individuals are now part of the Research and Learning Division and no longer help with collections decisions. With the announcement of the new library structure, the Content Development Department scrambled to distribute the stewardship of the collections among the much smaller department. Along with the added collections responsibilities, the department had to contend with the impending retirements of three experienced and knowledgeable librarians who are scheduled to retire within two years of the creation of the new department. These librarians specialize in the visual arts, the performing arts, and the humanities, three areas that demand strong subject expertise. It soon became evident that a thorough review of content development job responsibilities and succession planning was in order.

Job Responsibilities of the New Content Development Department

In order to begin succession planning, the librarians within the department identified common responsibilities. These included:

- Monitoring the changing nature of collections, including:

  - The changing practice of scholarly communication in all disciplines.

  - The changing nature of higher education and programs at KU.

  - Trends within the field of collection development: purchasing models, changes in publishing options.

  - New formats of scholarly products (e.g., journal articles linked to data sets, video).

- Collection Decisions:

  - Maintain awareness of curricular programs and research.

  - Monitor new faculty and research hires.

  - Manage approval plans.

  - Manage firm orders.

  - Select resources in all formats and platforms: monographs, serials, databases, data sets, streaming video, maps, scores, records, scripts, CDs and DVDs.

  - Consider scholarly communication patterns, including open access and local collections.

- Collection maintenance, including retention decisions.

- Collaborate with other library units and centers.

- Manage gifts by working with patrons to accept and review.

- Provide specialized instruction when extensive knowledge of collections is required.

- Provide consultation for in-depth subject questions.

- Participate in cooperative collection development projects with other

universities and the Western Regional Storage Trust (WEST).

Survey of the Environment

To truly understand how the KU Content Development Department would function in this new model required understanding the changing nature not only of KU, but also research libraries and higher education in general. "Bold Aspirations" and activities on campus indicated that research from freshman to highly recruited "Foundational Professors" would become a cornerstone of activities at KU. As such, the Libraries' content would become even more important and it would become imperative for those working in Content Development to understand the teaching and research activities on campus. A survey administered to graduate students and faculty at KU, as part of the Libraries' strategic plan, indicated that collections remained what they valued the most from the Libraries. This was not unlike the conclusions of the U.S. Faculty Survey 2012 administered by Ithaka (Schonfeld & Housewright, 2013). The other key finding from the KU survey was the increased desire for electronic resources, particularly serial back files and acquiring e-books. These key components of the KU survey provided us with important evidence that collections mattered.

Looking beyond KU, we focused on two main things: changes to collection acquisitions models and the research activities of different disciplines. Although KU Libraries' strategic plan indicated that we would continue to provide materials, the name change from collection to content indicated a sea change. While KU Libraries had implemented demand-driven acquisition (DDA) a few years prior to the reorganization, the new structure reinforced the abandonment of building collections for use in twenty years. The literature reinforced this concept. ARL's (2013) *Issue Brief: 21st Century Collections: Calibration of Investment and Collaborative Action* concisely states the problems faced by research libraries during this shift from institution-centered collections to those of a model focused on users—users who might be connected to the university or half-way around the world. This reinforced that KU needed to transition to a more streamlined selection process that was more agile and adaptable to new methods of providing information. Reports such as Lorcan Dempsey's (2013) *The Emergence of the Collective Collection: Analyzing Aggregate Print Library Holdings* gave us pause to think about how the collections at KU fit within the larger library community. As much as the responsibility of providing new sources to KU's scholars fell to this new department, so too did being stewards of what we had already collected. It was essential that staff in the new department and the administration understood that responsibilities included activities such as participating in WEST, reviewing collections for long-term storage and building other collaborative retention programs.

For over thirty years, KU had operated with a system of subject bibliographers. The new model abandoned this idea by assuming that generalists could answer reference questions and that the majority of collection decisions did not require expertise. Although true for areas that are dependent on journal packages and a monograph approval plan that results in automatic shipments of materials, this is not true for all areas, particularly the humanities. Interviews with librarians at other ARL libraries indicated that they recognize that subject knowledge in the arts and humanities remains key. As an institution, KU has long supported fields within the humanities. Hiring in these fields remains steady, classes in these fields generate the most profit, and KU remains committed to supporting these areas. The library has always collected extensively in the humanities. For example, interlibrary loan statistics indicates that the majority of KU's lending (particularly within the state) comes from the humanities. Numerous studies of specific disciplines' research habits and the services they need from the library reinforced that a blanket collection development approach, which might work for the social sciences, did not work for all members of the academy (Harley, Acord, Earl-Novell, Lawrence & King, 2010; Schonfeld & Rutner, 2012; Long & Schonfeld, 2013; Long & Schonfeld, 2014). These studies point to the fact that some areas simply require knowledge that a generalist cannot provide. The types of materials used in the humanities cannot be supplied by a general approval plan. Due to the variety of

formats used (i.e., scores, primary sources, museum publications) and the lack of electronic resources, significant sleuthing is necessary to adequately collect in these areas.

Subject Expertise

Through our review of the literature and consulting with colleagues at other schools, we concluded that to effectively provide our patrons with the information they needed, Content Development needed to retain these areas of expertise:

- History (currently divided between an American and world history).
- Art (visual art and history of art) and architecture.
- Music (performing arts).
- English literature.
- Language proficiency (specifically French, German, Italian).

This realization was particularly alarming, because, with the exception the American history content development librarian, all of this subject knowledge was contained in individuals who were either retiring or had temporary appointments. Consequently, the members of Content Development initiated an evaluation of why these areas needed to be filled once the individuals left KU.

World History—with one of the largest firm order funds, this discipline requires a knowledge of publishers worldwide and a variety of formats. To support this discipline requires selecting books in western European languages. The range of history researchers at KU requires knowledge of resources in ancient, medieval, Renaissance, and modern history.

Visual Art and Architecture—the visual arts require a deep knowledge of numerous vendors who supply resources in European art, Asian art, architecture, exhibition catalogues, and catalog raisonnes. Out-of-print dealers are also routinely checked. Resources are selected in multiple western European languages.

Performing Arts, with an emphasis on music—the librarian in this area must be familiar with a variety of vendors who supply books, serials, DVDs, CDs, scores, streaming video and music, monumental sets, and play scripts. A strong knowledge of older and contemporary composers is needed along with musicology, music theory, performance, and history.

English Literature—requires a deep knowledge of comparative literature, literature in translation, literary criticism, poetry, and works of fiction. An awareness of small presses and publishers worldwide is needed to cover the vast amount of literature published.

Language Proficiencies—To purchase literature in the humanities, librarians with proficiency in French, Italian, and German is instrumental to support these degreed programs.

These findings were summarized in the report "Environmental Assessment and Recommendations for Staffing the Content Development Department." Initially, it was shared with the assistant deans who were working on the establishment of the KU Libraries' new model for providing instruction and reference support. These library leaders agreed with the findings of the document and recognized these areas of specific knowledge in the larger library plan for assisting researchers at KU. The document was then forward to the Dean and Associate Deans. The timing was perfect because the library administration, during the summer of 2014, created a three year hiring plan.

Outcomes and the Future

There have been many positive outcomes to report. First, the Provost approved the hiring of a new Visual Arts Librarian and a new Performing Arts Librarian and searches for these positions should be launched early during the 2015 spring semester. Due to the possibility of a period of vacancy in these positions, the Head of Content Development has been training with the two librarians in the visual arts and performing arts. Both librarians say this is the first time their supervisor has known the specifics of what they do and the Head has picked up new knowledge of

vendors, publishers, and providers of resources in these subjects.

The Content Development Department is still trying to determine how they will provide collection development in areas that will have voids in the near future. Currently, a staff member in the Undergraduate Center, who is a Ph.D. candidate in English at KU, is responsible for collection development in English literature, but she is a temporary employee and her contract may not be renewed next year. We are also grappling with covering World History. Due to significant other responsibilities the American history librarian will not be able to devote significant time to this area of a collection. As a solution, we are changing established approval plans with European vendors to increase the parameters in order to decrease the time necessary for firm order selection. We are hopeful that the individuals hired for either the visual arts or performing arts positions will have language skills and will be able to incorporate these areas in their responsibilities.

In the fall of 2014, a search for a new African Studies librarian that will report to International and Area Studies began. The Head of Content Development was consulted so that preferred requirements in the position description would address other subject expertise needed by the Content Development Department. We hope to find candidates that have subject expertise in some of the disciplines mentioned above or language proficiencies in some of the Western European languages that are needed.

Overall, collection development at KU has become more focused in all of the disciplines. Because those now responsible for this important task truly believe in its importance, there is a better distribution of attention and time to the various subject areas. While four of the librarians in the department continue to provide instruction, two others do not. This has made it possible, at least for a portion of the team, to focus just on content development. This is critical as KU is dealing with budgetary woes. Today our main focal point is not on building collections, but making important decisions on what materials KU will retain.

References

Association of Research Libraries. (2012, March 10). *Issue brief: 21st century collections: Calibration of investment and collaborative action.* Retrieved from http://www.arl.org/storage/documents /publications/issue-brief-21st-century-collections-2012.pdf

Dempsey, L. (2013). *The emergence of the collective collection: Analyzing aggregate print library holdings.* Retrieved from http://oclc.org/content/dam/research/publications/library/2013/2013-09intro.pdf

Harley, D., Acord, S. K., Earl-Novell, S., Lawrence, S., & King, C. J. (2010). *Assessing the future landscape of scholarly communication: An exploration of faculty values and needs in seven disciplines.* Retrieved from http://www.cshe.berkeley.edu/publications/final-report-assessing-future-landscape-scholarly -communication-exploration-faculty

Long, M. P. & Schonfeld, R. C. (2014). *Supporting the changing research practices of art historians.* Retrieved from http://www.sr.ithaka.org/research-publications/supporting-changing-research-practices-art -historians

Long, M. P. & Schonfeld, R. C. (2013). *Supporting the changing research practices of chemists.* Retrieved from http://www.sr.ithaka.org/research-publications/supporting-changing-research-practices-chemists

Schonfeld, R. C., & Housewright, R. (2013). *US faculty survey 2012.* Retrieved from http://www.sr.ithaka.org/research-publications/us-faculty-survey-2012

Schonfeld, R. C., & Rutner, J. (2012). *Supporting the changing research practices of historians.* Retrieved from http://www.sr.ithaka.org/research-publications/supporting-changing-research-practices-historians

University of Kansas. (2012). Bold aspirations: The strategic plan for KU. Retrieved from http://boldaspirations.ku.edu/

———. (2013). Changing for excellence. Retrieved from http://cfe.ku.edu/index.php

University of Kansas Libraries. (2012). KU libraries strategic directions 2012–2017. Retrieved from http://www.lib.ku.edu/strategicplan/

———. (2013). KU libraries organizational structure. Retrieved from http://lib.ku.edu/orgstructure/

Remote Storage: Leveraging Technology to Maximize Efficiency and Minimize Investments

Eric C. Parker, Pritzker Legal Research Center, Northwestern University

Abstract

Libraries are increasingly using, or at least considering, remote storage facilities for their little-used materials in order to free up valuable on-campus library space for other purposes. This paper details the experiences of one library, Northwestern University's Pritzker Legal Research Center, in preparing for, then doing, this work. This type of work can be expensive in terms of staff time, particularly when staff is already being asked to do many additional things. Because extra staff could not be hired, Pritzker has experimented with alternative ways to get this work done, using relatively inexpensive and readily available technology, combined with the creativity of its staff, to accomplish this work with a minimum of time and other inputs while maintaining quality of work.

Introduction

Northwestern University's Pritzker Legal Research Center, located on the university's Chicago campus, is the law library for the Northwestern University School of Law (Northwestern Law). Additionally, as needed, we serve the research needs of the rest of the University, collaborating with the other Northwestern libraries on numerous initiatives. We are a large academic law library of over 600,000 volumes and equivalents. The library's history dates back to the 1890s; it has voluminous historical and current collections of law and law-related materials.

Planning for Off-Site Storage

Thinking about and planning for the possibility of remote storage of library materials began at Pritzker in late 2010. At that time, the librarians were asked by the then Associate Dean for Information Services to develop a plan detailing which materials would move off-site, assuming the Library were asked to give up 55% of its shelving capacity. After a process that took several months, the librarians established a series of rule-based decisions to follow for each part of the collection, folding those (and the inevitable exceptions) into a final plan in late spring, 2011.

While Pritzker's planning was being done, the University was in the process of building a state-of-the-art, climate-and temperature-controlled high-density library shelving facility with a capacity to house up to 1.9 million items in 12,000 square feet of space. This facility, named the Oak Grove Library Center, opened in fall 2011. It is located in Waukegan, Illinois, about 30 miles north of the University Library, and about 45 miles north of the Pritzker Legal Research Center. The University Library, along with the Galter Health Sciences Library, began sending portions of their collections to Oak Grove facility between 2011 and 2014. Pritzker did not send any materials to Oak Grove during the facility's first two years of operation.

A Change of Plans

In early spring, 2014, a construction project at Northwestern Law was slated to break ground. As the beginning of construction work loomed closer, the library became aware that about 5,000 volumes stored in the basement of the building would need to be moved to allow construction crews access to a particular area. As it turned out, these old print runs of reports from cases decided in state courts were materials we had identified in our 2011 plan to send off-site since the content is available to our users online, and the volumes are not heavily used. Like print periodical runs, individual volumes are not typically read cover-to-cover, but are accessed via citations to specific pieces of content.

However, we needed to come up with a plan of action for these materials in fairly short order—we had only a little more than one week before the first batch of empty totes was to be dropped off. Pritzker was fortunate in that we could tap into the experiences of our colleagues who had already been moving materials for several years. Materials are sent from Northwestern libraries to the Oak Grove facility via weekly van pickup. The van has a fairly limited capacity of 108 full totes' worth of materials. We calculated that this project would take three vans trips to move all 5,000 or so volumes we needed to move. We also knew that, since materials in Oak Grove are sorted and stored by size, the maintenance of call number order is really of no importance for materials going there. As long as each item has a barcode, it can be stored there, and retrieved whenever desired.

Getting Ready to Do the Work

As we understood the processes in place at other Northwestern libraries, they involve moving materials from the stacks to a processing station (consisting of a computer with barcode scanner), where the processing is done. Each book's barcode is either scanned or typed individually into a special piece of simple software, called Oak Grove Assistant, developed by Gary Strawn, Authorities Librarian at the University Library (see Figure 1). The software interfaces directly with the libraries' Voyager database, changing the item record for each scanned barcode so it has an Oak Grove location, changing the item type to the default type for Oak Grove locations, setting an item status of "In Transit" (which is subsequently removed at the Oak Grove facility as part of their ingest process), and, upon scanning of the last item record attached to a holdings record, changing the location code in the holdings record to an Oak Grove one (see Figures 2 and 3).

Figure 1. Oak Grove Assistant software.

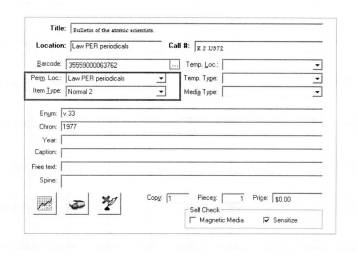
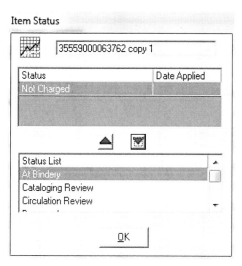

Figure 2. Voyager item record details before Oak Grove Assistant software processing.

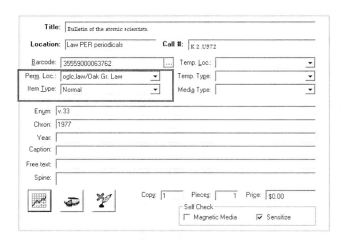

Figure 3. Voyager item record details after Oak Grove Assistant software processing.

Given that we had to carve extra time from already full staff workdays, we were concerned that we devote the absolute minimum amount of staff time and effort needed to accomplish the work accurately. So we tried to think of ways to lessen the workload, deciding that the fewer touches for materials, the better. We attempted to achieve this by taking several steps.

First, we asked Gary Strawn if he would be willing to modify the Oak Grove Assistant software to allow for batch processing of barcodes contained in a simple .txt file. Fortunately, that turned out to be a relatively easy task that he was willing to do for us. We ran some small test files of barcodes through the modified software, confirming that it would work in the ways we wanted. Next, we decided that, rather than take the work (e.g., each and every print volume) to the computer, it would be much easier to take the computer to the work. We use a pretty basic Dell laptop for our work, mostly because we have a couple extra of those on hand; however, almost any device that one can hook a barcode scanner up to, and create files of scanned barcodes that can be processed, would work fine. Additionally, to provide ample movement within the stack areas, we bought a couple of wireless barcode scanners to use with the laptop. These cost about $75 or so apiece. Finally, we had the empty totes delivered directly to the stack area we would be working in.

Doing the Work

With the above pieces in place, library assistants could pull each volume from the shelf, scan its barcode into a .txt file on the laptop, and then place the book directly into the bin. Full bins were stacked four-high (how they would be moved, and how they would fit into the van). Since every item going off-site needs a barcode, items lacking them would be set aside to have them added later, their barcode processed by the Oak Grove Assistant software, then placed into a bin. At the end of a shift, the library assistant would then email me the file or files containing the barcode numbers that had been scanned. I would then process these using the Oak Grove Assistant software. In essence, the packing up of materials and the changes to the Voyager database were not accomplished together, but batched and separated chronologically.

So, How Did It Work Out?

We were able to complete our initial move of, as it turned out, 5,300 volumes to off-site storage on time, and with an extremely small number of errors. Out of the 5,300 things that were sent, exactly one item came back from Oak Grove because it lacked a barcode. Maintaining accuracy is critically important due to the way materials are stored in a facility such as ours (e.g., not in any call number order). In regular library stacks, missing items can be searched for in ways that have some fair probability of the item being found; that probability goes down dramatically at a remote storage facility. While we do not have the ability to compare directly how this method compared with any other used at Pritzker, we believe that we were able to complete this initial project accurately and with a minimum of staff time and effort, since materials did not need to be pulled from shelves, placed onto carts, and then moved to a processing station.

Lessons Learned

The biggest lesson we learned: include staff that will do most of the work in the planning process, and really listen to their thoughts and suggestions. Library assistants are often way more creative problem solvers than we librarians are. So tap into those abilities! Because of space limitations in the stack aisles, I had initially thought that our process would involve filling bins by removing books from shelves on one side of an aisle at a time. Once that side was empty, and the full totes had been taken away, the shelves on the other side of the aisle would then be emptied and the totes filled. Fortunately, our library assistants are smarter than I, so they quickly figured out how to build in extra efficiencies that would not alter our need for accuracy. For example, rather than follow the above work pattern, they determined that it would be faster to scan materials in bulk, then go back and pack the materials into the totes. This would involve less turning, bending, and stooping to place materials into totes. When they asked me if this would be OK, I told them they should try it and see how it works out. In fact, it has worked out great!

Another efficiency that our staff approached me about involved the number of text files of barcode number to create each shift. Initially, I had asked them to create a separate file for each tote, so that, if problems were to develop, we could isolate which tote to look in for problem volumes. However, they found the creation of separate files to be cumbersome, and I found that the number of problems that required looking for in already-filled totes was exceedingly small. So we decided to try having each person create only one or two text files per shift. Again, in our case, the change has resulted in a faster process (less remembering

to open and close a lot of text files, and to be sure that barcodes were in the correct file) without really creating any problems with accuracy.

Finally, after we had completed our initial 5,300 volume project, and had begun work on the rest of the collection, I had a library assistant ask me why we couldn't just make the database changes without scanning each individual barcode. We are still working primarily with portions of our collection that are large print runs of serial titles—not an unusual thing in law libraries. So we have been trying out this modified approach. Essentially, this just shifts the time that quality checks are done. Instead of them being accomplished prior to materials leaving the building, they occur once the processing has happened at Oak Grove. I use a program, similar to Oak Grove Assistant, called Vger Location Changer, to bulk process these changes. Our colleagues at Oak Grove let us know when they have completed the processing of each week's batch. I then check to see which item records still say "In Transit," and resolve those that do. There have been a few hiccups in doing the work this way, but there have been very few cases wherein an item record did not transfer, or a piece lacked a barcode. So few, in fact, that it seems to be not worth the effort to scan each and every barcode at our end just to catch a handful of problems. It is easy enough for our colleagues at Oak Grove to send those materials back to us to handle.

As mentioned above, many of the materials sent thus far have consisted of long serial runs. I think our process, while efficient for handling these sorts of sets, will be less efficient when we turn our attention to the monograph portions of our collection. There, we will be dealing with many additional bibliographic and holdings records to represent the same number of volumes. We could produce reports of particular items to change through software to Oak Grove locations, etc. Since we will not be pulling contiguous volumes from shelves, we run a significantly greater risk of pulling and sending incorrect materials, or, at least, having many more corrections to make. Therefore, I would not be surprised if we determine that our earlier scanning and packing process, wherein we scan things and set them on their sides on the shelves, to be packed up a bit later, will work best in those areas. To me, it seems most important not to take a one-size-fits-all approach to any of this work, but to develop the best process that will fit the particular materials being sent.

As libraries are increasingly using, or at least considering, remote storage facilities for their little-used materials in order to free up valuable on-campus library space for other purposes, they face the often-daunting task of actually getting this work done. Often, that means getting the work done without many additional resources, such as extra staff. This paper has attempted to detail how one library has tried to approach this work. To date, this work has been successful, while allowing staff enough time to complete their many other additional responsibilities. At Pritzker, we expect the Oak Grove work to take about three years total to complete, but, as a result, we expect to have the ability to transform the collections we do keep on site, as well as the library space itself.

The Big Shift: How VCU Libraries Moved 1.5 Million Volumes to Prepare for the Construction of a New Library

Ibironke Lawal, Science and Engineering Collections Librarian, Virginia Commonwealth University
Patricia Selinger, Head, Preservation and Inventory Management, Virginia Commonwealth University
Barbara Anderson, Head, Metadata and Discovery, Virginia Commonwealth University

Abstract

Virginia Commonwealth University Libraries (VCUL) has been faced with serious space problems for more than a decade. Initiatives to correct this include the digital shift. VCUL's new policy stipulates that journal subscriptions should be electronic only, wherever available. Where publishers offer both print and online for the same price, the library donates the print instead of keeping them on the shelves. Replacing print series with the electronic version as they become available is another ongoing practice. Added to these is moving infrequently used or superseded materials to storage as a continuous activity. All these were short-lived measures until now. In the spring 2014, VCUL began the construction of a new library and the renovation of the old one on its Monroe Park Campus. When completed, it will have 63,000 square feet of renovated space and 93,000 square feet of new space. Both old and new will be 263 square feet. The new facility will alleviate overcrowding and add much needed study and collaborative spaces. The new space will have 25 new group study rooms, a 65-seat quiet reading room, a 110-seat graduate and faculty research center, an innovative media center, an expanded café, and a 300-seat public auditorium. Ninety percent of the new space will be for students. In order for the renovation to begin, it was necessary to release the space currently housing part of the collection. This involved moving, shifting, weeding, and deaccessioning a large number of materials in the collection. This paper describes the repurposing of space, reshelving, storing, and withdrawing approximately 1.5 million volumes, a process we call "The Big Shift." This is a major endeavor, one that will have an impact on Cabell Library for a long time to come. In the words of John Duke our Senior Associate University Librarian, "Virtually every book and media piece in the library will have to be touched, along with hundreds of thousands of bibliographic records" (Duke, 2013).

Introduction

Virginia Commonwealth University (VCU) is one of the nation's top research universities. It enrolls more than 31,000 students on two Richmond campuses—the Monroe Park Campus and Medical College of Virginia (MCV) campus. The VCU Medical Center including the university's health sciences schools, offers state-of-the-art care in more than 200 specialty areas and serves as the region's only Level I Trauma Center. Situated in the heart of Richmond the capital of Virginia, VCU serves an integral role in the economic health of the city—educating the current and future workforce, reaching out to the community, advancing research and enhancing patient care since 1838. VCU also has campuses in Northern Virginia, in Doha, Qatar, and in Charles City County, Virginia. VCU Libraries (VCUL), one of Virginia's outstanding research library systems, advances the university's teaching , research, service, and patient care mission with holdings exceeding 2.3 million volumes, 61,000 serials, 600,000 e-books and nationally prominent collections in the health and biological sciences, social work, the arts, the history of medicine, and comic book arts.

Literature Review

In order to put in perspective what VCUL is trying to achieve, it is important to understand the changes in structure and function of academic libraries through the ages. There has been a shift in the information-seeking behavior of students, faculty, and researchers. Contrast with the past, is rightly put by Freeman:

> "Unlike the medieval libraries, early academic libraries were both centers of learning and important gathering places for scholars. As a

'temple of scholarship', the library as place assumed an almost sanctified role, reflected both in its architecture and in its siting."

"Originally, academic libraries in the United States started as places to collect, access, and preserve print collections. Admission and use were a privilege, the interiors were dim, some books were locked down with chains, it was difficult to move around, and specialized services were only available to the very serious scholar. Collections were the main focus of these primarily static buildings. Given this long practice, it is no surprise the traditional library cannot serve today's needs. To meet today's academic needs as well as those of the future, the library must reflect the values, mission, and goals of the institution of which it is a part, while also accommodating myriad space needs to embody new pedagogies, including collaborative and interactive learning modalities. Significantly, the library must serve as the principal building on campus where one can truly experience and benefit from the centrality of an institution's intellectual community." (Freeman, 2005)

Freeman goes on to say:

"The library which is still a combination of the past (print collection) and the present (new information technologies), must be viewed with new perspective and understanding if it is to fulfill its potential in adding value to the advancement of the institution's academic mission and in moving with that institution into the future. With the emergence and integration of information technology, many predicted that the library would become obsolete. Contrary to that, usage has expanded dramatically, sometimes doubling or even tripling. Students at all levels of academic proficiency need and want to go to the library more than ever before. Going to the library adds value to their lives and offers many of the tools and experiences that will give them the competitive edge they will need to succeed after their formal education is completed. There is an expectation that the library is the place to be; it is where the action is. The faculty expect their students to use their time in the library thinking analytically, rather than simply searching for information. Faculty also see the library as an extension of the classroom, as a place in which students engage in a collaborative learning process, a place where they will it is hoped, develop or refine critical thinking." (Freeman, 2005)

One of the goals of this project is to provide the kind of space specified by Freeman, one that will help students to be creative to become innovators. In the age of interdisciplinary subjects, students need collaborative spaces to discover and create new knowledge.

According to Brown, Bennett, Henson, and Valk, (2014), learning spaces are directly connected, and that in many cases, the new services and programs in learning spaces have resulted in significant changes to library collections. In an Association of Research Libraries (ARL) survey, approximately 89% of survey respondents stated their collection was moved within the library as a result of learning space development. In the same survey, 71% reported their collection was moved to an off-site facility as a result of changes in learning spaces, 86% weeded their collection, and 57% were influenced to make transition from print to electronic resources (Brown, Bennett, Henson, and Valk, 2014).

Seeking more information about similar projects, we found that the literature features current renovations and construction of new library buildings, but each one is unique in its own way as tailored to the specific needs, goals, and aspirations of the parent institution. Kent State University, for instance, moved 600,000 books, about half the total collection to remote storage, in order to free four floors. Two of these floors became the home of the journal collection that was moved from the second floor to construct a 16,000 square foot Math Emporium. One floor houses the Emporium and the last floor is a new lounge study area for students. In what they called the smart pull, the 600,000 books represented those with low use and publication date before 1990, and those with very low use and publication date between 1990 and 2000.

On another note, North Carolina State University (NCSU) opened its brand new library, the focal point on the Centennial campus, in January 2013. The goal was to provide a place for different constituents to interact, collaborate, and innovate. In an unprecedented operation, part of their collection was moved into an automated book delivery system called bookBot. The bookBot can hold up to two million volumes and it serves as the primary storage facility. The bookBot, contains older and low use materials, the majority of which were transferred from the off-site storage facility.

In the case of VCUL, the need to renovate and construct a new library at this time cannot be overemphasized. The next section articulates the problem.

The Problem

VCUL over the years has been creative in dealing with inadequate space. James Branch Cabell Library surpassed its capacity several years ago, and optimum user space is lacking. The reason for this space shortage is in the history of Cabell. The first phase of Cabell, built in 1970, consisted of two floors, the basement and ground floor, both of which held 138,945, with a total capacity of 225,000 volumes. It was to grow at a rate of 25,000 volumes per year. Five years later, three additional floors were added for a total potential capacity of 750,000 volumes. If it continued to add 25,000 volumes per year, it would reach full capacity in 30 years. However, between 1975 and 2010, Cabell more than doubled that number. Between 1995 and 2009 alone, we added more than 813,000 volumes. VCUL converted user spaces to book stacks on a regular basis to accommodate the growth. Today, the collection stands at 2.3 million, and the level of overcrowding cannot be overstated.

As the collection grew so did the VCU community. According to the 1970-1971 *University Bulletin*, there were 672 full time faculty and 280 adjunct faculty. According to the same source, there were 12,350 undergraduate students that year (8,750 full time, 4,600 part time), and 800 graduate students. In another publication, the September 10, 1970 issue of the student paper,

Commonwealth Times, there were 1,616 students on the MCV campus. Enrollment increased by 144% between 1970 and 2012; and faculty grew by 300%.

Over the years, library patrons visiting the physical space have increased exponentially. In 2004, one million people visited the libraries. That number doubled to two million in ten years, as our collection keeps growing steadily.

Something had to be done, even if only temporarily, to relieve the crowded nature of the stacks. This was achieved in a number of ways. In 2002 and 2004, VCU Libraries purchased 17,289 linear feet of compact shelving which were installed on the basement floor of the building. This houses the collections that included journals dated prior to 2000, electronically replicated titles, particularly JSTOR titles, out of scope titles, and duplicates. With in-house storage, came the policy that all infrequently used materials be relocated to storage as an ongoing activity to release space for newer, more frequently used materials and for more comfortable user space. Also included, were titles considered by selectors to be candidates for storage using system generated lists. Criteria used were:

- Circulation over time.
- Age.
- Condition.
- Outdated subject matter.

Added to this were low-use nonbook materials of enduring value to the VCU community. The goals were to relieve overflowing in the stacks, reduce the frustration of our patrons and increase the usability of the collections.

This approach worked for the collection temporarily, but there was still a dire need to increase user space. In the LibQUAL results for 2008, users expressed their dissatisfaction with the inadequate study and collaborative spaces in Cabell. This prompted the university to acquire an offsite storage facility in 2009, repurposing part of a former grocery store. In 2010, the office of the Provost and VCU Libraries decided to construct a new Learning Commons on the second floor of

Cabell. The Commons would provide 18,000 square feet of study and work space for users.

In order to understand the shifting and moving, it is necessary to give the original layout of the library.

- 1st floor—reference collection and government documents, current periodicals, newspapers.

- 2nd floor—formerly bound journal collection (now the Learning Commons).

- 3rd floor—class number A-M, microfiche and microfilm collections, oversize collection, and Media Services.

- 4th floor—class number N-Z, Juvenile Literature, oversize collection, and Special Collections.

The decision to construct the Learning Commons on the second floor set in motion the monumental task of moving all the bound journals out of the second floor. In an effort to keep bound journals in the building, materials previously stored in the compact shelving on the basement floor, mostly electronically replicated abstracts and indexes and superseded reference sets, were moved to an offsite storage facility recently acquired by the university. Subsequently, part of the bound journal collection was moved to the basement. JSTOR journals were moved to offsite storage facility. Those with significant print characteristics or without electronic version were moved to the 1st floor, next to the current periodicals.

The new Learning Commons (LC) has 18,000 square feet of academic and collaborative workspace and a 1,100 square foot multipurpose room for instruction and more. This room can be reconfigured for different needs. The new LC also has seven new group study rooms with white boards, computer, large monitors, and other support for collaborative work, 438 new seats, 83 PCs, and 12 Macintosh computers, 18 mobile whiteboards, 20 new laptops to expand the already popular laptop loan program, electrical outlets throughout the facility for laptops and other mobile devices, ubiquitous, high speed wireless network access, and print stations for both color and black and white printing.

With the opening of the LC in the fall of 2010, Cabell became a very popular sanctuary on campus. Typical gate count in the fall is 10,000 per day. After the Learning Commons opened, gate count exceeded 15,000 per day for 17 days in one month, an increase of 50% over the typical gate count. Where there were 47 visits per patron per year eleven years ago, that number increased to 72 visits per patron per year in 2010-2011. This phenomenon of if you build it, they will come, is confirmed by ARL 2014 survey that found that 75% of responding libraries experienced an increase in gate counts and 35% experienced an increase in web traffic related to learning spaces, (Brown, Bennett, Henson, and Valk, 2014). The construction of the Learning Commons marked the end of one of our major initiatives. The project provided much-needed relief for some of our perennial space problems, but was it enough?

The LibQUAL results for 2011 showed significant satisfaction among users. However, it took just a couple of years before users started feeling the effect of overcrowding again. The survey results in 2013 show the overarching dissatisfaction with the space and accompanying infrastructure, such as electrical outlets and adequate number of seats. By 2013, in order to meet VCUL's aspiration and projected service goals for the next 20 years and beyond, it was imperative to build an addition to Cabell and renovate the old space. The announcement that the state had allocated funds for the construction of a new library could not have come at a more opportune time.

After the announcement and the architects released their drawings showing the size of the space to be renovated, work started in earnest. The first step was to review the collection in storage and make a decision about what to keep and what to withdraw from the collection to make room for materials to be moved out of Cabell stacks. For an easy workflow, collection management librarians marked the spine of the books to be withdrawn with a black line. Those withdrawn included duplicates, superseded editions, abstracts and indexes that have electronic versions, and out of scope titles. Staff members in the preservation department then took the books off the shelves and scanned their barcodes into Excel spreadsheet files. With a large number of materials to deaccession, it was easier and quicker to use a batch approach. Catalogers used these Excel files to generate and withdraw large sets of item records in ALMA (Ex Libris). This collection review released some space in both the in-house compact storage and the off-site storage. This space will eventually house the materials that will be moved out of Cabell stacks. Estimates showed that in order to create the space necessary for the renovation, as specified by the architects, it would be necessary to move approximately 200,000 volumes out of Cabell. When we realized this, we invested in high capacity compact shelving which brought the total capacity of our off-site storage close to 500,000 volumes. In order to install these shelves in the same space, we had to first move all the books on the current storage shelves into a holding place with the help of Richmond Commercial Services, and the shelves dismantled. During this period, we had to restrict access to the collection and update the item records to have the location of "Not available." After the installation of the high capacity storage shelves, the books were returned and the item records changed again. The next step was the review of the general collection. This was done in phases.

First Floor

Reference Collection

Starting from the first floor, it became imperative to reduce the size of our very large reference collection. Specifically, the collection has to be reduced significantly. We achieved this by integrating some essential reference tools with the circulating collection and deaccessioning outdated ones and electronically duplicated ones. For easy workflow, the subject specialists and liaison librarians devised a color scheme, whereby yellow stood for transfer to stacks and red stood for withdraw. During this period, we had to restrict access to the collection and update the item records to have the location of "Not available." All relocations entailed relabeling the spines and changing circulation policies.

Government Documents

Similarly, on the first floor, it is essential to reduce the government documents collection. VCU Libraries had been a 50-60% depository library for federal documents, therefore it had a relatively large collection. There were 5,640 linear feet of government documents. This needed to be reduced significantly. To accomplish this task, two processes ran simultaneously. One process was to remove those that were neither relevant to our mission nor our curriculum, 17,421 items total. These were deaccessioned and considered withdrawn from the collection. The second process was more involved. Working with the head of the Regional Center, we identified the superseded titles and deaccessioned those as well. The remaining in this category, were offered to other institutions according to the depository agreement, keeping to the depository regulation, of offering and waiting 45 days total. At the end of 45 days, if no institution requested them it would be safe to withdraw from the collection. 37, 695 items fit into this category.

In summary, 5,640 linear feet of shelving has been cut to 3,153.5 linear feet, a reduction of the space occupied by government documents by about 44%. The five remaining rows of shelving are, predicted to be stable, since there is minimal acquisition of physical government documents. This is a significant space saving towards our renovation. The government document reduction and realignment took one staff working 30 hours a week and three students working about 30 hours total a week for about three months. During the peak months of this project, a cataloging staff member also spent about 25-50% of her time processing the thousands of withdrawals. Since VCU is one of ASERL Centers of Excellence with a robust Master's program in Homeland Security, a 100% depository for Homeland Security documents (HS1) was the only collecting area retained at that level. The weeding of superseded documents will continue as needed, to ensure that the collection maintains relevance to curriculum needs. The space thus saved makes room for study spaces and construction of offices.

Still on the first floor, five rows of shelving housing current journals, bound journals, and foreign newspapers were taken down to make room for the temporary entrance, security post, and some study space. With space gained from weeding government documents and the reference collection, there was room to move part of the circulating collection to the first floor.

Third floor

Nonbook materials

There were over three million microforms, occupying 2,000 square feet of floor space. We decided to retain those holding the *Richmond Times-Dispatch*, *New York Times*, and *Washington Post*, or 35 cabinets in all. We consolidated others that have relatively moderate use into the compact upright storage cabinet and moved the remaining to our off-site storage facility. The third floor also held other nonbook collections such as CDs, DVDs, computer files, 16 mm films, vinyl recordings, and music scores. A review showed it was best to reduce the size of this collection significantly by deaccessioning obsolete formats, CDs accompanying outdated books, superseded software, old computer files, and items no longer relevant to VCU's curriculum. We ended up removing about 500 computer files and another 500 multimedia items from the collection. The remaining items were more manageable to review. Some lesser used ones were moved to storage, while we integrated CDs that come with monographs into the circulating collection alongside the parent monograph. We also re-shelved music scores, formerly in a separate location, with the rest of the general collection. Depending on the program requirements in the departments of music and film, we will still keep and protect some 16mm films and vinyl recordings.

Collection A-F

Previously, collection classes A-F resided on the third floor. With the shifting and renovation, they were relocated to the first floor. By removing this collection and a significant number of microforms, we claimed the space for the construction of administrative offices.

Fourth Floor

Previously, collection N-Z resided on the fourth floor. With the space gained on the third floor by moving A-F, we were able to move collection N to the third floor, while P-Z remain on the fourth floor.

Oversize Collection

A review of the oversize collection on both the third floor and fourth floor resulted in deaccessioning and storing part of the collection. As a result, we could consolidate both collections into one that now resides on the fourth floor.

The Shifting

With all the physical weeding completed, it is time for the shifting. First we shifted the bound journals to the space relinquished by the reference collection and part of government documents.

In the next phase, we moved the collection in Library of Congress classification A-E from the third to the first floor, while F-N moved to the third floor, followed by shifting and rearrangement of the shelves. The rest of the collection, P-Z, remains on the fourth floor. With class N moving out of the fourth floor, it was time to consolidate the space, shift the books, and remove the shelving to release the space that will become part of the Special Collections Department. Moving collections around could result in user confusion and frustration. There was a conscious effort to minimize this. Changing signage promptly was a priority.

Conclusion

Our endeavor to create functional spaces for today's learning patterns started in the late 1990s. This project is a significant phase, the one that satisfies today's needs and will prepare us for the future. We have repurposed our old space in such a way that our collections can be meaningful. Essentially, we touched over one million items. Not only did we move books physically to storage we also have to change their records. Books to withdraw had to be deaccessioned and the system updated. Work is not completed on the renovation, and work is still going on with the construction of the new building, but the part that involves the collection is over. The current configuration as far as collection goes is as seen in Table 1 below. Moving our construction forward involved about 90 staff, helpers, and volunteers in four major departments who, since last October, reviewed, touched, moved, shelved, stored, or withdrew 1.4 million volumes, with minimal disruption or inconvenience to users, a phenomenon we call "The Big Shift." Our community cannot wait to see the old and the new when it is all finished in the fall of 2015. It will give learning, teaching, and research on the Monroe Park campus a whole new meaning.

First Floor	Old	New
Collaborative Study and Computing	Reference Collection Government Documents Collection Information Services Group Study rooms Print Stations Self-service checkout Starbucks	Collaborative Study and Computing Bound Journals Collections A-E Reference Collection Government Documents Collection Information Services Group Study Rooms Print Stations, Photocopiers, and Digital Sender Self-service checkout Starbucks CD/DVD Collection Reserves
Second Floor	Bound Journals Photocopy station	Learning Commons, Collaborative Study and Computing Group Study rooms Print Stations, Photocopier and Digital Sender
Third Floor	Collections A-M, CD/DVD Collection Music Scores Microforms Media Center Reserves	Quiet Study Collections F-N Innovative Media Microforms Group Study Rooms
Fourth Floor	Quiet Study Collections N-Z Oversize Books N-Z Special Collections and Archives	Quiet Study Collections P-Z All Oversize Books Art Browsery Graduate/Faculty Study Room (will close in 2015 due to the construction) Special Collections and Archives Expanded

Table 1.

References

Anonymous. (1975). A library with room to grow. *VCU Magazine, 44*, 20.

Barry, J. (1970). New library is "service organization." *Commonwealth Times, 2*(2).

Brown, S., Bennett, C., Henson, B., and Valk, A. (2014). *Next-Gen learning spaces*. Washington, DC: Association of Research Libraries (SPEC kit 342).

Day, A.; Vickery, J. Davis, H. (2012). Accidental collection assessment: the NCSU library's collection move. *Charleston Library Conference Proceedings*. West Lafayette, IN: Purdue University Press.

Duke, J. K. (2013). The shift. Richmond, VCU Libraries, *Internal Memorandum*.

Freeman, G. T. (2005). *The library as place: Changes in learning patterns, collections, technology, and use.* In *Library as place: Rethinking roles, rethinking space*. Washington DC: Council on Library and Information Resources.

Klinger, T. (2012). Smart pull for remote storage: How to keep (mostly) everyone happy when making a large collection move to remote storage. *Charleston Library Conference Proceedings*. West Lafayette, IN: Purdue University Press.

Recovering Wet Materials: Disaster Plans and Recovery Workflows

Joshua Lupkin, Chief Bibliographer for the Humanities, Howard-Tilton Memorial Library, Tulane University

Sally Krash, Head of Acquisitions, Howard-Tilton Memorial Library, Tulane University

Eric Wedig, Chief Bibliographer for the Social Sciences, Howard-Tilton Memorial Library, Tulane University

Abstract

Careful documentation of collections and disaster planning can allow a library to recover physical collections after events with the best possible outcomes for condition, materials costs, outreach, and librarian/staff workflows. This paper describes how the Howard-Tilton Library at Tulane University (HTML) experienced a roof leak in February 2014 with attending need to manage the outsourced work of disaster recovery contractors for the remediation of more than 2,000 wet books, the reshelving of more than 20,000 displaced books, and the replacement of about 300 books within a two month period during the academic year. This paper describes successful methods of response, workflow considerations, and adaptations, as well as lessons learned. The paper concludes with recommendations about disaster policy implementation and includes an appendix with updated resources and a link to Tulane's revised policy.

The Precipitating Incident: How It All Began

Tulane received national attention for its response to catastrophic flooding and attendant collections losses in the aftermath of Hurricane Katrina in 2005 (Corrigan, 2010). Other recent incidents of large although still lesser scale have occurred, such as at Colorado State University in 1997 and University of Iowa in 2008 (Lunde & Smith, 2009). This paper pertains to a smaller disaster that may be more common or likely. Many libraries have aging infrastructure or periodically undertake renovation projects that can allow smaller but still serious floods of vulnerable collections.

Since October 2013, Howard-Tilton Memorial Library (hereafter HTML) had been in the midst of a construction project in which two floors were being erected above the existing floors of HTML. This build-back and hazard mitigation program was funded by the Federal Management Agency (FEMA) and through a long and heavily regulated process. The two floors being added above the existing four stories were meant to replace spaces destroyed after Hurricane Katrina in the basement of the library main building and in the basement of a neighboring library building for special collections (Corrigan, 2014).

A single mistake in the construction process, combined with the heavy precipitation characteristic of the Gulf Coast, left open the door to major damage. During the very early morning of February 21, 2014, water came into building through the roof above a top floor office where a cement subcontractor had been installing rebar into the existing concrete roof. The source of the problem, beyond a significant amount of rain, was apparently two holes mistakenly driven all the way through the roof. Matters were made worse by the fact that the rainfall on the roof was channeled to the very area where the holes were located, thereby forming a pool just above the holes. What stemmed the flow was the ending of the downpour and the mobilization of the university's Facilities Services staff onto the roof to cover the holes with a tarp. The holes were subsequently plugged and the subcontractor responsible for the holes was dismissed from the project.

Inside the building, the picture was hectic during the flood. Sometime after midnight, a student reported water coming through the roof during the rain storm. Facilities Services, the Tulane University Police Department and the Dean of Libraries were contacted by evening access service managers. The Dean arrived around 1:10

a.m. to find water pouring heavily through the roof at the northeast corner of the 4th floor. Students and staff in the building at the time responded to a public call to assist in the removal of books from the areas directly affected by the incoming water onto dry floor areas, forming human chains. Books on lower shelves elsewhere on the floor, though not wet, were also removed in order to allow the raising of the base of the shelves for proper drying of the carpet later.

The primary construction contractor hired a local recovery service to take initial steps to remove the water and dry the carpets. HTML staff, custodial staff, and Facilities Services cooperated to transfer wet and damp books to the basement. Thousands of dry books thought to be in harm's way near the wet areas of the floor were also transported to the basement. Under the direction of HTML's preservation librarian, HTML staff took appropriate measures to limit subsequent damage to the wet and damp materials.

The basement is a large 40,000 square space that was destroyed after Katrina and at the time of the 2014 roof leak was still gutted and unfinished. It provided a useful space to temporarily stage all the affected materials.

While roughly three double-sided ranges (6 sections each) experienced moisture from the roof, the wet book damage extended to other books handled in a sense of urgency and to their placement on floor areas that went from dry to moist as the volume of water increased. The very slight slope of the floor, which led water to accumulate most in areas at slight remove from the stacks, limited the damage from being more severe. At this stage, disaster management revolved around two classes of books: dry (<20,000) and wet (2500). After proper assessment of condition, 2200 were later determined to be salvageable and 300 unsalvageable.

The Initial Response

The initial response, including immediate onsite condition review and triage and collaboration with the recovery contractor, was crucial for moving forward with recovery in a timely way. Quick

identification of the number and character of books requiring replacement allowed staff in collections and technical services to begin the process of assessing value, requesting appropriate replacement funds, and beginning to source replacements.

On the morning after the leak, many senior staff went immediately to the affected floor to survey the damage. Many people had already been working for hours, engaged in gathering up the books and placing them on book carts so that they could be transported to a location (to be determined) in the building for review of their condition. HTML was fortunate to have large carts on hand from a moving company the library had contracted with to move books in another area of the building. It was quickly determined that the unoccupied and access-restricted basement of HTML was the best place for this review. Library staff transported materials to the basement and distributed them to tables based on their condition. Staff from Technical Services and Circulation worked under the direction of stacks management and the preservation librarian. Timely identification of essential supplies, including carts, tables, and dehumidifiers, greatly speeded this work.

An impromptu triage area in the basement, furnished with tables drawn from elsewhere in the library and on hand for public events, allowed the condition of 4th floor books to be reviewed. Most books were general history, medieval history, and history of the British Isles, in call number ranges D-DA 900s. HTML's preservation librarian organized an initial assessment of all of the books from the 4th floor affected area.

HTML Technical Services librarians, in particular the heads of the Library's Cataloging and Database Management units, worked with the preservation librarian to scan barcodes from most of the reviewed books and create a master list of all damaged books. The Library's Information Technology staff added a new category in the system admin module to reflect the changed location. Some books did not have barcodes and the technical services staff was able to manually add these books to the master list. The list of barcodes improved outcomes in a number of ways, as it allowed a timely update of the catalog to reflect the status of the items and maximum transparency to library users.

Books were initially identified as being either wet or dry, and then assessed for the type of damage incurred. They were placed in three categories: wet coated paper (to be replaced), wet uncoated paper, and dry (to be returned to shelf). Of greatest concern to those engaged in book triage were the volumes containing coated paper and glossy prints. While replacement was preferable to salvage in these cases, HTML could not dispose of them prior to working with the insurance adjuster on replacement funding. Ultimately, a number of books were identified as being a total loss, either too damaged to even be opened or containing unrecognizable photographs and prints. Many of books with damaged prints or photographs were books on the history of the British Isles, often documenting archaeological sites.

Initial Outsourcing and Communication Considerations

Tulane's familiarity with outsourcing damaged books informed crucial early responses. After Katrina, HTML had in its main building alone more than 700,000 individual print volumes and recordings submerged underwater, as were nearly 1.5 million individual pieces of microform such as microfilm reels and microfiche cards. In an adjacent building for special collections, 700,000 or so manuscript folders and other archival items also needed to be salvaged. A large disaster management firm called BELFOR was called to the scene within days for early reconnaissance, as part of Tulane's campus-wide emergency plan. Eventually BELFOR handled the salvage, building climate stabilization, and collections remediation tasks for the library as well as the University as a whole. One of the primary lessons the library learned from Katrina was that disaster management and remediation is its own profession with methods, techniques, and equipment that are continually evolving. Therefore in the event of real disasters it can be best to rely on qualified outside expertise. Moreover, extensive labor is required to acquire

and catalog replacement items or to process restored items for their return to the shelves, generally more extra labor than libraries have on hand. After Katrina, these tasks were outsourced as well, with labor brought in to the Library's temporary Recovery Center that also provided for the temporary storage of recovered materials until destroyed library spaces could be built. These operations were funded through a complex mixture of federal disaster assistance programs and the University's emergency recovery funds gathered from insurance, donations, and other sources. Eventually the Recovery Center processed more than 1 million physical items requiring restoration or replacement.

In the case of the smaller roof leak in 2014, the library still needed to organize a recovery funding and billing protocol and arrange for expert building remediation, professional treatment of wet materials, and outsourced labor for materials handling processing. This was handled by the Library's Associate Dean, who had overseen the Library's recovery planning and operations after Katrina. In this instance he worked closely with Tulane's Office of Risk Management, Department of Capital Projects & Real Estate, Facilities Services, Office of Environmental Health and Safety, the construction contractor, and insurance representatives. On the morning after the leak, the Office of Risk Management agreed to provide initial funds to bring in a qualified disaster firm. Although BELFOR was used in Katrina, engaged the services of by then a different company, BMS-CAT, with which it had a standing contract for these types of events. BMS-CAT responded relatively quickly to take over the drying and remediation of both the affected library space and its wet materials.

Within a few days all parties had agreed to allow BMS-CAT to ship the wet materials to a treatment facility in Texas and to provide funds for the library to hire an outside service provider to eventually process the returning restored materials. The service provider, LAC Group, had been used by the library to staff its Recovery Center post-Katrina. Handling and processing in this case included the reshelving of what turned out to be more than 20,000 dry books that had been pulled from lower shelves to assist with drying wet carpet underneath.

The Library's Recovery Center was still in operation at the time, with LAC Group staff finishing up the last of its Katrina recovery-related projects. In a long-established routine, books dried by the remediation vendor (in this case BMS-CAT) were returned for processing to the Recovery Center located at the Library's off-site storage facility off-campus, before they were eventually returned to their original shelves.

The thousands of dry books that had been moved from harm's way to the basement were reshelved in the 4th floor stacks area within eight days. This work was outsourced to the LAC Group and the library's Stacks Management Department supervised the work. Also, the faculty of several academic departments at Tulane (History, Political Science, Art and Anthropology) was informed about the actions taken by the library, and kept up to date as to the condition of the damaged books and when the dry books would be reshelved. In retrospect this was a very important step; keeping faculty members informed allowed them to work with their students, adjusting assignments related to the books in the affected area.

Ultimately 2,200 wet books were identified as needing restoration. These books were in usable condition, but needed to be stabilized and dried. These books were transported by BMS/CAT to their facility in Texas for drying and were ready to be returned to HTML by the end of March. It was determined that an additional 300 (mostly coated paper) books needed to be replaced. It would be the job of the Howard-Tilton Acquisitions staff to locate replacement copies. It was unclear if all, or a majority, could be replaced.

Replacing the Materials

While the disaster response effort involved many areas of HTML staff in some manner, technical services regarded the organization of collection recovery workflows in an acute manner. Technical Services Division managers, including those in Acquisitions, Cataloging, Database Management (DBM), and Stacks Maintenance, met to evaluate

the scope of recovery activities' impact and to evaluate the capacity of current departments to handle recovery-related activities. Managers who had been involved in recovery efforts after Hurricane Katrina provided insight into what had worked well and what had not worked well with recovery from that disaster event. LAC Group, which was used for that recovery effort, was still being used for a subsequent cataloging/records management project. Since the company had an established fiduciary relationship with Tulane University as well as experience with our collections and local technical services processes, it was a logical choice for this recovery effort.

Of direct impact on Technical Services were pressing questions about the very logistics and budgets of moving collections and assigning funds for replacements. As the books were lying in piles on tables in the basement, librarians had to ask vital questions in order to determine appropriate staffing needs and the attendant costs. Vital to this process was determining the number of books that were salvageable and the number that needed to be replaced. There was an initial estimate of 300 unsalvageable volumes, later including 94 volumes rejected after return from remediation, among 166 boxes of wet materials (approximately 2200 books). There were also 70 book trucks (approximately 30,000 books) with dry/undamaged books that needed to be brought back to shelves as soon as possible after the carpet dried.

Collections recovery presented important fiscal questions as well. While the construction contractor was insured for losses of this type, funds needed to be made available in the short term and before such claims were negotiated. Before substantial action could be taken, library managers needed to determine the source of funds for replacements and outsourcing and the timetable for receipt of these funds.

In line with lessons learned from the far larger Katrina recovery effort, it was determined that third-party disaster remediation firms and library service providers should play the primary role in every stage of collections recovery where the use of library staff would not have been possible or would have diverted staff from important normal work flows.

Departmental Workflows

Technical services departments needed to resolve questions of who could be involved in recovery efforts and to what extent they could handle increased activities. Different units had slightly varying latitude in their workflows. For some departments, the added work required a determination of whether outsourcing could be funded and whether a trusted contractor could be engaged to do the work.

Activities of the Library's Preservation Librarian, a member of the Technical Services division, have been mentioned earlier. As she was leading hands-on activities directly related to affected materials, the Associate Dean was working with other Tulane administrative departments in quickly identifying vendors who could be used in recovery efforts, and procedures and responsibilities for who in which university department would approve which kinds of expenses and handle and monitor billing and payments. He quickly got permission to use outsourced labor for reshelving dry materials.

At the time of the 2014 flood event, Stacks Management was actively involved in shifting materials in response to construction occurring in the building. This was in addition to regular shelving activities. The staff of four was not able to handle the increased workload involved in handling the more than 20,000 dry/undamaged books. The recovery contractor was used for this effort.

Acquisitions reviewed the kinds of materials (mostly books with some serials volumes) and dates of publication (1839–2013) to determine if replacement ordering could be done in-house in the midst of ongoing activities and commitments. In February, the acquisitions staff was already heavily involved in ordering processes after the cyclical 60% spend-down effort of funds, meaning that bibliographers are required to have 60% of their funds spent by the first week of February. Also considered was the department's wish not to repeat the recent experience of having corrected

over 10,000 records that were not properly handled after Katrina recovery, very specifically related to fund management and receiving. In the end, it was determined that replacement workflows would easily fit into current activities of the department and its complement of seven. Acquisitions staff handled replacement processes.

Cataloging and Database Management, in contrast, were not prepared to handle increased workloads in managing records related to books involved in the disaster, cataloging replacement materials, and physical processing of remediated and replacement materials. Although staff in these departments totaled 20, they were working through backlogs, a legacy project, and ongoing cataloging and records management of newly acquired materials. As such, employees of our Katrina recovery vendor were used for all outsourced activities except salvaging.

The end results were that the Library outsourced the reshelving of dry books and the remediation of 2200 books. A small group of the remediated volumes (94) were rejected as unacceptable and the list of additional titles was sent to Acquisitions for replacement processing. Acquisitions replaced a total of 390 volumes that were lost in this flood event, at an average of $48.70 per title. The initial replacement effort included 277 volumes, augmented by the volumes rejected after remediation. Among the 20 volumes that presented the most difficulty, only one—a serial volume from the 1970s—was never found. Most replacements were for British imprints and were found through Amazon and ABE in the US, Canada, and the UK. Acquisitions staff also had to contact societies and book vendors in the UK to obtain hard-to-find materials. This process led to important insights about the capacities and concerns of various vendors. Barter Books in the UK was the most helpful, as they were very responsive to queries about materials that were not included in their online bookshop. The biggest disappointment was in using ABE books, which presented issues with receiving and condition of materials. The materials most challenging to replace were those from the 1960s and 1970s.

It is worthwhile to note that prior to this event, disaster kits had been strategically located throughout the library building. Those kits included plastic sheeting which could have been used to cover bookshelves as an alternative to moving books from the shelves. It was clear that the library needed to address more clearly best practices in its disaster plan and reinforce this with training across the organization. The Preservation Librarian has since created a detailed disaster recovery plan that is now in place, and has provided training across the library.

Detailed workflows can be found at http://tults.pbworks.com/w/page/76901795 /Recovery_and_Remediation_2014.

Lessons Learned and Concluding Thoughts

While there is no shortage of vetted information available about best practices (Wilkinson, 2010; Wellheiser, 2002; Todaro, 2009; Wessely, 2010), the larger task for libraries may be to extend familiarity about such best practices and individual responsibilities to all of the different parts of the library that may be involved. Especially important in the case at hand was for such training to extend to new hires and those staffing the building on evenings/weekends.

Tulane's own experience after Katrina had suggested three primary lessons: having an effective means of communication after an event; relying on a qualified external disaster management firm and not overburdening normal workflows more than absolutely needed; and establishing liability beforehand as far as possible (Corrigan, 2010, p. 126).

The experience in 2014 suggested that our team benefited from these lessons. Once recovery began, we did communicate well with campus stakeholders and among ourselves. Our University had an established relationship with external contractors for book drying as well as sorting and reshelving, who were poised to act efficiently and with comparatively minimal diversion of regular staff duties. However, the University chose to use a different vendor for remediation efforts. In the end, all but one of the 2500 wet books was successfully restored or replaced within three months and procedures put into place that prevented a repetition of such water incursion.

Not everything was perfect, however. It was not enough simply to have a good disaster plan in place; rather, it is necessary to make sure that there is widespread training among all staff about its details and their personal role in the bigger picture. Although the contribution by building users in removing books from perceived harm speaks highly of public spiritedness on our campus, current plans more clearly state that the best practice would have been to leave affected books in place on shelves under readily available plastic sheeting until being removed by experienced contractors.

It would have been difficult for the Library to have done more to anticipate or prevent the water incursion. Despite careful oversight of the process by the University, the process of doing such fundamental construction on a continuously occupied building presented a consistent give-and-take between the interests of the contractors and subcontractors for speed and efficiency, and those of the Library for collections integrity and minimal disruption to building users. The event was a stark example of the construction project's complexity and low margin for error. One part of the Library also on the same floor, the special collections unit of the Latin American Library, had earlier relocated its rare materials in order to avoid the chance of damaging them. However, it would not have been possible to move all the collections housed on the 4th floor. After the incident, steps were taken to make sure that all potentially sensitive construction work above had multiple checks by more parties each day before the work site was vacated.

Wet books are not a new phenomenon for academic libraries, and many libraries have disaster plans on file, but the experience of the team at Tulane suggests the need for constant vigilance and training. Even at a time when many libraries are reevaluating the investment of staff and space for the maintenance of physical collections in their facilities, it remains highly relevant to devise and to raise awareness of plans to protect and recover their investments. It is beyond the scope of this presentation to discuss the distinct but equally pressing issues of response to "disaster" threats to digital collections, though there are some essential commonalities in principle (Breeding, 2012).

References

Breeding, M. (2012). From disaster recovery to digital preservation. *Computers in Libraries*, *32*(4), 22–25.

Corrigan, A. (2010). Case 3: Hurricane Katrina. In Wilkinson F. C., Lewis, L. K., & Dennis, N. K., *Comprehensive guide to emergency preparedness and disaster recovery* (pp. 117–127). Chicago: Association of College and Research Libraries.

Corrigan, A. (2014, March 31). Howard-Tilton Memorial Library build-back and hazard mitigation project: 4th floor update: Remediation and construction progress. Retrieved from http://html-addition .blogspot.com/2014/03/4th-floor-update-remediation-and.html

Lunde, D. B., & Smith, P. A. (2009). Disaster and security: Colorado State style. *Library & Archival Security*, *22*(2), 99–114. http://dx.doi.org/10.1080/01960070902869766

Todaro, J. B. (2009). *Emergency preparedness for libraries*. Lanham, MD: Government Institutes.

Wellheiser, J. G. (2002). *An ounce of prevention: Integrated disaster planning for archives, libraries, and record centres* (2nd ed.). Lanham, MD: Scarecrow Press.

Wessely, T. (2010). Preparing for the end of the world: Are you ready for a library disaster? *Access (10300155), 24*(2), 26–29.

Wilkinson, F. C. (2010). *Comprehensive guide to emergency preparedness and disaster recovery*. Chicago: Association of College and Research Libraries.

Appendix

Disaster Planning and Preservation Links

Public version of Howard-Tilton Memorial Library at Tulane University disaster plan
http://library.tulane.edu/sites/library.tulane.edu/files/documents/2014HTMLplan_public.pdf

The below lists are not exhaustive, but are meant as a starting point for researching and working on disaster preparedness at your institution.

All links below are also at http://libguides.tulane.edu/preservation

Tools and Resources for Disaster Preparedness

dPlan: "A free online tool that will help you simplify the process of writing a disaster plan. Enter information about your institution using the comprehensive fill-in-the-blank template. This template will guide you through the steps necessary for effective disaster planning."
http://www.dplan.org/

Council of State Archivists (CoSA) Framework for Emergency Preparedness
http://www.statearchivists.org/prepare/framework/index.htm

Pocket Response plan (PReP): "A concise document for recording essential information needed by staff in case of a disaster."
http://www.statearchivists.org/prepare/framework/prep.htm

American Library Association (ALA) Disaster Preparedness and Recovery
http://www.ala.org/advocacy/govinfo/disasterpreparedness

National Archives and Records Administration recovery and salvage vendor list
http://www.archives.gov/preservation/disaster-response/vendors.html

Amigos Library Services, "A Disaster Plan for Libraries and Archives"
"Designed to assist libraries and archives in preparing for emergency situations which may threaten the safety of persons, collections and facilities."
http://www.amigos.org/preservation/disasterplan.pdf

Connecting to Collections online course "Risk Evaluation: First Step in Disaster Planning" recordings available at http://www.connectingtocollections.org/courses/risk-evaluation/

Connecting to Collections online course "Protecting Your Collections: Writing a Disaster Response Plan" recordings available at http://www.connectingtocollections.org/courses/writing-a-disaster-plan/

California Preservation Program, library disaster plan template
http://calpreservation.org/wp-content/uploads/2013/05/CPTF_disaster_plan_2003.pdf

Getty Conservation Institute, "Building an Emergency Plan: A Guide for Museums and Other Cultural Institutions"
http://www.getty.edu/conservation/publications_resources/pdf_publications/pdf/emergency_plan.pdf

Salvage Instructions

National Parks Service Conserve O Grams: Disaster Response and Recovery
http://www.nps.gov/museum/publications/conserveogram/cons_toc.html#collectionpreservation

National Archives and Records Administration (NARA) Salvage Procedures
http://www.archives.gov/preservation/disaster-response/salvage-procedures.html

Northeast Document Conservation Center (NEDCC) Leaflets: Emergency Management
https://www.nedcc.org/free-resources/preservation-leaflets/overview

Association of Moving Image Archivists (AMIA), "Disaster Recovery for Films in Flooded Areas"
http://www.amianet.org/sites/all/files/Resource_Recovery_for_films_in_flooded_areas.pdf

AMIA, "Disaster Recovery for Tapes in Flooded Areas"
http://www.amianet.org/sites/all/files/Disaster%20Recovery%20for%20Tapes%20in%20Flooded%20Areas%20by%20Peter%20Brothers.pdf

Minnesota Historical Society Salvage Procedures for Wet Items
http://www.mnhs.org/preserve/conservation/emergency.php

Library of Congress, "What To Do If Collections Get Wet"
http://www.loc.gov/preservation/emergprep/dry.html

Sample Disaster Plans

Syracuse University Library Disaster Recovery Manual
https://library.syr.edu/about/departments/preservation/PDF/SULDisasterManual.pdf

University of Michigan Library Disaster Response & Recovery Plan for Library Collections
http://www.lib.umich.edu/preservation-and-conservation/university-library-emergency-response

Columbia University Libraries Disaster Response Manual for Care of Library Materials (2008 ed.)
https://library.columbia.edu/content/dam/librarywebsecure/behind_the_scenes/preservation/disaster-2008-edition.pdf

University of Washington Libraries Disaster Response Plan for Library Collections
https://www.lib.washington.edu/preservation/disaster/unit-plan

Patron-Driven Acquisitions and Interlibrary Loan

Patron-Driven Acquisition: What Do We Know about Our Patrons?

Monique A. Teubner, Project Manager, Utrecht University
Henk G. J. Zonneveld, Subject Specialist, Utrecht University

Abstract

This paper describes how Utrecht University Library is trying to reach a sustainable and efficient PDA model, offering more e-books to our users.

PDA e-books were made available in the catalog. We developed an efficient back office process for updates, deletions and financial administration. We did pilot programs to test PDA as an acquisition model. During the pilot anonymized user data was collected of patrons and their use of PDA e-books.

Due to heavy usage and too fast depletion of budget we had to adjust our PDA model. The collected data helped to understand the development of costs and to decide about the changes in the PDA model. After a year PDA pilot, we developed a predictable PDA model. However, for a sustainable model there are still challenges, not only due to dilemmas on restricting the PDA profile, but also due to publishers raising STL prices.

Introduction

In 2010 Utrecht University Library started buying e-books. A few packages at first, but in 2011 we started to order e-books separately at EBL. Next, Evidence Based Selection packages were acquired.

In order to build a good collection more efficiently, we started with PDA program pilots.

Goal of PDA Pilots

All pilots related to collection management in the last few years have been based on the same principles: 1. Develop a good book collection, 2. Respond to the needs of our users better (buy just-in-time), 3. Develop more efficient workflows for both front office and back office, 4. Develop a financially sustainable acquisition model.

We didn't want to spend less on books but spend less on librarians. This implies that we prefer unmediated PDA.

Broad Pilot 2013–2014

After a small pilot with specific PDA profiles by subject which didn't work out, we decided to conduct a broad pilot that lasted one year, paid for with the general library budget.

The budget was $41,000 per teaching period. For a whole year this was $164,000.

We didn't make a selection by subject, but decided to select these publishers from which Utrecht University Library buys publications on a regular basis. The list of publishers was compiled by asking all subject specialists to submit their top 10 publishers, complemented with EBL publishers from which we had bought books over the past year. Next, publishers with which we had already entered into agreements were excluded, such as Cambridge and Wiley.

Further restrictions were:

- Publication year: 2012–2013–2014.
- Language: only English.
- Exclude publishers with > 15% STL (for one day).
- STL price max. 30 dollars
- Listprice max. 280 dollars.
- Max. 3 books per 24 hours.
- 3 STLs, 4th STL was Auto Purchase

Catalog

By mid-August 2013 35,000 titles were imported into our catalog. Each week EBL additions, deletions and updates were processed. Titles purchased by subject specialists and gifts were automatically and immediately removed from the PDA profile in the EBL platform. This way the number of available PDA titles in the catalog and on the EBL platform fluctuated weekly, increasing to 48,000 titles by the end of May 2014.

Users

The basic principle was that we did not want the user to notice the difference between owned titles and PDA titles. At the same time we wanted to collect more data about the users to gain more insight into the use of (PDA) e-books. This way, we hoped to come to a sustainable model or at least control the costs as best we could. We were also interested in the ways in which faculty members from different faculties used e-books and the subjects they chose.

That is why we asked all users to complete a questionnaire the first time they borrowed an EBL e-book. EBL has an option to do so: the Patron Information Gathering Tool. Users were asked two questions: first, to which user category do they belong: student (master or bachelor), staff, or another category; second, to which faculty or department do they belong.

Each user got a token from EBL. This token is used in the EBL usage reports. This token was linked to data about category and faculty of the user as soon as he or she used a book. These anonymized data helped us to find out more about the use, divided into user and faculty categories.

Progress of the Pilot

From the start we suspected that the budget would be too limited in relation to the number of titles. These predictions came true just before Christmas, during the second teaching period. The budget for this period would be used up three weeks too early. Luckily it turned out that there was still $36,000 of funding available.

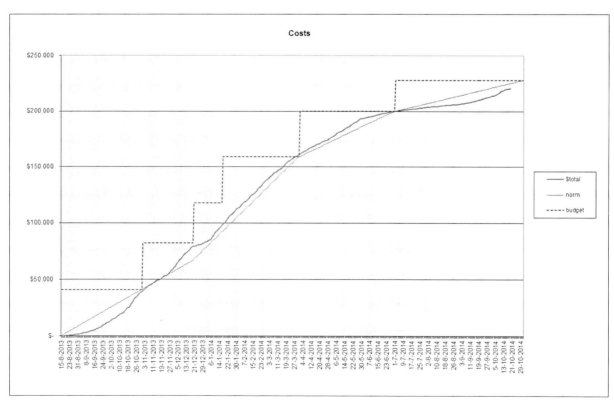

Figure 1. Development of costs during the PDA pilot.

Different Approach

In the course of teaching period 3 this situation seemed to repeat itself. Based on the costs curve it was obvious that we were not going to make it with the planned budgets per teaching period.

One option for managing the costs was to change to mediated PDA. Evaluating the results so far we concluded that PDA was efficient for the library because it saves subject specialists time and answered the needs of the users. Furthermore, the used titles were of the same academic level as the subject librarian would have chosen. And, compared with e-books bought by the library, purchased PDA titles were browsed more per title, more titles had loans and there were more loans per title (Table 1). So we concluded that the selection of useful books can be entrusted to our patrons.

	# Titles purchased	# Titles browsed	# Browses per title	# Titles with loans after purchase	# Loans per title
Auto Purchase	547	547	12,0	447	7,8
Ebook	1074	1044	4,8	375	5,8

Table 1. Use of AutoPurchased PDA e-books and e-books bought by the library (Ebook).

We decided to continue with unmediated PDA and try to find another way to stay within the budget.

We then looked at the publishers who were included in the profile. Taylor & Francis (T&F) had ten times as many STLs as the number 2 on the list of popular publishers in the EBL reports. T&F titles represented half of the available PDA e-books. It became clear to us that a large well-used publisher should not be part of our PDA profile. In this case another purchasing model, such as Evidence Based Selection, may be more profitable and the costs more predictable. PDA, we decided, can best be used for the group of smaller and new publishers.

We also decided to adjust our PDA goals. From considering PDA as a tool for collection development, we changed our view to making books available for our patrons. We decided to focus less on purchases and more on borrowing.

While maintaining a maximum STL percentage of 15% we decided (in week 13) to switch to Auto Purchase at the 9th STL. In Figure 2 you can see that since then, hardly a book was bought in the PDA.

Unfortunately we were not able to see if these two choices alone would lead to a sustainable PDA.

Just before we removed Taylor & Francis from our PDA profile, this publisher together with a number of other publishers was automatically removed from the profile because they had drastically raised their STL percentages to above 15%.

In June and July more publishers followed. In the end over 15 publishers were automatically removed, among which three of the four most popular publishers. As a result the number of available PDA titles was more than halved. Accordingly the number of STLs dropped, but not halved.

We were surprised by the reaction of our patrons. We expected to receive a lot of complaints from patrons missing books in the catalog. Beforehand we decided that subject specialists would immediately buy any PDA title they received complaints about.

This turned out to be a mere handful.

A possible explanation could be that patrons just use the books they can find in the catalog. Only the patrons who actively used a particular book complained when they couldn't find it anymore in the catalog after it had been removed.

Maybe some patrons found alternative titles within the PDA, because the relative number of STLs did not drop as much as the available titles.

Another explanation could be that they fell back on the print collection.

Prediction of the Use in One Year's Time

Despite the fact that one of the advantage of a digital library is that you can consult it 24/7 without having to visit the library building, you can see a clear connection with the number of visitors in the building. This is quite logical, because at the end of each teaching periods students are still using the library as a place to study and write their papers.

This way it is possible to estimate the costs over a certain period of time.

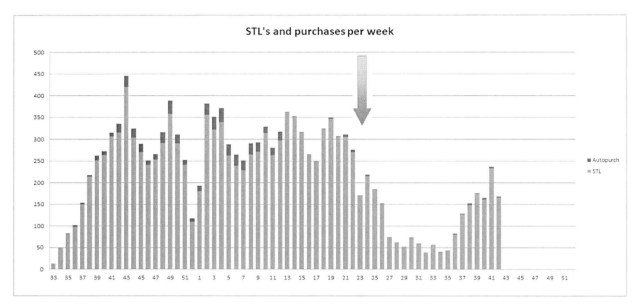

Figure 2. STLs and purchases per week. In week 23 T&F and other publishers were removed from the PDA pool.

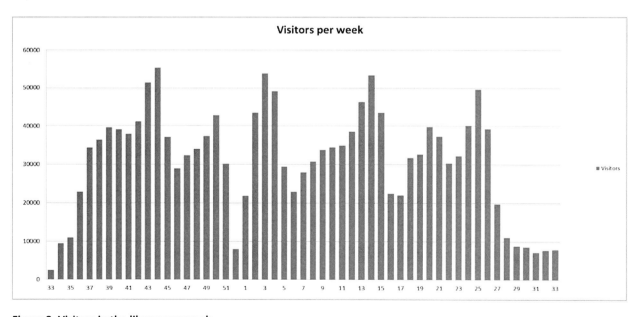

Figure 3. Visitors in the library per week.

Use by Disciplines

When we look at the usage by the members of different faculties, Humanities' large share becomes clear. The share of Humanities titles in the PDA pool was constantly around 38%, even though some publishers which are important for Humanities were removed from the PDA profile due to the high STL prices. There are relatively more humanities patrons and they do relatively more transactions. We see that this is consistent with their share of borrowed material from the print collection.

We noticed that the shares of transactions vary from one week to the next. The average share for Humanities is 53%, but one week this may be 40% and the other week may be 60%. A relationship with student activity is obvious.

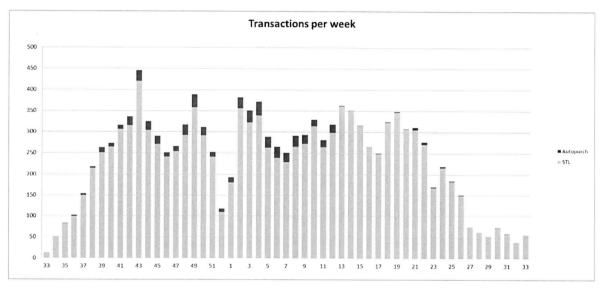

Figure 4. PDA transactions per week.

Who Uses Which Books

The assumption faculties make is that students only read the books that have been bought for their faculties, belonging to their discipline. Based on this assumption some faculties refuse to pay for titles outside their field of interest. Our usage statistics show that the situation is not as simple as that.

The next graph shows the use by faculty members of "faculty subjects." Almost all subjects are used by members of all faculties.

Faculty	% Patrons	% PDA titles on faculty subjects	% Transactions	% Costs
Geosciences	9%	0,4%	7%	7%
Humanities	43%	37,6%	53%	51%
Law, Economics & Governance	12%	14,4%	12%	14%
Medicine	3%	4,5%	2%	2%
Science	6%	9,6%	4%	4%
Social and Behavioural Sciences	11%	21,6%	8%	8%
Veterinary Medicine	1%	0,9%	1%	1%
Others	13%		14%	13%

Table 2. Shares of patrons, available titles, transactions, and costs per faculty.

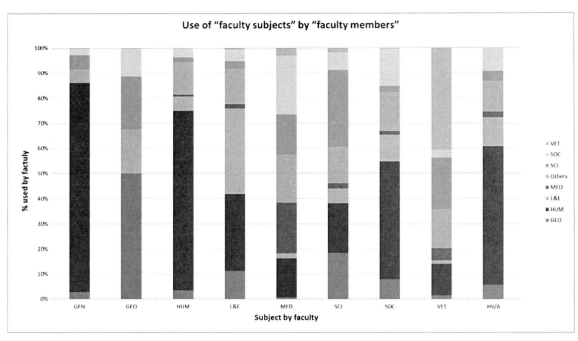

Figure 5. Use of "faculty subjects" by "faculty members."

During the presentation in Charleston we discussed the possibility that there would be a difference between different user groups: bachelor students would use more books from other faculties while master students and staff would be more focused on their own subject.But that is not true. In some cases it was just the staff that is using books outside their own collection profile.

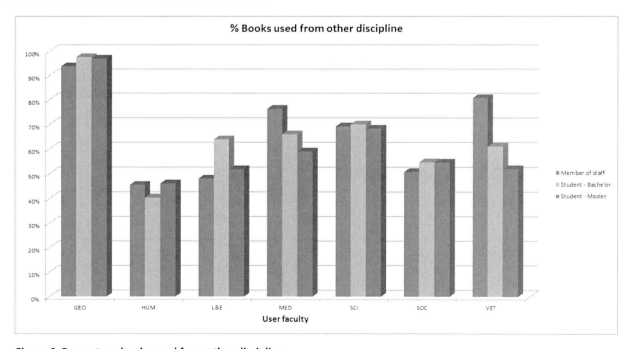

Figure 6. Percentage books used from other discipline.

What Else Did We Find Out, Using the Usage Reports from EBL?

Figure 7 shows that the different user categories not always follow the 4 teaching periods. At first sight the staff seems to use less e-books than the students. But if you compare their numbers (6500 staff) to the number of students (30,000), then their usage is considerable.

The long-standing idea that Humanities scholars read more pages of a book than other disciplines seems to be proved wrong if you look at Figures 8 and 9. However, it is possible that they look for a print book if they want to read the entire book.

The high average reading times for bachelor students from Science and Veterinary Sciences are probably caused by the fact that some books were used in a course.

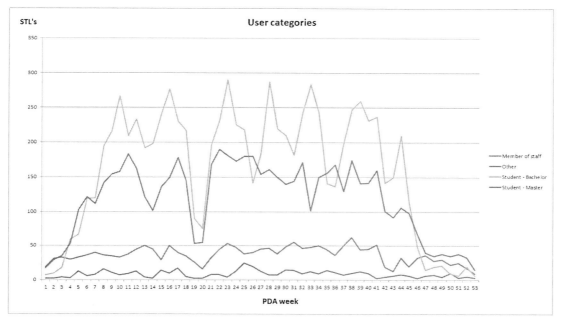

Figure 7. User categories.

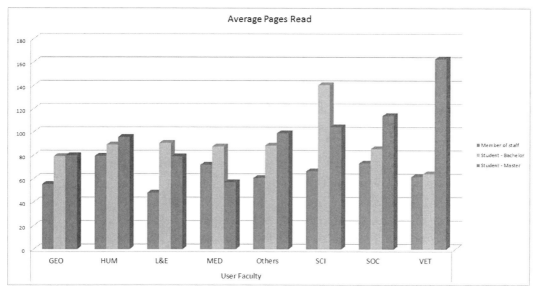

Figure 8: Average pages read.

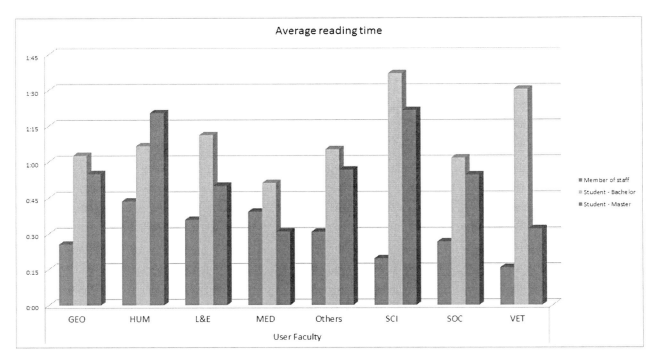

Figure 9: Average reading time.

In figures 10 and 11 you can see a clear difference in the use of e-books. Bachelor students print less and read much more online-only (without printing). Is this a development of another way people use e-books? Or Does their usage change during their scientific career? Time will tell.

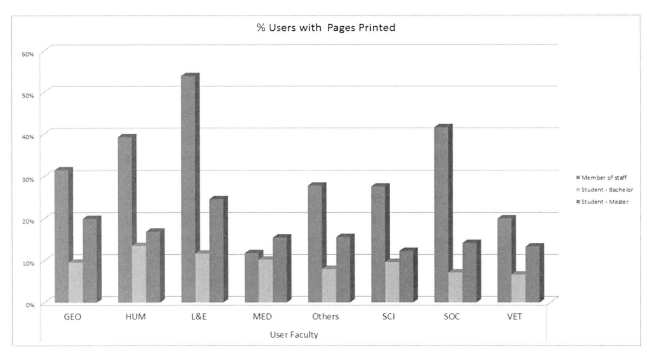

Figure 10. Percentage users with pages printed.

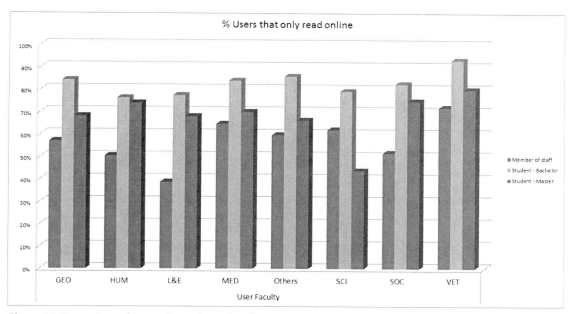

Figure 11. Percentage of users that only read online.

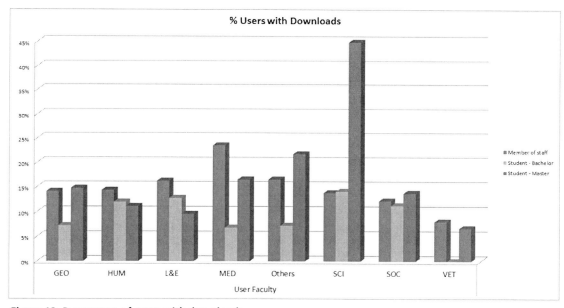

Figure 12. Percentage of users with downloads.

Due to the small number of STLs in Science, it was easy to discover that the high score for the Science master students was caused by two students who downloaded a lot of e-books on several subjects.

Moving Wall

An important question in our model with a moving wall is whether "old titles" are still used and how to deal with them.

The graph below shows the titles published in 2012 which we available for the entire time of the pilot. These books were used just as often in the beginning of the pilot as the end. So "less usage" cannot be an argument to remove older titles from the PDA pool. On the other hand, to make PDA sustainable, these books might have to be removed because they are still used and therefore cost money. We don't know what to do about this yet.

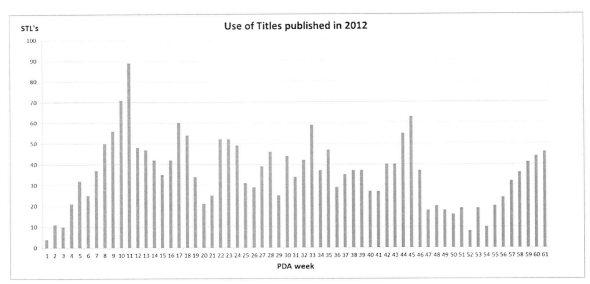

Figure 13. Use of titles published in 2012 per week.

Conclusions

The titles in our PDA model, based on a number of publishers, and available in the catalog, are heavily used by our users.

At the moment we have not dealt with our model long enough to be able to reach conclusions about sustainability in the long run. But if conditions remain the same, we will be able to control the costs of the PDA sufficiently.

Gathering usage data for a whole year did tell us more about the usage during all teaching periods and help us develop a sustainable type of PDA. The number of library visits proves to be a good indication for the usage of PDA titles.

Gathering data about the users and the usage in the long run can also help to reach a sustainable model for the PDA in your own situation. What

that model entails exactly and how that fits in with the collection development strategy and the collection may differ per library.

Insights into the usage per group show how patrons are using e-books and which subjects they choose. This can lead to a different approach to collection development. Why would you spend so much time on the collection profile if it turns out that your students get their books from all possible Dewey codes?

Gathering data however offers no guarantee if the financial conditions are changed by individual publishers. The drastic raising of the STL rates by a number of publishers has severely limited the possibility to come to a sustainable PDA model. It makes the model unpredictable, and unsustainable if you don't remove these publishers, or less efficient and less interesting for patrons if you do remove these publishers.

Turning a Crisis Into an Opportunity: DDA and PDA at UTA Libraries

Peter Zhang, University of Texas at Arlington Libraries

Abstract

Facing a 72% cut in our monographic acquisitions budget in FY13–14, University of Texas Arlington Libraries turned a crisis into an opportunity. We examined print monographs' circulation data and discovered the hard truth that the "just-in-case" acquisition model is neither sustainable nor serving our users well. Subsequently, our approval plan was put on a virtual mode: no more approval book shipments. We implemented demand-driven acquisition (DDA) programs for both electronic and print books and put broader patron-driven acquisition (PDA) programs in place to meet our users' needs.

The Crisis

University of Texas at Arlington Libraries have operated under a flat materials budget for four years in a row. During this time, however, serial prices steadily increased and, in some cases, increased dramatically (Bosh & Henderson, 2012). For instance, our Stat!Ref subscription through TexShare's "Big Deal" came with a 60% increase for the 2014 renewal. We have shrunk the monographic budget to shore up serials each year. At the beginning of fiscal year 2013, we had to cut 72% of the monographic fund to sustain existing serials.

At the same time, we discovered that close to 100,000 books the libraries purchased through approval plans from January 2004 to January 2014 never circulated. These books account for $4.4 million direct cost and another $3.8 million indirect cost based on the $4.26 per year estimate (Courant & Nielsen, 2010) to keep them on the open shelves. As our shrinking buying power has reached a crisis level, our monographs collection development is in a worse place. The just-in-case-someone-will-use-them-someday model has failed to address our users' needs and is unsustainable. We must change.

Opportunities

That close to 100,000 books we purchased in the past ten years never circulated is a tough truth, but it *is* the truth. It propels us to reexamine our overall collection development paradigm through the lens of "what a collection does rather than what a collection is," (Horava, 2010) and to seek opportunities to reprogram our monograph acquisition to meet our users' needs. As a result,

our service orientation has shifted from collection-centric to engagement-centric, and from librarian-predicting to patron driven. Recently, the library implemented a new liaison program that greatly expanded our outreach effort. There used to be five subject librarians making selections. Now almost 50 librarians and archivists are taking on liaison responsibilities. Requests from faculty and students are now driving our resource selection and acquisition. We have made a paradigm shift to patron-driven acquisition (PDA). Through the expanded liaison program and library's broader outreach efforts, the library formed several partnerships to support library resources. The College of Business, for example, contributed $113,000 to fund business databases purchases.

Programmatically, several measures have been put in place to facilitate PDA. First of all, approval plan shipments were stopped as soon as logistics permitted in November 2013. The approval plan was put on a virtual mode, which is available as a selection tool but does not generate new shipments and purchases. At the same time, we boosted our interlibrary loan (ILL) book-on-demand program. When ILL requests to borrow newly published books cannot be fulfilled with three attempts, we purchase them. The chance of an ILL borrowing request being fulfilled goes down with each attempt. Most libraries have polices that do not allow ILL lending for newly published books. Rather than hoping a borrowing request is fulfilled and prolonging the wait, we decide to cut the waiting time and meet our users' needs in time. More than enough savings were generated by stopping approval plan purchases. We are able to support the ILL on-demand purchase program without adding strain to the budget. Furthermore, these purchases have gone a long way for the library. We not only are able to address our users' needs in time, but also generate so much good will from our users. They are glad to have a much longer check-out time for these books than what would otherwise be allowed by ILL arrangements.

Next, based on NISO's best practices for demand-driven acquisition (DDA) of monographs (Kawecki & Levine-Clark, 2013), an electronic DDA program was implemented locally in February 2014. We selected to set up the e-book DDA program through Yankee Book Peddler (YBP) with Ebook Library (EBL). One compelling reason for us to use EBL is the nonlinear lending feature that has no single user restrictions. Three short-term loans (STL) are allotted before a purchase is made. We elected to have the 2014 front list and 2013 back file fitting our profiles in the consideration pool. Each week new consideration records are automatically retrieved, customized, and loaded. Markers are entered in the 590 field of the records for easy reporting and tracking of the title's status. The first STL was triggered a week after the program started. From February 2013 to August 2013, $158,659.36 was spent on approval books and 18.09% of them had at least one charge by September 8, 2014. In the same period for 2014, $9,425.14 was spent on the e-book DDA program, and 100% of them were used. Compared to the approval plan, the e-book DDA program saves us over 94% and takes out the guessing game for librarians.

Publishers have not made all books available in electronic format (Besen & Kirby, 2014). It is particularly true for front list titles. Users such as art and humanities faculty also report that certain materials about drawing, painting, and so forth are still desired in print. Driven by our patrons' demands, the library took another step forward. A print book DDA program was set up in September 2014. Consideration titles are limited to the art and humanities and social sciences portions of our profiles. Unlike e-book DDA, print DDA requires staff mediation. We try to minimize the mediation and shorten the turnaround time as much as possible. After considering several options, we

creatively tapped ILLiad as the user authentication mechanism. We gain a couple of advantages by doing so. Rather than handling patron accounts in a separate environment, ILLiad has built-in LDAP that communicates with campus user information. Users who have an ILLiad account do not have to reenter their personal information each time when making a request. ILLiad has built-in email capability. Patron information as well as bibliographic information are supplied automatically. Acquisition staff members do not have to re-enter them. We also take advantage of the OpenURL protocols to automatically populate the DDA request form in ILLiad with bibliographic information. The OpenURL link in each record is generated dynamically when consideration records are customized.

The library's Department of Access and Discovery that administers the DDA programs is a "get it" (Chadwell & Nichols, 2010) type of integrated multifunctional technical service unit. To streamline the workflow and therefore shorten the turn-around time for users, acquisition staff members are cross-trained in ILLiad, shelf preparation, and circulation. An Amazon Prime membership is purchased for alternative purchasing and shipping options when other vendors' pricing and shipping are not competitive. So far, we are able to keep the turnaround time from staff placing an order to delivery to users within five business days.

Conclusion

The library's monographic fund was cut 72% in fiscal year 2013–2014. At the same time, close to 100,000 books purchased in the last ten years through approval plans never circulated. Facing the challenge of a shrinking budget and failing to meet users' needs, the library made a paradigm shift from a librarian predicting what books to buy to patron-driven acquisition. Several programs have been put in place to turn a crisis to an opportunity where we are able to strategically spend our budget to meet our users' needs and, at the same time, make it financially sustainable. By the end of the fiscal year, the monographic fund stayed in the black and created a 28% savings to support the serials fund. Since approval plan shipments were stopped, the library spent only $50 on book binding. Savings from that is used to support a bindery for Special Collection items. Staff time has also been freed up from handling tens of thousands of approval books each year. Staff members now can assist digitization projects for unique local resources. Cross-training of staff in ILLiad, shelf preparation, and circulation enable a streamlined workflow that results in faster turnaround time.

References

Besen, S. M. & Kirby, S. N. (2014). Library demand for e-books and e-book pricing: An economic analysis. *Journal of Scholarly Publishing*, *45*(2), 128–141.

Bosch, S. & Henderson, K. (2012). Coping with the terrible twins. *Library Journal*, *137*(8), 28–32.

Chadwell, F. A. & Nichols, J. (2010, November 10). The "get it" department: Oregon State University's strategic realignment of collection services. *Proceedings of the Charleston Library Conference*. Retrieved from http://docs.lib.purdue.edu/cgi/viewcontent.cgi?article=1128&context=charleston

Courant, P. N. & Nielsen, M. B. (2010). On the cost of keeping a book. *The idea of order: Transforming research collections for 21st-century scholarship* (pp. 91–105). Washington, DC: Council on Library and Information Resources.

Horava, T. (2010). Challenges and possibilities for collection management in a digital age. *Library Resources and Technical Services, 54*(3), 142–152.

Kawecki, B. & Levin-Clark, M. (2013). Best practices for demand-driven acquisition of monographs: Preliminary recommendations of the NISO DDA working group. Retrieved from http://www.niso.org/workrooms/dda/

We're E-Preferred. Why Did We Get That Book in Print?

Ann Roll, Collection Development Librarian, California State University, Fullerton

Abstract

While California State University, Fullerton's Pollak Library has an e-preferred approval plan for all subject areas, the Library still continues to receive a number of print titles on approval. However, 25% of the print approval books received in the 2013–14 fiscal year were published by only eight publishers, all of which actively publish their books in e-format. This paper investigates the reasons why print books were supplied over potentially available e-versions. In some cases, individual titles were only published in print, while others were available as e-books, but could only be purchased within collections. Others were available for purchase as individual e-books, but not via the Library's primary aggregator. Options for approval profile adjustments to further reduce print approval receipts are offered.

Introduction

For the start of the 2013–14 fiscal year, California State University, Fullerton's Pollak Library transitioned to an "e-preferred" approval plan for all subject areas. The Library had made a concerted effort to increase electronically available collections, due not only to the rise in online course offerings, but also to the desire to repurpose space in the Library building. In order to provide access to more content at a lower total cost, the Library also wanted to move as much monograph acquisition as possible to a demand-driven-acquisition (DDA) model. Moving to an e-preferred approval plan more easily enabled this; all approval titles that were available as e-books from the Library's primary aggregator could be added to the DDA pool rather than purchased outright, regardless of whether they were profiled as books or as slips. An analysis of the print approval books received in the 2011–12 fiscal year showed that 33% had been simultaneously published as e-books, and so it was apparent that the move to an e-preferred approval plan would expand the Library's electronic holdings while reducing the space necessary for future print collections.

Over the course of the 2013–14 year, the Library did indeed add to its electronic collections, but also encountered some surprises concerning which titles were still being received in print. The Library received 3358 print books from 670 imprints, but 25% of those receipts were from only eight publishers, all of whom were known to actively publish in e-format. This paper explores the reasons why those books were supplied in print rather than electronically and suggests profile adjustments that could be made so that more titles would be supplied electronically.

The Transition to an E-Preferred Monograph Collection

With over 38,000 students, California State University, Fullerton (CSUF) is the largest campus is the 23-campus California State University (CSU) system. CSUF is a predominantly undergraduate and master's-level teaching institution, and Pollak Library is CSUF's sole library, located in the center of campus. Since 2010, when the Library initiated its first e-book DDA program with Ebook Library (EBL), Pollak Library has been gradually moving toward an e-preferred monograph collection. Transitioning the Library's existing approval plan with YBP Library Services (YBP) to be e-preferred by the start of the 2013–14 fiscal year was a logical step.

While the Library also firm ordered e-books from EBSCO and provided access to ebrary e-books via a CSU-wide subscription to the Academic Complete e-book collection, EBL remained the Library's preferred aggregator for the e-preferred approval plan. Since the Library had been providing access to EBL e-books since 2010, librarians and users were familiar with EBL's interface. EBL's Non-Linear Lending purchasing model was also desirable, since it allows for unlimited simultaneous users at a cost that is often similar to the cloth list price, while costs for unlimited simultaneous user access from other aggregators are often higher. The e-preferred approval plan was established with the guideline that any profiled title available as an EBL e-book would be supplied as such, and any title that was DDA eligible would be added to the DDA pool rather than purchased. Profiled titles that were not available as EBL e-books would continue to be supplied in print.

Books Received in Print

Based on the analysis of the 2011–12 approval receipts and knowing that a number of publishers, especially small publishers, either only publish their books in print or do not work with EBL, the Library expected to continue to receive a number of titles in print. What was surprising was that 852 titles (25% of the total print receipts) were from eight major publishers known to publish in e-format. The eight publishers, in order from the most print books received to the least, were:

1. Oxford University Press (195 print receipts).

2. Palgrave Macmillan (168 print receipts).

3. Cambridge University Press (113 print receipts).

4. Springer (106 print receipts).

5. Routledge (76 print receipts).

6. Yale University Press (66 print receipts).

7. HarperCollins (56 print receipts).

8. The University of Chicago Press (54 print receipts).

The electronic availability of these print books was investigated using GOBI[3], YBP's online selection and ordering system. In general, e-books were not provided for one of four reasons: 1) the book was available electronically via an e-book aggregator, but not from EBL; 2) the e-book version was only available on the publisher's online platform; 3) the book was only available for purchase from YBP in print format; 4) timing (the e-book was available on the EBL platform, but not within YBP's eight-week timeframe for simultaneous print and e-book publication). In addition, there were some anomalies in which an EBL e-book actually was available when the print book was supplied due to issues with the approval profile or errors.

Results by Publisher

Oxford University Press

The Library received more print books published by Oxford University Press than any other publisher. However, the majority of those books (62%) were available as e-books from either ebrary or EBSCO, and so more e-books would have been received if the Library had opted for a multi-aggregator option for the e-preferred approval plan. 16% of the print books were available as e-books, but only on the University Press Scholarship Online platform, and half of those could only be purchased as part of a collection. 15% were only available in print format, and the remaining 7% were available from EBL, but not in within the eight-week timeframe in order to be supplied on the approval plan. For Oxford University Press, the Library would have received a considerable number of the titles as e-books if the profile was broadened to include EBSCO, ebrary, and titles available for individual purchase from University Press Scholarship Online. However, while both EBSCO and ebrary also offer DDA options, costs for multi-user access from these two aggregators are typically higher than EBL, and University Press Scholarship Online does not currently provide a DDA option, a cost-saving method that is important to the Library.

Palgrave Macmillan

Timing was the most significant factor for the print books published by Palgrave Macmillan. 39% of the print receipts eventually became available as e-books on EBL's platform, but not until after the eight-week timeframe for simultaneous print and e-book publication had expired. Another 29% of the Palgrave Macmillan books were only available in print format. A number of books (22%) were available from either ebrary or EBSCO. However, timing would have also been a factor with many of these, and so even if the Library had a multi-aggregator option for the e-preferred approval plan, then not all of them would have been supplied.

In March 2014, it became possible to order individual e-books on Palgrave Macmillan's platform, Palgrave Connect, via GOBI[3]. Nearly all of the print titles that eventually became available for purchase as e-books from one or more of the aggregators (EBL, EBSCO, and ebrary) also became available for purchase directly on Palgrave Connect. Although, this may have been months after the Library received the titles in print, since March 2014 was late in the 2013–14 year. Of the Palgrave Macmillan books that the Library received in print, 71% eventually became available for purchase as e-books on one or more platforms. Only 6% of those were exclusively offered on the Palgrave Connect online platform; however, looking at the print receipts from March 2014 and later, it appears that Palgrave Macmillan intends to release e-books on Palgrave Connect simultaneously with the print publication, but continue to delay the release to the aggregators.

It appears that in the future, the Library could receive the majority of Palgrave Macmillan titles as e-books if Palgrave Connect was added to the approval profile as a platform option. However, the lack of an option for DDA, the requirement of minimum purchase, and the likelihood of high per-title costs based on institutional size, may make this an unreasonable option for the Library.

Cambridge University Press

Similar to the Palgrave Macmillan print receipts, the Cambridge University Press receipts also indicated a preference for the publisher's e-book platform over aggregators. 58% of the Cambridge University Press print receipts were available as e-books, but only on the publisher's platform. 17% were available only in print. Oddly, a substantial number (20%) of the print books received were available as EBL e-books at the time that the print book was profiled. Figure 1 shows an example in which the title was available as an e-book on EBL's platform on November 8, 2013, but on February 19, 2014, the Library was supplied with a print version on the approval plan. While timing is likely to be the factor for some of these, the individual titles need to be investigated more closely by both the Library and YBP to determine the cause. The remaining 5% of the Cambridge print receipts were either released on EBL after the simultaneous publication timeline expired, or they were available from ebrary or EBSCO.

Figure 1. Title available from EBL, but supplied on approval as a print book.

Similar to the possible solution for the Palgrave Macmillan titles, the Library could receive more Cambridge titles electronically by adding the publisher platform as an option in the approval profile. However, again, this would eliminate the option for DDA. Cambridge University Press does have an evidence-based acquisition model which could serve a similar function, but it would require the Library to acquire Cambridge University Press e-books outside of the approval plan and does not allow for the cost-savings of short-term loans, which the Library values.

Springer

Similar to the situation with the Oxford University Press print receipts, the Library would have received more Springer books electronically had the Library opted for a multi-aggregator option for the e-preferred approval plan. 57% of the Springer print books received were available from EBSCO or ebrary, but not from EBL. An additional 25% were available electronically on Springer's online platform, SpringerLink. However, these are only available for purchase in collections, and so if the Library prefers to receive the books via the approval plan, then print is the only option. Another 19% were available from EBL, but either timing or profiling issues caused them to be sent in print instead. Showing Springer's commitment to releasing content in e-format, all of the books that the Library received in print were available electronically in some form.

Expanding the Library's e-preferred profile to include EBSCO and ebrary would be a good next step to receive more Springer titles electronically via the approval plan. Since all of the content is available electronically, removing Springer from the approval plan entirely and purchasing SpringerLink collections would be another option. However, thus far, the Library's print Springer receipts have not fit neatly into any of the existing subject collections, and purchasing the full collection is unlikely to be cost effective or necessary for the CSUF community.

Routledge

Timing was the most notable factor for the Routledge print books received. 38% were released as EBL e-books after the eight-week window had come to a close. Another 38% appeared to be available as EBL e-books at the time the print version was profiled, and so these need further investigation by both the Library and YBP. However, it is likely that timing was a factor for some of them. 14% were only available in print. 9% were available from ebrary and EBSCO, but timing, and possibly the other factors that affected the EBL availability, would have also been a factor for those.

It appears that there is very little that the Library could adjust in order to receive more Routledge books electronically via the approval plan.

Yale University Press

More than for any other publisher, an adjustment to a multi-aggregator option would bring more Yale University Press e-books to the Library. 81% of the Library's Yale print receipts were available from either ebrary or EBSCO. The remaining titles were only available in print.

HarperCollins

Of the HarperCollins print receipts, one title became available from EBL after profiling, but all others were only available from YBP in print format. However, HarperCollins differs from the other publishers listed, in that academic libraries are not its primary market. For comparison, 84% of HarperCollins books that the Library received are available for purchase as e-books to the public and school library markets on Baker & Taylor's Axis 360 e-book platform. However, these books are not available from any of the e-book aggregators that work primarily with academic libraries. As such, there is little the Library could adjust in order to receive these titles electronically.

The University of Chicago Press

Again, the situation with The University of Chicago Press mimicked that of Oxford University Press. Had the Library selected a multi-aggregator option, then a significant number of the books received in print would have been received electronically. 61% of the University of Chicago print books were available electronically from either ebrary or EBSCO. An additional 20% were affected by timing, becoming available on the EBL platform after the print book had been profiled. The remaining books were only available in print. Opening the profile to include EBSCO and ebrary as options would have noteworthy impact for the University of Chicago Press titles

Discussion

Of the four primary factors that caused a book to be sent in print format rather than e-format, the choice of a single aggregator had the most impact on the Library's print receipts. As illustrated in Figure 2, 38% of the 852 print books received from these eight publishers were available from either ebrary or EBSCO, but not from EBL, the

Library's preferred aggregator. This change would be especially influential for books published by Oxford University Press, Springer, Yale University Press, and The University of Chicago Press.

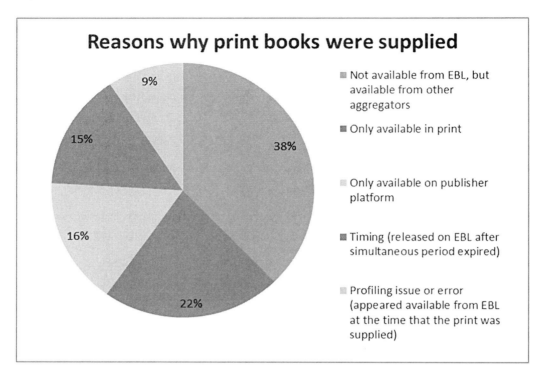

Figure 2. Reasons why 852 print books from eight publishers were supplied on Pollak Library's e-preferred approval plan.

In addition, 16% of the print books were available electronically on the publisher's own platform. While the majority (69%) of the titles that were only available on publishers' platforms were available for individual purchase via YBP, a subset of those titles that were published by Oxford University Press and Springer were only available in collections. If the Library had expanded the approval profile to include ebrary, EBSCO, and all publisher platforms, then nearly half (49%) of the 852 print books supplied from these eight publishers could have been supplied as e-books. However, 15% of the total print receipts were affected by the timing of the release of the book on the EBL platform. While multiple platforms would reduce the impact of timing since some publishers release the e-version on their own platform or that of a selected aggregator sooner, it would very possibly continue to be a factor even in a multi-

platform environment which includes the publisher platforms. There are also unknown factors which caused some books to be sent in print despite the availability of e-versions on the EBL platform within a reasonable timeframe. In total, these anomalies represented 9% of the total, and so the Library, along with YBP, will need to continue to investigate the causes. What remains is the 22% of the receipts for which no electronic version was available for purchase according to GOBI3. Only Springer had some electronic version available for every title that was supplied in print, while the other seven publishers each had some titles for which no e-book was available.

Conclusion

While Pollak Library had many reasons for its move to an e-preferred approval plan for the start of the 2013–14 fiscal year, the ability to save funds while providing access to more monographs via DDA was key. Because the Library had been using EBL as its primary e-book aggregator for DDA since 2010, it was a logical decision to continue with EBL as the preferred aggregator for the e-preferred approval plan. As this analysis has indicated, the number of approval books supplied in e-format would have increased notably if options for multiple aggregators and publisher platforms had been included. However, with minimum purchase or collection requirements on some publisher platforms, the options are reduced if the Library plans to continue the focus on DDA. To increase the number of approval books received in e-format, while maintaining DDA as a preferred method, a move to a multi-aggregator, e-preferred approval plan would be a good next step.

Earnestly Seeking Greater Flexibility:
The Pros and Cons of Pay-Per-View Journal Access

Marija Markovic, Acute Source
Steve Oberg, Wheaton College

Abstract

This presentation sheds light on a relatively new phenomenon that needs more earnest consideration from all kinds of libraries: the switch to a pay-per-view (PPV) access model for journals. The presenters, one from a corporate library background and one from an academic background, have extensive experience in utilizing PPV. They detail pros and cons of PPV and how it allows for greater access for users with more financial flexibility for acquisitions budgets. Discussions among acquisitions and collection development librarians in recent years have focused on demand-driven acquisitions (DDA) for e-books. The presenters believe that PPV for journals is in the same vein but even more far-reaching and beneficial.

The presenters started with an overview of PPV. Oberg reported that PPV access options were available across a versatile range of content types, from journal articles to e-book chapters or sections, to parts of content of reference works, and even streaming video. These PPV options are available via different pricing models. The most common is a prepaid token bundle purchase, in which the library prepays a set of (article) tokens. Typically, the higher the volume of the purchase, the lower is the price per (article) token. A less common model is a postpaid arrangement, in which the library sets up the PPV access, and is invoiced on a monthly or quarterly basis, whichever is preferred/negotiated. Other pricing models include access via an institutional credit card (on demand access), as well as a newer model of article rentals. Article rentals is an innovative concept where the library user can preview an article for a limited time before deciding whether to proceed with purchase.

Following different content and pricing models, libraries have a variety of implementation options. Oberg discussed available options and their variance both from the purely technical implementation and implementation directed by the library's budget model, i.e., whether the library absorbs all PPV costs or whether the library charges back users for any PPV transactions. The most optimal option, from the library user's perspective, is the one with the least access obstacles, when PPV is activated/open for all library users. A less user friendly option is one where access to PPV content is mediated by selected super users, who can be internal staff (library staff), or external contacts (in the case where the library is utilizing an external document delivery vendor).

Markovic continued the PPV overview by addressing different challenges libraries should be ready to encounter when planning PPV implementation. Estimating potential usage is critical, especially with the initial PPV purchase. It is essential to review previous document delivery/ILL usage and user demand for nonsubscribed content, for overestimating will result in overspending on a PPV account, and underestimating will result in overpayment on the per-token/per-item level of purchase. To make matters more complex, there is a lack of standardization among vendors in not only pricing models but nomenclature itself. Some vendors call their PPV options tokens; others Article Select; and others use bundle, prepaid article, etc. Additionally, the lack of standardization extends itself through the terms of use for PPV content. While some vendors allow nonexpiry on purchases, others make their PPV options valid only for a limited time (a year or two) after purchase. Moreover, vendors define actual usage differently. Some may allow archiving, use of articles by more than one user, while others do not. Another critical challenge is the the technical aspect of implementation which was mentioned earlier. In the user-friendly, open to all, implementation, there exists a potential for the

PPV account to be depleted more rapidly than in the mediated implementation. On the other hand, while the mediated option is more economically conservative, as the demand can be "controlled" by the super users, it is more complex from a technical standpoint. There are additional steps to set up access for super users, whether they are internal library staff or an external document delivery vendor.

Though the presenters agree that PPV access options have both pros and cons, they lean toward pros.

PPV access to nonsubscribed content is a perfect solution for shrinking budget trends, where libraries are not only less able to acquire new content, but often have to cancel subscriptions to content with moderate to high usage, all in an effort to accommodate budget limits. By offering PPV, library users' needs are fulfilled in a quick, easy way, where implementation can be so seamless that the users will remain unaware that they are accessing PPV content (vs. subscribed content). In addition, the cost per article via PPV is by rule lower than cost per article via a document delivery vendor, ILL, or directly through the publisher's web site (where no PPV has been established). Thus, in short, PPV fulfills users' content needs and provides cost savings for the library's budget.

Though PPV requires more ongoing oversight including troubleshooting, maintenance of access, and usage statistics review, it is a beneficial collection development tool. Collections can be assessed in a cost-per-use analysis to include cost per use for PPV access. Moreover, reviewing PPV access usage statistics over time provides great insights into usage trends and user behavior. Overall, PPV accounts are an excellent negotiation asset when negotiating annual contracts. Understanding and analysing PPV usage statistics is an excellent negotiation asset when negotiating renewal of PPV accounts.

One of the key cons that the presenters wanted to emphasize, especially for the vendors in attendance, was that although PPV is available across a range of content types, not all vendors support institutional PPV, and that needs to

change. As they stated in the session, the message they communicate to vendors is "something is better than nothing." If vendors only offer inflexible, bundled, and expensive subscriptions across their content portfolio, libraries will not be able to sustain them. If vendors offer institutional PPV, on the other hand, libraries will be able to provide them with some revenue.

Oberg next turned to a discussion of examples from the academic sector that focused on what is the end-user experience with journal article PPV. He noted the components of access include an end user A&I database (could include Google), an OpenURL resolver, and the publisher's website, and focused on the steps taken by end users to get to a PPV article in a nonmediated environment. Essentially, the principle at work is to make the end user barrier as invisible or seamless as possible. His first example showed PPV directly available to the end user, and his second example illustrated how PPV works for one publisher who doesn't support direct availability of the article to end users. In this second example, Oberg's library has modified a web form template to prepopulate with article metadata and include key end user contact detail. Once that form is submitted by the end user, a structured email is sent to a dedicated e-mail address, the article is purchased by the library's credit card, and the article is then emailed back to the end user within a set amount of time.

Markovic discussed examples from her extensive work in corporate libraries that focused on various budget and access models. She talked about the importance of a cost threshold whereby a PPV transaction might then be triggered as a less expensive option. Another key consideration is from where the money is allocated in a library's budget to pay for PPV versus subscriptions. This is particularly a problem when a library wants to shift money toward one type of access versus another, and it also has a significant impact on how PPV access might be implemented. In other words, if a library charges PPV costs back to users and the transactional portion of the budget is separate from subscriptions, it points toward a moderated PPV implementation. It also may mean ongoing difficulty if the PPV option increases in popularity versus subscriptions due to problems in shifting the money from a different budget area over time.

In closing, both presenters highlighted the major takeaways from their PPV experience:

- Greater flexibility (for library budgets).

- Greater access (for end users).

- A bit more for libraries to manage.

Markovic and Oberg asserted that the subscription-only, bundled journal model is no longer sustainable for all types of libraries. To (mis)use a famous advertising slogan, "A subscription isn't forever."

Supporting Rapidly Growing Online Programs in Times of Change

Mary Ann Mercante, Assistant Dean and Professor, Maryville University Library
Ying Lin, Electronic Resources Librarian and Assistant Professor, Maryville University Library

Abstract

In May 2012, Maryville University launched two online graduate Nursing programs. Twenty-eight months later, 2,321 students from across the United States were enrolled as online-only students in these programs. Two additional Nursing graduate programs are going online as well as an MBA program. Concurrently, Library space is being reconfigured to accommodate student support services from other areas and to provide more learning spaces for students. With less space for physical collections and more students to support, Maryville University Library is trying to find ways to provide better research support for all its students. How Maryville is handling these challenges and their impact on all aspects of library service (Interlibrary Loan, Collection Development for Journals, Books and Databases, and Reference) will be discussed in this paper.

Background

Maryville University is a small private university located in the St. Louis metropolitan area. Maryville's mission statement describes its mission as offering "an innovative liberal arts education leading to excellent academic and professional programs." In April, 2012, Maryville offered undergraduate degrees in programs similar to many four year small private institutions: Liberal Arts, Business, and Education. Maryville also had a robust School of Health Professions, offering degrees in Nursing, Physical Therapy, Occupational Therapy, Rehabilitation Counseling Services, and Music Therapy. Several graduate programs were offered, including an EdD and a clinical doctorate in Physical Therapy along with Masters degrees in various programs, including Nursing. All Maryville programs were on-ground. Maryville's official student population consisted of a headcount of 3,846 students with an FTE of 2,568.

On May 7, 2012, Maryville began three nation-wide online graduate Nursing programs: a Master of Science in Nursing for Adult/Geriatric Nurse Practitioner, a Master of Science for Family Nurse Practitioner, and a DNP degree (Doctor of Nursing Practice) program. In fall 2011 (the last student census prior to the beginning of the online programs) Maryville had no online students. The fall 2014 student census counted 2,321 online-only students.

At the same time as the growth in online students occurred, the physical space in the Library's two-story building was being reconfigured to increase first-floor student collaboration areas for on-ground students and to make way for offices from other areas of campus. By August 2014 all library collection materials needed to be consolidated on the Library's 2nd floor.

We thought we were prepared for the online programs. A librarian had been embedded in each course. An updated tutorial on using library resources for nursing was prepared. LibGuides were created for specific classes. We began a Nursing e-book PDA with EBSCO. What we (and the Nursing Program) didn't plan for was how many students there would be and how fast these programs would grow.

This paper will describe how the introduction and growth of the online student population coupled with the need to reduce the physical collection have impacted the library's collections and services.

Interlibrary Loan

ILL BOROWING	2011-2012	2013-2014	% Change
Articles requested	5,733	8,949	56.1%
Articles received	4,986	7,634	53.1%
Articles Average Turn-Around Time	n-a	4.14	

Table 1. ILL articles two-year borrowing comparison, 2011–2012 to 2013–2014.

Interlibrary Loan was the area in which change was most immediately noticeable.

This increase resulted in an increase in copyright fee payments from $1,873 in 2011–2012 to $11,984 in 2013–2014, an increase of 539%. The much larger percentage increase in dollars versus number of articles occurred because most of the articles received in 2011–2012 fell within our fair use allotment. Almost all of the articles making up the increase between 2011–2012 and 2013–2014 fell outside of our fair use allotment and fell within a very specific (and expensive in terms of copyright fees) subject set of journals.

The Copyright Clearance Center's Get-It-Now service was implemented during this time as a way of decreasing the time between a patron request and the patron receipt of an article. These numbers are included in the above calculations. We have not implemented unmediated Get It Now service as we find a significant number of article requests are from journals for which the Library has the article available in a database or a subscription.

The Library began a document delivery service to supply, via email, a scanned copy of an Interlibrary Loan requested article where the Library had the article available, but only within its physical holdings. In 2011–2012, 1,337 articles were delivered in this manner. In 2013–2014, 3,484 articles were provided via document delivery, a 161% increase.

Journals

The Library conducted a review of its physical journal collection from November 2013 through January 2014. A master spreadsheet was prepared with the following information:

- Title.
- Physical Holdings.
- Interlibrary Loan & Internal Document Delivery Usage of Our Physical Holdings (the scanning of articles from our physical collection & emailing to patrons).
- Vendor/Publisher for Electronic Availability.

- Online Backfile Coverage Available from Vendor/Publisher.
- Online Backfile Price.
- Online Coverage Currently Available via our Database Subscriptions & Title-by-Title Subscriptions.
- Subscription Price for a Current Online Subscription.
- Library's Current Physical Subscription Price.

For titles identified in this process as candidates for replacement with online, we further looked at questions of online format stability. This included factors such as whether paid content was preferable to free content when both were options and what the vendor or publisher's policy was regarding continued access to online content if a subscription was cancelled. Once decisions were reached as to which titles should have physical holdings replaced with online, we examined the economics of title-by-title subscription vs packages.

As a result of the review, back holdings for 194 titles were completely withdrawn and back holdings for 36 serial titles were partially withdrawn. In some instances, back files overlapped with current online availability in our databases and subscriptions; in other instances changes in programs and teaching methods meant that holdings were no longer relevant to our students' learning. Deep online back file purchases were made for 10 titles in Nursing. In our spring EBSCO annual renewal review, 79 print subscriptions were cancelled. Twenty were total cancellations while 59 were converted to online only. Of the 34 nursing journals to which we subscribed, only two remain in print as this point; the rest are online only.

The Library initiated subscriptions to three online journal packages for Nursing: the OVID I and II nursing collections from Lippincott, Williams, & Wilkins and the Clinics package from Elsevier. OVID I and II provided us with 28 new nursing titles and allowed us to replace print with online for 10 titles. The Clinics package provided current and back holdings for nine health titles, four of which were new and five of which replaced print titles. A site license for JAMA was also initiated.

Books

MOBIUS (the Missouri state-wide library consortium with membership including several major medical libraries and a robust delivery system), backed up by traditional Interlibrary Loan, has served our on-ground students well as a supplement to our physical book collection. This model does not work for an online program with students in 48 states. Students cannot come to the library to pick up books from ILL nor the MOBIUS delivery system, both of which are predicated on delivery to libraries, not individuals. Our online courses run on eight-week rather than the on-ground 16-week cycle, so the shipping of books from our library to students would not have provided a timely solution, even if we had the staff resources to handle this.

By May 2012, the Library had begun moving towards e-book as the preferential format for selected subject areas, including most of the Health Professions. Selection of e-books was done by librarians and faculty members in the disciplines. The PDA model had been investigated, but not adopted. The online Nursing programs propelled us into our first PDA, a targeted nursing PDA with EBSCO begun in May 2012.

We began the PDA by looking at the then-current EBSCO Nursing subject set, making additions and deletions to it based on a review of the title list by our reference librarians. We began with an initial set of 109 titles and a beginning deposit of $3,000 on a Thursday in May 2012. We had an initial scare when we came in the following Monday to discover that $780 had been purchased from the PDA during its first four days. The pace of spending did slow somewhat, since a book "purchased" by one user was frequently used by others.

Each spring, the PDA is redone. All titles not purchased are removed and a new PDA based on the latest EBSCO Nursing subject set is created. Titles we already own (through purchases outside the PDA) are identified and removed. Expensive titles ($350 or higher) are removed. The reference

librarians review the list of removed expensive titles and any they identify as relevant for our curriculum are added back. Starting in 2013, any requests for books during the year that are received from Nursing faculty are added to the PDA rather than being outright purchased, so we only pay for them if they are actually used. PDA statistics are summarized below:

PDA Statistics -- 2 and 1/2 years

Total PDA titles	273 titles
Purchased	155 titles
Usages	3,880 uses
Total Cost	$18,924
Cost per Title	$122.09
Cost per Usage	$4.88

Table 2. PDA Statistics for 2 ½ years.

In conjunction with the shift to e-books-only purchasing for the Health Professions, a major review of the print collection was conducted by nursing and library faculty. The Library weeding project was designated as a "community service" project for the University's Maryville Reaches Out day of community service when classes are cancelled on a day in September so that students, faculty, and staff can participate in service projects across the St. Louis area. Once Nursing and other Health and Sciences faculty had begun the project on this day, their interest in continuing to work on the project during the school year was easier to maintain. By year's end, 3,524 volumes had been withdrawn from the Health Sciences collection.

Databases

Full-text article databases are critically important in the support of online programs. The Maryville University Library upgraded several databases to the "Complete" versions to gain additional full-text titles. A highly specialized medical database, Up To Date, was added. In addition to full-text article databases, nontextual databases are important for online programs, such as EBSCO's SMARTImage collection of medical images. Databases of streaming video collections (such as the Alexander Street Press Nursing Education in Video and Academic Video Online) were added.

The rapid growth in the number of students impacted our FTE count for several databases which base pricing on FTE. This impact spilled over to other nonmedical subject areas in which database use the University's FTE to calculate pricing. Overall database spending has increased by 58% since the implementation of our online programs.

Reference Service

Maryville University Reference staffing prior to the online programs consisted of two full-time Reference librarians, supplemented by Circulation Desk staff paraprofessionals. Neither Reference librarian had medical librarian background or training, though both had gained sufficient experience to handle the on-ground undergraduate nursing students and the small number of on-ground graduate health professions graduate programs. The number of online nursing students and the increasingly complex nature of their research led to the hiring of one FTE medical librarian (filled initially by one full-time librarian and now by two part-time librarians).

Video tutorials on library resources and their usage are embedded in each online course as is a LibGuide specific to the class. Close communication with both the faculty teaching the online courses and the online course developers (not always the same personnel) is essential. Knowing logistical details such as the number of

students enrolled in a class and the schedule of due dates as well as the content of class assignments allows for better scheduling of library personnel to meet the ebbs and flows of student needs.

Ideally assignments should be vetted with reference librarians as the assignments are being developed to ensure that there are electronic resources available for students to find. During the first eight-week online course cycle, the Nursing Theory class was offered. Each student in this class completes a research project, including primary resources, on a present or past nursing theorist, picking from a list prepared by the instructor. This had been a successful assignment in the on-ground version of the course. However, with the large number of students in the online course, the instructor, not wanting duplication among the student choices, increased the number of names on the list. Unfortunately, primary resources in electronic format didn't exist for many of the newly added names, leading to student (and librarian) frustration. This list is now reviewed by a reference librarian when changes are made to it.

In 2012–2013, the Library implemented an online form for the collection of reference statistics. A comparison of 2012–2013 with 2013–2014 shows the shift in reference transactions as the online student population has grown.

REFERENCE STATISTICS		2012-2013	2013-2014	Change
	Total Questions	1,409	1,280	-9.16%
Communication Method	Email	159	407	155.97%
	In Person	864	432	-50.00%
	Phone	384	441	14.84%
Category	Reference	396	509	28.54%
	Research	528	691	30.87%
	Directional	54	27	-50.00%
	Technology	552	253	-54.17%
	Other	44	19	-56.82%
Length of Question	0-3	387	210	-45.74%
	4-10	669	458	-31.54%
	10-20	221	272	23.08%
	20+	132	340	157.58%
	Time spent (minutes)	12,539	17,801	41.97%

Table 3. Reference statistics two-year comparison.

E-mail and phone transactions increased as in-person transactions decreased. While the overall number of transactions has decreased, the number of transactions categorized as reference (under 20 minutes) and research (over 20 minutes) have increased. (The decrease in overall questions is due to the decrease in the number of technology questions directed to the Library as the campus's School of Adult and Online Education has geared up to handle technology issues.)

In looking at the time spent in transactions, the greatest growth is found in the 20 or more minutes category. The 10–20 minute category also increased as did overall time spent in transactions with patrons.

Future Plans

The Library will continue to shift its collections from print to online, transforming from a library with a primarily physical collection supplemented with online resources to a library with a primarily online collection supplemented with some physical resources. A chat reference service will be introduced in early 2015. We are looking at ways to reduce our turnaround time for Interlibrary Loan article delivery. While turnaround time for the internal document delivery service is a respectable 1.22 days, turnaround time for ILL article delivery is 4.14, days which is higher than we would like for classes on an eight-week cycle. The University will soon be adding two additional online Masters programs in Nursing and an online MBA program, so we know our growth and our learning experiences in the world of online support will continue.

What You Need to Know About Moving Collections and Acquisitions Into an E-Dominant Model!

Gerri Foudy, Manager of Collections, University of Maryland College Park

Lila A. Ohler, Head of Acquisitions, University of Maryland College Park

Lenore A. England, Assistant Director for Electronic Resources Management, University of Maryland University College

Abstract

Two different University of Maryland Libraries discuss how they have moved to an e-dominant model, the reasons why, and the new acquisitions strategies libraries can use in crafting an e-dominant collection. Whether your organization is a large ARL library like University of Maryland, College Park (UMD) Libraries or a nontraditional online library like the University of Maryland University College (UMUC) Library, there are many strategies for taking advantage of the new acquisitions environment and rethinking how to build collections in an e-dominant world. At UMD, adopting an e-dominant model has been a gradual change over time, allowing the library staff to develop new ideas about collection development and experiment with new tools and techniques for acquiring and managing the libraries' collection. As these changes have unfolded over time, staff began to develop a more comprehensive and holistic picture, becoming more aware of how their own work with e-resources impacts our colleagues, our patrons, and the wider library community. At the UMUC Library, the electronic resources management staff developed an e-model initiative that represents a fundamental shift for electronic resources management at UMUC. Electronic resources have become a critical, important, and fully integrated component in course development for the university and this is driving the direction of collection development for the Library. The main thrust of this shift has been the establishment of an E-Resources Initiative to replace the use of textbooks in print with e-resources, primarily open access, embedded within the learning management system (LMS) course modules.

Introduction

As more libraries move to an electronic model (e-model) for their collections, two libraries in the University System of Maryland and Affiliated Institutions (USMAI) consortium planned out their own approaches to this process: the University of Maryland, College Park (UMD) and the University of Maryland University College (UMUC). Planning for the change in processes at the two libraries emerged over time, as e-resources began to develop as the primary means of access for our patrons. The change in processes was dependent on the infrastructure and environmental influences within their libraries and at their institutions as a whole. Both also shared e-resources provided by several organized consortial organizations in Maryland and in the Washington, DC area. As will be discussed, while these two libraries have different foundations and stances on their paths to an e-dominant model, commonalities do emerge. The basic premises of

their approaches can help the UMD and UMUC librarians understand and share what they are doing at their institutions and learn from their experiences, ultimately enabling both to continue to develop improvements, effectively enhancing access to and management of their e-resources.

University of Maryland, College Park Libraries

Moving to an e-dominant model for collections means rethinking how our patrons use the collections we have, and more importantly, how they wish to use the collections we don't already own. Many have argued that in order to make this shift, libraries must overcome the traditional idea of building collections, particularly print collections, moving from a just-in-case model to a just-in-time model of offering materials at the point of patron need (Lehman, 2014). We argue that new acquisitions models like demand-driven purchasing, enhanced by network level discovery and the unbundling of scholarly content, are in fact the culmination of the traditional model of collections—one in which the library can finally achieve the hallowed goal of offering our patrons any material in the world, and all at the click of a button. But to do this well, the catch is to understand we are no longer in the business of building and managing collections. Instead we are managing collections services, and specifically a core suite of services that provide instantaneous access to anything, anywhere, and at any time. The success of that model is the degree to which any library can coordinate the work to be done in fulfilling those services, not only across its own organization and staff, but also out into the marketplace working with external vendors and cooperative partners (Dempsey et al., 2014).

At the University of Maryland Libraries, we recently underwent an organizational change, moving those departments that traditionally encompass collection development and technical services under one administrative division entitled Collection Strategies and Services. The close association between collection development and the support of collections that these traditional units provide is now seen as one coordinated service, or rather a suite of services. We have learned through our experiments with demand-driven acquisitions and the development of discovery tools that our goal must be to offer our patrons the best services we can to not only find what we already own, but also to find, access, purchase, or borrow anything else in the world of scholarly information they may need. That's a big job, and not one that any unit within a library can do by itself. Nor for that matter can the library do it without some significant help from our partners in the marketplace, including consortia, enterprise level system providers, book vendors, content providers, knowledge base companies, subscription agents, networked metadata providers, and so on.

The real key to moving to this kind of e-dominant collections model understands the difference between developing collections versus developing coherent collections' services across the entire marketplace. We no longer simply develop collections or acquire materials. Instead we might

manage the selection profile that pushes demand-driven books appropriate for our libraries' focus into the pool of available books for our patrons to see and potentially use. Or we might manage the metadata profile for potential collections, working with our vendors and content providers to ensure their materials are discoverable through our knowledgebase provider, even though we may never own the material. Or we might work with our vendors to negotiate the right to convert their original content into another format, offering streaming video to students who would rather watch a film for class from anywhere via the course reserves content management system than physically visit the media services library. Or we might negotiate access to a provider's content that would allow a faculty member to perform data mining research. Or we might work with our IT unit and our Interlibrary Loan Unit to develop a "buy or borrow" option, allowing our patrons to generate a request for nonowned content in the same way they currently do for ILL. This is a wholly different view of collections, and one that takes a larger amount of coordination between library staff than the traditional collections model.

It will come as no surprise that as a direct result of our experiences with developing and managing some of the new collections services we now provide, the staff working across the libraries have gained a healthy appreciation of what each of us does to support those services, and just how difficult the decisions are that we must make in this new environment. The work has been slow going at times, and has involved a lot of rethinking what we do and how we do it. Like many libraries, we're struggling to rethink our physical spaces. The largest challenge in this area is the disconnect between what some of our patrons, and even some of our own subject librarians, want us to preserve (physical books in a branch library that are rarely used) with what others desperately need us to develop (space for collaboration, makerspaces, learning and research commons, big data set repository). And again like almost every other library we know, we also struggle with our budgetary constraints. Do we continue to fund that "big deal" for journals from publisher X? And if we do, what are the opportunity costs we've lost in not repurposing those funds to develop an on demand article service that might ironically offer our patrons access to more content? And when it comes to selection and acquisition, our two greatest challenges continue to be 1) understanding the new role of selection and acquisition expertise in developing and evaluating new models for collections, and 2) developing both the internal and external infrastructure needed to support robust discovery and fulfillment services for the collections we want to offer. Anyone who has faced the wrath of a patron who does not understand why they cannot immediately access anything from anywhere at any time will understand what we mean here. Or the shock of finding out the knowledge base provider updated its global content over the weekend and overwrote our local data for certain publishers or local collections, followed quickly by the dawning panic that we have no really good way to notify our patrons that those links won't work for a bit while our external business partner quickly tries to fix it. The bar of expectation has been set high by the retail marketplace of content providers and fulfillment services (iTunes, Netflix, or any other commercial on-demand service) that can offer efficient and immediate consumption of content to our patrons. Our job has become figuring out how to connect the content sold in the library marketplace with our patrons in that same seamless and immediate fashion.

University of Maryland University College Library

UMUC was established as a distance education institution when originally founded in 1947, and continues today as one of the largest provider of online learning in the United States. Initially the UMUC Library provided resources mainly in print and then, about 20 years ago, switched gradually to electronic as this type of format became more readily available. There were UMUC libraries in Asia and Europe with more substantial print materials; these closed around 2007, primarily due to changes in locations of US bases. In 2013, the physical facility of the Library in the UMUC headquarters closed, albeit with a small volume of print materials, and the Library has been completely virtual since then.

It was a natural process for the UMUC Library to focus strictly on electronic materials. Our students and faculty are located worldwide, and access to a physical library is not always possible, especially to our patrons down range on bases and other military installations. As a result, the e-model for the Library was initiated very early on, more as a matter of necessity and unwittingly as a provider of e-resources using a model that all libraries are now developing according to their institutional requirements. In that sense, the UMUC Library represents the very end of the spectrum of an e-dominant model: the "only" e-model, with no focus on print collections, except to provide books in print from the USMAI institutions, on a lending basis to our students within the contiguous United States.

Management of electronic resources started out in 2001 with one part-time librarian, and in 2013 a library associate was hired to help with the increasing workload. The management of electronic resources is not a traditional career in the UMUC Library, since it is a new and burgeoning field, and this work has led the staff to carve out new pathways both beneficial for the Library and for the potential management of electronic resources at UMUC as a whole. In addition, the unique academic environment at UMUC has provided an even greater opportunity for innovation.

While the ERM Unit is modeled after a more traditional, but changing, technical services unit at an academic library, the workflows have not been traditional. The UMUC Library fully supports the acquisition, evaluation, and operations for ERM, but does not focus on cataloging. In fact, we do very little cataloging here for our electronic resources, instead focusing on access through our discovery tool, EBSCO Discovery Services (EDS). Even in EDS though, we do not load in our relatively small number of catalog records. Most of our students and faculty are located through the world and a library catalog that includes print materials that they cannot access nor borrow is not useful for them. In addition, the nontraditional environment has enabled the staff to think in very different ways of how to establish effective ERM workflows and overall operations, with a small number of personnel to manage all of it. The Core Competencies for Electronic Resources Librarians (http://www.nasig.org /site_page.cfm?pk_association_webpage_menu =310&pk_association_webpage=1225) serves as a basis for our work, especially for the life cycle of electronic resources, research and assessment, and effective communications. However, the trends for ERM at UMUC present many other challenges and we are faced with both understanding these trends and adapting to them in very different ways than we see at other academic libraries.

Adaptation is important for ERM at UMUC in order to prove relevancy of our subscribed resources. We need to reach out to our faculty in order to understand, explore, and participate in high-priority projects, such as analytics, to identify the most important learner interventions and new adaptive learning techniques. The ultimate goal is for our student success and retention of those students in their chose track of learning.

The main thrust of these changes have been the establishment of an E-Resources Initiative to replace the use of textbooks in print with e-resources, primarily open access, although we are seeing more of a trend of late of utilizing the Library's proprietary electronic resources as a means of directly supporting required course reading, embedded within the learning management system (LMS) course modules. This may seem to be similar to what is occurring in online academic courses at many other institutions, but there is a fundamental shift in ERM here at UMUC that is unique. Electronic resources are acquired not only by the Library, but by UMUC as a whole, and further have become a critical, important, and integrated component in course development. Electronic resources collection development is no longer limited to the library; many other departments have become involved at this very beginning stage and will continue to do so, with the expertise and help from the UMUC Library staff.

The E-Resources Initiative is part of a larger initiative now, Competency-Based Education (CBE), which is primarily defined by identifying competencies in program and providing students

with the means to prove those competencies as they progress towards the goal of obtaining their degrees. As a result of the ongoing competency-based education initiative, the E-Resources Initiative is evolving into the Online Learning Resources (OLRs) initiative. OLRs can be articles, e-books, videos, websites, and open access resources, as well as Library-subscribed resources. The word electronic does not necessarily define their inclusion; that is set by the importance of the resource for any given program. OLRs will mean a different view of licensing, access, linking, and analysis of their usage that we are just beginning to envision for ERM at UMUC.

There are four initiatives to develop and improve the e-model workflow for the UMUC Library and the entire university. All of these are intentionally reaching out beyond the Library's own systems to explore and develop the use of electronic resources within an innovative environment of online learning that ultimately supports our students' success and leads to improve retention within the various programs.

1. Utilizing existing content management systems that are integrated with our learning management system (LMS) for electronic resources management. We are thinking that using the same systems that are used for course management, instead of ERM systems built specifically for libraries, is the future of ERM at UMUC. The system we will work with is Equella, which will enable us to enter in important metadata about our resources, and track usage.

2. Working on how to improve access to electronic resources by better understanding both curricular needs and how students gain and organize their access to electronic resources. I am aiming to tie all of this into how our LMS is utilized by students and faculty in order to understand and develop a fully integrated ERMS with our LMS.

3. Developing a project to enable improved access to electronic resources within a Competency-Based Educational system. The ultimate goals are to initiate valuable

assessment of the use of electronic resources and how these resources can develop to track and aide in the educational process within this type of environment.

4. Developing a philosophical approach to learning with electronic resources, based on the Extended Mind theory proposed in 1998 (Clark & Chalmers). Pursuing the best intentions of this theory will lead the Library staff to a better understanding of how our students organize their environment to access electronic resources. This will help us develop improved means of setting up access for them.

Conclusions

At both UMD and UMUC, acquisition and collection development librarians find that shifting models for managing e-resources has fundamentally changed their role in managing library collections. Rather than build a collection, we now coordinate collection options for our users, from building to coordinating, sometimes in a rapidly changing environment. This change has meant a shift in focus from a more centric approach to a broader, patron-focused approach. While each library arrived at this approach for different reasons, the resulting goal for both libraries has been improving access for our patrons and experimenting with the best means to achieve that goal.

References

Clark, A., & Chalmers, D. (1998). The extended mind. *Analysis,* 58(1), 7–19.

Dempsey, L., Malpas, C., & Lavoie, B. (2014). Collection directions: The evolution of library collections and collecting. *portal: Libraries and the Academy*, 14(3), 393–423.

Lehman, K. A. (2013). Collection development and management: An overview of the literature, 2011–12. *Library Resources and Technical Services*, 58(3), 169–177.

An Evaluation of ReadCube as an Interlibrary Loan Alternative

Elizabeth J. Weisbrod, Auburn University Libraries

Abstract

Libraries are continually searching for more affordable ways to provide access to research materials. The rising costs of journal subscriptions, site licenses, and interlibrary loan have made libraries look for new methods of providing those materials. In 2014, Auburn University Libraries began a pilot project to test the feasibility of using ReadCube, an article delivery service, as a method of patron-driven acquisition for scholarly journal articles. ReadCube allows users immediate access to articles from Nature Publishing Group journals at a lower cost than document delivery, but with usage restrictions.

This case study evaluates ReadCube as an alternative to interlibrary loan by comparing the costs and usage of ReadCube Access to those of interlibrary loan. Users were also surveyed to determine their satisfaction with ReadCube. The results indicate that ReadCube is a cost-effective method of obtaining Nature articles, although some users have reservations about the usage restrictions.

Introduction

Auburn University Libraries began a project in 2014 with ReadCube Access, an unmediated document delivery service for articles in Nature Publishing Group journals. As in many libraries, Auburn's budget remains flat while journal subscription costs continue to rise and the Libraries are continually looking for ways to provide more access at a reasonable cost. ReadCube is one approach to providing access to research journals without the cost of a new subscription.

Before contracting with ReadCube, researchers at Auburn University used interlibrary loan (ILL) to acquire articles from unsubscribed Nature journals. While ILL provides reliable access to articles, it has certain drawbacks. Copyright costs for articles can be substantial, staff time is required to process requests, and delivery to users is not immediate. A report at the Charleston Conference in 2013 by Jones and England described a trial of ReadCube Access, a new model of patron-driven acquisition for journal articles, at the University of Utah (Jones & England, 2014). After analyzing ILL costs for Nature journals, the Libraries began a trial with ReadCube Access in January 2014. Although limited to Nature Publishing Group journals, ReadCube appeared to a good fit for the Libraries' needs, and the Libraries contracted with ReadCube in March 2014.

How ReadCube Works

ReadCube Access is a patron-driven document delivery service for libraries. Originally developed by Labtiva, ReadCube is owned by Digital Science, a division of MacMillan Publishers and a sister company of Nature Publishing Group ("Introducing ReadCube," 2014). The ReadCube platform is a group of products that includes ReadCube Access as well as the ReadCube client, a free reference management system, the ReadCube Web Reader, a PDF reader integrated into the Nature Publishing Group's journal websites, and other tools and services. ReadCube provides enhanced PDFs which have such features as clickable references, supplements and other related materials, and the ability to highlight and make notes in the PDF.

Currently, for libraries, only articles from Nature journals are available through ReadCube Access. Articles from over 100 Nature journals are offered through ReadCube and libraries may select which Nature journals are available to their users. ReadCube is IP-based and users must be on campus or use a proxy server or virtual private network (VPN) to download articles.

Three levels of download are offered. In exchange for lower costs, articles from the lower two tiers come with certain rights restrictions. The library subsidizes the rental or purchase price of articles and may choose which levels of download are presented to their patrons:

- 48-hour rentals ($3.99). The article must be downloaded and read in the ReadCube reader and is only available for 48 hours. No printing is allowed.

- Cloud purchase ($9.99). The article must be downloaded and read in the ReadCube reader. The article is saved indefinitely to the user's ReadCube cloud account. Printing is allowed.

- Unrestricted download ($25). The article is downloaded without digital rights restrictions and may be printed and saved.

When a user selects an article from a journal on the Nature Publishing Group website, he or she sees an icon indicating that an enhanced PDF is available. After clicking on the icon, the first page of the article is displayed and the user is given the choice of renting or purchasing an article (Figure 1). He is then prompted to log in to his existing ReadCube account or to establish one. After the user logs in to his account, download is immediate and the library is billed for the article. After the article is downloaded, ReadCube queries the Libraries' link resolver to check whether the article is available through subscription or an aggregator. If it is available, the library is not charged for the article. By going through a library's link resolver, ReadCube works as an unmediated document delivery service since libraries will not be charged for articles already available to users.

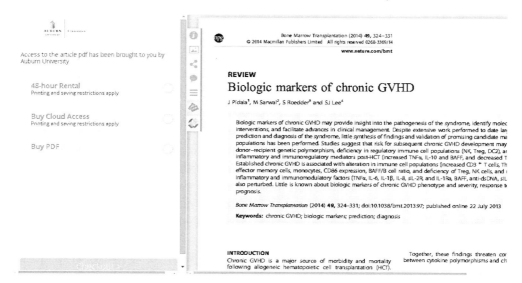

Figure 1. The ReadCube application showing the article purchase choices.

ReadCube offers much-reduced costs for Nature articles, especially when compared to ILL copyright charges. According to the CONTU (Commission on New Technological Uses of Copyrighted Works) guidelines, each year a library may borrow five articles published within the last five years from a journal without incurring copyright fees. However, for the sixth and subsequent articles, libraries must seek permission, usually through the Copyright Clearance Center, and pay copyright charges (United States Copyright Office, 2005). For Nature Publishing Group journals, the fee for each article

is $35.50. All three levels of download offered by ReadCube are less expensive than ILL after a title exceeds the five article request threshold.

The low price points are offered in exchange for usage restrictions on the two lower tiers of download (rental and cloud purchase). Rental articles may not be printed and both rental and cloud purchase articles must be read in the ReadCube client rather than downloaded as a PDF which can be saved anywhere. To libraries, despite the restrictions, ReadCube seems very appealing—lower costs and immediate access to articles for users. However, users may not view the restrictions as acceptable.

To evaluate the project, the Libraries wanted to answer several questions. Is ReadCube financially sustainable? Will users misuse the availability of the articles and download unacceptable numbers? Do researchers find the ReadCube platform acceptable? Is ReadCube an adequate substitute for ILL?

ReadCube and Auburn University Libraries

Auburn University is a land-grant institution located in Auburn, Alabama, with significant research programs in science and technology fields. The University has 25,000 students, of whom 5,000 are graduate students, 1,200 faculty, 140 undergraduate majors and graduate study in over 110 areas, and professional schools of Pharmacy and Veterinary Medicine. Auburn University Libraries is an ARL library with a serials budget of over $7,000,000.

The Libraries subscribe to 24 of the over 100 Nature journals listed on the nature.com website. The Libraries elected to provide ReadCube access to 83 Nature journals; that is, all Nature journals to which they do not subscribe or which are not completely available through open access or an aggregator. The Libraries chose to only offer the 48-hour rental ($3.99) and the cloud purchase options ($9.99).

In 2013, the Libraries received 91 ILL requests for articles from Nature journals and paid over $3,000 in copyright charges. By using ReadCube, the Libraries anticipated that usage would go up because of the convenience of no longer having to request articles through ILL, but believed that the costs would be manageable because of the reduced cost of each article.

ReadCube usage from March-September 2014 was compared to ILL requests for articles from Nature journals during March-September 2013. In 2014, the Libraries paid for 283 articles through the ReadCube application, 96 of which were 48-hour rentals and 187 of which were cloud purchases. (An additional 43 articles were downloaded but not paid for as they were available through aggregators or subscriptions. These articles were not included in the study.) During the same period in 2013, 42 articles were requested through ILL (Table 1). As expected, ReadCube usage was greater than ILL requests. Comparing the two years, the number of ReadCube purchases and rentals was nearly seven times the number of ILL requests.

The cost of ReadCube was also compared to the cost of copyright charges for ILL requests for Nature articles. Copyright fees for March-September 2013 ILL requests were $1,313.50 while ReadCube costs for the same period in 2014 were $2,251.17 (Table 1). The total price of purchases and rentals from Readcube in March-September 2014 was nearly twice that of the copyright charges paid for Nature articles during the same period in 2013. However, while the overall costs were higher, usage was greatly increased and the price per article was much lower for ReadCube. The average cost per article was $31.27 for ILL requests (not including staff costs or other charges) and $7.95 for ReadCube purchases, making the average cost of acquiring a Nature article through ILL nearly four times as expensive as downloading it through ReadCube.

Table 1

ReadCube uses and costs compared to ILL requests and costs

	March	April	May	June	July	August	Sept.	Total
2013 ILL Requests	4	7	9	3	8	7	4	42
2014 ReadCube Uses	19	65	37	29	34	40	59	283
2013 ILL Copyright Costs	$106.50	$248.50	$319.50	$35.50	$213.00	$248.50	$142.00	$1,313.50
2014 ReadCube Costs	$183.81	$595.35	$327.63	$265.71	$225.66	$261.60	$391.41	$2,251.17

Table 1. ReadCube uses and costs compared to ILL requests and costs.

Although the Libraries were initially concerned that individuals would download great numbers of articles because they were easily available, for the most part this turned out not to be a problem. Fifty-four percent of users downloaded only one article and 92% percent of users downloaded five or fewer articles (Figure 2). However, one user downloaded 32 articles for a cost of $279.72. With an unmediated system, potential for abuse exists, but the Libraries consider the overall level of usage acceptable.

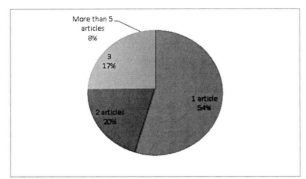

Figure 2. Number of ReadCube downloads per user. 92% of users downloaded five or fewer articles.

User Feedback

To assess the ReadCube project, a short survey was sent to all 153 registered users (Appendix 1). Eighteen responses were received for a return rate of 11%. While a small sample, it did provide some insight into users' impressions of ReadCube.

When the Libraries began the ReadCube project, it was promoted through email announcements, by subject librarians, and on the Libraries' website, but over half of the respondents reported learning about ReadCube only by seeing the icon on the journal article. One-third of the respondents reported having no difficulties using ReadCube but other users reported having problems such as difficulty printing and viewing articles, difficulty navigating the ReadCube application, and access links not working. When asked "What do you see as the greatest benefit to ReadCube?," the majority of the respondents mentioned having access to articles that they would not have access to otherwise. Another person mentioned that they liked the "highlighting, direct links to the references, and ability [to] save with notes" that are available in the ReadCube application. A

couple of other people, though, indicated that they preferred other reference managers. Another comment damned with faint praise. "I suppose if it's the only way to access a paper it's better—barely better—than having to request it through ILL."

In response to the question "What is the biggest challenge to using ReadCube?," half of the respondents mentioned problems with printing. Comments like "Unable to print some/all articles that I have accessed using it. Able to read but cannot print" were typical. Anecdotally, librarians reported that users had found printing a problem so these comments were not unexpected. Some of the ReadCube printing issues have been resolved, so user education may alleviate some of the difficulties.

A number of respondents questioned why they could not just download a PDF, rather than having to save a copy to the ReadCube reader or client. Comments such as "Printing and not being able to save a pdf. That is completely ridiculous. I shouldn't have to log on a website to access an IMPORTANT reference," and "It's good, but what's wrong with just viewing a PDF?" indicate that users do not understand why the Libraries are utilizing ReadCube. Some users may wonder, not unreasonably, why they are required to log in to an additional application when other journals require only a click to download a PDF. If the Libraries provided the more expensive unrestricted level of ReadCube download, users could download a PDF that could be saved anywhere. However, at $25 per download and at the current level of usage, ReadCube would no longer be financially sustainable. Education about how ReadCube works and the costs of journal subscriptions may help users understand the financial reasons why the Libraries are utilizing ReadCube.

Conclusion

Auburn University Libraries has found ReadCube Access to be an acceptable alternative to interlibrary loan. The Libraries believe ReadCube provides much more access at a reasonable cost. Although the amount spent to acquire Nature articles was nearly twice that of ILL costs in the previous year, users downloaded nearly seven times the number of articles at a much lower average cost per article. Very little abuse of the system was seen during the study and 92% of users downloaded five or fewer articles. While users have some concerns about the platform and usage restrictions, they appreciate the access to articles that they would not otherwise have. At the current level of cost and usage, the Libraries consider ReadCube financially sustainable and good value for the investment.

References

Introducing ReadCube. (2014). Retrieved from https://www.readcube.com/about

Jones, P., & England, M. M. (2014). An alternative mechanism for the delivery of scholarly journal articles: ReadCube access at the University of Utah. In B. R. Bernhardt, L. H. Hinds, & K. P. Strauch (Eds.), *Proceedings of the Charleston Library Conference* (pp. 563–570). http://dx.doi.org/10.5703 /1288284315325

United States Copyright Office. (2005). CONTU guidelines. Retrieved from http://www.copyright.com /Services/copyrightoncampus/content/ill_contu.html

Appendix

Readcube Survey

Welcome to the Readcube Survey for Auburn University Libraries.

Are you 19 years of age or older?

◯ Yes
◯ No

If No Is Selected, Then Skip to End of Survey

Have you used Readcube?

◯ Yes, I have successfully viewed and/or printed article(s) through Readcube
◯ I have tried to use Readcube but was not able to view and/or print the articles I needed
◯ No, I have not tried to use Readcube to view and/or print articles

If No, I have not tried to use... Is Selected, Then Skip to How did you learn about Readcube?

Please select any difficulties you have encountered while using Readcube.
Choose all that apply.

❑ Access links not working
❑ Problems with viewing articles
❑ Problems with printing articles
❑ Difficulty navigating Readcube app
❑ None
❑ Other (please specify) _____

How many articles have you viewed in Readcube during the past year?
◯ 0
◯ 1
◯ 2 to 3
◯ 4 to 6
◯ 7 to 10
◯ more than 10

How many articles have you printed from Readcube during the past year?

- ◯ 0
- ◯ 1
- ◯ 2 to 3
- ◯ 4 to 6
- ◯ 7 to 10
- ◯ more than 10

How did you learn about Readcube? Choose all that apply.

- ❑ From a librarian
- ❑ From a colleague
- ❑ From the library's website
- ❑ Saw icon on a journal article
- ❑ Other (please specify) _____

Have you used the Library's subject guide (http://libguides.auburn.edu/readcube) for Readcube?

- ◯ Yes
- ◯ No

What do you see as the greatest benefit to Readcube?

What is the biggest challenge to using Readcube?

What is your academic status?

- ◯ Undergraduate Student
- ◯ Graduate Student
- ◯ Staff
- ◯ Faculty
- ◯ Other (please specify) _____

With which college or department or research unit are you associated?
Please use this space if you would like to make any additional comments about Readcube, AU libraries, or this study.

Thanks for completing this survey!

ILL as Acquisitions: Implementing and Integrating POD in a Research Library

Edward F. Lener, Associate Director for Collection Management, Virginia Tech, Blacksburg

Ladd Brown, Head of Acquisitions, Virginia Tech, Blacksburg

Abstract

This paper describes Virginia Tech's implementation of a purchase-on-demand (POD) program designed to complement the traditional interlibrary loan workflow. POD can offer a way to obtain otherwise unavailable or unlendable content or to get many items at lower cost than a typical borrowing transaction. POD also offers another means of building the collection through purchases of materials we know will get at least one use. We share key details of our program from pilot phase to its broader integration into the acquisitions workflow.

Background

As a comprehensive research university, with over 225 undergraduate and graduate research programs, Virginia Tech regularly relies on interlibrary loan (ILL) to meet our patrons' needs and to supplement existing holdings and subscriptions. In May 2013 the University Libraries at began a pilot purchase-on-demand (POD) program for articles. This soon expanded to include books. The primary reason for implementing the program was to reduce the number of ILL transactions that were cancelled because they could not be filled through regular channels. In addition, all books acquired in this way are reviewed for the collection, making the POD program an integral part of our collection building.

The Collection Management unit moved to the Technical Services Department in July of 2009. By becoming integrated with acquisitions and serials, there is now a more centralized role for Collection Management in overseeing funds and making major purchasing decisions. This move also allowed for more cohesive and data-driven decisions based on assessment of cost, usage, and other metrics.

The University Libraries adopted an e-preferred policy in April 2012 that applied to all disciplines. While print books are still acquired for a variety of reasons, the default preference for new orders is to get an ebook version when available. Purchase strategies have changed in other ways including the acquisition of more ebook packages and a migration to demand-driven acquisitions (DDA) for many titles (Stovall, Lener, & Gilmore, 2013).

The Interlibrary Loan unit moved in early 2013 from Access Services to the Collections and Technical Services Department. There was a reduction in staff and this move entailed significant reworking of space and hardware. All ILL staff now report to the Head of Acquisitions. The service philosophy for the unit has changed to reflect their new place in the organizational structure by enhancing their ability to get materials by whatever means works best, including purchases where appropriate.

Launching Purchase on Demand

The University Libraries already had precedents for buying materials for Virginia Tech patrons at the point of need. For example, many engineering standards are acquired in this manner, with policies in place to cap the total cost of such expenditures per patron each year. Purchase on demand has resulted in considerable savings relative to our previous subscriptions to engineering standards. Similarly, POD is used to supply NTIS documents to our users when needed and also to acquire an occasional data set.

Interlibrary Loan decided to build upon these initial forays and launched a purchase on demand pilot program in May of 2013. The initial focus was on difficult to fulfill article requests (see next section for some examples). When ILL requests from our patrons couldn't be fulfilled by other channels, then POD was used to fill the need and reduce the number of cancelled transactions.

The POD pilot was soon expanded to include books. Again the focus was on titles that could not readily be borrowed through interlibrary loan such as new imprints or titles that were not widely held. Purchases included both e-books and print copies, with preference given to the electronic format when available. Since one goal was to match the speed on article delivery, print books were initially given directly to patrons rather than first passing through the cataloging process. This practice led to many questions and a mixture of patron reactions from delight to bewilderment.

Phase II of the POD pilot began in January 2014. A key goal at this time was to bring other units from the Collections and Technical Services Department into the process but to do so without slowing it down. Several changes were implemented following a discussion with a broader group from the CTS Department and regular meetings of key stakeholders. First, a process was put in place to have all print titles reviewed by Collection Management to determine in advance what to retain for the collection. Next, procedures were implemented to facilitate expedited ordering, processing, and fast cataloging of such materials. The stakeholders group also reviewed and updated the purchase criteria to make it as straightforward and simple to apply as possible. Finally, to facilitate better tracking, a new POD fund code was created for books and e-books beginning with fiscal year 2015.

What Gets Purchased?

For articles, certain types of requests have often proved problematic to fulfill through normal ILL channels. These included ahead-of-print articles, embargoed aggregator content, and recently cancelled journal subscriptions. Adding POD has provided a means to fulfill ILL requests from Virginia Tech patrons that otherwise might have been cancelled. The Get It Now service from the Copyright Clearance Center is the first choice for fulfilling these kinds of requests. There is a limit of $100 per request for all patron types although higher cost items may be approved at the discretion of the Head of Acquisitions.

For books, requested materials may be unavailable from another library (new imprints,

limited holdings, etc.) or they may simply be less expensive to purchase outright than to borrow through Interlibrary Loan. As with articles there is a limit of $100 per request for all patron types. Higher cost items may be approved by the Head of Acquisitions or the Associate Director for Collection Management. In some cases these more expensive requests may be charged to a specific subject fund code rather than to the generic 1POD fund.

The following represents a simplified version of the workflow shown in Figure 1 that we use now:

- ILL request arrives from VT patron.
- If available—fulfill normally.
- If unavailable for loan—use GOBI, Amazon, & Alibris for books or Get It Now for articles.
- If not available as POD or does not meet criteria—request cancelled.
- If available as POD:
    - Articles?—ordered and sent to patron,
    - Ebook?—ordered and added to collection.
    - Print?—retention decision made, then order is placed.

For books, an email template with bibliographic and patron information is generated by Illiad when a purchase on demand transaction is initiated by ILL staff. The request is reviewed by the Associate Director for Collection Management to determine what to keep for the collection. These decisions are usually made the same day and conveyed back to ILL and to the acquisitions staff. Most print books are kept but some items including celebrity biographies, religious instruction, travel guides, etc., may not fit our collection profile as an academic library. Print copies are ordered with rush shipping. Upon receipt, print books ordered via POD go through the "fast cat" process to add them to the collection or are routed directly to circulation so the patron may pick them up.

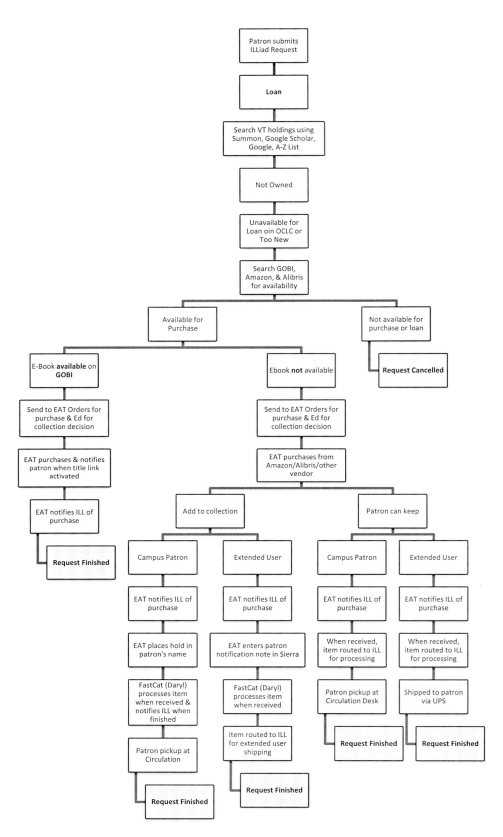

Figure 1. Purchase on demand workflow in Interlibrary Loan and Acquisitions.

POD Program Statistics (May 2013 to September 2014)

Books and E-Books

POD Collection Decision	FY 2013–2014	FY 2014–2015	Cumulative Total
Added	144	93	237
% Added	52.36%	94.90%	63.54%
Patron	131	5	136
% to Patron	47.64%	0.17%	36.46%
Total	275	98	373

POD Patron Distribution—Books	FY 2013–2014	% of Total (FY 2013–2014)	FY 2014–2015	% of Total (FY 2014–2015)	Since Inception	% of Total (Since Inception)
Faculty	107	38.91%	37	37.37%	144	38.50%
Graduate	133	48.36%	51	51.52%	184	49.20%
Undergraduate	13	4.73%	3	3.03%	16	4.28%
Staff	22	8.00%	8	8.08%	30	8.02%
Total	275		99		374	

POD Price Breakdown—Books	FY 2013–2014	FY 2014–2015	Since Inception	% of Total (Since Inception)
under $10	30	4	34	9.12%
$10–$24.99	130	44	174	46.65%
$25–$49.99	80	31	111	29.76%
over $50.00	35	19	54	14.48%
Total	275	98	373	

POD Price Breakdown—Books	FY 2013–2014	FY 2014–2015	Since Inception	% of Total (Since Inception)
under $10	30	4	34	9.12%
$10–$24.99	130	44	174	46.65%
$25–$49.99	80	31	111	29.76%
over $50.00	35	19	54	14.48%
Total	275	98	373	

Articles

POD Patron Distribution	Articles
Faculty	303
Graduate	572
Undergraduate	49
Staff	17

Overall

POD items	# Purchased	$ Spent
Articles	941	$ 31,782.79
Books	373	$ 10,397.36
Total	1314	$ 42,180.15

Future Goals and Program Considerations

We have already made considerable progress in the adoption of POD. An ongoing goal is to integrate content delivery processes more fully within the Collections and Technical Services Department, including functions such as acquisitions, ILL, serials, and collection management. Refining the data from ILLiad and our ILS will also help in better supporting collection-related decisions. While still under deliberation, we may also seek in the future to make subject-based fund code assignments for more POD orders.

References

Stovall, C., Lener, E., & Gilmore, T. (2013) Redesigning workflows and implementing demand driven. acquisition at Virginia Tech: One year later. In *Charleston Conference Proceedings, 2013*. West Lafayette, IN: Purdue University Press. Retrieved from http://docs.lib.purdue.edu/charleston /2013/Acquisitions/13/

Scholarly Communication

Engrossed, Enraged, Engaged:
Empowering Faculty in Transforming Scholarly Communication

Jen Waller, Interdisciplinary Librarian, Collections & Research Services; Miami University Libraries
Jennifer W. Bazeley, Interim Head, Technical Services; Miami University Libraries

Abstract

Librarians are deeply invested in the scholarly publishing lifecycle. This investment, in tandem with an evolving scholarly communication system, has encouraged librarians to become advocates for transformation in this landscape. At the same time, some faculty members have been slower to understand the complexities of the current system and its evolution. At Miami University, traditional communication methods weren't sufficient to meaningfully engage faculty in these evolving trends. As a response, several librarians designed and cofacilitated two Scholarly Communication Faculty Learning Communities (FLCs) for two academic years. These FLCs have been the most successful method of increasing faculty understanding about scholarly communication and academic publishing issues.

The FLCs brought together university community members comprised of faculty, staff, and graduate students interested in learning more about scholarly communication. Each group spent two semesters doing readings, attending panel presentations, and meeting for seminar-style discussions about current issues and trends in scholarly publishing. Over the course of the year, FLC members became more aware of the nuances in the lifecycle of scholarly publication and learned which scholarly communication issues affected them most. As a result, the cofacilitators saw a rapidly growing understanding about problems inherent in the current system of scholarly publishing, a substantial increase in faculty discussions on scholarly communication, and greater faculty-led advocacy for open access publishing. Additionally, community members appreciated the cross-disciplinary nature of the FLC, which afforded them the opportunity to escape traditional disciplinary silos. This article will discuss how the facilitators used the learning community format to successfully change faculty behavior about issues in scholarly communication and how these experiences altered librarian perceptions and improved interactions with faculty.

Background

About Miami University

Miami University, established in 1809, is a public university with a main campus in Oxford, Ohio (approximately 35 miles northwest of Cincinnati, OH) and four nearby regional campuses. In 2013, the university had a total undergraduate enrollment of approximately 21,000 students and a total graduate enrollment of 2,260 students. The University is residential and focuses primarily on undergraduate liberal education, offering bachelor's degrees in over 100 areas, master's degrees in more than 60 areas, and 12 doctoral degrees. Faculty positions are primarily tenure-track, but adjunct positions and clinical/lecturer positions have been rising in number in recent years.

The Challenge and Previous Efforts

Miami University has a large and active body of faculty members who perform research and publish regularly, yet the University community has been slow to recognize the changes occurring in the scholarly communication landscape.

In 2009, the former Dean and University Librarian formed a Scholarly Communication Working Group charged with supporting the formation and maintenance of the library's new institutional repository (called the Scholarly Commons) as well as to educate librarians, faculty, and the University community at large on current issues in scholarly communication. Members of the working group initially prepared presentations on open access, scholarly communication, and journal costs to present to individual departments on campus. Faculty were clearly interested in the issues at hand, yet the presentations had the unfortunate effect of generating hostility about subscription costs and open access rather than starting a dialogue among concerned stakeholders. An open access mandate was drafted and presented to the Council of Academic Deans (COAD) in 2010 but was not widely understood or accepted, and ultimately not implemented. Additionally, the working group created a LibGuide about open access and copyright, but it was not widely utilized by faculty or students. Some of the group's most successful efforts consisted of offering copyright seminars for faculty, increasing faculty participation in the institutional repository, and establishing a stronger scholarly communication presence on campus through social media and the celebration of Open Access Week.

While these successes helped to overcome some faculty skepticism, the group struggled with a way to educate researchers on campus in a focused and deliberate manner. At the end of 2011, the group discussed the idea of using a Faculty Learning Community (FLC) to educate a finite group of University community members on issues in scholarly communication. The FLC was an appealing idea for several reasons. The University community has a high participation rate in FLCs, because they are important additions to tenure-seeking faculty resumes, and because FLCs offer each participating member a $500 stipend to be used for educational materials or professional development. While some FLCs are restricted to faculty-only membership, the Scholarly Communication Working Group felt it would be more beneficial to open FLC applications to full- and part-time faculty, as well as administrative staff, librarians, and graduate students. This was done because scholarly communication issues affect many points in the research lifecycle, so the facilitators wanted to allow an opportunity for all relevant stakeholders to apply. With support from the library administration, three librarians volunteered as potential cofacilitators for the FLC, and moved forward in preparing a description and proposal for an FLC on scholarly communication for the 2012–2013 school year. In February 2012, the FLC proposal was accepted and a call for applications went out in March.

What Is an FLC?

A faculty learning community (FLC) is a community of interdisciplinary faculty, graduate students, and professional staff, comprised of 6–15 members, who engage in an active, collaborative, year-long program. Each FLC chooses a special topic that is relevant to some aspect of teaching and learning, and holds regular meetings and activities that provide opportunities to learn about and develop that topic. Participants in an FLC may select an individual or group project to identify innovations or assess student learning. Participants are also encouraged to present the results of their work to the university as well as at national and regional conferences.

At Miami University, FLCs are sponsored by the University's Center for Learning, Teaching, and University Assessment (CELTUA). CELTUA supports long-term and short-term FLCs, workshops, and seminars. They also offer grants and awards to support innovative teaching and help the university's programs in assessing their educational effectiveness. CELTUA organizes and hosts the annual Lilly Conference on College Teaching and also publishes several journals on teaching and learning.

Prior to the FLC on scholarly communication, the library hosted an FLC on information literacy from 2004 through 2012. In 2012, the Information Literacy FLC facilitator chose to retire the FLC after eight successful years. He agreed to assist in the creation of the Scholarly Communication FLC, taking responsibility during the first year for administrative duties and liaising with CELTUA.

This freed the two other facilitators to focus on content and projects, both of which are crucial to the success of a first-year FLC.

Creating an FLC

The process for preparing for and creating an FLC took approximately nine months:

- January: began prepping description/proposal.

- February (end): FLC proposal accepted by CELTUA.

- March: call for applications sent out.

- Mid-April: deadline for application submission.

- May: decisions on applicants made and invitations distributed.

- September: first FLC meeting.

Typical Application Questions

- Why do you wish to participate in this community?

- Please indicate areas in which you can contribute to the work of the community.

- How do issues of scholarly communication and open access to research apply to your academic focus/discipline?

- How do you believe that participation in this FLC will motivate you to educate your colleagues and/or students regarding communication and open access issues?

- Are you a member of a scholarly society? If so, which one and what is your involvement?

- Are you an editor of a scholarly journal? If so, which one?

Choosing Members

For both years, the Scholarly Communication FLC received between 12 and 16 applications from faculty (both full and part time, as well as faculty from both the main and regional campuses), administrative staff, librarians, and graduate students. Criteria for selection were based on answers to application questions and research interests. The facilitators looked for applicants who demonstrated genuine interest in objectives of FLC in relation to their role in the Miami University community. It was clear after the first year that some faculty applied to numerous FLCs using the same answers to the general questions, and so facilitators ranked thoughtful answers very highly. There was also a desire for equitable distribution across subject areas, since scholarly communication issues are significantly different for STEM researchers than for humanities scholars.

Original Objectives and Activities of the FLC

Original goals for the FLC were lofty:

- Raising awareness and increasing the intellectual depth and curiosity among faculty, staff, and students across disciplines regarding the changing state of scholarly communication.

- Strengthening student understanding of scholarly communication and research as part of Miami's emphasis on active, student-centered engagement.

- Exploring the impacts of digital technology on scholarly communication issues in a reflective manner.

- Generating interest among faculty on scholarly communication issues so that students engaging intensely with faculty on research will benefit from knowledge of these issues.

- Developing methods of integrating education regarding open access to scientific research and data into existing curricula.

- Developing knowledge among faculty working on federal grant proposals (e.g., NSF, NIH) regarding digital preservation and its role in their research.

Planned activities included:

- Seminar-style meetings five to six times per semester for approximately 1.5 hours.

- Panel presentation during Open Access Week (October).

- Conferences: FLC members to attend and potentially present at Lilly Conference in Oxford (November) and two to three members to attend and potentially present at the Scholarly Publishing and Academic Resources Coalition (SPARC) Open Access Meeting (March).

- CELTUA seminar: FLC members to plan and present a CELTUA workshop on a scholarly communication topic of interest to the Miami community.

FLC Programming and Meetings

The cofacilitators had a general sense of what they wanted to cover throughout the year and at each meeting. Even so, it was important for the cofacilitators to meet prior to each FLC meeting to plan and finalize the agenda and to choose readings for the group. During the first year, the facilitators assigned and posted readings one week prior to each meeting. Based on evaluations from the first year FLC, the facilitators began posting readings two weeks prior to meetings during the second year FLC.

Meeting Topics

Open access and the issues surrounding open access were extremely important topics throughout both years' FLCs; however, scholarly communication encompasses more than just open access. The groups spent time during the first FLC meetings discussing "What is Scholarly Communication?" to set the stage and to gather input from participants in the different disciplines represented. From there, FLC meeting topics included:

- Open Access.
- Data, Data Sharing, and Open Data.
- Open Peer Review.
- Predatory Publishers and Vanity Presses.
- Economics of Publishing and Funding Models.
- Institutional Repositories.
- Altmetrics.
- Author Rights.
- Creative Commons.
- Copyright.
- OER.
- Misconceptions about Open Access.
- Open Access Week Special Programming.

Engrossed

The cofacilitators chose three descriptive words for the title of this presentation—engrossed,

enraged, and engaged. Most meeting topics were successful, but some particularly stood out because of the effect they had on participants. FLC participants were particularly engrossed in the following topics and/or materials:

PhD Comics Video

Released in October 2012 during Open Access Week, Nick Shockey, Jonathan Eisen, and PhD Comics created an eight-minute video, "Open Access Explained!" The combination of the video's anecdotal style and its narration by a scientist makes it understandable but still authoritative. The facilitators didn't show this video when it was first released. Instead, they waited until it better fit into the FLC programming. Surprisingly, this video was one of the most successful tools at getting FLC members to relate to the problems with toll journals and the traditional publishing system, and FLC members highly recommended showing it earlier in the year. The video is freely available on YouTube, and the facilitators have one caveat: the video spends nearly no time on institutional repositories.

Journal Costs

Another successful meeting topic focused on journal costs and how libraries purchase subscriptions. For this meeting the facilitators created a homework assignment where members were asked to select three journals in their field and find the institutional subscription cost for each one. One of the facilitators is an expert in this area, as it is a substantial part of her job. She created a slide presentation outlining the subscription prices for each of the member-selected journals. She took consortia (OhioLINK) pricing and big deals into account and then provided revenue and profit charts for several major publishers. FLC participants were shocked and found the system extremely interesting. Until then they had been completely unaware of how librarians purchased journal subscriptions. Getting a glimpse into the system was eye opening and provided a call to action. Participants were eager to learn how traditional publishers spend their profits. Were they rolled back into the system? Were they used to gild publishers' executive offices? The content shared at this meeting crystallized participants' understanding of the publishing system, including how academics provide free labor to publishers who then lease it back to academic institutions. Prior to this meeting the FLC participants had not thought about the system in this way. This also led to a discussion about the importance of transparency and that faculty members do care about the cost of library resources.

Author Rights/Copyright

The meeting that covered author rights allowed the facilitators to discuss copyright in a way that was highly relevant to faculty. The facilitators modified an exercise from the ACRL Scholarly Communication Toolkit and asked each FLC member to bring in a publishing contract that they had signed. The members then broke into groups and examined their contracts for language that allowed them to retain their rights or required them to give away their rights. The facilitators also provided contracts from three publishers whose agreements ranged from very closed to very open. This exercise was eye opening for FLC members, because most of them had never bothered to read their publishing contracts. This topic also provided the facilitators with an easy way to introduce Miami's institutional repository, the Scholarly Commons. Later in the year, one member of the FLC shared an email exchange with the rest of the group in which she had used the techniques and language in this exercise to negotiate her rights with a publisher.

Open Peer Review

The topic of open peer review surprised the facilitators, because they hadn't anticipated that it leading to such a thoughtful and thought-provoking discussion. This was the first time many FLC members had heard about open peer review or had critically thought about the review process. In the past the review process was simply something they did or something that was done to them. The discussion of open peer review then led to a deeper dialog about privilege in the academy.

Enraged

The facilitators, perhaps naively, did not expect any of the FLC meeting topics to be contentious,

so they were surprised to get initial pushback from some of the FLC members about their views on open access. Many faculty members weren't used to thinking about a system in which they had been entrenched, so initial discussions were sometimes met with doubt or skepticism. Additionally, some members of the FLC had misconceptions, which were generally easier to handle.

However, during the second iteration of the FLC one member in particular remained skeptical throughout the entire year. Worse, she became defensive and disruptive to the community by alternately trying to "win people" to her side and then distancing herself from the group, both physically and intellectually. This FLC member's stance remains confusing to the facilitators. The faculty member is on the editorial board for two open access journals, yet she frequently protested that she was anti-open access. She was concerned about her work being broadly distributed for fear it would be misrepresented or fall into the "wrong hands." This member's attitude made community building in the second FLC very challenging.

During the second semester of the second FLC, the facilitators experienced another challenge (although they would not necessarily characterize it as "enraged"). Unfortunately, due to conflicting schedules among the FLC members there was no single time when the entire membership was available to meet. Instead of having meetings at a consistent day and time, the facilitators had to alternate meeting days. This meant that that for the second semester, the entire FLC membership was never together at the same meeting. This, in addition to the hostile faculty member, inhibited the community building that is a necessary part of most FLCs.

Engaged

In both years there were topics and meetings that the facilitators deemed beyond successful. These were meetings where members truly participated and engaged with the materials or process over and above the discussions. During these meetings members became actively involved, which was extremely gratifying to all. Some of the situations where members were more engaged included:

Member-Facilitated Discussions

As discussed above, one of the challenges during the second FLC was one faculty member's defensiveness and hostility. In addition to the above discussion, this member seemingly did not respect librarians or the facilitators' knowledge of scholarly communication issues. As a response, the facilitators changed their meeting strategy for the second semester. They asked FLC participants to pair up, choose from a list of topics (see "Meeting Topics" above), and select the date they would be responsible for leading the meeting. The facilitators provided each group with "seed readings," but the choice of what to read and how to run each meeting was left to the individual groups. This strategy, chosen as a response to a disruptive group member, actually ended up working better for everyone. FLC members made connections with a peer from outside their discipline, and the end-of-year evaluations specifically praised this format. The facilitators gave up some control in exchange for higher quality discussions that arose from an angle that made sense to the faculty presenters.

Learning Management System (LMS)

Many people don't think of a LMS as a place for engagement, but the LMS used for the Scholarly Communication FLCs worked well. Miami's LMS is called niihka ("friend" in the Myaamia language), and it is an instance of Sakai. For both years the facilitators added participants to niihka, organized meetings, made announcements, posted readings, and used the LMS as an email tool. This kept the content both organized and in one place. It allowed the facilitators to keep the two FLCs separate yet address them jointly when necessary. Additionally, it gave both FLC cohorts the ability to access all the material. During the second year of the FLC the facilitators added a Twitter feed to the FLC's front page, which enabled members to get a feel for Twitter and see its value. Finally, niihka contains an area for discussion forums, and the facilitators were gratified to learn that several FLC members were interested in using the forums to continue discussions and/or ask additional questions.

Panel on Data, Data Sharing, and Open Data

During the first year of the FLC the facilitators organized a panel discussion on data, data sharing, and open data. One panelist, a member of the FLC, was responsible for providing computing resources to support faculty research. He was eager to participate on the panel, because he had unique insights into the types of data that needed to be supported across the University. The two other panelists included a computational biologist and the Head of the Libraries Center for Digital Scholarship. These other two panelists became very interested in joining the FLC once they participated on this panel, and one of them is a member of the authors' current FLC on OER.

Getting Your Work "Out There"

Readings, discussion, and demonstration of altmetrics and alternative ways to distribute research involved an opportune coincidence with one of the FLC members. About a month before the "getting your work out there" discussion, the FLC member had published research that was then picked up by a major publisher's blog. She was asked to write a blog post, and in the process the publisher asked for her Twitter handle. This faculty member had never used Twitter, but she set up an account, because the publisher "made it seem like I had to." Unsurprisingly to some of us, this faculty member ended up getting tremendous value from Twitter. She began to get requests to weigh in on other research articles, and the Miami University Communication Department added her to their "list of experts." All of this increased her reach, and she was able to facilitate a discussion about impact and sharing through nontraditional channels from first hand experience.

Outcomes and Lessons Learned

Several months into the fall semester the cofacilitators realized that accomplishing all of the original goals in a single academic year was unrealistic. Some FLC members did attend the Lilly Conference, but the full FLC group did not have enough time to prepare a presentation for that conference. The goal of presenting a workshop was also postponed—the group's learning curve was different than expected.

Successes

As discussed above, many FLC meetings were successful. However successes went deeper than individual meetings. Some of the more successful outcomes included:

Open Access Week Panel Discussion—"Publish Don't Perish" (October 2013):

> This panel included four FLC members from the 2012–2013 FLC as well as one moderator. The panel discussion attracted a significant audience and resulted in an interesting and quality Q&A period afterwards.

Scholarly Communication Website:

> The final project for the 2012–2013 FLC was to develop the structure and content for a dynamic website on scholarly communication issues, tailored specifically to faculty and graduate students. This was accomplished through a series of multivoting exercises, discussions, and card-sorting activities. Members of the library's Scholarly Communication Committee were responsible for implementation of the site. Due to time constraints, creation and implementation of the website was pushed to spring 2015.

Faculty Behaviors Change:

> There were several very gratifying faculty behavior changes in both years of the FLC. One faculty member who was originally skeptical about open access ended up publishing articles in two different open access journals, both of which required article-processing charges that he paid for with grant funding. A second faculty member is currently working on the creation of an open access history of mathematics journal (hosted by the library), to be managed by his students in a particular course. The intention is to teach undergraduates about the lifecycle of research and scholarship by immersing them in peer review and editing.

Social Media Tools:

> Several members from year two worked together to create a comparison chart of academic social media-type tools that they felt were useful to academics and early career researchers. The chart compared features of each tool, pros and cons, and possible uses.

Breaking Down Silos

The primary takeaway for cofacilitators was in learning to identify and break down silos, and the diverse community demographics helped accomplish this:

- Status: Having graduate students in the FLC forced faculty and cofacilitators to think about publishing and scholarly communication from a different perspective and look forward at the next generation of researchers and teachers.

- Discipline: The interdisciplinarity of the community helped to engage members more completely and to identify more issues.

- Time at Miami University: Newer faculty and graduate students were the most willing to discuss issues and potential changes. These faculty and students spurred conversations with the less flexible or more skeptical faculty.

Awareness of Roles

Facilitators must be aware of members experience (or lack thereof) with different parts of the scholarly communication lifecycle. It's important not to overestimate faculty awareness of institutional subscription costs, journal economics, or the scholarly research lifecycle. As librarians, we are asking faculty to advocate for change in a system that they know only as authors, editors, and reviewers.

Topics and Programming

What librarians think are the most interesting discussion topics are not always the same as what group members find most interesting (e.g., the PhD comics video). Flexibility in topics and programming became immensely important.

While it is helpful to select topics in advance, it's also imperative to accommodate requests from members who want to discuss other topics. This keeps members of the group fully engaged and increases participation.

Anecdotal Experiences

There were several instances of group members sharing stories from different perspectives (especially experiences with predatory publishers and attempts at negotiating author's rights). These shared experiences fostered a tremendous amount of collegiality and "me, too!" conversations.

Assumptions about Community Formation

The final, and possibly most important, lesson is not to make assumptions about the community formation. The same tactics and community forming norms do not apply to every group. The second year of this FLC had a much harder time forming a community than the first year did.

DIY FLC

The authors recognize that not every college or university has a Faculty Learning Community program in place, but they also believe that this shouldn't limit others from trying to establish their own FLC or employing similar strategies. If readers wish to create an FLC at their institution, here are things they may wish to consider:

Funding and Funding Partners

As stated above, Miami's Center for the Enhancement of Learning, Teaching, and University Assessment (CELTUA) and the Miami University Libraries shared the cost of the FLC. By far, the biggest cost was for professional development funds for FLC participants. Each FLC participant received $500, and it was required that the funds be spent on items such as conference registration or travel, a piece of technology that enhanced their job, or some other tangible expense related to their professional development. This meant that approximately $7000 per year was budgeted for the FLC for participant professional development funds. It is probably not necessary to provide a $500 stipend,

but funding helps attract faculty members and lets them know their participation has value.

The second largest budgeted expense was for food, which is hospitable but also not critical. When FLC meetings fell during the breakfast or lunch time block, the facilitators felt it was necessary to provide a light meal. However, many of the FLC meetings fell during mid-morning or mid-afternoon when light snacks were more than adequate. For some meetings the University's catering service was used, but this service was also more expensive. More frequently the facilitators purchased fruit, bottled water, and other snacks at the local grocery store.

All of the FLC meetings took place in the library—mostly in the Center for Digital Scholarship. Therefore, no funding was directed to space in which to hold FC meetings.

As mentioned above, Miami University's CELTUA provides the administrative support and structure for FLCs. Other academic institutions may have similar offices that could also provide funding and other means of support, although they most definitely are known under a different name. The facilitators found units at other academic institutions with names such as the "Center for Teaching and Learning," "Faculty Professional Development Center," "Center for the Advancement of Teaching," and the "Center for Teaching Innovation and Excellence." Those interested in establishing a FLC at their own institutions may also look for support from the Scholarly Communication Office, the Provost's Office, the Research and Grants Office, or from grants themselves. In short, while this particular FLC received significant funding, the facilitators do not believe lack of funding should prevent others from forming a FLC on their own campus.

Marketing, Promotion, and Communication

CELTUA also provides support for Miami's FLCs by announcing calls for proposals and soliciting member applications through the CELTUA website and listserv. CELTUA's structure and timing is well known across Miami, and there are FLC applicants and participants every year. Yet the Scholarly Communication FLCs still required advertising and promotion on the part of the facilitators. For both years, the facilitators developed an email for liaison librarians to send to their faculty members and departments, and it was important for liaisons to be involved in FLC recruitment and—more importantly—be aware of FLC participants from departments they represent. Additionally, the facilitators developed a "pitch list," which consisted of names and email addresses of faculty who had already shown an interest in open access and scholarly communication issues. These faculty names were culled from email questions about copyright, author rights, and data management plans and from faculty who had already uploaded work to the institutional repository. After the pitch list was developed, the facilitators sent individual, targeted emails to every individual on the list (approximately 250 people). These emails generated a great deal of interest among faculty, many of whom applied or asked questions. In any case, it is unrealistic to expect that faculty will come running to apply once you've established your own FLC. Consider recruitment, and plan to spend time and energy recruiting members.

Scheduling and Meetings

Determining a schedule among 12–16 busy faculty members proved to be challenging, so to the extent possible, it is critical to establish a schedule as far in advance as possible. For both years of the FLC, the facilitators scheduled 5–6 meetings per semester, and each meeting lasted between one and one and a half hours. The facilitators began by looking at the course list and time blocks for each accepted participant. This bit of preplanning narrowed down the options, and sometimes a mutually available time block simply emerged. When more than one day/time was available,

facilitators distributed a Doodle poll to determine time preferences.

Meetings primarily took place in the Libraries' Center for Digital Scholarship, which was a newly constructed space first available in the spring of the first FLC iteration. Holding meetings in this new space provided a good way to showcase and promote the services of the Center and its staff. Wherever meetings are held, it is important that the furniture and room configuration be flexible enough to accommodate different programming and formats for each meeting. In this way, the room could be set up to assist in forming groups, viewing a web seminar, having a discussion, presenting a panel discussion, and other programs. Of course, the rooms were wired for Internet access, both via ethernet and wireless, and included monitors and screens for viewing content as well as whiteboards for noting "on the fly" ideas.

Conclusion

Reaching approximately 30 people over the course of two years may not sound like a significant impact. However, those 30 people are involved in faculty meetings, attend promotion and tenure meetings, and talk to their colleagues every day. In this way, information about scholarly communication spread naturally and organically among faculty in many different disciplines as opposed to being broadcast by librarians or a "top down" approach. The FLC facilitators have seen the impact these two Scholarly Communication FLCs have made on the Miami University campus, and—in fact—the FLCs have proved to be the most successful way of reaching the Miami community regarding open access and scholarly communication issues.

Peeling Apart the Layers: Library Services to Online Education Consortia

Amy D. Coughenour, Concordia University – Portland

Abstract

Universities and colleges have been forming online education consortia as one of many methods to better serve their students while reigning in the rising costs of higher education. While libraries' responses to these consortia vary, there are trends in the methods and standards being used. This paper reviews some of the literature published about library services in online education consortia, evaluates a selection of interstate and intrastate online education consortia, and provides information about the beginning stages of a library service model in a new online education consortium—Concordia Online Education. Because Concordia Online Education is new, the library services across the partner schools are not yet fully defined, nor are they an official part of the consortial agreement. By taking into account the information from the literature and the websites, we've been able to begin a foundation to frame our collaboration with partner schools and develop recommendations for how to move forward.

Higher education has been tackling the conundrum of educating more students with less funding by forming online education consortia. These consortia lower many of their operating costs due to shared sourcing, along with the use of technology. Libraries' responses to online education consortia vary depending on available resources and services. In all cases, libraries strive to meet the "access entitlement principle" from the *Standards for Distance Learning Library Services*:

> Every student, faculty member, administrator, staff member, or any other member of an institution of higher education, is entitled to the library services and resources of that institution, including direct communication with the appropriate library personnel, regardless of where enrolled or where located in affiliation with the institution. (Association of College & Research Libraries, 2008)

What Are Online Education Consortia?

The phrase *online education consortia* often comes with different meanings for different stakeholders. To some, such consortia are collaborative groups that share best practices and training opportunities, and for others, they are shared service entities. In *State U Online,* Fishman (2013) breaks down the types of online education consortia into five "steps" based on services provided to students: 1) "clearinghouse," 2) "shared contracts," 3) "shared student services,"

4) "shared and articulated credentials," and 5) "shared credentials beyond state borders" (p. 9). These steps take a consortium from:

- A base level of providing a gateway to courses taught by institutions in the consortium.

- To a second level of pooling funds to share costs of licensing and contracts.

- To a third level of sharing point-of-contact support services, such as advising, etc.

- To a fourth level of providing a method for "easy transfer of credit among institutions and shared credentialing."

- Finally, to a fifth level, where the institutions in the consortium provide the resources and services from the previous steps "and allow students to move freely beyond state borders" (Fishman, 2013, p. 9).

When reviewing the literature about online education consortia and examining the websites of a selection of interstate and intrastate consortia, these "steps" work well as definitions to determine the service levels provided by each consortium. The "steps" also provide a lens for viewing libraries' roles within the consortia. For example, a consortium at the base level has little to no evidence of library involvement in a centralized capacity. Whereas, a consortium at the third level of "shared student services" may potentially have more collaboration between the libraries at the participating institutions.

Libraries Roles in Online Education: From Individual Institutions to Consortia

In *Standards for Distance Learning Library Services,* the Association of College and Research Libraries (ACRL, 2008) provides in-depth recommendations and best practices for how libraries should serve distance learning students and online education programs. Such services "must be equivalent to those provided for students and faculty in traditional campus settings" (ACRL, 2008). The ACRL (2008) goes on to specify the importance of "direct human access" for online students and faculty, emphasizing the need for librarians to be actively involved "through instruction, interaction, and intervention . . . in the provision of library services and in facilitating successful use of library resources."

At the same time, libraries don't provide these online services in a vacuum. We provide better services when we collaborate with other departments who serve online students, such as teaching faculty, instructional designers, and student services. The ACRL (2008) recognizes this need for collaboration in its recommendation to "involve library and other personnel in all stages of the detailed analysis of planning, developing, evaluating, and adding or changing of the distance learning programs." The ACRL goes on to recommend that librarians become active "in the curriculum development process and in course planning for distance learning" while also communicating with faculty, administration, and related community members.

These standards are also applicable to libraries' roles in online education consortia because the ACRL (2008) places the responsibility of library service provision on the institution that enrolls students "in its courses, unless an equitable agreement for otherwise providing these materials has been made." Many libraries in online education consortia follow this model of the "home institution . . . provid[ing] access to library resources," such as the Web-based

Information Science Education (WISE) consortium (Montague and Pluzhenskaia, 2007, p. 38).

Interstate Online Education Consortia

When evaluating the websites of several interstate online education consortia, only one out of eight consortia listed information about library services on its website. The Great Plains Interactive Distance Education Alliance (Great Plains IDEA, 2012) states that "students will have access to the online library system of their home institution. Students may receive access to library resources at the teaching institution if the instructor expects students to utilize such resources."

Adams and Cassner (2010) surveyed libraries in the Great Plains IDEA consortium to determine types and levels of services provided by each library. Their survey found that most of the consortial libraries provided reference services with some type of communication, usually via email or an ask-a-librarian service (Adams & Cassner, 2010, pp. 420-421). At the same time, Adams and Cassner found a disconnection in the libraries' awareness of the Great Plains IDEA consortium as it related to online education programs occurring on their campuses. "Unfamiliarity may be partly due to the complexity of large academic organizations. The name of the consortial program may differ from the name of the administrative home department that offers courses" (Adams & Cassner, 2010, p. 423).

Because the other interstate online education consortia did not list library services on their websites, it is difficult to know what the expectations are for library services in relation to online courses offered within the consortia. Further research would be needed to reach out to the libraries at the participating institutions with a survey or other research instrument.

Intrastate Online Education Consortia

When evaluating the websites of several intrastate online education consortia, six out of eleven consortia listed information about library services on their websites. Of those six consortia, two provide links to statewide library databases, one provides a link to a statewide reference service, one provides a link to a statewide library catalog, and four provide links to individual libraries. (However, one of the consortia has working links to less than half of the individual libraries.)

These access points to individual libraries correlate with the ACRL's (2008) recommendation for "originating institutions" to provide library services for their own students. While reviewing the progression of a distance education library services task force in Indiana, Haynes and Mannan (2006) highlight the focus of using the collaborative nature of an online education consortium "to facilitate and enhance what individual institutions would do. It was seen as a multi-layered, networked approach" (p. 206). Thus, the libraries focus their service provision on their own users while reaching out to other libraries in the consortium for resources, assistance, and best practices.

At the same time, some of the online consortia are beginning to branch out into Fishman's (2013) "shared contracts" and "shared student services" models by providing access to statewide databases and a statewide reference service, respectively. However, it is unknown if the online education consortia played a role in the statewide databases and statewide reference service, or if those shared services would have been in place, regardless.

Traditionally, intrastate online education consortia have often had a geographic advantage in that the participating institutions are closer to each other. This benefits distance learners who reside in the state because there are more opportunities to physically visit participating libraries if needed (Subramanian, 2003, p. 40). As more students enroll in online courses cross-country, more research will be needed to determine whether this advantage will continue.

Challenges and Opportunities

There are challenges and opportunities whenever groups of people work together. Adding distance to the mix because of the nature of online education consortia can either magnify or obscure some of these situations. Several common challenges and opportunities that appear in the literature are: communication, institutional cultures and expectations, and staffing ability.

While lack of communication can cause complications, strong communication skills can increase collaboration and benefit everyone involved in the consortium. Adams and Cassner (2010) state that "open communication has been essential to shared curriculum development and local institutional practice. . . . Including distance librarians in meetings with Great Plains IDEA faculty and administrative staff could be beneficial" (p. 423). Kayler and Pival (2004) echo the benefits of communication as a method of preventing problems from "escalat[ing] and undermin[ing] the project" (p. 209). Montague and Pluzhenskaia (2007) echoed these views from the perspective of "coordination between schools" (p. 38).

Montague and Pluzhenskaia (2007) also brought up the need to discover other institutions' "cultures and expectations" when collaborating in an online education consortium (p. 38). Devlin, Burich, Stockham, Summey, and Turtle (2006) repeated the idea of "institutional cultures" affecting decisions as related to the development of a memorandum of understanding (pp. 155, 161-162). "Each institution wants to maintain its own culture and identity, and each wants to take advantage of the benefits of working together" (Devlin et al., 2006, p. 162). While there are many procedures and skills that we share as librarians, it helps to keep in mind that institutions develop their own cultures, which then proceed to make their way into library services and policies.

Finally, having the ability to staff online education library services can be both a challenge and an asset. Devlin et al. (2006) note the ability for individual libraries to "determine [their] own staffing and scheduling needs, training requirements, and . . . technical configurations" (p. 162). For libraries that have enough librarians, this works well. However, Ferguson, Fowler, Hanley, and Schafer (2002) point out the challenge of not having enough staff to fully implement the UMass Digital Library project. Without funding for additional personnel, the future of the project was uncertain (Ferguson et al., 2002, p. 331), and as of the submission of this article, it appears that the UMass Digital Library project either changed into something else or did not make it further than their "proof of concept."

Concordia Online Education: Developing Library Services

Concordia Online Education is an interstate online education consortium in its early stages of shared services provision. At the moment, it consists of three partner schools: Concordia University-Portland, Concordia College – New York, and Concordia University, Nebraska. As of the submission of this article, the library services are not part of a contract or memorandum of agreement between the schools. However, the library at Concordia University – Portland has been supporting our online students and faculty for several years.

We decided to review the literature about library services for online education consortia, along with an evaluation of the websites of both interstate and intrastate versions of such consortia. Our goals were to develop a broad perspective of best practices, trends, and common challenges and opportunities faced by libraries in these consortia.

We found that the services we offer to our students fall in line with best practices: interactive individual reference via phone, chat, text, email, and the learning management system (LMS); on-demand instruction via tutorials, videos, and a frequently asked questions site; and embedded librarians in the LMS. We have also taken care to keep track of student enrollment numbers to make sure we have a sufficient number of distance education librarians on staff to serve the online students and faculty. Another aspect of library staffing that we discovered was the need for additional interlibrary loan staff. While we have full-text article databases, the increase in online student enrollment has brought with it an increase in interlibrary loan requests.

Even though the library is not formally or officially part of the agreement in Concordia Online Education, we are invited to operations meetings, which provides us with updates from other participating departments. We have also started the process of developing guidelines for online library services at participating schools in the consortium. We compiled statistics to form a foundation of recommendations for best practices in regard to access, instruction, and the learning management system. For access, we looked at the need for students and faculty to be able to contact librarians, access electronic resources, and locate a library website. For instruction, we laid out the different models: individual, on-demand, research guides, and FAQs. For the learning management system, we proposed both links to resources and the ability of distance education librarians to be embedded in courses and provide advice in the development of curriculum.

We have also been reaching out to the libraries at the partner schools to share information and provide encouragement. While we're currently working in a model of each institutional library serving its own students and faculty, we remain open to the possibility of a more centralized service. The collaboration between the libraries is still in its early stages, though.

Conclusion: Plans for the Future

While we have performed research into how library services perform in online education consortia, these services are constantly changing. We continue to explore new ways to leverage our strengths to better serve our students and faculty. We try to use a combination of different opportunities: new collaborative partnerships, taking advantage of technology where possible, and keeping our eyes open for innovative educational resources and services.

References

Adams, K. E., & Cassner, M. (2010). Library services for Great Plains IDEA consortial students. *Journal of Library Administration, 50,* 414-414. http://dx.doi.org/10.1080/01930826.2010.488584

Association of College & Research Libraries. (2008, July 1). *Standards for distance learning library services.* Retrieved from http://www.ala.org/acrl/standards/guidelinesdistancelearning

Devlin, F. A., Burich, N. J., Stockham, M. G., Summey, T. P., & Turtle, E. C. (2006). Getting beyond institutional cultures: When rivals collaborate. *Journal of Library Administration, 45,* 149-168. http://dx.doi.org/10.1300/J111v45n01_08

Ferguson, J., Fowler, J., Hanley, M., & Schafer, J. (2002). Building a digital library in support of distance learning. *Journal of Library Administration, 37,* 317-331. http://dx.doi.org/10.1300/J111v37n03_26

Fishman, R. (2013). *State u online.* Retrieved from *New America Foundation* website: http://education.newamerica.net/sites/newamerica.net/files/policydocs/FINAL_FOR_RELEASE _STATE_U_ONLINE.pdf

Great Plains IDEA. (2012). Student services. Retrieved from http://www.gpidea.org/students/services/

Haynes, A., & Mannan, S. (2006). Indiana's statewide distance education library services task force: Past, present, and future. *Journal of Library Administration, 45,* 201-213. http://dx.doi.org/10.1300 /J111v45n01_11

Kayler, G., & Pival, P. R. (2004). Working together: Effective collaboration in a consortium environment. *Journal of Library Administration, 41,* 203-215. http://dx.doi.org/10.1300/J111v41n01_15

Montague, R.-A., & Pluzhenskaia, M. (2007). Web-based information science education (WISE): Collaboration to explore and expand quality in LIS online education. *Journal of Education for Library and Information Science, 48,* 36-51. Retrieved from http://www.alise.org/jelis

Subramanian, J. M. (2003). The growing and changing role of consortia in providing direct and indirect support for distance higher education. *The Reference Librarian, 37*(77), 37-60. http://dx.doi.org/10.1300/J120v37n77_05

Appendix

Online Resources

List of Interstate Online Education Consortia

- Alliance for Cooperative Course Exchange in the Plant Sciences (ACCEPtS)
  http://www.accecpts.uark.edu/index.html

- Great Plains Interactive Distance Education Alliance (Great Plains IDEA)
  http://www.gpidea.org/

- Nursing Education Xchange (NEXus)
  http://www.winnexus.org/

- Natural Resources Distance Learning Consortium (NRDLC)
  http://nrdlc.usu.edu/

- National Universities Degree Consortium (NUDC)
  http://www.nudc.org/

- University Engineering Alliance (UEA)
  http://www.universityengineeringalliance.org/

- Western Interstate Commission for Higher Education Internet Course Exchange (WICHE ICE)
  http://wiche.edu/ice

- Web-based Information Science Education (WISE)
  http://www.wiseeducation.org/

List of Intrastate Online Education Consortia

- University of California Online (UC Online)
  http://www.uconline.edu/

- Cal State Online
  http://calstateonline.net/

- Florida Virtual Campus
  https://www.flvc.org/home

- Georgia's College Core-Curriculum Online (eCore)
  https://ecore.usg.edu/

- Indiana College Network (ICN)
  http://www.icn.org/

- Iowa Community College Online Consortium (ICCOC)
  http://www.iowacconline.org/

- Louisiana Online
  http://louisianaonline.org/

- Open SUNY (The State University of New York)
  http://open.suny.edu/

- Oregon Community College Distance Learning Association (OCCDLA)
  http://occdla.net/

- University of Texas Online Consortium (UTOC)
  http://utcoursesonline.org/index.html

- Wyoming Course Locator & Support Services (WyCLASS)
  http://wyclass.wy.edu/

Libraries Leading the Way on the Textbook Problem

Marilyn Billings, Scholarly Communication and Special Initiatives Librarian, UMass Amherst
William M. Cross, Director, Copyright and Digital Scholarship Center, NCSU Libraries
Brendan O'Connell, Libraries Fellow, NCSU Libraries
Greg Raschke, Associate Director for Collections and Scholarly Communication, NCSU Libraries
Charlotte Roh, Scholarly Communications Resident Librarian, UMass Amherst

Abstract

Escalating textbook costs and continually evolving technologies for delivering course content have combined to place the "textbook problem" at a boiling point ripe for systemic change. This article describes two efforts to address the "textbook problem" by offering incentive grants to faculty members who adopt, adapt, or create open educational resources (OERs) to replace costly textbooks. It describes programs at UMass Amherst and North Carolina State University and discusses the role of the library as a campus leader, educating faculty on new textbook models and investigating and providing incentives to incubate change.

Introduction: The Textbook Problem

The increase of textbook costs combined with the continual evolution of technologies that deliver course content has made the "textbook problem" ripe for systemic change. According to the 2014 College Board *Trends in College Pricing* study, college students spend an average of $1,200 a year on textbooks.[1] While course materials are a vital part of the higher education system, cost increases well above the general rate of inflation have increased dissatisfaction with standard textbook publishing and delivery models. Though traditional textbook publishers rightly note that students can spend less than the College Board reports through ebooks and rentals, the escalation of textbook prices well above the overall rate of inflation continues unabated. The Government Accountability Office estimates that from 2002 to 2013 prices increased by 82%, three times the rate of increase in overall consumer prices.[2] This unsustainable rate of increase is driven by a variety of factors, but at its core stems from a generally inelastic market where consumers (students) and providers (publisher/vendor /bookstore) are separated by an intermediary (professor) who is not directly exposed to price.

Though inelastic in structure, the significant rate of increase in costs has helped increase awareness and dissatisfaction among participants in the textbook market. From this crossroads of unsustainable costs, emerging delivery technologies, and growing dissatisfaction—the long-term evolution of systems for delivering course materials will be shaped by a complex mix of economic, political, pedagogical, and technological factors, along with a diverse set of players that includes students, faculty, publishers, open educational resource providers, central information technologists, and librarians.

The immediate problem facing academic libraries of all types is what, if anything, they can or should do about textbooks. Libraries, particularly in North America, have traditionally taken a hands-off approach to the textbook problem. No library has the funding or mandate to purchase textbooks at the scale needed to serve an entire institution of students. As neither the ones selecting nor using textbooks, libraries have not been principal agents

---

[1] College Board. (2014). Trends in college pricing. Retrieved from https://secure-media.collegeboard .org/digitalServices/misc/trends/2014-trends-college -pricing-report-final.pdf

[2] General Accountability Office. (2013). College textbooks: Students have access to textbook information. Retrieved from http://www.gao.gov/assets/660/655066.pdf

in the textbook market. That traditional stance on textbooks, however, is rapidly changing.

As hubs of higher education institutions, libraries have a natural connection to students and their growing dissatisfaction with textbook costs. Libraries also work closely with faculty across the life cycle of their research and teaching. Library service provision and engagement with pedagogical tools such as electronic reserves and course management systems increased engagement with digital tools for delivering course materials. More libraries are putting together the pieces of student dissatisfaction, faculty interest in new pedagogical approaches, established relationships with both students and faculty, and the burgeoning open educational resource (OERs) market to move into the middle of the textbook conversation, and become leaders in offering solutions to the "textbook problem."

OERs and alternative market driven options such as Flat World Knowledge and OpenStax created opportunities for libraries to come off the sidelines of the "textbook problem" and start participating in developing, promoting, and disseminating alternatives to traditional textbooks. While academic libraries do not exert central authority or market power to drive solutions, they do have both physical centrality on campuses and important visibility and goodwill in the academy.

Further, there are strategies available for librarians to move the needle from problem to affordability, access, and piloting new spaces to incubate change. From utilizing existing systems of reserves, to innovating in the use of course management systems, to developing incentive programs for incubating alternatives to traditional textbooks—libraries are fostering change by providing educational resource solutions to their students and faculty. This paper highlights efforts at the libraries of the UMass Amherst and NC State University to move into leadership roles in fostering innovation and cost savings in the delivery of educational resources.

Libraries Leading the Way at UMass-Amherst

The UMass Amherst Libraries have been engaged in seeking open alternative models in scholarly communication since 2006. These alternative models included the development of an institutional repository for UMass Amherst scholarly materials, the introduction of library publishing services, and partnership with the University Press. When the textbook affordability "crisis" was brought to the attention of librarians at the Scholarly Publishing and Academic Resource Coalition (SPARC) forum during the American Library Association (ALA) midwinter in 2009 and again during a SPARC phone conversation in February 2011, we realized that this was an exciting opportunity to participate actively within the teaching and learning community and aligning with our open mission, seeking open alternatives to high cost textbooks. During the SPARC phone conversation, Steven Bell, Associate University Librarian for Research & Instructional Services at Temple University, outlined the alternative textbook project they had established and willingly shared the materials they had developed.

The Director of Libraries, Jay Schafer approached the Provost to seek that level of support and engagement as we envisioned the Open Education Initiative. Building upon Temple's success and our own active partnerships with Academic Computing, the Center for Teaching and Faculty Development, and the academic IT Minor Program, we created an innovative new Open Education grant program in April 2011 that began with 10 $1,000 grants to incentivize faculty who were interested in pursuing alternatives to high cost textbooks. Within a year, we realized that we were not attracting faculty who were teaching large general education classes of over 200 students so we added 2 $2500 grants to the program. Now in its fifth round of funding, the program has attracted faculty from across the university, included courses from general education to graduate level, and saved students over $1 million in textbook costs.

The Open Education Initiative

Many libraries already purchase access to materials that are excellent substitutes for materials that educators currently use in their teaching. Some of the items are actually identical to adopted course materials. The shift from paper to digital means that, instead of one book on reserve at the library counter, an e-book could be available to a hundred students at once. For many educators, this is a shift in access that is not within their personal experience. They are familiar with course packs, reserve materials, and the campus bookstore. They are aware of library databases in their own research. Through the Open Education Initiative, grant recipients are made aware of the wealth of materials that libraries offer and how licenses have been negotiated so that the maximum number of students can have access to a research. This can at times be tricky, since we have different contracts with different vendors. But it can also be an eye-opening experience for professors, who in our workshops often say, "I didn't know the library had that." While the OEI workshop is not billed as such, it is really an opportunity to showcase the value of the library and its subscribed resources, to the benefit of the library, faculty, and students.

The OEI workshop also includes an introduction to open access resources, which have greatly matured in the last five years. The UMass Amherst Libraries keeps an extensive list of resources through its LibGuide at http://guides.library.umass .edu/oer. The list can be overwhelming, as there are many initiatives around the country and none that offer comprehensive coverage. However, this is also a sign that open education resources are part of a growing movement, and it does take effort. During training, it is important to stress the availability of the scholarly communication and subject liaison librarians and guides and consultants to finding open education resources.

The Office of the Provost has been an important partner and supporter since the beginning of the Open Education Initiative. The Provost funds half of the grants every semester, sends out the email announcing the request for proposal, and is vocal regarding the impact of the program and its benefits.

Another important campus partners for open education at UMass Amherst is the Information Technology (IT) office, which already holds workshops to help faculty with instructional and classroom technologies, from embedding videos in Moodle to creating a wiki. For example, Professor Hossein Pishro-Nik worked with IT on his statistics and probability e-book http://www.probabilitycourse.com/. It includes videos and calculators within the text for an interactive experience. A few professors have worked with the Center for Educational Software Development, which is an interactive quizzing/homework service.

As a consequence of new technologies and methods, there are some who discover that, having made their lecture slides into the course materials, they now must learn how to flip their classroom to an interactive one. We partner with the Center for Teaching & Faculty Development, who works with professors in order to teach using new models. This taps into the innovative learning trends that are happening on campus, such as the new academic classroom building on campus that is built specifically to encourage nonlecture styles of teaching and learning.

The most recent partner in the UMass open education efforts has been students. Individual students and those affiliated with MASS PIRG have written articles, spoken to their own professors, advocated on Facebook, and even spoken to the Faculty Senate as part of a panel presentation. Student advocacy around open education is a growing and important voice for any institution who is looking to establish an open education program. In 2015, student PIRG chapters across the state of Massachusetts plan to make open education their central campaign, and will work towards having departments commit to seeking affordable alternatives to expensive textbooks.

The last piece of the Open Education Initiative is assessment. In terms of cost savings, the program is a quantitative success. As of spring 2014, projected savings based on initial proposals were approximately $750,000. An online survey was sent out asking participants when and where they had implemented the grant, and it was realized that there was an ongoing impact due to materials being used in semesters after the initial launch. For example, the aforementioned Professor Pishro-Nik has now used his textbook nine times, resulting in a savings of $50,000 for just one grant recipient. We estimate that students have saved over $1 million in textbook costs.

The qualitative feedback is just as compelling. In a recent informal survey for the fall 2014 semester, 83% of students in the OEI program indicated they were happy with the course materials. Professors have told us that since they are more engaged with the material, students are more engaged with material. They are seeing more prepared students and greater participation in class discussion. It's clear that the OEI program has been a catalyst for shaking up, not just the traditional textbook adoption model, but also the structure of teaching and learning.

Libraries Leading the Way at NCSU

The NCSU Libraries has long recognized the danger posed to student outcomes and the education mission of higher education, and investigated several strategies for addressing the problem. Recognizing limitations in market and bargaining power, and respectful of faculty member's academic freedom to make decisions regarding curriculum and instruction, the Libraries began with a strategy based on developing resources, infrastructure, and support for faculty and students.

Beginning in the early 2000s, the Libraries approached the problem in three ways: by supporting learning technologies, offering education, and providing resources. Support for both instruction and technology has always been a core mission of the Libraries, so ramping up and synthesizing that support for faculty instructors looking beyond textbooks was a natural fit. Similarly, as the Libraries worked to advocate for open access, advocacy for open education followed naturally. We developed our own expertise in open education, offered

consultations, and developed web materials and a white paper describing the textbook problem. Through these efforts, we hoped to inform faculty members about the issue and support them when and in the ways that they were most comfortable engaging.

Along with our work engaging faculty instructors, the Libraries also developed strategies for reducing the high cost of textbook for students at NCSU. We offered online and physical course reserves and worked with faculty to license materials—both traditional print and digital/audiovisual materials. The Libraries also partnered with our campus bookstore to reduce the burden on students. We adopted a policy of purchasing at least one copy of every assigned textbook, to be placed on reserve for students to use. This program is incredibly popular today, with rising use every semester driving greater use of other Library resources.

Despite these efforts, however, textbook costs continue to be a major issue for our students. As such, the Libraries were increasingly persuaded that direct action was also needed to empower faculty and support student access. In 2011, we partnered with the Physics Department to pilot an open physics textbook for our large Physics 211 and 212 courses.[3] Serving more than 1,300 students, the book was a massive success, making one of the most expensive textbooks free for students to read and available for print-on-demand for $45. We also offered market alternatives through hosting faculty materials and investigating both FlatWorldKnowledge and OpenStax. In 2014, the Libraries finally decided to enter the Open Education environment directly, by launching the Alt-Textbook Project. This project follows on the success of programs at UMass Amherst and Temple, offering individual faculty members grants as an incentive to replace costly traditional textbooks with open alternatives.

Like most supporters of open education, we were keenly aware of the cost of textbooks, and this cost both drove our efforts and helped us

---

[3] http://chronicle.com/blogs/wiredcampus/north-carolina-state-u-gives-students-free-access-to-physics-textbook-online/21238

articulate the problem to faculty members and to our own funders, the NC State Foundation. Most studies suggest that the cost issue has several facets.[4] The unsustainable rate of growth—80% in the past decade and more than 800% in the past 30 years—dwarfs the rising cost of both home prices and medical care, two areas that have been recognized as areas in crisis. The actual cost per student—more than $1,200 per year, was also a concern since textbooks are often purchased with student loans, leaving many students with final costs much greater than even that alarming number. We also saw this cost as a social justice issue, pricing many of the most vulnerable students out of an education that our public, land grant mission is especially attuned to.

This issue of cost also played into our concerns about educational outcomes. More than 70% of students have admitted to going without a required textbook based on cost, so it should come as no surprise that open educational materials are more effective. Indeed, we have been encouraged by the growing body of research on the efficacy of OERs, confirming empirically our anecdotal experience that open works are more effective.[5] After all, you can't learn from a book you can't afford to read.

We also believe that efficacy is improved when faculty are fully engaged and empowered to make and use resources that reflect their own instruction. For this reason, we were equally excited by the opportunity to engage our faculty members with library services and empower them to create better models for instruction. Along with questions of cost, we expected to see great return on our investment in faculty teaching. Libraries spend millions of dollars every year on research, from acquiring materials and hosting repositories to managing data and tracking impact. We strongly believe that similar support should be provided for faculty instruction, which impacts the next generation of researchers, as well as the millions of students who will go on to work outside of the academy. As discussed below, faculty shared these sentiments and we're often

tremendously inspired to create materials that leveraged library resources to do something a print textbook just couldn't do.

Our decision to enter this space was made easier by the rich and growing OER community. The ability to point faculty members to existing resources such as Merlot-, OpenStax-, and Creative Commons-licensed works gave them a foundation on which to build and reinforced our belief that work done in our program would resonate far beyond our campus. Our project itself was supported by the generosity of colleagues at peer institutions, who shared materials, strategies, and tips for launching the program. Armed with advice, resources, and a passionate faculty base, we launched the Alt-Textbook Project in the spring of 2014.

The NCSU Alt-Textbook Project

From the start, we took a team-based approach to this project. We wanted the Alt-Textbook Project to really be a tool, not just to save students money, but also to promote the full range of library materials and services to our faculty. The Alt-Textbook Project, then, is not just a grant award but an outreach opportunity for us to introduce faculty to materials and services they might not be aware that we offer. We've pitched grant awards to our faculty as the beginning of a semester-long process in which many of our librarians will work closely with them to help them locate and evaluate the quality of existing OER resources, using our course management system Moodle with library resources, e-reserves, licensing content for course use, exploring digital publishing tools, and incorporating streaming video into courses.

Will Cross, Brendan O'Connell, and Kim Duckett (Associate Head, Research & Information Services) founded the project in late 2013, and applied for and received a $15,000 campus grant to build the Alt-Textbook Project. After receiving the grant, we added the Associate Head of Digital Library Initiatives Jason Casden and Associate Head of

---

[4] General Accountability Office. (2013). College textbooks: Students have access to textbook information. Retrieved from http://www.gao.gov/assets/660/655066.pdf

[5] Robinson et al. (2014). The impact of open textbooks on secondary science learning outcomes, *Educational Researcher, 43*(7), 341-351.

Access and Delivery Services Sydney Thompson to our team to bring expertise in web content delivery, and e-reserves, respectively. This team-based approach allows us to leverage a large range of library services to aid faculty award recipients, from Kim's expertise in e-learning and course management systems, Will's expertise in copyright, fair use, and licensing content, and Sydney's skills in e-reserves, to name a few examples.

We knew from early on that for this project to succeed, we had to get buy-in from staff. We were interested in asking staff to partner with faculty awardees throughout the semester, which would which mean more work, so we had to make sure to get them on board first. We decided to conduct outreach visits to department meetings for the most likely departments that faculty grant recipients would be working with—Collection Management and Research and Information Services, where the majority of our subject specialists are located. We also wanted this to be a recruitment effort, and asked our colleagues to help us seed great project proposals by promoting the grants to faculty they already have relationships with.

We promoted the project through emails to a number of faculty listservs, a press release, social media, and a gallery image in the artbox on our homepage. An important component of our outreach to faculty members was a series of information sessions on the project. We held two faculty info sessions, one in collaboration with our campus Office of Faculty Development, which holds a well-attended workshop series. We held an additional info session at D. H. Hill Library.

We've also ended up meeting for individual consultations with almost every faculty member who attended our workshops, again demonstrating the effectiveness of open information sessions as a way to attract interest in the project, and invite faculty members to seek further consults with us.

We've built a diverse peer review team, including students, faculty members, campus partners, and librarians to evaluate faculty applications. We believe it's extremely important to bring all stakeholders to the table on a project like this that affects the entire campus, and especially to include student voices in our review process.

We're also currently working on developing partnerships on and off campus. Representatives of DELTA (Distance Education and Learning Technology Applications) and OFD are on our peer review team, and our campus bookstore has offered print-on-demand services at cost for our project. We're fortunate that our campus bookstore is not an external for-profit entity, as many are, so in our case they're extremely concerned about the cost of textbooks for students and are an enthusiastic supporter of efforts to promote textbook affordability.

We've also been in discussions with Lumen Learning and OpenStax about using their platforms to publish some of our alt-texts, as well as the University of North Carolina system press. This represents a very potent partnership for us, as our library doesn't offer digital publishing infrastructure, so for some of our more ambitious applicants we plan to partner with UNC Press to publish open alt-textbooks.

In the fall of 2014 we completed our applications and peer review process, and a common thread, not surprisingly, was that our faculty applicants are dissatisfied with commercial textbooks. Obviously our applicants are a self-selecting group of faculty members, but we believe OER faculty incentive programs like this one on other campuses will find a receptive audience among faculty members. Many of our faculty members propose to create resources that incorporate existing practices in their courses—making instructional videos, crowdsourcing knowledge, and developing lab notes into a durable alt-textbook, but are requesting library help to publish them.

We were actually surprised to see how many of our faculty members were interested in creating totally new alt-textbooks, instead of adopting existing OERs. We're confident that we'll be contributing a great deal to the broader OER landscape by working with faculty members to publish all these new alt-textbooks on emerging, interdisciplinary, or specialized subjects.

Finally, we've built assessment into our project, with plans to assess learning outcomes for students using OERs, continued use of OERs by faculty after the grant award period, and making improvements to our website based on comments and feedback.

Lessons Learned and Joining the Party

Both Amherst and NCSU have learned important lessons from our experience with these programs. Libraries can, and must, take an active role leading their institutions to make changes to a broken textbook market. We have the necessary expertise, a historical mission to marshal resources for the benefit of our stakeholders, and we offer a trusted space on campus for innovative, interdisciplinary work to be done.

Having run a grant-based program on campus, both institutions also believe that this sort of program, offering financial support for faculty who adopt, adapt, or create open educational resources is a powerful and effective way to spark change. In many cases, even a relatively modest investment can give faculty the ability to hire a graduate student, license resources, or acquire software needed for transformative practice. Even in cases where faculty members do not need to meet specific line-item costs, a small financial incentive can be the push faculty need to focus their attention on this sort of project. In either case, returns on an investment can be expected to be exponential in terms of dollars, and immeasurable in terms of faculty and student outcomes.

We have also learned the value of meeting faculty on their terms using library strengths. Some faculty members may be tech-savvy or knowledgeable about OERs. Others may be neophytes. Wherever faculty are, if they have a sincere desire to be better instructors and improve outcomes for students, libraries can best-

help them succeed be making space for contributions from instructors of all levels. This can be done by leveraging library expertise and building on the strengths of your own institution. Both Amherst and NCSU have strong copyright and instructional support, so leveraged those to empower faculty. Other institutions may have a mature repository, deep relationships with subject specialists, or an affiliated university press. Any program interested in addressing the textbook problem should identify the strengths within the library and across campus and use those as a foundation to build on.

At the same time that library strengths bolster an OER program, an OER program can also support traditional library practices. Raising the issue of instruction with faculty, particularly in the context of grant funding, reinforces the value of all library services around instruction, from course design and CMS use to the licensed resources that libraries offer, often at great cost. For example, both institutions have seen numerous faculty members come forward with a proposal for "open" materials that fit comfortably within our standard electronic reserves system. An OER program also creates a welcoming context for faculty-library interaction, forging new relationships and partnerships that will resonate with other projects and remind faculty that the library is a place with a wide variety of services and support, as well as a space that values their instructional work, too often work that is trivialized by other campus stakeholders.

Because the open education community is increasingly rich, a host of tools, templates, and examples are being developed to support best practice. SPARC offers an overview of open education that includes fact sheets, videos, and other resources.[6] The November 2014 issue of *Against the Grain* offers a series of articles on the changing role of textbook content.[7] SPARC is also offering an institute on open educational resources at the ALA Midwinter Meeting 2015 in Chicago that will build and further expand

---

[6] http://www.sparc.arl.org/issues/oer

[7] http://www.against-the-grain.com/2014/11/changing-roles-in-providing-textbook-content/

librarian expertise and seed even better resources.[8] As a critical mass of faculty members begins to engage with open education and OERs,[9] there has never been a better time for your library to start leading the way on your own campus.

---

[8] http://www.ala.org/acrl/oerinstitute

[9] Babson survey on open educational resources available at http://www.onlinelearningsurvey.com/oer.html

Building Capacity in Your Library for Research Data Management Support (Or What We Learned From Offering to Review DMPs)

William M. Cross, Director, Copyright and Digital Scholarship, NCSU Libraries
Hilary M. Davis, Interim Head, Collection Management & Director of Research Data Services,
NCSU Libraries

Abstract

In our evolving effort to build infrastructure and support around research data management needs, we found traction in launching a data management plan review service. In doing so, we have been able to achieve multiple goals: 1) support the research process; 2) create active learning situations for subject liaisons to engage in and learn how to support data management planning; 3) find resonance with campus-sponsored research officers; 4) collaborate with other campus research support groups including campus IT, the institutional review board, and statistical consulting; 5) and participate in the national dialogue about the tensions of data management.

Introduction

Many models of supporting research data management needs exist. Some libraries invest in spaces to showcase and deliver services for researchers who need support managing data. Examples include the new Research HUB at the University of North Carolina-Chapel Hill, which includes consultation space, workshop space, hands-on data wrangling, deposit, and visualization support. Some libraries have a web presence typically defined by a web guide or libguide that may or may not have librarian support associated with the guide. This approach, while potentially more hands-off, is also low-cost. And a few libraries have taken the approach of hiring a dedicated team of data curation specialists (with deep expertise in data curation and/or data wrangling), with or without dedicated space. This approach centralizes the support in a few library staff experts. In its efforts to provide research data management support at North Carolina State University (NCSU), the NCSU Libraries took a hybrid approach. We started with a web guide, then built up support across our subject liaison librarians, guided by a core team composed of subject liaisons, technology-focused librarians, and curation/preservation librarians. We have iteratively rolled out workshops, presentations, and a data management plan (DMP) review service as part of our growing portfolio. This paper will describe the components

of our data management plan review service as a means for building capacity for supporting research data management at our campus. We will explain how different stakeholders participate in the process, and how subject liaisons learn to engage in research data management to lend insights for leveraging subject liaisons in research engagement. We end with a view to the future and explore ways to tap into a broader networks at your own institutions and nationally.

Components of Our Research Data Management Support Portfolio

The mainstays of the NCSU Libraries' support for research data management includes our digital repository services which focus on ETDs, scholarly publications, and technical reports, but have very limited support for datasets. We extend deep expertise in issues and guidance around copyright, intellectual property, open data, and the publishing landscape. Our consultation support provides help to researchers to find and gain access to datasets (with dedicated librarians for geospatial and social science data services). As partners for Dryad (biosciences data repository), we provide technical infrastructure and systems administration for researchers who leverage Dryad. Since 2011, we developed and have maintained a data management planning guide and adopted the DMPTool in 2012.

We deliver this support primarily through workshops and presentations to both broad groups as well as specific academic departments; via consultations to individuals and lab groups; and through referrals directed to our librarians from other units on campus or from the Libraries to other units on campus with specific expertise on issues such as statistical consulting, data security, and institutional review board protocols.

All of this activity is coordinated by the NCSU Libraries' Research Data Committee, which acts as a hub for the research data management support. The committee is composed of eight subject specialist and digital technologies librarians from across the Libraries.

In August 2013 we launched DMP Review service because we wanted to engage more fully in the active phase of planning a data management strategy. We heard from the Research Administration unit on campus that there was an imminent need to help researchers design their initial DMPs to make their data available and manage their data. No other unit provided this hands-on assistance to researchers and we were confident that we could fill that gap. We recognized that it could be a technical conversation (what is data and how to manage it) and that we could help researchers explore those questions.

Equally important, we wanted to know how to support the active phase of data management planning ourselves and we needed to provide practical experiences for our subject liaison librarians to gain skills to better support researchers' data management needs.

Nuts and Bolts of the Data Management Plan (DMP) Review Service

Recognizing the need for a DMP review service and the components of our portfolio, we designed our service to be team-based, light, and nimble. In order to review the DMP's we knew we would need expertise from several fields and that we would not have a full-time research data librarian, so we gathered experts from across the Libraries who could work together and share knowledge on the Research Data Committee (RDC). This gave us

a team that, working together, could cover most of the substantive issues around data management and sharing—from filetypes to funder mandates. It also meant that the RDC would have established relationships with many departments, creating a broad network for outreach across campus.

This team-based approach also served as a training ground where experts could share their knowledge with the rest of the RDC, so all members could learn from one another. In the past year, we have also begun to rotate new members onto the RDC, sending trained librarians back "into the field" and bringing in new members for this "on-the-job training" in data management and sharing. Rotating members in and out of the RDC has also continued to expand our network with stakeholders across campus and created new relationships for the RDC to build upon.

The process for reviewing a DMP begins with a submission of a draft DMP by the researcher to a library web form that is forwarded to an internal RDC email distribution list. Members of the RDC monitor the distribution list and the first person who has the ability to reply back to the researcher reaches out to gather the relevant bits of information needed to review the DMP. The first responder also coordinates with relevant subject specialists and creates a simple Google document of the draft DMP that all RDC members and subject specialists can contribute to. Each member reviews the DMP, adding comments that would improve the DMP or, where appropriate, raising questions that could be best answered by another RDC member with relevant expertise.

Once all comments have been made, the team leader compiles and synthesizes them into a manageable format. We are conscious of the danger of overwhelming a researcher with too many comments or comments that are daunting or overly complex. Our aim is to offer comments that are detailed enough to be put into practice and offer actionable suggestions for the researcher. Generally, these comments do not exceed a single page. To support both DMP review and drafting feedback, we have compiled several documents describing established practice based on our own past experience as well as materials from other scholars such as Dorothea Salo.

Having offered the service for more than a year, we have also begun some preliminary assessment. Measuring success can be complex, and we want to be particularly sensitive to the time of the researchers who have reached out to us. Since our earliest users have been some of our most active researchers, a time-consuming or detailed survey might be an unwelcome addition to their already busy schedule. Our DMP review service also deals with content that requires confidentiality as well as impacting funding and promotion/tenure decisions, so we want to be mindful of avoiding any questions that might be uncomfortable for our researchers to answer. Because our initial group of researchers would offer a small sample size, we also rejected seeking any quantitative outcomes measurements.

These complications, along with fundamental questions about what constitutes a "successful" program, have led us to rely on a basic set of questions about how our researchers experienced the review. We asked them simply to let us know if the service was helpful for them. Early results have been very positive, with several researchers noting that they appreciated the service in strong terms. "The service was GREAT," one wrote "It really helped me craft a strong data management plan for the project!" Other researchers make it a point to indicate specific suggestions they found helpful, such as data security guidance and help locating repositories for data storage. We will continue to consider strategies for and conduct assessment, but at this stage the project seems to be valued highly by researchers and is certainly valuable for us in the Libraries as we engage with these important issues.

What We Learned From Our DMP Review Service

Supporting the Research Process

Through the DMP Review service and other consultations we have conducted, we have a better picture of where we can have impact on the research process. We have found a lot of momentum in helping to train graduate students

in data information literacy and have been invited to deliver presentations to academic departments about the fundamentals of data management planning. As part of more robust and in-depth effort to increase data literacy for researchers and students in NCSU College of Agriculture and Life Sciences, several of our subject liaison librarians are actively developing and delivering customized hands-on training for those stakeholders.

By reviewing and providing feedback about DMPs, we have found synergy in establishing connections with other experts across campus, including statistical consultation support, institutional review board (IRB) compliance officers, data security experts, and the technology transfer unit.

In many ways, we act as advocates for researchers with publishers (e.g., to help researchers maintaining the rights they need to comply with funding public and open science mandates), and with grant funding agencies (e.g., working as mediators between our NIH-funded researchers and the NIH compliance group to work out trouble spots in the NIH submission system). Most close to home, we help to shape the campus-wide dialogue and drive action toward creating a system that supports activities like assigning author identifiers, DOI minting, providing short- and long-term data storage, and establishing policies or expectations for data sharing, data integrity, and data security.

Creating Learning Opportunities for Librarians

Our goal is for subject liaisons to learn to engage in research data management in a collaborative, supportive environment. Our approach has emphasized the importance and value of leveraging subject liaisons in research engagement. Since we started integrating subject liaisons into our RDM support strategies (July 2013), we have held training sessions/workshops on institutional review board (IRB) protocols, directives for public access to federally funded research, reviewing example DMPs (repeated multiple times), data rights and ownership, data management for students, and statistical consulting services across campus. We are planning a session with our campus IT to have a discussion with us about supporting data security.

The main component lacking in all of these sessions was real-life examples to build skills and drive home the value of being able to engage with researchers in RDM. The DMP Review service offered exactly that in a safe environment where subject liaisons could engage in the process on their own terms, learn from one another, and gain an understanding of the various components of support across campus.

Early reactions from subject liaison librarian were mixed: some were more comfortable observing the process, while others adopted the new role more readily. As subject liaisons had opportunities to get involved directly with reviewing DMPs, presenting workshops on research data management fundamentals, and consult with researchers, they see the value in being able to handle those conversations and have grown into their new roles in an organic, iterative way.

List of Most Common Mistakes (aka Learning Opportunities for Librarians)

The process of reviewing a DMP might be a little daunting to the uninitiated, but the learning curve is not as difficult to overcome as some might think. When we review DMPs, liaisons can observe and learn from the group process and get involved as much as they are comfortable. Once they have a foot in the door, they can learn how to handle some of the common mistakes. That generates confidence in their ability to take part in the conversation about RDM, and gives them a foundation to build on.

Some of the more common mistakes are listed as follows with opportunities for librarians to offer a value-added level of support:

- Forgetting to review the list of expected components—funding agencies expectations vary, even within different divisions of the same funding agency; the value that librarians bring is to review the specific requirements of the funding source that a researcher is applying for and let the researcher know which are missing. We have found it extremely

useful to review the funding agency guidelines for every DMP that has been submitted to us for review and feedback.

- Neglecting to be more specific about types of data being produced by the research—DMP requirements dictate more specificity beyond just "observational" or "experimental" data; the value that librarians can bring is to help elucidate the data types by asking the researcher questions that get at what types of data will be produced.

- Proprietary vs. nonproprietary formats—it has happened to every one of us: we try to open a file that is in a format for which we don't have the right software or the right version on our computers. Researchers don't often think about converting final data files into non-proprietary formats, but librarians do because we help our patrons overcome this problem all of the time. We help the researcher think ahead and figure out which formats will achieve their goals of future compatibility and ease of sharing.

- Data? I don't have data—several of the DMPs we have reviewed start with "no data will be generated from this project" and then they go on to describe the software code that will be created and the analyses that will be conducted to test models. The value that librarians bring is to remind the researcher about what is considered data and what isn't. We make sure the researchers are aware of this and help them think through their plan for active and ongoing management and sharing of their software code or other data that they don't realize is considered a research asset to funders.

- Describing data—most of the DMPs we have reviewed do not say much more than "we will provide documentation for the data produced." The value that librarians bring is that we recognize that this is too vague to pass muster and we can make easy suggestions about standard schema to use and even offer consultation to help set up a schema.

- Providing data on request or promising to post it on a researcher's website—this is sometimes considered inadequate, depending on the community of interest. Some PIs are unaware that disciplinary data repositories exist. We have helped connect researchers with disciplinary repositories and often do the legwork to find out logistics, cost, and policies up front.

- Sharing the publications—after reviewing some DMPs, we have suggested that researchers leverage our institutional repositories (text or data or both); if your repository is really only set up for text objects as opposed to data, you can still encourage the researcher to deposit their version of their article into your repository to enhance discovery and uptake. This will also open the door to some useful conversations about author's rights.

- Expectations for re-use by others—we have seen researchers that do not address how they might expect others to re-use their data and we have seen cases where researchers try to write a contract for re-use in the DMP. Librarians can guide researchers to some easily digestible options and take this opportunity to address the balance that can be struck between sharing and intellectual property rights while helping to reinforce data citation practices so that researchers get credit for their data too.

Once we have subject liaisons go through a couple of actual DMP review experiences, they have a better sense of what it takes to have conversations about researchers and their data. We have experts that can help them go the extra mile once the conversation reaches a more advanced level (e.g., metadata generation) and we can leverage other experts on campus (e.g., IRB group).

Finding Resonance With Campus-Sponsored Research Officers

In conjunction with our work with subject specialists, we have developed an important working relationship with our Sponsored Programs and Regulatory Compliance Services (SPARCS). In particular, the College Research Officers (CROs) have been critical contacts since CROs are the people who are on the ground supporting PIs in both the pre-award and post-award phases. Although CROs are not typically involved in writing the DMPs themselves, they are valuable for spreading the word about our support. As research moves from design to grant application and through the process it has been important to establish clear lines of responsibility and coordination, so research can be "handed off" to the appropriate body through recommendations and word of mouth.

This relationship is natural, of course, since we have the shared objective of supporting researchers. Indeed, our creation of our Data Management Planning Guide arose from a SPARCS request. As our project has continued to develop, we hope to continue to find opportunities for collaboration. SPARCS and the CROs have been particularly useful because they have an established infrastructure for information sharing that we have been able to tap in to. From access to listservs and mentions in their presentation to invitations to offer full workshops to their researchers, we have been able to share information about our service through this channel. Although we have not seen substantial adoption of our services directly by CROs, the real value has been putting our name into the ears and onto the tip of the tongues of the people who work directly with and advise researchers.

Collaboration With Other Campus Research Support Groups

We have had similar success with other partners across campus, particularly our campus institutional review board (IRB) and IT teams. As with SPARCS and CROs, we have worked to build lines of communication with these stakeholders so we can share information and tap into a broader collaborative network. In particular, we have served as the canary in the coal mine for these stakeholders, taking the pain points from the DMPs and using them to make a pitch to campus for improved support and services. Where appropriate, we are able to use the examples from our service to create case studies and document examples where current services leave our researchers unprepared or in need of greater support.

As with our partnership with CROs, we have also offered workshops on IRB issues and Statistical Consulting Services, and held ongoing conversations about what we can learn from one another's experiences supporting research. We have not always been able to persuade these stakeholders to address our concerns—researchers currently face a major gap on campus around networked storage—but by raising those issues and keeping lines of communication open we believe we are continuing to build a case based on evidence we gather about the needs of researchers in this area.

What Is the Next Step/Future for Library Support RDM?

In terms of our next steps for local engagement, we are continuously exploring ways to enhance support for research data management and find the right fit and investment of our already overstretched subject liaison librarians. Dedicated space configured and promoted specifically for digital scholarship is an area of current investment to support needs such as consultation and collaboration space, hands-on data wrangling, and visualization support.

As we continue to push efforts and integrate into campus dialogue regarding enterprise-wide data storage and sharing infrastructure, we also are exploring ways to more formally become part of the grant application workflow (e.g., the DMPTool has a feature to enable researchers to request review of their DMPs) as well as the Responsible Conduct of Research (RCR) program at NC State.

We also recognize the importance of engaging at the regional and national level. So far, our role has focused on serving as a bridge, connecting

national projects with local practice on campus. We work to remain abreast of developing best practices and new tools and bring those to campus. We also regularly share updates about open data mandates and requirements, offering workshops, updates, and consultation about the ongoing response to the White House Office of Science and Technology Policy's Directive on open access. These have covered the development of practitioner-driven solutions such as SHARE and CHORUS as well as the new mandates from executive agencies such as the DOE.

We also work to share local concerns with national stakeholders. By maintaining relationships and lines of communication with researchers and librarians on campus, we are able to draft well-informed responses to calls for comment, requests for information, amicus briefs, and similar federal outreach opportunities. We also use information gathered through this service to inform conference presentations, scholarly writing, and active participation in discussions about open data and data sharing.

Along with this national engagement, we have focused on developing regional networks in our area. The North Carolina Research Triangle has a strong core of academic libraries, each with data management and data sharing programs, and we have worked to leverage those relationships into regular meetings and, where appropriate, partnerships.

These collaborations at the regional and national level will be critical as libraries across the profession work to develop infrastructure needed to support open access to research and research data envisioned by the OSTP Directive, other open data mandates, and subsequent policies and legal requirements. Projects like SHARE, in particular, are predicated on a robust, interoperable network of libraries, repositories, and practices. Without those networks of services and relationship, open access and open data would be much more difficult to manage. By developing them at our institution, we hope to empower our researchers, engage our library services, and facilitate more complete, transformative data sharing.

SELF-e 101: A Lesson for Academic Libraries in Connecting Self-Published Authors and Readers

Corrie Marsh, SFASU

Mitchell Davis, BiblioBoard

Meredith Schwartz, Library Journal

Etta Verma, Library Journal

Eleanor Cook, East Carolina University

Abstract

SELF-e is an innovative collaboration between *Library Journal* and BiblioBoard that enables public libraries to provide curated self-published e-books to library readers in a simple and elegant way. The session will give an overview of how the program was conceived, how it works and lessons academic libraries can take as it has been implemented across the country. Representatives from BiblioBoard, *Library Journal* and NC Live will discuss how SELF-e can represent certain populations on campus—that is, student, alumni, or faculty. Ms. Cook will discuss Issues in collecting Self-Published Books for Academic Libraries. Ms. Marsh will lead exploration with the panelists on how peer review can be incorporated into these types of publishing ecosystems.

BiblioBoard Platform and Technology

Bibliolabs has created a publishing program design for authors to independently publish electronic books. The SELF-e platform enables public libraries to accept self-published submissions from their local authors and make those e-books available to patrons via participating libraries throughout their state. Libraries can make these e-books available to patrons with no checkouts or returns, and no multiuser limitations. The platform is easy to use and can accommodate any author. Authors can use the simple submission process for PDF or ePUB manuscript formats.

How *Library Journal* Got Involved

LJ has heard from librarians that they need a way to find the best self-published books. Libraries don't want to ignore this market, but desperately need guidance on a vast segment of publishing that's only minimally covered by review journals. Libraries also struggle to meet the demands of local authors who wish to sell their materials to the collection, while still purchasing traditionally published materials that are in high demand. *LJ* has a need here too: self-published materials usually don't meet their review criteria, and *LJ* needs an alternative method of informing librarians about them.

For the past year, *LJ* worked with BiblioBoard to develop SELF-e, an e-book platform that provides the solution for self-published works for libraries. Self-published authors can submit their fiction books directly to the platform. *LJ* editors read them and identify the best ones, and these are made available to all subscribing libraries in genre modules in SELF-e. Books that are not selected for these modules can still be uploaded to a section of SELF-e that hosts books and makes them available to libraries in that state. In the future, they hope to expand SELF-e to cover nonfiction and materials for children.

How Can SELF-e and BiblioBoard Be Used in Academic and Public Libraries?

Eleanor Cook of East Carolina University Library addressed possible uses of BiblioBoard in academic libraries. The NC Live consortium (www.nclive.org) licensed BiblioBoard for all of its public and academic library members. Wake Forest University has already started planning new uses for the platform. Cook discussed how the platform could be used for faculty authors to create open textbooks and how the platform could be used for archival and repository support. One librarian at the presentation from Baltimore County Public Library expressed how useful SELF-e is for serving local indie authors and connecting them with library patrons. She explained that authors are constantly contacting them about getting their books to the local readers and SELF-e puts the tools in the hands of authors for e-book production. New e-books can automatically become part of the collections offered by BiblioLabs. SELF-e is now in beta test at the Los Angeles Public Library, San Diego County Public Library, Ohio's Cuyahoga County Public Library, the Arizona State Library (through Reading Arizona), and the State of Massachusetts (through the Massachusetts eBook Project).

Mitchell Davis, founder and Chief Business Officer of BiblioLabs, is eager for libraries to begin using the system. "This local library aspect is the part of SELF-e that accepts every author, no matter what self-publishing service they use or whether or not their book is accepted into the LJ-curated Module. It's a space to celebrate the state's local talent and enhance the community of a region's authors and readers. We're honored to be working with such great libraries for the initial release of the service."

Los Angeles Public Library's Catherine Royalty sees SELF-e as a way to develop the library's literary community in the digital sphere. Royalty says,

"We are very excited to be partnering with *Library Journal* and BiblioBoard to showcase emerging self-published authors at the library. We plan to use the product to foster a community of local authorship and to provide our patrons with access to exciting new literary voices."

Cook agreed that these concepts of outreach to local authors could also be utilized by academic libraries. The pilot project at East Carolina University is not yet off the ground but could be modeled after the NC Live site. This portal is called "Home Grown eBooks" and includes both fiction and non-fiction e-books from North Carolina publishers. Cook has been working with a couple of faculty authors at ECU who have published consumer-oriented books on such topics as financial literary for students and health care topics such as vegan diets for nursing mothers, for example. These topics are of general interest to the local population as well as to those on campus, but are not considered typical faculty research. Cook hopes that continued outreach to faculty about open publishing trends may present opportunities to utilize the BiblioBoard platform for materials that otherwise might go unpurchased. Academic libraries that specifically collect materials on a specific region and/or authors from their area might find the platform of use, especially since self-published materials are more likely to be available as e-books only in the future.

Techie Issues

Realizing Potential: Innovation Beyond the Cliché

Howard Burton, UNC Greensboro
Christine Fischer, UNC Greensboro

Abstract

How well have we been doing at exploiting the fruits of modern technology to develop truly innovative and impactful educational products for the university student and educator? How might we do better still? In this joint paper, Burton (creator of *Ideas Roadshow*) argues that a vital first step towards a more promising future lies in adopting a "first principles" methodology: identifying the specific pedagogical challenge before subsequently investigating how technology might productively address it, rather than unreflectively applying technological advances to existing frameworks. Meanwhile, Fischer, Head of Acquisitions at UNCG, responds to these claims by providing an independent librarian's perspective.

Taking Stock

All too often technological progress gets confused with contextual innovation. When the context in question is strictly technological (the production of a newer, better smartphone, say), there is naturally no difference between the two. But for those who work outside the domain of technological development per se, it is essential to consistently ask how new advances in technology might be most productively applied to their particular environments.

This straightforward, common-sense notion can sometimes be harder to apply in practice than one might naively expect, particularly for librarians and other purveyors of high-level intellectual and educational content. In a world where "information consumers" are madly scrambling towards the widely hyped "next best thing," holding one's head above the fray to deliberately investigate best practices and calmly explore substantive possibilities can often prove to be extremely challenging. Yet it is little short of essential in order to make fundamental progress.

Lessons From the Past

Historians of science will point out that there is often a pronounced delay between the discovery of new forms of technology and their direct

application towards the creation of truly transformative (i.e., disruptive) products. Inevitably, in the first instance at least, modern technologies are simply unthinkingly applied to older, established idioms.

So it was, for example, that the advent of television initially resulted in the none too riveting spectacle of news presenters being filmed reading their reports as if on radio. Half a century later, we see a strikingly similar phenomenon occurring within the educational sphere, as the development of widely affordable, high-resolution video cameras has principally resulted in merely recording standard talks and lectures.

So much, so familiar. But an added complication arises in the modern context: that of the increasingly democratizing effect of contemporary information technologies. Whereas in the past, the transition from radio to television was an opportunity exclusively in the purview of those select view who could afford to own a television station or run a film studio, the barrier to entry for both production *and* dissemination of high-quality videos has effectively been reduced to zero.

Meanwhile, a very different challenge exists for the modern librarian: with so much broadly similar material "out there," how to choose?[1] What are the appropriate criteria for determining

---

[1] Much has been written on the modern challenges academic librarians have of curating appropriate content. See, for example, Walters, T., and Skinner, K. (2011, March), "New roles for new times: Digital curation for preservation," *Report prepared for the American Association of Research Libraries*;

Wolfe, J., Naylor, T., and Drueke, J. (2010), "The role of the academic reference librarian in the learning commons." *Faculty publications, UNL Libraries*. Paper 221; Bell, J. and Shank, J. (2004), "The blended librarian," *College and Research Libraries News, 372.*

the maximum utility of existing films, multi-media and video material? What sorts of highly relevant content might already exist, buried in archives or in huge, aggregated collections?

Locating overlooked jewels is one thing. But, as noted above, by far the greatest opportunity for long-term impact lies in developing innovative, transformative products that directly capitalize on the potential that the new technology suddenly makes possible.[2]

Might it be possible for librarians to take a more proactive role in this key activity, dynamically influencing matters so that increased numbers of highly innovative products get created in the first place?

First Principles

In order for librarians to elevate themselves to a more active position as innovation catalysts, it is essential to take a step back and focus on first principles of the teaching and educational experience.

What are the core challenges of today's academic environment? What sorts of products might concretely address those challenges? How might they be used and accessed? By whom?

Answers to these questions will inevitably vary widely from institution to institution and from individual to individual. But we believe that the following represent three widespread concerns:

1. Intimacy: As class sizes swell and communications technology extends the academic environment (real or virtual) to ever-increasing numbers of participants, a constant concern is how to preserve (or in some instances, reestablish, or even create) a key sense of intimacy between student and faculty member. Might it be possible to harness the very technology that is in some ways structurally weakening these bonds of intimacy to

create specific tools that will explicitly redress this?

2. Flexibility: The modern academic experience is much less rigidly structured than it once was, both in terms of an increasing overlap between previously segmented subject areas and an ever-expanding profile of the "typical student" (together with that of the "typical professor or expert"). How might we create new tools to explicitly assist this natural trend towards a more flexible approach to the academic experience, both in terms of subject areas and their participants?

3. Critical thinking: The quest to instill rigorous critical-thinking skills in students is hardly particular to the modern era, yet remains the sine qua non of the academic experience and a vital measure by which all academic institutions are judged. In an age of substantially increased distractions to all participants, it is very much worth examining how we might use modern technology to develop enhanced critical-thinking tools.

The *Ideas Roadshow* Experience

These, then, are three fundamental concerns that we are convinced are common to all in today's higher education space. Doubtless there are more. But in the interests of providing a concrete example of the prospective utility of this "first principles" approach to the development of new pedagogical tools, we describe how this framework clearly maps onto our motivations in creating *Ideas Roadshow*.

1. Intimacy by proxy: Recognizing that the technological advances responsible for small, affordable, high-quality video cameras entail an inherent portability, we concluded that a productive way to establish a strong sense of intimacy between student and faculty was by developing informal recordings, one-on-

---

[2] See, for example, Zheng (John) Wang. (n.d.). "Co-Curation: New strategies, roles, services, and opportunities for libraries in the post-web era and the digital media context," *Libri*. http://dx.doi.org/10.1515/libri-2013-0006

one conversations with leading domain specialists in the comfort and privacy of their homes or offices. While this technique is clearly distinct from actual exchanges between students and professors, and is obviously not meant as a substitute for such interaction, our experience is that it nonetheless can provide an added measure of intimacy that is increasingly lacking in the contemporary academic realm. By explicitly constructing a dynamic of dialogue between a curious non-specialist and a domain specialist, we establish a proxy for the student so that he can feel some sense of genuine participation in the discussion. Meanwhile, by chatting in a relaxed fashion about her ideas in a familiar environment, the expert naturally projects a more accessible and less formal demeanor, excited by the prospect of simply focusing on the subject matter devoid of any other personal or administrative constraints. The goal is thus to develop a substantial treatment of ideas combined with personal anecdote in such a way that the student will naturally find both deeply motivating and fully accessible.

2. Flexibility through interdisciplinarity: Academic administrators have long recognized and encouraged interdisciplinary thinking, to the extent that it is something of a near-tautology to claim that truly innovative ideas almost always occur on the boundaries between disciplines. But stating such sentiments is quite different from understanding how, precisely, to move forwards: how to concretely navigate between the Scylla of specialized, impenetrable silos and the Charybdis of some naive, wooly "everything is connected" worldview. After all, disciplinary boundaries exist for a reason: studying medieval history is obviously different from studying molecular biology or music theory or mathematics. How, then, to make connections while rigorously maintaining high standards? How to pursue academic

excellence while encouraging flexibility? We concluded that the challenge can be met in two largely overlapping ways: by choosing a mode of engagement that would naturally highlight the benefits of interdisciplinary thinking, while actively selecting interlocutors who were particularly successful role models of flexible, multidisciplinary approaches throughout their own highly productive research careers. By combining a naturally multidisciplinary format with the opportunity to engage naturally broadminded and wide-ranging participants, we consciously aspired to create a flexible, multidisciplinary outcome in a straightforward, uncontrived way.

3. Critical thinking from substantive questioning: All educators focused on the development of critical-thinking skills value the importance of questioning received wisdom as an essential aspect of personal intellectual development. Yet however broad-based the understanding might be that students ought to routinely engage their curiosity through active questioning, the modern curriculum is typically so charged with content that there is scant opportunity for the professor to properly cover core material, let alone stimulate additional student questioning. Moreover, even when such occasions exist in principle, the social dynamics of an undergraduate experience often make it extremely problematic for students to indulge in any fundamental questioning that might inadvertently expose them to ridicule from their peers. For all that the time-honored mantra, "There's no such thing as a stupid question" is consistently invoked in classroom settings throughout the nation and around the world, most educators will agree that the barrier to spontaneous student interaction is usually still prohibitively high. Ideas *Roadshow* explicitly addresses this issue by creating a format where the students' proxy unhesitatingly asks probing, often basic,

questions to the domain expert, thereby triggering a wealth of supplementary content while tangibly demonstrating to the students the efficacy of open, honest engagement. Moreover, our experience is that most guests clearly value the opportunity to clarify and justify their views through an open and respectful exchange, even to the point of admitting that the conversational format helped them better frame, and sometimes even better appreciate the subtleties of, their respective positions.

Conclusions and Future Possibilities

Whether or not the reader is convinced that *Ideas Roadshow* achieves all that we set out to do is, of course, not the essential point of this paper. The methodology inherent in this "first principles" approach naturally transcends any one product or producer; and different institutions will unquestionably have different educational needs and correspondingly different pedagogical priorities.

But what is much less debatable in our mind is that the time is clearly ripe for individual institutions to drive the innovation process forwards by *first* focusing on their specific pedagogical needs and desires and *then* explicitly harnessing technology as an active enabler of those needs.

Such an attitude will also require, we believe, a subtle shift in the interactions between librarians, professors, and students, requiring all to be considerably more entrepreneurial and engaged in the production of innovative educational materials. Many postsecondary institutions already contain a wealth of practical and theoretical talent on their own campuses at the student, staff, and faculty level (computer gaming, modeling, ICT, film schools) that could, and should, be leveraged to produce high-level bespoke products at many distinct levels.

Prospective philanthropists and community representatives from the ICT sector (a growing force in philanthropic support and governance) could play an increasing participatory role with

both targeted funding and in-kind assistance. Student and faculty feedback on existing materials and suggestions for enhanced products should be actively solicited, together with a variety of practical student research projects to dynamically test the waters. This article is primarily concerned with educational and pedagogical materials, but, of course, the same principles apply to more ostensibly research-related content, many of which would naturally lend themselves to this framework.

What does all this mean, specifically, for libraries and librarians?

We believe that librarians could, and likely should, play a much more active role as interinstitutional coordinators and purveyors of innovative content, proactively seeking out productive partnerships with forward-thinking publishers when the occasion demands, and going it alone when it doesn't.

By both experience and disposition, librarians are highly sensitive to specific anxieties and frustrations of both faculty and students, and thus are ideally poised to make active contributions towards innovative solutions, rather than simply finding themselves in a fundamentally reactive position of sifting through a steady bombardment of often inappropriate mass-market solutions.

Moreover, as the information-content centers unwedded to any particular subject area, yet responsible for all, academic libraries are ideally placed to take a more active leadership role on behalf of the entire institution to directly drive the creation of the next generation of innovative products that will explicitly serve that specific community's teaching and research interests.

Of course, not all such resources will be produced locally; and there are many occasions when librarians will naturally opt to seek out productive partnerships with external vendors to most productively improve the faculty and student experience.

But whether such solutions are developed internally or externally, we maintain that the primary determining factor to success lies in adopting the aforementioned first principles approach of *first* identifying key educational needs before *then* turning one's attention to how current technology might specifically meet it.

—*Howard Burton, CEO, Open Agenda Publishing*

A Librarian's Response

Academic librarians seek ways of working with faculty and students to enhance and support the learning process through instruction, services, and collections. There is value in first determining educational needs and then looking at how technology can help to fulfill those needs. Librarians listen to faculty and students and then seek out effective solutions. Sometimes that can be promoting services or resources that are already available. It could mean developing internal technology projects or finding the right provider externally. Networking with publishers, vendors, and other content providers offers opportunities for librarians to share expectations and needs of the academic community.

How Do We Know the Needs of Faculty and Students?

At the University of North Carolina at Greensboro (UNCG), classified by The Carnegie Foundation as a Research University with High Research Activity and serving 16,000 FTE students, the librarians actively connect with faculty. Faculty members talk to librarians about changes in their curriculum or in methods of instruction by working directly with Library Liaisons. It can be fairly informal situations as well, where a librarian may be working on a campus committee or serving in some other way that leads to conversations in which a problem is shared, and the library can respond.

Assessment is a key method for determining campus needs for users of all kinds. In 2008 and 2012 the University Libraries conducted LibQual+ surveys that included comment sections that were very helpful in identifying areas of service that needed improvement or were newly recognized. The library worked cooperatively with campus IT and the Office of Research to conduct a faculty

survey on research and data needs, including data storage and data management plans. Other surveys and assessment methods are used, so that in conjunction with personal interactions, informal conversations, meetings with departments, and direct requests, librarians can partner with faculty to answer needs.

Climate in Higher Education

In all aspects of our culture, organizations are expected to be nimble, responsive to consumer desire for customized experiences and products, and able to incorporate the latest technology in serving users.

The *NMC Horizon Report: 2014 Higher Education Edition* offers a look at trends and challenges in higher education technology. The New Media Consortium and EDUCAUSE produced the report, and several of the issues raised can inform the process of identifying a need and then using technology to develop a solution. One of the developments described in the *Horizon Report* is the flipped classroom model. Students watch streaming films or clips, listen to online lectures or podcasts, consult open educational resources, and work in online communities with fellow students prior to class, so that classroom time can be spent on adapting what they've learned to practical, collaborative projects and discussion. Academic libraries support this by providing resources and also services that go beyond information literacy to teaching and supporting media literacy and digital literacy in conjunction with the activities of the faculty.

Media at UNCG

The media component of our collections is evolving quickly. The need for streaming film accelerated in the summer of 2013 when a significant number of language classes were moved from face-to-face instruction to online instruction. We very quickly learned about streaming rights and added new streaming platforms. Faculty needed to be able to offer streaming for films they had formerly shown from DVDs in the classroom. The flipped classroom model demands that libraries offer a variety of streaming film options to accommodate classroom instruction that is augmented by preparation outside of class. With that model in mind, it is clear that the Ideas Roadshow films could be successfully incorporated into curricula. The films have a question and answer approach but are truly more of a conversation than an interview. The films could inspire local conversations and film production as well.

There are numerous payment models available for streaming film including one-time purchase with hosting fees, licensing for a semester or a year or more, evidence-based with use statistics determining the make-up of future collections, and patron driven acquisition. UNCG offers many streaming film platforms, and all those payment models are in use. Just this month the Ideas Roadshow films became available via the Kanopy platform, which now makes it possible for students and faculty to access the titles.

Striving to solve the needs of faculty for streaming film has resulted in the University Libraries testing a variety of models for licensing streaming media because the providers and platforms needed by faculty to serve their curricular needs cannot be handled by one primary vendor. Actively communicating with the providers offers an opportunity for librarians to share the needs of the academic community, and providers gain information that informs further innovation.

—*Christine Fischer, Head of Acquisitions Department, UNCG*

References

Johnson, L., Adams Becker, S., Estrada, V., Freeman, A. (2014). *NMC horizon report: 2014 higher education edition*. Austin, TX: The New Media Consortium. Retrieved from http://cdn.nmc.org/media/2014 -nmc-horizon-report-he-EN-SC.pdf

You've Licensed It. Now What?

Sarah E. McCleskey, Head of Access Services, Film and Media, Hofstra University
Christine M. Fischer, Head of Acquisitions, University of North Carolina at Greensboro
Steven D. Milewski, Social Work and Digital Media Technologies Librarian, University of Tennessee Knoxville
Jim Davis, President of Docuseek, LLC

Abstract

While libraries face challenges in building usage of a new medium like streaming video, strategic, active marketing by libraries, with support from vendors, can overcome these challenges. Time-tested marketing strategies, as well as leveraging new promotional tools can help the library attain the usage that justifies the investment in new media. If you license, with a little help, they *will* come.

Unfortunately, the "build it and they will come" phenomenon does not apply to library media collections. The active marketing of new library resources is one of the necessary chores to ensure that patrons know about and use the resources. This is especially true about new media formats, and in particular the relatively new resource of streaming media. This paper will look at the challenges libraries face in promoting the use of streaming media collections, and strategies employed by academic libraries to meet that challenge.

A Framework for Thinking About Library Marketing

Much of the literature related to the marketing of electronic resources for libraries mentions the SWOT analysis (Dubicki 2009, Smith 2011). A SWOT analysis is a structured planning method used to evaluate the strengths, weaknesses, opportunities and threats involved in a project (Rogers, 2001).

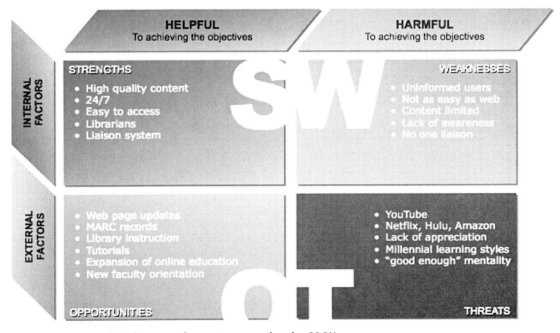

Figure 1. SWOT Analysis by www.showeet.com used under CC BY.

It involves specifying the objective of the project (in our case, marketing to the library's primary users, faculty and students) and identifying the internal and external factors that are favorable and unfavorable to achieve that objective (in our case, increased use of licensed video content). Strengths and weaknesses are internal factors: strengths are characteristics of the project that give it an advantage over others; weaknesses are characteristics that place the project at a disadvantage relative to others. Opportunities and threats are external factors: opportunities are elements that the project could exploit to its advantage, and threats are elements in the environment that could cause trouble for the project. Identification of these critical elements provides a foundation for strategic marketing planning.

When looking at marketing streaming video resources, the strengths are easy to outline: Libraries offer high quality, authoritative content in easy-to-access, 24/7 format; skilled librarians are available to teach users about these resources; many libraries have a liaison system in place where liaisons serve as marketers to faculty, etc.

Weaknesses are unfortunately even easier to outline: users may need training, the content is not as easy to use as other web resources, we can't own or offer access to everything, there is a lack of awareness on part of students and faculty, many libraries have subject liaisons for each department or school, but video content does not have a particular liaison (so typically the media librarian must try to reach all departments and schools, rather than targeting a select few).

The library's opportunities are many. The library's home page and LibGuides can be constantly updated to reflect new acquisitions. MARC records, offered by most vendors, make the videos available via our online catalogs and discovery platforms for "one stop shopping." These resources can be highlighted in library instruction sessions, and librarians have the opportunity to create classes or tutorials specifically geared to video resources. Online education is expanding and thus the need for streaming content should be increasing. Librarians

have opportunities to reach out to new faculty in orientation sessions and so on.

Threats, however, are also many. Online services like YouTube, Netflix, Amazon Prime, Hulu, as well as file sharing sites are familiar and easier to use and perhaps more convenient than the library's video offerings. Students don't automatically appreciate the library's resources as superior research tools. Millennial learning patterns (e.g., peer-to-peer teaching and self-teaching behavior) and the "good enough" mentality also present obstacles (Smith 2011).

So given that libraries take the leap of faith and license as many titles as possible, what are strategies that libraries can use to maximize the use the resources they have assembled? How can they maximize the strengths, leverage the opportunities, minimize the weaknesses and counter the threats facing the media collection?

The University of North Carolina at Greensboro Case

The University Libraries of the University of North Carolina at Greensboro have offered streaming film options to their users for years, and recently the resources offered have increased in response to research needs, student use of media, expansion of online instruction, shifting of face-to-face instruction to online classes, and the flipped classroom model with students viewing films outside of class for later discussion as a group. Faculty need to know the range of options available to them. In a continuing economic climate of reduced collections budgets, getting the maximum use from resources is crucial.

Information on licensed streaming media is gathered in a LibGuide that includes lists of resources, help for faculty on embedding links in the learning management system, acquisition policies, and notes on public performance rights. A copyright guide for the campus has a section devoted to instructors. It offers guidance on Fair Use, the TEACH Act, and video in the classroom. When librarians receive inquiries from faculty, the LibGuide and copyright information can be shared to help with planning how media is used in the curriculum as well as for campus events.

At the start of the 2014-15 academic year, the University Libraries arranged for webinars by representatives from Docuseek2, Kanopy, and Alexander Street Press. Library Liaisons to academic departments and any staff who work with faculty on acquiring or scheduling media were invited. The sessions offered a chance to see what kinds of films and which producers were available from each source. The method that the Libraries use to acquire and pay for each platform varies—evidence based, patron driven acquisition, and purchase with annual hosting fees—and the group conversation made that easier to understand.

Following the webinar sessions Library Liaisons were able to share information with faculty representatives from the departments, offering links to specific films or collections and simply promoting the streaming films to encourage use.

A Spotlight section on the University Libraries home page includes graphics and links to streaming film platforms in rotation with other current awareness items as a means of reaching visitors to the web site.

In early spring 2015, the University Libraries will host a Faculty Center Takeover event. These opportunities for faculty to gather informally to meet, socialize, share food and drink, and learn about services and organizations across campus are scheduled one afternoon each month. The Libraries' event will include a demonstration on streaming film.

One of the Libraries' priorities for the academic year strategic plan includes promoting streaming films to faculty to increase awareness and usage. Formalizing the effort in that way makes it clear that the Libraries intend to take action in marketing those resources. The response from faculty will be invaluable in making future selection decisions.

The University of Tennessee in Knoxville Case

The University of Tennessee in Knoxville is a public land grant university with an FTE of 26,000. While most classes at UT are still predominantly face-to-

face, the number of online classes is growing and several programs are online. Online, blended, distance, and even flipped classes need electronic resources from the Library, including streamed video. The UT Libraries has been working to meet these needs. The question with video streaming (and many other library resources) is: If you license it, will they use the resources? The answer is a qualified "yes."

While there is a need, and many times an articulated need, there is often a disconnect between what is available and student and instructor awareness of availability. So, they will only use it if there is a need, if it is accessible, *and above all, if they are aware that the Library has it.*

The UT Libraries licenses video collections from vendors such as Alexander Street Press, Films Media Group, Kanopy, and Criterion-on-Demand USA. Individual titles are licensed on platforms from Docuseek2, Residence Life Cinema, and New Day Digital. In addition, the Libraries has its own server for showing licensed steaming files, vendor provided or digitized in house, from Ambrose, Bullfrog, Insight Media, Kino, and many others.

Because these types of offerings are relatively new, at least in streaming format, colleges and universities find themselves in the position of having to promote their own materials. While new services have always needed to be promoted, users are often surprised and uninformed about the range of e-resources now available through libraries. For this reason, academic libraries are using more resources and techniques toward promoting the use of materials in an online environment. This promotes use and improves return on investment. Many vendors are aware of this need and have been supplying resources to aid in promoting the use of their products.

At the UT Libraries, these resources are still promoted in many of the traditional ways. Instructor requested titles remain one of the best ways to guarantee usage. Word of mouth advertising works but is unpredictable. Including the titles and links in the Library's catalog with MARC records, and in some cases individual cataloging, increases discoverability. LibGuides both promote collections and provide contact information for questions or problems. The UT Libraries' databases site also lists all video streaming collections and platforms at the collection level.

There are other strategies for advertising collections and for encouraging the promotion of streaming collections. First, doing a trial of a video streaming collection can be useful in increasing awareness, especially if it is requested by a subject librarian or a discipline-based faculty member. Never assume that simply linking to a trial will get the resource noticed. Subject librarians, in general, are good resources for promoting video streaming resources and enlisting them for this purpose ensures they themselves are aware of the collections. One successful way of promoting streaming collections internally has been to hold a "brown bag" session for librarians to learn about collections and platforms and to discuss how they might be used. A quick lunchtime presentation about new streaming resources is a relaxed way to introduce new types of resources in an informal environment.

Directly marketing to new faculty and graduate teaching assistants through orientations is another way to encourage the use of video streaming in the classroom. These are often groups who are interested in learning about resources for teaching support and may be more likely to readily adopt technology. At the UT Libraries, streaming collections are promoted as an important teaching resource in venues such as: new faculty orientation, Summer Teaching Institute (for new faculty and instructors), graduate teaching assistant (GTA) orientation, and the "Best Practices in Teaching Program" (teacher training program for GTAs). New faculty and GTAs are often more receptive to resources if they can see them in action. For this reason, we created a Prezi presentation demonstrating how streamed video could be integrated into a student's presentation, an assignment, and specific teaching situation.

Collections are also promoted to students. UT Libraries has two of its own Open Houses, one for graduates students and another for undergraduates for which video streaming gets its own table to show and tell about these resources. If possible, it is best to set up a monitor display to demonstrate films and special features to the students. Additional venues for reaching undergraduate students include: "Taste of Tennessee New Student Orientation," and other student events aimed at showcasing resources and services.

The Library also makes significant attempts at outreach and is fortunate to have two librarians dedicated to student outreach. Ingrid Ruffin has created a "Library Takeout" program focused on the Residence Halls and actively promotes some video collections to students in the dorms. Each month she also creates a marketing and communications display with chalk markers on a window in the central corridor of Hodges Library to help promote the feature film streaming collections.

While the library does create promotional materials, streaming vendors themselves often provide posters, fliers, image files, and other resources to help promote their video products. They are either available from their site, or by request from vendor representatives. Some vendors, like Films on Demand, have even created "Usage Booster" widgets that are subject-focused search boxes for their products that can be embedded in web pages. The important thing is to ask. While not all vendors have marketing kits and widgets, many have posters and handouts. Some don't, but most do.

While there is no "silver bullet" for video streaming promotion, it is important to be proactive in this endeavor so that more patrons can learn of existing resources. This will also encourage them to begin to look for and use other streaming resources.

The Docuseek2 Case

From the vendor perspective, there is obviously a financial interest in helping libraries promote their streaming collection. The rough math is summed up in the equation

$$usage = renewals$$

With the subscription licensing model, the vendor shares a mutual interest with the library of maximizing use of the resources.

There may be other considerations for vendors, though, besides the economic ones. From the perspective of the curator, whether at the library or the vendor, each title embodies a voice and an intention. The resources are intended to be (in the case of video) watched and appreciated. Viewing the films (and the same would hold true of other media) in theory will inform and enrich, and maybe even enthuse the viewer. The world, hopefully, will be a better place. The vendor and the librarian are two conductors on the road from the author to reader or producer to watcher.

The vendor can assist the library in promoting its materials in several ways. The minimal assistance is to provide MARC records, as well as other forms of metadata for third party discovery services that the library may use. The content must be discoverable before it can be found. Custom add-on tools, like Films Media Group's widgets can further enhance discoverability of the content. Once discovered, it is also essential for the vendor to provide easy to use tools to support integration into course pages and course management systems to facilitate use. Usability and reliability are important to ensure that the viewing experience is a positive one, and the patron returns for more.

The vendor can also actively assist the library in the promotion of content. The vendor can provide promotional materials, for example, in the form of flyers as mentioned above. Vendor-sourced tutorials and webinars provide another set of tools for the librarian-as-marketer.

Another level of support can come from website tools to assist not only the librarian-marketer, but users as well to leverage social media to spread the word about library content. This might include options to broadcast information about a resource via Twitter or Facebook, or to use email to share information about a specific resource or group of resources. Docuseek2, for example, provides a tool for librarians to email search results from within its web application. The librarian can search for titles on, say,

environmental anthropology, and send the results to a professor, with the library's links to the resources.

Still another level of marketing support consists of direct communication between the vendor and faculty and students at the institution. Vendor direct mail or direct email marketing, as well as other forms of marketing to faculty is a traditional way of raising awareness of specific resources. Vendor presence at academic conferences is another traditional way of building interest in resources. These activities are typically undertaken to drive presale or prelicense interest. But similar activities can be undertaken to drive "post-sale" interest—driving use of the resource after it has been licensed.

For example, Docuseek2 has been experimenting with such postsale marketing campaigns. Its distribution partners attend academic conferences, and collect the names of faculty interested in their films. Docuseek2 then emails the faculty at institutions that have licensed its content with specific instructions on accessing the films on their campus. Proactively, the company has screen-scraped faculty names and emails from institutional directories, focusing on key disciplines that match the foci of the Docuseek2 content. The company then individually emails faculty to alert them of the resource available to them, with links to the library's collection. In addition, the company has collected emails and social media information of student organizations in related areas. For example, the Docuseek2 streaming media collection includes a concentration of films about the environment and current environmental issues, so it looked for student organizations focused on the environment. The emails included search results for the organization's focus, including the campus link to the resources. Preliminary results of this campaign have been encouraging, with a strong increase in the number of views at the target institutions.

This experiment points to the potential of social media tools in micro-marketing to specific segments of the institutional audience and even individuals about single resources or logical groups of resources. These tools are relatively inexpensive to deploy, and the upside (e.g., the potential of a resource "going viral" on the campus) is great. The main cost associated with using social media tools is labor, and this can be an area where the vendor can help out.

Conclusion

While libraries face challenges in building usage of a new medium like streaming video, strategic, active marketing by libraries, with support from vendors, can overcome these challenges. Time-tested marketing strategies, as well as leveraging new promotional tools can help the library attain the usage that justifies the investment in new media. If you license, with a little help, they *will* come.

The accompanying slides for this presentation are available at http://misc.docuseek2.com/files /Charleston_2014_combined.pptx

References

Dubicki, E. (2007). Basic marketing and promotion concepts. *Serials Librarian*, *53*(3), 5-15.

Rogers, Stuart C. (2001). *Marketing strategies, tactics, and techniques: A handbook for practitioners*. Westport: Quorum Books.

Smith, D. A. 2011. Strategic marketing of library resources and services. *College & Undergraduate Libraries*, *18*(4), 333-349.

Metadata Challenges in Library Discovery Systems

Pascal Calarco, Associate University Librarian, Research and Digital Discovery Services, University of Waterloo

Lettie Conrad, Executive Manager, Online Products, SAGE

Rachel Kessler, Product Manager, Primo Central, Ex Libris

Michael Vandenburg, Associate University Librarian, Queens University

Abstract

With discovery systems such as Summon, EDS, and Primo Central, patrons can search nearly all of their libraries' resources from a single platform. In order to create this experience, data from disparate sources must be normalized and unified into one index.

In this session, we discussed some of the metadata challenges facing each of the parties involved in library discovery; the library, the publisher, and the discovery system provider. Libraries must normalize their bibliographic records to make them compatible with the discovery system's schema. Publishers need to create mechanisms to regularly export records with meaningful metadata, and the discovery system provider must integrate metadata from these sources while ensuring the best possible user experience.

We also touched on the recent guidelines of the NISO Open Discovery Initiative. The guidelines include goals such as "to streamline the process by which information providers, discovery service providers, and librarians work together to better serve libraries and their users." The session will explore how these guidelines can be implemented along with some of the challenges and will include a discussion with the audience.

Introduction

With discovery systems such as Summon, EDS, and Primo Central, patrons can search nearly all of their libraries' resources from a single platform. In order to create this experience, data from disparate sources must be normalized and unified into one index.

In this session, we discussed some of the metadata challenges facing each of the parties involved in library discovery; the library, the publisher, and the discovery system provider. Libraries must normalize their bibliographic records to make them compatible with the discovery system's schema. Publishers need to create mechanisms to regularly export records with meaningful metadata, and the discovery system provider must integrate metadata from these sources while ensuring the best possible user experience.

We also touched on the recent guidelines of the NISO Open Discovery Initiative. The guidelines include goals such as "to streamline the process by which information providers, discovery service providers, and librarians work together to better serve libraries and their users." The session will explore how these guidelines can be implemented along with some of the challenges and will include a discussion with the audience.

For Publishers

SAGE sees our participation in library discovery services as critical to our success as a member of the scholarly communication supply chain. New resources at SAGE enable closer partnership with other members of this supply chain, to openly share our vision and product strategy, to listen to peers in other organizations, to understand their needs and priorities, and to collaborate toward solutions to share challenges—such as those we're all experiencing with the metadata required for discovery of scholarly content.

To optimize the visibility and performance of SAGE content in discovery systems, like Primo, we dedicate a good deal of resource to operationalize distribution of high-quality metadata. These come in the form of:

- Content architecture—to ensure the full text of our content is well structured and fully marked up.

- Industry standards—it's important to SAGE that we're in compliance with the proper data standards.

- Systems development—for storage and delivery.

- Dedicated staff—SAGE has put a library discovery work group in place, made up of product and technical analysts along with reps from across the business.

This new group at SAGE recently conducted a SWOT of our metadata in order to crystalize our understanding of the challenges and changes we're facing. Here are the highlights:

- New content types—for SAGE, when we decide to add new types of content to our publishing programs, we struggle to establish metadata expertise, define process and develop our human and systems workflows.

- Manual versus automated—like many companies, these new workflows often begin by significant hand-wrought metadata, so we must eventually invest in systems development to automate these new process.

- Accuracy—keeping an eye on data accuracy along the way and developing appropriate QA routines that don't slow down publication.

- Industry standards—NISO and others are doing yeoman's work to establish clear protocols for metadata, but there isn't a published standard for every single metadata entity that we publish, so we sometimes find ourselves tripping a bit in the standards gaps.

For the most part, journals metadata is the most mature and the most automated, and has the benefit of the greatest number of industry standards. However, there are still moving targets, as the industry continues to evolve. Chief among these are around open access. Hybrid OA is a challenge for all members of the supply chain. So far, we've not hit on a great way to identify open articles in traditional subscription journals—largely because we've not arrived at a standard metadata element to indicate OA status and license types in our FT XML. Our prevailing journal markup protocol (now JATS) does not yet have an agreed upon identifier for OA articles or terms.

For SAGE, we're seeing a range of challenges around article-level workflows. Most of our systems—and our indexing partners' systems—are organized around the traditional issue/volume model. So, ahead-of-print articles, hybrid OA articles, and any other new model publishing at an article level create challenges for assembly, storage, and distribution of journal metadata.

Metadata for e-books and e-reference have some unique challenges. First, we don't have the benefit of journals' consistency in content structures—instead, in this category, we're dealing with encyclopedias, dictionaries, handbooks, monographs, case studies, and others, none of which share the similar formats. Some have abstracts, some don't. Some have references, some don't. These diverse types of content demand a good deal of manual work and limit our ability to automate some metadata creation and delivery steps.

Since you can't really set your watch to e-books metadata, the indexing routines and practices of our discovery partners is also diverse and variable. This further undermines our ability to standardize and automate our own processes. Some indexers—like Google Scholar—just won't touch scholarly ebooks with a 10-foot pole due to the chaotic landscape of e-books metadata.

Not surprisingly, e-books and e-reference data standards are also variable. There is no JATS for books—would that be BATS?—so everyone along the supply chain is struggling and you might say "storming" toward more consistency routines and data protocols.

Finally, I want to touch on both data and video metadata—what we sometimes joke is still the "wild west" of metadata. I don't mean to oversimplify either type of content, but these each have very similar patterns at the moment. If ebooks/e-reference metadata are diverse, then metadata for data and video content is pure anarchy. When we ask indexers and standards bodies for guidance on marking up these formats, we get a lot of head scratching—understandably so. Some things are becoming clear over time—such as the fact that both data and video assets require rich text-based content to make search and discovery remotely possible. But, we're still dealing with a void of standards for video transcripts or narratives to accompany datasets. And the published guidelines for standard identifiers—such as DOIs or ISBNs—are still lacking clarity in handling these new forms of scholarly output.

So what is a poor publisher to do with all these steep hills to climb? At SAGE, we believe it's vitally important for all vested parties to actively participate in the standards formation process. We are NISO voting members and active in committees such as the Open Discovery Initiative. We conduct original research into discovery and metadata practices, we publish whitepapers on these topics, in an effort to share our knowledge and continually learn from our industry peers.

We're also ramping up our internal metadata practices with more formal routines for generating and enhancing our content metadata. That Library Discovery WG mentioned earlier is now meeting more regularly to develop rubrics for assessing our data quality and compliance. We're also developing some internal standards and guidelines. For example, after a great deal of research conducted this year, we're putting together guidelines for all SAGE teams to use in our application and use of DOIs and other identifiers.

In general, though, we're practicing the art of flexibility, keeping our ears to the ground and working toward more agility reacting to developing standards and new protocols as metadata continues to evolve.

For Discovery Systems

The key challenge is to pull content from disparate sources and normalize it into a uniform database that contains records that are "useful" to library patrons. While "useful" is a vague term, the objectives of normalization can be broken down into three main goals:

1. *To make the content discoverable*—users must be able to surface the records. If the associated metadata is incorrect, for example, the record could be difficult to find.

2. *To facilitate delivery*—while many consider the primary function of a discovery system to be the enabling of finding relevant materials, the ability to actually reach the full text of that content is equally important. After all, most researchers will not find a citation useful if they cannot actually access the material. If the metadata is insufficient to allow users to access material via a link resolver or other means, the record is not considered "useful."

3. *To maintain a visually appealing interface*—content should be scannable to facilitate easy skimming of result sets. Additionally, metadata should be uniform in order to maintain a uniform, professional appearance.

The achievement of these objectives is often dependent on the quality of the metadata supplied by data providers. Below are three examples of poor quality metadata supplied to Ex Libris Primo by various providers.

Example 1

"Microsoft's antitrust fine—Sin of omission"

Information in publication title field:

[t][The economsst]

This obvious typo can affect all three of the above objectives and despite the fact that it is clearly a mistake can be difficult to catch among one billion records.

Example 2

"Valuation of mangrove services of Andaman and Nicobar Islands, India"

Information in the date field:

date=1013

The full text of this article lists the date as 2013. These types of errors are relatively easy to catch as rules can be created to flag records with dates from before a given year, i.e., 1450, the year the printing press was invented.

Example 3

"Book review corner"

Information in the resource type field:

<cto:doctype>cp</cto:doctype>

("cp" stands for conference proceeding!)

This document is clearly a book review and not a conference proceeding. Checks can be performed to catch some errors, i.e., does the title of the article contain the words "book review?" However, many mislabeled resource types go unnoticed if there are no obvious cues in the metadata.

Another area where discovery providers find it challenging to normalize data is authors. In addition to authority challenges, a standard has not yet been set for the format in which the data should be delivered. Simple issues such as punctuation and spacing can be easily fixed through normalization. However, how the names themselves are reported in the xml structure, can be more problematic. In the following example, you can see three different ways of providing the same information.

Provider 1

<author>

Lei Yang, Yajuan She, Shihua Zhao, Shihai Yue,

Qian Wang, Aiping Hu, Wei Zhang

</author>

Provider 2

700 1 {{[a][Hu, Aiping]}}

700 1 {{[a][She, Yajuan]}}

700 1 {{[a][Wang, Qian]}}

700 1 {{[a][Yang, Lei]}}

700 1 {{[a][Yue, Shihai]}}

700 1 {{[a][Zhang, Wei]}}

700 1 {{[a][Zhao, Shihua]}}

Provider 3

<preferred-name>

<ce:initials>L.</ce:initials>

<ce:indexed-name>Yang L.</ce:indexed-name>

<ce:surname>Yang</ce:surname>

<ce:given-name>Lei</ce:given-name>

</preferred-name>

<preferred-name>

<ce:initials>Y.</ce:initials>

<ce:indexed-name>She Y.</ce:indexed-name>

<ce:surname>She</ce:surname>

<ce:given-name>Yajuan</ce:given-name>

</preferred-name>

The more the fields are broken down, the easier it is for discovery providers to understand what they are receiving. Provider 3's data, for example, contains no ambiguity regarding which is the first name and which is the last or where one name begins and the other ends. This makes it easier for discovery providers to normalize the data and reduces the chance of parsing errors. An author name, which is normalized incorrectly, can lead to issues with all three objectives listed above. Ex

Libris is beginning to index ORCIDs within Primo Central records, which should disambiguate author names as ORCID's popularity rises.

It would also be exceedingly helpful to discovery services if a standard cataloging unit was created for discovery. The best way to explain this point is by means of an example.

The journal *Mass Communication and Society*, volume 6 issue 4, includes an umbrella article called, "Book Reviews," which unsurprisingly includes many book review subarticles. Provider 1 sent a record for the entire umbrella article with a start page of 453 and end page of 461. Provider 2 sent records for the individual subarticles. If we take the subarticle, "American Television News: The Media Marketplace and the Public Interest," the start page is 457 and the end page is 458.

If a user discovered the record from Provider 2 but had access to full text from provider 1, the linking could very well fail. The OpenURL sent from Primo to the link resolver would include the start and end page for the subarticle. These values would then be sent in the TargetURL to Provider 1's platform. However, since Provider 1 indexes the entire umbrella article and not the subarticles, Provider 1 would, accordingly, expect the start and end pages of the entire article and not the subarticle, thus causing the link to fail.

To work around this issue, Ex Libris created a feature called "Source to Target Matching" for its link resolver, SFX. This functionality allows libraries to define the preferred Target to be the provider of the source record if full text is available to the library from that provider. This will minimize the number of failed links that occur as a result of the above issue since it is more likely that Primo will send metadata that will result in a successful link if the Target is the same as the Primo Central data provider.

These few examples are merely a glimpse into the challenges faced by discovery systems when attempting to integrate content from many resources. In general, the solution to overcoming these challenges can be broken into three directions:

1. Rigid standards
   a. Discovery systems create their own standards to normalize data regardless of how it appears when initially received.
   b. We rely on the industry to set standards and on publishers to abide by these standards to minimize the amount of manipulation needed.

2. Cooperation with data providers—of course, positive relationships with providers is critical. These relationships encourage data providers and discovery providers to tweak their own processes to better serve the actual data.

3. Technological enhancements—technology can both help to improve data quality and provide solutions for dealing with data problems that cannot be easily solved, as was the case with the book review cataloging issue above.

In short, discovery providers face many challenges as a result of having to unify data from disparate sources. Some of these issues are easy to solve and other are more difficult. We rely on our relationships with data providers and the industry as a whole in order to provide our users with the level of service they expect.

For Libraries

Discovery related challenges associated with metadata have been apparent to libraries since well before the advent of the current generation of discovery layers. At Queen's University, prior to implementing a discovery layer, LibQUAL and other feedback consistently showed that our users ranked the ability to find information resources highest in terms of their expectations, but lowest in overall perception of services delivered. By 2010, user expectations had become informed by their experience with the tools they interacted with daily on the open web, and the rigid application and interpretation of library metadata in the traditional OPAC was increasingly seen as a barrier to access to information.

To help address this issue, Queen's implemented Summon in summer 2010. It was a deliberately streamlined implementation taking approximately eight weeks, and this early feedback ranging from very positive to very negative, prompted the formation of a discovery layer assessment project:

"SUMMON = AMAZING!!!!!"

"As a graduate student heading into my 'research & paper writing' year I am pleased to see the efforts being spent on making the library tools as user-friendly and intuitive as possible. Thanks for the investing in this area of Queen's infrastructure!!"

"Not only is Summons an idiot version for searching, it doesn't work."

The two primary goals of the discovery layer assessment were to:

1. Investigate how students, faculty, and library staff are using Summon to determine its impact at Queen's.

2. Recommend best practices for incorporating Summon into our broader suite of research tools, and evaluate the role of a discovery layer at Queen's.

As part of the assessment, in 2011-12 we worked with the University's Office of Institutional Research and Planning to develop and conduct a survey for students, faculty, and library staff. Much of the feedback from this can be tied to metadata challenges with the discovery layer.

Undergraduate Student Feedback

Undergraduate feedback was quite positive. Where we saw negative feedback, it generally wasn't about the ability to find articles but about problems getting from the discovery layer to full text. Undergraduate feedback included the following comments, highlighting common points raised by this group:

"It's on the front page and always just finds what I'm looking for with zero effort on my part."

"Easy to use. It brings up relevant information and is very helpful in finding academic sources to complete course assignments."

"There have been numerous times that full text of an article is not available online even if it is indicated that this is the case."

Looking at issues of the sort raised in the final quote, we found that the problem was often that records didn't contain the metadata needed to generate an OpenURL that would successfully link to full text. Underlying problems include insufficient metadata, incorrect metadata, and inconsistent application of metadata—all issues raised by my copresenters.

In many cases it simply boiled down to the way that different vendors interpret the OpenURL standard. In 2011, Serials Solutions stopped depending solely on OpenURL and began linking directly to full text for many providers. This has resulted in a significant decrease in broken links, but removes the users' option to choose between multiple providers in the OpenURL resolver where we subscribe on more than one platform.

Graduate Student Feedback

Graduate student feedback was also generally positive, but more critical of the structure of search results. A reoccurring theme in graduate student feedback was the request to improve relevance. Graduate student feedback included the following comments:

"The option to type in keywords without having to modify them by using asterisks and symbols I'm not familiar with and tend to forget . . . is simply superb."

"Improve the relevance function because sometimes relevant articles don't appear near the top of the search results."

"Irritating to have done a search which results in lots of hits, only to find that many of them are just citations which are not in the library's collection."

The underlying metadata challenge in the second comment is that of creating a unified index from records with vastly differing levels of quality. When records with full text indexing appear high in the results list, but users don't see their search terms in the metadata that's displayed in on screen, it reduces their confidence in the discovery layer. It's also difficult for librarians and other staff at public service points to explain these results to users, and having to fall back on an explanation that the term must be somewhere in the full text isn't very satisfying. Thankfully we've seen significant improvements in relevance ranking in since 2011.

The last comment here points to a metadata related challenge we face about whether to continue subscribing to A&I indexes, and if so how to integrate them into the discovery layer when they don't really respect the "limit to resources outside of the library" filter.

Postgraduate Student Feedback

Postgrads had positive feedback about the interdisciplinary nature of the discovery layer, and how it provides a good general starting place for research.

They also pointed out a metadata challenge around comprehensiveness. Postgraduate student feedback included the following comments:

> "I like having a centralized search tool that searches a range of source material. With so many discipline specific and complementary journal sources to choose from, as well as printed material, its often hard to start anywhere but a general search."

> "It would be helpful to know how comprehensively it searches, so I could get a sense of whether I am missing information out there on a topic."

It's difficult to gauge the scope of the index in our discovery layer since search result don't indicate when a well-known resource related to a topic has not been indexed. With the Open Discovery Initiative, we hope to see better and more open relationships between discovery layer vendors and the information providers whose resources they represent so that information about resources we subscribe to isn't kept out of discovery layers because of competition between vendors. Another issue with comprehensiveness is our inability to get metadata for many resources we subscribe to, particularly e-book and

multimedia packages. This can have less to do with competitive practice, and more that producing quality metadata is an afterthought, especially for vendors of new and emerging formats.

Faculty Feedback

Faculty feedback was similar to the students, but more critical. They noted the difficulty in being able to limit results to particular formats. Faculty feedback included the following comments:

> "It is much faster for me to find information using Summon."

> "Summon is great for cross-disciplinary research."

> "I find useful information using Summon, but not all papers that I find are readily available online."

> "Often I'm looking for an author and year of publication (e.g., Smith, 2005) and Summon turns reviews or articles that its Smith, 2005. Just give me Smith, 2005 please!"

> "Sorry, I don't know what Summon is."

The metadata challenge in the fourth quote is one noted by Rachel in her presentation—that of being able to distinguish between articles and reviews where we can't count on high quality metadata being available in the index. Although it isn't represented in our survey comments, another issue we've noticed with faculty is that their knowledge of the literature in their field makes them more aware than students of when they're facing metadata issues in the discovery layer. They are more likely to notice when articles from the most recent issue of a key title in their field are missing from results lists, making them more likely to dismiss the discovery layer and go to subject specific databases. The metadata issue we face here is with the connection between publishers, aggregators, and discovery layer vendors. An important element of the cooperation recommended by the ODI is the timeliness of information sharing between content providers, discovery layer providers and libraries, and standardization of the methods of sharing. No one should have to screen scrape records to populate an index.

Finally, one of the main differences between student and faculty feedback was that many faculty hadn't heard of the discovery layer. In many cases this was because it hadn't been promoted by library staff, who were finding the transition from the OPAC to the discovery layer challenging. For many this is because they were expert users of the OPAC and familiar with our ILS and cataloging standards, but not as well-versed in electronic resource management and e-resource troubleshooting.

Staff Feedback

Whereas most library staff felt comfortable helping users experiencing problems with our OPAC, many reported that they were often unable to explain what was happening when students and faculty came to service desks to report issues they had while using the discovery layer. Staff feedback included the following comments:

> "Where I do find Summon to be useful is as a broad discovery tool."

> "It's a great first step to help me figure out more targeted, sophisticated searches."

> "Rarely used for teaching or reference work— unpredictable, lacks precision, confusing links to resources—not a pleasure to show students."

> "There are a lot of mysteries in the functioning of this software in our environment."

Whereas library staff are generally well versed in the way metadata is applied in the search results of our OPAC, many of our library staff don't feel that they possess expert knowledge of how content in the discovery layer is indexed or how relevancy is determined, and as a result don't feel

as confident in their ability to play the role of an expert user with Summon.

One of the most common issues that has been raised was that they are unable to determine what is and isn't indexed and how frequently new content is added to the index. The tools provided by our discovery layer vendor to show users what content they've indexed are not user friendly, and don't give an indication of how quickly new content is added after publication. Like faculty, library staff have been most likely to avoid the discovery layer when they know we subscribe to content and are aware of new articles that should be available in Summon, but are unable to find them in results lists. If ODI recommendations for consistent and transparent methods of content exchange are respected, it should be possible to have new content indexed in all discovery layer platforms as soon as possible once it is published, which would ameliorate this issue.

Library staff recommendations for improving the discovery layer include the following comments:

> "Better indication of why results are being retrieved."

> "Better indexing, particularly when harvesting records from QCAT. Serials Solutions MARC records are sometimes quite minimal with no subject headings."

> "Get MARC records in QCAT (and hence Summon) for e-books faster than currently is the case."

These comments are quite relevant to the issues being addressed by the recommendations of the Open Discovery Initiative, and we are hopeful that if all parties follow those recommendations, that many of the metadata related barriers to effective use of our discovery layer will be removed, making it an effective tool in our broader suite of information resources.

"Happiness Is . . . Library Automation": The Rhetoric of Early Library Automation and the Future of Discovery and Academic Libraries

Lauren Kosrow, University of Illinois at Urbana-Champaign
Lisa Hinchliffe, University of Illinois at Urbana-Champaign

Abstract

During the second half of the twentieth century, the professional literature of academic librarianship imagined, speculated, and envisioned how impressive technological advancements might affect the future of academic libraries and the profession as a whole. Technology and automation, stalwarts of the Space Age, were portrayed as the panacea for librarians burdened with growing collections and overwhelming clerical processes. Many voices chimed in to predict how mechanization and automation would impact collections, communication, and information retrieval, as well as the role of academic libraries in the future. In this paper, we examine how library professionals predicted technology would influence the role of academic libraries in the past and in light of current conversations about collections, discovery, competition, and the future of academic libraries. By examining the rhetoric of past conversations through the lens of present dialogs, we hope to bring a new perspective, informed by the past, to the professional discourse as ideas regarding collections, discovery, and the future of academic libraries continue to be discussed.

Introduction

> The taste for such things grows on what it feeds, and the librarian who has invented an appliance for supplying his readers with books . . . by means of an automatic ticket-in-the-slot machine will not be happy until he has invented one which will, by the touching of a button, shoot the book into the reader's home.
>
> —J. Y. W. MacAlister, 1897

> Surrounded as we are by an exploding technology which constantly increases the flood of library materials and library service demands, we may be hurriedly unaware that we in the midst of a recent but astonishing accelerated technology of our own. . . . Library technology sprints ahead. We must run if we hope to see it fully and intelligently used for the sake of the book.
>
> —R. Kingery, 1959

With references to exploding technology, increasing flood of materials, and rising demand for services, the quotation above could easily be describing the current milieu of academic libraries. However, instead of sparking discussions surrounding the integration of e-books and innovative discovery systems, as one might expect, Kingery was championing the use of the Xerox copier, punched cards, and a sorting machine. The article, appearing in the May 1959 issue of *Library Journal*, utilized rhetorical strategies that, upon closer examination, are rampant in the professional literature throughout the following decade. Amidst the glamour and glorification of technology during the Space Age, librarians like Kingery recognized the relationship between emerging technologies and library services, envisioned the role of automation in library services, and, most importantly, speculated about how these impressive technological advancements might affect the future of academic libraries and the profession as a whole.

The desire to predict the future of academic libraries is not new, and professional librarians have consistently engaged in this speculative practice for decades, contemporary company not excluded. In the introduction to the *Ithaka S + R Library Survey 2010: Insights from U.S. Academic Library Directors*, the authors acknowledged, "many studies have tried to re-imagine the future of the academic library." They continued on to assert the "purpose of the *Ithaka S + R Library*

Survey is to provide data that will focus these questions about the future of the library" (Long & Schonfeld, 2010). In July 2014, *portal: Libraries and the Academy*, published by Johns Hopkins University Press, dedicated an entire special issue, titled "Imagining the Future of Academic Libraries" to the popular practice. In this issue, guest editor Damon E. Jaggars explains that authors "from different sectors of academia, publishing, and technology share their thoughts about the future" and "explore the possibilities of what academic libraries might become." Similarly, in 1956, *Library Trends* distributed a special issue titled "Mechanization in Libraries" in hopes that "the articles presented here will not only supply useful information on the subject but that they will stimulate ideas and experiments which will provide further impetus to the trend towards mechanization of library operations" (Trotier, 1956). In both the second half of the twentieth century and the first half of the twenty-first, librarians have recognized the intimate connection between the technological breakthroughs of the period and the future projection of academic libraries. We too are in an age of exploding technology, and, surrounded by giants like Google and Amazon, librarians are seeking to understand how technology today will impact the future of academic libraries. However, as technology "sprints ahead," librarians do not always agree on what it means for academic libraries to run after it—or if libraries should even be in the race.

In the promising years after the invention of the computer and surrounding the launch of the first online catalog by OCLC in 1971, the late 50s to early 70s were a unique period that stimulated wild speculation, hopeful visions, and harsh criticisms of how technology would impact the role of academic libraries. On the one hand, technology and automation, stalwarts of the Space Age, were portrayed as the panacea for librarians burdened with growing collections and overwhelming clerical processes. Others cautioned and, at times, scathingly criticized, what was perceived as the pursuit of automation simply for the sake of automation. Many voices chimed in to predict how mechanization and automation would impact academic libraries, the role of librarians, and information retrieval in the future.

This paper will examine how library professionals predicted technology would influence the future of academic libraries and the role of librarians in the past, with current conversations about collections, discovery, and competition in mind. This paper will draw on an analysis of the rhetoric in the professional literature, primarily from articles, editorials, and letters to the editor in popular publications such as *Library Journal*, *Library Trends*, and *College & Research Libraries*, in order to gain perspective of this issue from the widest audience. Additional relevant journals, as well as conferences held on library automation, were also consulted. The scope for this project focuses on the 1960s to 1970s as this period reveals the shift from conceptualization of automated libraries to implementation. In order to focus specifically on early automation rhetoric, conversations regarding microfilm and other technologies during this period are considered outside the scope of this paper. By examining the rhetoric of past conversations through the lens of present dialogs, this paper will bring a new perspective, informed by the past, to the professional discourse as ideas regarding collections, discovery, and the future of academic libraries continue to be discussed.

The Library of Tomorrow

In the 1956 special issue of *Library Trends* titled "Mechanization in Libraries," editor Arnold Trotier posed the introductory question, "Does automation offer any possibilities in the foreseeable future with respect to any major library operations?" Over the next decade, librarians flooded the professional landscape with discussions of how, when, and, most importantly for this discussion, why libraries should pursue automation projects. Early arguments for automation focused primarily on mechanization processes that would improve circulation procedures, serial handling, acquisition, and accounting, in response to swelling collections and escalating clerical tasks.[1] The solution? Automation. "By automating," proclaimed Rodney Waldron in a 1958 issue of College & Research Libraries, "librarians can spend more time with their books and their contents—returning to the age when the librarian was an intellectual, a knower of language, and spent less time with clerical mechanics." Similar rhetoric continued throughout the decade in an attempt to push libraries to adopt automation. In 1966, Douglas Bryant, on the pages of *Library Association Record*, urged readers to "look forward to the time when machines will have freed the human members of library staffs to do more of those things that only a human being can do with is mind. When this day comes, and I believe it will come sooner rather than later," he suggested, "librarians will be free to devote their energies and time to the sensitive book selection and provision of reference and bibliographic assistance of closer application to the scholars with whom they are associated." The appeal of alleviating the repetitive, clerical tasks required of librarians was a consistent argument for why libraries should embrace early mechanization efforts, invest in automated systems, and, ultimately, purchase computers for their libraries.

Visions of what automation might do for the mechanization of clerical processes quickly escalated to dreams of what computers could do for information retrieval. In a 1962 issue of *Library Journal,* Marjorie Griffin, librarian of the Advanced Systems and Research Library at IBM and member of *Library Journal*'s editorial consultants, wrote an article titled, "The Library of Tomorrow." In her essay, she describes libraries of the future as "pulsating communication centers where transmission hook-ups with regional, national, and international centers will make current information as immediately available as information of the past." Griffin predicted that by the late 1970s, not only would technology in libraries "have surmounted the present hurdles in library service"—including backlogs in cataloging, redundancy in catalogs, and lack of shelf space—

but "we can expect technology to be so far advanced that a vast transmission network will make into a reality the possibility of calling upon total global resources to locate information." Expectations were fueled by the early success of projects such as the National Library of Medicine's MEDLARS project, an input and conversion system that required indexers to enter unit records into a computer, which then stored the information on reels of magnetic tape and was used to retrieve journal information. By the early 60s, the MEDLARS project was producing the *Index Medicus*, an index of over 2,000 journals that was distributed to medical libraries across the country (Schiller, 1963). The MEDLARS project solidified earlier conjectures that computers, indeed, had a role to play in libraries and became a launching point from which speculations of how computers might be used in the future were discussed.

Griffin, as both a librarian and an employee of IBM, characterizes the relationship between librarians and the technology industry that was cultivated by both parties during this period. Two conferences, the first of their kind, held in 1963 represented how librarians and the technology industry sought to create a more formal space in which members of both professions could engage in a dialogue around computers, data processing, automation, and the future of academic libraries. Both the Airlie Conference on Libraries and Automation, sponsored by the Library of Congress, the National Science Foundation, and Council on Library Resources, and the Clinic on Library Applications of Data Processing, hosted by the Graduate School of Library and Information Science at the University of Illinois, addressed the need for a meaningful dialogue between technologists and librarians in order to inform expectations of computer technology and explore its relevance to libraries. Presentations by librarians, IBM representatives, and other industry leaders celebrated the limited success of computer implementation into clerical processes and looked forward to more ambitious applications such as machine indexing, SDI

---

[1] See Waldron, R. K. (1958). Implications of technological progress for librarians. *College & Research Libraries, 19*(2), 118-164; Griffin, M. (1962). The library of tomorrow. *Library Journal, 87*; Kraft, D. H. in Goldhor, H. (Ed.). (1963).

Proceedings of the 1963 clinic on library applications of data processing. Urbana: University of Illinois at Urbana-Champaign IDEALS.

systems, and information storage, specifically by those outside of librarianship.[2] In his presentation at the University of Illinois, Burton W. Adkinson, Head of the Office of Science Information Service at the National Science Foundation, remarked that, although the "relatively low-level use" of library applications of computers had been helpful, the "present day applications represent the crawling stage of development. . . . We must always look forward to the running stage" (1963). As librarians and technologists collaborated and occupied the same professional space, the push toward more advanced automation processes continued to influence and shape librarians' expectations for what computers could do for the future of the profession.

Library Automation: "Rosy Prospects and Cold Facts"

While the titans of technology championed the computer and its expected role in revolutionizing library processes, there were members of the library profession who cautioned against the rising expectations for automation and predicted the difficulty of automating work that dealt with dynamic components such as ideas and language, specifically in terms of information retrieval. In a 1956 issue of *Library Trends*, Melvin Voigt remarked, "Regardless of how well a machine can store information and in how little space, it is of little value unless it is possible to put information in the machine easily and efficiently, and, more important, retrieve it in usable form just as easily." In an accurate description of future struggles in information retrieval, J. R. Pierce predicted that, until computers were more advanced, library users "would smother under the flood of information and misinformation it would produce." In anticipation of a vast network of information, Pierce argued, "What the person who consults the library needs is not everything about a subject, but the best information about it or about the part of it in which he is interested"

(1963). Remarkably, before automated retrieval was possible, library professionals predicted foundational issues with retrieving relevant information. More broadly, Jesse Shera, in a 1961 issue of *Library Journal*, warned readers that the "overselling of an idea when it is still in its experimental stage will lead to sketchy and ill-defined programs, the prostitution of ideals, and a sacrifice of quality to the end that mechanization per se may be discredited and condemned for faults that are not inherent in it."

Like Shera predicted, as the decade progressed, many initial attempts to mechanize remained stalled in the conceptualization phase and frustration with earlier promises heightened the rhetoric around library automation.[3] In 1967, Harrison Bryan, an Australian librarian, toured the United States in hopes of reporting on the wave of automation projects. "Projects which have all the recorded confidence of operating schemes turn out to be projects indeed," he stated. "Systems reported in the full flush of initial optimism are found abandoned or modified out of recognition" (1967, p. 189). His observations were confirmed by many reports at conferences and in the professional literature during the second half of the decade.[4] In his 1968 article in *Library Journal* titled, "Automation: Rosy Prospects and Cold Facts," Daniel Melcher confirmed Bryan's report. "I don't want to give the impression that we are disillusioned about the ultimate potential of the new technologies," he informs readers, "but it is awfully easy to read the literature and the conference reports and get the idea that things are further along than they are" (p. 1105).

"Kicking the Ostrich"

As initial automation projects lagged behind hopeful expectations, two camps formed within the profession in the eyes of those who desired library automation—"those who espouse the future and the mechanization and automation

---

[2] See Adkinson, B. W., Griffin, M., & Kraft, D. H., in Goldhor, H. (Ed.). (1963). *Proceedings of the 1963 clinic on library applications of data processing*. Urbana: University of Illinois at Urbana-Champaign IDEALS.

[3] "See Parker, R. H. (1963). In Goldhor, H. (Ed.). (1963). *Proceedings of the 1963 clinic on library applications of*

data processing. Urbana: University of Illinois at Urbana-Champaign IDEALS.

[4] In addition to Byrn's remarks, see also Fielding, D. (1969). American automation updated: A second report on automation in action by a librarian 'down under. *Library Journal, 94*.

which will surely come, and those who look toward the past and cling mightily and forlornly to the manual methods which they have known for so many years" (Wright, 1964). Although efforts to automate libraries had been largely unsuccessful up to that point, proponents of library automation continued to look forward to what computers would do for libraries in the future and described those who did not gaze favorably upon automation as backwards, narrow-minded, reluctant to change, and suffering from "psychosomatic myopia" (Kaiser, 1962). Metaphors ranged from the demise of the ancient Aztec empire to those who failed to immediately embrace the horseless carriage or ostriches with their heads in the sand.[5] Regardless of the rhetorical technique, the message was the same—unless libraries changed and adapted, they would be left behind. "If librarianship does not meet this challenge and fill the need for professional knowledge," predicted Robert Hayes at the 1964 Clinic on Data Processing in Libraries, "someone else will."

A Gentleman's Opinion

However, by the late 1960s and early 1970s, the high cost of automation, perceived inefficiency of failed automation projects, and lack of widespread success of library automation promised at the beginning of the decade brought scathing critiques of library automation as a whole. This sentiment is best captured in Ellsworth Mason's contentious article in a 1971 issue of *College & Research Libraries* titled, "The Great Gas Bubble Prick't; Or, Computers Revealed—By a Gentleman of Quality." After completing a seven-month report on computers and library processes at ten large university libraries, Mason concluded, "all the promises offered in its name are completely fraudulent" and "it has been wrapped so completely in an aura of unreason that fine intelligences are completely uprooted when talking about it" (1971). Draped in his infamously harsh, yet entertaining, diatribe against the use of

computers in libraries, Mason fundamental assertion was that, as a profession, librarians "were ignorantly imitating industrial research and development, which comprise our systems programming, and that we were wasting money on a faith the exact equivalent of a witch's faith in flying ointment" (1972, p. 5). To either the robust applause or profound vexation of many of his colleagues, Mason's numerous criticisms brought an interesting discussion to the forefront of the field—were libraries simply imitating industry? What was the end goal of automation? Was the price tag of automation projects ultimately worth it?

"Information Now": The Users' Role in Shaping the Library of the Future

Mason's attack on automation efforts occurred at a critical moment, appearing just as this period of conceptualization was shifting toward implementation, signaled by the success of the first online catalog through OCLC the very same year. A closer look at the literature toward the end of the 1960s and in the early 1970s reveals an important shift in the rhetoric surrounding library automation that could—and did—respond. Stern rebukes such as Mason's, rooted in rising costs and inefficiency, urged those advocating for automation to refocus the rhetoric on users. Without discrediting the cost of automation, Wright revealed this shift by asking, "Isn't our responsibility to our public, whoever that public may be, much greater than our responsibility to our institution? Is service not more important than cutting costs?" At the Meeting on Automation in the Library, held at Purdue University in 1964, C. D. Gull insisted it was critical for the profession moving forward "to define what we wish to accomplish by automating libraries and information services and equally important to discover what users want of libraries today and of automated libraries tomorrow." As a result, visions surrounding the future of academic libraries and the role of librarians shifted towards projected user needs and demands. At the

---

[5] For metaphorical references, see Kaser, D. E. (1962). Automation in libraries of the future. *Tennessee Libraries*, *14*, 79-84; Wright, J. H. (1964). Kicking the ostrich. *Library*

Journal, *89*; Melcher, D. (1971). Cataloging, processing, and automation. *American Libraries*, *2*, 701.

Preconference Institute for Library Automation before ALA Annual in 1967, Joseph Beck, in his keynote address, predicted the impact of future technological developments on expectations of users for libraries: "the ability to broadcast information to those who need it when they need it is likely to turn libraries and information centers into communication centers." In his article titled, "Library of the Future," J. G. Kemeny envisioned the impact of future information retrieval methods on the librarian's role within an academic library. "Once we have perfected the search technique, I am certain that a session of ten minutes at a terminal could accomplish more than hours of poring through library catalogs and thumbing laboriously through books," Kemeny asserted. This system, he predicted, would not eliminate the need for reference librarians, but would substantially change their role. "It would no longer be their job to find items for customers but instead to aid them in the computer search" (Kemeny, 1972).

In addition to adjusting predictions for the future to align with user needs, it was also critical that librarians recognized the agency of users in the present and, more importantly, in the future. "The library's clientele is changing its expectations," argued Allen Veaner at the Preconference Institute in Library Automation before ALA Annual in 1973, "the public will no longer be satisfied with any kind of library response that smacks of being plodding or bureaucratic. People want information *now,* not tomorrow or next week. If they can't get what they want from the library, they'll go to the computer facility." This sense of competition with other information sources did not dissuade librarians, but motivated them to pursue automation in order to meet their users' changing expectations. In response to a *Library Journal* article echoing Mason's sentiments on the enormous costs of automation, I. A. Warheir wrote a letter to the editor to address why library automation must persist: "The stockbroker today is completely dependent on his cathode ray tube terminal to bring him instantaneous, up-to-date information. He can not rely on yesterday's *Wall Street Journal.*" According to Warheir, the cost of automation was, in fact, worth reaching the end

goal. Why automate? "To make library services available to more people" (Warheir, 1971).

Conclusion

In a 1967 article title "Librarians and the Everlasting Now," L. Quincy Mumford, Librarian of Congress, pondered the cyclical nature of the issues that plague libraries. "Our problems repeat themselves over and over in every age," he mused. "It seems probable, for instance, that medieval monks were plagued with a temperature problem." On a more serious note, Mumford stated, "Challenges which will face the librarians of the future have been outlined more or less in detail by other prophets." The desire to look forward to predict the future of academic libraries is prevalent in our profession, but so should the practice of reflecting on past conversations. In regards to automation, discovery, and competition, the themes that emerged within the professional discourse during the 1950s to the 1970s seem, at times, to be prophetic of the current professional landscape. Although the "push for automation" looks quite different, the rhetoric surrounding fear of being left behind or considered irrelevant is remarkably similar. Also emerging from this decade of conceptualization is the need for librarians to continuously reinvent themselves, the profession, and role of the library in order to compete with other information sources, such as "the computer facility." During the present "Amazonification" of libraries, questions about discovery system, costs, and user expectation echo from earlier conversations on automation: are libraries simply imitating industry? What is the end goal? Is the price tag of automation projects ultimately worth it? Do we need to compete? Can we? If libraries exist only to serve users, as Vickery asserted in his 1966 article, "Future of Libraries in the Machine Age," then "it is the user who must decide—what is the cost to him of our *not* being automated?"

More work needs to be done in order to fully explore what these past conversations mean for the future of academic libraries today. As in decades past, library technology continues to sprint ahead—"we must run if we hope to see it fully and intelligently used for the sake of the book" (Kingery 1959).

References

Adams, S. (1963). Medical libraries are in trouble. *Library Journal, 88,* 2615.

Adkinson, B. W. in Goldhor, H. (Ed.). (1963*). Proceedings of the 1963 clinic on library applications of data processing.* Urbana: University of Illinois at Urbana-Champaign IDEALS.

Becker, J. in Salmon, S. (Ed.). (1967). Papers presented at the Preconference Institute in Library Automation. San Francisco, California.

Berman, S. (1971). Let it all hang out: A think piece for Luddite librarians. *Library Journal, 96.*

Bryan, H. (1967). An Australian librarian takes a look at American automation in action. *Library Journal, 92,* 189.

Bryant, D. W. (1966). University libraries and the future. *Library Association Record, 68,* 2–8.

Byrn, J. (1969). Automation in university libraries—A state of the art. *Library Resources and Technical Services, 13.*

Fielding, D. (1969). American automation updated: A second report on automation in action by a librarian 'down under. *Library Journal, 94.*

Gull, C. D. in Andrews, T. & Morelock, M. (Eds.). (1964). *Papers presented at the meeting on automation In the library—When, where, and how.* Lafayette, IN: Purdue University Press.

Griffin, M. (1962). The library of tomorrow. *Library Journal, 87.*

Griffin, M. in Goldhor, H. (Ed.). (1963). *Proceedings of the 1963 clinic on library applications of data processing.* Urbana: University of Illinois at Urbana-Champaign IDEALS.

Hayes, R. M. in Goldhor, H. (Ed.). (1964). *Proceedings of the 1964 clinic on library applications of data processing.* Urbana: University of Illinois at Urbana-Champaign IDEALS.

Jaggers, D. E. (2014). We can imagine the future, but are we equipped to create it? *portal: Libraries and the Academy, 14*(3), 319–323.

Kaser, D. E. (1962). Automation in libraries of the future. *Tennessee Libraries, 14,* 79–84.

Kingery, R. (1959) New library technology. *Library Journal, 84,* 1387–1391.

Kemeny, J. G. (1972). Library of the future. *Library Bulletin,* 1250–1260.

Kraft, D. H. in Goldhor, H. (Ed.). (1963). *Proceedings of the 1963 clinic on library applications of data processing.* Urbana: University of Illinois at Urbana-Champaign IDEALS.

Kraft, D. H. in Andrews, T. & Morelock, M. (Eds.). (1964). *Papers presented at the meeting on automation In the library—When, where, and how.* Purdue University, Lafayette, IN.

Long, M. P., & Schonfeld, R. C. (2010). Ithaka S + R library survey 2010: Insights from U.S. academic library directors. *Ithaka S + R.* Retrieved from http://www.ithaka.org/ithaka-s-r

MacAlister, J. Y. W. (1897). *Transactions and proceedings of the second library conference held in London, July 13–16, 1897* (pp. 10–11). London.

Markuson, B. E. (Ed.). (1963). *Proceedings of the conference on libraries and automation.* Warrenton, VA: Airlie Foundation.

Mason, E. (1971). The great gas bubble prick'd. *College & Research Libraries. 32*(3), 183–196.

Mason, E. (1971). Along the academic way: A report of a seven-month study project, November 1, 1969 to May 21, 1970. *Library Journal, 96.*

Mason, E. (1972). Perspective on libraries and computers: A debate. *Library Resources and Technical Services, 16*(1), 5.

Melcher, D. (1968). Automation: Rosy prospects and cold facts. *Library Journal, 93,* 1105.

Melcher, D. (1971) Cataloging, processing, and automation. *American Libraries, 2,* 701.

Mumford, L. Q., (1966). Librarians and the everlasting now. *Library Journal, 91.*

Parker, R. H. (1963). In Goldhor, H. (Ed.). (1963). *Proceedings of the 1963 clinic on library applications of data processing.* Urbana: University of Illinois at Urbana-Champaign IDEALS.

Schiller, H. (1963). What is MEDLARS? *Library Journal, 88.*

Shaw, R.R. (1955). Implications for library services. *Library Quarterly, 25,* 344.

Shera, J. (1961). The librarian and the machine. *Library Journal, 86.*

Trotier, A. (Ed.). (1956). Mechanization in libraries. *Library Trends, 4.*

Veaner, A. B., Martin, S. K., & West, M. W. (Eds.) (1973). *Library automation: The state of the art II: Papers presented at the preconference institute in library automation.* Las Vegas, Nevada.

Vickery, B. C. (1966). Future of libraries in the machine age. *Library Association Record, 68,* 252–260.

Voigt, M. J. (1956). The trend toward mechanization in libraries. *Library Trends, 4.*

Waldron, R. K. (1958). Implications of technological progress for librarians. *College & Research Libraries, 19*(2), 118–164.

Wright, J. H. (1964). Kicking the ostrich. *Library Journal, 89.*

Collection Development and Data Visualization: How Interactive Graphic Displays Are Transforming Collection Development Decisions

Paulina Borrego, Science and Engineering Librarian, University of Massachusetts Amherst

Rachel Lewellen, Assessment Librarian, University of Massachusetts Amherst

Abstract

Given the changing collection management landscape a clear tool for evaluating purchase decisions is needed to help selectors make the most of budget allocations. The UMass Amherst Libraries uses the business intelligence software Tableau to help selectors more clearly see the connection between monograph purchases and circulation data. Using dashboards, subject selectors can see the impact of monograph selections within a discipline, across the collection, and over a period of time. Graphic visualizations are easier to understand than previously used text and numerical based spreadsheets for data analysis and facilitate exploration at different levels. This paper discusses how data visualizations are used to effectively communicate monograph purchasing, circulation, and expenditures. Interactive dashboards help transform abstract ideas into a solid holistic understanding of the collections and in turn provide a common language to facilitate collection development discussions, decisions, and policies.

Introduction

	Budget Code	Order Group	Pct	Cost	Nbr	Pct	Cost	Nbr	Pct	Cost
2202	SELECTOR PAULINA BORREGO-2009	CompSci	24%	$534.66	8	89%	$491.91	1	11%	$42.75
2203	SELECTOR PAULINA BORREGO-2009	Geoscience	50%	$83.19	1	100%	$83.19	0	0%	$0.00
2204	SELECTOR PAULINA BORREGO-2009	MathStat	17%	$285.81	3	50%	$146.60	3	50%	$139.21
2205	SELECTOR PAULINA BORREGO-2009	Microbio	9%	$126.65	1	100%	$126.65	0	0%	$0.00
2206	SELECTOR PAULINA BORREGO-2009	Physics	15%	$334.95	2	50%	$54.45	2	50%	$280.50
2207	**SELECTOR PAULINA BORREGO-2009**	Total	24%	$2,876.00	27	64%	$1,773.83	15	36%	$1,102.17
2208	SELECTOR PAULINA BORREGO-2010	Biology	0%	$0.00	0	0%	$0.00	0	0%	$0.00
2209	SELECTOR PAULINA BORREGO-2010	Biology	0%	$0.00	0	0%	$0.00	0	0%	$0.00
2210	SELECTOR PAULINA BORREGO-2010	ChemEng	33%	$99.95	0	0%	$0.00	1	100%	$99.95
2211	SELECTOR PAULINA BORREGO-2010	Chemistry	27%	$328.74	3	100%	$328.74	0	0%	$0.00
2212	SELECTOR PAULINA BORREGO-2010	CompSci	0%	$0.00	0	0%	$0.00	0	0%	$0.00
2213	SELECTOR PAULINA BORREGO-2010	CompSci	9%	$28.49	1	100%	$28.49	0	0%	$0.00
2214	SELECTOR PAULINA BORREGO-2010	Geoscience	0%	$0.00	0	0%	$0.00	0	0%	$0.00
2215	SELECTOR PAULINA BORREGO-2010	MathStat	16%	$145.29	1	33%	$47.49	2	67%	$97.80
2216	SELECTOR PAULINA BORREGO-2010	Microbio	0%	$0.00	0	0%	$0.00	0	0%	$0.00
2217	SELECTOR PAULINA BORREGO-2010	Physics	0%	$0.00	0	0%	$0.00	0	0%	$0.00
2218	SELECTOR PAULINA BORREGO-2010	Physics	27%	$211.74	3	75%	$156.64	1	25%	$55.10
2219	**SELECTOR PAULINA BORREGO-2010**	Total	17%	$814.21	8	67%	$561.36	4	33%	$252.85
2220	SELECTOR PAULINA BORREGO-2011	Astronomy	44%	$674.35	6	38%	$210.18	10	63%	$464.17
2221	SELECTOR PAULINA BORREGO-2011	ChemEng	0%	$0.00	0	0%	$0.00	0	0%	$0.00
2222	SELECTOR PAULINA BORREGO-2011	ChemEng	0%	$0.00	0	0%	$0.00	0	0%	$0.00
2223	SELECTOR PAULINA BORREGO-2011	Chemistry	22%	$121.30	2	100%	$121.30	0	0%	$0.00
2224	SELECTOR PAULINA BORREGO-2011	Chemistry	40%	$3,179.88	11	35%	$1,092.88	20	65%	$2,087.00
2225	SELECTOR PAULINA BORREGO-2011	CompSci	18%	$160.38	2	100%	$160.38	0	0%	$0.00
2226	SELECTOR PAULINA BORREGO-2011	CompSci	8%	$296.96	0	0%	$0.00	4	100%	$296.96
2227	SELECTOR PAULINA BORREGO-2011	Education	0%	$0.00	0	0%	$0.00	0	0%	$0.00
2228	SELECTOR PAULINA BORREGO-2011	ElecEng	0%	$0.00	0	0%	$0.00	0	0%	$0.00
2229	SELECTOR PAULINA BORREGO-2011	ElecEng	50%	$211.83	0	0%	$0.00	2	100%	$211.83
2230	SELECTOR PAULINA BORREGO-2011	Engin, Gen	100%	$154.83	1	100%	$154.83	0	0%	$0.00
2231	SELECTOR PAULINA BORREGO-2011	MathStat	23%	$176.29	3	100%	$176.29	0	0%	$0.00
2232	SELECTOR PAULINA BORREGO-2011	MathStat	11%	$864.31	8	57%	$397.25	6	43%	$467.06
2233	SELECTOR PAULINA BORREGO-2011	Physics	22%	$51.89	2	100%	$51.89	0	0%	$0.00
2234	SELECTOR PAULINA BORREGO-2011	Physics	24%	$974.68	9	50%	$528.09	9	50%	$446.59
2235	SELECTOR PAULINA BORREGO-2011	PolymerSci	0%	$0.00	0	0%	$0.00	0	0%	$0.00
2236	**SELECTOR PAULINA BORREGO-2011**	Total	22%	$6,866.70	44	46%	$2,893.09	51	54%	$3,973.61
2237	SELECTOR PAULINA BORREGO-2012	Astronomy	17%	$22.50	1	100%	$22.50	0	0%	$0.00
2238	SELECTOR PAULINA BORREGO-2012	Biology	9%	$355.94	1	33%	$30.88	2	67%	$325.06
2239	SELECTOR PAULINA BORREGO-2012	Chemistry	68%	$2,101.51	1	8%	$169.13	12	92%	$1,932.38

Figure 1. Sample Microsoft Excel spreadsheet of monograph purchase data provided to selectors.

Librarians have long

sought to understand the extent to which monograph purchases meet the needs of users. Circulation is one indicator that can be captured and analyzed. This paper describes how the UMass Amherst Libraries use the business intelligence software Tableau to help librarians review monograph purchases with circulation data and expenditures to inform purchasing decisions.

Challenges of Spreadsheets

Before using dashboards, library collection data was typically shared with selectors in a Microsoft Excel spreadsheet (Figure 1). It was then up to the individual selector to manipulate the data, trying to review multiple worksheets, different data points and ultimately make sense of, and glean, trends. One of the problems with this practice is that not all library personnel are skilled with Microsoft Excel manipulation features or feel comfortable dealing with the sometimes massive spreadsheets that are created and shared. While this was very useful data, and regardless of Excel manipulation skills, it is still hard to make connections and see trends in this text and numerical based environment.

The next evolution in spreadsheet use was to provide data with subtotaling, filtering, and some of the other Excel features employed. These enhancements were greatly appreciated and made it easier for some to use the data but it still did not address the issue of discerning trends within the large amounts of data. It was still difficult to view data over time since each fiscal year was in a separate worksheet.

Advantages of Data Visualization

First introduced to Tableau at the 2011 Charleston Conference, the UMass Amherst Libraries use Tableau Desktop, Tableau Server, and Tableau Public to analyze, interact with, and communicate collection data as well as other library data. Positive aspects of Tableau products for the Libraries include an intuitive web interface that makes it easy for staff to absorb and interpret data. The ability to connect to and at times blend multiple data sources provides context and shows relationships between data sources. For example, Figure 2 shows walk-in traffic, proxy activity, and circulation counts within a single dashboard.

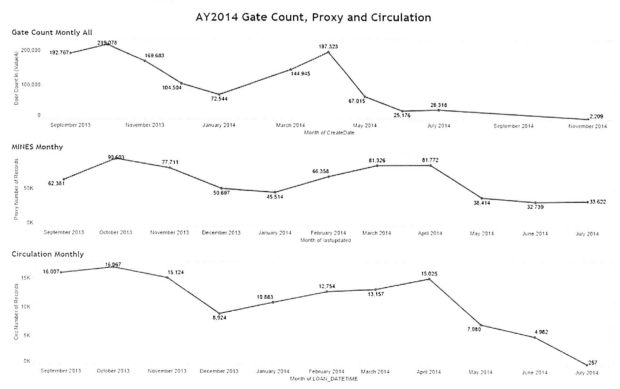

Figure 2. Gate count, proxy, and circulation dashboard.

Live interaction with real-time data and automatic updating is also beneficial. Multiple chart and graph options (bar, line, pie, map scatter plot, Gantt, Bubble, etc.) support a variety of analysis needs and learning styles. Options for private and public dissemination ensure protection of sensitive data and facilitate sharing of unrestricted data.

Using Tableau has increased the capacity for staff to use and understand data across many data sources these include: monographs, e-books, proxy traffic, gate counts, service desk interactions, instruction, space use, ARL statistics and more.

One Selectors' Collection Practice and Awakening with Tableau—Paulina Borrego

Soon after joining the staff at the UMass Amherst Science and Engineering Library Paulina Borrego was given the responsibility of selecting monographs for her various liaison departments. Being a new librarian, following a career change from teaching high school chemistry for nearly twenty years, she was unfamiliar with many library practices and had much to learn. She took her role as monograph selector seriously and tried to make the best use of the allocated budget for each of her liaison departments.

Monograph allocations were based on a number of factors including enrollment of undergraduates and graduate students as well as faculty FTE (full-time equivalent). A budget was assigned to each department and that amount was used to support the research and instruction needs of that department. The collection development policy outlines materials that are out of the scope of purchase, such as textbooks. The UMass Amherst Libraries is also part of the Five College Consortium with a shared online catalog striving to avoid unnecessary duplication of materials across the consortium.

As a selector Ms. Borrego tried to choose monographs that aligned with the faculty research area in her departments along with the overall mission of the University. She spent a great deal of time examining faculty webpages for current research interests so that she could make

monograph purchase decisions that supported those interests. This exercise of researching and noting faculty research areas was very time consuming and in the end did not guarantee that a monograph purchase decision would prove helpful or ultimately circulate. She also spent considerable time reviewing new title lists, book reviews, and current science trends to better inform her monograph purchase decisions. In hindsight, she felt she was somewhat naïve in thinking that she could accurately predict those items that would be of interest or circulate.

After her initial year of purchases she received the annual spreadsheets with circulation and duplication data. She tried to the best of her ability to deal with the massive spreadsheets to extract information dealing with each of her liaison departments, hoping to find trends and evidence to support purchasing decisions. Oftentimes she felt her Excel skills were lacking and she needed help to sort and filter the massive spreadsheets effectively. She was also frustrated with the formatting, finding that data points were hard to associate with one another and make connections. Overall, lacking the necessary computer skills to manipulate the data, along with the inability to visualize data trends given the format of the data, she felt disadvantaged in making successful selector decisions. What she wanted was indisputable evidence to make wiser collection development decisions.

Various Excel enhancements were of some help, providing an easier way to sort and filter the monograph use data, but still lacked the ability to visualize impact of seeing overall trends. Without data in a format she could reasonably use, Ms. Borrego continued to make monograph purchase decisions based on faculty research and instruction areas. Her hope was that the items purchased would satisfy the needs of the community and ultimately circulate. For some time she continued this individual collection development practice and tried to evaluate the circulation data available to make small adjustments as needed. She was mindful of trying to make informed decisions and to use her monograph allocation budget with a sense of fiscal responsibility.

Then Came Tableau, and That Changed Everything!

The same Excel spreadsheet data, previously shared with selectors, was used to create multiple dashboards and visualizations with Tableau. Selectors could now choose from multiple variables to create custom views.

When Ms. Borrego used the interactive dashboards to explore her data she found it both horrifying and freeing at the same time. She visually interacted with the data in a format that was fully understandable. Whereas before she had tried to make connections between the data points (monograph purchase decisions and circulation data) in the Excel spreadsheets, interactive dashboards presented the data in a form that was clear, simple, and undeniable.

The Order Group Dashboard (Figure 3) allowed selectors to choose the groups that correspond to their liaison departments. There is also the option to view a single year or multiple years. Horizontal bars showed monograph purchase data clearly delineated for circulated and noncirculated items. Expenditure totals along with percentages are tabulated and displayed alongside each bar. The Non Circ with Duplication Status display indicates information for monograph purchases either duplicated or unique as part of the Five College Consortium. Other dashboards allow selectors to drill down and view title level data, make comparisons to other order groups, and see trends for parts or the collection as a whole. Since the dashboards can display data for all selectors and order groups, transparency is built into the system allowing selectors to draw conclusions on many levels.

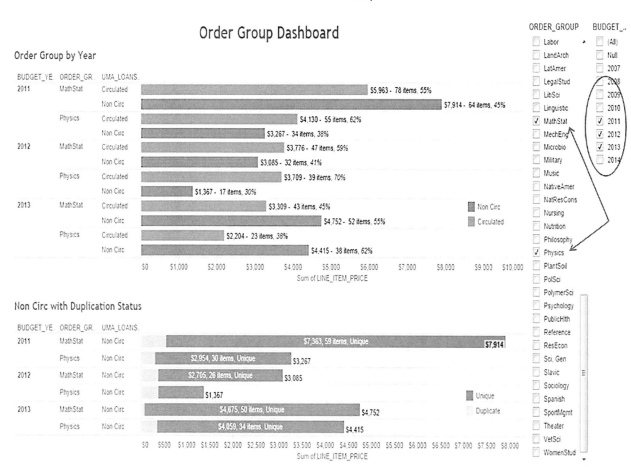

Figure 3. Sample order group dashboard of monographic purchase data in tableau format.

In dashboard form Ms. Borrego could quickly and easily see where monograph purchase decisions, no matter how informed, were not circulating. She also came to understand that in the interest of nonduplication within the Five College Consortium, she was selecting "unique" items but they were not circulating (Figure 4). Overall, she was horrified to see that the monograph titles she put so much work and effort into selecting based on research and instruction areas were not being used. Data visualization was fundamental in helping her to make this realization—clear, undeniable evidence that her monograph collection practices were not as effective as expected.

On a larger level seeing the data so clearly caused Ms. Borrego to question the practice of individually selecting titles for potential use and she immediately changed her personal collection development practice to purchasing only those monograph titles directly requested. Interacting with the data in Tableau provided the information in a format that was directly accessible and straightforward. It shaped her decision to change her approach to selection. Being able to make such a clear decision based on the data was very freeing. She now had the evidence she needed to change her course of action.

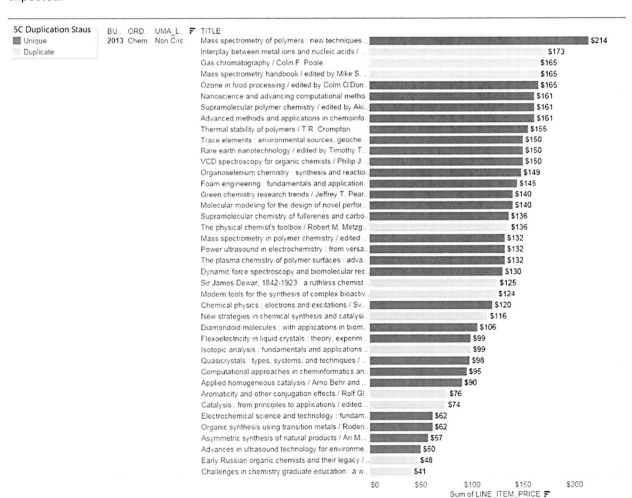

Figure 4. Titles purchased with circulation and consortial duplication status.

Visualizations and Dashboards Facilitate a Shared Perspective

Visualizations have improved how data is communicated, established a common language for discussion and contributed to decision making. Due to the transparent nature of the dashboards, selectors are free to explore their individual monograph purchase data as well as make comparisons at other levels. Visual displays highlighted comparisons between library purchase programs such as approval plans, Books on Demand (BODEM), *New York Times* (NYT), and monographs purchased for reserves (Figure 5). These displays facilitated discussion and decision making. For example, approval plans and BODEM purchases were expanded.

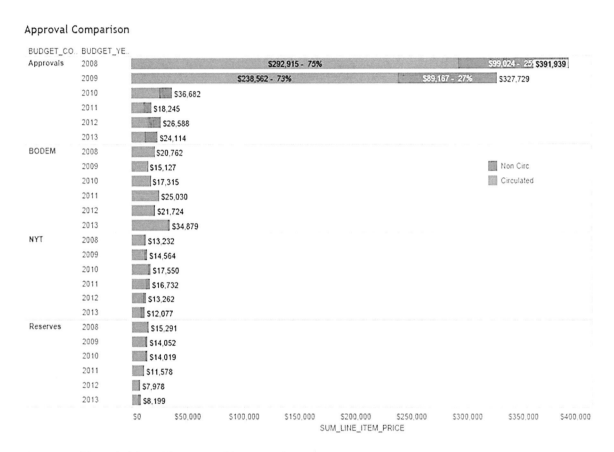

Figure 5. Tableau dashboard for various library purchase plans.

Visualizations allow selectors to drill down to view their individual order group purchase data as well as view the collection data on a larger Library of Congress (LC) scale (Figure 6). This ability to drill down as well as see the entire collection helps selectors understand their individual role in building the monograph collection as a whole. Being able to view one's individual data as part of the collective picture helps to establish a sense of community and create a common understanding of the entire collection. Having an understanding of an individual role in the entire monograph collection is vital when budgeting and allocation methods are reviewed. Overall, these displays have helped to provide a shared assessment of the monograph collection so that discussions and decisions can be based on a common perspective and more easily interpreted data.

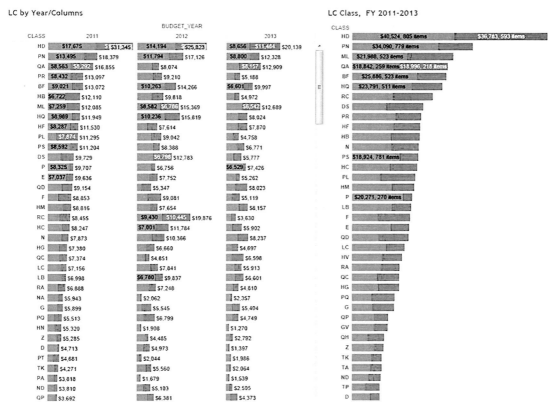

Figure 6. Tableau dashboard for monograph purchases by Library of Congress.

Data Visualizations as an Effective Communication Tool With Library Stakeholders

In the same way dashboards have helped to inform and educate library staff, they to help tell the Library story to stakeholders. Across campus, dashboards can be used on many levels, for example with faculty and deans, to effectively communicate relevant library data. Using dashboards it is easier for faculty to see how book purchasing, spending, and use relate to each school and college (Figure 7). This mode of communication provides information that may be unfamiliar in a clear, understandable, and visually powerful format. Expenditure dashboards demonstrate transparency and fiscal responsibility.

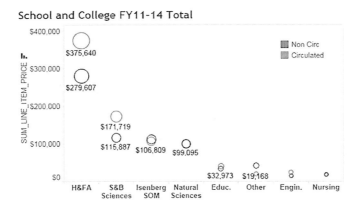

Figure 7. Spending and circulation by school and college.

Conclusion

Data visualizations enabled selectors to review monograph purchases, track and assess spending, and communicate effectively with library staff and campus stakeholders. These assessments impacted collection practices and are changing how collections are analyzed. The UMass Amherst Libraries use Tableau as the preferred way of interaction with data and it is a major component of the Libraries' assessment program. This has increased the capacity for staff to interact with, understand, and communicate data.

Recycling Database Records

Lars-Håkan Herbertsson, Chalmers University of Technology
Marie Widigson, Chalmers University of Technology
Rolf Johansson, Chalmers University of Technology
Lari Kovanen, Chalmers University of Technology

Abstract

"Our users are used to searching and don't care for A-Z lists. We don't want to maintain a separate database of databases. Let's catalog the database record once, recycle it and use the discovery API to build a database search feature." Those were our thoughts when introducing our new web site.

When filtering on databases Summon API was called and a relevancy ranked list was presented. But immediately voices were raised from researchers and post-graduates that they had difficulties using the tool.

So, we decided to build a more traditional database list yet keeping the main principles:

- To search databases from the general library search box.

- To maintain in one place only.

- To retrieve the records through several search services.

To build a tool that facilitates discovery and provides additional features we had to use a source with more stringent metadata. Thus we dropped the Summon API and instead used the API from the original source, the national catalog of Sweden, Libris.

A team of librarians and IT developers developed a database search feature and list that better met the needs of both students, faculty, and librarians. We, the librarians, got an understanding about APIs. We also learned by painful experiences that to make MARC records at least a bit machine readable we need to catalog with thorough control. The IT developers learned about the MARC reality we still live in.

Background

With a central search box for all of the library's information resources, and with the discovery system Summon as the underlying engine, Chalmers library new website was a radical break with the past at launch in February 2013. Usability and responsive design was the catchwords during development. To get a clear target it was decided at an early stage that it would be a web for undergraduate students rather than for faculty. Based on user interviews, there were three imaginary users, personas, who wished for simple and clear search systems and to find "everything" in one place.

Our definition of "a database" is broad, including large encyclopedias, platforms, search services, etc. On the old web, they were presented through a separate search tool with A-Z list and broad subject areas. A stand alone, static database of databases. Easy to maintain for the librarians and practical for those of the users who knew where to look, but hardly good for anyone else, particularly not the personas. The databases were not found in the national catalog Libris, in the OPAC or in Summon. In the new, discovery centered environment, we had to find another solution.

To meet the request for simplicity on the new web, the OPAC was hidden and no A-Z lists for journals or databases were set up. A large search box received a dominant place on all web pages. When entering a term in the search box the user was taken to Summon and could continue there. Nevertheless, we recognized a need to be able to search on journals and on databases separately.

This paper will describe the process of developing the database search.

Main Principles for the Database Search

These were the ideas that governed the development:

- *Findable through the library search box.*
  The databases should be found from the general search tool, both when searching "everything" (in Summon) and when filtering on databases (in Chalmers library web interface).

- *Maintenance in one place only, Libris.*
  In Sweden libraries are encouraged to enter holdings of all resource types in the national catalog (Libris). Recently libraries have begun to catalog databases there

Cataloging of bibliographics record are done directly in Libris. It is a collaborative process; everyone can make corrections and changes. Thereafter, records are downloaded to local catalogs.

- *Catalog once—use anywhere.*
  The same records should be recycled and transferred to other applications; to avoid double workload, differing information and broken links.

- *Use of discovery API for several search features.*
  The idea was to benefit from the enriched discovery index and to build specialized library services on this API; journal search, database search and possibly others. The focus should be on search & discover more than on browsing hierarchical lists.

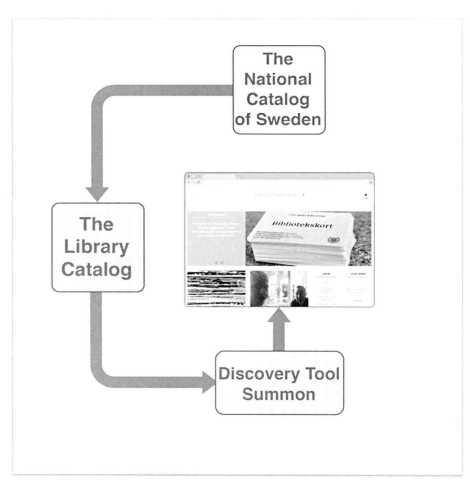

Figure 1. Data flow from Libris to database search via Summon.

First Attempt—Focus on Search

We cataloged around 200 databases in Libris and put our own proxy links in the locally controlled holdings record. Everything else was in the bibliographic record. The records were transferred to our local catalog, the same way as all MARC records are. They were then ingested into the Summon discovery tool with content type database.

Without filtering you were in theory able to find the database record in Summon, but as databases are not highly ranked they are hard to find in the giant index. A click on the filter icon in the library search box instead took you to a part of the library web using Summon API and only databases were retrieved.

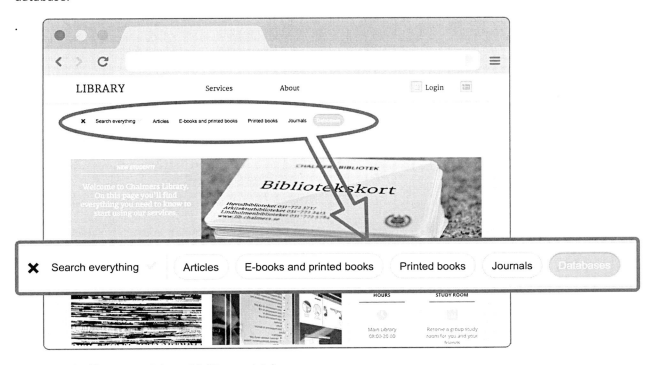

Figure 2. The library search box with filter on databases.

With a filtered search for a database name, a subject or a word in the description, a relevance ranked list was presented. Summon API works just like Summon itself, i.e., the search results can be sorted by relevance or date but not alphabetically. We chose to sort by relevance.

User Reactions

Of course, when big changes are made it takes time for users to adapt and you cannot expect only to get praise. But we were taken by surprise by the strong negative feedback from several researchers and experienced users regarding the lack of A-Z lists. Their everyday work tool was gone and they could not understand the benefits

of using a general search box, trying to find their database in a seemingly random result list.

Reactions from students regarding the new web were generally positive, but we understood that they also had difficulties using the search tool. They did not know where to start and got no overview of what we offered.

The search worked quite well if the user knew the exact title, or was lucky enough to enter a search term that matched a subject term or the description. But not when the user only had a vague idea of the database name, did not find a good search term or wanted to be sure that all relevant databases were retrieved.

Both English and Swedish subject terms and descriptions were indexed, which enriched the searchability but often produced confusing results.

We also found that relevance ranking, for this small amount of results, was not useful. Summon algorithms does not know which database is most important for a certain subject. Alphabetical sorting may seem more logical for a small number of results.

Putting Out the Fire

Ad hoc, we quickly compiled a manual A-Z list of the most important databases. This was soon replaced by an A-Z list made from the Libris API, which allowed alphabetical sorting.

Now the database search queried Summon API while the A-Z list queried Libris API. The same metadata was used, but from different sources, thus resulting in slight differences in content and update frequency. Not an ideal situation, but it worked while figuring out how to proceed.

User Studies

Chalmers Library website was made with undergraduates in focus, but databases are mainly used by graduates and researchers. So, in subsequent user tests we decided to focus on the latter. We tested our current search, ideas for development as well as database search features at a few other library sites.

Results of user studies:

Finding databases: On the whole, users had problems finding databases. Nobody found the Search Box filter. Without filter, the user ended up in Summon where databases are not highly ranked and thus not found. The built in Summon feature "Database recommender" was not seen, and when pointed to, not understood.

Guidance: All users expressed the need for an overview, somewhere to start. For inexperienced users this was essential as the concept of "database" itself is vague. They wanted to be able to easily find the most relevant information source for their own need. Many asked for some kind of ranking or top list.

Descriptions: It is difficult to take in information about databases you do not already know. However, browsing gives an opportunity to explore more if the items are attractively presented with short unbiased descriptions. Long sales-like texts were not appreciated.

Subject terms: This proved to be a catch 22. Broad terms—too many results. Narrow terms—too few. When finding a relevant narrow subject entry, whether in a hierarchy or just as a clickable term in the description, the user was happy but tended to miss that large general databases were omitted.

Database types: When pointed there, users really enjoyed browsing for specific material types such as images, patents, etc., while more abstract types such as "bibliographic" were just cluttering the interface.

Limitations With the Summon API

When records are transferred to Summon, related MARC fields are merged into larger field groups, which are used by the Summon API. This makes it difficult to distinguish between different kinds of titles, subject terms or to make use of specific note fields.

DocumentTitle	245$a
DocumentTitleAlternate	130$a $d $f $k $l $m $n $o $p $r $s,210$a $b,240$a $d $f $k $l $m $n $o $p $r $s, 242$a $b $n $s $p, 246$a $b $f $n $p,600$t,610$t,611$t,630$a $d $f $h $k $l $n $o $p $r $s,730$a $d $f $k $l $m $n $o $p $r $s,740$a $n $p
Notes	020$z, 022$z $y $l, 362$a $z, 500$a, 502$a $b $c $d $g $o, 510$a $b $c, 511$a, 518$a, 530$a $b $c $d,533$a $b $c $d $e $f $m $n,534$p $a $b $c $e $f $k $l $m $n $t,538$a $i,583$a $b $c $d $e $f $h $i $j $k $l $n $o $x $z

Figure 3. MARC fields merged into Summon field groups.

Delay in data update due to use of a nonprimary source was also an issue. From Libris to our local catalog it is one day delay. The data is uploaded to Summon the next day but the indexing takes 2-10 days. We wanted changes made much sooner.

Second Attempt—Focus on Search AND Browse

A cross-functional team was assembled with metadata librarians and IT developers. User stories were written and prioritized together with colleagues at the information literacy department.

Redirected Flow of Data

Abandoning the principle of using Summon API, we decided to use the API from the primary source, Libris. As the records were now coming directly from Libris, changes were visible the next day and we had access to granular metadata.

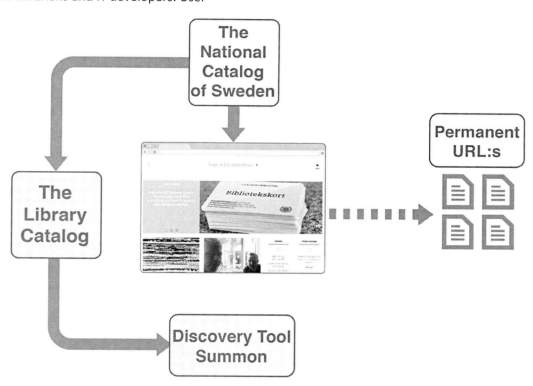

Figure 4. Redirected data flow.

Local Control of Collaborative Records

To make use of the new possibilities that came with access to original MARC fields, we needed to rethink and recatalog the databases completely. The only way to gain control of the selection and metadata was to work with our holdings records, which are not changeable by anyone else.

We strived to enable browsing in various ways and to distinguish English descriptions from Swedish. Another intention was to enter data that could be used to display information not normally found in catalog records (login information, etc.)

Entry Page

An entry page was created with A-Z, subject areas and types of content. We highlighted a few recommended starting points: general encyclopedias and large multidisciplinary databases. As a courtesy to alumni and other nonaffiliated users, we also included a premade search for free databases. When at the entry page, the filter on databases was automatically applied, to enable further searching.

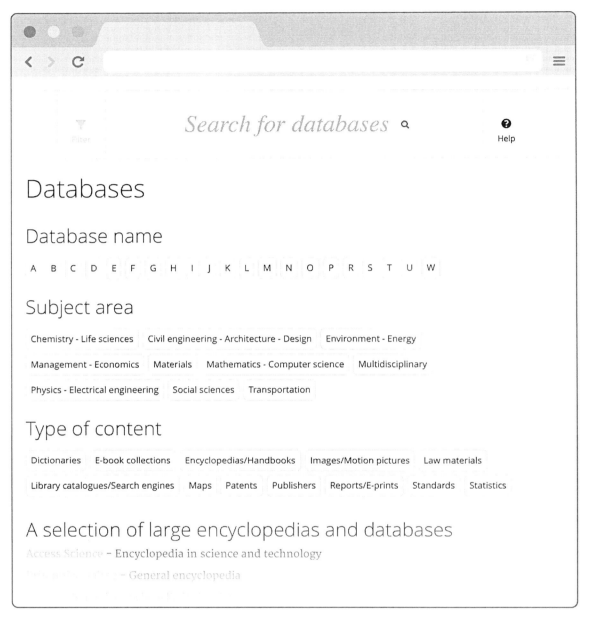

Figure 5. Entry page for database search & browse.

Useful Information About the Database

A great deal of work was demanded to write short and concise descriptions of each database in both languages, not being influenced by vendor phrases. Swedish descriptions were displayed but omitted from the search index as mixing of languages returns peculiar results.

A note field was committed for linking to the ERMs Terms of Use page. This link is displayed

under a Terms of Use tab in the result list. Nothing fancy, just taking the interested user to 360 Resource Manager license terms page.

We also dedicated a note field for useful information, to be displayed under the Hints tab. This could contain information about special software needed, login information, or, as in the case below, limits in the open access. When no information is entered, the tab is not displayed.

Description Terms of use Type of database | Hints

Most material is available for free. An exception is review and commentary content in the six flagship journals (Journal of Biology, Genome Biology, Genome Medicine, Arthritis Research and Therapy, Breast Cancer Research, and Critical Care)

Subject: *Chemistry - Life sciences*

Figure 6. A record with Hints tab displayed.

The Work With Subject Terms and Database Types

Subject terms are difficult in many ways. The user studies confirmed the risk of building a hierarchy of subject terms, as users go for the most narrow term and tend to miss general resources.

Subject terms are unequally ambitiously entered in Libris and Swedish terms are not as common as English. It is an overwhelming task to enter narrow terms on all databases, as many of them are covering very large areas. Also, there is no language distinction built into MARC fields, only an indication of the source of the term. As Swedish terms made retrieval unreliable, we needed to omit them even though it meant that some good English terms were omitted in the process.

A strict list of broad subject categories was deployed and used for populating the holdings records. This way we hope to achieve browsing on broad terms while using the narrower terms mainly for descriptions. We will continue to work with enhancing the bibliographic records while also benefitting from the work by other libraries.

For general databases we use the category "multidisciplinary." As user testing confirmed our expectations that nobody bother to click on this category, we gave these databases several other categories as well. We still need to figure out a way to show general resources in a better way.

"Database type" is used both as a pedagogical description and as browse feature. However, some descriptive types such as "bibliographic" or "articles" are meaningless to browse on and were removed from the entry page but kept at each record description.

Machine Readable Cataloging Records Are Not Machine Readable

Reflecting the old card catalog, cataloging rules state standardized punctuation. The punctuation depends on the subsequent subfield. For example, the title in the subfield 245#a is ended by a colon if there is a subtitle in 245#b, but with a slash if the subfield #a is directly followed by 245#c with creator. A nightmare for programmers. A whole bunch of if-clauses had to be programmed to avoid punctuation to turn up unexpectedly.

As we use some MARC fields in ways they are not intended for and as a programmed application is very unforgiving, every wrongly entered or left out indicator, subfield code or misspelled text could wreck the retrieval and display. In addition to carefully complying with the normal catalog standards, metadata librarians put together a detailed cataloging manual for databases, which is followed meticulously.

Avoiding Broken Links in LibGuides and Other Web Pages

The best way of avoiding double maintenance is not to link to other pages but to the database list itself, with a pre made search if needed. But in reality there will always be need for promoting specific titles and make a custom description for a defined user group. Therefore, we created a template for persistent URLs and encouraged colleagues to use those instead.

Improving Discoverability in the Discovery Tool

The Summon feature Database recommender is based on search results. It is a good intention but often gives rather peculiar results and we therefore decided to turn it off. Instead we use another Summon feature called Best Bets. Here you may enter links to web pages that you want to promote, with a short text and searchable tags. An entry has been made for each database in Best Bets, with alternative titles and possible misspellings. The persistent URLs are used for them as well.

What We Learned

We Love Recycling

To catalog once and use the same records in many places works really well. But, to be frank, there is still some double maintenance since we want to promote resources at web pages, LibGuides or in the discovery tool.

Use a Good Data Source That Suits the Purpose

We need controlled and granular data to build a good application. Also, keeping as close as possible to the primary source to avoid delays in update and distortion of metadata may be self-evident, but was a lesson learned by us.

Do Not Underestimate the Need to Browse

Our assumptions that, at least, students live in a search centered world may be true. But we strongly experience that the need for browsing is there anyway, especially when trying to make new acquaintances or to find something you may recognize but are not sure how to search for.

Collaborative Cataloging— And the Need for Local Control

To benefit from collaborate cataloging is great, but when using selected records to build additional search features, we need to have more local control. We solved this by using holding records for essential fields and to follow a detailed manual when cataloging.

Pragmatic Cataloging—Following Strict Rules

There is a need to be pragmatic, to find fields suitable for the information we want to share while at the same time not breaking cataloging rules. For efficient programming there has to be exact criteria as to when and how to display a specific text. It is an interesting balance between those worlds.

Another aspect is the future. The somewhat old fashioned MARC standard is still in use, despite of the not very machine readable format. Tomorrow, there will be another context with BIBFRAME and linked data. We cannot wait to develop applications but we also try to avoid messing up for the future.

Be Agile: Think—Test—Rethink

A search feature may be used differently by different user groups. It is a challenge to develop something that suits everyone. When finding that we had misjudged user needs, we had to be truly agile and rethink completely.

In this project, as well as in several others, we have found that cross-functional teams with librarians and IT-developers mutually benefit of shared experiences and gain a deeper understanding of limitations and possibilities. Agile Scrum teams are now the base for the new organization at Chalmers library.

Technical Specifications

The solution consists of an Umbraco controller that downloads MARC-XML data from Libris XSearch (the Swedish national catalog) and transforms it into SOLR XML. The controller can be triggered to do an update, to delete all or to delete a single record. Via a scheduler, a daily update is triggered and a librarian can trigger delete or update on demand. The created index contains every database record with details about subject, genre, title, URL, description and much more.

Using an Umbraco macro we create faceted lists for initials, subjects and genres on an overview page. The lists then trigger searches that use another macro for displaying the database results in a list. The user can also freely search the SOLR index via this macro. The controller is built in Microsoft.NET and runs in Umbraco, which is an open source CMS from Denmark. SOLR is an open source search platform from Apache Lucene project.

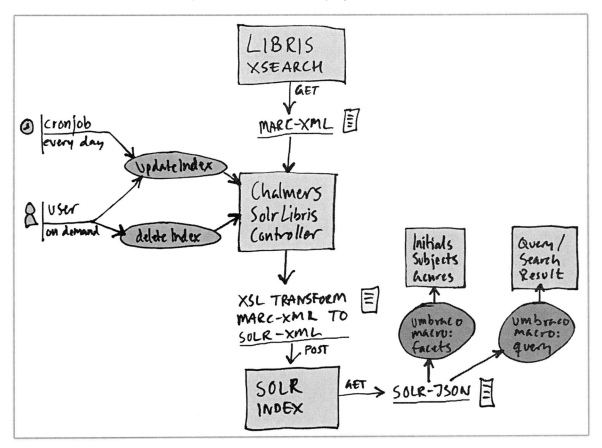

Figure 7. Technical description.

References

Chalmers Library Database Search. http://www.lib.chalmers.se/en/search/databases/database -list/?filter=2166&query=

Chalmers Library discovery tool Summon limited to databases. http://chalmers.summon.serialssolutions.com/#!/search?ho=t&fvf=ContentType,Database,f&q=&l=en

Examples on search strings on Chalmers Library web site. http://www.lib.chalmers.se/en/search/ Click on Encyclopedias/Handbooks, Patents, or Standards

The agile method scrum guide. http://www.scrumguides.org

Student Workers as Library Programmers:
A Case Study in Automated Overlap Analysis

Matthew W. Goddard, California Baptist University

Abstract

This paper describes a single solution to two very different problems. The first problem is that undergraduate students who aspire to careers in programming or software development need real-world work experiences that are not always readily available. The second problem is that in considering whether to acquire large e-book packages, libraries need to be able to answer the question, "How many of these do we already have?" Currently, most ILSs do not include a built-in feature to address the need for this kind of overlap analysis. In order to develop a simple, low-impact technical solution to this second problem, the library at California Baptist University also helped to address the first. We hired one upper division Electrical and Computer Engineering student to create a method to easily assess the redundancy of titles between large e-book packages and current holdings. The objective of this paper is twofold: to advocate for increased high-level use of student workers enrolled in computer science or computer engineering programs, and to share one simple, affordable way for libraries to assess the feasibility of large e-book packages.

In the earliest days of American higher education, undergraduate students were scarcely allowed to use their university's libraries, let alone work in them. Even when hiring of academic library student workers picked up steam in the 1910s and 1920s, there was grumbling from some quarters about what was seen as a tilt away from professional standards (White, 1985). By now, however, the widespread dependence of nearly all academic libraries on student workers is a long-standing fact of life. But these undergraduate students, particularly those enrolled in upper division courses with content relevance to library operations, often have so much more to offer than libraries are willing to accept. These students are also acutely aware that they will be entering a job market where relevant work or internship experience is viewed as more important than academic achievement across "all industries and hiring levels" (Fischer, 2013). By entrusting these students with projects that create value for the library and provide meaningful experience to the student, libraries can create an ideal win-win scenario.

Literature Review

The typical responsibilities of student workers are commonly known and fairly standard across academic libraries. Shelving, circulation, and the scanning component of digitization are representative of the relatively low level of responsibility entrusted to library student workers. Tasks requiring manual labor are prominent, and help desk duties are often limited to answering the most basic questions. Even as the historical trend has been toward giving student workers more responsibility, libraries remain reluctant to assign tasks requiring a high level of responsibility (Gruen & Wooden, 2011). There is a smattering of examples of more advanced projects in the library literature. In the late 1980s, Texas A&M hired students fluent in Chinese to assist in cataloging Chinese language materials (Gomez & LaGrange, 1990). At Virginia Commonwealth University in the 1990s, art students were hired to catalog art exhibition catalogs (Guidarelli & Cary, 1999). More recently, University of Michigan and Coastal Carolina University have implemented peer reference services, recruiting undergraduates to help other undergraduates with their research (MacAdam and Nichols; Faix et al.). Finally, many institutions with LIS programs offer graduate assistantships in a wide range of areas (Silver and Cunningham).

In all of these examples, students were recruited for the particular skills they brought to the project. In the first two examples, it was necessary to hire undergraduate student workers with particular skills because those skills were not sufficiently represented by the library staff. The project discussed in this paper focuses on student workers with career aspirations in programming and/or web development. For small libraries without the budget capacity for hiring library developers or programmers, these students are a rich and underutilized resource.

The Project

The Annie Gabriel Library is the sole library serving California Baptist University (CBU), a mid-sized private university in Riverside, California. Like every other academic library, we employ many student workers without whom our operations would quickly spin into chaos. They process, shelve, circulate and repair books, they scan archival materials, and they keep our printers full of paper. They do much else, but the preponderance of these responsibilities are similarly low on the scale of complexity and responsibility.

With significantly more e-books in our collections than print books, the library depends on licensing large packages of e-books from publishers and aggregators, ranging in size from several hundred to tens of thousands. With the rapid growth of our e-book collection, and continued acquisitions of print books, it becomes increasingly important for us to effectively evaluate the redundancy between the many and varied e-book packages available to us and our current holdings. Only with this analysis can we accurately calculate important values like the cost per unique title. So we decided to take advantage of the expertise represented in the CBU School of Engineering's Electrical and Computer Engineering Bachelor of Science degree program by hiring one upper division undergraduate student to tackle this project.

The results of his efforts was a simple utility (dubbed "Osiris" after its creator) to quickly and easily compare any list of books to a library's current bibliographic holdings. It is a short, relatively simple 343-line Perl script that checks the status of any given CSV file of titles against our local ILS holdings using a catalog search service included in the standard Symphony Web Services module provided by our ILS vendor, SirsiDynix. While it was designed with the primary purpose of

evaluating e-book packages as described above, it can also be used to evaluate large donations of print materials, as well as verifying that subscribed e-book packages are fully represented in the local catalog. After describing some general guidelines for small libraries considering hiring student workers to apply their programming or development expertise to library projects, this paper will conclude with a brief description of the utility itself.

The first recommendation is that the main project should be relatively low priority. Learning on the job is a significant aspect of the student's experience, so projects that require quick turnaround on tight deadlines are not ideal. The student and supervising librarian may decide to establish project milestones in advance, with particular dates as deadlines, but these dates should be merely provisional. The student's experience, and the project itself, will benefit most when the student has ample time to tinker.

Second, it is good to have additional, smaller and simpler projects or tasks for the student to pursue, even if they have nothing to do with programming. This practice benefits both the student and the supervising librarian. For the student, these kinds of tasks may provide a welcome change of pace from the main project and allow the student to continue working even when progress on the main project is halted for whatever reason. For the librarian, they provide some of the benefits of a traditional student assistant in getting more things done. Some examples of peripheral tasks completed during our project include verifying activation of e-journal access, creating library signage, updating library tutorial videos, and providing manual collection analysis.

Third, the supervising librarian should frequently be available for questions. The student will learn by doing, by reading, but also by interacting with the supervising librarian. Many questions will naturally arise over the course of a project, so being available to answer questions will prevent misunderstandings and wasted time. We tried to schedule the student's hours to overlap with the librarian's hours as much as possible, and both worked in the same office. Thus, it was an ideal environment for open communication.

Fourth, the supervising librarian should regularly check in on progress. The sharpest, most assertive students will ask all of the questions they need in order to effectively complete their project. However, either because they are shy or cocksure, some students will not. Regularly checking in on the student's progress not only provides accountability, but also provides an opportunity to communicate more deeply about the project. When everyone has a good understanding of how the project is proceeding, ideas can be shared about the best ways of proceeding. In our project, regular communication provided opportunities to discuss problems and combine our knowledge to identify the best solutions.

Finally, hiring students who are near the beginning of their senior year is a good idea for two reasons. First, these students will generally be the most experienced in the kind of programming and development they'll be asked to perform, even if only from their coursework. Secondly, relatively short-term employment ensures that in the unlikely event the arrangement ends up not being the win-win both parties expected, it will at least be only for a predetermined period of time. We have hired seniors for three consecutive years; each year, the graduating senior helps pick his successor. Using this method we have had great success in finding students who are sharp and committed.

The End Product

"Do we have this book?" is surely among the most basic questions that can be asked of a library, not to mention the most common. It is trivial for most people to answer this question for themselves. However, the task of automating this process in order to answer it for thousands of books at once reveals just how complex it really can be. Does "have" mean hold in print, or do e-book licenses count? Does "this book" mean this specific edition, or will any edition do? For the purposes of identifying overlap, we wanted to know if we held any edition, irrespective of format. This requirement limited the value of International Standard Book

Numbers (ISBNs), which are assigned to specific editions in specific formats (many newly published books will have five different ISBNs: for hardcover, softcover, and three different e-book formats (EPUB, MOBI and PDF). So the much simpler question, "Is this ISBN indexed in our catalog?" is not sufficient to answer our broader question, "Do we have this book?"

Other identifiers naturally suggested themselves as alternatives, foremost among them OCLC numbers; however, OCLC numbers are very rarely used by vendors, and thus are unlikely to be included in e-book package listings. So in spite of their shortcomings, ISBNs remained the best option for a unique identifier to look up, but further steps were needed to catch those cases where there is a match between titles, but not editions or format.

Thus, the script uses a two-step process. First, it searches for the ISBNs included in the source data file. Since many vendors include multiple ISBNs for each title, the script first looks up one, then the other only if the first does not find a match. If either ISBN is found in the local catalog, the script prints the result to the output file and moves on to the next title.

If neither ISBN is found, the script moves on to the second step, searching by title and author. Essentially, it performs a traditional known-item search, among the simplest tasks for a human operator. However, because the exact expression of titles and authors can vary in subtle but impactful ways, this step is more complicated than the first. We made an effort to find an optimal balance between two competing values: precision (i.e., accuracy—the proportion of matches that are made that accurate represent a match of the same title) and recall (i.e., comprehensiveness—the proportion of actual matches that are successfully identified as such).

The problem of precision arises in particular when the source data does not include author names, and/or when titles are extremely short or general. For example, if all we know about a title is that its title is Biology and its author is Smith, it is extremely likely to find results (there are many books written by a Smith with "biology" in its title), regardless of whether any of those results are actually the title in question.

The various complications that had to be considered related to recall included:

- Source data that includes edition information in the title field, which is not indexed in the local catalog.

- Author names that include initials (such as those specified in APA style) rather than spelling the name out.

- Author names that include middle names or titles that are not indexed in the local catalog.

- Other minor differences of spelling or punctuation that may impact the search.

While some of these cases have no elegant solution using the tools and limitations of the project, our overall approach was to strike an optimal balance wherein titles that are held are most likely to be identified as such, without creating unnecessary cases of titles that are not held being identified as held. To that end, we decided to exclude subtitles of books, to exclude stop words, to remove certain special characters that may affect the search, and to remove volume information that may be included in the title field. We also decided to avoid complications in author names by only including the author's last name.

To maximize the script's flexibility and reduce the workload necessary to run it, the operator is first asked to provide a number of inputs. These inputs provide information on the formatting of the source data so that that data does not need to be extensively manipulated prior to running the script. Specifically, the operator is prompted to provide the name of the source file, the name of the output file, the separator value (typically comma or pipe), and which columns contain the title, author, and ISBNs. There is also a prompt asking whether the author's first and last names are combined in one column or separated into two, and if the former, the order of those names ("First Last" or "Last, First").

After the script completes, it outputs the overall number and percentage of unique titles, the runtime, and any errors that may indicate titles that should be checked manually. It also creates an output file in CSV format that lists details of each title's status, number of hits, and the item type of the first hit. While it's not always perfectly accurate, this information has already proven invaluable for analyzing the viability of prospective e-book collections.

Conclusion

The future of library technology will be developed by individuals currently enrolled in IT/CS programs at our institutions. Employing these students now exposes them to the value and relevance of libraries, as well as our unique needs and challenges. While a consideration of the differences between the computer science/information technology paradigm and the library/information science paradigm is well beyond the scope of this paper, it might be noted that librarians have an opportunity to augment the dominant computer science paradigm in which they're being inculcated with the library perspective that places a great emphasis on privacy, ethical behavior, and traditional sources of information.

At the same time, bringing a computer science or information technology student to work in the library introduces a valuable source of fresh and innovative thinking that may sometimes be lacking in academic libraries. The result of this project was so valuable to the library, and the experience of it so valuable to the student worker, that we expect to continue to employ one senior from the Electrical & Computer Engineering Program to pursue similar projects in the future. It is hoped that other academic libraries with staffing limitations might learn from this experience. By creating a flexible environment that fosters creativity, by giving the student time to pursue his or her own ideas, and by helping projects along with suggestions when they hit a wall, libraries can create a win-win scenario that will pay dividends for both student and library, far into the future.

References

Faix, A. I., Bates, M. H., Hartman, L. A., Hughes, J. H., Schacher, C. N., Elliot, B. J., Woods, A. D. (2010). Peer reference redefined: New uses for undergraduate students. *Reference Services Review, 38*(1), 90-107.

Fischer, K. (March, 2013). The employment mismatch. *Chronicle of Higher Education*. Retrieved from http://chronicle.com/article/The-Employment-Mismatch/137625

Gomez, J. & LaGrange, J. (1990). A Chinese challenge: Utilizing students for special cataloging projects. *Cataloging & Classification Quarterly. 12*(1), 87-102.

Gruen, C. M. & Wooden, A. M. (2011). Student assistants 2.0: Utilizing your student assistant's capabilities. In Baudino, F. (Ed.), *Brick and click libraries: An academic library symposium, Northwest Missouri State University, Friday, November 4, 2011* (pp. 18-26). Maryville, MO: Northwest Missouri State University. Retrieved from http://files.eric.ed.gov/fulltext/ED526899.pdf

Guidarelli, N. & Cary, K. (1999). Untapped resource: Art students cataloging art exhibition catalogs at Virginia Commonwealth University." *Cataloging & Classification Quarterly, 26*(4), 63-75. http://dx.doi.org/10.1300/J104v26n04_05

MacAdam, B. & Nichols, D. P. (1989). Peer information counseling: An academic library program for minority students. *Journal of Academic Librarianship, 15*(4), 204-209.

Silver, S. L., & Cunningham, V. P. (2008). *The impact of the USF Tampa Library graduate assistant program on career and professional development*. Retrieved from ERIC database. (ED500319).

White, E. C. (1985). Student assistants in academic libraries: From reluctance to reliance. *The Journal of Academic Librarianship, 11*(2), 93-97.

Advanced Data Analysis: From Excel PivotTables to Microsoft Access

Christopher C. Brown, University of Denver
Denise Pan, University of Colorado Denver
Gabrielle Wiersma, University of Colorado at Boulder

Abstract

Most librarians run for the hills when they hear about Microsoft Excel PivotTables and relational databases such as Microsoft Access. PivotTables can be a powerful analysis tool. However, Microsoft Access can move beyond PivotTables by exploring more complex relationships between datasets. Building from the morning session, participants learned additional Excel functions including PivotTables and PivotCharts, as well as Access tables, queries, forms, and reports. The session was held in a classroom with computers, so attendees received sample data to create PivotTables, PivotCharts, and their own relational database during this hands-on workshop. Readers of this proceeding may request sample data for the Excel PivotTable presentation by email correspondence with the lead author (denise.pan@ucdenver.edu).

Introduction

In 2013, librarians from the University of Colorado (CU) Boulder and Denver campuses collaborated to offer an Excel workshop at the 2013 Charleston Conference. They frequently used Excel in their work and would share what they learned with one another. In turn, the librarians thought that others would also find these tips and tricks useful. By no means do they claim to know everything about Excel. Rather, they are sharing what they have learned from self-taught trial and error. While the 2013 session was well-attended and received, the speakers tried to cover too much information in one session. As a result, for the 2014 Preconference, they created another session for PivotTables and invited a University of Denver librarian to introduce Microsoft Access. Including Access seemed to be a natural next step in their data analysis workshop because at a certain point the data becomes too cumbersome to analyze in an Excel worksheet, and a relational database is needed. Specifically, this proceeding gives an introduction to Excel PivotTable features and functions.

Excel Worksheet Data for PivotTables and Pivot Charts

To make the workshop relevant to acquisitions and collection development librarians, the participants evaluated data for a fictitious journal cancellation project using information available in an Excel worksheet. It is assumed that that the data has been prepared in advance by exporting a journal title list and cost data from an Integrated Library Management System, and several years of usage data has been added into the worksheet. By including relevant data in a worksheet, it can be summarized, analyzed, and visualized with PivotTables and PivotCharts. For information on how to import data using VLookup, see the 2013 and 2014 Excelling with Excel Proceedings. The screenshot below shows the first 15 rows of data provided to session participants. Please note, instructions are provided for Microsoft Excel 2013.

	A	B	C	D	E	F	G	H	I	J	K	L	M
1	Journal Title	Order Record	Print ISSN	Online ISSN	Subject	Librarian	Fund	2013 Sub Cost	2011 Usage	2012 Usage	2013 Usage	2013 Cost per use	Total Usage
2	Aerospace Engine	2703828	5277-7728	3513-1053	Engineering	Jack	4444805	$2,584.00	9	9	11	$234.91	29
3	Anthropology Jou	290326x	6017-6218	4949-9377	Anthropolo|	George	4444137	$476.00	0	0	0	$476.00	0
4	Art Catalogue	2802284	3230-2654	3771-7393	Art	Ashley	4444987	$95.00	18	82	92	$1.03	192
5	Art Review	2703361	2394-4926	2951-8957	Art	Ashley	4444987	$101.00	13	43	27	$3.74	83
6	Biography Journal	2703993	7649-8742	9644-1556	General/Int|	Jill	4444397	$399.00	5	2	5	$79.80	12
7	Book Review Wee	2802259	7816-2614	3049-5471	Literature	Barbara	4444370	$500.00	6	4	3	$166.67	13
8	Business	2703889	9843-9957	6507-6796	Business	Philip	4444247	$168.00	0	0	0	$168.00	0
9	Chemical Reactior	2703300	3843-3646	7716-6704	Chemistry	Jack	4444765	$1,569.00	0	0	0	$1,569.00	0
10	Chemistry Journa	2703695	5768-7163	9426-5179	Chemistry	Jack	4444765	$1,427.00	2	5	3	$475.67	10
11	Classics Review	2703890	7500-6558	4534-7813	Classics	Jill	4444038	$283.00	6	6	19	$14.89	31
12	Computer Science	2703725	6530-3171	3282-7349	Computer S	Jack	4444924	$1,489.00	6	4	2	$744.50	12
13	CS Journal	2703981	4328-7461	3079-3250	Computer S	Jack	4444924	$2,543.00	8	6	6	$423.83	20
14	Dancer Quarterly	2685851	3747-1602	5787-3237	Dance	Jill	4444061	$191.00	4	7	7	$27.29	18
15	Earth Sciences Jou	2734072	5306-4002	2172-1495	Earth Scienc	Jack	4444412	$961.00	83	149	134	$7.17	366

Figure 1. Excel worksheet data.

When making an Excel worksheet and before creating PivotTables, make sure that there are no blank or unlabeled columns in the worksheet. Excel will not be able to generate a PivotTable. Without a header the field is undefined. Other best practices including the following:

- Use short and unique phrases in headers.

- Avoid using special characters because some characters will cause Excel to ignore that particular column.

- If you sum totals in the bottom row of a table, avoid including the total row in your source data. Otherwise, the total row will be included in your PivotTable as if it is another row of data or journal title.

- Excel can only pivot or analyze the rows or values that already exist in your worksheet. Therefore, derived valued (e.g., Cost per Use and Total Use) must be calculated in advance of inserting a PivotTable.

Creating PivotTables

Create a PivotTable from an existing Excel worksheet.

Instructions

1. Select ALL contents of the worksheet (Ctrl+A or click triangle in corner of A1). Or select a specific range of data ($A$1:$L$100).

2. Click on the PivotTable button in the Insert tab.

3. This will open the Create PivotTable window. Click OK to create new worksheet (default).

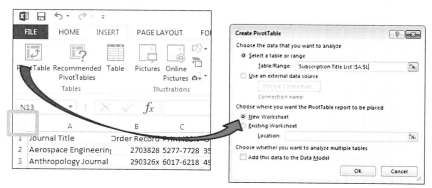

Figure 2. Create PivotTable.

Summary by Subject

This first example demonstrates how to answer the question "What is the count and cost of journals by subject?" with a PivotTable. It is possible to use Excel filters to sort and display a particular subject area. However, PivotTables will summarize the data in one table. Specifically, this scenario highlights the following aspects of PivotTables:

- Subtotal and summarize data by categories and subcategories.

- Expand and collapse levels of data to focus your results.

- Drill down to details from the summary data.

- Summarize data with a calculation type (e.g. sum, count, average, max, min, and product).

Instructions

1. Create new PivotTable worksheet (see *Creating PivotTables* section).

2. Rename worksheet as "by subject."

3. Drag and drop fields into the report.

   a. Rows: Subject and Journal Titles.

   b. Values: Journal Title and 2013 Sub Cost (Note: Report Filter will be blank and Columns will default to Values).

4. For 2013 Sub Cost in Values, click down arrow and select Value Field Settings.

5. Change Value Field Settings to Sum for Subscription Cost. Then click Number Format button to display the data in Accounting format ($X.XX). Click OK, OK.

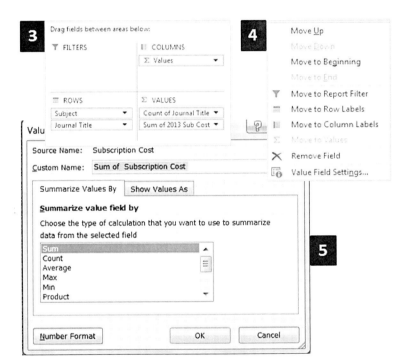

Figure 3. Summary by subject fields and values.

Analysis by Fund Code or Subject Librarian

The next example answers the question, "What is the total and average cost by fund or librarian?" It is also an opportunity to demonstrate how to pivot rows and also use the "average" calculation type.

Instructions

1. Create new PivotTable worksheet.

2. Rename worksheet as "by Fund."

3. Drag and drop fields into the report.

   a. Rows: Fund and Librarian.

   b. Values: Journal Title, 2013 Sub Cost **twice**.

4. Change Value Field Settings for first Subscription Cost to sum change the number format to Accounting.

5. For second Subscription Cost to average change the number format to Accounting.

6. Make a copy of "by Fund" worksheet and rename as "by Librarian."

7. Move Librarian up and Fund down.

Top 10 and Zero Use Titles

In the next example we will use filters to show the journal titles with the Top 10 highest used titles and all of the Zero use titles. The PivotTable can be used to answer the question—Which journal titles are used most/least?

Instructions

1. Create new PivotTable worksheet Rename worksheet as "Top 10."

2. Drag and drop fields into the report.

   a. Row Labels: Journal Titles.

   b. Values: 2013 Cost per use, and Total Usage.

3. Change Value Field Settings for Subscription Cost to **sum** and change the number format to Accounting; and 2012 Usage to **sum.**

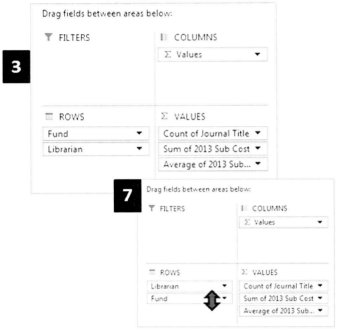

Figure 4. Analysis by Fund or Librarian fields and values.

Figure 5. Top 10 and Zero Use Titles filters.

4. Select the filter ⟨🔽⟩ icon in Row Labels, select Value Filters, and Top 10.

5. In the Top 10 Filter (Journal Title) window change the drop down to Sum of Total Usage.

6. Make a copy of "Top 10" and rename as "Zero Use."

7. Select the filer icon in Row Labels, select Value Filters, and Equals.

8. In the Value Filter (Journal Title) window change drop downs to display Sum of Total Usage equals 0.

Chart Usage by Subject

Charts provide a visual representation of your data. They show big picture trends and relationships between different series of data in a graphical format. Similarly, PivotChart can help you see comparisons and patterns from PivotTable report summary data. For our example we will create a PivotChart to look at the usage over time by subject area.

Figure 6: Create PivotChart.

Instructions

1. Create PivotChart worksheet by selecting "PivotChart" from the Insert tab.

2. Rename worksheet "Historical Usage."

3. Drag and drop fields into the report.

    a. Axis (Categories): Subject.

    b. Values: 2011 Usage, 2012 Usage, 2013 Usage.

4. Change Value Field Settings for all of the usage values to sum.

5. Excel will build the PivotTable and PivotChart. while you are changing the PivotTable Field List.

6. Customize the look and feel of the PivotChart from the PivotChart Tools > Design Tab > Change Chart Type (e.g., Stacked Line).

Figure 7. Change Chart Type.

PivotTable to PivotChart

Excel automatically creates a PivotChart when you are building a PivotTable.

Instructions

1. Make a copy of a worksheet that already has a PivotTable (e.g., Zero Use).

2. Rename the worksheet as "Chart Zero Use."

3. Click in the PivotTable to display the Analyze tab (Options tab in Excel 2010) PivotTable Tools, and then click the PivotChart Button.

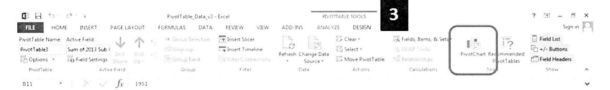

Figure 8. Create PivotChart from PivotTable.

4. The Insert Chart window will display. Select the type of chart you want to use (e.g., Column). OK.

5. Excel will create the PivotChart. Use Design tab in PivotChart Tools to customize the chart.

Conclusion

PivotTables and PivotCharts allow librarians to summarize, analyze, explore, visualize, and present data from their Excel worksheets. They are able to see comparisons, patterns, and trends. As a result, they have knowledge to make informed decisions about collection data. This session highlighted the following Excel features:

- Subtotal and summarize data by categories and subcategories.

- Expand/collapse levels of data.

- Summarize data with a calculation type (sum, count, average, max, min, product).

- Flip or pivot data.

- Filtering to limit results (Top 10 and zero use).

- Creating Pivot Charts.

In turn, these functions enabled participants to answer the following questions about their sample journal and cost data:

- What is the count and cost of journal by subject?

- What is the total and average cost by fund or librarian?

- Which titles are used most or least?

- What is the usage over time by subject area?

This presentation and paper demonstrated the power and possibilities of using PivotTables and PivotCharts in Acquisitions and Collection Development assessment activities.

Part 2. Microsoft Access

Christopher C. Brown

Most librarians run for the hills when they hear about Microsoft Excel PivotTables and relational databases such as Microsoft Access. PivotTables can be a powerful analysis tool. However, Microsoft Access can move beyond PivotTables by exploring more complex relationships between datasets. This session begins with an overview of Microsoft Access and its relational capabilities. Then we work through a five-part exercise. This stepped approach allows users to start anew in a new folder with a clean version of the project just in case they got lost or behind from the previous steps. Hopefully participants will be motivated to continue learning to use Access for statistical analysis.

Introduction

There are some library statistical projects for which Microsoft Excel is not powerful enough. Microsoft Access can be used to perform these more powerful functions. The problem is that Access can be quite challenging to learn; it's not intuitive to just start using Access. The Charleston Conference preconference and proceedings provide a basic introduction to what Microsoft

Access is and how it can be used for some basic statistics functions. After giving some background information about Access, we provide an exercise with five separate steps in which we use various Access skills. It is hoped that these exercises will give people enough of an initiation to delve into the many other aspects of Access queries, forms, and reports.

Because the data sets for the practice exercises are quite large (56 MB), flash drives were distributed during the preconference session. However, readers of these proceedings may request access to the data by email correspondence with the author (christopher.brown@du.edu).

Excel or Access—Which to Use When?

Microsoft Excel is an extremely powerful tool when used in analyzing library collection statistics, but there are some functions that require more power. Microsoft Access can be used for larger data sets, when more complex querying is required, and when one-to-many or many-to-many relationships need to be expressed.

Excel	Access
One-to-one relationships	Possible one-to-many relationships
1,048,576 rows by 16,384 columns (Office 2010)	2GB database size limit
Best for small amounts of data	Better for larger amounts of data
Simple displays and sorts	Complex queries
Best for mostly numeric data	Best when textual data included
Best for calculations and basic statistical comparisons	Useful for more complex comparisons
Flat structure keeps all data together—easier to migrate	Relational means data lives in many tables—hard to migrate
Pivot Tables	Cross-tabulation queries

Table 1. Excel and Access compared.

Understanding Access Object Types

People find Access intimidating from the outset for many reasons. First of all, you can't even begin to use Access without naming your database and saving it to a specific location. This model differs from that of Microsoft Word, Excel, and PowerPoint, where you simply open the application and begin doing things. With Access beginners have no idea where to start. With that in mind it is helpful to define the object types within Access and how they relate to each other.

Access Structure

Access Forms and Reports can be based on tables or queries, but my advice is: always base them on queries.

Queries allow for functions such as sorting, limiting with parameters, calculations, and dynamic URL links.

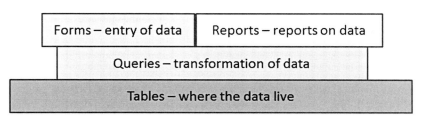

Figure 1. Microsoft Access basic object types.

The basic underlying object type is the table. All data ultimately are stored in tables and other objects like queries, forms, and reports are built off of the data stored in tables. Queries are useful for transforming data: transformations such as sorting and calculating numbers. Queries can also be used to make other tables, append records to tables, and update data in tables. We will be using each of these query types in this workshop.

Forms and reports can be built of off either tables or queries, but I very highly recommend that you only build them off of queries. Building forms and reports off of queries gives you much greater flexibility as your database project evolves. Forms can be used to enter data (in the case of ongoing projects) and display data (as in charts). Reports can be used to summarize data, group data and even output into book format.

Flat World Versus Relational World

Excel represents data in a "flat" manner, but Access is capable of representing data in a relational manner. The best way for me to communicate the differences is for us to imagine together that we are building a personal address book. We need certain data fields to hold our data. We will certainly need a LastName field, a FirstName field, and perhaps a MiddleName (or initial) field (at least when thinking of the structure of names in our culture). This means that every record in our database will have a MiddleName field whether or not every person has a middle name. We also would need appropriate address fields (Addr1, Addr2, City, State, Zip, and perhaps country).

But now we need to include information for contact information such as phone numbers. We might construct a field for HomePhone, WorkPhone, and perhaps Fax. But many people have more phone numbers than this. They may have multiple cell phone numbers, for example. We could include email address, but again, many people have a work email address, and very more than two personal email addresses. In the flat database world things are already getting overly complicated. We can continue to add multiple fields to accommodate all of these phone

numbers and email address, all the while increasing the size of our database for fields that will only be used in some of the cases.

The flat database world requires us to keep adding additional fields to our personal address database, whether we need them all of not, just to accommodate the numerous varieties of contacts we encounter today. But now let's do the same project in a relational database environment. We could construct a related table, a contacts table that could accommodate any number of contacts, from zero to an endless number. We only add a field if it is called for given the shape of the data.

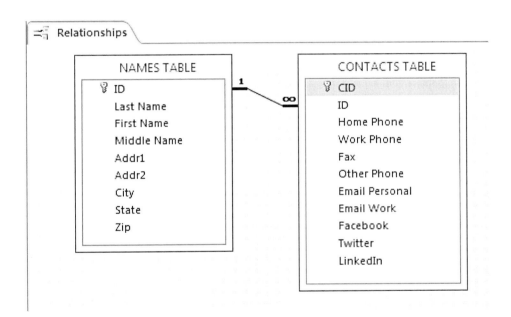

Figure 2. Relational database structure suggestion for an address book.

This simple example shows the power of a relational database such as Microsoft Access.

When working with data projects it is essential to think of the shape of the data. What kinds of relationships exist among the various fields? Consider field types: do you need number fields, text fields? Do you need binary Y/N fields, or would this information be better represented in a text field? Librarians have special considerations to consider like standard numbers (ISBN, ISSN)— fields that even though they appear to be

numbers, actually require text fields because of leading zeros, check digits, and hyphens.

In library data projects you often don't have the luxury of planning a data project from the ground up. Often you are given data sets from vendors, your ILS, or colleagues. You may need to compare data sets from dissimilar sources; for example, print circulation statistics from your ILS and counter statistics for ebooks from a vendor. Access is particularly strong at manipulating, transforming data from these different sources.

Example of a Relational Database

To give an example of what Access can do in terms of complex relationships I present a database project I did several years ago for United Nations Centre for Regional Development publications. The UNCRD is a United Nations field office headquartered in Nagoya, Japan. The database serves as an index to their books, book chapters, journal articles, conference proceedings, and other publications. I built the database from the ground up by systematically working through publications located in their Nagoya library. I needed Access because of the complexity of relationships. One item (article, paper, chapter) could have one or many authors, and any individual author could, in turn, have one or many published items.

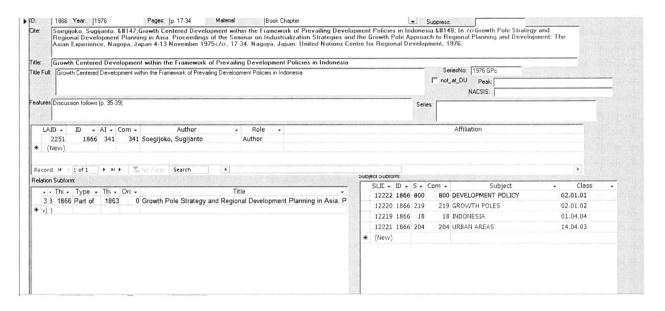

Figure 3. UNCRD database entry form.

The form in Figure 3 shows the main form with title and descriptive information in the upper section, with related subforms for author, relationship, and subject terms in the lower section.

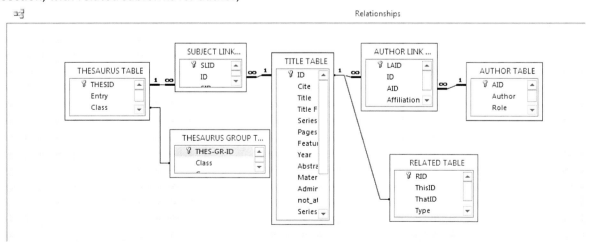

Figure 4. UNCRD database relational structure.

Figure 4 shows the relationships that exist in the UNCRD database, The Title Table is the central idea. Since it is only possible to have one-to-many relationships between any two tables, an additional table is inserted between the Title Table and the Author Table. Here is a one-to-many relationship between Title and the Author Link Table, and a one-to-many relationship between the Author Table and the Author Link Table. Thus we now have a many-to-many relationship between the Title Table and the Author Table, thanks to the intervening table. The same kind of relationship exists between the Title Table and the Thesaurus Table.

Most library statistical project won't need this kind of complexity within Access. I only provide this illustration to show the potential of a relational database in a library context.

Exercises

The best way to learn Access is to jump right in. With this in mind, I have prepared a series of datasets (JR1 reports) from eight academic libraries. All of the data has been anonymized.

This project involves comparing journal use from a particular big deal vendor across these eight academic libraries. The problem is that no two libraries have exactly the same list of journal titles. We need to figure out a way to compare data from dissimilar lists. We will do this by placing all ISBNs from each of the eight libraries into a new table, and then de-duplicating the ISSNs, thus creating a master list of ISSNs. Then we will build up the table with the usage data from each of the eight libraries. Finally we will examine cost-per-use for each library by importing yet another file. This series of exercises will require the use of select queries, make table queries, append queries, and update queries. Time will not permit us to get into forms or reports.

Step 1: Clean up Excel files by removing intro rows and totals row. Import files into Access.

Go to the folder labeled Step 1 and for each of the Excel files, remove the extra rows as shown in green in Figure 5. This is necessary before importing into Access.

	A	B	C	D	E	F	G	H	I
1	_JR1 Number of Successful Full-Text Article Requests by Month and Journal (Year 20								
2									
3	Page by:								
4	Account: Lib04								
5									
6	Journal	Publisher	Platform	Print ISSN	Online ISSN	Jan-2010	Feb-2010	Mar-2010	Apr-2010
7	Total					33,756	42,533	46,575	47,203
8	ACC Current Journal Review	Elsevier	ScienceDirect	1062-1458		1	3	1	(
9	Accident Analysis & Prevention	Elsevier	ScienceDirect	0001-4575		27	46	151	14(
10	Accident and Emergency Nursing	Elsevier	ScienceDirect	0965-2302		3	2	3	:
11	Accounting Forum	Elsevier	ScienceDirect	0155-9982		2	1	0	(
	Accounting, Management and Information Technologies	Elsevier	ScienceDirect	0959-					

Figure 5. Preparing the file for importing.

Now we are ready to import each of these files into Access as separate tables. Click the External Data tab in Access and select the Excel button.

Then navigate to each of the Excel files in the Step 1 folder and import them into Access as illustrated in Figure 6.

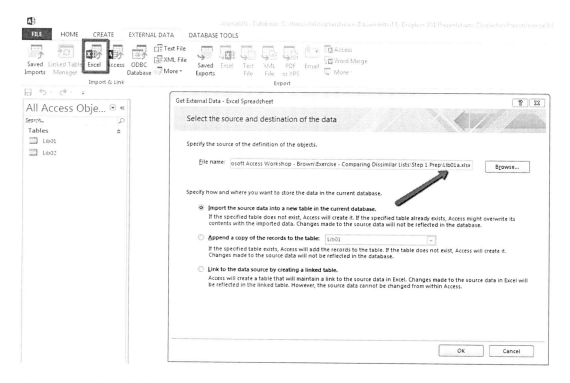

Figure 6. Importing a file from Excel.

Just in case you didn't understand how to do this, the Access database in Step 2 has all the data files already imported for you.

Step 2: Create a master ISSN Table containing all ISSNs from each of the eight files.

Be sure to navigate to the Step 2 folder within the data folder. This step involves using a query to do a make table query operation, followed by append operations. There are eight files that you need to place into a new table. The first operation will be

to take the first file and use a make table query. Create a new query and drag the Print ISSN and Journal fields into the grid as illustrated in Figure 7. Then, change the query type from a select query to a make table query. You will be asked to name your new table, so create a name of your choosing. Note that this operation has already been done for you for illustrative purposes. When you are ready to create your table, click the Run button within the query. You will then see your new table when you view your existing tables.

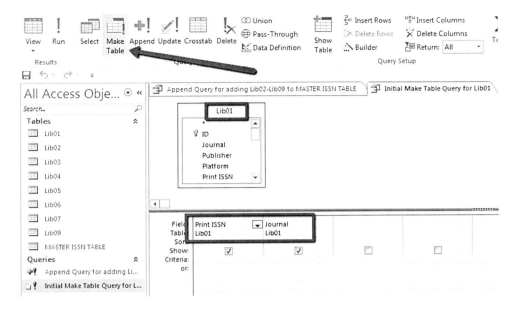

Figure 7. Creating Master ISSN Table to hold all ISSNs.

Now that the first file has been imported with a make table query, add the others with an append query as illustrated in Figure 8. These subsequent steps are similar to the make table operation, except that we want to add (append) the same fields from the other tables to your new Master ISSN Table.

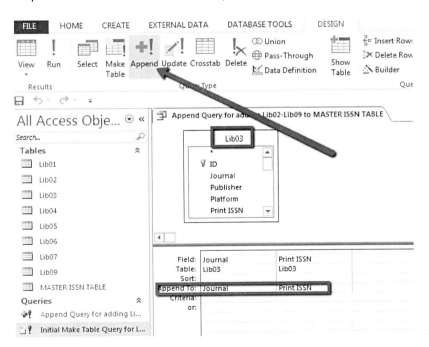

Figure 8. Appending ISSNs to Master ISSN Table.

Step 3: Deduplicate the Master ISSN Table.

Go now to the Step 3 folder. For this operation you need to create a query based on the Master ISSN Table.

When you create a new query, the default query type is the select query. In design mode of your newly created query, open the Property Sheet and select Unique Values = Yes, as illustrated in Figure 9. To see the results of this, click the View button to see your select query. You will see that what you have is just the unique ISSNs without all the duplicates.

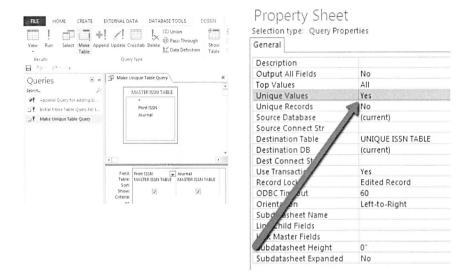

Figure 9. Make a new query, based on the Master ISSN Table, with only unique values showing.

Now use this query to make a table called Unique ISSN Table. After clean-up you should have something like 2,603 rows.

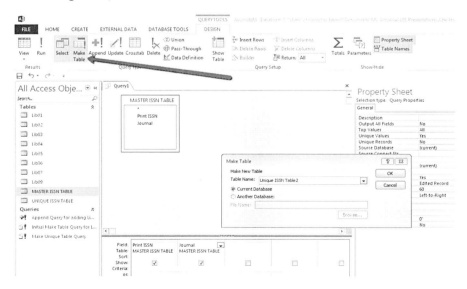

Figure 10. Make a new table containing only unique ISSNs.

Step 4: Update Query. You will first need to create fields for each of your "Libs" in your newly created Unique ISSN Table.

Open the newly created Unique ISSN Table in design view, and add fields for each of your eight

.

libraries as shown in Figure 11. Make the data type Number Double to match the format in each of the Lib tables. This step creates the empty fields into which we will place the matching data from the individual library data tables that you imported in Step 1.

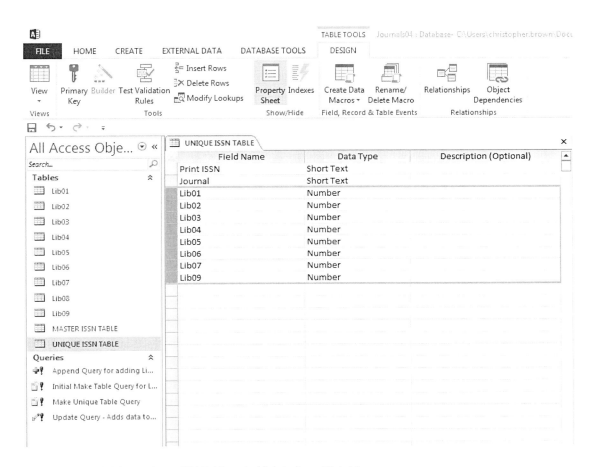

Figure 11. Add field to Unique ISSN Table to hold data from Lib tables.

Now we need to get the data from the individual "Lib" tables into the corresponding fields in the Unique ISSN table. To do this we need a new query that contains both the Unique ISSN Table (the target) and each, in turn, of the "Lib" tables (the source). Then, create a query linking on the ISSN as shown. You will then make this into an update query to update the respective "Lib" fields in the Unique ISSN table. You then need to make the link between the Print ISSN field in the Unique ISSN Table and the "Lib" table by dragging a line from one to the other, the result of which is

shown in Figure 12. Also, make sure your grid is as shown in Figure 12. This is the field that will be updated when we change the query from a select query to an update query. After you have changed the query to an update query and everything is set up as in Figure 12, you are ready to "run" the query (by hitting the run button).

You will do this same operation for each of the remaining Lib tables. Keep in mind that you can go to the next step to see these operations already completed for you.

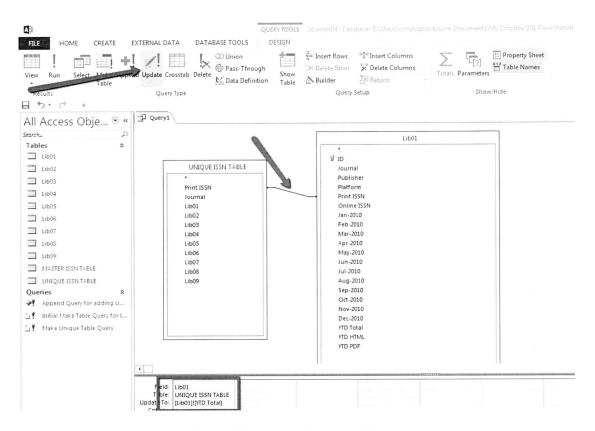

Figure 12. Prepare update query to bring Lib data into Unique ISSN table.

We now have solved our initial problem. All libraries have use data matched up against a unique list of ISSNs, with a uniform basis of comparison among all eight libraries.

Step 5. Import cost data.

But now we want to take things a step further. We want to see the cost-per-use for each journal. To do this we have supplied you with a data set. You will see a Cost Data Excel file in the Step 5 folder. Import this Excel file into your Access database. Next, create a linkage between your cost table and any of the tables in your database. You can use an individual library, or you can use the newly created Unique ISSN Table with all the work you have just completed.

To derive cost-per-use, create calculations in your query. First, calculate Cost-per-Use:

CostPerUse: [Cost]/[YTD Total].

Next, use this calculation to create a properly formatted series of cells:

PerUse: Format([CostPerUse],"Currency").

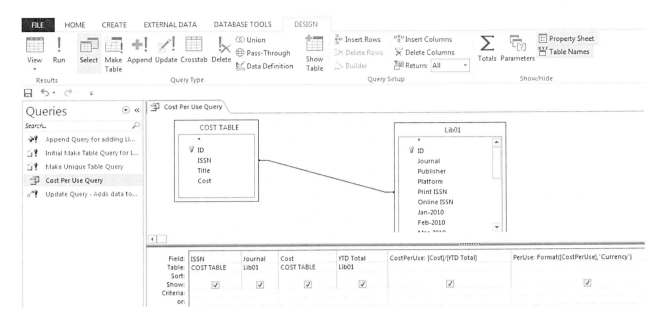

Figure 13. Link cost-per-use data with existing usage data.

Your final result will look like Figure 14.

ISSN	Journal	Cost	YTD Total	CostPerUse	PerUse
1062-1458	ACC Current Jo		3		
0001-4575	Accident Analy	$2,604.00	508	5.1259842519685	$5.13
0965-2302	Accident and E	$526.00	9	58.4444444444444	$58.44
0155-9982	Accounting For	$438.00	22	19.9090909090909	$19.91
0959-8022	Accounting, Ma	$1,023.00	3	341	$341.00
0361-3682	Accounting, Or	$2,815.00	97	29.020618556701	$29.02
0094-5765	Acta Astronaut	$5,881.00	116	50.698275862069	$50.70

Figure 14. Cost-per-use calculated in Access.

Review

We have performed many of the essential Access skills: importing data, work with make table queries, append queries, update queries, and select queries. We created linking to related fields. Being accomplished with Access involves years of building on previously learned skills and moving on the new ones. These exercises have only touched upon a few of the basic Access skill sets. There are many expensive Access guidebooks in your local bookstores, but I recommend the following one because it focuses on the skill sets needed by librarians.

Alexander, Michael. *Microsoft Access 2007 Data Analysis*. John Wiley & Sons, 2012. ISBN 9780470104859. Although Alexander's book is based on Access 2007, it's more than adequate for all subsequent versions of Access.

Part 3. Advanced Excel Functions for Collection Analysis

Gabrielle Wiersma

Microsoft Excel 2013 offers useful features and formulas that facilitate data manipulation and collection analysis. Using journal cancellations as a workplace scenario, this paper will provide an overview of how to organize data and complete basic calculations with Excel. The paper includes instructions for importing and exporting data, combing and comparing data from different sources, and formatting data to communicate results more effectively. It also describes how to use several advanced Excel functions including Flash Fill, VLOOKUP, and other formulas

Introduction

Librarians have access to a multitude of data about collections and usage. However, it can be difficult to connect and combine data from various sources because they are often saved in different files and formats. Using a hypothetical journal cancellation scenario, this paper highlights some of the features, functions, and formulas in Excel 2013 that make it a powerful tool for data manipulation and collection analysis. The tools and techniques described in the paper could be applied to other collection analysis projects such as evaluating renewals, marc record reconciliation, or comparing print and online usage.

This session was originally offered as a preconference workshop during the 2013 Charleston Library Conference. The session was well attended and the presenters were asked to repeat the workshop at the 2014 Conference. The 2014 preconference workshop and these proceedings build upon the 2013 presentation and paper and incorporates feedback that was received during and after the 2013 session. In addition, this paper includes additional information about new features in Excel 2013 with updated screen shots. For more information, please see the 2013 Charleston Library Conference proceedings by Denise Pan and Gabrielle Wiersma, "Excelling with Excel: Advanced Excel Functions for Collection Analysis" available online: http://dx.doi.org/10.5703/1288284315327

The following instructions will teach users how to create an Excel spreadsheet with information from various data sources, calculate cost-per-use, and analyze a set of journals based on usage. Readers could apply the same techniques to include other data such as impact factor or faculty input.

Project Goals

The most important first step in collection analysis is defining project goals and objectives. The goal of the workshop was to use Excel to identify journal titles for cancel within one hypothetical journal package. The objective was to cancel approximately $7,000 or 8% of the package based on cost per use data and usage trends.

Gathering and Importing Data

The next step is considering what types of data to collect. For a serials review project, data sources may include payment info from the Integrated Library System (ILS) and Journal Citation reports for impact factor in text format (.txt), and usage data or price lists from publishers that can be downloaded in Excel format (.xls). If the data is only available as a text file, it will need to be imported into Excel using the **Text Import Wizard**.

Importing Data

Excel can import data from Access, websites, text, and other sources like XML or SQL.

Click on the **Data tab → Get External Data → From Text** and select the text (.txt) file to open.

Figure 1. Import data from text.

Text Import Wizard

Step 1 of 3

1. Is your data **Fixed Width** or **Delimited**?

2. Was the data created in a specific character set? CU Boulder's ILS data is encoded in Unicode, UTF-8; other data sources like Serials Solutions provide the option of downloading in UTF-8 or Latin 1 encoding. Selecting the appropriate file origin will ensure that special characters and diacritics display properly in your spreadsheet.

3. Select **My data has headers** if the information in the first row contains columns headings.

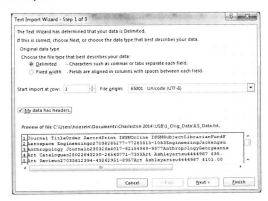

Figure 2. Text Import Wizard step 1.

Step 2 of 3—Delimited

For Delimited data you need to tell Excel which character delimits your data.

Use the **Data Preview** window to see how each character will affect your data (you can select space or enter a letter in the Other box to see how different delimiters separate the data).

Step 2 of 3—Fixed Width

Fixed width data contains data in fields of comparable or equal size. Use the preview window to add, move, or delete a column break.

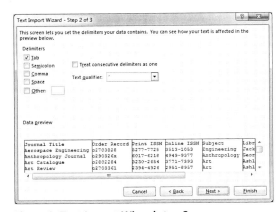

Figure 3. Text Import Wizard step 2.

Step 3 of 3

Format the data in each column: **General** converts numeric values to numbers, date values to dates, and all remaining values to text; Select **Text** for Print and Online ISSN, **General** for other columns and **Finish.**

Tell Excel where you want to paste the data. Default is Existing worksheet =$A$1.

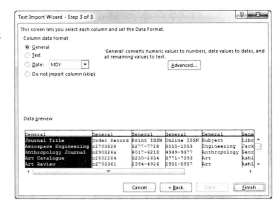

Figure 4. Text Import Wizard step 3.

Text to Columns

After data has been exported, it can be further separated using **Text to Columns**. Text to Columns can only separate one column of data at a time.

1. Insert column or columns to the right of the column that you want to separate.

2. Highlight the column of data that you want to separate.

3. Click on the Data tab **Data → Text to Columns.**

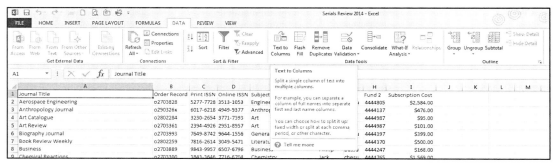

Figure 5. Text to Columns.

Create a copy of your data

Creating a copy of your data allows you to preserve a copy of your original data in one sheet and creates another copy of your data that you can clean up and manipulate. You can refer back to the original data or create additional copies as needed.

TIP: Create copies of your original data (you can only undo (CTRL+Z) so much!) Right-click the Sheet tab to copy, rename, or change tab color.

To create a copy of an Excel sheet:

1. Double Click or Right-click on **Sheet1 → Rename ILS Data** (or original data).

2. Right-click on **Sheet1 → Move or Copy.**

3. Select the **Create a copy** option.

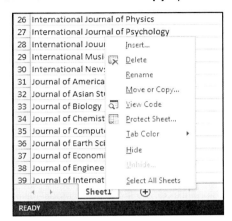

Figure 6. Move or copy a sheet.

Figure 7. Create a copy.

Figure 8. Organize sheets.

4. Rename the copy **Data Analysis.**

5. **OR** use the **Format Menu Home →** Format **→** Organize Sheets: Rename Sheet, Move or Copy Sheet, Tab Color.

Tables

By converting data into a table, Excel creates a relationship between the data and automatically adds several features that will make it easier to format and analyze the worksheet.

For example, the first row of the Table is automatically frozen so that it will continue to display as you scroll down the spreadsheet. In addition, the Table Tools Design tab includes options to make the Header Row and/or Last Column bold, and a variety of Table Styles to change the color and shading of the Table. This menu also includes Table Style Options like Banded Rows or Columns and functions like adding Filter Buttons to the first row and a Total Row on the last row. Total Rows are useful for inserting many simple formulas such as subtotals (sum), average, counts, min, and max in any column.

To insert a Table:

1. Click on the **Insert** tab**→ Table (Ctrl + T)**.

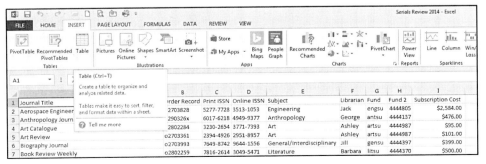

Figure 9. Insert a Table.

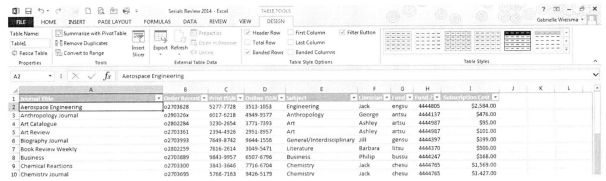

Figure 10. Table Tools and Design.

2. Table Design and Style.

    a. Click on the **Design tab/Table Tools** → Header Rows, Banded Rows, Filter buttons, Total Rows and Table Styles (colors and shading).

    b. Freezing the first row allows you to see the first row as you scroll down: **View → Freeze Panes** (1ˢᵗ row is automatically frozen in a Table; you can also freeze the first column or a select number of panes).

TIP: add a numbered column so that you can revert back to your original

Sorting, AutoFill, and Flash Fill

Sorting data is a basic but useful feature in Excel. Numeric data can be sorted smallest to largest or vice versa and text can be sorted alphabetically in ascending or descending order. If your data is was originally sorted alphabetically or by a simple numeric system you may be able to return to your original sort order. However, if you are working with data that was sorted by an alphanumeric schema like LC call number or another complex way Excel may not be able to sort the data in the correct order. Creating a numbered column with the original sort orders ensures that you can revert to the original sort order if needed.

Create a numbered column with original sort order

1. Right click on cell A1 and insert a table column to the left of column A .

2. Start numbering the series 1,2,3 and then use the fill handle ⬜ to **AutoFill** the series down the column (drag down or double click on the square in the bottom right of the fill handle until it turns into a +).

3. Sort data by text (A to Z or Z to A), numbers (smallest to largest or largest to smallest), dates and times (oldest to newest and newest to oldest).

4. Sort by Subject, Librarian, Subscription Cost; font or fill color.

Flash Fill

Flash Fill is a new feature in Excel 2013 that looks for patterns in adjacent cells to format your data. It can be used to clean up data or format it in different ways. For example, it can be used for:

- changing text casing from ALL CAPS to Upper and lowercase.

- formatting numbers (ISSN ####-#### instead of ########).

- combining text (First Name Last Name → Last Name, First Name).

To use Flash Fill:

1. **Right Click** and **Insert** a column to the right of the column that you want to format.

2. Start typing the data in the format you want to display (e.g. lowercase instead of caps or a specific number format).

3. Press **Enter** when Excel recognizes the pattern to fill down OR use **Ctrl + E.**

4. See also: **Home → Fill Down/Series/Flash Fill.**

TIP: Use Flash Fill to clean up data with inconsistent casing or combine

Filtering

Filtering is another basic but extremely useful function. Filtering creates a subset of data by displaying only data that meets your criteria and hiding all of the other data.

1. Numeric fields: try filtering to find the Top 10 or 20, Above Average, Below Average journals based on subscription costs.

   a. Filter → Number Filters → Top 10, Averages.

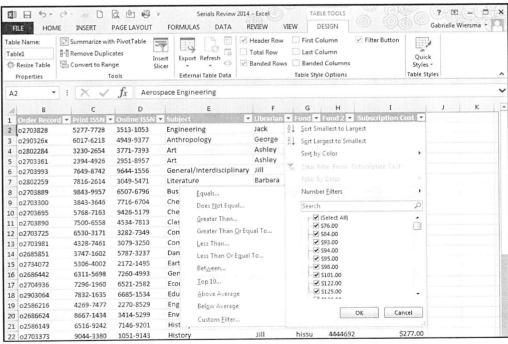

Figure 11. Number filters.

   b. Text fields: look for fields that contain, equal, start with, or end with certain terms.

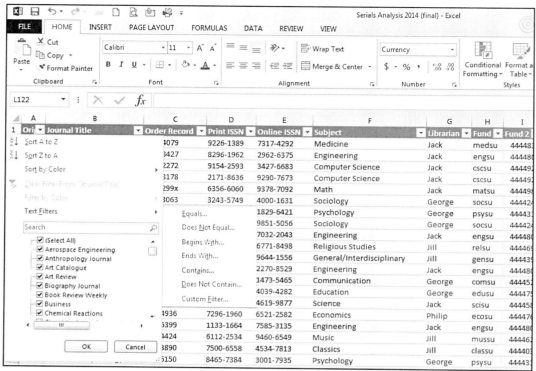

Figure 12. Text filters.

    c. To clear filters, use the Clear Filter option from the dropdown or go to **Home → Sort and Filter → Clear** to clear all filters in the Table.

Highlighting and Removing Duplicates

Data sources may have duplicate values that need to be identified and removed. In the ILS data the journal title, order record numbers, and ISSNs should be unique values while the subject area, librarian, fund, and even cost may be repeated. There are two different ways to find and remove duplicate values. Use Conditional Formatting to highlight duplicate values within a column and manually delete duplicates. Use the Remove Duplicates function in Table Tools to automatically detect and delete duplicates.

1. Find duplicate values using **Conditional Formatting.**

    a. Select columns that may have duplicate values (e.g. Journal Title and Order Record).

    b. **Home → Conditional formatting→ Highlight Cell Rules → Duplicate Values.**

    c. **Sort** or **Filter by color** to see the duplicates.

    d. **Right Click on Row** and **Delete** OR use **CTRL-**

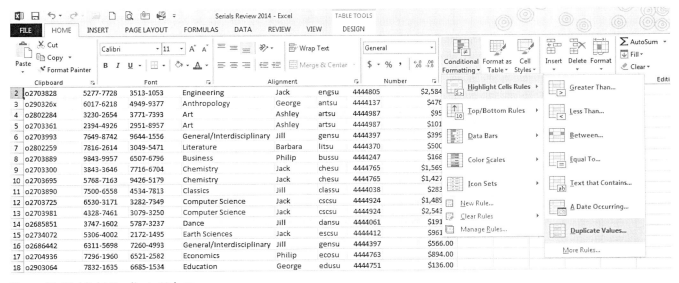

Figure 13. Highlight Duplicate Values.

2. Remove Duplicates with Table Tools.

    a. Design/Table Tools → Remove Duplicates.

    b. Select columns that may have duplicate values.

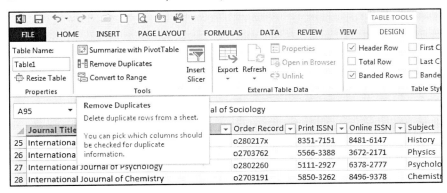

Figure 14. Remove duplicates.

Combining Data From Multiple Spreadsheets

Librarians often need to connect data from different sources during journal cancellation projects. For example, a title list with pricing information from a publisher or ILS data with COUNTER usage stats. VLOOKUP is a formula that you can use to look up values in one spreadsheet and pull them into another sheet. It searches for a value in a table and returns a corresponding value

from another column in the same row. VLOOKUP works best if there is a unique identifier to connect the data. Fortunately, most ILS data, title lists from publishers, and COUNTER usage reports include ISSNs which can be used as a match point to identify the same journal in different spreadsheets. Using the ISSN as the unique lookup value, VLOOKUP can find and enter the YTD usage statistics from a COUNTER JR1 report into a spreadsheet with your ILS data. In Excel, click on the **Formulas** tab → **Lookup & Reference** → **VLOOKUP**.

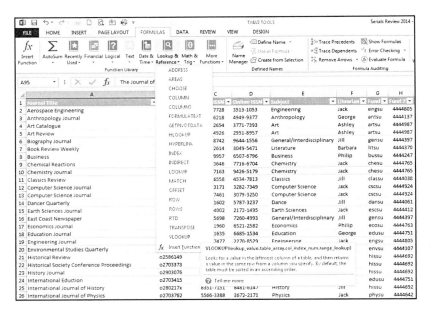

Figure 15. VLOOKUP formula.

Function Arguments:

3. **Lookup_value** is the unique identifier or key that is in both spreadsheets (click on the **Print ISSN** value in the first row).

4. **Table_Array** tell Excel where to look for the data (select the data starting with the Print ISSN of the first journal in the JR report and highlight all of the data across to YTD total and down to the end of rows).

5. **Col_Index_Number** which column to you want to pull data from and display in your spreadsheet (In COUNTER 4 reports, total is 3 columns away from Print ISSN; in older reports it is 15).

6. **Range lookup.**

    a. TRUE approximate match (can be used to match text fields like title but is not always accurate).

    b. **FALSE** exact match (this is useful if you only want an exact match and works well if you are using a numerical match point like ISSN).

Figure 16. VLOOKUP function arguments.

Analyzing the Data

Cost per use is one metric that can be useful for evaluating journal packages. Excel can calculate cost per use by dividing the subscription costs by the YTD usage stats. However, if a journal had 0 use Excel will display an error message, #DIV/0! because it cannot divide the subscription costs by 0. This error message can be interpreted as a title with 0 use, but it is also possible to use another Excel formula called IFERROR to calculate cost per use and change the display of the error message. For example, IFERROR can display another value like n/a, -, or the actual subscription cost instead of displaying #DIV/0!.

Calculate cost per use:

1. Create a new column for **2013 Cost Per Use.**

2. Type the formula =subscription cost/use into the formula bar.

3. If you use the simple formula to divide subscription costs by use (=subscription cost/use) then you will get the **#DIV/0!** error for titles with 0 use.

4. Use the **IFERROR formula** to calculate cost per use and insert subscription costs for 0 use titles.

5. **Formulas → Logical → IFERROR.**

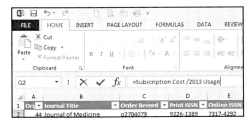

Figure 17. Formula bar.

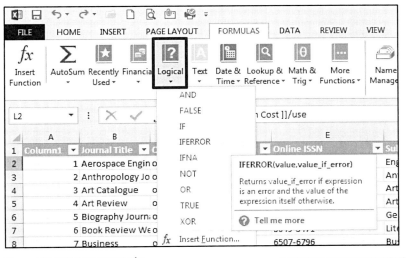

Figure 18. IFERROR Formula.

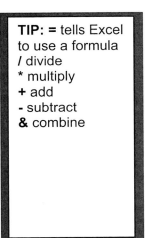

> **TIP: =** tells Excel to use a formula
> **/** divide
> ***** multiply
> **+** add
> **-** subtract
> **&** combine

Function Agreements:

Value: Subscription Cost/2013 Usage.

Value_if_error: Subscription Cost OR type in another value (e.g. 0, n/a, zero).

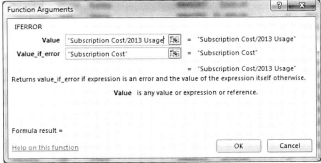

Figure 19. IFERROR Function Arguments.

Presenting the Data

In addition to highlighting duplicate values, conditional formatting can also be used to highlight other data aspects and create graphic representations of the data. For example, Excel can create data bars that represent how much each journal title costs compared to the total subscription costs. Conditional formatting also contains various icons that can be used to visually to represent data intervals. For example, red, yellow, and green icons can be added to cost-per-use to indicate high (>$30), medium ($11-29), and low values (<$10) compared to average Interlibrary Loan or pay-per-view article costs. It can also highlight the top/bottom which is useful for identifying the most expensive journals and the journals with the highest cost-per-use, which would be likely candidates for cancellation. Adding graphics and icons to data helps quickly identify patterns and interpret the data without having to create separate graphs or charts.

Conditional Formatting

6. Add Data Bars for subscription costs.

    a. **Highlight** the data in the Subscription Cost column → **Conditional Formatting** → **Data Bars.**

7. Add **Icon Sets** for cost per use.

    a. **Highlight** the data in the Cost Per Use column → **Conditional Formatting** → **Icon Sets**→ **More Rules.**

    b. **Reverse Icon Order.**

        i.   Red when value is >= 30.

        ii. Green when value is >= 10.

    c. **Highlight Top 8%** to identify titles for cancellation.

    d. **Sort by Color** to see the highlighted titles at the top of the column.

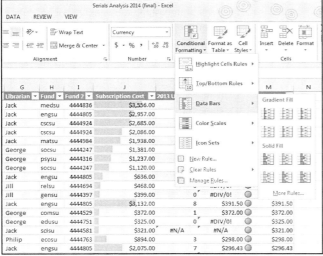

Figure 20. Conditional formatting: Data bars.

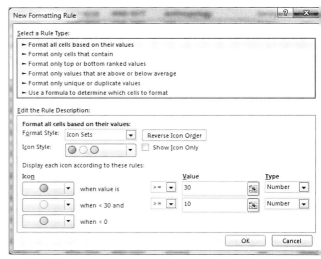

Figure 21. Conditional formatting rules: Icons.

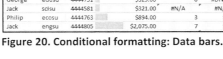

TIP: Use metrics like average ILL costs to analyze the data

Visually Filter Data With Slicers

Slicers are tools that can be used to quickly filter data. Slicers are an optional feature of PivotTables in Excel 2010 and are now available for regular Tables in Excel 2013. Slicers work like regular filters; they create subsets of the data based on the criteria selected. Multiple slicers can be inserted so that you can filter data in different columns. In addition, the size, color, and placement can be customized in the Slicer Tools options. Slicers are another option to add visual interest to your spreadsheet and create an easy way for to users to interact with the data.

8. **Design/Table Tools → Insert Slicer.**

9. OR Insert → Slicer.

10. Add Slicers for Subject, Librarian, Fund.

11. Use **Ctrl + click** to select more than one filter.

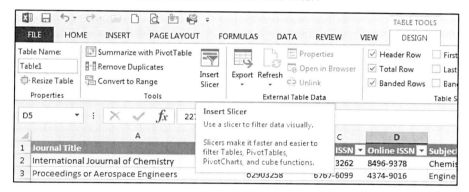

Figure 22. Insert Slicer.

Conclusion

The final spreadsheet can be sorted, filtered, and sliced to determine which journals should be cancelled. Sorting by subscription cost and highlighting journals with high cost per use will identify some of the best candidates for cancellation. Slicers give subject librarians a quick way to review the journals in each area and conditional formatting provides visually clues to help analyze and interpret the results.

This paper demonstrated how Excel can be used to collect, format, and analyze data from various sources. The Excel tools, formulas, features, and functions used in this paper could be used for a many different collection analysis projects.

Figure 23. Slicers.

Final Spreadsheet

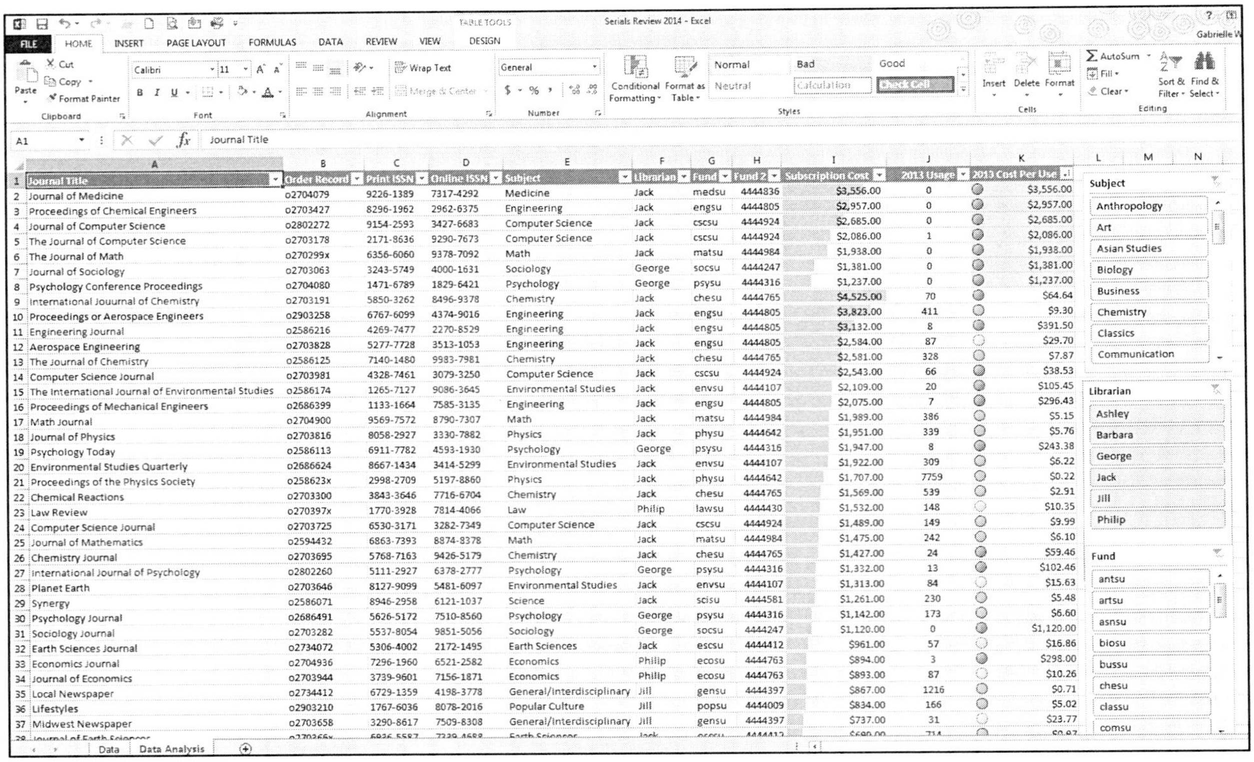

Journal Title	Order Record	Print ISSN	Online ISSN	Subject	Librarian	Fund	Fund 2	Subscription Cost	2013 Usage	2013 Cost Per Use
Journal of Medicine	o2704079	9226-1389	7317-4292	Medicine	Jack	medsu	4444836	$3,556.00	0	$3,556.00
Proceedings of Chemical Engineers	o2703427	8296-1962	2962-6375	Engineering	Jack	engsu	4444805	$2,957.00	0	$2,957.00
Journal of Computer Science	o2802272	9154-2593	3427-6683	Computer Science	Jack	cscsu	4444924	$2,685.00	0	$2,685.00
The Journal of Computer Science	o2703178	2171-8636	9290-7673	Computer Science	Jack	cscsu	4444924	$2,086.00	1	$2,086.00
The Journal of Math	o270299x	6356-6060	9378-7092	Math	Jack	matsu	4444984	$1,938.00	0	$1,938.00
Journal of Sociology	o2703063	3243-5749	4000-1631	Sociology	George	socsu	4444247	$1,381.00	0	$1,381.00
Psychology Conference Proceedings	o2704080	1471-6789	1829-6421	Psychology	George	psysu	4444316	$1,237.00	0	$1,237.00
International Jouurnal of Chemistry	o2703191	5850-3262	8496-9378	Chemistry	Jack	chesu	4444765	$4,525.00	70	$64.64
Proceedings or Aerospace Engineers	o2903258	6767-6099	4374-9016	Engineering	Jack	engsu	4444805	$3,823.00	411	$9.30
Engineering Journal	o2586216	4269-7477	2270-8529	Engineering	Jack	engsu	4444805	$3,132.00	8	$391.50
Aerospace Engineering	o2703828	5277-7728	3513-1053	Engineering	Jack	engsu	4444805	$2,584.00	87	$29.70
The Journal of Chemistry	o2586125	7140-1480	9983-7981	Chemistry	Jack	chesu	4444765	$2,581.00	328	$7.87
Computer Science Journal	o2703981	4328-7461	3079-3250	Computer Science	Jack	cscsu	4444924	$2,543.00	66	$38.53
The International Journal of Environmental Studies	o2586174	1265-7127	9086-3645	Environmental Studies	Jack	envsu	4444107	$2,109.00	20	$105.45
Proceedings of Mechanical Engineers	o2686399	1133-1664	7585-3135	Engineering	Jack	engsu	4444805	$2,075.00	7	$296.43
Math Journal	o2704900	9569-7572	8790-7307	Math	Jack	matsu	4444984	$1,989.00	386	$5.15
Journal of Physics	o2703816	8058-2927	3330-7882	Physics	Jack	physu	4444642	$1,951.00	339	$5.76
Psychology Today	o2586113	6911-7782	4593-1930	Psychology	George	psysu	4444316	$1,947.00	8	$243.38
Environmental Studies Quarterly	o2686624	8667-1434	3414-5299	Environmental Studies	Jack	envsu	4444107	$1,922.00	309	$6.22
Proceedings of the Physics Society	o258623x	2998-2709	5197-8860	Physics	Jack	physu	4444642	$1,707.00	7759	$0.22
Chemical Reactions	o2703300	3843-3646	7716-6704	Chemistry	Jack	chesu	4444765	$1,569.00	539	$2.91
Law Review	o270397x	1770-3928	7814-4066	Law	Philip	lawsu	4444430	$1,532.00	148	$10.35
Computer Science Journal	o2703725	6530-3171	3282-7349	Computer Science	Jack	cscsu	4444924	$1,489.00	149	$9.99
Journal of Mathematics	o2594432	6863-7393	8874-8378	Math	Jack	matsu	4444984	$1,475.00	242	$6.10
Chemistry Journal	o2703695	5768-7163	9426-5179	Chemistry	Jack	chesu	4444765	$1,427.00	24	$59.46
International Journal of Psychology	o2802260	5111-2927	6378-2777	Psychology	George	psysu	4444316	$1,332.00	13	$102.46
Planet Earth	o2703646	8127-9099	5481-6097	Environmental Studies	Jack	envsu	4444107	$1,313.00	84	$15.63
Synergy	o2586071	8946-2958	6121-1037	Science	Jack	scisu	4444581	$1,261.00	230	$5.48
Psychology Journal	o2686491	5626-5172	7510-8560	Psychology	George	psysu	4444316	$1,142.00	173	$6.60
Sociology Journal	o2703282	5537-8054	9851-5056	Sociology	George	socsu	4444247	$1,120.00	0	$1,120.00
Earth Sciences Journal	o2734072	5306-4002	2172-1495	Earth Sciences	Jack	escsu	4444412	$961.00	57	$16.86
Economics Journal	o2704936	7296-1960	6521-2582	Economics	Philip	ecosu	4444763	$894.00	3	$298.00
Journal of Economics	o2703944	3739-9601	7156-1871	Economics	Philip	ecosu	4444763	$893.00	87	$10.26
Local Newspaper	o2734412	6729-1359	4198-3778	General/Interdisciplinary	Jill	gensu	4444397	$867.00	1216	$0.71
Lifestyles	o2903210	1767-6036	8078-2016	Popular Culture	Jill	popsu	4444009	$834.00	166	$5.02
Midwest Newspaper	o2703658	3290-8617	7509-8308	General/Interdisciplinary	Jill	gensu	4444397	$737.00	31	$23.77

Figure 24. Final spreadsheet with conditional formatting for subscription cost and cost per use and slicers for subject, librarian, and fund, and the journals with the top 8% cost per use highlighted in red.

Streamlining and Advancing Collection Development With GOBI: Bringing Your Collection Into the 21st Century

Christa E. Poparad, College of Charleston
Lindsay H. Barnett, College of Charleston
Sarah Hoke, YBP Library Services

Abstract

Based on a desire to transition from a paper-based acquisitions system to a completely online system, College of Charleston Libraries have used the features in YBP Library Services' GOBI[3] (Global Online Bibliographic Information) to streamline firm order selections, to expedite and make more transparent the firm order process, and to advance our collection development efforts.

Introduction

There are three key components in our firm order process: the liaison structure between the College of Charleston Libraries and the teaching faculty, our approval plan, and GOBI.

Liaison Structure

Each department at the College is appropriated a portion of the firm order budget to purchase library materials based on the department's student enrollment and faculty research needs. To facilitate communication, each academic department chair appoints a member of the teaching faculty as a departmental liaison while the Assistant Dean for Technical Services and Collection Development appoints a librarian or library staff member as a library liaison to spend the money allocated in each fund. The departmental liaison solicits materials to order from the faculty and passes these orders to the library liaison who selects the materials in GOBI. In addition, library liaisons suggest potential materials of interest to the faculty using the tools available in GOBI.

Approval Plan

In recent years, the College of Charleston has put a great deal of effort into refining our YBP approval plan. It has become the launching pad for expanding and advancing collection development services. YBP works with a number of publishers and profiles thousands of titles each year. We have been satisfied with the quality and range of titles available through this service, and

began receiving our print approval plan titles fully cataloged and shelf-ready in 2012. Our approval plan profile, which incorporates our collection development goals, librarian input, and YBP bibliographer recommendations, identifies content of interest based on our stated collection development needs. Profiles are built on key pieces of data, including library generated specifications concerning series, publishers, subject areas, price, format, and other criteria. In addition to continually providing automatic shipments for print books of interest, e-book content can also be provided. Furthermore, an approval plan profile can be used to drive notification slips to help library liaisons and faculty find additional titles of interest and to drive the content for a demand-driven acquisitions (DDA) program.

The titles covered on approval carry typical bibliographic data, but also include information provided by YBP's book-in-hand (and now sometimes book-on-screen when e-books are available) profiling process. Each title is reviewed thoroughly to determine additional details about the content of the title, such as whether a title is more appropriate for research purposes, whether a title was edited by someone of interest, if an author has affiliation with a specific university, and whether a title has a focus on a special topic (like environment or religion) that may not be evident in its classification number. The tags supplied by YBP and the parameters of the library's profile combine to determine whether a title is fit to be purchased automatically, if it is best to review the title before purchase (i.e., to send a notification slip), or whether it would be best to exclude the title altogether. We were also able to create a faculty-specific approval plan with YBP at the College of Charleston, and when any of our faculty produce content with the publishers YBP profiles, those titles are auto-shipped to us on a separate subaccount.

Setting up GOBI[3]

GOBI is YBP's portal to review and purchase content of interest. With a variety of features and workflow options, it is important to collaborate with YBP to find the best workflow, and customize the GOBI setup to reflect that workflow. Key component links in GOBI for the College of Charleston's daily workflow are the following: purchase history including library catalog holdings, whether a title is part of DDA, table of contents when available, book reviews, and library activity.

Logins can be provided for an unlimited number of users, as long as they have an institutional email address. User profiles allow the flexibility to provide certain features such as requesting titles or allowing the ability to order titles or manage other GOBI users. At the College of Charleston, all of our liaisons have "Select Only" status, which allows them to submit title selections only. Our Acquisitions Manager is the only person with permissions to place orders, which has been a great help to us in reducing error and preventing duplication of effort. Custom user profiles can be created allowing users to define their own workflow based on what they have the capability to do.

Some key options in use at the College of Charleston to optimize GOBI include the following:

Preferences

Under "General Cart Preferences," setting the "default title view for list results" to "full" displays links to features such as library activity and reviews. These can aid in determining whether to select a particular title. In addition, under "Basic Search Preferences," the default search field and Boolean operator can be configured.

GobiTween

YBP Library Services can work with a consortium to allow individual users to view what has been purchased by other member libraries. In the past year, this has also expanded to identify print versus E-Book purchases, member library versus consortium purchases, titles active in DDA, and titles that were purchased as part of an e-collection. There is a GobiTween view in place for the Partnership Among South Carolina Academic Libraries (PASCAL), of which the College of Charleston is a part, to see which items other member libraries have purchased.

Peer Group

Each user can create a peer group of other institutions with purchase activity at YBP which will allow the user to see if a title under consideration has been purchased by comparable or aspirational peers. While GobiTween is pre-configured by YBP, a peer group is customized by the individual user. This feature is helpful when evaluating titles that may be considered for accreditation and collection assessment purposes.

Templates

Templates speed the selection process for liaisons by prepopulating fields such as subaccount, fund code, quantity, and selector initials. This feature is especially useful when prompted to enter order details.

Streamlining Firm Order Selections

Our workflow is configured with the library liaisons as selectors in GOBI. Departmental liaisons inform the library liaisons regarding titles they would like to have in the collection. The library liaison then researches the titles, selects, and submits them in GOBI. The orders are then reviewed and placed by the Acquisitions and Electronic Resources Manager.

Slips

Slips are lists of titles sorted by fund code that are delivered electronically in GOBI which can be automatically distributed to faculty and staff by email using the notification process. Slips are based on our YBP approval profile and represent areas in which we may be interested in purchasing books but do not wish to have titles shipped automatically. Library liaisons deliver slips to their assigned departmental faculty, and many faculty members use these lists as a method of identifying books they would like us to purchase as firm orders. This is an effective way to build the collection while ensuring that the titles we purchase are high quality and serve the research needs of our institution. In some subject areas, the number of slips can be overwhelming. In these areas, the librarians can assist faculty by using the special features in GOBI to email a selection of pertinent titles.

Searching for Titles

When faculty make requests, the following are used most often for selecting titles.

Basic Search

For individual titles, basic searching by keyword, ISBN, title, author, subject, and table of contents is available from the initial screen.

Add Titles by ISBN

This feature allows a GOBI user to add a number of ISBNs to a list in GOBI at one time. For example: if a collection list is available outside GOBI, the ISBNs for the titles of interest may be added to either a folder, the select cart, or the order cart. This removes the lengthy process of typing each individual ISBN into the basic search, finding the title, and then adding it to a folder or cart in GOBI. This feature is especially useful when faculty members email lists of titles or send catalogs with circled items to their library liaisons.

Advanced Search

The advanced search feature has been invaluable to us as we attempt to recognize and develop underserved areas of our collection. This is the most powerful tool for collection building in specific areas as it provides a number of limiters to define your search. You can limit your search to a specific format, LC range, subject, YBP select level, and publication date, among others. We have heavily used the advanced search tool to find books in less popular academic areas and interdisciplinary studies. In addition, the ability to

save search parameters saves time when it is necessary to run a specific search many times during the year.

Evaluating Titles

The following assist librarians and faculty members in evaluating titles under consideration for selection.

YBP Select Levels

YBP Select Levels describes the tag that YBP bibliographers assign to titles to help librarians be better informed about the titles they are selecting for their collections. Tags include "Basic-Essential," "Basic-Recommended," "Research-Essential," "Research-Recommended," "Specialized," "Supplementary," and "Not a Select Title." The profiling system, in addition to the title summaries and peer reviews contained in many GOBI records, has allowed us to better and more efficiently select quality titles for our collection. Rather than browsing through multiple publisher catalogs on a weekly basis for titles, we can now use GOBI and *Choice* reviews almost exclusively to make book selections. Our librarians have been satisfied with the quality of the titles we have purchased based on YBP Select Levels.

Reviews

When available, links within GOBI to reviews from *Choice, Doody's Book Reviews, Library Journal, Publisher Weekly, Book News*, and *Booklist* speed the evaluation process.

Library and Peer Activity

Library activity details the quantity sold to all libraries via YBP giving an indication of the popularity of a title. Local ISBN catalog holdings loads and purchase history help prevent duplicate ordering. GobiTween details orders among consortium member institutions. User created peer groups allow us to see which titles have been purchased by institutions to whom we compare especially for accreditation and collection assessment purposes.

Expediting the Firm Order Process

Export Cart

Using the export cart to place orders has streamlined and simplified our ordering process immensely. One major benefit of the export cart is that it acts as a storage facility for all the orders we intend to place, and orders can be manipulated, added, and deleted from the export cart prior to placing the order. GOBI also offers the ability to save records in the export cart as a PDF or email them, making paperless record keeping easier than ever.

"Batch" Import of Records

The most important feature of the export cart at the College of Charleston, however, is the capability to batch import records into our local ILS. The presence of extensive bibliographic information in GOBI such as full LC call number and subject headings indicates we will receive quality MARC records when the titles are imported into our catalog. Prior to using GOBI, our acquisitions staff imported MARC records from OCLC Connexion one by one before placing an order, entering in order details manually. With the use of the export cart, we can now import large orders, often 300 titles or more, into our ILS in one stroke and then FTP them to YBP. Order details are included in the export and order records are created when the data is ingested in our system. There is still some work to be done after the batch import—if our system matches a book with an individual or series title already in our catalog it will list the order with a status of pending, which will not allow it to be FTP'd. While these titles must be edited manually, this process is still far less time consuming and error prone than importing records individually from OCLC.

Multilibrary Campuses

GOBI also offers ease in managing purchases for multilibrary campuses. At the College of Charleston, we have several specialized libraries in addition to the Addlestone Library, which houses our general collection. The Marine Resources Library serves our Marine Biology graduate students, the Avery Research Center collects materials specific to African American culture in the South Carolina Lowcountry, and the North Campus Library serves working adults and traditional students seeking educational advancement. Each library has its own collection goals, and the acquisitions staff at the Addlestone Library manages collection development for all libraries. In GOBI, purchases for all libraries are displayed in one place, and librarians can create separate funds or subaccounts for each branch's purchases, making it easy to keep purchases organized. GOBI also offers a wealth of data for e-book titles that assists in making purchases for multi-library campuses. Most platform and purchasing options are listed on each e-book record, allowing the librarian to determine which level of access is most appropriate for his or her campus. Librarians can also purchase multiple copies of a title at once, if more than one library collects similar materials.

Transparency

Order Status Visible in GOBI

Another benefit of GOBI is that it creates an opportunity for library liaisons to be more involved in the acquisition process. All librarians in our institution have access to GOBI (though only the Acquisitions Manager can place orders), and can easily search by title or fund code to determine the status of any orders they have submitted. GOBI offers real-time tracking of orders, allowing users to see both when an item was shipped and its anticipated delivery date. This has been incredibly useful to us in the months leading up to the fiscal year end as we try to determine how much of our on-order materials will be received before the end of the year.

Invoices Posted

GOBI also acts as a storage system for all of our invoices for orders placed through YBP, on all of our subaccounts (firm orders, approval, DDA, e-book firm orders, etc.). This has allowed us to keep paperless records of invoices in one easily retrievable place.

Easy to Track Fund Expenditures

YBP keeps a record of all actions taken in GOBI for the last three years, allowing us to easily calculate how much money has been spent on the approval plan, in firm orders, and in DDA in any given time period. Older data is available upon request, as well. This has proven extremely useful for end-of-year reporting.

Advancing Collection Development

Firm Order E-Books

Prior to using GOBI, purchasing access to e-books was a difficult and time-consuming process that our staff tended to avoid unless absolutely necessary. We typically had to purchase e-books directly from publishers, which not only meant less flexibility in platform selection but also signing any licenses required by the publisher and in some cases browsing through pages of legal documents to understand our rights in using the material. With GOBI, YBP facilitates contact between us and the content provider and we only have to sign one license with each provider that then allows us to make as many single-title e-book purchases as we wish. The invoices are delivered from YBP through GOBI, allowing for better purchase tracking and record keeping.

DDA

DDA only became a possibility to us recently because of the advanced purchasing ability and expenditure tracking made available to us through GOBI. We began a full-scale e-book DDA plan in the 2013-2014 fiscal year using YBP and ebrary. Our e-book profile was based on our existing approval profile and we had already completed a license with ebrary, so some of the essential elements of the plan were already in place. While we encountered many issues along the way with the plan that required creative problem solving,

we ultimately consider the program a success as we spent approximately $20,000 of our allotted $30,000 budget within five months. We have decided to continue with the DDA program permanently, with a $50,000 budget on a 12-month plan in the 2014-2015 fiscal year. Depending on the success of our program this year, we are also considering expanding into DDA for other material types, such as print and streaming media.

Consideration of E-Approval Plan

The success of DDA has inspired us to consider other methods of building a stronger e-book collection, which we feel is a valuable service to our patrons. We have been researching the possibility of establishing an e-approval plan, with the hopes of using this plan specifically to enhance interdisciplinary areas which are becoming increasingly popular fields of study. The fact that librarians can view titles for a period of time on the approval bookshelf before the order is completed allows for a great deal of flexibility in building a quality e-book collection, especially considering the breadth of academic subjects interdisciplinary studies cover.

Conclusion

GOBI offers a suite of services to help libraries manage almost all aspects of the acquisitions process. Libraries may wish to analyze their acquisitions workflow to determine how GOBI can assist them in reaching their goals. At the College of Charleston, we found that GOBI offered the tools we needed to expand, improve, and streamline our services, and to advance and update our collection.

References

Jones, D. (2011). On-demand information delivery: Integration of patron-driven acquisition into a comprehensive information delivery system. *Journal of Library Administration, 51*(7/8), 764-776. http://dx.doi.org/10.1080/01930826.2011.601275

Pickett, C., Tabacaru, S., & Harrell, J. (2014). E-approval plans in research libraries. *College & Research Libraries, 75*(2), 218-231.

Poparad, C. E., Barnett, L. H., & Hoke, S. (2014, November). *Streamlining and advancing collection development with GOBI©: Bringing your collection into the 21st century*. Concurrent session presented at the 2014 Charleston Conference Issues in Book and Serial Acquisition, Charleston, SC. Retrieved from http://goo.gl/7MQlkh

YBP Library Services. (n.d.). *GOBI tutorials*. Retrieved from http://www.gobi3.com/hx/Falcon.ashx ?location=welcome

Bringing GOKb to Life: Data, Integrations, and Development

Kristen B. Wilson, North Carolina State University Libraries

Abstract

The Global Open Knowledgebase (GOKb) project is developing a repository of freely available data that describes electronic journals and books as they are offered in the academic publishing supply chain. Since the first partners release in May 2014, the project has taken major steps toward realizing its goals. This article will include a general project overview and update, followed by discussion of data collection, integration, and development initiatives that are already underway among the project partners. Readers will also learn about next steps for GOKb and opportunities for broader community involvement.

Why GOKb?

Electronic resources knowledge bases are essential tools for libraries, providing management information and powering public-facing discovery services. Most libraries spend significant amounts of time managing knowledge base data, not only in their primary knowledge base but also in related tools like the integrated library system (ILS), electronic resources management system (ERMS), and subscription agent platform. My own experience at North Carolina State University Libraries illustrates both the extent of work required to management a knowledge base and the duplication of effort that can accompany this process.

Like most large libraries, NC State uses a commercial knowledge base product. We often notice that the holdings information in our knowledgebase changes unexpectedly, introducing errors into our systems. Sometimes, large groups of titles disappear from a package. Or the coverage dates for a certain package are replaced with incorrect data. Whenever possible, we investigate these issues, figure out what the correct information should be, and send it back to our knowledgebase vendor. To their credit, our vendor is able to fix the majority of the problems we report. However, we often hear the same explanation for these errors: they come from the publisher, and sometimes the publisher sends the same errors again and again. In the past, staff in my unit have tried contacting publishers directly and asking them to fix faulty data, but haven't gotten very far with this approach. Dealing with data issues tends not to be a priority for most

publishers, and that's understandable given that they are the business of selling content—not metadata. Still, isn't it worth thinking about how we might address these data errors at their source? And consider this—when an individual library finds problems and reports them to a knowledge base vendor, it is doing a service for all the customers of that vendor. But what about libraries that use a different vendor? I have to imagine there are many librarians out there spending a lot of time correcting knowledge base errors and potentially duplicating one another's effort. Why not harness their efforts in a central location to benefit the entire community?

These questions get to the heart of what the Global Open Knowledgebase (GOKb) project hopes to accomplish. First, to harness the power of the library community, who in many cases are already doing significant knowledge base work, to create a repository of high quality metadata about electronic resources. And second, to engage publishers and vendors to help improve the quality of this data across the supply chain.

To these ends, GOKb (http://gokb.org) is a freely available, community-managed data repository that contains key publication information about electronic resources as represented within the supply chain from content publishers to suppliers to libraries. The community management aspect of GOKb means that librarians can directly influence the quality of the data and contribute their work back to a central repository. And the fact that GOKb's data is freely available under a Creative Commons 0 (http://creativecommons.org /publicdomain/zero/1.0/) can be used by anyone, for any purpose, without attribution. These two features, taken together, uniquely position GOKb to become a central knowledge base that is managed by its users, independent of any one commercial product, and freely available to any organization that can benefit from its data.

GOKb Data

Data Processing and Workflow

Data is the heart of the GOKb project. By collecting and curating essential metadata about electronic resources, GOKb will provide a valuable service to libraries and vendors who wish to use that data in local projects or to improve the quality of an existing data set. GOKb's data is contributed by project partners and flows through several stages of processing to become part of the knowledge base.

The starting point for data management in GOKb is a tool called OpenRefine (http://openrefine.org). OpenRefine is open source software used for cleaning, transforming, and enhancing data. The GOKb development team has built a custom extension for OpenRefine that allows users to take

title list files that have been created by publishers or vendors and validate them against a predefined set of rules before loading them into GOKb. These files are currently downloaded from publisher web sites, but in the future they may be harvested in an automatic way or contributed directly by publisher partners themselves.

Once data has been loaded into OpenRefine, the GOKb extension identifies errors like blank fields, incorrectly labeled data, and ISSN conflicts. A series of error and warning messages appear in the OpenRefine interface, along with tools that help automatically address problems or single out values that are problematic (see Figure 1). Users can work through each error, and when they are all resolved, OpenRefine will present an option allowing the user to ingest the data into GOKb. The OpenRefine extension can be used for any file type, although the formatting will determine how much work is needed to complete the validation process. GOKb has been designed to work especially well with KBART-compliant files (http://www.niso.org/workrooms/kbart), and the project strongly supports industry adoption of this best practice.

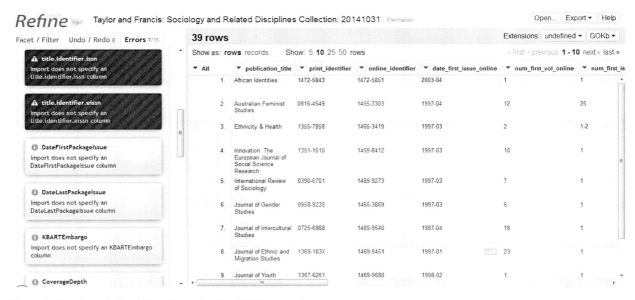

Figure 1. The OpenRefine client featuring the GOKb extension.

Once data has been ingested from OpenRefine, it becomes part of the GOKb knowledge base and is accessible to users via a web application. Within this application, data can be edited further. Upon

ingest, GOKb will generate a series of review tasks to identify possible errors that could not be detected at the OpenRefine stage. Each review task is assigned to the user who completed the initial ingest, although it can be reassigned to another user if desired. Users will resolve any review tasks generated by an OpenRefine ingest before approving the file for public use. There are also additional data quality activities that will take place in the GOKb web application, such as creating title history metadata or documenting information about open access rights. These activities, however, are large projects that will be addressed through a variety of methods as the knowledge base matures.

Data Model

GOKb's data model contains many of the same record types as traditional knowledge bases, along with a few unique features that improve on these existing concepts. Some of the key entities within the GOKb data model are the title, package, platform, title instance package platform (TIPP), and organization. Each of these records supports a variety of metadata elements, as well as a series of relationships created by establishing linkages between the different record types.

The title record in GOKb describes an electronic resource at the work level. It includes basic administrative metadata, including some fields that help users see the status of the title and whether or not it has been approved by an editor. This record also includes extensive title history metadata. A set of published from and to dates show the years that a title was actively publishing, and a series of title history events can be used to link titles together. Each event describes the situation before and after a change occurs. Figure 2 illustrates a title family that contains a simple title changes and a title split. The title record also contains identifiers for the title, a list of current and past publishers, and a list of all the packages to which the title belongs.

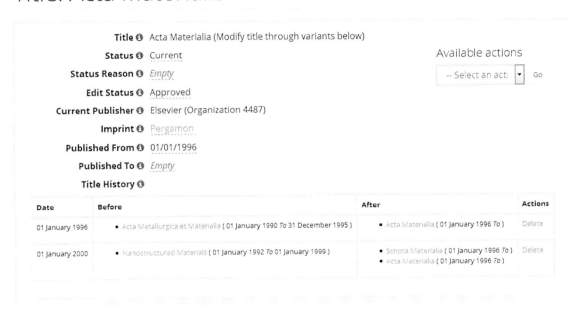

Figure 2. A GOKb title record with two title history events.

Like most knowledge bases, GOKb contains records to represent packages and platforms. The package record brings together a set of titles that are commonly sold as a group by their publisher or a third party. The platform record represents a web site where electronic resources content is hosted. GOKb links together the combinations of title, package, and platform to form another record called the title instance package platform, or TIPP. The TIPP record represents what might be traditionally thought of as a holding—the unique, salable entity that libraries purchase and manage.

By creating the TIPP record, GOKb can not only store metadata about this entity, such as URL and coverage dates, but also assign it an identifier and make statements about its relationships to other records.

GOKb also creates linkages between the records mentioned above and organization records. Organizations represent the key players involved in making e-resources available to libraries: publishers, content providers, platform providers, vendors, and licensors. Organizations within GOKb can assigned one or more of these roles, and associated with resources with respect to which they play those roles. Organizations also mark the start of GOKb's foray into linked data. Thanks to contributions from on an organization name linked data project done at NCSU (http://www.lib.ncsu.edu/ld/onld/), we have been able to prepopulate GOKb's organization records with a rich set of metadata, including alternate names and URIs for other linked data sets like the Library of Congress Name Authority File (http://id.loc.gov/authorities/names.html) and the Virtual International Authority File (http://viaf.org/).

Integrations

While the GOKb web application is a useful tool in itself, GOKb's data is also available via an API, which will allow users to create integrations with local systems. GOKb's current partners, Kuali OLE (http://www.kuali.org/ole) and Knowledge Base + (http://www.kbplus.ac.uk/kbplus), have already been working on creating integrations with GOKb. The API and coreferencing service allow any user to do the same at a variety of scales—from a full-scale integration with a downstream system to a simple queries using a tool like OpenRefine.

The primary function of GOKb's API is to allow external systems to extract data from GOKb. The API can be used to retrieve data such as the list of titles in a package, along with their associated metadata, or the title history information for a particular title. GOKb uses the Open Archives Initiative Protocol for Metadata Harvesting (http://www.openarchives.org/pmh), so users familiar with that standard should find GOKb's APIs easy to adopt. Additionally, authorized users will be able to send updates back to GOKb via API.

This piece of the API will become critical for partners who find themselves interacting with GOKb's data primarily through a downstream system.

Integration between GOKb and KB+ is currently under development. KB+ is a service developed by Jisc Collections (https://www.jisc-collections.ac.uk) to help libraries in the United Kingdom manage their electronic resource purchases. KB+ provides information about publications, subscriptions, and licenses. Data managers for the KB+ project have been building their own knowledge base of information about UK-specific journal packages within their local environment. The ultimate goal for KB+ is to shift from managing these packages locally and instead manage the global data in GOKb, while continuing to allow libraries to customize the data to match their individual entitlements in KB+. This model gets back to the earlier point about reducing duplication of effort. By doing part of their work in GOKb, the KB+ data managers can maximize the impact of their efforts by contributing them to a central community system that feeds many other projects in addition to their own.

The integration between GOKb and KB+ is still under development, but enough work has been completed to convey clearly how the functionality will work. Within KB+, a user can access a list of all of the packages available through GOKb. This information is brought into KB+ using the GOKb API. The user can choose to create a new local package in KB+ based on a GOKb package, or to merge GOKb's package information with an existing package in the system. Creating or merging a package will pull in information from GOKb for all the titles in the package, including identifiers, coverage dates, URLs, and other details. Once a package has been established with a link to GOKb, users will receive updates whenever new information is available about that package or its titles, and they will have the option to accept or reject each change.

GOKb's other partner, Kuali OLE, is planning to integrate its product with GOKb using a very similar model to KB+. Kuali OLE is a full library management system, which includes traditional functionality like acquisitions, cataloging, and circulation, in addition to e-resources management. In the Kuali OLE model, GOKb data will be used to create records like bibs, holdings, organizations, and platforms. Users will receive updates through a central change management dashboard, where they can choose which updates to apply or reject.

In addition to its API, GOKb offers a coreferencing service that will allow users to create crosswalks between identifiers. Users will be able to search GOKb for any identifier and return a list of all the other identifiers associated with that some component. Users can also search for within in specific namespaces, such as ISSNs or a publisher's proprietary identifier. This coreferencing service is available through the GOKb web interface and can also be accessed using JSON or XML queries sent by an external system.

Users can take advantage of the coreferencing service by using a lightweight tool like OpenRefine to retrieve additional identifiers for a data set. It's common that a user may have data that contains only a single identifier, for example the ISSN. Within OpenRefine, the user can add another column to her project based on a URL—in this case a URL that queries the GOKb coreferencing service. This new column will display a block of JSON code provided by GOKb. Within this code, the user will see any additional identifiers associated with an entity, such as an e-ISSNs or a publisher's proprietary identifier (see Figure 3). Tools like OpenRefine or Excel can be used to parse that information from the JSON code and make it into more regular or eye-readable data. As GOKb begins to collect more data and store more identifiers, this service should become extremely useful, and may aid in processes like system implementations or migrations.

Figure 3. Using OpenRefine to query GOKb's co-referencing service.

GOKb Development

GOKb has received a second round of funding from the Andrew W. Mellon Foundation to support development of the project from October 2014 through December 2015. During this period, the development team will focus on enhancing existing functionality and exploring new directions.

There are several areas of ongoing work that will receive enhancement during Phase 2 of the project. The first area of development will be to continue to streamline the data loading process through OpenRefine. While the OpenRefine client goes a long way toward guiding users through this process, there are still improvements to be made. Phase 2 will see the OpenRefine software become simpler to download and install, with more quick resolution options and tools that allow users to create reusable rules for specific packages and providers. We also want to look at the possibility of automating the data ingest process even further, so that data managers can focus more on data quality work instead of ingest.

Second, GOKb needs more features to support community management. Planned enhancements to the web application include editor dashboards that will allow for better monitoring of the general health of the system. These dashboards will highlight new contributions that need to be vetted and identify areas of missing or low quality data so they can be targeted for improvement. Editors will also need a snapshot view of open review tasks, so they can address or reassign outstanding work. We also plan to implement rules and options that will prompt review of high-value items and allow users to escalate problems to an editor.

Finally, GOKb will continue to develop ways to improve its overall data quality. One of the biggest areas of ongoing work needed to maintain any knowledgebase is documenting title histories and making sure that holdings are consistent with the years a title actually existed. During Phase 2, we plan to bring in more title history data from sources like KB+ and union catalogs, and to create review queues where users can focus on working through errors or conflicts related to this data.

During Phase 2, GOKb will also be exploring new areas of development. One of the project's charges is to begin integrating ebook metadata into the knowledge base. We're hoping to collaborate with librarians, vendors, and publishers who area already the experts in this area to expand our data model to accommodate ebooks. We are also planning to expose data about all of GOKb's major entities as linked data, which will allow us to make connections with existing vocabularies and create new terms to describe concepts not currently covered. Linked data is one of the first priorities for development

and something we hope to accomplish fairly early on in Phase 2. Finally, GOKb hopes to collect more data about open access publications and to begin some investigations into the ways that this data might support other open access initiatives. This work will likely begin with an environmental scan and user research to discover what data is considered most valuable.

Community Building

Perhaps the biggest challenge for GOKb is that of collecting a significant amount of knowledge base data in a way that is scalable and effective. In addition to new technical development that will make the process easier, we also need to identify new partners who can contribute resources and expertise. Many of partnership use cases I will describe here are only in the beginning stages of development, but they represent powerful ways that GOKb can work with the community to build a robust knowledge base while also providing benefits to its partners.

Library partners will be key collaborators. Our current libraries partners include the Kuali OLE institutions, who are in the early stages of working on data collection and data quality activities. In the most basic model, these partners are getting title list files from publisher web sites, loading them into GOKb using OpenRefine, and working on cleaning up data problems in the web application. We'd like to find more library partners who would be interested in taking part in some or all of these activities—either because they'd like to use GOKb for a specific local project or because they see broader value the data we're providing to the community.

Another avenue for library partners that we'd like to explore is management of consorital packages. Often consortia struggle to keep track of the titles that are part of their custom deals and to communicate that information across members and to other knowledge bases. GOKb can serve as a central environment to host these custom title lists. It provides a publicly accessible location where all members of a consortium can go to download lists for internal use or distribution. Plus, any work that consortiums put into cleaning up the titles, platforms, and organizations related to their packages will benefit the broader community.

Publisher partners are also important to GOKb, as they're the source of much of the data that makes up the e-resources metadata supply chain. There are a number of ways that GOKb can benefit publishers and the broader community at the same time. If a publisher is interested providing KBART-compliant files to knowledge base vendors, but doesn't have the time or expertise to implement the best practice themselves, GOKb data managers can help with the process by reformatting, vetting, and enhancing publisher metadata. GOKb can also function as a useful place to for publishers to host their KBART files so that they don't have to maintain them on their own web sites. The beauty of this model is that, once their data is properly formatted and stored in the GOKb, publishers can distribute this data to other knowledge base vendors, thereby pushing out high-quality data across the supply chain.

Finally, GOKb is also interested in partnering with library vendors, particularly other knowledgebase providers. GOKb is not a competitor to these services, but rather a collaborator that can help others working in the same space supplement their data. As GOKb grows, knowledgebase vendors are welcome to repurpose GOKb's data for their own products, and we especially hope they will include GOKb identifiers as a part of their data sets—and maybe even contribute their identifiers to GOKb in return. Sharing identifiers will help improve GOKb's co-referencing service, and allow users to crosswalk their data in situations like system implementations and

migrations. We also may be able to help other knowledge bases improve their overall data quality by pushing out files that have been vetted by the community, or even helping to clean up specific data sets in exchange for making them publicly available through GOKb.

Next Steps for GOKb

GOKb will make its web application, APIs, and co-referencing service available to the community as part of a public preview period scheduled to begin in early 2015. The preview will showcase the latest version of the GOKb software and contain a small amount of seed data illustrating the different record types. Additional data will continue to be added to the system throughout Phase 2 as more partners join the project. While we recognize that there is still a great deal of work to be done before GOKb has enough data to be truly useful to the community, we believe it's important to open up the service to a wider audience early on so we can incorporate feedback from potential users and contributors. During the public preview, users will be invited to use GOKb to search and browse metadata, export package information, and experiment with the system's API and coreferencing service. We are very interested in receiving comments and suggestions from users during this time.

Information about the GOKb public preview will be made available at http://gokb.org in early 2015. For more information about the project, please contact Kristen Wilson at kristen_wilson@ncsu.edu.

Collection Data Visualization: Seeing the Forest Through the Treemap

Geoffrey P. Timms, Systems Librarian, Mercer University Libraries
Jeremy M. Brown, Associate Director for Technical Services and Systems, Mercer University Libraries

Abstract

Collection management is one of the more complicated responsibilities in librarianship. In this task, the librarian must simultaneously synthesize the needs, desires, and aspirations of the institution, departments, and individuals. While much of this is elusive qualitative data that may not yield a definitive answer, we also have increasingly accessible hard data from our integrated library systems (ILSs) that we can synthesize to complement it. In the latest generations of ILSs, this information is readily available to use for statistical analysis and visualization. When it comes to our increasingly limited materials budgets, it is important to make sure that we make the best decisions possible, thus it is advantageous to analyze all the data at our disposal. We introduce a web application that produces live statistics from the ILS. The system uses data points, including collection use and metrics, which describe a collection (e.g., age, quantity). This system goes beyond traditional charts and graphs by employing several visualization techniques that lend a unique perspective to these data points. The particular techniques allow collection managers to visualize multiple data points simultaneously and reveal data correlations that might not otherwise be obvious.

Manually analyzing data from the Integrated Library System (ILS) is a challenging task. As we move from broad data points deeper into the classification system to study particular subsets of the collection, the numbers seem incessant and the data is hard to translate into an understanding of the collection's characteristics and use. This is where data visualization techniques can be applied to graphically describe data in a meaningful way, conducive to human interpretation. When data is presented graphically the absolute numbers, while used to generate the graph, are not the focus of the output. The emphasis of data represented graphically is identifying trends and comparing data points. For the purpose of comparing subsections of our library collection, we focused on two techniques for representing data graphically: treemaps and cartograms.

A treemap is a constrained proportional graphical representation of data. Perhaps the most-recognized treemap is the squarified treemap where a square represents the data in its entirety and individual subsets of data are proportionally represented by scaled rectangles contained therein and sorted from top left to bottom right in diminishing size order. In addition, a second tier or subset of data can be proportionally represented

within each of those rectangles as another series of scaled rectangles. In theory this could continue ad infinitum but in reality, it is hard to derive meaning from more than two tiers of data presented simultaneously. A second data point can be represented using varying shades of color. An example of a treemap representing votes cast by county, state, and recipient (Obama [blue] vs. Romney [red]) in the US Presidential Elections of 2012, is demonstrated in Figure 1.

A cartogram is constructed on similar visual principles to a treemap insomuch as data can be represented graphically and a second data point can be represented with shades of color. The primary distinction between a cartogram and a treemap is that a cartogram can be any shape and may be distorted in its entirety to represent data proportionally. This is not necessarily always the case, however, as the overall shape of the image can be maintained by using noncontiguous graphics to represent the first tier of data within the confines of the overall image. An example of a contiguous area cartogram is a map of the United States, with each county rescaled in proportion to its population. Colors refer to the results of the 2012 U.S. presidential election, as demonstrated in Figure 2.

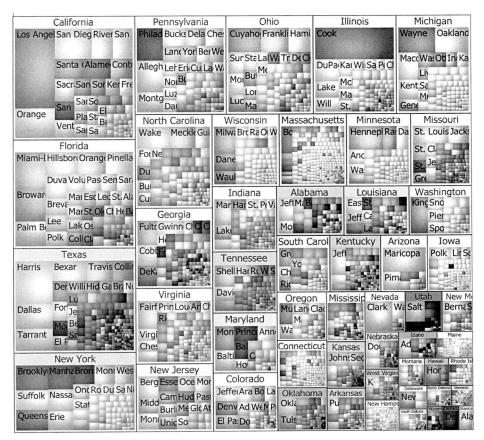

Figure 1. Treemap of votes by county, state, and locally predominant recipient (Obama blue, Romney red in the US Presidential Elections of 2012). Reprinted from Treemapping, In *Wikipedia*, 2012, Retrieved October 28, 2014, from http://en.wikipedia.org/wiki/Treemapping. Copyright 2012 by Luc Girardin. Reprinted with permission. CC BY 3.0.

Figure 2. Cartogram of the United States, with counties sized according to their population and colors demonstrating the percentage of votes cast for Obama (blue) and Romney (red) in the 2012 U.S. presidential election. In *Maps of the 2012 US Presidential Election Results,* 2012, Retrieved October 28, 2014, from http://www-personal.umich.edu/~mejn/election/2012/. Copyright 2012 by Mark Newman. Reprinted with permission. CC BY 2.0.

Application Design

Mercer University Libraries' Systems and Technical Services Unit operates Innovative Interfaces Sierra ILS. With our recent upgrade to Sierra, we gained the opportunity to query elements of the database to access data about the collection. This can be performed in dynamically, using scripted procedures initiated from within a web interface. We undertook to develop a web application which would provide the user with the opportunity to choose two data points describing the collection and its use, and which would then query the database and generate either a squarified treemap or a hybrid cartogram to visually represent the data.

The web application is created in Python with a lightweight underlying CherryPy web framework. The squarified treemap coordinates are generated from the raw data using Uri Laserson's Squarify Python library (https://github.com/laserson /squarify) and both the treemap and cartogram are drawn and color-enhanced using Python Imaging Library (http://www.pythonware .com/products/pil/). The treemap is a squarified graphic sorted in diminishing order by primary data point size, while the cartogram simulates ranges of library shelves and maintains sorting in call number order.

As an academic library, our collection is organized using Library of Congress (LC) call numbers. In order to facilitate convenient visual interpretation we only present one tier of data at a time, starting with the primary call numbers A, B, C, etc. We enable the user to proceed to the next tier of call number data by clicking on the graphic. Thus, by selecting P, for example, a new graphic will be drawn presenting the data for call number P and its subsets P, PA, PB, etc. The user can continue further into the third tier, PA for example, where

the data will be subdivided into call numbers 0-999, 1000-1999, 2000-2999, and so on. These can be further subdivided into 100s and 10s.

We provide the user multiple data points by which to evaluate and describe the collection. Each of these can be represented either by size or shade of color on the graphic. The data points available are:

- Collection size (item count).
- Last year's total use.
- Last year's average use.
- Year to date total use.
- Year to date average use.
- Average publication year (relative age indicator).
- Renewal total.
- Renewal average.
- Total usage (all years).
- Average total use (all years).
- Average number of uses per item.
- Percentage of items with no circulations.
- Percentage of items with at least one circulation.
- Percentage of items with more than one circulation.

Data Interpretation

Figures 3 and 4 demonstrate the treemap and cartogram respectively, presenting the same two select data points on the graphics. In this example, *collection size* is chosen as the primary data point and *percentage of collection circulated at least once* as the secondary data point.

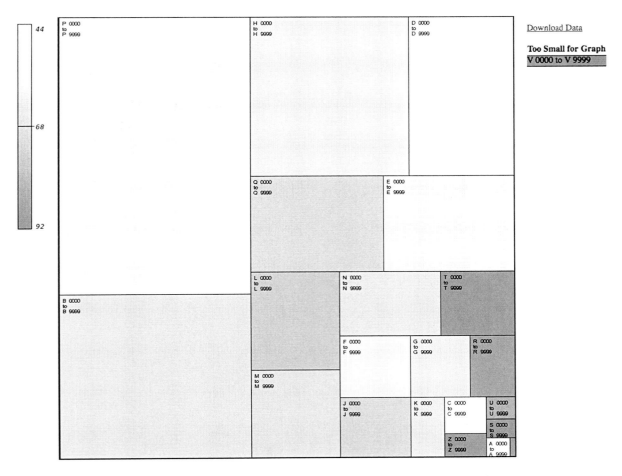

Figure 3. Treemap with size representing collection size (item count) and color representing percentage of items circulated at least once.

The primary data point, represented by the relative size of the boxes in the treemap and of the shelf sections (which may span more than one shelf range) in the cartogram, demonstrates the relative size of each call number range in the context of the total collection size. The treemap presents the call number ranges in order of diminishing item count, emphasizing the largest call number range at the top left of the treemap with the largest box and the smallest call number range at the bottom right with the smallest box. The cartogram maintains the alphabetical call number order with the section size varying in situ.

The secondary data point, represented by the shade, demonstrates the percentage of items circulated at least once in each call number range and ranges from white to a deep orange with increasing percentage value. This is true regardless of the data type. In this example, the shade represents the percentage of items circulated at least once. Therefore, white represents the lowest percentage of items circulated at least once and full-intensity orange represents the highest percentage of items circulated at least once, for the collection assessed.

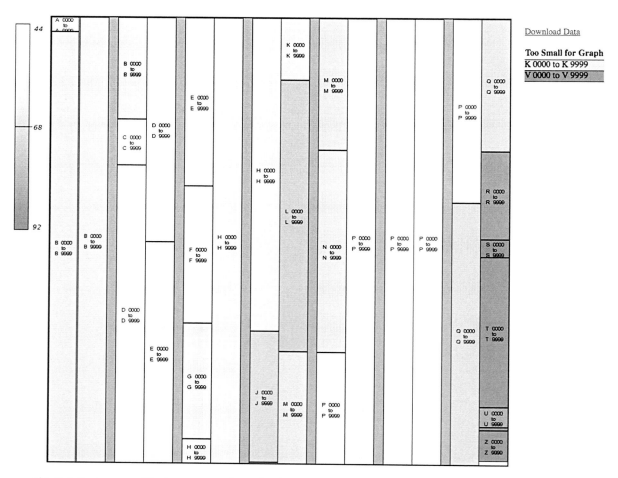

Figure 4. Cartogram with size representing collection size (item count) and color representing percentage of items circulated at least once.

Similarly, if the shade is chosen to represent percentage of items uncirculated then white represents the lowest percentage of items uncirculated and full-intensity orange represents the highest percentage of items uncirculated for the collection assessed. Even though the two concepts described have a completely inverse relationship, the color is determined by percentage value increasing, from white to orange. It is, therefore, very important to maintain awareness of what is actually being represented by the graphic.

The gradient scale to the left of the image identifies the lowest and highest values as well as

the median value to assist with interpretation. The values may be absolute or percentages depending upon the secondary data point selected. In either case the lowest value, represented by white, is not zero unless the lowest absolute or percentage value represented is actually zero. Similarly, if percentages are represented, the highest percentage represented by intense orange is not always 100% unless the highest value represented is actually 100%. It will always represent the highest absolute or percentage observed in the data. We see from the gradient scale that, of the call number ranges assessed, the lowest percentage of items circulated at least once is 44% and the highest is 92%.

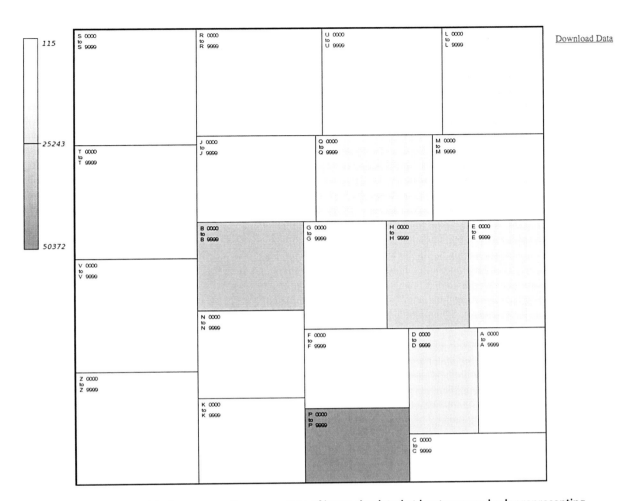

Figure 5. Treemap with size representing percentage of items circulated at least once and color representing collection size (item count).

A particularly interesting perspective on the size and use of the collection is to reverse the primary and secondary data points, as seen in Figures 5 and 6. In doing so, size represents the percentage of items circulated at least once and color represents collection size. No new information is presented compared to Figures 3 and 4, but the different perspective on the same information is notable.

To assist with interpretation of the visual information, we provide a link to download the raw data used to create the graphic as an Excel spreadsheet. This adds context to the analysis of the graphics. The data used to generate Figures 3-6 is shown in Table 1.

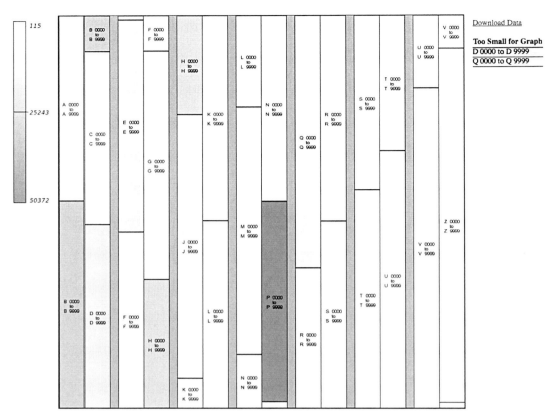

Figure 6. Cartogram with size representing percentage of items circulated at least once and color representing collection size (item count).

Challenges

At the beginning of this project, we encountered some interesting obstacles. Once we had adequately described the problem we were attempting to help solve, and what kinds of visualizations we wanted to implement, we prepared to tackle those.

Call Number	Percent with 1+ Circulations	Count
A	47	438
B	62	30178
C	44	1434
D	48	16115
E	54	12016
F	54	4231
G	58	3576
H	58	24162
J	67	4048
K	60	1978
L	71	8361
M	63	7545
N	61	6241
P	51	50372
Q	66	12162
R	88	2724
S	92	546
T	90	4611
U	84	627
V	90	115
Z	90	965

Table 1. Raw data showing percentage of items circulated at least once and collection size by call number.

Data acquisition was of primary importance. While Sierra can be queried directly, the volume of data being queried is large and structured in such a way that that any data query would take just under two minutes to run. At that point, we would begin to be able to conduct calculations upon that data to produce visualizations, and that is an unacceptable amount of time. To mitigate this issue, we created a PostgreSQL database on another server and provided sufficient indexes to optimize the queries used in the application. As a result, the query run time was reduced to a fraction of a second. The data stored in Postgres is refreshed periodically by querying Sierra using a system cron job. This still takes nearly two minutes to run, but with transactions, a user can continue to work on old data while the data is being refreshed. The application, therefore, does not query Sierra in real time but utilizes data that is sufficiently current for our purposes.

With proportional representation of data on the graphic and call numbers written within each section to identify the range covered, it was inevitable that some sections would be too small in which to list the call numbers. We elected to provide a table to the side of the graphic to list those sections. This was particularly important, as each section of the graphic is clickable to enable the user to delve deeper into the data. We made the items listed in the table clickable also, so that the user could be sure to access the desired data.

Larsen's Squarify Python library did not account for zero-value data, which certainly occurs within the data points utilized. Some subsections of the collection, for example, did not see any use. This resulted in calculation errors in generating the data used to draw the treemap. We adapted the script to extract and exclude data that would result in a zero-size square, presenting it in the table along with sections where the insufficiently sized sections were represented.

Future Enhancements

Opportunities exist to optimize data analysis performance further. When we added the last three data columns: percent of items with no circulation, items with circulations, and items with more than one circulation, we encountered a problem. The original query merely aggregated data, either by summation or average, and it ran in under a half second. Producing data for each of the final three items requires each to run as separate queries. Each of those would require approximately a half second to run, and when run over all of the rows in the original query, we added seconds on to the original run time. We mitigated much of the performance issues by running it on more robust hardware, but further work on the query or postprocessing available data might speed that up to run in under a second.

Although we provide two different visualizations and a Microsoft Excel export option, many users might prefer other visualization methods. Some users will prefer something like a bar graph, or perhaps pie charts. Some users might prefer an in-browser tabular data display as well. All of these visualization methods are implementable, given sufficient time.

Our query is specific to the Innovative Sierra database schema. However, we designed the program to make it easy to adapt to other integrated library systems. The data extraction is compartmentalized in its own Python object, and each charting object's data needs are minimal and uniform. That is, each graphed call number range is represented by a data tuple with three elements: the call number range, data for the first element, and data for the second element. This is passed to the data objects as a list of tuples.

LoC call number ranges representing sub-disciplines are comprehensive and specific. We would like to map the call number ranges to their subject descriptors and use that structure to define the data divisions displayed in the graphics by discipline and sub-discipline. The task of making the structure of call numbers and descriptors programmatically traversable, however, is of significant magnitude.

Conclusion

Data visualization does lend a unique perspective to the analysis of a library collection. It is important to note that context is the filter through which visual data must be interpreted and, therefore, data visualization alone does not paint the entire picture. It serves best to highlight areas of a collection where further investigation might be prudent in order to ascertain whether a change in collection development strategy is needed. Pairing visual (relative) data with raw data will help the librarian determine a more complete picture of the nature and use of the collection. With modest investment of time and skills, a data visualization tool can be developed to serve the needs of librarians who address collection development and analysis.

Index

University of Colorado - Denver, 571
University of Denver, 571
University of Florida, 304–310
University of Hong Kong, 358
University of Illinois at Urbana-Champaign, 311, 541
University of Kansas, 74–79, 344–349, 414
University of Maryland, 239–244, 470–474
University of Massachusetts, 38, 504, 549
University of Michigan Libraries, 3, 8, 336
University of Michigan Press, 2–11
University of Nevada, Reno, 272–276
University of North Carolina, Greensboro, 272, 276–279, 371, 528–529
University of North Florida, 316
University of North Texas, 291
University of Tennessee, 405, 529–530
University of Waterloo, 533
University System of Georgia, 219
Use factors, 377–380
Users
    changing perceptions of e-books, 304–310
    delivering wow for, 35–36
    disabled, 172–179
    discovery methods used by, 322–327
    engagement, 16, 319–320
    marketing digital resources to, 298–303
    mobile device use, 333–335, 350–355
    music library, 314
    patron-driven acquisition and, 152–155, 443–452
    preferences, 34
    self-published authors and, 518–519
    services crowd sourcing, 95–105
Utah State University, 74–79
Utrecht University, 322, 443–452

V

Vaillancourt, Shawn, 146
Vandenburg, Michael, 533
Vaughn, John, 20–29
Veaner, Allen, 546
Vendors, 47–58, 85–87
    post- purchase activities and ROI, 371–376
Verma, Etta, 518
Verminski, Alana, 295
Vickery, B. C., 546
Video collections, streaming, 398–404
Virginia Commonwealth University, 187–192, 425
Virginia Tech, 368, 482

Virtual Library of Virginia, 200–212
Visualization, data, 549–556, 614–622
Voigt, Melvin, 544

W

Waller, Jen, 488
Warheir, I. A., 546
Waters, Don, 2
Watkinson, Anthony, 123–127
Watkinson, Charles, 2–11
Wedig, Eric, 433
Weeding, 219–222
    serials deselection project, 409–413
Weighted collection development allocation formula, 381–383
Weisbrod, Elizabeth J., 475
Welsh, Don J., 287
West, Don, 268
Western Oregon University, 254–258
Westervelt, Ted, 260
Westlaw, 42
Wet materials, recovery of, 433–438
Wheaton College, 462
White, Meg, 47–58
Whittier College, 230–235
Widigson, Marie, 557
Wiersma, Gabrielle, 571
Wikipedia, 95–96
Wilders, Coen, 322
Wiley e-books, 167–171
Wilson, Kristen B., 607
Wolters Kluwer, 333
Woodward, Hazel, 123–127
WorldShare Management Services (WMS), 392–397

Y

Yale University Press, 457, 459, 460
Yelp, 96
Young, Frederick, 146
YouTube, 317
Yue, Paoshan W., 272

Z

Zagat reviews, 96–97
Zonneveld, Henk G. J., 443
Zsulya, Carol, 252, 258–259
.